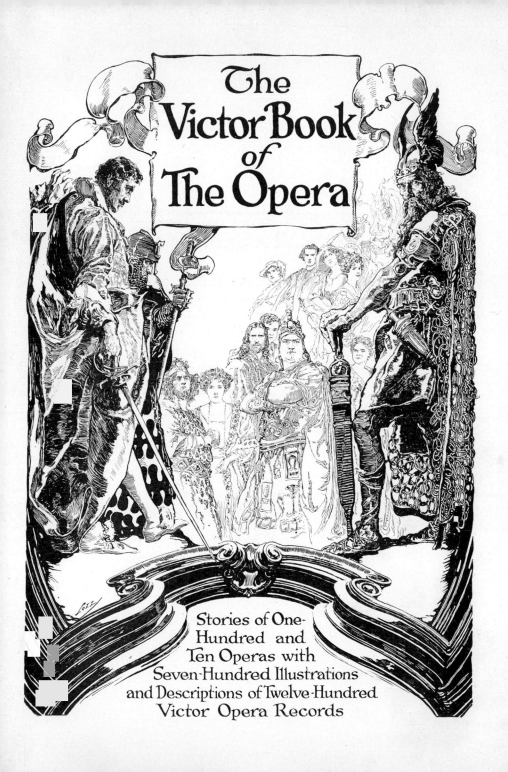

The Victor Book of The Opera

Stories of One-Hundred and Ten Operas with Seven-Hundred Illustrations and Descriptions of Twelve-Hundred Victor Opera Records

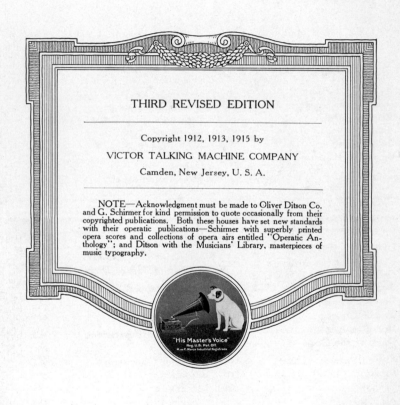

Index

ALTHOUGH the Opera Stories in this book are in alphabetical order, under the most familiar of the various titles, this index will be found convenient for quick reference.

Africana, Africaine	9	Forza del Destino, La	164
Aida	15	Fra Diavolo	169
Amleto	198	Freischutz, Der	172
Andrea Chenier	28		
		Germania	176
Ballo in Maschera	308	Gioconda, La	179
Barbiere di Siviglia	30	Götterdämmerung	188
Bartered Bride	38	Griselidis	196
Bohême	41	Guglielmo Tell	548
Bohemian Girl	48	Guillaume Tell	548
Boris Godounow	51		
		Hamlet	198
Carmen	53	Hansel and Gretel	202
Cavalleria Rusticana	71	Hernani	109
Chimes of Normandy	77	Hérodiade, Herodias	206
Contes d'Hoffman	474	Huguenots, Les	211
Cristoforo Colombo	78		
		Iris	219
Damnation of Faust	79		
Daughter of the Regiment	83	Jewels of the Madonna	221
Dinorah	85	Juggler of Notre Dame	224
Don Carlos	87		
Don Giovanni, Don Juan	89	King of Lahore, The	446
Donne Curiose	95	King of Ys	417
Don Pasquale	97	Konigskinder	226
Dusk of the Gods	188		
		L'Africana, L'Africaine	9
Elisir d'Amore (Elixir)	103	Lakmé	230
Erminie	107	Linda di Chamounix	234
Ernani	109	Lobetanz	235
		Lohengrin	237
Falstaff	118	Lombardi, I	251
Faust	120	Louise	253
Favorita, La	145	Lucia di Lammermoor	254
Fidelio	150	Lucrezia Borgia	262
Flauto Magico	272		
Fledermaus	153	Madama Butterfly	265
Flying Dutchman	155	Magic Flute, The	272
Force of Destiny	164	Manon (Massenet)	278
		Manon Lescaut (Puccini)	287

(*Index continued on page 5*)

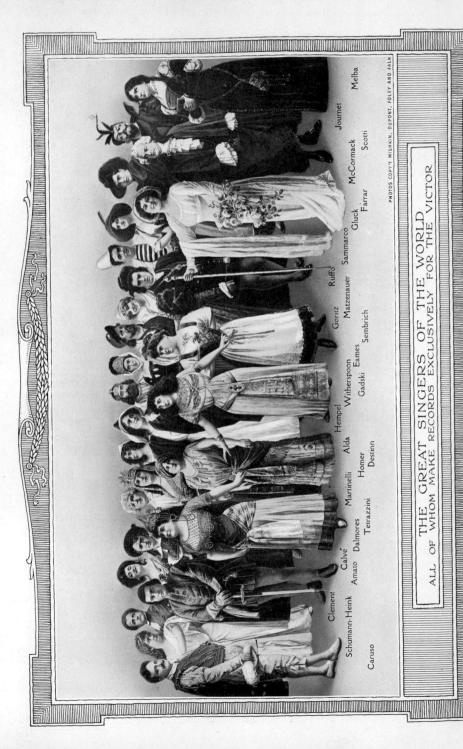

THE GREAT SINGERS OF THE WORLD
ALL OF WHOM MAKE RECORDS EXCLUSIVELY FOR THE VICTOR

PHOTOS COPY'T MISHKIN, DUPONT, FOLEY AND FALK

Melba
Journet
Scotti
McCormack
Farrar
Gluck
Sammarco
Ruffo
Matzenauer
Goritz
Sembrich
Eames
Gadski
Witherspoon
Hempel
Alda
Destinn
Homer
Marinelli
Tetrazzini
Dalmores
Calvé
Amato
Schumann-Heink
Clement
Caruso

Index ~ continued

Maritana 291	Rinaldo 441
Marriage of Figaro 293	Robert le Diable 442
Martha, Marta 300	Robert the Devil 442
Masked Ball 308	Robin Hood 444
Mefistofele 315	Roi de Lahore, Le 446
Meistersinger, Die 321	Roi d' Ys 417
Mephistopheles 315	Romeo and Juliet 447
Mignon 329	Rustic Chivalry 71
Mikado 336	
Mireille 339	Samson and Delilah 454
	Samson et Dalila 454
Nabucco 341	Segreto di Susanna 457
Natoma 343	Semiramide 458
Norma 347	Shepherd King, The . . . 416
Nozze di Figaro 293	Sicilian Vespers 532
	Siegfried 460
Oberon 350	Snegourotchka 469
Orfeo ed Euridice 353	Snow Maiden, The . . 469
Orpheus and Eurydice . . 353	Sonnambula, La . . . 471
Otello 356	
	Tales of Hoffman 474
Pagliacci 361	Tannhäuser 478
Parsifal 376	Thaïs 489
Patience 393	Tosca 493
Pearl Fishers 395	Traviata, La 502
Pearl of Brazil 399	Tristan und Isolde . . . 511
Pêcheurs de Perles, Les . 395	Trömpeter von Säkkingen . . 531
Pescatori di Perle . . . 395	Troubadour, The 519
Pinafore 400	Trovatore, Il 519
Pique Dame 402	Trumpeter of Sackingen, The 531
Pirates of Penzance 403	
Profeta, Prophète 405	Ugonotti, Gli 211
Prophet, The 405	
Puritani, I 410	Valkyrie, La 533
Puritans, The 410	Vascello Fantasma, Il . . . 155
	Verkaufte Braut, Die 38
Queen of Sheba (Goldmark) 413	Vespri Siciliani, I 532
Queen of Sheba (Gounod) 414	
	Walküre, Die 533
Regina di Saba 413	Werther 546
Rè Pastore, Il 416	William Tell 548
Rheingold, Das 419	Zauberflöte, Die 272
Rigoletto 425	Zaza 557

METROPOLITAN, NEW YORK

METROPOLITAN, PHILADELPHIA

FRENCH OPERA, NEW ORLEANS

THE AUDITORIUM, CHICAGO

THE COLON THEATRE, BUENOS AIRES

BOSTON OPERA HOUSE.

FAMOUS AMERICAN OPERA HOUSES.

ROYAL OPERA, BERLIN

COVENT GARDEN, LONDON

LA SCALA, MILAN

ROYAL OPERA, MADRID

THE OPÉRA, PARIS

FAMOUS OPERA HOUSES OF EUROPE

CARUSO AS VASCO DI GAMA

SCENES FROM L'AFRICAINE

Vasco before the Council—Act I
Scene in the Prison—Act II

The Massacre—Act III

The Indian Paradise—Act IV
The Fatal Tree—Act V

(Italian)
L'AFRICANA
(Laf-ree-kah' nah)

(French)
L'AFRICAINE
(Laf-ree-kahn)

(German)
DIE AFRIKANERIN
(Dee Ah-free-kah'-ner-in)

(English)
THE AFRICAN

OPERA IN FIVE ACTS

Text by Scribe; music by Meyerbeer. First produced at the *Opéra*, Paris, April 28, 1865. First London production in Italian, under the French title, at Covent Garden, July 22, 1865; and in English at the Royal English Opera, Covent Garden, October 21, 1865. First American production December 1, 1865, with a cast including Saxe, Batteo, Naudin and Faure, and the opera has since been absent from New York but a few years at a time. Minnie Hauk, Mme. Moran-Oldin, Mme. Bettaque, Mme. Breval, Lillian Nordica and Mme. Litvinne are some of the famous *prima donne* who have appeared as *Selika;* and *Vasco di Gama* has been sung by Campanini, Giannini, Perotti, Grienauer, Dippel, de Reszke and Tamagno. Produced at the New Orleans Opera December 18, 1869. Some noted Metropolitan revivals were in 1901 with Breval, de Reszké, Adams, Plançon and Journet; 1906, with Caruso (his first appearance in the rôle), Fremstad, Plançon and Journet.

Strangely enough, Scribe gave Meyerbeer the libretto in 1838, and part of the music was written then, but the two could not agree as to alterations, and it was not until 1852 that Scribe furnished a revised book. The work was not completed until 1860, nor produced until 1865, two years after Meyerbeer's death.

FAURE AS NELUSKO, 1865

9

Characters in the Opera

SELIKA, (*Say-lee'-kah*) a slave, formerly an African princess . . . . Soprano
INEZ, (*Ee'-nez*) daughter of Don Diego . . . . Soprano
ANNA, her attendant . . . . Contralto
NELUSKO, (*Nay-loos'-koh*) a slave, formerly an African chief . . . . Basso
DON PEDRO, (*Don Pay'-droh*) President of the Royal Council . . . . Basso
GRANDE INQUISITORE . . . . Basso
DON DIEGO, (*Don Dee-ay'-goh*) Member of the Council . . . . Basso
HIGH PRIEST OF BRAHMA (*Brah'-mah*) . . . . Basso
DON ALVAR, Member of the Council . . . . Tenor
VASCO DI GAMA, (*Vahs'-koh dee Gah'-mah*) an officer in the Portuguese Navy, Tenor
Chorus of Counsellors, Inquisitors, Sailors, Indians and Attendant Ladies.

The action occurs in Portugal, on Don Pedro's ship at sea, and in India.

ACT I—*Council Chamber of the King of Portugal*

The first scene occurs at Portugal, in the King's Council Chamber, whither *Vasco di Gama* has come to announce his discovery of a strange land, producing two of the native slaves, *Selika* and *Nelusko,* as proof. In this scene is given the noble and stately chorus

Dio che la terra venera (Thou Whom the Universe Adores)

By La Scala Chorus (*In Italian*) *62614 10-inch, $0.75

Don Pedro, President of the Council, who wishes to marry *Vasco's* sweetheart, *Inez,* influences that body to discredit the explorer's tale and throw him into prison with his slaves.

ACT II—*Prison of the Inquisition*

As the curtain rises *Vasco* is seen asleep on a bench, while *Selika* watches over him. She gazes at the sleeping youth and sings a beautiful lullaby.

SCENE, ACT II

* *Double-Faced Record—See page 13.*

PHOTO NADAR   KRAUSS AS SELIKA

The slave, seeing her master's grief over his inability to find the route to the unknown country, reveals to him the location of the coveted land. *Vasco*, overcome with gratitude, embraces her, and the duet follows.

Sei l'angiol diletto (Oh! Guardian Angel!)

By Tina Farelli, Soprano, and Gino Martinez-Patti, Tenor

(*In Italian*) *62407 10-inch, $0.75

Inez consents to marry *Don Pedro* in order to save *Vasco*, who is released, but too late to prevent his enemy from sailing in search of the unknown land, carrying with him *Vasco's* private papers and maps as well as the two slaves, *Selika* and *Nelusko*. The latter, who loves *Selika*, has discovered her attachment for *Vasco*, and through jealousy offers to guide *Don Pedro* to his country. The young officer secures a ship and goes in pursuit.

ACT III—*Deck of Don Pedro's Ship*

Preludio (Prelude to Act III)

By La Scala Orchestra   *62614 10-inch, $0.75

Act III shows the decks of *Don Pedro's* vessel. *Nelusko*, who is secretly plotting to destroy the ship, is brooding over his plans; and his gloomy bearing being noticed by the sailors,

SCENE, ACT III

* *Double-Faced Record—See page 13.*

11

they banter him, and finally ask him to relate the old legend of Adamastor, king of the seas.

Adamastor, re dell' onde profonde (Ruler of Ocean)

By Pasquale Amato, Baritone, and Chorus
    (*In Italian*) 88490 12-inch, $3.00
By Francesco Cigada, Baritone
    (*In Italian*) *62407 10-inch, .75

NELUSKO:
Adamastor, monarch of the pathless deep,
Swift o'er foaming waves
To sound of fierce winds tramping;
When his dark steeds vex the misty sea,
Beware, mariner! Beware, mariner!
When the gale rolls o'er the deep,
Then beware, then beware!
See, the lightning's flash reveals to thine eye,
How the dark waves seek the storm-laden sky.
All hope now is lost,
For the doomed wretch no tomb,
None, none but a watery grave!

A storm is threatened, and amid the preparations for resisting the elements a ship is seen, which proves to be *di Gama's*. He rashly comes on board, is promptly seized by *Don Pedro* and is about to be executed, when *Selika* draws her dagger and threatens to kill *Inez* unless her lover is released. The tyrant reluctantly yields, but afterward orders *Selika* to be flogged. The storm breaks, and

PHOTO BERT

AMATO AS NELUSKO

in its midst the ship is boarded by Indians, fellow-countrymen of *Nelusko*, and the entire ship's company are either killed or made prisoners.

ACT IV—Temple of Brahma

Act IV represents the Temple of Brahma in the country of *Selika* and *Nelusko*. The act opens with the weird and striking Indian March.

Marcia Indiana (Indian March)

By La Scala Orch. *68027 12-inch, $1.25

The priests, who have crowned *Selika* their Queen, announce the immediate execution of all the prisoners except *Vasco* ; and he too is condemned to die. The priests and people disperse and *Vasco* enters, guarded by soldiers. He is entranced with the beauty of this wonderful land, of which he had dreamed, and voices his admiration in the celebrated air, "*O Paradiso.*"

O Paradiso! (Oh Paradise!)

By Enrico Caruso, Tenor
    (*In Italian*) 88054 12-inch, $3.00
By Giovanni Martinelli, Tenor
    (*In Italian*) 74440 12-inch, 1.50
By Florencio Constantino
    (*In Italian*) 74085 12-inch, 1.50
By Evan Williams
    (*In English*) 74148 12-inch, 1.50

COPY'T DUPONT   CARUSO IN AFRICAINE

VASCO:
Hail! fruitful land of plenty, beauteous garden, hail!
An earthly paradise art thou!
Oh Paradise on earth!
Oh azure sky, oh fragrant air

All enchant my heart;
Thou fair new world art mine!
Thee, a radiant gift,
On my native land I'll bestow!
O beauteous country—mine thou art at last!

Double-Faced Record—See page 13.

SCENE, ACT IV

The soldiers are about to kill *Vasco*, but he is saved by *Selika*, who announces that he is her chosen husband. *Nelusko* is forced to remain silent by threats that *Selika* will destroy herself. *Vasco*, forgetting *Inez*, yields to the spell and weds the Queen by the native rites.

ACT V—SCENE I—*The Queen's Gardens*

At the beginning of the last act, *Inez*, who had escaped from the prison, is captured and brought before the Queen, who becomes convinced that *Vasco* still loves the Portuguese maiden. In a moment of generosity she sacrifices her own feelings and assists the lovers to escape.

SCENE II—*Promontory Over the Sea*

The final scene shows a promontory from which *Selika* is watching the ship bearing *Inez* and *Vasco* toward Portugal. As the vessel disappears from view she advances toward the deadly mancanilla tree, the fumes of which are death.

SELIKA:
Aye! here I look upon the mighty sea—boundless—infinite
As is my woe!
Its waves in angry fury break, and then anon their course renew,
As doth my sorrowing heart!

(*Observing the mancanilla tree.*)
Thou leafy temple, thou vault of foliage dark,
After life's weary tumult I now come
To seek repose of thee, and find oblivion from my woes,
Yes! thy shade eternal is like the darkness of the tomb!

Gathering the fatal flowers, she inhales their perfume, sadly saying: "Farewell, my Vasco, I forgive thee," and is soon overcome and sinks unconscious beneath the tree. *Nelusko*, who has come in search of her, finds her dying; and in a frenzy of grief, also inhales the deadly blossoms and falls lifeless by her side.

DOUBLE-FACED L'AFRICAINE RECORDS

Marcia Indiana (Indian March)	By La Scala Orchestra	68027	12-inch,	$1.25
Traviata—Preludio	*By La Scala Orchestra*			
Adamastor, re dell' onde profonde (Adamastor, Ruler of the Ocean)	By Francesco Cigada, Baritone (*In Italian*)	62407	10-inch,	.75
Sei l'angiol di letto (Oh, Guardian Angel!) By Tina Farelli, Soprano; G. Martinez-Patti, Tenor (*In Italian*)				
Dio che la terra venera (Thou Whom the Universe Adores!)	By La Scala Chorus (*In Italian*)	62614	10-inch,	.75
Preludio—Atto III	By La Scala Orchestra			

HOMER AS AMNERIS

(Italian)

AIDA

(*A h-ee'-dah*)

OPERA IN FOUR ACTS

Text translated from the French of Locle by Antonio Ghislanzoni. Music by Giuseppe Verdi. First produced in Cairo, December 24, 1871; at La Scala, Milan, under the direction of the composer himself, February 8, 1872; at Naples in March, 1872; at Parma, April, 1872; Berlin, 1874; in Paris, at the *Theatre Italien*, April 22, 1876; revived at the same theatre in 1878; and given at the Opéra, March 22, 1880, where it has since been one of the most popular of all operas. First London production at Covent Garden, June 22, 1876; produced at St. Petersburg, in Russian, 1879. First performance in America at the Academy of Music, New York, November 26, 1873, the cast including Torriani, Cary, Campanini and Maurel. Produced in Philadelphia, December 12, 1873; and at the New Orleans Opera, December 6, 1878. The opera has always been a favorite one in America, and but few seasons have passed since 1873 without from ten to thirty performances. In 1904 Caruso made his first appearance at the Metropolitan as *Rhadames*. A highly impressive open air production was given in 1912 at the foot of the pyramids of Egypt.

Characters of the Drama

AIDA, an Ethiopian slave .... Soprano
THE KING OF EGYPT.. Bass
AMNERIS, (*Am-nay'-iss*) his daughter....................... Mezzo-Soprano
RHADAMES, (*Rahd'-ah-maze*) Captain of the Guard..................... Tenor
AMONASRO, (*Am-oh-nahz'-roh*) King of Ethiopia .... Baritone
RAMFIS, (*Rahm'-fiss*) High Priest .... Bass
A MESSENGER .... Tenor

Priests, Priestesses, Ministers, Captains, Soldiers, Officials, Ethiopian
Slaves and Prisoners, Egyptians, etc.

The scene is laid in Memphis and Thebes, in Pharaoh's time.

© MISHKIN   CARUSO AS RHADAMES

This opera was written by request of the Viceroy of Egypt, who wished to celebrate the opening of his new Opera House at Cairo by the production of a work upon an Egyptian subject from the pen of the most popular composer of the time. It is one of the longest of all operas, lasting four hours and forty minutes when given without cuts. No opera of Verdi's has proved more popular than Aida, with the possible exception of Trovatore, and it is beloved by opera-goers the world over. The story originated with Marietta Bey, the famous Egyptologist, and seems to have inspired Verdi to unusual efforts.

Aida, daughter of *Amonasro*, King of Ethiopia, has been captured by the Egyptians and is a slave at the Court of Memphis, where she and the young soldier *Rhadames* have fallen in love with each other. *Rhadames* goes to the Egyptian war, and during his absence the *King's* daughter, *Amneris*, discovers his attachment and is furious, as she herself loves *Rhadames*.

Rhadames returns, covered with glory and bringing many prisoners, among them *Amonasro*, *Aida's* father. The *King* releases all the prisoners except *Amonasro*, and bestows his daughter on the unwilling *Rhadames*.

In the next scene *Amonasro* forces his daughter to persuade *Rhadames* to become a traitor. The latter's love for *Aida* and his distaste for the approaching union with *Amneris* lead him to consent. *Amneris*,

15

however, has overheard the plot, and after vainly trying to induce *Rhadames* to abandon *Aida*, she denounces him as a traitor, and he is condemned to be buried alive. When the vault is sealed he discovers *Aida*, who had concealed herself there that she might die with him; and the lovers slowly suffocate in each other's arms.

Prelude

By Vessella's Italian Band   *17729 10-inch, $0.75

This short prelude is too little known to the music-loving public, one reason being that an audience is seldom seated when it is played, and the music is too delicate for it to be properly heard amid the confusion.

ACT I

SCENE 1—*A Hall in the Palace. Through the grand gate at the back may be seen the Pyramids and the Temples of Memphis*

The curtain rises, showing a hall in the palace of the King of Memphis, where *Rhadames* and the High Priest, *Ramfis*, are discussing the coming invasion of Ethiopia; and *Ramfis* hints that some young and brave warrior may be chosen to command the expedition. *Rhadames*, left alone, hopes that he himself may gain the coveted honor, and promises to lay his triumphs at the feet of his *Aida*.

Celeste Aida (Heavenly Aida)

By Enrico Caruso, Tenor
(*In Italian*) 88127 12-inch, $3.00

By Giovanni Martinelli, Tenor   (*In Italian*) 74424 12-inch, $1.50

By Leo Slezak, Tenor   (*In German*) 64113 10-inch, 1.00

By Paul Althouse, Tenor
(*In Italian*) *55045 12-inch 1.50

COPY'T MISHKIN

SLEZAK AS RHADAMES

He voices these hopes in the splendid gem of Act I, the *Celeste Aida*, beginning

Ce - le ste A - i - da,   for - ma di vi - na,— mi - sti • co ser - to   di lu - ce e fior
Heav'n-ly A - i - da,   beau ty re-splen-dent,—Ra - di - ant flow-er, bloom-ing and bright

in which he chants the praises of the peerless *Aida*. It is seldom enjoyed at the opera, especially in America, as it occurs almost immediately after the rise of the curtain, and is invariably marred by the noise made by late comers. With the Victor, however, it may be heard in all its beauty and the fine renditions by Caruso, Slezak, Martinelli and Althouse fully appreciated.

COPY'T DOVER ST. STUDIOS

MARTIN AS RHADAMES

RHADAMES:
Heavenly Aida, beauty resplendent,
  Radiant flower, blooming and bright;
Queenly thou reignest o'er me transcendent,
  Bathing my spirit in beauty's light.
Would that thy bright skies once more behold-
    ing,
  Breathing the soft airs of thy native land,
Round thy fair brow a diadem folding,
  Thine were a throne next the sun to stand!

* *Double-Faced Record—See page 27.*

GADSKI AS AIDA

The *King's* daughter, *Amneris*, enters, and seeing the young warrior's glowing enthusiasm, delicately hints of her secret affection for him, saying:

AMNERIS:
What unwonted fire in thy glance!
With what noble pride glows thy face!
Worthy of envy—oh, how much—
Would be the woman whose beloved aspect
Should awaken in thee this light of joy!

Rhadames begins to explain his hope of securing the command of the expedition, when *Aida* enters, and the young soldier's expressive glance reveals to *Amneris* his love for the Egyptian slave.

The *King* and his guards enter and receive a messenger, who reports that Egypt has been invaded by the Ethiopian army, under the command of *Amonasro*. ("My father!" exclaims *Aida* aside.) Amid great excitement *Rhadames* is appointed leader of the army, and is presented with a banner by *Amneris*.

The *King* begins another trio, urging the Egyptian forces to guard with their lives the sacred Nile.

Su! del Nilo (Nilus' Sacred Shores!)

By Elena Ruszcowska, Soprano; Maria Cappiello, Mezzo-Soprano; Tapergi and Davi (*In Italian*) **88266   12-inch, $3.00**

Following the trio comes a grand chorus:

To battle! We'll hunt the invader down.
On! Rhadames, thy brow may laurels crown!

All depart to prepare for the expedition, while *Aida,* left alone, gives way to her grief and sings the beautiful *Ritorna vincitor,* expressing her conflicting emotions.

Ritorna vincitor (Return Victorious!)

By Johanna Gadski, Soprano   (*In Italian*)   **88137   12-inch, $3.00**

AIDA:
Return victorious! And from my lips
Went forth the impious word! Conqueror
Of my father—of him who takes arms
For me—to give me again
A country; a kingdom; and the illustrious name
Which here I am forced to conceal!
The insane word forget, O gods;
Return the daughter
To the bosom of her father;
Destroy the squadrons of our oppressors!. . .
What am I saying? And my love,
Can I ever forget
This fervid love which oppresses and enslaves,
As the sun's ray which now blesses me?
Shall I call death on Rhadames—
On him whom I love so much?
Ah! Never on earth was heart torn by more
cruel agonies!

She gives way to her emotion for a brief moment, then sings the lovely and appealing

I sacri nomi (The Sacred Names)

**By Celestina Boninsegna, Soprano
88223   (*In Italian*)   12-inch, $3.00**

Rousing herself she calls on her gods for aid and goes slowly out as the curtain falls.

EAMES AS AIDA

LANDE

The Return of Rhadames—Act II

SCENE II—*The Temple of Vulcan—in the centre an altar, illuminated by a mysterious light from above*

Ramfis, the High Priest, and the priests and priestesses have assembled to bless the expedition. The chant in praise of *Ptah* is heard from an invisible choir. *Rhadames* enters and receives the consecrated veil.

RAMFIS:
Mortal, beloved of the gods, to thee
Is confided the fate of Egypt. Let the holy
  sword
Tempered by the gods, in thy hand become
To the enemy, terror—a thunderbolt-death!

RHADAMES:
God, who art leader and arbiter
Of every human war,
Protect thou and defend
The sacred soil of Egypt!

Nume, custode e vindice (God, Guardian and Avenger)

By Antonio Paoli, Tenor; Perello de Segurola, Bass; and
Chorus   (*In Italian*)   88268   12-inch, $3.00

Ramfis then sings the closing invocation, in which *Rhadames* joins. He is invested with the sacred armor, and as the priestesses perform the mystic dance the curtain slowly falls.

ACT II

SCENE I—*A hall in Amneris' apartments*

The curtain rises, showing the Princess and her slaves, who are adorning her for the triumphal festival in honor of *Rhadames,* just returned with his victorious army. *Amneris* and the slaves sing the ode to the returned hero.

Chi mai fra (His Glory Now Praise)

By Maria Capiello, Mezzo-Soprano,
  and Chorus   (*In Italian*) *55005 12-inch, $1.50

Seeing *Aida* approaching, the Princess dismisses her slaves and prepares to enjoy her revenge.

This scene is expressed in a splendid duet, given here in two records by Mmes. Gadski and Homer, and in condensed form by two La Scala artists.

Fu la sorte dell' armi ('Neath the Chances of Battle)

By Johanna Gadski, Soprano, and Louise Homer,
  Contralto   (*In Italian*)   89024   12-inch, $4.00

Alla pompa, che s'appreste (In the Pageant Now Preparing)

By Johanna Gadski, Soprano, and Louise Homer,
  Contralto   (*In Italian*)   89025   12-inch, $4.00

PHOTO BERT

HOMER AS AMNERIS

Ebben qual nuovo fremito (What New Alarm?)

By Elena Ruszcowska, Soprano, and Bianca Lavin de Casas,
  Mezzo-Soprano   (*In Italian*)   88263   12-inch, $3.00

Amneris pretends to sympathize with the afflicted girl, saying:

AMNERIS:
The fate of arms was deadly to thy people.
Poor Aida! The grief
Which weighs down thy heart I share with
  thee.
I am thy friend;
Time will heal the anguish of thy heart,
And more than time—a powerful god-love.

AIDA:
Oh! love immortal! oh! joy and sorrow,
Sweetest delirium, dark doubts and woes!

As in thy trials new life I borrow,
A heav'n of rapture thy smiles disclose.

AMNERIS (*aside*):
This death-like pallor, this strong emotion,
Plainly reveal the fever of love!
(*To Aida*):
Among the braves who fought so well,
Has someone a tender sorrow haply waken'd
  in your heart?

AIDA:
What say'st thou?

* *Double-Faced Record—See page 27.*

OBER AS AMNERIS

AMNERIS:
Tremble! I read thy secret,
Thou lov'st him! lie no longer!
I love him too—dost thou hear?
I am thy rival, daughter of kings Egyptian.

AIDA:
Thou my rival? 'tis well, so be it—
Ah, what have I said? forgive and pity,
Ah, let this my sorrow thy warm heart move.
'Tis true I adore him with boundless love—
Thou art so happy, thou art so mighty,
I cannot live hence from love apart!

AMNERIS:
Tremble, vile minion! be ye heartbroken,
Warrant of death this love shall betoken!
In the pomp which approaches,
With me, O slave, thou shall assist;
Thou prostrate in the dust—
I on the throne beside the King;
Come, follow me, and thou shalt learn
If thou canst contend with me!

AIDA:
Ah, pity! What more remains to me?
My life is a desert;
This love which angers thee
In the tomb I will extinguish!

Always a highly impressive number, this duet is doubly so when given by such famous exponents of the parts of *Aida* and *Amneris.* Mme. Gadski's *Aida* is one of her most effective rôles—splendidly acted and vocally perfect; while Mme. Homer's impersonation of the Egyptian Princess is always a dramatic one, and she sings the noble music with thrilling power.

The rendition by the two La Scala artists, Mme. Elena Ruszcowska and Mme. Bianca Lavin de Casas, is one of the finest which has come to us from Milan.

SCENE II—*Without the City Walls*

The scene changes to a gate of the city of Thebes. The King and his court are assembled on a magnificent throne to receive the conquering army. A splendid chorus is sung by people and priests. The Egyptian troops, preceded by trumpeters, enter, followed by chariots of war, ensigns, statues of the gods, dancing girls carrying treasures, and finally *Rhadames,* under a canopy borne by twelve slaves; the procession headed by bands of musicians playing the famous Triumphal March.

CARUSO AS RHADAMES

Grand March (Triumphal March)
By Vessella's Italian Band   *35265   12-inch, $1.25

Vessella has admirably produced the familiar effect of the two bands playing, at first separately, and then together.

KING (*descending from the throne to embrace Rhadames*):
Saviour of our country, I salute thee.
Come, and let my daughter with her own hand
Place upon you the triumphal crown.
(*Rhadames bows before Amneris, who places the crown upon him.*)
Now ask of me
What thou most wishest. Nothing denied to thee
On such a day shall be—I swear it
By my crown, by the sacred gods!

The prisoners enter, including *Amonasro,* who is dressed as an officer. *Aida* sees him and cries, "What do I see! My father!" All are surprised, and *Amonasro* signals to *Aida* not to betray his rank. *Amonasro* then sings his recital:

* *Double-Faced Record—See page 27.*

Quest' assisa ch'io vesto (This Dress Has Told You)

By Ernesto Badini, Baritone; Sra. Fabris, Soprano; Lavin de Casas, Mezzo-
Soprano; Egidio Cunego, Tenor   (*In Italian*)   88264   12-inch, $3.00

AMONASRO:

I am her father. I went to war,
Was conquered, and death I sought in vain.
(*Pointing to his uniform*)
This habit I wear may tell you
That I have defended my king and my coun-
try.
Fate was hostile to our arms;
Vain was the courage of the brave!
At my feet, in the dust extended,

Lay the King, transfixed by many wounds;
If the love of country is a crime
We are all criminals—all ready to die!
(*Turning to the King with a supplicating
accent*)
But thou, O King, thou powerful lord,
Be merciful to these men.
To-day we are stricken by Fate,
To-morrow Fate may smite thee!

LANDE

THE GREAT CONSECRATION SCENE

The people and prisoners appeal to the *King* for mercy, while the priests demand that the captives be put to death. *Rhadames,* seeing the hesitation of the *King,* reminds him of his vow, and demands life and liberty for the captured Ethiopians. The *King* yields, stipulating only that *Aida* and her father be held as hostages, and then announces that *Rhadames* shall have the hand of *Amneris* as his reward.

The magnificent finale then follows, *Aida* and *Rhadames* gazing at each other in despair, *Amneris* glorying in her triumph, and *Amonasro* swearing secret vengeance against his captors. The curtain falls amid general rejoicing.

ACT III

SCENE I—*A moonlight night on the banks of the Nile—the Temple of Isis can be
seen, half concealed by palm trees*

As the curtain rises on this beautiful scene, a chorus within the Temple is heard in a chant of praise.

COPY'T MISHKIN

DESTINN AS AIDA

O tu che sei d'Osiride (Oh, Thou Who Art Osiris)

By Maria Cappiello, Soprano, and Chorus (*Double-faced—see page 27*) (*In Italian*) 55005 12-inch, $1.50

A boat approaches, bearing *Rhadames* and *Amneris*, who go into the Temple.

CHORUS (*in the temple*):
O Thou who art of Osiris,
Mother immortal and spouse,
Goddess who awakens the beatings
In the heart of human creatures,
Come piteous to our help,
Mother of eternal love.

AMNERIS:
I will pray that Rhadames may give me
His whole heart—as mine to him
Is consecrated forever!

Aida, veiled, cautiously enters, hoping that *Rhadames* will come thither, and sings a tender and despairing song of that lovely land which she may never see again.

(*Italian*)   (*German*)   (*English*)

O patria mia—Mein Vaterland—My Native Land

By Johanna Gadski, Soprano
(*In Italian*) 88042 12-inch, $3.00
By Emmy Destinn (*In Italian*) 88469 12-inch, 3.00
By Emmy Destinn (*In German*) 92058 12-inch, 3.00
By Celestina Boninsegna
(*In Italian*) 88239 12-inch, 3.00
By Lucy Isabelle Marsh
(*In Italian*) 60098 10-inch, .75

AIDA:
O native land, no more to thee shall I return!
O skies of tender blue, O soft airs blowing,
Where calm and peaceful my dawn of life pass'd o'er,
O hills of verdure, O perfum'd waters flowing,

O home beloved, I ne'er shall see thee more!
O fresh and fragrant vales, O quiet dwelling,
Promise of happy days of love that bore.
Now hope is banish'd, love and yonder dream dispelling,
O home beloved, I ne'er shall see thee more!

Five fine renditions of this air, one of the most effective in the opera, are given here by four celebrated prima donnas, three of whom have been seen in America in this rôle.

Aida is about to depart when she is astonished to see her father. *Amonasro* reproaches his daughter with her love for his enemy *Rhadames,* telling her with significant emphasis that she may behold her native land again if she wishes. He tells her that his people have risen again, and proposes that she shall influence *Rhadames* to betray the plans of his army in the new campaign. She at first refuses, but he bids her be true to her country, and pictures the sufferings of her people.

Ciel! Mio Padre! (Heaven! My Father!)

By Johanna Gadski, Soprano, and Pasquale Amato, Baritone
(*In Italian*) 89067 12-inch, $4.00

Rivedrai le foreste imbalsamate (Thou Shalt See Again the Balmy Forests)

By Elena Ruszcowska and Giuseppe Maggi
(*Italian*) 88267 12-inch, $3.00

LANDE

DESTINN AND SCOTTI IN AIDA

AIDA:
Heaven! My father!

AMONASRO:
Grave affairs lead me to thee, Aida.
Nothing escapes my sight; thou art destroying
Thyself with love for Rhadames; He loves thee
And here thou waitest him.
The daughter of the Pharoahs is thy rival—
An infamous race, abhorred and fatal to us!

AIDA:
And I am in her power! I, the daughter of
Amonasro.

AMONASRO:
In her power! No! If thou wishest,
This powerful rival thou shalt defeat,
And country, and throne, and love all shall
be thine.
Thou shalt see again the balmy forests,
The fresh valleys, our temples of gold!

AIDA (with transport):
I shall see again the balmy forests,
Our valleys, our temples of gold!

AMONASRO:
Thou rememberest that the merciless Egyptian

Profaned our houses, temples and altars;
Mothers, old men and children he slew.

AIDA:
Ah! well I remember those unhappy days.
I remember the grief that my heart suffered.

AMONASRO:
Then delay not. In arms now is roused
Our people—everything is ready—
Victory we shall have. It only remains for me
to know
What path the enemy will follow.

AIDA:
Who will be able to discover it? Whoever?

AMONASRO:
Thyself!

AIDA:
I?

AMONASRO:
Rhadames will come here soon—he loves thee—
He leads the Egyptians. Dost thou understand?

AIDA:
Horror! What dost thou counsel me? No, no!
Never!

Su, dunque! (Up, Then!)

By Johanna Gadski and Pasquale Amato   (*Italian*)   89068   12-inch, $4.00

With growing excitement he describes the consequences of her refusal.

AMONASRO (with savage rage):
Up, then!
Rise, Egyptian legions!
With fire destroy our cities—
Spread terror, carnage and death.
To your fury there is no longer check!

AIDA:
Ah, father!

AMONASRO (repulsing her):
My daughter
Dost thou call thyself?

AIDA (terrified and suppliant):
Pity!

AMONASRO:
Rivers of blood pour
On the cities of the vanquished—
Seeth thou? From the black gulfs
The dead are raised—
To thee they point and cry;
For thee the country dies!

AIDA:
Pity!

AMONASRO:
A horrible ghost
Among the shadows to us approaches—
Tremble! the fleshless arms
Over thy head it raised—
It is thy mother—recognize her—
She curses thee!

AIDA (in the greatest terror):
Ah, no! Father!

AMONASRO (repulsing her):
Go, unworthy one! Thou'rt not my offspring—
Thou art the slave of the Pharaohs!

AIDA (yielding):
Father, their slave I am not—
Reproach me not—curse me not;
Thy daughter again thou canst call me—
Of my country I will be worthy!

AMONASRO:
Courage! he comes—there, I shall hear all.
(*Conceals himself among the palm trees.*)

Rhadames now enters and tries to embrace her, but she repulses him, saying bitterly:

AIDA:
The rites of another love await thee,
Thou spouse of Amneris!

He protests that he loves *Aida* alone, but she bids him prove his affection by fleeing with her.

Fuggiam gli ardori (Ah! Fly With Me)

By Lucy Marsh, Soprano, and Paul Althouse,
Tenor   (*Double-Faced—See page 27*)
(*In Italian*)   55058   12-inch, $1.50

AIDA:
Ah! fly with me, and leave behind
These deserts bare and blighted;
Some country, new and fresh to find,
Where we may love united.
There, 'mid virgin forest groves,
By fair sweet flow'rs scented,
In quiet joy contented, the world will we
forget!

COPY'T MISHKIN

ZEROLA AS RHADAMES

He finally consents, and reveals to her that the army will go by the pass of Napata. *Amonasro*, who has overheard, now enters, and *Rhadames* is horrified at the knowledge that he has betrayed the army to the King of Ethiopia.

Amneris, coming from the temple, pauses behind a pillar and overhears the final words. Mad with jealousy, she rushes in and denounces the guilty trio. *Aida* and *Amonasro* escape but *Rhadames* is taken in custody as a traitor.

ACT IV

SCENE I —*A room in the Palace—on one side a door leading to Rhadames' prison cell*

PHOTO HALL

RHADAMES DENOUNCED AS A TRAITOR

The curtain rises, disclosing *Amneris* in an attitude of despair. She is torn between her love for *Rhadames* and a desire for vengeance, and finally orders the prisoner brought before her.

AMNERIS (*bitterly musing*):
> My rival has escaped me—
> And Rhadames awaits from the priests
> The punishment of a traitor.
> Traitor he is not, though he revealed
> The high secret of war. He wished to fly—
> To fly with her—traitors all!
> To death, to death!
> Oh, what am I saying? I love him—
> Oh! if he could love me!
> I would save him—but how?
> Let me try. Guards, Rhadames comes.

Rhadames enters, and the first great duet of the act occurs.

Gia i sacerdoti adunansi (The Priests Assemble)
By Louise Homer and Enrico Caruso   (*In Italian*)   89050   12-inch, $4.00

Aida a me togliesti (Aida Thou Hast Taken)
By Louise Homer and Enrico Caruso
(*In Italian*)   89051   12-inch, $4.00

Amneris offers to save his life if he will renounce *Aida.* He scorns her proposal, resolving to die rather than be false to his Ethiopian Princess.

AMNERIS:
> Renounce her forever
> And thou shalt live!

RHADAMES:
> I cannot do it!

AMNERIS:
> Wouldst thou die, madman?

RHADAMES:
> I am ready to die.

AMNERIS:
> Who saves thee, O wretch,
> From the fate that awaits thee?
> To fury hast thou changed
> A love that had no equal.
> Revenge for my tears
> Heaven will now consummate!

The guards now appear and conduct *Rhadames* to the judgment room. The ensuing scene is a highly dramatic and impressive one.

COPY'T MISHKIN

DALMORES AS RHADAMES

Ohimè! Morir mi sento (Ah, me! Death Approaches!)

By Lavin de Casas, Mezzo-Soprano; Rizzo Sant' Elia,
Bass; and Chorus   (*In Italian*)   88270   12-inch, $3.00

Amneris, seeing *Rhadames* taken out by the Priests, repents her harshness and sinks down desolate on a seat.

AMNERIS (*falling on a chair, overcome*):
Ah me! Death's hand approaches! who now
  will save him?
He is now in their power.
His sentence I have sealed—Oh, how I curse
  thee,
Jealousy, vile monster, thou who hast doomed
  him
To death, and me to everlasting sorrow!
(*Turns and sees Ramfis and the Priests, who
  cross the stage and enter the subterranean
  hall.*)
What see I? Behold of death
The ministers fatal, his merciless judges.

PRIESTS:
Defend thyself!

RAMFIS:
Rhadames, Rhadames: and
  thou hast played
The part of a traitor to King,
  and to honor!

PRIESTS:
Defend thyself!

RAMFIS:
He is silent.

ALL:
Traitor vile!

RAMFIS:
Rhadames, we thy fate have
  decided,
Of all traitors the fate shall
  be thine—
'Neath the altar whose God
  thou'st derided
Thou a sepulchre living shall
  find.

AMNERIS:
Find   a   sepulchre   living!
  Hated wretches!
Ever   vengeful,   blood-thirsty
  and blind!

Ah, let me not behold those white robed
  phantoms!
(*Covers her face with her hands.   The voice
  of Ramfis can be heard within.*)

RAMFIS:
Rhadames, Rhadames: thou hast betrayed
Of thy country the secrets to aid the foeman:

PRIESTS:
Defend thyself!

RAMFIS:
Rhadames, Rhadames: and thou wast absent
From the camp the very day before the
  combat!

SCOMPARINI

THE DESPAIR OF AMNERIS—ACT IV

Sacerdoti, compiste un delitto! (Priests, a Crime You Have Enacted!)

By Lavin de Casas, Mezzo-Soprano; F. Rizzi, Bass; and
Chorus   (*In Italian*)   88323   12-inch, $3.00

The priests now enter from the crypt and pass across the hall. The wretched woman denounces them.

Priests of Heaven, a crime you have enacted,
Tigers even in bloodshed exulting,
Earthly justice and Heaven's you are insulting,
On the guiltless your sentence will fall!
PRIESTS: (*Departing slowly.*)
  None can his doom recall!

AMNERIS:
Impious priesthood, curses light on ye all!
On your heads Heaven's vengeance will fall!
(*Exit wildly.*)

This is one of the most impressive records of the *Aida* series. The despair of the wretched *Amneris,* and the solemn reply of the unbending priests are wonderfully expressed by Verdi.

© MISHKIN

CONSTANTINO AS RHADAMES

SCENE II—*Interior of the Temple of Vulcan—below a Subterranean Apartment*

"The work finishes in serenity and peace, and such terminations are the most beautiful. Above, the temple full of light, where the ceremonies continue immutable in the sanctuary of the indifferent gods; below, two human beings dying in each other's arms. Their song of love and death is among the most beautiful of all music."—Camille Bellaigue.

When we hear the expression "the duet from Aida," our thoughts always instinctively turn to this number at the close of the work. There are other duets in the opera, some of them fine numbers, but this is the *great* one—perhaps the most intensely dramatic and melodiously beautiful of all Verdi's writings.

La fatal pietra (The Fatal Stone)

By Johanna Gadski, Soprano, and Enrico Caruso, Tenor (*In Italian*) 89028 12-inch, $4.00

By Nicola Zerola, Tenor (*Part of scene—* "To die, so pure and lovely!") (*In Italian*) 74225 12-inch, 1.50

This last scene is a highly picturesque one. Above we see the splendid Temple of Ptah, where priests and priestesses are chanting their strange songs. Below, a dark vault, in whose depths *Rhadames* is awaiting with patience a slow death by starvation.

RHADAMES (*despairingly*):
The fatal stone upon me now is closing!
Now has the tomb engulf'd me!
The light of day no more shall I see!
No more behold Aida!
Aida, where art thou now?
Whate'er befall me, may'st thou be happy!
Ne'er may my frightful doom be told to thine ear!
(*Then suddenly in the shadows he sees a form—it is Aida, who has secreted herself in the crypt that she may die with her lover.*)
What moan was that?
Is't a phantom, or vision dread?
No! 'tis a human being!
Heaven! Aida!
AIDA: Yes!
RHADAMES (*in great desperation*):
Thou, with me here buried!
AIDA:
My heart foreboded this, thy dreadful sentence,
And to this tomb that shuts on thee its portal,
I crept, unseen by mortal.
Here, free from all,
Where none can more behold us,
    Clasp'd in thy arms, love,
    I resolved to perish!
RHADAMES: To die! so pure and lovely!
To die! thyself thus dooming,
In all thy beauty blooming,
Fade thus forever!
Thou, whom the gods alone for love created;
Yet to destroy thee, was my love then fated!
Thou shalt not die! so much I love thee,
Thou art too lovely!
AIDA (*transported*):
See'st thou where death, in angel guise,
With heavenly radiance beaming,
Would waft us to eternal joys,
On golden wings above!

I see heaven's gates are open wide
Where tears are never streaming,
Where only bliss and joy reside.
The bliss and joy of never fading, endless love!

FROM AN OLD PHOTOGRAPH

CAMPANINI AS RHADAMES

The lovers sing their plaintive farewell to earth in hauntingly lovely strains, while in strange contrast the heathen chanting continues above.

O terra addio (Farewell, O Earth)

By Johanna Gadski, Soprano, and Enrico Caruso, Tenor

(*In Italian*) 89029 12-inch, $4.00

By Lucy Isabelle Marsh, Soprano, and John McCormack, Tenor

(*In Italian*) 74398 12-inch, 1.50

AIDA AND RHADAMES:

Farewell, O earth,
Farewell, thou dark vale of sorrow,
Brief dream of joy,
Condemned to end in woe!

See, brightly opens for us,
Brightly opens now the sky, and endless morrow,
There, all unshadow'd, shall eternal glow!

(*Curtain*)

DOUBLE-FACED AND MISCELLANEOUS AIDA RECORDS

Chi mai fra (His Glory Now Praise) By Maria Cappiello, Mezzo-Soprano, and Chorus (*In Italian*) O tu che sei d'Osiride (Oh, Thou Who Art Osiris) By Maria Cappiello, Mezzo-Soprano, and Chorus (*In Italian*)	55005	12-inch,	$1.50
Celeste Aida (Heavenly Aida) *Trombone* By Arthur Pryor *Il Guarany Overture* By Pryor's Band	35030	12-inch,	1.25
The Fatal Stone *Cornet-Trombone* By Arthur Pryor, Emil Keneke and Pryor's Band Serenade (*Titl*) *'Cello-Flute* By Louis Heine and Darius Lyons	35150	12-inch,	1.25
Aida Fantasia By Police Band of Mexico *Cascades of Roses Waltz* By Police Band of Mexico	35047	12-inch,	1.25
Aida Selection By Pryor's Band *Attila—Grand Trio* (*Verdi*) By Kryl's Bohemian Band	35195	12-inch,	1.25
Aida Selection (Finale, Act II) By Pryor's Orchestra	31359	12-inch,	1.00
Aida—Grand March Vessella's Italian Band *Rondo Capriccioso* (*Mendelssohn*) Vessella's Italian Band	35265	12-inch,	1.25
Marcha Triunfal (Triumphal March) By Garde Republicaine Band *Tosca—Tosca divina!* (*In Italian*) By Gustavo Berl-Resky, Baritone	62409	10-inch,	.75
Prelude Vessella's Italian Band *Traviata—Prelude* Vessella's Italian Band	17729	10-inch,	.75
Celeste Aida (Heavenly Aida) (*In Italian*) Paul Althouse *Standchen (Schubert)* (*In German*) Paul Reimers	55045	12-inch,	1.50
Fuggiam gli ardori (Ah! Fly With Me) (*In Italian*) Lucy Marsh and Paul Althouse *Madama Butterfly—O quanti occhi fisi* (*In Italian*) Olive Kline and Paul Althouse	55058	12-inch,	1.50
Gems from "Aida"—Part I Victor Opera Company Chorus, "Almighty Phtha"—Solo, "Heav'nly Aida" (Celeste Aida)—Women's Chorus, "Come Bind Thy Flowing Tresses"—Soprano Solo, "Love, Fatal Power"—Duet and Chorus, "On to Victory" Gems from "Aida"—Part II Victor Opera Company Chorus, "Glory to Isis"—Solo, "My Native Land" (O Patria Mia)—Solo and Chorus, "O King in Thy Power Transcendent"—Finale, Duet and Chorus, "Fatal Stone"	35428	12-inch,	1.25

(Italian)

ANDREA CHENIER

(Ahn-dray'-ah Sheh-neay')

OPERA IN FOUR ACTS

Libretto by Luigi Illica; music by Umberto Giordano. First produced at La Scala, Milan, March 28, 1896. First performance in Berlin in 1898; in London, April 26, 1903, by the Carl Rosa Company, in English. Given in Italian some years afterward, with Strakosch, de Cisneros, Zenatello and Sammarco. Produced in Paris at the Théâtre Sarah Bernhardt, June 3, 1905. First American production at the Academy of Music, November 13, 1896, with Durot, Ughetto and Bonaplata-Bau. Revived in 1908 by Oscar Hammerstein's Manhattan Opera Company, the cast including Mme. Eva Campanini, Bassi, Sammarco, Zeppili and de Cisneros.

GIORDANO

Characters

ANDREA CHENIER	Tenor
CHARLES GERARD	Baritone
COUNTESS DE COIGNY	Soprano
MADELEINE, her daughter	Soprano
BERSI, her maid	Mezzo-Soprano
ROUCHER	Bass
MATHIEU	Baritone
MADELON	Soprano
FLEVILLE	Tenor
THE ABBE	Tenor
SCHMIDT, jailer at St. Lazare	Bass
A SPY	

Ladies, Gentlemen, Servants, Pages, Peasants, Republican Soldiers, Masqueraders, Judges, Jurymen, Prisoners, etc.

Time and Place: Paris; during the French Revolution.

The story tells of *Andrea Chenier,* a patriot, poet and dreamer, who was born in Constantinople, coming to Paris for his education. The French Revolution was in full swing, and being a worshipper of liberty and a hater of monarchs, he took vigorous sides, and was arrested, imprisoned and finally guillotined on July 25, 1794. Illica's plot, however, is almost wholly pure fiction.

ACT I

SCENE—Hall in the Castle of Coigny

As the curtain rises the servants of the castle are preparing for a ball, and among them is *Gerard,* afterward to become the leader of the Revolution. As his old father enters, bent under the weight of a load of furniture, the young man wistfully sings the *Son sessant' anni :*

Son sessant' anni (My Aged Father)

By Ernesto Badini, Baritone   (*In Italian*) *45012   10-inch, $1.00

The guests arrive, including *Andrea Chenier,* the young poet, and during the festivities *Madeleine* coquettishly asks *Chenier* to improvise upon the theme of love.

*Double-Faced Record—See page 29.

28

Improvviso—Un di all' azzurro spazio   (Once O'er the Azure Fields)

By Enrico Caruso, Tenor   (*In Italian*)   88060   12-inch, $3.00

In this air *Chenier* sharply criticises the aristocracy, and speaks of the pride of the rich and its effect upon the poor.   The guests are displeased at his lack of taste, and later, when *Gerard* appears with a crowd of ragged men and women, *Chenier* supports him and goes with the party when it is ordered from the castle

ACT II

SCENE—*A Café on the Seine, Paris.   Five years later*

Bersi and a spy are dining at one of the tables, while at another table nearby is *Andrea*. *Roucher* enters and tells the young man that he is in danger and is being watched, giving him a pass which will enable him to escape in case of necessity.   *Andrea*, however, tells *Roucher* that he has a rendezvous that evening with an unknown lady, and the latter begs him not to go.   *Bersi* goes into the café with the spy, but presently returning, mingles with the crowd and speaks to *Chenier*, begging him to await a lady whom she calls *Speranza*.

As darkness falls *Madeleine* appears and is recognized by both *Chenier* and the spy, who is concealed and watching from a distance.   He hurries away to report to *Gerard*, and the young girl begs *Chenier* to save her from *Gerard*.   They avow their love and are about to fly together when *Gerard* intercepts them and tries to drag *Madeleine* away, but *Roucher* interferes and escorts the girl to her home, while *Chenier* and *Gerard* draw their swords. *Gerard* is wounded, and warns *Chenier* that he is proscribed and begs him to save *Madeleine*. *Chenier* flees and the mob surrounds the wounded *Gerard*, while he declares his assailant is unknown to him.

ACT III

SCENE—*At the Tribunal*

At a meeting of the people at which *Gerard* is spokesman, a spy enters and tells him that *Chenier* has been arrested and that *Madeleine* is not far away.   The spy urges him to denounce *Chenier*, and after much hesitation he consents to draw up the necessary papers. He signs them and hands them to the spy, when *Madeleine* appears and offers herself in exchange for *Andrea's* life.   *Gerard* is touched by the young girl's grief and promises to do what he can.

Andrea is brought before the judges and jury and denounced as a traitor, whereupon he speaks with deep feeling and defends himself with brilliancy.

Si, fui soldato (I Was a Soldier)

By Egidio Cunego, Tenor (*Double-Faced—See below*) (*Italian*)   45012   10-inch, $1.00

Gerard, regretting that he has signed the papers which condemned *Andrea*, rushes forward and testifies for him, but the people demand more victims, insisting upon the death sentence, and the prisoner is led away.

ACT IV

SCENE—*The Prison of St. Lazare*

Andrea is in his cell, writing verses by the light of a lamp.   *Madeleine* succeeds in getting into the prison by impersonating a recently pardoned prisoner, and by bribing his jailer.   *Gerard* conducts her to *Andrea* and then goes for a last appeal to Robespierre.   The lovers cling to each other in a last embrace, and at dawn, when the death wagon comes for *Andrea*, *Madeleine* goes to the guillotine to die with him.

DOUBLE-FACED ANDREA CHENIER RECORDS

Son sessant' anni (My Aged Father)   By Ernesto Badini, Baritone   (*In Italian*)
Si fui soldato (I Was a Soldier)   By Egidio Cunego, Tenor   (*In Italian*)   45012   10-inch, $1.00

SETTING OF ACT I, SCENE I, AT LA SCALA

(Italian)

IL BARBIERE DI SIVIGLIA

(Eel Bahr-beay'-reh dee See-veel'-yah)

(English)

BARBER OF SEVILLE

COMIC OPERA IN TWO ACTS

Text by Sterbini, a Roman poet; founded on the celebrated trilogy of Beaumarchais. Music by Rossini. First presented at the Argentina Theatre in Rome, February 5, 1816. The opera was at first called "Almaviva, or the Useless Precaution," to distinguish it from Paisiello's "Barber of Seville." First London production March 10, 1818. At Paris, in Italian, 1819; in French, 1824. First production in Germany at Brunswick, October 30, 1820. Produced at Vienna, December 16, 1820; Berlin, June 18, 1822. First New York production November 29, 1825, by Manuel Garcia and his company; sung at the New Orleans Opera, March 9, 1828. Many notable revivals have occurred in America of recent years—for Melba, who made her first American appearance as *Rosina*, January 28, 1898; for Sembrich, who made her farewell operatic appearance in this work; in 1908 by Oscar Hammerstein, for Tetrazzini; and the New Theatre production with Lipkowska.

Cast

COUNT ALMAVIVA (*Ahl-mah-vee'-vah*)..................................Tenor
BARTOLO, (*Bahr'-toh-loh*) physician ....Bass
ROSINA, his ward ....Soprano
BASILIO, (*Bah-seel'-yoh*) music master................................Bass
MARCELLINE (*Mar-chel-lee'-neh*)...............................Soprano
FIGARO (*Fee'-gah-roh*)...Baritone
FIORELLO, servant to the Count.....................................Tenor
A Notary, Chorus of Musicians, Chorus of Soldiers

Scene and Period: Seville, the seventeenth century.

Rossini's opera is a marvel of rapid composition, having been written in about fifteen days! This seems almost incredible, but the fact is well authenticated. The composer had agreed to write two operas for the Roman carnival of 1816, the first of which was produced December 26, 1815, and on that day he was told that the second would be required on January 20, 1816.

He agreed to have it completed, although he did not even know what the subject was! The libretto was given to him by Sterbini in sections, and he wrote the music as fast as the verses were furnished. While the opera did not achieve an instantaneous success, it gradually found favor with opera-lovers on account of its brightness and the manner in which the humor of its action is reflected in the music.

The plot of *Barber of Seville* is very simple. The *Count Almaviva* loves *Rosina*, the ward of *Dr. Bartolo*, a crusty old bachelor who secretly wishes to wed her himself. *Almaviva* persuades the village barber, *Figaro*, to arrange a meeting for him, and gains entrance to the house disguised as a dragoon, but is arrested by the guardian.

Not discouraged, he returns, pretending to be a substitute for *Rosina's* music teacher, who, he says, is ill. The appearance of the real *Don Basilio* spoils the plan, and the Count retreats for the second time, having, however, arranged a plan for elopement.

Bartolo finally arouses *Rosina's* jealousy by pretending that the Count loves another, and she promises to forget him and marry her guardian. When the time for the elopement arrives she meets the Count, intending to reproach him, but he convinces her of the treachery of *Bartolo*, and the lovers are wedded by a notary, just as *Bartolo* arrives with officers to arrest the Count.

Overture to Barber of Seville
By La Scala Orchestra, Milan   *68010   12-inch, $1.25

ACT I
SCENE I—*A Street in Seville. Day is Breaking*

The Count, accompanied by his servant *Fiorello* and several musicians, enters to serenade the beautiful *Rosina*. Accompanied by the mandolins, he sings his serenade, *Ecco ridente*, considered one of the most beautiful numbers in the opera.

Ecco ridente (Dawn, With Her Rosy Mantle)
By Fernando de Lucia, Tenor *(Piano acc.)*   *(In Italian)*   76000   12-inch, $2.00

COUNT:
Lo! smiling in the Orient sky,
Morn in her beauty breaking,
Canst thou, my love, inactive lie—
My life, art thou not waking?
Arise, my heart's own treasure,
All that my soul holds dear;
Oh! turn my grief to pleasure!
Awake, my love, appear!

But, hush!—methinks I view that face,
And all my doubts are vanished;
Thine eyes diffuse soft pity's grace.
And all my fears are banished.
Oh, rapturous moment of delight!
All other blisses shaming;
My soul's content, so pure and bright,
On earth no equal claiming!

Even such a lovely serenade as this fails to bring a response from the window, but the Count still lingers, concealing himself in the shadow as he sees *Figaro*, the jack-of-all-trades of the village and general factotum in the house of *Bartolo*. *Figaro* unslings his guitar and sings that gayest and most difficult of all airs, the joy or despair of baritones the world over, which has been recorded for the Victor by three famous singers.

Largo al factotum (Room for the Factotum)

By Pasquale Amato, Baritone
     (In Italian)   88329   12-inch, $3.00
By Emilio de Gogorza, Baritone
     (In Italian)   88181   12-inch, 3.00
By Titta Ruffo, Baritone
     (In Italian)   88391   12-inch, 3.00

Figaro is thoroughly satisfied with himself, and gives a long list of his numerous accomplishments, of which the following is a sample:

FIGARO: Room for the city's factotum here,
La, la, la, la, la.
I must be off to my shop, for the dawn is near.
La, la, la, la, la, la.
What a merry life, what pleasure gay,
Awaits a barber of quality.
Ah, brave Figaro; bravo, bravissimo, brave.
La, la, la, la, la, la.
Of men, the happiest, sure, art thou, bravo.
La, la, la, la, la, la, etc.

COPY'T DUPONT
CAMPANARI AS FIGARO

* *Double-Faced Record—See page 37.*

31

"Oh! what a happy life," soliloquizes the gay barber, "what pleasure awaits a barber of quality!"—Oh, bravo, Figaro, bravo, bravissimo: thou art sure the happiest of men, ready at all hours of the night, and, by day, perpetually in bustle and motion. What happier region of delight; what nobler life for a barber than mine! Razors, combs, lancets, scissors—behold them all at my command! besides the snug perquisites of the business, with gay damsels and cavaliers. All call me! all want me!—dames and maidens—old and young. My peruke! cries one—my beard! shouts another—bleed me! cries this—my billetdoux! whispers that. Figaro, Figaro! heavens, what a crowd. Figaro, Figaro! heavens, what a tumult! One at a time, for mercy sake! Figaro here: Figaro there: Figaro above: Figaro below. I am all activity: I am quick as lightning; in a word—I am the factotum of the town. Oh, what a happy life! but little fatigue—abundant amusement—with a pocket that can always boast a doubloon, the noble fruit of my reputation. So it is: without Figaro there's not a girl in Seville will marry; to me the little widows have recourse for a husband: I, under excuse of my comb by day, and under favor of my guitar by night, endeavor to please all in an honest way. Oh, what a life, what a life!"

Three fine records of this great air are given here. Ruffo, in his rendition, proves himself possessed of an admirable sense of humor, and this, with his powerful and flexible voice, enables him to attack this difficult solo in the true opéra-bouffe vein. The result is as fine a performance of the *Largo* as one would wish to hear. The extreme difficulties are made a vehicle for the display of the baritone's ample vocal resources, which sweep everything before them; he is indeed a little free with the text, and sings snatches of the accompaniment out of sheer bravado, while bits of comic characterization peep out at every available opportunity. Amato's rendition is a fine example of how the music of this air should be sung, and is a veritable triumph for the singer.

Signor de Gogorza's version differs from the others in many respects. It is one of the finest records he has made for the Victor, and exhibits his splendid voice and wonderful execution to perfection.

The Count now accosts *Figaro,* asking him to arrange a meeting with *Rosina,* telling him that his rank must not be known and that he has assumed the name of *Lindor.*

COPY'T MISHKIN

HEMPEL AS ROSINA

PHOTO CAMINAOA

RUFFO AS THE BARBER

Il mio nome? (My Name?)

By Fernando de Lucia, Tenor   (Piano acc.)   (In Italian) 66000 10-inch $1.50

Figaro consents to become his ally. *Rosina* and her guardian come to the balcony, and *Rosina,* perceiving the Count, manages to drop a note, which he secures. *Bartolo* leaves the house and orders that no one be admitted.

Figaro now says that he is expecting a military friend to arrive in the village, and suggest the Count dress himself as this soldier and thus gain admittance to the house. He agrees, and retires to assume the disguise.

SCENE II—*A Room in Bartolo's House*

Rosina is discovered holding in her hand a letter from the Count. She is agitated and expresses her feelings in her celebrated entrance song, four records of which, by four celebrated singers are offered by the Victor.

Una voce poco fa (A Little Voice I Hear)

By Marcella Sembrich, Soprano	(In Italian)	88097	12-inch,	$3.00
By Luisa Tetrazzini, Soprano	(In Italian)	88301	12-inch,	3.00
By Maria Galvany, Soprano	(In Italian)	87060	10-inch,	2.00
By Giuseppina Huguet, Soprano	(In Italian)	*68144	12-inch,	1.25

* *Double-Faced Record—See page 37.*

MELBA AS ROSINA

The number is in the form to which most Italian composers of the period adhered—a slow opening section (here accompanied by occasional chords for the orchestra) succeeded by a quicker movement culminating in a coda which presents many opportunities for brilliant vocal display. Musically the aria is full of charm, and is deservedly popular with those singers whose method enables them to deliver it with the requisite lightness and bravura.

> ROSINA: A little voice I heard just now:
> Oh, it has thrill'd my very heart!
> I feel that I am wounded sore;
> And Lindor 'twas who hurl'd the dart.
> Yes, Lindor, dearest, shall be mine!
> I've sworn it, and we'll never part.
>
> My guardian sure will ne'er consent;
> But I must sharpen all my wit:
> Content at last, he will relent,
> And we, oh, joy! be wedded yet.
> Yes, Lindor I have sworn to love!
> And, loving, we'll our cares forget.

A bewildering array of artists have essayed this charming song, and Victor audiences can choose whether they will have it sung by an Italian, Polish or Spanish prima donna.

Rosina runs out as her guardian and *Don Basilio* come in. *Bartolo* is telling *Basilio* that he wishes to marry his ward, either by love or force. *Basilio* promises to help him, and says that the Count is trying to make *Rosina's* acquaintance. They decide to invent some story that will disgrace him. "A calumny!" says *Basilio*. *Bartolo* asks what that is, and *Basilio*, in a celebrated air, gives his famous description, which is a model of its kind.

La calunnia (Slander's Whisper)
By Marcel Journet, Bass

(In Italian) 74104 12-inch, $1.50

> BASILIO: Oh! calumny is like the sigh
> Of gentlest zephyrs breathing by;
> How softly sweet along the ground,
> Its first still voice is heard around.
> So soft, that sighing amid the bowers
> It scarcely fans the drooping flowers.
> Thus will the voice of calumny,
> More subtle than the plaintive sigh,
> In many a serpent-wreathing find
> Its secret passage to the mind;
> The heart's most inmost feelings gain,
> Bedim the sense, and fire the brain.
> Then passing on from tongue to tongue,
> It gains new strength, it sweeps along
> In giddier whirl from place to place,
> And gains fresh vigor in its race;
> Till, like the sounds of tempests deep,
> That thro' the woods in murmurs sweep
> And howl amid their caverns drear,
> It shakes the trembling soul with fear.
> Thus calumny, a simple breath,
> Engenders ruin, wreck and death;
> And sinks the wretched man forlorn,
> Beneath the lash of slander torn,
> The victim of the public scorn!
> *(They go out.)*

Rosina and *Figaro* return, and the barber tells her that her guardian is planning to marry her. She laughs at the idea, and then asks *Figaro* who the young man was she observed that morning. *Figaro* tells her his name is *Lindor*, and that he is madly in love with a certain young lady, whose name is *Rosina*.

Dunque io son (What! I?)
By Maria Galvany, Soprano, and Titta Ruffo, Baritone *(In Italian)* 92501 12-inch, $4.00

COPY'T DUPONT

SEMBRICH AS ROSINA

ROSINA:
What! I? or dost thou mock me?
Am I, then, the happy being?
(But I all the scheme foreseeing,
Knew it, sir, before yourself.)

FIGARO:
Yes, Lindor loves you, lady;
Oft he sighs for his Rosina,
(As a fox she cunning seems,
Ah, by my faith, she sees thro' all).

ROSINA:
Still one word, sir—to my Lindor
How shall I contrive to speak?

FIGARO:
Poor man, he but awaits some sign
Of your affection and assent;
A little note, a single line,
And he himself will soon present.
To this, what say you?

ROSINA:
I do not know.

FIGARO:
Take courage, pray you.

ROSINA:
I could not so—

FIGARO:
A few lines merely.

ROSINA:
I blush to write.

FIGARO:
At what? Why really—may I indite?
Haste, haste, your lover quick invite.
(*Going to the desk.*)

TETRAZZINI AS ROSINA

ROSINA:
A letter! Oh, here it is.
(*Calling him, she takes a note from her bosom,
which she gives him.*)

FIGARO (*astonished*):
Already written! What a fool

Was I to think to be her master!
Much fitter that she me should school:
Her wits, than mine, can flow much faster.
Oh, woman, woman, who can find,
Or fathom, all that's in thy mind?

(*Exit Figaro.*)

NIELSEN AS ROSINA

Bartolo comes in and accuses *Rosina* of dropping a note from the balcony, and when she denies it he shows her ink marks on her finger and calls attention to a cut pen and a missing sheet of paper. She says she wrapped up some sweetmeats to send to a girl friend, and cut the pen to design a flower for her embroidery. *Bartolo* then denounces her in another famous air:

Manca un foglio (Here's a Leaf Missing)

By Arcangelo Rossi, Bass

(*In Italian*) *68144 12-inch, $1.25

BARTOLO:
To a doctor of my rank,
These excuses, Signorina,
I advise another time
That you better should invent.
Why is the paper missing?
That I would wish to know.
Useless, ma'am, are all your airs—
Be still, nor interrupt me so.
Another time, sweet Signorina.

When the doctor quits his house
He will carefully provide
For the keeping you inside.
And poor innocent Rosina,
Disappointed then may pout:
In her room shall she be locked,
Till I choose to let her out.
(*He goes out in a rage, followed
by Rosina, who is laughing.*)

A loud knocking is heard at the street door—it is the Count in his soldier disguise. He pushes his way in, and insists that the commandant has ordered him to put up in *Bartolo's* house. A long scene follows, full of comedy, finally ending in the arrest of the Count, who, however, privately informs the officer who he is; and the astonished official salutes respectfully and takes his soldiers away. *Bartolo* is in such a rage that he can hardly speak, and the act ends with the famous quartet:

* *Double-Faced Record—See page 37.*

THE COUNT GIVES ROSINA A MUSIC LESSON

Guarda Don Bartolo
(Look at Don Bartolo)

By Giuseppina Huguet, Soprano; Antonio Pini-Corsi, Baritone; Gaetano Pini-Corsi, Tenor; Ernesto Badini, Baritone
*63171 10-inch, $0.75

ACT II

SCENE—*A Room in Bartolo's House*

Bartolo is discovered musing on the affair of the soldier, and as he has learned that no one in the regiment knows the man, he suspects that he was sent by the Count.

A knocking is heard and the Count is ushered in, dressed as a music master. He greets *Bartolo,* beginning the duet, *Pace e gioia.*

Pace e gioia (Heaven Send You Peace and Joy)

By Antonio Pini-Corsi, Baritone, and Emilio Perea, Tenor *(In Italian)*
*62105 10-inch, $0.75

COUNT:
Peace and happiness be with you!
BARTOLO:
A thousand thanks; don't trouble yourself.
COUNT:
Peace and happiness for thousands of years.
BARTOLO:
Upon my word, I am obliged to you.

COUNT:
Peace and happiness, happiness and peace!
BARTOLO:
Enough—heavens! what an annoyance!
COUNT (*aside*):
The old fellow knows me not. How fortunate for me! Within a few moments I shall freely converse with my beloved.

Bartolo says he is much obliged for these kind wishes and wonders who this can be. The Count explains that *Don Basilio* is ill and he has come in the music master's place to give *Rosina* a lesson. He shows *Bartolo* the note *Rosina* had written, saying he found it at the inn, and offers to make *Rosina* believe the Count has shown her note to another lady. *Bartolo* is pleased with the idea and calls *Rosina.* Then occurs the celebrated "Lesson Scene" in which *Rosina* usually interpolates an air. Rossini wrote a trio for this scene, but in some manner it was lost.

Figaro now comes in to shave *Bartolo,* and in the course of the scene contrives to secure the key to the balcony. At this moment all are petrified at the entrance of *Don Basilio,* who is supposed to be confined to his bed. *Figaro* sees that quick action is necessary and asks him what he means by coming out with such a fever. "Fever?" says the astonished music master. "A raging fever," exclaims *Figaro,* feeling his pulse. "You need medicine," says the Count, meaningly, and slips a fat purse in his hand. *Don Basilio* partially comprehends the situation, looks at the purse and departs.

The shaving is renewed, and *Rosina* and the Count pretend to continue the lesson, but are really planning the elopement. *Bartolo* tries to watch them, but *Figaro* manages to get soap in the Doctor's eye at each of his efforts to rise. He finally jumps up and denounces the Count as an impostor. The three conspirators laugh at him, and go out, followed by *Bartolo,* who is purple with rage.

Bertha, the housekeeper, enters, and in her air, *Il vecchietto,* complains that she can no longer stand the turmoil, quarreling and scolding in this house.

* *Double-Faced Record—See page 37.*

THE SHAVING SCENE

Il vecchietto cerca moglie (The Old Fool Seeks a Wife)
By Emma Zaccaria
(*In Italian*) *62105 10-inch, $0.75

"What kind of thing is this love which drives everybody crazy?" she asks. This air used to be called in Rome *Aria di sorbetto* (sherbet), because the audience used to eat ices while it was being sung!

BERTHA: There is always noise and clamor in this house! There is nothing but disputing, weeping and threatening. There is not a single hour of peace with this old, avaricious wrangler! Oh! what a house of confusion! The little old man seeks a wife; the girl sighs for a husband; the one is all eagerness, the other a dotard. Neither of them should be suffered to go loose; but what can this love be that makes everyone go mad? It is a universal evil, a fury, a thing that tickles, that pesters, that torments! Unhappy that I am, I also feel it, and know not what remedy to seek. Ah, cursed old age! I am despised by all; and furious and desperate, I feel ready to die with chagrin.

Don Bartolo now desperately plays his last card, and shows *Rosina* the note, saying that her lover is conspiring to give her up to the *Count Almaviva*. *Rosina* is furious and offers to marry *Bartolo* at once, telling him that he can have *Lindor* and *Figaro* arrested when they arrive for the elopement. *Bartolo* goes after the police, and he is barely out of sight when *Figaro* and the Count enter by means of the key which the barber had secured. *Rosina* greets them with a storm of reproaches, accusing *Lindor* of pretending to love her in order to sacrifice her to the vile *Count Almaviva*. The Count reveals himself and the lovers are soon clasped in a fond embrace, with *Figaro* in a "Bless you, my children," attitude.

Don Basilio, who had been sent for a notary by *Bartolo,* now arrives. The Count demands that the notary shall wed him to *Rosina*. *Basilio* protests, but the sight of a pistol in the Count's hand soon silences him.

SAMMARCO AS FIGARO

* Double-Faced Record—See page 37.

BARTOLO ARRIVES WITH THE SOLDIERS—FINALE, ACT II

This scene is rudely interrupted by the arrival of *Bartolo* and the soldiers. The officer in charge demands the name of the Count, who now introduces *Signor and Signora Almaviva* to the company. *Bartolo* philosophically decides to make the best of the matter. However, he inquires of *Basilio* :

BARTOLO:
But you, you rascal—
Even you to betray me!

BASILIO:
Ah! Doctor,
The Count has certain persuasives
And certain arguments in his pocket,
Which there is no withstanding!

BARTOLO:
Ay, ay! I understand you.
Well, well, what matters it?
Go; and may Heaven bless you!

FIGARO:
Bravo, bravo, Doctor!
Let me embrace you!

ROSINA:
Oh, how happy we are!

COUNT:
Oh. propitious love!

FIGARO:
Young love, triumphant smiling,
All harsher thoughts exiling,
All quarrels reconciling,
Now waves his torch on high!

(Curtain)

DOUBLE-FACED BARBER OF SEVILLE RECORDS

Barber of Seville Selection	By Pryor's Band		
Prophete Fantasie	By Pryor's Band	35125	12-inch, $1.25
Overture	By La Scala Orchestra		
Don Pasquale—Sinfonia (Donizetti)	By La Scala Orchestra	68010	12-inch, 1.25
Manca un foglio (Here's a Leaf Out)	By A. Rossi, Bass		
Una voce poco fa	By Giuseppina Huguet, Soprano	68144	12-inch, 1.25
Guarda Don Bartolo (Look at Bartolo)	By Huguet,		
A. and G. Pini-Corsi, and Badini	(In Italian)		
Fra Diavolo—Agnese la Zietella By Pietro Lara	(In Italian)	63171	10-inch, .75
Il vecchietto cerca moglie By Emma Zaccaria	(In Italian)		
Pace e gioia By A. Pini-Corsi and Perea	(In Italian)	62105	10-inch, .75

(English)   (Bohemian)
BARTERED BRIDE   PRODANA NEVESTA
(German)
DIE VERKAUFTE BRAUT

COMIC OPERA IN THREE ACTS

Libretto by Sabina. Music by Friedrich Smetana. First performance, Prague, May 30, 1866, where the success of the work led to Smetana's appointment as director of the Prague opera. Produced at the Vienna Music Festival 1892, from which time its fame really dates, and it is now to be found in the repertoire of nearly every German opera house. First London production, Drury Lane, June 26, 1895, and at Covent Garden in 1907. First heard in America at the Metropolitan Opera House, New York, February 19, 1909, with Destinn, Jörn, Didur and Reiss, under the direction of Gustav Mahler.

When Director Schubert produced this work for the first time before a German-Austrian public in 1892, the surprise of the audience was great, and on all sides was heard: "How is it possible that such genius has not been recognized in Germany and Austria?"

SMETANA

Cast of Characters with Original American Cast

KRUSCHINA, a peasant.....................Baritone.......Robert Blass
KATHINKA, his wife.......................Soprano.....Marie Mattfeld
MARIE, their daughter....................Soprano.....Emmy Destinn
MICHA, a land owner.........................Bass..Adolf Muehlmann
AGNES, his wife....................Mezzo-Soprano.Henrietta Wakefield
WENZEL, their son........................Tenor.......Albert Reiss
HANS, MICHA'S son by first marriage..........Tenor........Carl Jörn
KEZAL, a marriage broker.......................Bass......Adam Didur

Smetana, a pupil of Liszt, composed altogether eight operas, besides a set of symphonic poems called "Mein Vaterland." For ten years prior to his death (1884) he was totally deaf, yet some of his best work was written during this period.

The *Bartered Bride* was intended by its composer to be typical of Bohemian life and character—to be a national opera, and so it really is. The work illustrates accurately Bohemian

MISHKIN

DESTINN AS MARIE

GORITZ AS KEZAL

village life, and is based on a simple story full of mirth and sometimes almost farcical.

Marie, daughter of *Kruschina*, a rich peasant, is betrothed to *Hans*, her father's servant. *Hans* and *Marie*, however, are threatened with separation because the maiden's father has determined she shall marry *Wenzel*, a half-witted, stuttering lad, who is the son of *Kruschina's* old friend, *Micha*. *Kruschina* and *Kezal* endeavor to arrange this marriage, but the girl flatly refuses to give up her old lover. *Kezal* finally offers *Hans* three hundred crowns if he will renounce *Marie*. At first the offer is indignantly rejected, but later *Hans* consents, insisting on a rather strange condition—that these words be inserted in the agreement, "that *Marie* shall only be married to a son of *Micha*." *Kezal*, although he does not understand the reason for this, gladly agrees, and shortly afterward the paper is signed, the entire village being called in to witness the signature.

Marie refuses to believe that her lover has sold her for three hundred crowns, but is compelled to realize the truth when the marriage broker produces *Hans'* receipt for the money. The young girl meets her ruthless lover, who seems remarkably joyous over the affair, and still declares his love for her. The mystery is not explained until *Micha* and his wife arrive and recognize *Hans* to be their long-lost eldest son. So *Hans* not only wins his bride, but gains 300 crowns, for *Kezal* has agreed that *Marie* "shall marry only a son of *Micha*." As the money remains in the family no one objects save *Kezal*, who departs in wrath.

The famous *Overture* to *Bartered Bride* is a work of delightful melody, and has had

SCENE IN THE ZOPPOTER WALDTHEATER PRODUCTION

numberless performances as a concert number. It is delightfully spontaneous and highly interesting, containing parts of the national airs of Bohemia.

{ Overture	By Arthur Pryor's Band }	35148	12-inch, $1.25
{ Madam Butterfly Selection (Puccini)	By Pryor's Band }		

INTERIOR OF METROPOLITAN OPERA HOUSE, NEW YORK

<table>
<tr><td>(French)</td><td>(English)</td></tr>
</table>

(French)

LA BOHÊME
(Lah Boh-ehm')

(English)

THE BOHEMIANS

OPERA IN FOUR ACTS

Text by Giacosa and Illica; music by Puccini; being an adaptation of part of Mürger's *La Vie Bohême,* which depicts life in the *Quartier Latin,* or the Students' Quarter, in 1830. First produced at the Teatro Reggio, Turin, February 1, 1896, under the direction of Toscanini. In English, as "The Bohemians," at Manchester (Carl Rosa Company), April 22, 1897, and at Covent Garden with the same company, October 2d of the same year. At the *Opéra Comique,* Paris, June, 1898. In Italian at Covent Garden, July 1, 1899. First production in the Americas at Buenos Ayres in 1896. First U. S. production at San Francisco, March, 1898, by the Royal Italian Opera Company, following their tour of Mexico. The company later sang the opera in New York, Wallack's Theatre, May 16, 1898. Given in English by the Castle Square Opera Company at the American Theatre, New York, November 20, 1898. The first important production in Italian was that given by Melba's Company in Philadelphia, December 29, 1898. Produced in 1907 at the Metropolitan, with Caruso, Sembrich and Scotti.

Characters

RUDOLPH, a poet...Tenor
MARCEL, a painter...Baritone
COLLINE, a philosopher......................................Bass
SCHAUNARD, a musician.......................................Baritone
BENOIT, an importunate landlord.............................Bass
ALCINDORO, a state councilor and follower of Musetta........Bass
MUSETTA, a grisette...Soprano
MIMI, a maker of embroidery.................................Soprano

Students, work-girls, citizens, shopkeepers, venders, soldiers, waiters, etc.

Scene and Period: Paris, about 1830.

COPY'T DUPONT

CAMPANARI AS MARCEL

THE STORY

The principal characters in Puccini's delightful opera are the inseparable quartet described by Mürger, who with equal cheerfulness defy the pangs of hunger and the landlord of their little garret. In the scenes of careless gaiety is interwoven a touch of pathos; and the music is in turn lively and tender, with a haunting sweetness that is most fascinating.

Rudolph, a poet; *Marcel,* a painter; *Colline,* a philosopher; and *Schaunard,* a musician, are four friends who occupy an attic in the *Quartier Latin,* where they live and work together. Improvident, reckless and careless, these happy-go-lucky Bohemians find a joy in merely living, being full of faith in themselves.

ACT I

SCENE—*A Garret in the Quartier Latin*

The opening scene shows the four friends without money or provisions, yet happy. *Marcel* is at work on a painting, "Passage of the Red Sea," and remarks, beginning a duet with *Rudolph,* that the passage of this supposedly torrid sea seems, owing to the lack of fuel in the studio, to be a very cold affair!

Questo mar rosso (This Red Sea)

By Gennaro de Tura and E. Badini   (*In Italian*)   88233   12-inch, $3.00

Rudolph says that in order to keep them from freezing he will sacrifice the bulky manuscript of his tragedy. *Marcel* holds the landlord at bay until *Schaunard* arrives with an unexpected store of eatables. Having dined and warmed themselves, *Marcel, Colline* and *Schaunard* go out, leaving *Rudolph* writing. A timid knock at the door reveals the presence of *Mimi,* a young girl who lives on the floor above. She has come to ask her neighbor for a light for the candle, which has gone out. They enter into conversation, and when *Mimi* artlessly asks *Rudolph* what his occupation is, he sings the lovely air usually termed the "Narrative."

Racconto di Rodolfo (Rudolph's Narrative)

By Enrico Caruso, Tenor
  (*In Italian*)   88002   12-in., $3.00
By Herman Jadlowker, Tenor
  (*In Italian*)   76023   12-in.,   2.00
By Giovanni Martinelli, Tenor
  (*In Italian*)   74381   12-in.,   1.50
By John McCormack, Tenor
  (*In Italian*)   74222   12-in.,   1.50
By Florencio Constantino, Tenor
  (*In Italian*)   74106   12-in.,   1.50
By Evan Williams (*Eng.*) 74129   12-in.,   1.50

THE FOUR BOHEMIANS

Puccini has never written a more interesting air than this narrative. It is one of the great numbers of the opera, and always arouses an audience to a high pitch of enthusiasm. The tender sympathy of the opening—"Your little hand is cold"; the bold avowal—"I am a poet"; the glorious beauty of the love motive at the end—and the final brilliant high note, are all extremely effective.

CARUSO AS RUDOLPH

Mi chiamano Mimi (My Name is Mimi)

By Nellie Melba, Soprano
(*In Italian*) 88074 12-in., $3.00

By Lucrezia Bori, Soprano
(*In Italian*) 88475 12-in., 3.00

By Geraldine Farrar, Soprano
(*In Italian*) 88413 12-in., 3.00

By Alice Nielsen, Soprano
(*In Italian*) 74062 12-in., 1.50

Then follows the charming *Mi chiamano Mimi*, in which the young girl tells *Rudolph* of her pitifully simple life; of how she works all day making artificial flowers, which remind her of the blossoms and green meadows of the country; of the lonely existence she leads in her chamber up among the housetops.

O soave fanciulla—Duo and Finale, Act I (Thou Sweetest Maiden)

By Nellie Melba, Soprano, and Enrico Caruso, Tenor 95200 12-inch, $5.00

By Lucrezia Bori and John McCormack
(*In Italian*) 87512 10-inch, 2.00

"*Mimi's delicate perfection enchanted the young poet—especially her little hands, which in spite of her menial work, she managed to keep as white as snow.*"—Mürger's La Vie de la Bohême.

This lovely duet occurs just after the *Mi chiamano Mimi*. The young girl having finished her story, *Rudolph* hears the shouts of his friends in the courtyard below. He opens the window to speak to them, letting in a flood of moonlight which brightens the room. The Bohemians go off singing. As *Rudolph* turns to *Mimi* and sees her in the moonlight, he is struck with her beauty, and tells her how entrancing she appears to him.

SEMBRICH AS MIMI

Love awakens in the heart of the lonely girl, and in this beautiful duet she pledges her faith to the handsome stranger who has come into her life. The lovely motive with which the duet begins is associated throughout the opera with the presence of *Mimi*, and is employed with touching effect in the death scene in Act III.

Mimi consents to go to the *Café Momus*, where his friends are to dine, and after a tender scene at the door they go out, and the curtain slowly falls.

GILLY AS MARCEL

ACT II

SCENE—*A Students' Café in Paris*

This act represents the terraces of the *Café Momus*, where the artists are holding a carnival. Puccini has pictured with masterly skill the noisy, bustling activity of this scene, and the boisterous merriment of the gay revelers. The Bohemians of Act I are seated at a table with *Mimi*, when *Musetta*, an old flame of *Marcel's*, appears

COPY'T DUPONT
FARRAR AS MIMI

with her latest conquest, a foolish and ancient beau named *Alcindoro.* *Marcel* pretends not to see her, but *Musetta* is determined on a reconciliation, and soon gets rid of her elderly admirer and joins her old friends.

The gem of this gay scene is the charming waltz of *Musetta,* which Mme. Viafora sings here with spirit and delightful abandon.

Musetta Waltz

By Gina C. Viafora, Soprano
(*Italian*) 64085 10-inch, $1.00
By Guido Gialdini (*Whistling*)
*16892 10-inch, .75

The fun now becomes fast and furious, and *Musetta* is finally carried off on the shoulders of her friends, while the foolish old banker, *Alcindoro,* is left to pay the bills of the entire party.

ACT III

SCENE—*A City Gate of Paris*

This act begins in the cheerless dawn of a cold morning at the city gates, the bleakness of the scene being well expressed in Puccini's music. The snow falls, workmen come and go, shivering and blowing on their cold fingers. *Mimi* appears, and asks the

COPY'T MISHKIN
GLUCK AS MIMI

officer at the gate if he will find *Marcel*—that good and kind-hearted Bohemian painter being now located at the inn on the Orleans Road and painting, not landscapes, but tavern signs, in order to keep body and soul together. *Marcel* enters and is surprised to see *Mimi,* whom he supposes to be in Paris. Noticing that she is melancholy and apparently ill, he kindly questions her and learns her sad story.

Mimi, Io son! (Mimi, Thou Here!)

By Geraldine Farrar, Soprano, and
Antonio Scotti, Baritone
(*In Italian*) 89016 12-inch, $4.00
By Dora Domar, Soprano, and Ernesto
Badini, Baritone 88228 12-inch, 3.00

Mimi tells her friend that she can no longer bear the jealous quarrels with *Rudolph,* and that they must separate. *Marcel,* much troubled, goes into the inn to summon *Rudolph,* but before the latter comes, *Mimi* secretes herself, and when he enters she hears him again accuse her of fickleness.

Mimì è una civetta (Cold-hearted Mimi!)

By Laura Mellerio, Soprano; Gennaro
de Tura, Tenor; and Ernesto Badini, Baritone
(*In Italian*) 88227 12-inch, $3.00

A distressing fit of coughing reveals her presence, and she appears and sings the sad little air which is one of the features of this act.

PHOTO BERT
FARRAR AND SCOTTI AS MIMI AND MARCEL
(ACT III)

* Double-Faced Record—See page 47.

44

THE SCENE OF THE BARRIER—ACT III

Addio (Farewell)

By Nellie Melba,
Soprano (*Italian*)
88072 12-in., $3.00
By Geraldine Farrar,
Soprano (*Italian*)
88406 12-in., 3.00
By Alma Gluck,
Soprano (*Italian*)
64225 10-in., 1.00

Most pathetically does the poor girl's "Farewell, may you be happy" come from her simple heart, and she turns to go. *Rudolph* protests, something of his old affection having returned at the sight of her pale cheeks.

Musetta now enters and is accused by *Marcel* of flirting. A furious quarrel follows, which contrasts strongly with the tender passages between *Mimi* and *Rudolph* as the lovers are partially reconciled.

Quartet, "Addio, dolce svegliare" (Farewell, Sweet Love)

By Geraldine Farrar, Gina C. Viafora, Enrico Caruso and Antonio
Scotti   (*In Italian*) 96002 12-inch, $6.00
By Dora Domar, Annita Santoro, Gino Giovannelli and Ernesto
Badini   (*In Italian*) 89048 12-inch, 4.00

THE QUARTET—ACT II

Like the Rigoletto Quartet, this number is used by the composer to express many different emotions: The sadness of *Mimi's* farewell to *Rudolph;* his tender efforts to induce her to remain; the fond recollections of the bright days of their first meeting—and contrasted to these sentiments is the quarreling of *Musetta* and *Marcel,* which Puccini has skillfully interwoven with the pathetic passages sung by the lovers.

Two brilliantly sung and perfectly balanced renditions of this great concerted number are offered to music lovers by the Victor.

ACT IV
SCENE—*Same as Act I*

"At this time, the friends for many weeks had lived a lonely and melancholy existence. Musetta had made no sign, and Marcel had never met her, while no word of Mimi came to Rudolph, though he often repeated her name to himself. Marcel treasured a little bunch of ribbons which had been left behind by Musetta, and when one day he detected Rudolph gazing fondly at the pink bonnet Mimi had forgotten, he muttered: 'It seems I am not the only one!'"—Mürger.

Act IV shows the same garret in which the events of Act I took place. Bereft of their sweethearts, the young men are living sad and lonely lives, each trying to conceal from the other that he is secretly pining for the absent one.

In the opening scene, *Marcel* stands in front of his easel pretending to paint, while *Rudolph,* apparently writing, is really furtively gazing at *Mimi's* little pink bonnet.

SAMMARCO AS MARCEL

CONSTANTINO AS RUDOLPH

Ah Mimi, tu piu (Ah, Mimi, False One!)
By Enrico Caruso, Tenor, and Antonio Scotti, Baritone
(*In Italian*) 89006 12-inch, $4.00
By McCormack and Sammarco (*Italian*) 89044 12-inch, 4.00
By Da Gradi and Badini (*In Italian*) *45013 10-inch, 1.00
By Murphy and Werrenrath (*In Italian*) 60108 10-inch, .75

The friends, however, pretend to brighten up when *Schaunard* and *Colline* enter with materials for supper, and the four Bohemians make merry over their frugal fare. This scene of jollity is interrupted by the unexpected entrance of *Musetta,* who tells the friends that *Mimi,* abandoned by her viscount, has come back to die.

The poor girl is brought in and laid on *Rudolph's* bed, while he is distracted with grief. The friends hasten to aid her, *Marcel* going for a doctor, while *Colline,* in order to get money to buy delicacies for the sick girl, decides to pawn his only good garment, an overcoat. He bids farewell to the coat in a pathetic song, which Journet delivers here with much feeling.

THE DEATH OF MIMI

46

Vecchia zimarra (Coat Song)

By Marcel Journet *(In Italian)* 64035 10-inch, $1.00

Colline goes softly out, leaving *Mimi* and *Rudolph* alone, and they sing a beautiful duet.

Sono andati? (Are We Alone?)

By Maria Bronzoni, Soprano, and Franco de Gregorio, Tenor *(In Italian)* *45013 10-inch, $1.00

The past is all forgotten and the reunited lovers plan for a future which shall be free from jealousies and quarrels. Just as *Mimi,* in dreamy tones, recalls their first meeting in the garret, she is seized with a sudden faintness which alarms *Rudolph,* and he summons his friends, who are returning with delicacies for *Mimi.* But the young girl, weakened by disease and privations, passes away in the midst of her weeping friends, and the curtain falls to *Rudolph*'s despairing cry of "Mimi! Mimi!"

COPY'T MISHKIN

DE SEGUROLA AS MARCEL

DOUBLE-FACED AND MISCELLANEOUS BOHÊME RECORDS

Bohême Fantasie *'Cello* By Victor Sorlin		
Calm Sea and Happy Voyage—Overture	35132 12-in., $1.25	
By Pryor's Band		
Bohême Selection By Pryor's Band		
Jolly Robbers Overture (*Suppé*)	35077 12-in., 1.25	
By Pryor's Band		

Bohême Selection	By Pryor's Band	
Mimi's Aria, " My Name is Mimi," Act I—Duet, " Thou Sweetest Maiden," Act I	35353 12-inch, $1.25	
Madame Butterfly Fantasia *'Cello*	By Rosario Bourdon	
Ah, Mimi, tu più By Da Gradi and Badini *(In Italian)*	45013 10-inch, 1.00	
Sono andati? By Bronzoni and de Gregorio *(In Italian)*		
Musetta Waltz (*Whistling Solo*) Guido Gialdini	16892 10-inch, .75	
Carmen Selection *Xylophone* Wm. H. Reitz		

CIPOLLA'S PAINTING OF THE DEATH SCENE

* *Double-Faced Record—See above list.*

THE ABDUCTION OF ARLINE—ACT I

THE BOHEMIAN GIRL

OPERA IN THREE ACTS

Text by Bunn, who took his plot from a ballet written for Ellsler, the dancer, by Saint-Georges, but transferred the scene from Scotland to Hungary. Music by Balfe. First produced at Drury Lane Theatre, London, November 27, 1843, the cast including Harrison, Rainforth, Betts, Stretton and Borrani, and the opera had an unprecedented run of one hundred consecutive performances. An Italian version was brought out at Drury Lane, February 6, 1858. First American production November 25, 1844, with Frazer, Seguin, Pearson and Andrews. The work, after its English success, was eventually translated into almost every language of Europe, and during the next twenty years was produced in Italy as *La Zingara* (at Trieste, February 12, 1854); in Hamburg as *La Gitana*; in Vienna as *Die Zigeunerin*, where it was at one time played at three houses simultaneously; and in Paris as *La Bohémienne*. This French version, for which Balfe added several numbers, besides enlarging it to five acts, was written by Saint-Georges, and produced at the Théâtre Lyrique, Paris, December 30, 1869, gaining for the composer the Legion of Honor decoration.

Characters

ARLINE, daughter of Count Arnheim............................Soprano
THADDEUS, a Polish exile.......................................Tenor
GYPSY QUEEN..Contralto
DEVILSHOOF, Gypsy leader.......................................Bass
COUNT ARNHEIM, Governor of Presburg.........................Baritone
FLORESTINE, nephew of the Count................................Tenor

Retainers, Hunters, Soldiers, Gypsies, etc.

Time and Place: Presburg, Hungary; nineteenth century.

48

ACT I
SCENE—*Country Estate of Count Arnheim, near Presburg*

The story of this opera is quite familiar, and can be dismissed with a brief mention. *Thaddeus*, an exile from Poland, is fleeing from Austrian troops, and to facilitate his escape he casts his lot with a band of gypsies, headed by *Devilshoof*. As the tribe is crossing the estate of the Governor of Presburg, *Count Arnheim*, *Thaddeus* is enabled to rescue the little daughter of the Count from a wild stag, and in his gratitude the Count invites the gypsies to the hunting dinner. In the course of the festivities *Thaddeus* refuses to drink the health of the Emperor, and is about to be arrested when *Devilshoof* interferes and is himself confined in the Castle, while *Thaddeus* is permitted to go. *Devilshoof* climbs from a window and steals the little *Arline*, making his escape good by chopping down the bridge across the ravine as the soldiers pursue him.

ACT II
SCENE—*The Gypsy Camp in the Outskirts of Presburg*

Twelve years elapse and we see the camp of the gypsies, among whom *Arline* has grown to be a beautiful maiden of seventeen. *Thaddeus*, who has fallen in love with the young girl, now tells her of his affection, and in a melodious duet the lovers plight their troth. The *Gypsy Queen*, herself enamored of *Thaddeus*, is forced to unite him to *Arline*, but secretly plans vengeance. Her opportunity soon comes, as she contrives to have *Arline* accused of stealing a medallion from the young nephew of *Count Arnheim*, who has come to the fair at Presburg, near where the gypsies are camped. *Arline* is arrested and taken before the *Count*, who in the course of the examination recognizes her as his daughter, from the scar made in her childhood by the wild stag.

ACT III
SCENE—*Castle of Count Arnheim*

The third act shows *Arline* restored to her position, but still secretly pining for her gypsy lover. *Devilshoof* contrives to get *Thaddeus* into the castle and he secures an interview with *Arline*. They are interrupted, however, by the *Count's* approach, and *Thaddeus* hides in a closet as the guests arrive for a reception in honor of the newly-found heiress.

The *Queen*, still bent on revenge, now enters, and in a dramatic denunciation reveals the hiding place of *Thaddeus*. The *Count* asks for an explanation, and *Arline* declares she loves *Thaddeus* even more than her father. The *Count*, enraged, is about to attack *Thaddeus*, when the young man reveals his history and proves himself to be of noble blood. The *Count* then gives his consent and all ends happily.

Many of the most effective numbers from this pretty opera have been recorded by the Victor, besides the brilliant potpourri made by the Opera Company, which includes no less than seven of the most tuneful bits.

THE VENGEANCE OF THE QUEEN—ACT III

BOHEMIAN GIRL RECORDS

{Overture to Bohemian Girl { *La Czarine Mazurka* (Ganne)	Pryor's Band} *Pryor's Band*}	16287	10-inch,	$0.75
{I Dreamt I Dwelt in Marble Halls {Then You'll Remember Me	Elizabeth Wheeler} Harry Macdonough}	16398	10-inch,	.75
The Heart Bow'd Down	Clarence Whitehill	74407	12-inch,	1.50
{The Heart Bow'd Down Herbert Goddard (*Piano acc.*)} { *Good Bye, Sweetheart* Herbert Goddard}		16064	10-inch,	.75
{The Heart Bow'd Down { *Home to our Mountains*	Alan Turner} *Morgan and Macdonough*}	16407	10-inch,	.75
{Fair Land of Poland { *Rob Roy—Song of the Turnkey*	Reed Miller} *Wilfred Glenn*}	17383	10-inch,	.75
{Then You'll Remember Me { *I'll Sing Thee Songs of Araby* (Clay)	Frederic Freemantel} *Harry Macdonough*}	35048	12-inch,	1.25
Then You'll Remember Me	George Hamlin	74134	12-inch,	1.50
{Then You'll Remember Me {I Dreamt I Dwelt in Marble Halls	Harry Macdonough} Elizabeth Wheeler}	16398	10-inch,	.75
{Then You'll Remember Me { *Vilia Song*	Harry Macdonough} *Elizabeth Wheeler*}	35082	12-inch,	1.25
{Fantasia of Principal Airs Wm. H. Reitz (*Xylophone*)} { *Jig Medley* (*Rollinson*) *Pryor's Band*}		16505	10-inch,	.75
{Selection from Bohemian Girl { *Yelva Overture* (Reissiger)	Pryor's Band} *Pryor's Band*}	35081	12-inch,	1.25

Gems from Bohemian Girl

Part of Overture—Chorus, "In the Gypsy's Life"—Chorus, "Come with the Gypsy Bride"—Entr'act Waltz—Chorus, "Happy and Light"—"Then You'll Remember Me"—Finale, "Oh, What Full Delight"

By the Victor Light Opera Company   31761   12-inch, $1.00

PHOTO BYRON

THE CARNIVAL AT PRESBURG—ACT II

BORIS GODOUNOW
(Boh'-rees Goo'-doo-noh)
OPERA IN THREE ACTS

Text arranged by Moussorgsky, based on a historical drama by the famous Russian poet, Poushkin. Music by Modeste Moussorgsky. Portions of the opera were given at St. Petersburg in February, 1873, but the production of the work in its entirety was delayed until January 24, 1874. Produced at Moscow in 1889. In 1896 the orchestration was somewhat revised by the composer's friend, Rimsky-Korsakoff. Given at Paris in 1908 by a Russian opera company, with Chaliapine in the title rôle. First American production at the Metropolitan Opera House, New York, November 19, 1913, with the original costumes and scenery painted for the Paris production. First Philadelphia production, March 10, 1914, when Mme. Ober appeared for the first time in the rôle of *Marina*.

© MISHKIN   HOMER AS MARINA

Characters
(With the Cast of the First American Production)

BORIS GODOUNOW, Regent of Russia
....Adamo Didur
XENIA, his daughter........Leonora Sparkes
THEODORE, his son........ ......Anna Case
THE NURSE.................Maria Duchene
MARINA....................Louise Homer
CHOUISKY....................Angelo Bada
DIMITRI....................Paul Althouse
VARLAAM..............Andrea de Segurola
MISSAIL....................Pietro Audisio
TCHELKALOFF.........Vincenzo Reschiglian
PIMENN.......................Leon Rothier
A SIMPLETON.................Albert Reiss
A POLICE OFFICER...........Giulio Rossi
TWO JESUITS.........{Louis Kreidler
                    {Vincenzo Reschiglian

Time and Place: About 1600; on the border of Poland.

Moussorgsky's masterly opera is intensely Russian in character, and relates actual events in the history of Russia during the reign of the Czar Féodor, son of Ivan the Terrible, while Boris Godounow was acting regent. Moussorgsky has simplified Poushkin's text somewhat, and has written a prologue to precede the drama, which has scarcely anything in common with Poushkin's book.

Boris, the acting regent, has caused the murder of *Dimitri,* the younger brother of *Ivan the Terrible,* to whom the throne would have passed on *Ivan's* death, but he is remorseful for his act and has entered a monastery on the outskirts of Moscow. At the opening of the opera the people are urging him to declare himself *Czar.* In the second scene the guilty ruler overhears *Pimenn,* an old monk, relating to a young novice, *Gregory,* the story of the murder, which fires *Gregory's* imagination so that he escapes from the cell, flees to the Lithuanian border and declares himself to be *Dimitri,* whom he insists was never slain.

In the next scene *Boris* is in the Czar's private apartments in the royal palace, having yielded to the demands of the people and declared himself ruler. His daughter, *Xenia,* and

PHOTO BOYER & BERT

CHALIAPINE AS BORIS

51

OBER AS MARINA

her young brother are with him, but when *Chouisky*, his old accomplice, arrives, he sends the children away. *Chouisky* has brought alarming news—the people are revolting and an impostor, calling himself *Dimitri*, has appeared. *Boris*, overcome, is once more a prey to remorse.

In the next scene *Marina*, betrothed to the imposter *Dimitri* (*Gregory*), is urged by *Rangoni* to try to influence the young usurper to convert the heretics of Moscow. Failing to move the girl, he appeals to the pretended *Dimitri*, who is waiting in the garden for *Marina*. The young girl appears, and the scene closes with a love duet.

The scene now changes to the country, with the people in open revolt. Cries of "Death to *Boris*" can be heard, and the usurper passes through the forest, drawing the crowd with him. As the stage is emptied, the village idiot is left sitting alone in the falling snow, singing a heart-rending ditty on the hopeless condition of Russia.

We now see a hall in the imperial palace. *Chouisky* arrives and later *Boris*, haggard from the terrible visions that are haunting him. *Pimenn* enters and relates a miracle which has happened at the tomb of *Dimitri*. He tells how a blind man, commanded in a dream to appear at *Dimitri's* tomb, has his vision restored when he kneels at the grave. A cry of agony interrupts the old monk. It is *Boris*, who, feeling himself dying, asks for his son, and in a few moments expires, begging his son to rule wisely and always protect his sister, *Xenia*.

Moussorgsky's masterly opera has made one of the greatest successes in the history of the Metropolitan, and it is with pleasure that the Victor is able to present the beautiful duet in Act III by the same artists who appeared in the Metropolitan production. It is astonishing that so fine a work should have been neglected for nearly forty years—for *Boris* was produced in 1874—and the Western musical world, as one critic has aptly remarked, must have been "dozing." However, the Metropolitan has made amends somewhat by giving a magnificent presentation of Moussorgsky's opera, with a cast that could not be equaled anywhere in the world.

The duet occurs in the scene representing the garden of the castle of *Michek* in Poland. *Marina*, the beautiful daughter of *Michek*, spurred on by both love and ambition, urges *Dimitri* to conspire against the throne.

This lovely number is admirably given by these singers, Mme. Ober's dramatic but richly sympathetic contralto blending exquisitely with Mr. Althouse's pure tenor.

ALTHOUSE AS DIMITRI

Finale, Act III (Garden Scene)

By Margarete Ober, Contralto,
and Paul Althouse, Tenor
(*In Italian*) 76031 12-inch, $2.00

CARMEN'S DEFIANCE—ACT IV

CARMEN
(Kar'-men)

OPERA IN FOUR ACTS

Text by Meilhac and Halévy, founded on the novel of Prosper Mérimée. Music by Bizet. First production at the Opéra Comique, Paris, March 3, 1875. First London production June 22, 1878. First American production October 23, 1879, with Minnie Hauk. First New Orleans production, January 14, 1881, with Mmes. Ambre and Tournie. Some notable revivals in New York were in 1893, being Calvé's first appearance; in 1905 with Caruso; and the Hammerstein revivals of 1906, with Bressler-Gianoli, Dalmores, Gilibert, Trentini and Ancona, and in 1908 with Calvé. The supreme event of the recent brilliant Metropolitan season was the sumptuous revival with an "all-star" cast, including Farrar, Caruso, Alda and Amato.

Characters

DON JOSE, (*Don Ho-zay'*) a Brigadier.............................Tenor
ESCAMILLO, (*Es-ca-meel'-yoh*) a Toreador ....Bass
DANCAIRO, (*Dan-ky'-roh*) ⎱ Smugglers ⎰ ....Baritone
REMENDADO, (*Rem-en-dah'-doh*) ⎰ ⎱ ....Tenor
ZUNIGA, (*Tsoo-nee'-gah*) a Captain.................................Bass
MORALES, (*Moh-rah'-lez*) a Brigadier..............................Bass
MICAELA, (*Mih-kah-ay'-lah*) a Peasant Girl.......................Soprano
FRASQUITA, (*Frass-kee'-tah*) ⎱ Gypsies, friends of Carmen ⎰ .... Mezzo-Soprano
MERCEDES, (*Mer-chay'-deez*) ⎰ ⎱ .... Mezzo-Soprano
CARMEN, a Cigarette Girl, afterwards a Gypsy..................Soprano
An Innkeeper, Guide, Officers, Dragoons, Lads, Cigar Girls, Gypsies, Smugglers.

Scene and Period: Seville, Spain; about 1820.

CALVE AS CARMEN

BIZET

Georges Bizet was a native of Paris, where he was born on October 25, 1838. Like Gounod and Berlioz, he won the *Prix de Rome* (*Pree d' Roam'*); in this case in 1857, the year that his first opera, *Docteur Miracle,* was produced. Among other productions came *Les Pecheurs de Perles,* in 1863, an opera recently revived at Covent Garden with Mme. Tetrazzini as *Leila.* Carmen was produced in 1875, and this most Parisian of all operatic works was received at its production with a storm of abuse. It was immoral, it was Wagnerian—the latter at that time being a deadly sin in France! Nevertheless, the supreme merits of Carmen have won it a place among the two or three most popular operas in the modern repertory.

The talents of Bizet are shown by his remarkable lyric gifts; the power of writing short, compact and finished numbers, full of exquisite beauty and convincing style, at the same time handling dramatic scenes with the freedom demanded by modern opera. His music is more virile, concentrated and stimulating than perhaps any other French composer.

It was probably not a little owing to the hostile reception of this, his finest work, that its composer died three months later. The music Bizet has written, however, is likely long to survive him, and chief among the works into which he ungrudgingly poured his life's energy was Carmen.

THE PLOT

I

Carmen has its opening scene in a public square in Seville, showing at one side a guard-house, where *Jose,* a young brigadier, keeps guard. *Micaela,* a peasant girl whom he loved in his village home, comes hither to seek him with a message from his mother. As *Jose* appears, the girls stream out from the cigarette factory hard by, and with them their leading spirit in love and adventure, *Carmen,* the gypsy, reckless and bewitching. Heedless of the pressing throng of suitors, and attracted by the handsome young soldier, *Carmen* throws him a flower, leaving him dazed and bewildered at her beauty and the fascinating flash of her dark eyes. A moment later a stabbing affray with a rival factory girl leads to the gypsy's arrest, and she is placed in the care of *Jose* himself. A few more smiles and softly-spoken words from the fascinating *Carmen,* and he is persuaded to allow her to escape. There is a sudden struggle and confusion—the soldier lets go his hold—and the bird has flown!

II

Act II takes place in the tavern of *Lillas Pastia,* a resort of smugglers, gypsies and questionable characters generally. Here arrives *Escamillo,* the toreador, amid the acclamations of the crowd, and he, like the rest, offers his homage to *Carmen.* Meanwhile, the two smugglers, *Dancairo* and *Remendado,* have an expedition afoot and need *Carmen* to accompany them. But she is awaiting the return of the young soldier, who, as a punishment for allowing her to escape, had gone to prison, and she will not depart until she has seen him. The arrival of *Jose* leads to an ardent love scene between the two. *Carmen* dances her wild gypsy measures before him; yet, in the midst of all, he hears the regimental trumpets sounding the retreat. While *Carmen* bids him remain and join her, the honor of a soldier urges him to return. The arrival of his captain, who orders him back, decides *Jose.* He defies his officer, who is bound by the smugglers, and deserts his regiment for *Carmen.*

III

The next scene finds *Jose* with the smugglers in a rocky camp in the mountains. The career of a bandit, however, is one to which a soldier does not easily succumb. His distaste offends *Carmen,* who scornfully bids him return home, she also foreseeing, in gypsy fashion, with the cards, that they will end their careers tragically together. In the midst of this strained situation two visitors arrive: *Escamillo,* the toreador, who has also followed *Carmen;* and *Micaela,* with a message from *Jose's* dying mother. The soldier, frustrated in his attempt to kill *Escamillo,* cannot resist the girl's appeal and departs, promising to return later for his revenge.

IV

The final act takes place outside the *Plaza de Toros,* at Seville, the scene of *Escamillo's* triumphs in the ring. *Carmen* has returned here to witness the prowess of her new lover, and is informed by her friends that *Jose,* half crazed with jealousy, is watching, capable of desperate deeds. They soon meet, and the scene between the maddened soldier and the gypsy is a short one. The jealous *Jose* appeals to her to return to him, but she refuses with scorn, although she knows it means death. In a rage *Jose* stabs her, and thus the end comes swiftly, while within the arena the crowd is heard acclaiming the triumph of *Escamillo.*

Prelude (Overture)

By La Scala Orchestra	*68052	12-inch, $1.25
By La Scala Orchestra	*62617	10-inch, .75
By Victor Herbert's Orchestra (1st part only, preceded by First Intermezzo)	70067	12-inch, 1.25
By Victor Herbert's Orchestra (Last part—Andante—only, followed by Third Intermezzo)	70066	12-inch, 1.25

The Prelude to Carmen opens with a quick march in 2-4 time, of an exceedingly virile and fiery description, which is taken from the music preceding the bull-fight in the last act. Following this stimulating march comes the "Toreador's Song," leading to the march theme again. These two sections, complete in themselves, are now followed by a short *andante* in triple time indicating the tragic conclusion of the drama. Here, the appealing notes of the brass, heard beneath the tremolo of the strings, gives poignant expression to the pathos which lies in the jealous love of the forsaken *Jose,* and expresses the menace of the future death of *Carmen.* This movement breaks off on a sudden detached chord of the diminished seventh as the curtain rises.

ACT I

SCENE—*A Public Square in Seville*

The curtain rises on a street in Seville, gay with an animated throng. In the foreground are the military guard stationed in front of their quarters. The cigarette factory lies to the right, and a bridge across the river is seen in the background.

MAIRET   SETTING OF ACT I

Among the crowd which throngs the stage a young girl may be seen searching for a familiar face. It is *Micaela,* the maiden whom *Jose* has left behind in his native village. The soldiers accost her, and from them she learns of her lover's absence. She declines the invitation to remain, and departs hastily.

The cigarette girls now emerge from the factory, filling the air with the smoke of their cigarettes, and with them *Carmen,* who answers the salutations of her admirers among the men by singing the gay *Habanera.*

Habanera (Love is Like a Wood-bird)

By Jeanne Gerville-Réache, Contralto	(*In French*)	88278	12-inch,	$3.00
By Emma Calvé, Soprano	(*In French*)	88085	12-inch,	3.00
By Maria Gay, Mezzo-Soprano	(*In Italian*)	92059	12-inch,	3.00
By Geraldine Farrar, Soprano	(*In French*)	87210	10-inch,	2.00
By Sophie Braslau, Contralto	(*In French*)	64469	10-inch,	1.00

Though often attributed to Bizet, the air was not original with him, but was taken from Yradier's "*Album des Chansons Espagnoles.*" The refrain:

is a particularly fascinating portion of the number.

* *Double-Faced Record—See page 70.*

CARMEN SINGING "HABANERA"—ACT I

HABANERA.—"Love is Like a Wood-Bird Wild."

CARMEN:

Ah! love, thou art a wilful wild bird,
And none may hope thy wings to tame,
If it please thee to be a rebel,
Say, who can try and then reclaim?
Threats and prayers alike unheeding;
Oft ardent homage thou'lt refuse,
Whilst he who doth coldly slight thee,
Thou for thy master oft thou'lt choose.

Ah, love!
For love he is the lord of all,
And ne'er law's icy fetters will he wear,
If thou me lovest not, I love thee,
And if I love thee, now beware!
If thou me lovest not, beware!
But if I love you, if I love you, beware!
beware!

Several records of this charming air are offered—by Calvé, whose *Carmen* is universally accepted as one of the greatest of all impersonations of the rôle; by Gerville-Réache, whose *Carmen* is a fine character study on quite original lines; by Miss Farrar, the latest of famous *Carmens*, who has made one of the greatest successes of her career in the recent revival; and by Miss Braslau, the youngest of the Metropolitan contraltos.

The men invite *Carmen* to choose a new lover, and in reply she flings a flower in the face of the surprised *Jose* and laughingly departs.

Mia madre vedo ancor (My Mother)
By Fernando de Lucia, Tenor, and Giuseppina Huguet, Soprano (*In Italian*) 92052 12-inch, $3.00

Parle-moi de ma mere (Tell Me of My Mother) (*Same as above*)
By Lucy Marsh, Soprano, and John McCormack, Tenor (*In French*) 74345 12-inch, $1.50

Now *Micaela* returns, and finds the soldier she seeks. Her song tells of the message of greeting she brings *Jose* from his mother, and with it a kiss. The innocence of *Micaela* is here a foil to the riper attractions of the gypsy, and the music allotted to the maiden possesses the same simple charm; the conclusion of *Micaela's* air being a broad sustained melody of much beauty. *Jose* takes up the strain, as the memories of his old home crowd upon him, and the beautiful duet follows.

GAY AS CARMEN

CÉCILE THÉVENET
OPÉRA, PARIS

GERMAINE BAILAC
OPÉRA-COMIQUE

DELNA

DE NUOVINA

GALLI-MARIÉ
THE ORIGINAL CARMEN

DAVELLI
OPÉRA COMIQUE

MARIÉ DE L'ISLE

MÉRENTIÉ
OPÉRA, PARIS

ELENA SANZ

CHARLOTTE WYNS

BRESSLER-GIANOLI
OPÉRA COMIQUE

Some Famous Carmens of the Past

COPY'T DUPONT

CALVÉ AS CARMEN

JOSE: Ah! tell me of her—my mother.
MICAELA:
 Faithful messenger from her to thee,
 I bring a letter,
 And some money also;
 Because a dragoon has not too much.
 And, besides that—
JOSE: Something else?
MICAELA:
 Yes, I will tell you.
 What she has given, I will to thee render.
 Your mother with me from the chapel came,
 And then, lovingly, she kissed me.
 "My daughter," said she, "to the city go:
 When arrived in Seville,
 Thou wilt seek out Jose, my beloved son;
 Tell him that his mother,
 By night, by day, thinks of her Jose:
 For him she always prays and hopes,
 And pardons him, and loves him ever.
 And then this kiss, kind one,
 Thou wilt to him give for me."
JOSE: A kiss from my mother?
MICAELA: To her son.
 Jose, I give it to thee—as I promised.
 (*Micaela stands on tip-toe and kisses Jose—
 a true mother's kiss.—Jose is moved and
 regards Micaela tenderly.*)
JOSE:
 My home in yonder valley,
  My mother lov'd shall I e'er see?
 Ah fondly in my heart I cherish
  Mem'ries so dear yet to me.
MICAELA:
 That one sweet hope,
 'Twill strength and courage give thee.
 That yet again thou wilt thy home
 And thy dear mother once more see.

Micaela leaves him after a tender farewell, and *Jose* begins to read his mother's letter, but is interrupted by a commotion within the factory. *Carmen* has stabbed one of her companions, and is arrested and placed under the guard of *Don Jose.* The soldiers drive away the crowd, and *Carmen,* left alone with *Jose,* brings her powers of fascination to bear on the young soldier, partly to facilitate her escape, and partly because he has attracted her attention. Here she sings the *Seguidilla,* a form of Spanish country dance.

Seguidilla (Near the Walls of Seville)

 By Geraldine Farrar,
  Soprano (*In French*)
   88511 12-inch, $3.00
 By Maria Gay, Contralto (*In Italian*)
   91085 10-inch, 2.00
 By Margarete Matzenauer,
  Contralto (*In French*)
   87103 10-inch, 2.00

CARMEN AND ESCAMILLO AT THE INN—ACT II

The *Seguidilla* is one of Spain's most beloved dances, and its rhythm is most fascinating. Bizet has given us a brilliant example in this dainty number, which he has set to Michael Carre's words.

CARMEN (*airily*):
 Nigh to the walls of Sevilla,
 Soon at my friend Lillas Pastia
 I'll trip thro' the light Seguidilla,
 And I'll quaff Manzanilla,
 I'll go seek out my friend Lillas Pastia.

(*Plaintively, casting glances at Jose*):
 Yes, but alone one's joys are few,
 Our pleasures double, shared by two!
 So just to keep me company,
 My beau I'll take along with me!

THE INN OF PASTIA—ACT II

Although *Jose* says to himself that the girl is only amusing herself, and whiling away the time with her gypsy songs, the words which fall on his ear—of a meeting-place on the ramparts of Seville—of a soldier she loves—a common soldier, all these play upon the feelings of *Jose* and rouse in him a love for the changeful gypsy, who is fated to be the cause of his downfall.

He unties her hands, and when the soldiers are conducting her to prison she pushes *Jose*, who falls, and in the confusion she escapes.

{(a) **First Intermezzo** } By Victor Herbert's Orchestra   70067   12-inch, $1.25
{(b) **Prelude—1st Part** }

ACT II

SCENE—*A Tavern in the Suburbs of Seville*

The second act opens amid the Bohemian surroundings of the tavern of Lillas Pastia ; the wild tune with which the orchestra leads off depicting the freedom and gaiety with which the mixed characters here assembled are wont to take enjoyment and recreation.

Les tringles des sistres (Gypsy Song)

By Geraldine Farrar, Soprano
　　　　　(*In French*)   88512   12-inch, $3.00
By Emma Calvé, Soprano
　　　　　(*In French*)   88124   12-inch,   3.00

Carmen again leads them with her song, another lively gypsy tune, in the exulting refrain of which all join, a picture of reckless merriment resulting.

COPY'T DUPONT

CALVÉ SINGING THE GYPSY
SONG—ACT II

> Ah! when of gay guitars the sound
> On the air in cadence ringing,
> Quickly forth the gipsies springing,
> To dance a merry, mazy round.
> While tambourines the clang prolong,
> In rhythm with the music beating,
> And ev'ry voice is heard repeating
> The merry burthen of glad song.
> Tra la la la, etc.

But *Carmen* is thinking of the soldier who went to prison for her sake and who, now at liberty, will shortly be with her. Her musings are interrupted by the arrival of a procession in honor of *Escamillo,* whose appearance is followed by the famous "Toreador Song," the most popular of all Carmen numbers.

Cancion del Toreador (Toreador Song)

By Titta Ruffo, Baritone, and La Scala
   Chorus   (*In Italian*) 92065 12-inch, $3.00
By Emilio de Gogorza, Baritone, and New
   York Opera Chorus
         (*In French*) 88178 12-inch, 3.00
By Pasquale Amato, Baritone
         (*In Italian*) 88327 12-inch, 3.00
By Giuseppe Campanari, Baritone
         (*In Italian*) 85073 12-inch, 3.00
By Alan Turner, Baritone
         (*In English*) *16521 10-inch,   .75
By Francesco Cigada, Giuseppina Huguet,
   Inez Salvador and La Scala Chorus
         (*Italian*) *62618 10-inch,   .75

Note.—The Toreador Song also occurs in the records of the Prelude—See page 56.

DE LUSSAN AS CARMEN

After *Escamillo's* departure, *Carmen's* comrades invite her to depart upon a smuggling expedition, but she refuses to stir until she sees the soldier for whom she is waiting.

Jose's voice is now heard in the distance, and *Carmen* and her friends all look through the shutters.

FRASQUITA:
   What a handsome dragoon!
MERCEDES:
   Indeed a gallant fellow!
DANCAIRO:
   Faith, he would make a fine smuggler!
REMENDADO:
   Bid him join us.
CARMEN:
   No, he will refuse.
DANCAIRO:
   Come, you can tempt him.
CARMEN:
   Well, go; I will try.

Carmen pushes her companions from the room, and greeting *Jose* with joy, questions him about his two months in prison.

EMMY DESTINN AS CARMEN

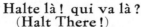

DALMORES AS DON JOSE

Halte là! qui va là?
(Halt There!)

By Geraldine Farrar, Soprano, and Giovanni Martinelli, Tenor
         (*In French*) 88536 12-inch, $3.00

Carmen then tries her fascinations on the stolid soldier to induce him to join the band of smugglers, and dances for him while he watches her with fascinated gaze. However, her efforts are useless, as he is reminded of his duty when he hears the bugle in the distance summoning him to quarters.

* *Double-Faced Records—See page 70.*

Au quartier pour l'appel (To Your Quarters?)

By Geraldine Farrar and Giovanni Martinelli (*French*) 88532 12-inch, $3.00

"Then go, I hate you!" says *Carmen,* and mocks him, singing

Ah, this is too mortifying!
All to please you, sir, I gaily sang and danced.
(*Aside.*) But now ta ra ta! he hears the trumpet call!
And off he flies, like a guest to a feast!

She is furious, and pitches at him his cap and sabre, and bids him begone.

(French)   (Italian)   (English)

Air de la fleur—Romanza del fiore—Flower Song

By Enrico Caruso, Tenor
  (*In French*) 88208 12-inch, $3.00
By Enrico Caruso, Tenor
  (*In Italian*) 88209 12-inch, 3.00
By Charles Dalmores, Tenor
  (*In French*) 85122 12-inch, 3.00
By Herman Jadlowker, Tenor
  (*In French*) 76027 12-inch, 2.00
By Fernando de Lucia, Tenor
  (*In Italian*) 76001 12-inch, 2.00
By Evan Williams, Tenor
  (*In English*) 74122 12-inch, 1.50
By John McCormack, Tenor
  (*In Italian*) 74218 12-inch, 1.50

Desperate at the thought of losing her forever, *Don Jose* shows her the flowers she threw him at their first meeting, and which he had preserved, then sings this lovely romance, beginning:

BRESSLER-GIANOLI AS CARMEN

Andantino. (♩ = 69.)
p con amore.

La fleur que tu ma-vais je - te - e Dans ma pri - son m'e-tait res - té - e
This flow'r you gave to me, de - grad - ed 'Mid pri - son walls I've kept tho' fad - ed

The struggle between love and duty which has been distracting the unfortunate lover is now seemingly forgotten, and he pours out his heart in this romanza, telling only of his great passion for the beautiful but heartless gypsy.

DON JOSE:
This flower you gave to me, degraded
'Mid prison walls, I've kept, tho' faded;
Tho' withered quite, the tender bloom
Doth yet retain its sweet perfume.
Night and day in darkness abiding,
I the truth, Carmen, am confiding;
Its loved odor did I inhale,
And wildly called thee without avail.
My love itself I cursed and hated,
* * * * * * * * * * *
Then alone myself I detested,
And naught else this heart interested,
Naught else it felt but one desire,
One sole desire did it retain,
Carmen, beloved, to see thee once again!
  O, Carmen, mine! here as thy slave, love
    binds me fast,
        Carmen, I love thee!

From Schirmer score. Copy't G. Schirmer

COPY'T DUPONT

CARUSO AS DON JOSE—ACT III

Carmen then paints the joys of the gypsies' life which might be *Jose's,* if he would desert his regiment and follow her.

Las bas dans la montagne (Away to Yonder Mountains)
By Emma Calvé, Soprano, and Charles Dalmores, Tenor

                                 (*In French*)   **89019**   12-inch, **$4.00**

By Geraldine Farrar, Soprano   (*In French*)   **88513**   12-inch, **3.00**

    The soldier listens with half-willing ears, his voice joining hers at the close, in a lovely duet passage.

CARMEN:
  For roof, the sky—a wandering life;
  For country, the whole world;
  Thy will thy master;
  And above all—most prized of all—
  Liberty! freedom!
  Up yonder, up yonder, if thou lov'st me,
  To the mountains, together we'll go.

JOSE:
  Carmen!
CARMEN:
  Wilt come with me?
  Up yonder, up yonder, thus will we go
  Away, if thou lov'st me, together!

    However, in spite of *Carmen's* fascinations, *Jose* is about to return to his duty, when the appearance of his superior officer *Zuniga*, who orders him back, decides the matter. *Don Jose* resents the overbearing tone his captain uses and defies him. *Zuniga* is finally overpowered and bound by the gypsies, and the smugglers all depart on their expedition.

Second Intermezzo
By Victor Herbert's Orchestra   **60067**   10-inch, **$0.75**
By La Scala Orchestra   (*Double-faced—See page 70*)   **62102**   10-inch,   **.75**

    The retreat in the mountains is musically described by this pastoral intermezzo. A dreamy melody given to the flute, with a *pizzicato* accompaniment, is taken up by the other instruments in turn, the strings joining in the coda.

Andantino quasi allegretto.

    This is one of the finest records made by the Herbert Orchestra, who have given an artistic and finished rendering of the interlude.

PHOTO MAIRET

MICAELA PLEADS WITH JOSE—ACT III

© DUPONT   FARRAR IN ACT I

© MISHKIN   CARUSO AS DON JOSE

PHOTO WHITE   FARRAR IN ACT II

© DUPONT   FARRAR AS CARMEN—ACT III

Cast of the Metropolitan "All-

PHOTO WHITE   ALDA AS MICAELA

© MISHKIN   AMATO AS THE TOREADOR

PHOTO WHITE   THE QUINTET—ACT II

Star" Carmen Revival of 1915

BYRON

CARD SCENE—ACT III

ACT III

SCENE—*A Wild and Rocky Pass in the Mountains*

As the curtain rises, the smugglers are seen entering their rocky lair. Here occurs the famous sextette, a portion of which is given in the "Gems from Carmen" (*page 70*).

The smugglers prepare to camp for the night. It is evident that *Jose* is already repenting of his folly, and that *Carmen* is tiring of her latest lover. After a quarrel with *Jose*, she joins *Frasquita* and *Mercedes*, who are telling fortunes with cards.

Voyous que j'essaie (Let Me Know My Fate)

PHOTO REUTLINGER

THE CARDS PREDICT CARMEN'S DEATH
(EMMA CALVÉ)

———

* *Double-Faced Record—See page 70.*

By Geraldine Farrar, Soprano
(*In French*) 88534 12-inch, $3.00
By Lavin de Casas, Mezzo-Soprano
(*Piano acc.*)
(*In Italian*) *62617 10-inch, .75

Carmen tells her own fate by the cards, reading death, first for herself and then for her lover. In vain she shuffles and re-tries the result; the answer is ever the same.

This highly dramatic air, one of the most impressive numbers in Bizet's opera, is effectively sung by Miss Farrar.

The neighboring camp being ready, the smugglers retire, and the stage is once more deserted.

Je dis que rien ne m'epouvante (Micaela's Air," I am not Faint-Hearted")

By Luisa Tetrazzini, Soprano
(*In Italian*) 88503 12-inch, $3.00
By Geraldine Farrar, Soprano
(*In French*) 88144 12-inch, 3.00
By Frances Alda, Soprano
(*In French*) 74353 12-inch, 1.50
By Alma Gluck, Soprano
(*In French*) 74245 12-inch, 1.50

Into this strange and wild scene now enters *Micaela*, the peasant sweetheart of *Don Jose*, who has forgotten her in his fascination for the wayward *Carmen*. *Micaela* has braved the dangers of the road to the smugglers' retreat, whither *Don Jose* has followed *Carmen*, to carry to the soldier a message from his dying mother. The innocent girl is frightened by the vast and lonely mountains, and in her aria appeals to Heaven to protect her, ingenuously confessing her love for *Don Jose* and her detestation of the woman who has led him away from his duty.

MICAELA:
> I try not to own that I tremble;
> But I know I'm a coward, altho' bold I
>   appear.
> Ah! how can I ever call up my courage,
> While horror and dread chill my sad heart
>   with fear?
> Here, in this savage retreat, sad and weary
>   am I,
> Alone and sore afraid.
> Ah! heav'n, to thee I humbly pray,
> Protect thou me, and guide and aid!
> I shall see the guilty creature,
> Who by infernal arts doth sever
> From his country, from his duty,
> Him I loved—and shall love ever!
> I may tremble at her beauty,
> But her power affrights me not.
> Strong, in my just cause confiding,
> Heaven! I trust myself to thee.
> Ah! to this poor heart give courage,
> Protector! guide and aid now me!

The young girl, hearing a shot fired, runs into a cave in fright. *Jose,* who is guarding the smugglers' effects, has seen a stranger and fires at him. It proves to be *Escamillo*, the toreador, who has come to join *Carmen*. He appears, examining his hat with rueful gaze, as *Jose's* bullet had gone through it. "Who are you?" says the latter. "I am *Escamillo*, toreador of Granada!" replies the bull fighter.

COPY'T MISHKIN
TRENTINI AS FRASQUITA

The duet which follows is given here by two famous artists of the Paris *Opéra*.

Je suis Escamillo   (I am Escamillo!)

By Léon Beyle, Tenor, and Hector Dufranne, Baritone
   (*Double-faced – See page 70*) (*In French*) *62750 10-inch, $0.75

The two men compare notes, and learning that they are rivals, *Jose* challenges the other to a duel with knives, which is interrupted by the timely arrival of *Carmen* herself. This dialogue, with the fiery duet at the close, well depicts this exciting scene.

A popular-priced rendition by Beyle and Dufranne, of the *Opéra*, is listed above.

Finale—"Mia tu sei"   (You Command Me to Leave You)

By Antonio Paoli, Tenor; Giuseppina Huguet, Soprano;
   Inez Salvador, and Francesco Cigada   (*In Italian*)   92035   12-inch, $3.00

A dramatic scene between *Carmen* and *Jose* is interrupted by *Micaela*, who begs *Jose* to return to his mother; and *Carmen*, with fine scorn, echoes her request. Thus to leave his rival in possession of the field is too much for the soldier, who swears never to be parted from the gypsy until death.

CARMEN (*to Jose*):
> Go, and go quickly; stay not here;
> This way of life is not for thee!

JOSE (*to Carmen*):
> To depart thou dost counsel me?

CARMEN:
> Yes, thou shouldst go—

JOSE (*fiercely*):
> Yes, that thou mayst follow
> Another lover—the toreador!
> No, Carmen, I will not depart!

MICAELA:
> Be not deaf to my prayers;
> Thy mother waits thee there.
> The chain that binds thee, Jose,
> Death will break.

JOSE (*to Micaela*):
> Go from hence;
> I cannot follow thee.
> (*To Carmen.*)
> Mine thou art, accursed one!
> And I will force thee to know
> And submit to the fate
> That both our lives unites!

The message from his dying mother, however, decides him; he will go, but vows to return. In this wild and tumultuous number the jealous anger of *Jose* gives rise to some highly dramatic singing, delivered with extreme intensity and power by Paoli, the tragic theme at the close being introduced with meaning effect. The Toreador chorus indicates the triumph of *Escamillo* in the gypsy's attentions, and this with the orchestral close slowly sinking to rest brings the powerful act to a finish.

JOSE PLEADING WITH CARMEN—ACT IV

Third Intermezzo
By La Scala Orchestra
*62101   10-inch, $0.75
By Victor Herbert's Orchestra
(Preceded by the last part
of Prelude to the Opera)
70066   12-inch,   1.25

This short intermezzo is a quick bustling one, only the plaintive oboe solo indicating the tragedy which is soon to occur. The playing of this striking prelude is on the same artistic level which marks each of the renditions by these famous orchestras.

ACT IV
(*A Square in Seville, with the walls of the Bull Ring shown at the back*)

The fourth act opens with a momentary brightness. Outside the *Plaza de Toros*, in Seville, an animated crowd awaits the procession about to enter the ring.

This scene, as the orange sellers, hawkers of fans, ices and the rest, press their wares on the waiting crowd, is extremely gay, and affords welcome relief from the intensity of the drama.

Escamillo, who has returned to take part in the bull-fight, now enters, and all join in the refrain of the Toreador Song in his honor.

Si tu m'ames   (If You Love Me)
By Geraldine Farrar, Soprano; Pasquale Amato, Baritone;
with Metropolitan Opera Chorus   (*In French*)   89086   12-inch, $4.00
By Inez Salvador, Mezzo-Soprano, and Francesco Cigada, Baritone
(*In Italian*) *62102   10-inch,   .75

Escamillo takes farewell of *Carmen* before entering the arena. He promises to fight the better for her presence, and she, half conscious of what is coming, avows her readiness to die for him. This number is full of lovely melodies and one of the most beautiful records of the Carmen series.

PHOTO BYRON

THE DEATH OF CARMEN—ACT IV

Double-Faced Record—See page 70.

As the procession passes on, the warning comes to *Carmen* that *Jose* is here, to which she replies that she fears him not.

Duetto e Finale   (Duet and Finale)
By Maria Passeri, Soprano; Antonio Paoli,
   Tenor; and La Scala Chorus 92050 12-inch, $3.00

C'est toi!   (You Here?)
By Geraldine Farrar, Soprano, and Giovanni
   Martinelli, Tenor (*French*) 88533 12-inch, 3.00

Je t'aime encore   (Let Me Implore You)
By Geraldine Farrar, Soprano; Giovanni
   Martinelli, Tenor; with Metropolitan
   Opera Chorus   (*French*) 88531 12-inch, 3.00

Jose now enters and makes a last appeal, which is dramatic in its intensity. It takes the form of a swinging melody to an insistent triplet accompaniment. To each request of her lover, *Carmen* adds her disdainful negative, reckless of the danger which threatens her.

COPY'T DUPONT

MARTIN AS DON JOSE

JOSE (*in desperation*):
   Now thou refusest my prayers,
   Inhuman girl! For thy sake am I lost!
   And then to know thee shameless, infamous!

Laughing, in his arms, at my despair!
No, no! it shall not be, by Heaven!
Carmen, thou must be mine, mine only!
CARMEN (*proudly*): No, no, never!
JOSE: Ah! weary am I of threats.
CARMEN: Cease then,—or let me pass!
CHORUS (*in bull ring*): Victory! victory!
   Viva Escamillo!
JOSE: Again I beseech thee, Carmen,
   Wilt thou with me depart?

Carmen's last refusal, as she flings him back his ring, rouses the soldier's jealousy to madness and he stabs her to the heart. As she falls the success of the *Toreador* in the arena is announced by the singing of his well-known refrain. The last notes of the opera are a few pitiful tones from the stricken *Jose* addressed to the mute form of his beloved.

DON JOSE AND CARMEN

DOUBLE-FACED AND MISCELLANEOUS CARMEN RECORDS

Carmen Selection   By Pryor's Band 31562 12-inch, $1.00
   Prelude to Act I—Toreador Song, Act II—"Habanera," Act I—Chorus from Act IV.

{ Carmen Selection   By Sousa's Band }
{ Freischutz—Overture   By Sousa's Band } 35000 12-inch, 1.25

{ Carmen Selection   By Pryor's Band }
{ Opening of Act I—"Habanera," Act I—Chorus of Street }
{   Boys, Act I—Carmen's Defiance, Act IV   } 16575 10-inch, .75
{ Manon—Ah! fuyez douce image!   By M. Rocca, Tenor }

The selection begins with the brilliant and animated Prelude, the first part of which is given, including the refrain of the famous "Toreador Song." Then is heard (as a cornet solo) the quaint "Habanera,"

Allegretto quasi Andantino.

L'a - mour est un - oi - seau re - bel - le Que nul ne - pent ap - pri - voi - ser
Love is like an - y wood-bird wild, That none can ev - er hope to tame,

with its curiously varied rhythm, its chromatic melody and the changes from minor to major which are so effective. With the last note the full band takes up the rollicking chorus of street boys from Act I, and after a few measures there appears suddenly the weird strain from Act IV when *Carmen* hurls at *Don Jose* her last defiance.

Ti bre elle est née let ti bre elle mour - rai
Free I was born, And free I will diet

The spirited introductory strain returns, closing the selection.

DOUBLE-FACED AND MISCELLANEOUS CARMEN RECORDS—Continued

Gems from Carmen

Chorus, "Here They Are"—Solo and Chorus, "Habanera" (Love is Like a Bird)—Duet, "Again He Sees His Village Home"—Sextette, "Our Chosen Trade"—Solo and Chorus, "Toreador Song"—Finale.

By Victor Opera Company   (*In English*)   31843   12-inch, $1.00

Quite a number of the most popular bits of Bizet's masterpiece have been crowded into this attractively arranged potpourri.

Toreador Song By Alan Turner, Baritone (*In English*) Trovatore—Tempest of the Heart By Alan Turner, Baritone (*In English*)	16521	10-inch,	$0.75
Prelude (Overture) By La Scala Orchestra Damnation of Faust—Hungarian March By Sousa's Band	68052	12-inch.	1.25
Prelude (Overture) By La Scala Orchestra Scena delle carte (Card Song) By Lavin de Casas, Mezzo- Soprano (*Piano acc.*) (*In Italian*)	62617	10-inch,	.75
Canzone del Toreador (Toreador Song) By F. Cigada, Bari- tone; G. Huguet, Soprano; I. Salvador, Mezzo-Soprano; La Scala Chorus (*In Italian*) Cavalleria Rusticana—Intermezzo By Pryor's Orchestra	62618	10-inch,	.75
Intermezzo—Acto III, Aragonaise La Scala Orchestra, Milan Se tu m'ami (If You Love Me) By Inez Salvador, Mezzo- Soprano; F. Cigada, Baritone (*In Italian*)	62102	10-inch,	.75
Je suis Escamillo (I Am Escamillo!) By Léon Beyle, Tenor; Hector Dufranne, Baritone (*In French*) Valse des Roses (*Métra*) By Mlle. Lucette Korsoff, Soprano (*French*)	62750	10-inch,	.75
Preludio, Acto IV By La Scala Orchestra Norma—Mira o Norma—By Ida Giacomelli, Soprano; Lina Mileri, Contralto (*In Italian*)	62101	10-inch,	.75
Carmen Selection (*Xylophone*) By Wm. Reitz Bohême—Musetta Waltz (*Whistling*) By Guido Gialdini	16892	10-inch,	.75

A FAMOUS OPEN-AIR PRODUCTION OF CARMEN IN FRANCE

(Italian)

CAVALLERIA RUSTICANA

(Kah-vahl-lay-ree'-ah Roos-tih-kah'-nah)

(English)

RUSTIC CHIVALRY

OPERA IN ONE ACT

Libretto adapted from the book of Verga by Targioni-Torzetti and Menasci; music by Mascagni. First production in Rome, May 17, 1890; in Germany, at Berlin, October 21, 1891; Paris, January 19, 1892; London, 1891. First United States production in Philadelphia, September 9, 1891.

Cast

SANTUZZA, *(San-toot'-zah)* a village girl..........................Soprano
LOLA, *(Low'-lah)* wife of Alfio...........................Mezzo-Soprano
TURIDDU, *(Too-ree'-doo)* a young soldier ....Tenor
ALFIO, *(Al'-fee-oh)* a teamster..........................Baritone
LUCIA, *(Loo-chee'-ah)* mother of Turiddu ....Contralto
Chorus of Peasants and Villagers. Chorus behind the scenes.

The scene is laid in a Sicilian village. Time, the present.

THE COMPOSER

Pietro Mascagni, son of a baker in Leghorn, was born December 7, 1863. Destined by his father to succeed him in business, the young man rebelled, and secretly entered the Cherubini Conservatory. He began composing at an early age, but none of his works attracted attention until 1890, when he entered a contest planned by Sonzogno, the Milan publisher. Securing a libretto based on a simple Sicilian tale by Verga, he composed the whole of this opera in eight days, producing a work full of dramatic fire and rich in Italian melody, and easily won the prize. Produced in Rome in 1890, it created a sensation, and in a short time has become one of the most popular of operas.

NOTE—*The quotations from Cavalleria Rusticana are given by kind permission of G. Schirmer. (Copy't 1891.)*

CARUSO AS TURIDDU

THE STORY

Turiddu, a young Sicilian peasant, returns from the war and finds his sweetheart, *Lola*, has wedded *Alfio*, a carter. For consolation he pays court to *Santuzza*, who loves him not wisely but too well. Tiring of her, he turns again to *Lola*, who seems to encourage him. *Santuzza*, in despair, confides all to *Turiddu's* mother, and when *Alfio* returns tells him all. He is furious, challenges *Turiddu* and kills him.

Prelude

By La Scala Orchestra *35104 12-inch, $1.25

The Prelude takes the form of a fantasia on the principal themes of the opera. During the number *Turiddu's* voice is heard in the charming *Siciliana*, in which he tells of his love for *Lola*:

O Lo la, bian ca co me fior di spi no,
Oh, Lo la, with thy lips like crim son ber-ries!

Siciliana (Thy Lips Like Crimson Berries)

By Enrico Caruso, Tenor   (*Harp acc.*)

	(*In Italian*)	87072	10-inch, $2.00
By Enrico Caruso, Tenor (*Piano acc.*)	(*In Italian*)	81030	10-inch, 2.00
By George Hamlin, Tenor (*Harp acc.*)	(*In Italian*)	64387	10-inch, 1.00
By Leo Slezak, Tenor	(*In German*)	61202	10-inch, 1.00

It is sung behind the scenes, before the rise of the curtain, making it peculiarly effective. At the close of the number *Turiddu's* voice is heard dying away in the distance. This delightful serenade is almost the only bright spot in Mascagni's passionate and tragic operatic melodrama.

SCENE—*A Square in a Sicilian Village*

After the *Siciliana* the chorus of villagers is heard, also behind the scenes, and during this chorus the curtain rises, showing a square in the village, with the church at one side and the cottage of *Turiddu's* mother on the other.

Gli aranci olezzano (Blossoms of Oranges)

By New York Grand Opera Chorus
      (*In Italian*)   64048 10-inch, $1.00
By La Scala Chorus
      (*In Italian*) *68218 12-inch, 1.25

This beautiful chorus is rendered here both by the famous organization of La Scala, Milan, and the New York Grand Opera Chorus.

It is Easter Day and crowds of villagers cross the square and enter the church. *Santuzza* enters, and knocking at *Lucia's* door, asks her if she has seen *Turiddu*. His mother replies that he is at Francofonte, but the jealous girl refuses to believe it, and suspects that he is watching for *Lola*.

The cracking of a whip and shouts of the villagers announce *Alfio*, who appears and sings a merry song.

Il cavallo scalpita (Gayly Moves the Tramping Horse)

By Pasquale Amato, Baritone   (*with Metropolitan Opera Chorus*)
      (*In Italian*) 87097 10-inch, $2.00
By Renzo Minolfi, Baritone
      (*In Italian*) *45003 10-inch, 1.00

PHOTO BERT, PARIS
AMATO AS ALFIO

*Double-Faced Record—See page 76.

GADSKI AS SANTUZZA

He is happy and free, his wife *Lola* loves him and guards his home while he is gone—this is the burden of his air.

The peasants disperse and *Alfio* is left with *Lucia* and *Santuzza.* When he says he has just seen *Turiddu, Lucia* is surprised, but at a gesture from *Santuzza* she keeps silent.

After *Alfio* has entered the church, the Easter music is heard within and all kneel and join in the singing.

Regina Coeli (Queen of the Heavens)

By La Scala Chorus (*In Italian*) *68218 12-inch, $1.25

All go into the church except *Lucia* and *Santuzza,* and the agitated girl now sings her touching romanza, beginning:

as she pours out her sad history to the sympathetic *Mamma Lucia.* This is one of the most powerful numbers in Mascagni's work.

Voi lo sapete (Well You Know, Good Mother)

By Margarete Matzenauer, Contralto	(*In Italian*) 88430	12-inch, $3.00
By Emma Calvé, Soprano	(*In Italian*) 88086	12-inch, 3.00
By Emma Eames, Soprano	(*In Italian*) 88037	12-inch, 3.00

Stung with the remembrance of her great wrong she sings of vengeance, but love overpowers revenge, and in spite of herself, she cries: "I loved him! ah, I loved him!" Then the thought of her rival, *Lola,* returns and she gives way to despair, throwing herself at the feet of the gentle mother of *Turiddu,* who is powerless to aid her and who can only pray for the wretched woman.

SANTUZZA.

Well do you know, good mother,
Ere to the war he departed
Turiddu plighted to Lola his troth,
Like a man true-hearted.
And then, finding her wedded

Loved me!—I loved him!—
She, coveting what was my only treasure—
Enticed him from me!
She and Turiddu love again!
I weep and I weep and I weep still!

Lucia tries to comfort her and passes into the church just as *Turiddu* appears. He asks *Santuzza* why she does not go to mass. She says she cannot, and accuses him of treachery, which puts him in a rage, and he tells her brutally that she is now nothing to him.

Tu qui, Santuzza (Thou Here, Santuzza!)

By B. Besalù, Soprano, and G. Ciccolini, Tenor (*Italian*) *55022 12-inch, $1.50

No, No, Turiddu

By Besalù and Ciccolini (*In Italian*) *55022 12-inch, $1.50

This scene is now interrupted by *Lola's* voice, heard behind the scenes.

LOLA (*behind the scenes*):
My king of roses,
Radiant angels stand
In Heav'n in thousands;

None like to him so bright
That land discloses,
My king of roses!—

She enters, and divining the situation, shows her power by taking *Turiddu* into the church with her. Frantic with jealousy, *Santuzza* turns to *Alfio,* who now enters, and tells him that his wife is false. Two records are required to present this powerful scene.

Turiddu mi tolse (Turiddu Forsakes Me!)

By B. Besalù and E. Badini	(*In Italian*) *55021	12-inch, $1.50
By Joanna and Minolfi	(*In Italian*) *45002	10-inch, 1.00

Ad essi io non perdono ('Tis They Who Are Shameful)

By Clara Joanna and Renzo Minolfi (*In Italian*) *45002 10-inch, $1.00

Double-Faced Record—See page 76.

SANTUZZA: None should go
But those who have not sinned!
LOLA: Thanks be to the Almighty,
I vow before you!

Alfio swears vengeance, while *Santuzza* already regrets her disclosure, but is powerless to prevent the consequences of her revelation. They go out, leaving the stage empty, and the beautiful Intermezzo follows.

Intermezzo

By Victor Herbert's Orchestra

	60074 10-in.,	$0.70
Pryor's Orchestra	*62618 10-in.,	.75
Victor Orchestra	4184 10-in.,	.65
Victor Concert Orch	*17311 10-in.,	.75

The instantaneous popularity of this selection was remarkable, and in no small measure helped to make *Cavalleria Rusticana* the tremendous success that it was. These records bring out the beautiful melody—the harp lending a lovely background of peaceful harmony—and makes the *Intermezzo* a tone picture of exquisite coloring.

After the storm and passion of the first scene, this lovely number comes as a blessed relief. The curtain does not fall during the playing of the Intermezzo, although the stage is empty.

PART II

A casa, a casa (Now Homeward)

By La Scala Chorus

(*In Italian*) *45014 10-inch, $1.00

SANTUZZA PLEADING WITH TURIDDU—ACT I
(DESTINN AND CARUSO)

The services being over, the people now come from the church, and *Turiddu*, in a reckless mood, invites the crowd to drink with him, and sings his spirited *Brindisi*.

Double-Faced Record—See page 76.

Brindisi (Drinking Song)

By Enrico Caruso, Tenor	(*In Italian*)	81062	10-inch, $2.00
By George Hamlin, Tenor	(*In Italian*)	64245	10-inch, 1.00

In striking contrast to the prevailing tragic tone of Mascagni's opera comes this merry drinking song, which *Turiddu* sings as gaily as if he had not a care in the world, although at that moment the culminating tragedy of the duel was close at hand. The *Brindisi*, which has a most fascinating swing, begins:

Larghetto (♩ = 80 TURIDDU.)

viva il vi - no spu meg gian - te,   nel bic - chie - re scin - til - lan - te
Hail the red wine rich - ly flow - ing,   In the beak - er sparkling, glow-ing

TURIDDU:
Hail the red wine richly flowing,
In the beaker, sparkling, glowing,
Like young love, with smiles bestowing,
Now our holiday 'twill bless.

Hail the wine that flows and bubbles,
Kills care, banishes all troubles,
Brings peace, pleasure it redoubles,
Causes sweet forgetfulness!

Alfio now enters, and when *Turiddu* offers him a cup, he refuses. *Turiddu* throws out the wine, saying carelessly, "Very well! suit your pleasure!."

The seriousness of this scene is not lost on the peasants, who now leave the young men together. A challenge is quickly given and accepted after the Sicilian fashion, *Turiddu* viciously biting *Alfio's* ear, and they arrange to meet in the garden.

Turiddu now calls his mother from the cottage, and asks for her blessing, bidding her, if he does not return, to be a mother to *Santuzza*.

Addio alla madre (Turiddu's Farewell to His Mother)

By Enrico Caruso, Tenor	(*In Italian*)	88458	12-inch, $3.00
By Riccardo Martin, Tenor	(*In Italian*)	88277	12-inch, 3.00
By Gennaro de Tura, Tenor	(*In Italian*)	76015	12-inch, 2.00
By G. Ciccolini, Tenor	(*In Italian*)	*55021	12-inch, 1.50

Finale to the Opera

By Mmes. Joanna, Rumbelli and Chorus	(*In Italian*)	*45003	10-inch, $1.00

Lucia is distressed and bewildered, and calls after him despairingly. Confused cries are now heard and a woman screams "*Turiddu* is murdered!" *Santuzza* and *Lucia* sink down senseless, and the curtain slowly falls.

THE DEATH OF TURIDDU

Double-Faced Record—See page 76.

DOUBLE-FACED AND MISCELLANEOUS CAVALLERIA RECORDS

Gems from "Cavalleria Rusticana"
   "Blossoms of Oranges"—"Alfio's Song"—Lola's Ditty, "My King of
   Roses"—"Santuzza's Aria"—"Drinking Song"—"Easter Chorus"
             By Victor Opera Company (In English)
   Gems from "Pagliacci" By Victor Opera Company (In English)
	35343	12-inch,	$1.25

Turiddu, mi tolse (Turiddu Forsakes Me!) By
   B. Besalù, Soprano, and E. Badini, Baritone (In Italian)
 Mamma, quel vino è generoso (Mother! the Wine
   Cup too Freely Passes) By G. Coccolini, Tenor (In Italian)
	55021	12-inch,	1.50

Tu qui Santuzza (Thou, Santuzza) By Besalù and Ciccolini No, No, Turiddu By Besalù and Ciccolini (In Italian)	55022	12-inch,	1.50
Prelude By La Scala Orchestra Selection ("Alfio's Song," "Easter Chorale," "Intermezzo") Pryor's B	35104	12-inch,	1.25
Gli aranci olezzano—Coro d' Introduzione By La Scala Chorus (In Italian) Regina Coeli By La Scala Chorus (In Italian)	68218	12-inch,	1.25
Turiddu, mi tolse l'onore (Turiddu Forsakes Me!) By Clara Joanna and Renzo Minolfi (In Italian) Ad essi io non perdono—By Joanna and Minolfi (In Italian)	45002	10-inch,	1.00
Finale dell' Opera—By Clara Joanna, Soprano; Sra. Rumbelli, Mezzo-Soprano; and La Scala Chorus (In Italian) Il cavallo scalpita By Renzo Minolfi, Baritone (In Italian)	45003	10-inch,	1.00
A casa, a casa (Now Homeward!) La Scala Chorus (Italian) Guglielmo Ratcliff—Padre Nostro Mussini and Molinari (Italian)	45014	10-inch,	1.00

Intermezzo   By Pryor's Orchestra
   Carmen—Toreador (Bizet)
          By Cigada, Huguet, Salvador and Chorus (In Italian)
	62618	10-inch,	.75

Intermezzo Victor Concert Orchestra Tales of Hoffman—Barcarolle Victor Concert Orchestra	17311	10-inch,	.75

LANDE   CARUSO   TOSCANINI   DESTINN   GATTI-CAZZAZA   MARTIN
                                          HOMER

A REHEARSAL OF CAVALLERIA AT THE METROPOLITAN OPERA HOUSE, NEW YORK

(French)

LES CLOCHES DE CORNEVILLE

(English)

THE CHIMES OF NORMANDY

COMIC OPERA IN THREE ACTS

Text by Clairville and Gabet; music by Robert Planquette. First produced at the *Folies Dramatiques,* Paris, April 19, 1877, where it ran for four hundred continuous performances. First New York production at the Fifth Avenue Theatre, October 27, 1877.

ROBERT PLANQUETTE

Characters

HENRI, the Marquis of Valleroi.................Baritone
GRENICHEUX, a young villager....................Tenor
GASPARD, a miser...............................Bass
SERPOLETTE, the good-for-nothing..............Soprano
GERMAINE, the lost Marchioness ....Mezzo-Soprano
SHERIFF..Bass

Time and Place : Normandy ; time of Louis XV.

The Chimes of Normandy abounds in striking numbers, and the music is full of gayety and French grace. It has had no less than six thousand performances, a testimony to its enduring place in popular appreciation.

The opera opens in an old Norman village, where a fair is in progress. *Henri, the Marquis of Valleroi,* has just returned to his native town after an absence of many years. The village gossips are discussing with vehemence scandals about *Serpolette,* the village good-for-nothing, who arrives just in time to vindicate herself by turning the tables on her traducers. *Gaspard,* the miser, has a plan for marrying his niece, *Germaine,* to the sheriff, but the young girl objects, telling him that if she must wed she feels it her duty to marry *Grenicheux,* a young villager, in gratitude for his saving her life. To escape the marriage, which is distasteful to both *Germaine* and *Grenicheux,* and to fly from the vengeance of *Gaspard* and the sheriff, she and *Grenicheux* take advantage of the privileges of fair time and become servants of the *Marquis.*

In the second act the ghosts are reported to be roaming the Castle of Valleroi. The *Marquis* does not credit these stories and soon discovers it is only old *Gaspard,* the miser, who, when found out, goes crazy through fear of losing the treasures he has concealed there. In the last act the castle is restored to its former splendor and the *Marquis* is giving a fête to which he invites all the villagers, including the crazy *Gaspard.* *Serpolette* is there as a fine lady with *Grenicheux* as her factotum. After a love scene between the *Marquis* and *Germaine,* it is discovered that the latter is the rightful heiress and true claimant to the title of Marchioness. The story comes to a fitting conclusion with the betrothal of the *Marquis* and *Germaine,* over whom the bells of Corneville ring out sweetly and gladly to tell the happy news.

The Victor offers three band records of the principal airs, and an unusually effective selection of five of the most popular numbers in the opera by the Victor Light Opera Company.

Gems from " Chimes of Normandy "

Chorus, "Silent Heroes"—"Just Look at This, Just Look at That"—"Cold Sweat is on My Brow"—"That Night I'll Ne'er Forget"—"Bell Chorus"—Finale.

By the Victor Light Opera Company   31788   12-inch, $1.00

Selection of the Principal Airs

By Sousa's Band   31180   12-inch, 1.00

{Selection of the Principal Airs	By Sousa's Band}	35134	12-inch, 1.25
{ Naila Intermezzo (Pas des Fleurs)	By Pryor's Band}		
{Selection of the Principal Airs	By Pryor's Band}	16385	10-inch, .75
{ Poet and Peasant Overture (von Suppe)	By Pryor's Band}		

CRISTOFORO COLOMBO
LYRICAL DRAMA IN FOUR ACTS AND EPILOGUE

Text by Luigi Illica. Music by Alberto Franchetti. First produced at Genoa in 1892; and a revised version was brought out at La Scala December 26, of the same year. Produced in Hamburg, October 5, 1893. First American production at Buenos Aires, July 21, 1900. First in the United States at the Metropolitan Opera House, Philadelphia, November 20, 1913, by the Philadelphia-Chicago Opera Company, the cast including Titta Ruffo, Rosa Raisa, Amedeo Bassi, Gustave Huberdeau, Henri Scott, Ruby Heyl and Federeci Venturini, Warnery, Nicolay, Erolle, Fosetta and de Keyser.

Characters

COLUMBUS...Baritone
QUEEN ISABELLA...Soprano
DON GUEVERA.. :...Tenor
DON RONALDO XIMINES.......................................Baritone
RODERIGO DI TRIANA...Baritone

PHOTO MATZENE COPY'T   THE DEATH OF COLUMBUS

The libretto, by Luigi Illica, presents in a simple manner some episodes from three periods in the life of the discoverer of America, and takes sufficient liberties with historical fact to give the story a romantic touch and an effective ending in the death of *Columbus* at the tomb of *Isabella*.

The first act portrays a square in Salamanca, before the Council chamber, in 1485, and shows *Columbus* rejected by the Council and broken in spirit. He is finally befriended by the *Queen*, who, as a dramatic and sympathetic ending to the scene, takes the crown from her head and presents it to him as he falls at her feet overcome with gratitude.

The second act takes place on the Santa Maria in 1492. The sailors, discouraged at the apparent failure of the long voyage, are about to throw *Columbus* into the ocean, when land is sighted, and all are soon rejoicing.

The next act takes place in America. An Indian, husband of *Queen Anacoana*, is murdered by the Spaniards, and the Queen pretends to be in love with his murderer, *Rolando,* in order to be revenged. The Indians revolt against the Spaniards, but are soon subdued, and *Rolando* hands *Anacoana* over to the Spanish general to be deported as a captive to Spain. *Guevera,* in love with the Queen's daughter, *Janika,* tries to save the princess from being deported but, as the Indian rebels are being burned, the young girl throws herself into the flames and perishes with her people.

In the Epilogue the action returns to Spain, showing *Guevera* and *Columbus* among the tombs of the kings of Castile. *Guevera* goes in search of *Queen Isabella,* while maidens bearing wreaths enter the crypt. *Columbus* is so shocked to learn that his beloved Queen has died and is buried there that he loses his reason and dies of grief near the tomb,

Upon this Franchetti built an effective score with passages of real melody and several instrumental climaxes of genuine power. The best number in the score is this fine air for *Columbus,* which Mr. Ruffo sings with a glorious outpouring of his noble voice and much dramatic power.

Aman lassu le stelle (Our Love is Like the Stars)
By Titta Ruffo, Baritone   (*In Italian*)   88486   12-inch, $3.00

DAMNATION OF FAUST—FOURTH SCENE—PARIS OPÉRA

(French)

LA DAMNATION DE FAUST
(Lah Dam-nah-seeohn' d'h Fowst)

(DAMNATION OF FAUST)

Hector Berlioz's dramatic legend in four parts; book based on de Nerval's version of Goethe's poem, partly by Gandonniere, but completed by Berlioz himself. First performed December 6, 1846, at the *Opéra Comique*, Paris, in concert form. In New York under Dr. Leopold Damrosch, February 12, 1880. It was given at Monte Carlo as an opera February 18, 1893, with Jean de Reszke as *Faust*. Revived there March, 1902, with Melba, de Reszke and Renaud. First American performance of the operatic version in New York, 1908.

Cast

MARGUERITE (*Mahr-guer-eet'*)..................................Soprano
FAUST (*Fowst*)..Tenor
MEPHISTOPHELES (*Mef-iss-tof'-el-leez*) ....Baritone or Bass
BRANDER..Bass

Place : A German village.

No one to-day doubts the genius of Berlioz, and critics are almost unanimous in praising his originality, his spontaneous force and immense creative power. But, like many another genius, he had to die to be appreciated! His *La Damnation de Faust* was quite coldly received by the French public. Ten years after his death, however, what a change began! A Berlioz memorial in Paris, at the Hippodrome, where thousands were turned away; Berlioz monuments erected in Grenoble and other cities of France; the first performance of Damnation of Faust as an opera at Monte Carlo in 1893, amid scenes of the wildest enthusiasm; and finally a magnificent production in Paris in 1903, on the hundredth anniversary of Berlioz's birth, the cast including Calvé, Alvarez and Renaud.

In his "Faust" Berlioz has given us a musical legend which has all the picturesqueness of the original work.

Whatever severe critics may say of its merits in the highest artistic sense, it is nevertheless a wonderful work. Strange eccentricities and rare beauties are found side by side; even the wild orgie of fiends called "Pandemonium," which almost transgresses the license of genius, must be admired for its astounding orchestral effects. On the other hand, there are melodies of purest beauty, such as the numbers for *Marguerite*. However, the most striking numbers

AUERBACH'S BEER CELLAR IN LEIPSIC—ACT II

in the opera are those written by Berlioz for *Mephistopheles,* two of which have been most effectively rendered for the Victor by Plançon and de Gogorza.

THE OPERA

Berlioz, disregarding Goethe's poem, located the opening scene on a plain in Hungary simply to excuse the interpolation of the Rakoczy March. We quote Berlioz himself here: "The march on the Hungarian Rakoczy theme, written one night at Vienna, made such a sensation at Pesth that I introduced it into my Faust score, taking the liberty of putting my hero in Hungary and making him witness the passage of a Hungarian troop across the plain where he is wandering in reverie." But Raoul Gunsbourg, who adapted the cantata for the stage, changed the first scene to a room with open windows showing the peasants dancing and the military passing by to the strains of the Hungarian March. Here *Faust* soliloquizes on the vanity of all things, while the people make merry outside, and the march of the soldiers makes an inspiring finish to the scene.

RENAUD'S STRIKING CON-
CEPTION OF MEPHISTO

Hungarian (Rakoczy) March

By Sousa's Band (*Double-faced, see p. 82*)	68052	12-in., $1.25
By Sousa's Band	31424	12-in., 1.00
By Pryor's Band	4314	10-in., .60

This is Berlioz's treatment of the famous "Rakoczy March," known as a national Hungarian melody for a hundred years. Its stirring measures so fascinated the composer that, contrary to his original intention, he laid the scene of his "Faust" legend in Hungary in order that he might make use of this wild and pulse-quickening melody. His treatment of it is brilliant in the extreme, and it remains one of the most effective portions of his "Faust."

In this connection it is interesting to remember that Liszt, although a warm friend of Berlioz, considered himself aggrieved and wrote to Mme. Tardieu in 1882: "My transcription of the Rakoczy March * * * is twice as long as the well-known version of Berlioz, and it was written *before* his. Delicate sentiments of friendship for the illustrious Frenchman induced me to withhold it from publication until after his death. * * * In writing it he made use of one of my earlier transcriptions, particularly in the harmony."

Scene II shows *Faust* alone in his study, as in the Gounod version. He is about to take poison, when the strains of the Easter hymn come from the adjoining church and arrest his purpose. *Mephistopheles* then appears and suggests that they go forth and see the world together, to which *Faust* consents.

In the third scene *Faust* and *Mephistopheles* go to a beer cellar in Leipsic, where students and soldiers are carousing. *Brander* sings his song of the rat, which as in the Gounod opera, meets with but ironical praise from *Mephistopheles,* and he volunteers his famous "Romance of the Flea," a curiosity of music as effective as it is difficult to render.

Chanson de la puce (Song of the Flea)

By Pol Plançon, Bass   (*In French*)   81087   10-inch, $2.00

Gounod's *Mephistopheles* is mild and innocent by the side of the strange utterances of the Devil as portrayed by Berlioz.

This is one of the most interesting numbers in the work, for Berlioz has described, by means of clever forms in the accompaniment, the skipping of the flea in various directions. The words are most fantastic—

Once a king, be it noted, had a fine and lusty flea,
And on this flea he doted, cherish'd him tenderly,
So he sent for his tailor, and to the tailor spake:
"Please to measure this youngster, and coat and breeches make!"

In velvet and in satin
He now was duly drest
Had jewels rare his hat in,
And medals deck'd his breast!

Faust dislikes the scene, and the two vanish from the gaze of the astonished students amid a fiery glow.

LE THÉÂTRE

DANCE OF THE SYLPHS

We next discover *Faust* asleep in a lonely forest on the banks of the Elbe, where the demon murmurs a softly penetrating melody into his ear, lulling him to slumber with these seductive words—

'Mid banks of roses, softly the light reposes,
On this fair, fragrant bed, rest, O Faust, rest thy head—
Here slumber, while lovely visions haunt thy dream
Of radiant forms, rare lips and eyes that fondly beam!

while the gnomes and sylphs dance through his dreams, and the vision of *Marguerite* is seen for the first time.

The next scene corresponds to the Garden Scene of Gounod, and shows a room in *Marguerite's* cottage.

The demon now summons the will-o'-the-wisps in this evocation:

Ye spir-its of in-constant fire, Hast-en here, on the wings of air!

The sprites come flying to *Marguerite's* door, and the demon continues:

> Ye spirits of caprice and of evil, conspire
> To enchant and subdue, and win a maiden soul.
> Now dance, ye sons of Evil, dance in the name of the devil,
> Will-o'-the-wisp and gnome, dance, or away you go!

Then, after the dance of the will-o'-the-wisps, *Mephistopheles* sings his serenade:

Serenade—Mephistopheles

By Emilio de Gogorza, Baritone	(*In French*) 88447	12-inch, $3.00
By Pol Plançon, Bass	(*In French*) 81034	10-inch, 2.00

De-vant la mai - son De ce - lui qui t'a do - - - re, de ce lui, de ce - lui qui t'a do re
Dear Kath'rine, why to the door - of thy lov - - - - - - er, to the door, to the door of thy lov - er

in the accompaniment of which Berlioz has reproduced the peculiar effect of the guitar by *pizzicato* crescendos for strings.

MEPHISTOPHELES:
> Dear Katherine, why to the door of thy lover,
>   Drawest thou nigh?
> Why there timidly hover? why art there?

> Oh, sweet maiden, beware;
>   come away do not enter;
> It were folly to venture.
>   Refrain, nor enter there!

Berlioz's *Mephistopheles* is a much more sardonic and less gentlemanly devil than the one we are accustomed to see in Gounod's opera.

While the sprites dance *Marguerite* apparently sleeps, but soon comes from the house in a kind of trance. She tries to enter the church, but the influence of *Mephistopheles* prevents, and she returns to the house and falls into the arms of *Faust*.

The last act contains four scenes. Scene I shows a moonlit room where the unhappy *Marguerite* sings her lament. This changes to a rocky pass where *Mephistopheles* informs *Faust* that *Marguerite* is about to be executed for the murder of her mother. *Faust* demands that she be saved, but is first required by *Mephistopheles* to sign the fatal contract which pledges his soul to the Devil. Summoning the infernal steeds *Vortex* and *Giaour,* the wild Ride to Hell commences, shown by a striking moving panorama, while at the close the angels are seen hovering above the town to rescue the soul of the pardoned *Marguerite*.

DOUBLE-FACED DAMNATION OF FAUST RECORDS

{Hungarian March	By Sousa's Band}	68052	12 $1.25
{ Carmen—Prelude	By La Scala Orchestra}		
{Menuet des Follets	By l'Orchestre Symphonique}	35462	12 1.25
{ Marche Hongroise	By l'Orchestre Symphonique}		

L'ART DU THÉÂTRE

THE RIDE TO HELL—ACT V

(English)

DAUGHTER OF THE REGIMENT

(French)

LA FILLE DU REGIMENT

(*Lah Feeyeh deh Rezh'-ee-mong'*)

COMIC OPERA IN TWO ACTS

Words by Bayard and St. Georges. Music by Donizetti. First produced at the *Opéra Comique*, Paris, February 11, 1840; Milan, October 30, 1840; Berlin, 1842, at the Royal Opera, and during the next sixty years it had two hundred and fifty performances on that stage. Produced in London, in English, at the Surrey Theatre, December 21, 1847, and during the same year, in Italian, with Jenny Lind. The first American performance of which the Editor has knowledge was that at the New Orleans Opera, March 7, 1843. Jenny Lind, Sontag, Lucca and Patti have all appeared here as *Marie*. Revived in 1902-03 at the Metropolitan Opera House for Sembrich, the cast including Charles Gilibert as *Sulpizio*. Produced by Oscar Hammerstein in 1909, with Tetrazzini, McCormack and Gilibert.

Characters

TONIO, a peasant of Tyrol... Tenor
SULPIZIO, Sergeant of the 21st .... Bass
MARIE, Vivandière of the 21st .... Soprano
MARCHIONESS OF BERKENFIELD .... Mezzo-Soprano

The scene is laid in the Swiss Tyrol.

Up to 1840 Donizetti had written no less than fifty-three operas, and during that year five new ones were created by him. His *Daughter of the Regiment* is a brilliant little opera, with its rollicking songs, its drums, its vivacious heroine and its comic old *Corporal*. Few works are so rich in melody or possess a more entertaining plot, which tells of the Tyrolese peasant, *Tony,* who enters a regiment to win the heart of its *vivandiere,* or daughter.

DONIZETTI

The opera was first produced in 1840 at the *Opéra Comique,* and was the fifty-third work of Donizetti. At first it was not a success, and it was not until after its German and Italian triumphs that French opera-goers took to the work.

At the beginning of the opera *Marie* is a beautiful girl of seventeen, who had been found on the battlefield as an infant, and brought up by *Sulpizio* as the daughter of the regiment. *Marie* is loved by *Tonio,* a young peasant, who had saved her life in the Alps and who follows the regiment to be near her. The young girl returns his affection, and they decide to appeal to *Sulpizio.*

In asking for *Marie's* hand in marriage *Tonio's* suit is brought before the regiment, which decides that he may have the *Vivandière* providing he joins the army, which he promptly does. *Sulpizio* meets the *Marchioness of Berkenfield* and gives her a letter which he had found addressed to her at the time the baby *Marie* was found on the battlefield.

The *Marchioness,* who had married a French army captain far beneath her own rank, immediately recognizes the young girl as her daughter. The marriage had been a secret one and the child was confided to her father's care at her birth. Not wishing to acknowledge this marriage even now, the *Marchioness* declares *Marie* to be her niece, and dismisses *Tonio* as a totally unfit person to wed a high-born maiden.

Marie assumes her proper position in society, her "aunt" selecting a wealthy Count as

83

JENNY LIND AS MARIE

TETRAZZINI AS MARIE

a future husband for her. However, in the midst of all her beautiful surroundings *Marie* continues to long for her sweetheart *Tonio*. Her mother, still pretending to be her aunt, endeavors to persuade her to give up *Tonio* and marry the Count, but *Marie* flatly refuses. In desperation the *Marchioness* reveals herself as the girl's own mother, and the maiden then agrees to accede to her wishes and marry the Count. Touched by *Marie's* filial devotion, the *Marchioness* consents to allow her to marry *Tonio,* who in the meantime, through rapid promotion, has reached a high rank in the French army under Napoleon.

The Victor offers five records from this charming opera; the first being the tuneful *Per viver vicino,* the song of the lover *Tonio.* Mr. McCormack gives a spirited performance of this delightful *Romanza.* The rôle of *Marie* is one of Mme. Hempel's favorite ones, and she has sung for the Victor the famous Adam variations, which display the brilliancy and flexibility of her voice in a marked degree. Mlle. Heilbronner gives a splendid rendition of the *Salut à la France.* Two fine band records are also offered—a Pryor's Band rendition of the gay and spirited *Overture* and a Vessella Band record of the principal airs in the opera.

Per viver vicino (To Be Near Her)
By John McCormack, Tenor (*In Italian*) 74221 12-inch, $1.50

MC CORMACK AS TONIO

Variations on an Air from "Daughter of the Regiment" (Arr. by Adolphe Adam)
By Frieda Hempel, Soprano (*In French*) 88404 12-inch, 3.00

Salut à la France! (Hail to France!)
By Mlle. Heilbronner, Soprano
(*Double-Faced—See below*) (*In French*) 35409 12-inch, 1.25

DOUBLE-FACED AND MISCELLANEOUS DAUGHTER OF THE REGIMENT RECORDS

Overture to Daughter of the Regiment By Pryor's Band *Dance of the Serpents* (*Boccalari*) By Pryor's Band	35065	12-inch, $1.25
Principal Airs of the Opera By Vessella's Band *Fra Diavolo Selection* (*Auber*) By Vessella's Band	35191	12-inch, 1.25
Salut à la France! (Hail to France!) By Mlle. Heilbronner, Soprano (*French*) *Madame Butterfly*—*Sur la mer calmée* By Mlle. Heilbronner, Soprano (*In French*)	35409	12-inch, 1.25

DINORAH
(Dee-noh'-rah)

OPERA IN THREE ACTS

Libretto by Barbier and Carré.   Music by Giacomo Meyerbeer.   First production Paris, *Opéra Comique*, April 4, 1859.   First London production, under direction of Meyerbeer, July 26, 1859.   First American production, November 24, 1864, with Cordier, Brignoli and Amodio.   Sung by Ilma di Murska at Booth's Theatre in 1867; in 1879 with Mariman and Campanini; and in 1882 with Patti.   Revived in 1892 for Marie Van Zandt, and by Oscar Hammerstein in 1907 for Mme. Tetrazzini.

Cast

HOËL, a goatherd .... Bass
CORENTINO, bag-piper .... Tenor
DINORAH, betrothed to Hoël................................. Soprano
HUNTSMAN .... Bass

Place: Breton village of Ploërmel.

© DUPONT   ANCONA AS HOËL

Although the name of Meyerbeer is usually associated with *Robert le Diable, Prophéte* and *Huguenots,* his opera, *Pardon de Ploërmel* (afterwards revised and renamed *Dinorah*), was at one time a favorite work with opera-lovers.

The revival of Meyerbeer's sparkling opera during the last Manhattan season was most welcome, not only for its tunefulness, but because it was an ideal medium for the exhibition of Mme. Tetrazzini's marvelous gifts. Old opera goers in America will remember the productions of the past—that arranged for Marie Van Zandt in 1892; Patti's famous performance a dozen years before; and the fine impersonations of Gerster, di Murska and Marimon. But it is safe to say that no exponent of the part of the wandering Breton shepherdess has ever excelled Mme. Tetrazzini in the rôle.

The plot is utterly absurd—its demented goat-girl, seeking a runaway lover; the lover himself, who contrary to operatic precedent is a baritone, and who spends a year chasing an imaginary treasure; a weak-kneed bag-piper.   These are the principal characters.

But in the music Meyerbeer has atoned for the triviality of the libretto, and the audience listens to the delightful melodies and pays little attention to the plot. The action is laid in Brittany.   *Dinorah,* a maiden of the village of Ploërmel, is about to be wedded to *Hoël,* a goat-herd, when a storm destroys the house of the bride's father.   *Hoël* resolves to rebuild it, and goes off to seek treasure in a haunted region, while *Dinorah,* thinking herself deserted, loses her reason, and wanders through the country with her faithful goat, seeking the absent *Hoël.*

ACT I

As the curtain rises, *Dinorah* enters in her bridal dress, seeking her goat, and finding the animal asleep, sings this lullaby to him.   So lovely an air is worthy of a better object.

Si, carina caprettina (Yes, My Beloved One)

By Giuseppina Huguet, Soprano   *(In Italian)*   35180   12-inch, $1.25

Slumber, darling, sweetly slumber,
Sleep, my belov'd one, sleep!
Soft the evening breeze is playing,
'Neath the cooling shadows here
Flows a streamlet, fresh and clear,
Swift, among the flowers straying,
Alas! six days has she been away,
Nor yet returns!

Perchance she has wandered on the hills
Amid the thorns!
Ah! wert thou to be seized by the wolf—fear not!
I will be there to defend thee—fear not!
Yes, darling sleep in peace,
Sweet little birds your warbling cease,
My beauteous one must sleep.
Awake her not!   Yet softer still!

Corentino, a bag-piper, enters and is terrified at the sight of *Dinorah,* believing her to be an evil fairy about whom he had heard, who causes the runaway traveler to dance till he dies. *Dinorah,* in a spirit of mischief, makes him dance until he is exhausted, and runs away laughing.

Hoël enters, still seeking the treasure, and confides in *Corentino,* telling him that the wizard with whom he had lived for a year had instructed him to seek for a white goat which would guide him to the gold. The bell of *Dinorah's* goat is heard, and *Hoël* pursues it, dragging with him the terrified *Corentino.*

ACT II

The second act begins with the famous shadow dance, for which Meyerbeer has furnished some most beautiful music. *Dinorah* enters, and seeing her shadow in the moonlight, imagines it is a friend and sings and dances to it.

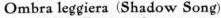

Ombra leggiera (Shadow Song)

By Luisa Tetrazzini, Soprano 88298   12-inch, $3.00
By Maria Galvany, Soprano 88222   12-inch,   3.00
By Olive Kline, Soprano
(*In Italian*) 55047   12-inch,   1.50

Light flitting shadow, companion gay
    Go not away!
Play here beside me, dark fears betide me
When thou dost go far from me!
Ah! go not away, go not away!

Each coming morn I thee would find,
Ah prithee stay and dance with me!
If thou wilt stay, nor go away,
Thou thus shalt hear me sing.

Know'st thou not that Hoël loves me?
That as his bride he claims me!
Love well hath known
Our two hearts to unite!
(*A cloud passes over the moon—the shadow disappears.*)

This dance is accompanied by a waltz, which is full of the most brilliant vocal effects, including a florid cadenza for voice and flute, as in Lucia.

The act closes with the rescue of *Dinorah* by *Hoël* when the bridge, on which she was crossing a ravine, gives away.

ACT III

Act III opens with the famous "Hunter's Song," long a favorite concert number.

Chant du Chasseur (Hunter's Song)

By Pol Plançon, Bass   (*Piano acc.*)
(*In French*)   81065   10-inch, $2.00

Hoël enters, bearing the form of *Dinorah,* who is still senseless. Thinking her dead, he bitterly reproaches himself in the great air, *Sei vendicata.*

COPY'T FOLEY

TETRAZZINI AS DINORAH

Sei vendicata assai (Thou Art Avenged!)

By Titta Ruffo, Baritone   (*In Italian*) 88366   12-inch, $3.00
By Pasquale Amato, Baritone   (*In Italian*) 88473   12-inch,   3.00

HOËL:
'Twas on this self-same spot—a year ago
When from the tempest an asylum my Dinorah
   sought;
Within these arms I pressed her; and now!
Dead!—ah! heaven, I'll not believe it yet!
Look up again, dear angel, thy pardon I im-
   plore!

(*He anxiously watches Dinorah, who gradu-
ally recovers.*)
Great heaven! my pray'r hath risen unto thee!
Yes! she breathes again; her eyes she opens!
But why thus fixedly they gaze upon me?
O heaven, I had forgotten
That grief of reason had bereft her!

Dinorah now opens her eyes and recognizes *Hoël,* her reason having been restored by the shock. The reunited lovers go to the village, are greeted by their friends, and the curtain falls on preparations for the wedding.

SCENE FROM DON CARLOS

DON CARLOS
(Don Kahr'-los)
OPERA IN FOUR ACTS

Libretto by Mèry and Du Locle; music by Verdi. First produced at Paris, March 11, 1867; in London, at Her Majesty's Theatre, June 4, 1867. Although it was revised and improved by Verdi in 1883, it is seldom given nowadays. Revived at La Scala, Milan, in 1912 and recently at Monte Carlo for Ruffo.

Original Paris Cast

PHILIP II	Obin, *Bass*
DON CARLOS	Morère, *Tenor*
MARQUIS DE POSA	Faure, *Baritone*
GRAND INQUISITOR	Belval, *Bass*
ELIZABETH DE VALOIS	Sass, *Soprano*
PRINCESS EPOLI	Gueymard, *Soprano*

Don Carlos belongs to the intermediate stage of Verdi's career as a composer. After his Trovatore, Traviata and Masked Ball had been produced, the younger musicians, influenced by the doctrines of Wagner which had reached Italy, began to protest against the current style of Italian opera. Verdi, however, had already taken a step forward in Don Carlos, written for the Paris *Opéra*, and it was enthusiastically received.

Schiller's magnificent drama gave Verdi great opportunities for dramatic writing, and some of his greatest arias, notably the fine *Per me giunto*, may be found in this opera.

The libretto is based on Schiller's drama of Don Carlos, and tells of the erratic and morbid son of Philip II of Spain, who was engaged to Elizabeth of France, but subsequently became her stepson. The conduct of *Don Carlos* finally became so scandalous that his father placed him under arrest and confined him in the Madrid prison, where he died in 1568, at the age of twenty-three.

The same plot had previously been used by Bona, Milan, 1847; Costa, London, 1844; Moscuzza, Naples, 1862; and also by Ferrari. Operas with the same title but a different plot

BASSANI, MILAN   DON CARLOS AT LA SCALA, MILAN—ACT II, SCENE II

were those of Duplessis (Paris, 1780) and Deshayes (Paris, 1800). John Towers also mentions still others, Barthe (1828) and Nordal (1810).

Don Carlos, son of Philip II of Spain, is in love with Elizabeth of Valois, daughter of the French King, Henry II. For state reasons, however, Henry has arranged that his daughter

FAURE AS DON CARLOS

shall marry King Philip, and accordingly the royal ceremony takes place. The passion which Carlos feels for his young stepmother is as intense as ever, and he confides in Rodrigo, Marquis of Posa, who entreats the Prince to leave the Spanish Court in the hope that he will forget his love. Carlos begs the Queen to obtain Philip's permission for him to join the Flemings in their struggle against the cruelties of the Spaniards. Time seems to have but strengthened the mutual affection of the pair, and the Queen is unable to conceal from Carlos the fact that her love for him is greater than ever.

Princess Eboli, who is herself in love with Carlos, learns of the Queen's affection for the Prince. Her jealousy is aroused and she tells all to Philip. This maddens the King, who is already angry with his son for his sympathy with the Flemings, and, on the advice of the Grand Inquisitor, Carlos is thrown into prison. Rodrigo visits the Prince there, and is shot by friends of the King, who suspect him of helping the Flemings. Carlos is freed and goes to St. Just Monastery to keep a tryst with Elizabeth. The King surprises them there, and his anger being once more aroused, he hands over Carlos to the Officers of the Inquisition, who bear him away to his death as the curtain falls.

The Victor presents three of the most famous of the numbers—the dramatic duet between Carlos and Rodrigo, which Caruso and Scotti have sung in a masterly manner; the great air for Rodrigo, given by Ruffo; and the famous march, played by Sousa.

Dio che nell' alma (God in My Soul)
By Enrico Caruso and Antonio Scotti   (In Italian)   89064   12-inch, $4.00

Per me giunto è il di supremo (The Supreme Day)
By Titta Ruffo, Baritone   (In Italian)   92038   12-inch,   3.00

DOUBLE-FACED DON CARLOS RECORD

{ Grand March   By Sousa's Band }
{ Tannhauser—Pilgrims' Chorus (Wagner)   Victor Brass Quartet } 17133   10-inch, $0.75

(Italian)
DON GIOVANNI
(Don Joh-vahn'-nee)

(Spanish)
DON JUAN
(Don Huahn)

OPERA IN TWO ACTS

Libretto by Lorenzo da Ponte.   Music by Wolfgang Amadeus Mozart.   First produced at Prague, October 29, 1787; at Vienna, May 7, 1788; at Berlin, 1791; Paris, 1811.   First London production April 12, 1817; produced in New York May 29, 1826. First New Orleans production May 9, 1853.   Some notable revivals occurred in 1889 at Metropolitan Opera House, with Reichmann, Kalisch, Behrens and Fischer; in 1898 with Sembrich, Nordica, Eames and Plançon; in 1900 with Sembrich, Nordica and de Reszke; and at the Manhattan Opera in 1909 with Russ, Donalda, Bonci and Renaud.

At the great Mozart Festival performance of 1914 in Salzburg, the composer's birth-place, the cast (made up almost entirely of Victor artists), included Lilli Lehmann, Farrar, de Segurola, McCormack and Forsell.

Cast

DON GIOVANNI, a licentious young nobleman.....................Baritone
DON OCTAVIO, (*Oct-tah'-vee-oh*) betrothed to Donna Anna...............Tenor
LEPORELLO, (*Lep-oh-rel'-loh*) servant of Don Giovanni...................Bass
DON PEDRO, (*Pay-droh*) the Commandant.............................Bass
DONNA ANNA, his daughter......................................Soprano
MASETTO, (*Mas-set'-toh*) a peasant................................Bass
ZERLINA, (*Zer-lee'-nah*) betrothed to Masetto.......................Soprano
DONNA ELVIRA, (*El-vee'-rah*) a lady of Burgos......................Soprano
Peasants, Musicians, Dancers, Demons.

Scene and Period: Seville, in the middle of the seventeenth century.

Mozart's Don Giovanni was written in 1787 and produced during the same year at Prague.   Da Ponte, the librettist, was a Viennese Court dramatist, who had also written Le Nozze di Figaro.   The plot of the opera was probably founded upon a play entitled *El Burlador de Sevilla y Convidada de piedra,* attributed to Tirso de Molina, a Spanish monk and prior of a monastery at Madrid.   This had also served as a basis for numerous other "Don Juan" plays and operas by Fabrizzi, Gardi, Raimondi, Carnicer and latterly Dargomyszky, the Russian composer.

ACT I

SCENE I—*The Courtyard of the Commandant's Palace at Seville.   It is Night*

The wicked *Don Giovanni,* ever pursuing his gay conquests, attempts to enter *Donna Anna's* apartments. She cries for help and he tries to escape, but is pursued by the angry girl, who endeavors to

EDOUARD DE RESZKE
AS LEPORELLO

COPY'T DUPONT

SCOTTI AS DON GIOVANNI

penetrate his disguise. Her father comes to the rescue and is mortally wounded by the *Don*, who makes his escape, followed by *Leporello*, his servant. *Donna Anna* is overcome with grief, and charges her betrothed, *Don Octavio*, to avenge her father's death.

OBER AS ELVIRA

SCENE II—*An Inn in a Deserted Spot Outside Seville*

Don Giovanni and *Leporello* enter and conceal themselves as a lady approaches in a carriage. Hoping for a new conquest, the *Don* comes forward, hat in hand, but is surprised to find that it is *Donna Elvira*, a young woman whom he has lately deceived and deserted. She denounces him for his baseness and he makes his escape, leaving *Leporello* to explain as best he can. *Leporello* rather enjoys the situation, produces his diary, and adds to the lady's anger by reading a list of the mistresses of the *Don*. This list is recited by *Leporello* in the famous *Il catalogo*.

RENAUD AS DON GIOVANNI

Madamina, il catalogo (Gentle Lady, this List)
By Arcangelo Rossi   (*Double-faced—See page 94*)   (*Italian*)   62623 10-inch, $0.75

CLICHE DU GUY   LEPORELLO

Nella bionda (The Fair One)
By Marcel Journet, Bass
(*In Italian*)   74191   12-inch, $1.50

LEPORELLO:
Ev'ry country, ev'ry township, fully confesses
Those of the sex whom to his rank he presses.
Gentle lady, this my catalogue numbers
All whose charms lent my master beguiling.
'Tis a document of my compiling,
An it please ye, peruse it with me.
In Italia,—six hundred and forty:
Then in Germany,—double fifty seem plenty;
While in old Spain here,—we count thousands three!
Some you see are country damsels,
Waiting-maids and city ma'amselles,
Countess', duchess', baronesses,
Viscount'—ev'ry kind of 'esses.
Womenfolk of all conditions,
Ev'ry form and ev'ry state!

Leporello is a unique character, who always stands forth as an admirable foil to the polished villainies of the suave and distinguished *Don*. This great buffo number, usually called the *Catalogue Song*, is full of the broadest humor, and is given by these artists with all the sly humor, gaiety, irony and sentiment which it requires.

Donna Elvira is horrified and drives off, swearing vengeance.

SCENE III—*In the Suburbs of Seville. Don Giovanni's Palace Visible on the Right*

A rustic wedding party comprising *Zerlina, Masetto* and a company of peasants are enjoying an outing. *Don Giovanni* and *Leporello* appear, and the *Don* is charmed at the sight of so much youthful beauty. He bids *Leporello* conduct the party to his palace and give them refreshments, contriving, however, to detain *Zerlina. Masetto* protests, but the *Don* points significantly to his sword and the bridegroom prudently decides to follow the peasants.

The *Don* then proceeds to flatter the young girl and tells her she is too beautiful for such a clown as *Masetto.* She is impressed and coquettes with him in the melodious duet, *La ci darem,* the witty phrases and delicate harmonies of which make it one of the gems of Mozart's opera.

La ci darem la mano (Thy Little Hand, Love!)

By Geraldine Farrar, Soprano, and
Antonio Scotti, Baritone
(*In Italian*) 89015 12-inch, $4.00

VANDYK, LONDON
NIELSEN AS ZERLINA

By Emma Eames, Soprano, and Emilio de Gogorza, Baritone
(*In Italian*) 89005 12-inch, $4.00
By Graziella Pareto, Soprano, and Titta Ruffo,
Baritone (*In Italian*) 92505 12-inch, 4.00

This celebrated number, which has been sung by many famous artists during the one hundred and twenty-eight years since its first hearing, is one of the best examples of the many sparkling concerted numbers which Mozart has written. Always interesting, it is wholly delightful when sung by such artists as those who have rendered it for the Victor. Not less than three versions, by famous exponents of the characters of *Zerlina* and *Don Giovanni,* are presented here.

DON GIOVANNI:
    Nay, bid me not resign, love, coldly the hand
        I press,
    Oh! say thou wilt be mine, love, breathe but
        that one word "yes."

ZERLINA:
    I would and yet I would not, I feel my heart
        misgive,
    Shouldst thou prove false, I could not become
        thy scorn and live.

DON GIOVANNI:
    Come then, oh come then, dearest.

ZERLINA:
    Yet should thy fondness alter.

DON GIOVANNI:
    Nay, love, in vain thou fearest.

BOTH:
    Yes, hand and heart uniting, each other's
        cause requiting,
    Our joy no bounds shall know!

PHOTO CLIFTON, BRISTOL

JEAN DE RESZKE AS DON GIO-
VANNI. HIS DÉBUT AS A
BARITONE (LONDON, 1875)

Giovanni is about to lead *Zerlina* away, when *Donna Elvira,* who has been watching, rescues the young girl and carries her off, to the chagrin of the *Don. Donna Anna* now enters with *Octavio,* who asks the help of his friend *Don Giovanni* in tracing the murderer of *Donna Anna's* father. The *Don* assures them of his devotion, and goes to his palace, while *Donna Anna* tells her lover that she recognizes by his voice that *Don Giovanni* is the one who slew her father.

They depart, and *Leporello* and the *Don* enter. The servant tells his master that when *Donna Elvira* and *Zerlina*
arrived at the palace, and *Elvira* attempted to tell the
peasants the truth about the *Don,* he led her gently outside the gate and then locked it. He is complimented
by his master, who bids him prepare for the feast of the
evening. Left alone, the gay *Don* sings his brilliant
Drinking Song, famous in every land.

Fin ch' han dal vino (Wine, Flow a Fountain)

By Titta Ruffo, Baritone,
(*In Italian*) **87174   10-inch, $2.00**

DON GIOVANNI:
 Wine, flow a fountain!
 Every vestal, bid to the festal.
 Quickly repair. All that are witty,
 All that are pretty,
 Provide each one with excellent fare.
 Then, set them tripping it, wilful or willing;
 Some minueting, some seguidilling,
 Some for bolero only may care!
 I shall enjoy in slyly decoying
 One or another, love to declare;
 My list adorning, long ere the morning,
 Fully with twenty names of the fair!

Ruffo's dashing portrayal of the *Don* is famous in
Europe and South America, and was one of his greatest
successes here. He sings this lively *brindisi* with brilliancy
and abandon.

PHOTO BERGER

ABOTT AND RENAUD AS ZERLINA AND
DON GIOVANNI

The scene changes to *Don Giovanni's* garden. *Zerlina* is
endeavoring to make her peace with *Masetto,* but he is sulky. She then sings her lovely *Batti, batti.*

Batti, batti, o bel Masetto (Scold Me, dear Masetto)

By Marcella Sembrich, Soprano   (*In Italian*) **88026   12-inch, $3.00**

This gentle number is in striking contrast to the brilliant writing in the lighter bits of
Zerlina's music.

Chide me, dear Masetto,
 Chide Zerlina at your will;
Like the patient lamb I'll suffer,
 Meek and mute and loving still.
Ah! I see, love, you're relenting,
 Pardon, kneeling, I implore!
Night and day, to thee devoted,
 Here I vow to err no more.

COPY'T DUPONT

MAUREL AS DON GIOVANNI

Masetto is only half appeased, but goes in to
dance with his bride.
Donna Anna, Donna Elvira
and *Don Octavio,* disguised
and masked, enter and sing
a trio, in which they pledge
themselves to have revenge
on the traitor.

The scene changes to
the interior of the palace,
where the ball is in progress. *Don Giovanni* con-
tinues his efforts to get
Zerlina away from her jealous and watchful lover,
and finally succeeds, but
Zerlina calls for help and
Masetto and the three conspirators rush to her assist-

PERIER AS DON JUAN
(OPÉRA COMIQUE)

ance. They denounce *Don Giovanni*, who defies them with drawn sword, and makes his escape from the palace.

ACT II

SCENE I—*A Square in Seville. Donna Elvira's Residence on the Left. It is a Moonlight Night*

Don Giovanni, followed by his servant, enters, wrapped in a mantle and carrying a mandolin. He has heard of a pretty servant whom *Donna Elvira* possesses, and is plotting to get the mistress out of the way. As *Elvira* sits at her window, he addresses her, pretending to be repentant, but when she comes out he pushes *Leporello* forward to impersonate him. While they are conversing, the *Don* makes a great outcry and the pair run off in fright.

The coast clear, the *Don* sings his famous *Serenade* to the fair waiting maid.

Serenata, "Deh vieni alla finestra" (Open Thy Window, Love)

By Antonio Scotti, Baritone
    (*In Italian*)   88194 12-inch, $3.00
By Emilio de Gogorza, Baritone
    (*In Italian*)   88447 12-inch, 3.00

CLEMENT AS DON OTTAVIO

By Titto Ruffo, Baritone   (*In Italian*)   87112 10-inch, $2.00
By M. Hector Dufranne, Baritone   (*In French*) *45011 10-inch, 1.00
By Giuseppè de Luca, Baritone   (*Piano acc.*) (*In Italian*) *62623 10-inch, .75

> DON GIOVANNI:
> Ope, ope thy casement, dearest,
>   Thyself one moment show;
> Oh, if my pray'r thou hearest,
>   Wave but that arm of snow.
> Canst thou my ceaseless sighing
>   With cold indif'rence greet?
> Ah! wouldst thou see me dying
>   Despairing, at thy feet?
> Thy sigh were balm amid a heav'n of flowers;
>   Oh, for one kiss, this soul would perish!

Ruffo's impersonation of *Don Giovanni* is admirable in every respect. He is the profligate nobleman and irresistible wooer to the life, and sings the difficult score with ease. This famous serenade is given by Scotti with the grace and ease which never fail him; while Mr. De Gogorza, whose concert audiences are very fond of the number, sings it with dash and spirit. Two records by famous European baritones are also offered by M. Dufranne, well known in America, and Signor de Luca, who is about to join the Metropolitan forces.

His amours are rudely interrupted by *Masetto,* who appears with a company of villagers, all armed with muskets, seeking the villain. The *Don,* pretending to be *Leporello,* offers to put them on the right track. Then follows a series of amusing situations, ending with the capture of the supposed *Don* by the three conspirators, but it proves to be *Leporello,* who takes advantage of the situation to make his escape.

The next scene shows the Cathedral Square, with the statue of the murdered Commandant in the centre. The *Don* and *Leporello* enter, and are discussing the events of the evening, when the statue speaks to them. *Leporello* is terrified, but the *Don* defies all spirits and boldly invites the statue to supper.

The scene changes to the banquet hall, where in the midst of the festivities a loud knocking is heard. The guests flee in terror, as the gigantic figure of the Commandant

* *Double-Faced Record—See page 94.*

PHOTO FELIX

VIX AS ELVIRA (OPÉRA COMIQUE)

appears. *Leporello* cowers in terror, but *Don Giovanni* is defiant until the ghost seizes his hand, when he feels for the first time a terrible fear. The statue sinks, flames appear on all sides, and demons rise and seize the guilty libertine.

DOUBLE-FACED DON GIOVANNI RECORDS

THE GHOST

Minuet from Act I	By Victor Dance Orchestra	35060	12-inch, $1.25
Forward March—*Two Step*	By Victor Dance Orchestra		
Sérénade By M. Hector Dufranne, Baritone (*In French*)		45011	10-inch, 1.00
Si j'étais Roi—Un regard de ses yeux!—Leon Beyle, Tenor (*French*)			
Madamina, il catalogo—By Arcangelo Rossi, Bass (*In Italian*)		62623	10-inch, .75
Serenata—Deh! vieni alla finestra (Open Thy Window, Love) By Giuseppè de Luca, Baritone			

ELVIRA, LEPORELLO AND THE DON—ACT II

DONNE CURIOSE—"THE CLUB," ACT I

(German)
DIE NEUGIERIGEN FRAUEN

(Italian)
LE DONNE CURIOSE
(*Don-neh Koo-ree-oh'-seh*)

(English)
INQUISITIVE WOMEN

MUSICAL COMEDY IN THREE ACTS

Libretto by Luigi Sugana, after Carlo Goldoni; music by Ermanna Wolf-Ferrari. Produced in Munich November 27, 1903, as *Die Neugierigen Frauen*. First United States production, at the Metropolitan Opera House, New York, January 3, 1912, with Farrar, Jadlowker, Scotti, Fornia and Murphy.

Characters

OTTAVIO, a rich Venetian	Bass
BEATRICE, his wife	Mezzo-Soprano
ROSAURA, his daughter	Soprano
FLORINDO, betrothed to Rosaura	Tenor
PANTALONE, a Venetian merchant	Buffo-Baritone
LELIO, } his friends	{ Baritone
LEANDRO, }	{ Tenor
COLOMBINA, Rosaura's maid	Soprano
ELEANORA, wife to Lelio	Soprano
ARLECCHINO, servant to Pantalone	Buffo-Bass

Servants, gondoliers, men and women of the populace.

Time and Place : Venice ; the middle of the eighteenth century.

FARRAR AND JADLOWKER
AS ROSAURA AND FLORINDO

Le Donne Curiose is a genuine comedy. The plot is very simple, and deals with the scheming of *Beatrice, Rosaura, Eleanora* and *Colombina* to gain entrance to the Friendship Clubhouse, of which their husbands and lovers are members. Over the door of the club may be seen the motto, "No Women Admitted." Each woman has her own theory as to the doings behind closed doors, and they seek in various ways to gain an entrance. In reality the men are enjoying themselves with simple masculine pleasures, and chuckling over the intense curiosity of their wives and sweethearts.

With the help of *Colombina* and *Arlecchino*, and by luring the keys from the pocket of one of the members, the ladies finally succeed in making an entrance within the sacred walls, and are surprised to find the men enjoying themselves harmlessly at dinner. On being discovered by the husbands they are forgiven, and the evening ends happily with a merry dance.

The Victor offers an air from Act II—the love duet of *Rosaura* and *Florindo,* sung after the former has induced her fiancée to give her the keys.

Il cor nel contento (My Heart, How it Leaps in Rejoicing)

By Geraldine Farrar and Herman Jadlowker   *(Italian)* 88359 12-inch, $3.00

SCENE FROM ACT III

THE GARDEN—ACT III

(Italian)

DON PASQUALE

(Don Pahss-quah'-leh)

COMIC OPERA IN THREE ACTS

Text and music by Gaetano Donizetti. Libretto adapted from the older Italian opera *Ser Marc' Antonio*, by Camerano. First presented at the *Théâtre des Italiens*, Paris, on January 4, 1843. First production in Paris, in French, 1864. First London production June 30, 1843. First New York production March 9, 1846, in English, and in 1849 in Italian.

Recently revived at the New Theatre, New York (December 23, 1909), with di Pasquali, Bonci, Scotti and Pini-Corsi; at the Metropolitan with Sembrich, Scotti and Rossi; and at the Boston Opera House with Nielsen, Bourrillon, Antonio Pini-Corsi and Fornari.

Characters

DON PASQUALE, an old bachelor....................................Bass
DR. MALATESTA, his friend, a physician ....Baritone
ERNESTO, nephew of Don Pasquale ....Tenor
NORINA, beloved of Ernesto ....Soprano
A NOTARY...Baritone
Chorus of Valets and Chambermaids, Majordomo, Dressmaker and Hairdresser.

Scene and Period: Rome;   the beginning of the nineteenth century.

This brightest of genuine lyric comedies always appeals to that class of opera-goers who find the present-day comic opera or musical comedy to be cheap, gaudy and lacking in genuine humor. *Don Pasquale* is pure entertainment, nothing else, the true spirit of comedy being found in the music as well as the plot; and both are delightful when the opera is presented by such artists as the Victor has assembled for this series.

Overture to Don Pasquale
By La Scala Orchestra
*68010   12-inch, $1.25

ACT I
SCENE—*A Room in Don Pasquale's House*

The *Don* is eagerly awaiting the arrival of *Dr. Malatesta*, who has promised to obtain for him a young and lovely bride.

Son nov'ore ('Tis Nine O'clock !)
By Pini-Corsi and Badini
(*In Italian*) *68273   12-inch, $1.25

The *Doctor* enters, declares he has found the bride, and proceeds to describe the charmer. The *Don* is overjoyed, and insists on seeing the lady at once. When the *Doctor* leaves, *Pasquale* gives vent to his feelings in an amusing air.

Un foco insolito (A Fire All Unfelt Before)
By Pini-Corsi and Badini
(*In Italian*) *62104   10-inch, $0.75

PASQUALE:
A fire, all unfelt before,
Burns in my heart's core:
I can resist no more—
I'll strive no longer.
Of old age enfeebling me,
Forgot is the misery,
Feeling still young to be—
Than twenty much stronger.

© MISHKIN

BORI AS NORINA—ACT I

His nephew enters, and is again urged by his uncle to give up *Norina,* whom the uncle calls a vain, coquettish widow. *Ernesto* refuses, and *Don Pasquale* announces his intention of marrying and disinheriting his nephew. The young man, at first incredulous, is finally convinced that his uncle is in earnest and gives way to despair, beginning his first air:

Sogno soave e casto (Fond Dream of Love)
By Giuseppe Acerbi, Tenor   (*In Italian*) *62624   10-inch, $0.75

ERNESTO:
Sweet holy dreams I loved to cherish
Of early youth, adieu! ye vanish!
If I e'er long'd for riches, splendor,
It was but for thee, love;

But now, poor and abandon'd, I,
Reduc'd from my condition high,
Sooner than thee in misery see,
Dearest, I'll renounce thee.

Before leaving his uncle, *Ernesto* begs him to consult *Dr. Malatesta* for advice, but *Don Pasquale* says it was the *Doctor* himself who proposed the plan and offered his own sister as the happy bride. *Ernesto* is astonished to hear that the *Doctor,* who he thought was his friend, had deserted him.

SCENE II—*A Room in Norina's House*

Norina is reading a romance, and at the beginning of her air quotes from the book:

Quel guardo (Glances so Soft)
By Giuseppina Huguet, Soprano   (*In Italian*) *68272   12-inch, $1.25

She then declares that she too knows the value of a glance and smile.

Cavatina—So anch'io la virtù magica (I, Too, Thy Magic Virtues Know)
By Amelia Pollini, Soprano   (*In Italian*) *62103   10-inch, $0.75

NORINA:
I, too, thy magic virtues know,
Of glance well tim'd and tender,
A gentle smile, born to beguile,
I know—an old offender!
A hidden tear, a languor near,

I know the mode, oh, dear,
Of love's bewitching wiles,
His facile arts and guiles. . . . .
To lure with wanton smiles,
I know the modes, oh, dear!

Double-Faced Record—See page 102.

A servant gives her a letter from *Ernesto,* just as the *Doctor* enters and informs her that he has conceived a scheme to force her lover's guardian to consent to the marriage. *Norina* declares she will have nothing to do with it, bidding him to read *Ernesto's* despairing letter, in which the young man tells her he is disinherited and will leave Rome, bidding her a last farewell.

The *Doctor* soothes her, telling her he will induce *Ernesto* to remain, and then reveals the details of the plot against *Don Pasquale,* in which he proposes to play on the vanity of the old bachelor, by pretending to find him a young and lovely wife. They decide that *Norina* shall play the part of this girl, and go through a mock marriage with *Don Pasquale.* *Norina* is delighted and begins to rehearse her new rôle. This takes the form of a charming duet, which ends the first act and which is always greatly admired. Two records of this sprightly duet are cataloged here.

Pronta io son (My Part I'll Play)

By Marcella Sembrich, Soprano, and Antonio Scotti, Baritone

(*In Italian*) 89002 12-inch, $4.00

By Giuseppina Huguet, Soprano, and Ernesto Badini, Baritone

(*In Italian*) *68272 12-inch, 1.25

NORINA:
My part I'll play, if not offending
Against my lover's repose and quiet;
Well the plot with me will fare!
DOCTOR:
Our plot but tends, you may believe,
Don Pasquale to deceive.
NORINA:
We're quite agreed, and I'm enlisted.
Would you have me gay or tearful?
DOCTOR:
Listen, and you'll all be told;—
You must play simplicity.
NORINA:
I'll lessons give—leave that to me.

"I'm so confused—I'm young, you know—
Thank you—Your servant,—Yes, sir,—Oh!"
DOCTOR:
Bravo, bravo, capital!
It can't be better—all goes well!
NORINA:
Head turned aside—"Oh fie! oh fie!"
DOCTOR:
Pursed-up mouth—"Ashamed am I."
NORINA:
"I'm quite confus'd, my thoughts take wing—"
DOCTOR:
Oh, clever creature! Just the thing!
BOTH:
Of this old fool, all sense who spurn'd;—
This time the head will be quite turn'd!

The scene is continued in another sprightly duet, which closes the act.

Vado corro (Haste We!)

By Giuseppina Huguet and Ernesto Badini   (*Italian*) *62097 10-inch, $0.75

ACT II

SCENE—*A Richly Furnished Hall in Don Pasquale's House*

Don Pasquale, in the most youthful of wedding garments, enters and struts up and down, admiring himself, until the *Doctor* arrives with *Norina,* who is closely veiled. She pretends to be shrinking and frightened, and the *Doctor,* beginning a delightfully humorous trio, the first of the concerted numbers in this act, begs her to have courage.

The pretended notary now arrives, and another comical scene ensues as the mock ceremony is performed. *Pasquale,* so much in love that his judgment is clouded, is not only induced to sign over one-half his property to his wife, but agrees that she shall be absolute mistress of the house. As *Norina* is signing, *Ernesto's* voice is heard outside demanding admittance, having come to bid his uncle farewell. He is amazed to see *Norina* posing as the *Doctor's* sister and about to be wedded to his uncle, and tries to interfere, but is restrained by *Malatesta.*

The moment *Norina* affixes her signature to the contract her manner changes, and when *Pasquale* attempts to embrace her she coldly asks him not to be so rude. *Pasquale* is astonished and *Ernesto* laughs, which enrages the old man so that he orders his nephew from the room. *Norina* stops him and says that as *Don Pasquale* is too old, fat and feeble to attend a young wife, she must have a young cavalier to attend her, and signifies that *Ernesto* is her choice. *Don Pasquale* is thunderstruck and attempts to protest, but *Norina* warns him that if her words are not sufficient to keep him in his place she will beat him! This is the last straw, and the bewildered old man stands in a daze, his brain refusing to comprehend what has happened!

This tableau is followed by the quartet, *E rimasto.*

Double-Faced Record—See page 102.

E rimasto la impietrato (He Stands Immovable)

By Linda Brambilla, Soprano; Antonio Pini-Corsi, Baritone; Gaetano Pini-Corsi, Tenor; Agusto Scipioni, Bass

(*In Italian*) *16566 10-inch, $0.75

PASQUALE:
Dream I? Sleep I? What's amiss?
Kicks—cuffs: good—a fine pretext—
'Tis well she warn'd me now of this—what's
  that mean?
We shall see what's coming next!
I, Don Pasquale, she'd think meet
To trample underneath her feet!

NORINA AND ERNESTO:
He stands petrified, and seems—

To know not if he wakes or dreams!
He's like a man by lightning struck!
No drop of blood runs in his veins.

MALATESTA:
Take heart, Pasquale, my old buck,
Don't be discouraged, use your brains.

NORINA:
Now then, at least, my worthy friend,
You must begin to comprehend.

The great finale to Act II then follows, and the curtain always descends amid a gale of laughter from the audience. *Norina* rings a bell, summoning the servants, and announces that she is now sole mistress of the house. She orders new servants engaged, two carriages, new furniture, etc., planning expenditures on a lavish scale. *Don Pasquale* attempts to protest, but is silenced, and in a voice choked with rage and astonishment begins the finale.

Son tradito (I Am Betrayed!)

By Giuseppina Huguet, Soprano; Antonio Pini-Corsi, Baritone; Gaetano Pini-Corsi, Tenor; Agusto Scipioni, Bass

(*In Italian*) *62097 10-inch, $0.75

PASQUALE:
I am betray'd, trod down and beat,
A laughing stock to all I meet;
Oh! with mingled rage and spite
I am suffocating quite!

NORINA (*to Ernesto*):
Now you see, ungrateful heart,
How unjust was your suspicion:
Love, to bring him to submission,
Counsell'd me to play this part.

ERNESTO (*to Norina*):
You are justified, dear heart;
Momentary my suspicion.
Love, to bring him to submission,
Counsell'd thee to play this part.

ALL (*pointing to Don Pasquale*):
Don Pasquale, poor, dear wight,
Is nearly suffocated quite!

MALATESTA (*to Pasquale*):
You're a little heated, really—
Do go to bed, dear Don Pasquale.
(*To Norina, in a tone of reproof.*)
On my brother-in-law to play
Thus, I'll not endure, I say!
(*To the lovers, who are embracing behind Don
  Pasquale's back.*)
Silly ones, for Heaven's sake, pray,
Don't, I beg, yourselves betray!

ACT III

(*Same as Act I—On the floor and furniture are piled up dresses, bandboxes, furs, etc., in great profusion. Servants are running to and fro with bustle and excitement*)

Don Pasquale is seen amid the confusion, looking with utmost consternation at a huge pile of bills. He throws them down in despair, and as *Norina* approaches resolves to make one last attempt to remain master in his own house.

Signorina in tanta fretta (My Lady, Why This Haste?)

By Emilia Corsi, Soprano, and Antonio Pini-Corsi, Baritone

(*In Italian*) *68273 12-inch, $1.25

She is dressed to go out, and is hastening to her carriage when *Don Pasquale* begins:

PASQUALE:
Prithee, where are you running in such haste,
Young lady, may I beg you will inform me?

NORINA:
Oh! that's a thing that very soon is told:
I'm going to the theatre to divert me.

PASQUALE:
But the husband, with your leave—excuse me
Saying so—may perchance object to it.

NORINA:
The husband sees, and wisely holds his tongue:
For when he speaks there's no one listens to
  him.

PASQUALE (*with rising warmth*):
Not to put me to the trial, Madame,—
It is for your own good that I advise you—
You'll to your chamber go, this very instant—
Remain content at home—stay in the house.

NORINA (*ironically*):
Oh, really!

(*With great heat.*)
Why, you impertinent!
But there—take what you well deserve, sir!
(*Boxes his ears.*)

PASQUALE:
Ah!
(It is all over with you, Don Pasquale!
All that now remains for you to do
Is quietly to go and drown yourself!)

NORINA:
(I must confess, 'tis rather hard a lesson;
Yet was required to have its due effect.)
(*To Don Pasquale*):
I'm going now, then—

PASQUALE:
Oh, yes, certainly!
But do not take the trouble to return.

NORINA:
Oh, we shall see each other in the morning.

PASQUALE:
A face of wood—a closed door, you will find.

*Double-Faced Record—See page 102.

As she goes out she intentionally drops a note which *Don Pasquale* seizes and peruses. He is petrified to find that it reads:

BORI AS NORINA—ACT II

"Adored Sophrania—
Between the hours of nine and ten
I shall be at the bottom of the garden—

This is too much, and the unhappy man runs in search of *Malatesta*. *Ernesto* and the *Doctor* enter, discussing the plot, and the young man, after being instructed to be at the garden rendezvous at nine that evening, goes out.

Pasquale returns, and going solemnly up to the *Doctor*, exclaims: ' Brother-in-law, in me, alas, you see a dead man, walking upright," and tells him of the contents of the note. *Malatesta* pretends to sympathize and proposes that they lie in wait for the guilty lovers that evening and teach them a severe lesson. *Pasquale* gloats over his coming triumph, and begins the duet.

Aspetta aspetta cara esposina (Wait, Wait, Dear Little Wife)

By Antonio Pini-Corsi, Baritone, and Giovanni Polese, Baritone (*Double-Faced—See page 102*) (*In Italian*) 62103 10-inch, $0.75

PASQUALE:
Wait, wait, dear little wife,
I soon reveng'd will be:
E'en now 'tis near, my life.
This night, without delay,
Thou must the reckoning pay!

MALATESTA (*aside*):
Oh, the poor fellow!
Vengeance he's prating;
Let the dolt bellow—
He knows not what's waiting!

SCENE II—*Don Pasquale's Garden—It is Night—Ernesto is Discovered Waiting*

This scene begins with the beautiful *serenade*, the most melodious of the airs in Donizetti's work.

Serenata—Com' e gentil (Soft Beams the Light)

By Enrico Caruso, Tenor (*In Italian*) 85048 12-inch, $3.00
By Aristodemo Giorgini, Tenor, and La Scala Chorus
　　　　　　　　　　　　　　　　　　(*In Italian*) 76010 12-inch, 2.00

ERNESTO:
Oh! summer night, thy tranquil light
Was made for those who shun the busy day,
Who love too well, yet blush to tell
The hopes that led their hearts astray!
All now is still, on dale, on hill,
And none are nigh, with curious eye;
Then why, my love, oh, why delay?
Your lattice open to the starry night,
And with your presence make the world more
　　　　bright!

Norina joins *Ernesto*, and they are reconciled in a duet, *Tell Me Again*. *Pasquale* and the *Doctor*, with dark lanterns, enter softly and hide behind the trees, but the irate old man can contain himself no longer and rushes out to denounce the lovers. *Ernesto* vanishes and *Norina* calmly declares there was no one with her, that she had merely come out to get fresh air. *Pasquale* is so beside himself with rage and chagrin that *Malatesta* considers it time to end the farce, and proposes to rid *Pasquale* of his bride by marrying her to *Ernesto*, revealing that the first marriage was not a real one, and that the lady was not his sister but *Norina*. *Pasquale* is so glad to be rid of such an extravagant termagant that he pardons the deception, consents to the union, and settles an income on the happy pair.

DOUBLE-FACED DON PASQUALE RECORDS

Signorina in tanta fretta (My Lady, Why This Haste?) By Emilia Corsi and Antonio Pini-Corsi (*In Italian*) Son nov' ore ('Tis Nine O'clock!) By Antonio Pini-Corsi and Ernesto Badini (*In Italian*)	68273	12-inch,	$1.25
Quel guardo, un sorrisetto (Glances So Soft) By Giuseppina Huguet, Soprano (*In Italian*) Pronta io son (My Part I'll Play) By Giuseppina Huguet and Ernesto Badini (*In Italian*)	68272	12-inch,	1.25
Overture By La Scala Orchestra *Barbiere di Siviglia—Manca un foglio* By La Scala Orchestra	68010	12-inch,	1.25
Un foco insolito (A Fire All Unfelt Before) By Antonio Pini-Corsi and Ernesto Badini (*In Italian*) Vado, corro (Haste We!) By Emilia Corsi, Soprano, and Ernesto Badini, Baritone (*In Italian*)	62104	10-inch,	.75
E rimasto la impietrato (He Stands Immovable) By Linda Brambilla, Soprano; Antonio Pini-Corsi, Baritone; G. Pini-Corsi, Tenor; Scipioni, Bass (*In Italian*) *Elisir d'amore—Io sonno ricco* (*I Have Riches*) By Passeri, Soprano; A. Pini-Corsi, Baritone; and Chorus (*In Italian*)	16566	10-inch,	.75
Cavatina—So anch'io lo virtù magica (I, Too, Thy Magic Virtues Know) By Amelia Pollini, Soprano (*In Italian*) Aspetta aspetta cara esposina (Wait, Wait, Dear Little Wife) By Antonio Pini-Corsi, Baritone, and Giovanni Polese, Baritone (*In Italian*)	62103	10-inch,	.75
Sogno soave e casto (Fond Dream of Love) By Giuseppe Acerbi, Tenor (*In Italian*) *Faust—Coro de soldados* (*Soldiers' Chorus*) La Scala Chorus	62624	10-inch,	.75
Vado corro (Haste We) By Giuseppina Huguet, Soprano, and Ernesto Badini, Baritone (*In Italian*) Son tradito By Giuseppina Huguet, Soprano; Antonio Pini-Corsi, Baritone; Gaetano Pini-Corsi, Tenor; Agusto Scipioni, Bass (*In Italian*)	62097	10-inch,	.75

LANDE

SCENE FOR ACT II AT METROPOLITAN OPERA

(Italian)
L'ELISIR D'AMORE
(*Ay-lee-zeer' dam-oh'-reh*)

(English)
THE ELIXIR OF LOVE

OPERA IN TWO ACTS

Text by Romani. Music by Gaetano Donizetti. First produced in Milan, May 12, 1832;
Barcelona, 1833; Paris, 1839; Berlin, 1844. First London production December 10, 1836.
First American production at the New Orleans Opera March 30, 1842. Given in Boston in
English by the Seguins shortly afterward.

Cast

ADINA, a wealthy and independent young woman ....Soprano
NEMORINO, a young peasant, in love with Adina....................Tenor
BELCORE, sergeant of the village garrison............................Bass
DOCTOR DULCAMARA, a quack doctor.............................Buffo

A Landlord, a Notary, Peasants, Soldiers, Villagers.

Scene and Period: A little Italian village ; the nineteenth century.

This delightful example of Donizetti's work is a real *opéra bouffe,* and while simple and
unconventional in plot, it has always been a favorite because of its lovely music.

Adina, a lively village beauty and heiress, is loved by a young peasant, *Nemorino,* who
although handsome and manly, is afraid to press his suit; but while the beauty treats him
rather coolly she is by no means indifferent to his love.

ACT I
SCENE—*The Homestead of Adina's Farm*

Adina and her companion are seated under a tree reading. *Nemorino* is near, pensively
observing his *innamorata,* and sings his first *Cavatina.*

Quant'e bella ! (Ah! How Lovely)

By Emilio Perea, Tenor   (*In Italian*)   *62626   10-inch, $0.75

NEMORINO:
Ah! how lovely! ah! how dear to me!
While I gaze I adore more deeply;
Ah! what rapture that soft bosom
With a mutual flame to move.
But while reading, studying, improving,
She hath learning and every attainment,
While I can nothing do but love!

Adina then reads to her friends a legend of a cruel lady who coldly treated a knight
who loved her, and only smiled on him when he gave her a love potion. *Nemorino* wishes
he could find the receipt for this potent elixir.

Martial music is heard and *Belcore,* a dashing sergeant stationed near the village,
appears with a bouquet for *Adina.* She has but few smiles for the military man, which
cheers *Nemorino* somewhat, and when *Belcore* departs he renews his suit, but the fair one
tells him that it is useless.

A commotion among the villagers is heard, and *Dulcamara,* a quack doctor, comes on
the scene, riding in a splendid carriage. He announces his wonderful medicines in a famous
song, *Udite, udite o rustici,* always the delight of *buffos.*

Udite, udite o rustici (Give Ear, Ye Rustics)

By Antonio Pini-Corsi, Baritone   (*In Italian*)   *68152   12-inch, $1.25
By Arcangelo Rossi, Bass   (*In Italian*)   *62626   10-inch,   .75

* *Double-Faced Record—See page 105.*

103

After the Doctor has recited the wonderful effects of his medicines, saying:

> DULCAMARA:
> I cure the apoplectical,
> The asthmatical, the paralytical,
> The dropsical, the diuretical,
> Consumption, deafness, too,
> The rickets and the scrofula—
> All evils are at once upset
> By this new and fashionable mode!

Nemorino exclaims, "Heaven itself must have sent this miraculous doctor to our village!" He draws the quack aside, and asks him if he has an elixir that can awaken love. The Doctor, of course, says that he is the original inventor of the liquid, and soon has *Nemorino's* last coin in exchange for the coveted potion, which is in reality a bottle of strong wine. This scene is in the form of an amusing duet, *Obbligato*.

Obbligato, obbligato (Thank You Kindly)

By Fernando de Lucia and Ernesto Badini   (*In Italian*)   91079   10-inch, $2.00

As soon as the Doctor has departed *Nemorino* drinks the elixir, and at once feels a new courage in his veins. He begins to sing and dance, and *Adina,* coming in, is astonished to see her love-sick swain so merry. Feeling sure that the potion will bring the lady to his feet, he pays no attention to her, which piques her so much that when the sergeant arrives and renews his suit, she consents to wed him in three days. *Nemorino* laughs loudly at this, which further enrages the lady, and she sets the wedding for that very day. This sobers *Nemorino,* who fears that the marriage may take place before the potion works, and he pleads for delay. *Adina* and *Belcore* laugh at him, and the curtain falls as preparations for the wedding are begun.

ACT II

SCENE I—*Interior of the Farmhouse*

The wedding feast is in progress, but the notary has not arrived. *Dulcamara* is present, and produces the latest duet from Venice, which he asks *Adina* to sing with him.

Io sono ricco e tu sei bella (I Have Riches, Thou Hast Beauty)

By Mme. Passeri, Soprano; Antonio Pini-Corsi, Baritone; La Scala Chorus
(*In Italian*) *16566   10-inch, $0.75

This amusing dialogue, supposed to occur between a rich old man and a young girl, is given here by two well-known singers of La Scala, supported by the chorus.

The company now goes to an adjoining room to dance; all but the Doctor, who says he doesn't know when another free dinner will come his way, and therefore remains at the feast. *Nemorino* enters, distracted, and tells the Doctor that the elixir has not yet taken effect.

"Take another bottle," says the Doctor, "only twenty crowns." *Nemorino* says he has no money, so the Doctor promptly pockets the bottle and goes in to the dancers, telling the unhappy youth to go out and raise the amount.

Belcore, the sergeant, comes in, and learning that *Nemorino's* distress is caused by lack of money, suggests that he enlist as a soldier and be richer the fee of twenty crowns. *Nemorino* jumps at the chance, signs the articles, runs in search of the Doctor, and drinks the second bottle!

The peasant girls, having heard that the death of *Nemorino's* uncle has just made him rich, begin to pay him attentions. The Doctor tells *Nemorino* that this popularity is the result of the elixir he has just sold him. *Adina,* woman-like, when she sees her lover in such demand, promptly regrets having treated him so coldly, and runs out on the verge of tears. *Nemorino,* noting her downcast looks, feels compassion for her, and gazing after her sadly, sings the lovely *romanza,* famous in every land.

Una furtiva lagrima (Down Her Cheek a Pearly Tear)

By Enrico Caruso, Tenor		(*In Italian*) 88339	12-inch, $3.00
By Enrico Caruso, Tenor	(*Piano acc.*)	(*In Italian*) 81027	10-inch, 2.00
By John McCormack, Tenor		(*In Italian*) 74219	12-inch, 1.50
By Florencio Constantino, Tenor		(*In Italian*) 74065	12-inch, 1.50
By Emilio Perea, Tenor		(*In Italian*) *68152	12-inch, 1.25
By Charles Harrison, Tenor		(*In English*) *35354	12-inch, 1.25

* *Double-Faced Records—See page 105.*

A GERMAN REHEARSAL OF ELISIR D'AMORE

Neglected as the opera, as a whole, has been for many years, this lovely romanza, the song which *Nemorino* sings to the tear that stood in his *Adina's* eye, will always keep the opera from being forgotten. This is one of the most famous of the Caruso records, and his exquisite singing of this beautiful number is something to be long remembered.

> Down her soft cheek a pearly tear
>   Stole from her eyelids dark,
> Telling their gay and festive cheer,
>   It pained her soul to mark;
> Why then her dear presence fly?
> When all her love she is showing?
> Could I but feel her beating heart
>   Pressing against mine own;
> Could I my feeling soft impart, and mingle
>   sigh with sigh,
> But feel her heart against mine own,
> Gladly I then would die,
> All her love knowing!

Mr. McCormack's rendition is also a most attractive one. Very few English singers are able to sing an Italian aria in a manner that would be acceptable to Italian audiences, but McCormack is one of these, and his rendering of Donizetti's exquisite air is an example of this mastery of the old school of vocalization.

The crafty *Dulcamara* now suggests to *Adina* that she try the wonderful elixir in order to win back her lover, but she says she needs not such aids.

ADINA:
With respect to your elixir,
One more potent, sir, have I—
Through whose virtues Nemorino,
Leaving all, to me will fly!
DULCAMARA (*aside*):
Oh! she's far too wise and cunning;
These girls know even more than I.

ADINA:
With a tender look I'll charm him—
With a modest smile invite him—
With a tear or sigh alarm him—
With a fond caress excite him.
Never yet was man so mulish,
That I could not make him yield.
Nemorino's fate's decided!

When *Nemorino* has sung his air *Adina* comes on with the soldier's contract, which she has bought back, and tells him that he must not go away. All misunderstandings are now cleared away, and *Belcore* arrives to find his bride-to-be embracing another. However, he is philosophical and saying, "There are other women!" marches off, while the villagers tell *Adina* and *Nemorino* of the latter's good fortune. The Doctor claims credit for the reconciliation, and the curtain falls as he is relieving the peasants of their wages in return for bottles of his wonderful *Elixir of Love !*

DOUBLE-FACED L'ELISIR D'AMORE RECORDS

Udite, udite o rustici (Give Ear, Rustics!) By A. Pini-Corsi, Baritone (*In Italian*) Una furtiva lagrima (A Furtive Tear) By Emilio Perea, Tenor (*In Italian*)	68152	12-inch,	$1.25
Quant'è bella! (Ah, How Lovely!) By Emilio Perea, Tenor (*In Italian*) Udite, udite o rustici—By Arcangelo Rossi, Bass (*In Italian*)	62626	10-inch,	.75
Io sono ricco e tu sei bella (I Have Riches, Thou Hast Beauty) By Maria Passeri, Pini-Corsi and Chorus (*Italian*) Don Pasquale—*Quartet, Act II* By Linda Brambilla, Pini-Corsi, Gaetano Pini-Corsi and Augusto Scipioni (*In Italian*)	16566	10-inch,	.75
Una furtiva lagrima (A Furtive Tear) By Charles Harrison (*In English*) Faust—*All Hail Thou Dwelling* By Charles Harrison (*In English*)	35354	12-inch,	1.25

SAN CARLO NAPLES

LA SCALA, MILAN

FAMOUS OPERA HOUSES OF EUROPE

PHOTO BYRON   SCENE FROM ORIGINAL PRODUCTION OF ERMINIE

ERMINIE

COMIC OPERA IN TWO ACTS

Text by Claxson Bellamy and Harry Paulton; music by Edward Jakobowski. First production at the Comedy Theatre, London, November 9, 1885. First American production at the Casino, New York, March 10, 1886, where it had the unprecedented run of more than twelve hundred performances at that house alone. The operetta has had a number of successful revivals in recent years.

Characters and Original Cast

CADEAUX, ⎫
RAVANNES,⎭ two thieves.................................. ⎧Francis Wilson
⎩W. S. Daboll

MARQUIS DE POMVERT....,......................................Carl Irving

ERMINIE, his daughter.......................................Pauline Hall

JAVOTTE...Marie Jansen

EUGENE MARCEL, the Marquis' secretary....................Harry Pepper

CHEVALIER DE BRABAZON, Marquis' guest.................Max Freeman

CERISE MARCEL, Eugene's sister...........................Marion Manola

PRINCESS DE GRAMPONEUR..........................Jennie Weathersby

VICOMTE DE BRISSAC.......................................C. L. Weeks

Sergeant, Soldiers, Peasants, Acrobats, Clowns, Lords, Ladies, etc.

Time and Place: France; the last century.

The story of Erminie is founded on an old melodrama, "Robert Macaire," by Selby, and the opera has been as popular as was the play in its time. Though Jakobowski has produced other operas—"Paolo," "The Three Beggars," "Dick," "Mynheer Jan" and "A Venetian Singer"—none has approached the great success of Erminie.

At the opening of the opera *Ernst de Brissac*, a young nobleman, is on his way to the home of his prospective fiancée, *Erminie*, whom he has never seen. At a turn of the road he is attacked by two clever thieves, *Ravannes* and *Cadeaux*, who tie him to a tree and carry off his clothes. Later the two rogues arrive at the betrothal festivities, *Ravannes* passing himself off as *de Brissac*, and introducing his companion, *Cadeaux,* as another nobleman. *Erminie* is already in love with *Eugene,* her father's secretary, and *Ernst* is in love with *Cerise, Eugene's* sister. When the prospective suitor escapes from his predicament and appears at the banquet, in great disorder, the imposters cry "Sieze the villian!" declaring that *Ernst* is the highwayman who attacked them that morning.

By promising to help *Erminie* secure the man she loves, *Ravannes* gains the young girl's confidence, and she unwittingly aids him in his plan to rob the house. In the end, however, the plan is frustated, and as the curtain falls the robbers are arrested and the union of *Eugene* and *Erminie* is assured.

The Victor offers three records from this popular opera—a splendid potpourri containing no less than eight of the favorite numbers; a complete record of the favorite "Lullaby" from Act II; and a brass quartet record of the "Good Night Quartet" from Act II.

Gems from "Erminie"

Opening Chorus, "A Soldier's Life"—Solo and Chorus, "When Love is Young All the World is Gay"—Chorus, "Join in the Pleasure"—Solo, "What the Dicky Bird Says"—Chorus, "Lullaby"—Chorus, "Deign to Cheer Each Heart"—Solo and Chorus, "Marriage is a Holy Union"—Finale, "Away to the Chateau"
By the **Victor Light Opera Company** } 35451 12-inch, $1.25

Gems from "Florodora" *By the Victor Light Opera Company*

{ Lullaby By **Elsie Baker, Contralto**
  Message of the Violet *By Olive Kline, Soprano* } 17345 10-inch, .75

{ Good Night Quartet By **Victor Brass Quartet**
  First Heart Throbs *(Bell Solo)* *By Wm. H. Reitz* } 17238 10-inch, .75

SCENE FROM A FAMOUS REVIVAL OF ERMINIE

ERNANI RESCUES ELVIRA FROM THE KING—ACT I

(Italian)   (French)
ERNANI   HERNANI
(*Ayr-nah'-nee*)   (*Her-nah'-nee*)

OPERA IN FOUR ACTS

Libretto adapted by Maria Piave; from Victor Hugo's drama "Hernani"; music by
Giuseppe Verdi. First production in Venice, March 9, 1844. First London production at
Her Majesty's Theatre, March 8, 1845. First New York production, 1846, at the Astor Place.
First New Orleans production April 13, 1858. At its Paris production, January 6, 1846, the
libretto was altered at Victor Hugo's request, the characters being made Italians and the
name of the opera changed to *Il Proscritto*.

Cast of Characters

DON CARLOS, King of Spain . . . . Baritone
DON RUY GOMEZ DE SILVA, a Grandee of Spain . . . . Bass
ERNANI, a bandit chief . . . . Tenor
DON RICCARDO, an esquire of the King . . . . Tenor
IAGO, (*Ee-ah'-goh*) an esquire of Don Silva . . . . Bass
ELVIRA, (*El-vee'-rah*) betrothed to Don Silva . . . . Soprano
GIOVANNA, (*Jeoh-vah'-nah*) in attendance upon her . . . . Mezzo-Soprano

Chorus of mountaineers and bandits, followers of *Don Silva*, ladies of *Elvira*, followers of
the King, Spanish and German nobles and ladies, electors and pages.

Scene and Period: Aragon; about 1519.

ACT I

SCENE I—*The Mountains of Aragon*

Elvira, a Spanish lady of rank, is about to be married to the elderly *Don Gomez de Silva*, a Grandee of Spain. *Ernani*, a bandit chief (in reality John of Aragon, become a brigand after his estates were confiscated), loves *Elvira* and resolves to prevent this unwelcome marriage. The first scene shows a mountain pass where *Ernani's* men are encamped.

Beviam, beviam (Comrades, Let's Drink and Play)

By La Scala Chorus   (*In Italian*) *35168 12-inch, $1.25

The opera opens with this spirited chorus of bandits and mountaineers, who are drinking and gambling in their stronghold. With reckless satisfaction in their lot they sing:

COPY'T DUPONT

SEMBRICH AS ELVIRA

VAN DYCK AS ERNANI

"What matters to the bandit
If hunted and branded
So wine be his share!"

Ernani, their chief, appears on a neighboring height with a melancholy brow. His men remark at his gloomy appearance, and he tells them that he is powerless to prevent the marriage of his betrothed to the aged *Silva* on the morrow. He describes the peerless *Elvira* in a fine aria, The Sweetest Flow'r.

Come rugiada al cespite (The Sweetest Flow'r)

By Luigi Colazza, Tenor
(*In Italian*)
*62627 10-inch, $0.75

The bandits offer their lives, if need be, in the service of their chief, and it is decided to rescue *Elvira* that night.

O tu che l'alma adora (O Thou, My Life's Treasure)

By Martinez Patti, Tenor, and La Scala Chorus (*In Italian*)
*16567 10-inch, $0.75

Ernani, in this passionate aria, sings of the charms of his beloved.

ERNANI:
Oh thou, my life's sole treasure,
Come, come to my arms adoring,
Death at thy feet were pleasure,
The joy of heav'n is mine where'er thou art.

I love thy starry glances,
Thy smile my heart entrances,
Most blessed he of mortals
To whom thou gav'st thy heart!

Ernani and his men depart in the direction of *Silva's* castle and the scene changes.

SCENE II—*Elvira's Apartment in the Castle*

Elvira is discovered alone, brooding over the prospect of the sacrifice, which she seems powerless to prevent.

ELVIRA:
'Tis near the dawning, and Silva yet returns not! Ah! would he came no more—with odious words of loving, more deeply confirming my love for Ernani!

---

* *Double-Faced Record—See page 117.*

PHOTO LARCHER

ELVIRA'S APARTMENT—ACT I

Ernani involami (Ernani, Fly with Me)

By Marcella Sembrich, Soprano   (*In Italian*)   88022   12-inch, $3.00

By Frieda Hempel, Soprano   (*In Italian*)   88383   12-inch,   3.00

By Maria Grisi, Soprano   (*In Italian*)   *63173   10-inch,   .75

In this beautiful but despairing number she calls on her lover to save her, singing:

> Ernani, fly with me;
> Prevent this hated marriage!
> With thee, e'en the barren desert
> Would seem an Eden of enchantment!

Three brilliant renditions of this famous number are given—by Mme. Sembrich and Mme. Hempel; and by Mme. Grisi, of La Scala.

Elvira's ladies-in-waiting now enter, bringing her wedding gifts, and in the graceful chorus with which this record begins, congratulate her.

Quante d'Iberia giovani (Noble Hispania's Blood)

By Ida Giacomelli and La Scala Chorus   (*In Italian*)   *16567   10-inch, $0.75

She thanks them, saying: "Each kindly wish awakes a response in my own heart"; then sings, aside, a second number, "*Tutto sprezzo che d'Ernani,*" in which she tells of her hope of rescue. The chorus joins in the concluding strain.

Da quel di che t'ho veduta (From the Day when First Thy Beauty)

By Angela de Angelis, Soprano; Francesco Cigada, Baritone

(*In Italian*)   *35168   12-inch, $1.25

* Double-Faced Record—See page 117.

111

We come now to one of the greatest scenes in the opera. *Elvira,* who has left the room with the ladies, returns and is amazed to discover in her boudoir the King, who has been secretly in love with her. She appeals to his honor, saying:

"In pity, sire, leave me!"

The record begins with the dramatic dialogue between *Carlos* and *Elvira.* *Carlos* then declares his love in the aria *"Da quel di"* leading up to a dramatic duet, which concludes this sixth number.

Tu se' Ernani! (Thou Art Ernani!)

By Giacomelli, Martinez-Patti and Pignataro (*Italian*) *16568 10-inch, $0.75

The King, maddened by *Elvira's* resistance, is about to carry her away by force. She snatches a dagger from *Carlos'* belt and cries: "Go, or with this dagger I will slay us both!" The King is about to summon his guard, when suddenly a secret panel door opens and *Ernani* appears. *Carlos* recognizes him and exclaims: "Thou art Ernani, the assassin and bandit," and in the spirited trio which follows the rivals declare their hatred, while *Elvira,* almost distracted, endeavors to protect her lover.

Infelice e tu credevi (Unhappy One!)

By Marcel Journet, Bass	(*In Italian*)	74008	12-inch,	$1.50
By Perello de Segurola, Bass	(*In Italian*)	*55007	12-inch,	1.50
By Aristodemo Sillich, Bass	(*In Italian*)	*63421	10-inch,	.75

In the midst of this thrilling tableau now appears *Silva,* who does not recognize the King and who is naturally astounded to find two rivals in the apartments of his future bride, quarreling for her possession. He summons his squires and soldiers, then addresses himself to *Elvira* and reproaches her in this well-known and impressive *Infelice,* one of the most beautiful of bass arias. Three records of this favorite number are available—by Journet, by de Segurola and by Sillich.

The editor regrets that he is unable to give satisfactory English translations for the majority of the *Ernani* airs, but most of the available translations of *Ernani* are so distorted as to be almost meaningless. The few extracts which are given have been revised and made somewhat intelligible. "Opera in English," about which we hear so much nowadays, cannot be permanently successful without new translations for some of the older works. For instance, here is a specimen translation of the text of this very air of *Infelice :*

Ah, to win, to win back summer's blossom
In my breast were tho't too gainless,
Winter lords it within this my bosom.
Far congealing, far congealing to the core,
Far congealing unto the core,
Far congealing unto the core.
Winter lords it in this bosom.
Far congealing, far congealing to the core,
Unto the core, congealing unto the core!

Now anyone who can tell just what this means is certainly a highly gifted individual!

In this connection, however, it should be stated that several American music publishers are entitled to praise for their efforts to improve opera translations, especially G. Schirmer, with many beautiful new editions of the older operas and collections of opera airs; and Oliver Ditson Company, whose Musicians' Library, a splendid piece of music typography, contains many new translations. The editor of this catalogue is indebted to both these firms for permission to quote from their new translations.

THE KING PLEADS HIS LOVE

* *Double-Faced Record—See page 117.*

Vedi come il buon vegliardo (Well I Knew My Trusty Vassal)

By Maria Grisi, Soprano; Carlo Ottoboni, Bass; Remo Sangiorgi, Tenor;
and Giuseppi Sala, Baritone (*In Italian*) *35169 12-inch, $1.25

Having reproached his bride for her supposed treachery, *Silva* thinks of vengeance, and calling for his armor and a sword, demands that the intruders follow him to combat. Before they can reply, the King's squires enter and salute their sovereign. The astounded *Silva*, though secretly enraged, kneels to his King, saying: "Duty to my King cancels all offences." The great finale then begins with *Carlos'* solo, sung aside to his squires:

> "Well I knew my trusty vassal
> Fierce in hate, in passion tender
> Would his wrath and love surrender
> In the presence of his King."

This is one of the most impressive records of the Ernani series.

Finale, Act I

By Maria Grisi, Soprano; Carlo Ottoboni, Bass; Remo Sangiorgi,
Tenor; and Giuseppi Sala, Baritone (*In Italian*) *16568 10-inch, $0.75

The finale to Act I is continued in this record. The situation at the close of the act may be understood by these quotations from the words the librettist has given to the various characters:

CARLOS (*to Ernani*):
I will save thee!
(*Aloud to Silva*):
Let this trusty friend depart.
ERNANI.
I thy friend? Never! unto death my vengeance will pursue thee!
ELVIRA:
Fly, Ernani, let love teach thee prudence!

CARLOS:
Power, dominion and love's delights,
All these are mine—all my will must obey!
SILVA:
From my eyes a veil has fallen . . .
I can scarce believe my senses!
COURTIERS:
Well doth Silva hide his anger
But within it still doth smolder!

Ernani yields to *Elvira's* pleadings and in the confusion makes his escape. The curtain falls on an impressive tableau.

ACT II
SCENE—*A Hall in Silva's Castle*

After his escape from the castle, nothing has been seen of *Ernani*. *Elvira* believes the rumors of his death and despairingly consents to wed *Don Silva*.

Esultiam (Day of Gladness)

By La Scala Chorus (*In Italian*) *16569 10-inch, $0.75

The first scene of Act II occurs in a magnificent hall in the castle. The company of knights and pages of *Silva*, and ladies in attendance on *Elvira* sing the opening chorus in praise of the noble *Silva* and his peerless bride.

Oro quant' oro (I am the Bandit Ernani)

By Maria Bernacchi, Soprano; Luisi Colazza, Tenor; and Torres de Luna,
Bass (*In Italian*) *16569 10-inch, $0.75

Silva, attired as a Grandee, enters. His squire, *Jago*, announces a holy man, who craves the hospitality of the castle. *Ernani*, disguised as a pilgrim, enters, then throws off his disguise and exclaims, beginning this fine trio:

> "I am the bandit Ernani . . . My men are dead or in chains . . . My enemies are without the castle . . . Seize me and deliver me up, for I am weary of life!"

Silva, however, refuses to betray one whom he has received as a guest. The trio, which is one of the great scenes of the opera, then follows.

La vedremo, o veglio audace (I Will Prove, Audacious Greybeard)

By Ernesto Caronna, Baritone, and Torres de Luna, Bass
(*In Italian*) *16570 10-inch, $0.75

* *Double-Faced Record—See page 117.*

113

CASTLE OF SILVA—ACT III

The retainers bring news that the King and his warriors are without the castle. *Silva* hides *Ernani* in a secret passage and orders that the King be admitted. *Don Carlos* inquires, with irony, why *Silva's* castle is so well guarded, and demands that he surrender *Ernani* or lose his own life. *Silva* refuses. The soldiers are ordered to search the castle. This duet then occurs, beginning:

CARLOS: I will prove, audacious greybeard,
If thou'rt loyal to thy King!
In my wrath I will destroy thee!
SILVA: Oh King, be just; I cannot yield!

Vieni meco (Come, Thou Dearest Maiden)

By Maria Grisi, Soprano; Francesco Cigada, Baritone; Carlo Ottoboni, Bass; and La Scala Chorus *(In Italian)* *16570 10-inch, $0.75

This record begins with a chorus of soldiers, who have explored the castle but have found no trace of *Ernani*. The King is about to torture *Silva* into revealing the secret, when *Elvira* rushes in and begs the mercy of his Majesty. *Carlos* turns to her, and sings consolingly of the bright future before her as his Queen, and in the great trio which follows the conflicting emotions of those in the scene are expressed in Verdi's fiery music.

A te scegli, seguimi (Choose Thy Sword, and Follow!)

By Luigi Colazza, Tenor, and Torres de Luna, Bass
(In Italian) *35169 12-inch, $1.25

The King, his followers, and the *Lady Elvira* having retired, *Silva* exclaims: "Hell cannot hate with the hatred I bear thee, vile King!" He then takes down two swords from the armory, and releasing *Ernani* from his hiding place, challenges him to combat. *Ernani* refuses, saying that his life belongs to *Silva*, who has saved it. *Silva* taunts him with cowardice and *Ernani* consents to fight, but asks for one look at *Elvira*. *Silva* replies that the King has taken her away. "Fool!" cries *Ernani* to the astonished Grandee, "the King is our rival!" and agrees to combine with *Silva* against their mutual foe. Once their

Double-Faced Record—See page 117.

114

revenge is accomplished, *Ernani* agrees to yield his life at *Silva's* call, and gives him a hunting horn which shall be the signal for his (*Ernani's*) death. For this magnificent number Verdi has written some of his most dramatic music.

In arcion, cavalieri (To Horse, Ye Warriors)
By Giuseppi Sala, Tenor; Cesare Preve, Baritone; and La Scala Chorus
(*In Italian*) *16571 10-inch, $0.75

The act closes with the spirited duet and chorus by *Ernani*, *Silva* and the warriors of the Don, who prepare to pursue the King to the death.

THE TOMB OF CHARLEMAGNE—ACT IV

ACT III
SCENE—*A Vault in Aix-la-Chapelle Cemetery*

O de' verd' anni miei (Oh Bright and Fleeting Shadows)
By Mario Ancona, Baritone   (*In Italian*) 88062 12-inch, $3.00

The third act occurs in the Tomb of Charlemagne at Aix-la-Chapelle. *Carlos* conceals himself in the tomb of his ancestor to witness the meeting of the conspirators who are plotting against him. He is depressed and melancholy, and sings this famous *O de verd*, in which he pledges himself to better deeds should the Electors, then in session, proclaim him Emperor.

Si ridesti il leon di Castiglia (Rouse the Lion of Castile)
By La Scala Chorus   (*In Italian*) *16571 10-inch, $0.75

The conspirators, among whom are *Ernani* and *Silva*, assemble at the tomb. *Ernani* is chosen to assassinate *Carlos*, and greets the decision with joy, exclaiming that his dead father will at last be avenged. The great ensemble then follows.

O sommo Carlo (Oh, Noble Carlos)
By Mattia Battistini, Baritone; Emilia Corsi, Soprano; Luigi Colazza,
Tenor; Aristodemo Sillich, Bass; and La Scala Chorus
(*In Italian*) 92046 12-inch, $3.00
By Maria Grisi, Remo Sangiorgi, Francesco Cigada and La Scala Chorus
(*In Italian*) *35170 12-inch, 1.25

* *Double-Faced Record—See page 117.*

The booming of cannon having announced that *Carlos* is proclaimed Emperor, he comes from the tomb and surprises the conspirators. At the same time the Electors and the King's courtiers enter from a secret door. *Carlos* condemns the plotters to death, when *Elvira* rushes to him and asks for mercy. The Emperor heeds her, pardons them all, and unites *Elvira* and *Ernani*. In this great finale all glorify the Emperor except *Silva*, who still secretly cries for vengeance.

FÊTE AT ERNANI'S PALACE OF ARAGON

ACT IV

SCENE—*Terrace of a Palace in Aragon*

Festa da ballo (Hail, Bright Hour of Gladness)

By La Scala Chorus   (In Italian) *16572 10-inch, $0.75

The lovers are now happily united, and this scene shows them at *Ernani's* palace, which, with his estates, has been restored to him. A chorus of ladies, masks and pages greets the happy pair.

Ferna, crudel estinguere (Stay Thee, My Lord!)

By Maria Bernacchi, Soprano; Luigi Colazza, Tenor; and Torres de Luna,
Baritone   (In Italian) *35170 12-inch, $1.25

Elvira and *Ernani* are alone on the terrace, oblivious to all but each other, when a blast from a horn is heard. *Ernani* awakes from his dream of bliss and recognizes the sound of

* *Double-Faced Record—See page 117.*

his own hunting horn, which he had given to *Silva* as a pledge to die when the revengeful Don should demand his life. The distracted *Elvira* pleads with *Silva* for her husband, but in vain. After an affecting farewell *Ernani* fulfills his vow, stabs himself and dies, while *Elvira* falls lifeless on his body. The curtain falls as the cruel and remorseless *Silva* is gloating over his terrible revenge.

DOUBLE-FACED ERNANI RECORDS

Infelice e tu credevi By Perelló de Segurola, Bass Puritani—*Sorgea la notte* By Perelló de Segurola, Bass (*In Italian*)	55007	12-inch,	$1.50
Ferna, crudel *By Maria Bernacchi, Soprano ; Luigi Colazza, Tenor ; and Torres de Luna, Bass (*In Italian*) O sommo Carlo By Maria Grisi, Soprano ; Remo Sangiorgi, Tenor ; Francesco Cigada, Baritone ; and Chorus (*Italian*)	35170	12-inch,	1.25
Ernani Selection By Pryor's Band *Meistersinger—Prize Song* By Victor Sorlin, '*Cellist*	35111	12-inch,	1.25
A te scegli, seguimi By Luigi Colazza, Tenor, and Torres de Luna, Bass (*In Italian*) Vedi come il buon vegliardo By Maria Grisi, Soprano ; Remo Sangiorgi, Tenor ; Giuseppi Sala, Tenor ; and Carlo Ottoboni, Bass (*In Italian*)	35169	12-inch,	1.25
Beviam, beviam By La Scala Chorus (*In Italian*) Da quel di che t'ho veduta By Angela de Angelis, Soprano, and Francesco Cigada, Baritone (*In Italian*)	35168	12-inch,	1.25
O tu che l'alma adora By Martinez-Patti, Tenor, and Chorus (*In Italian*) Quante d'Iberia giovani By Ida Giacomelli, Soprano, and Chorus (*In Italian*)	16567	10-inch,	.75
Finale, Act I By Maria Grisi, Soprano ; Carlo Ottoboni, Bass ; Remo Sangiorgi, Tenor ; and Giuseppi Sala, Tenor Tu se' Ernani By Ida Giacomelli, Soprano ; Martinez-Patti, Tenor ; and Enrico Pignataro, Baritone (*In Italian*)	16568	10-inch,	.75
Esultiam! By La Scala Chorus (*In Italian*) Oro quant' oro By Maria Bernacchi, Soprano ; Luigi Colazza, Tenor ; and Torres de Luna, Bass (*In Italian*)	16569	10-inch,	.75
La vedremo By Ernesto Caronna, Baritone, and Torres de Luna, Bass (*In Italian*) Vieni meco By Maria Grisi, Soprano ; Francesco Cigada, Baritone ; Carlo Ottoboni, Bass ; and Chorus (*In Italian*)	16570	10-inch,	.75
In arcion, cavalieri! By Giuseppi Sala, Tenor ; Cesare Preve, Bass ; and Chorus (*In Italian*) Si ridesti il leon di Castiglia By La Scala Chorus (*Italian*)	16571	10-inch,	.75
Festa da ballo "O come felici" By La Scala Chorus (*In Italian*) *Hamlet—O vin, discaccia la tristezza* By Francesco Cigada, Baritone, and Chorus (*In Italian*)	16572	10-inch,	.75
Ernani involami (Ernani, Fly with Me) By Maria Grisi, Soprano (*In Italian*) *Ballo in Maschera—O Figlio d' Inghilterra* By Huguet, Salvador, Cigada, Sillich, and Chorus (*In Italian*)	63173	10-inch,	.75
Infelice e tu credevi (Unhappy One!) By Aristodemo Sillich, Bass (*In Italian*) *Manon—Oh, Manon, sempre la stressa* By Giorgio Malesci, Tenor (*In Italian*)	63421	10-inch,	.75
Come rugiada al cespite By Luigi Colazza (*In Italian*) O tu che l'alma adora By Martinez-Patti, Tenor, and Chorus (*In Italian*)	62627	10-inch,	.75

SCENE—ACT IV

(Italian)

FALSTAFF

(Fahl'-stahf)

COMIC OPERA IN THREE ACTS

Text by Boito, taken from Shakespeare's comedy, *The Merry Wives of Windsor.* Music by Verdi. First production, Milan, March, 1893. First Berlin production June 1, 1893; Vienna, June 21, 1893; Buenos Aires, July 9, 1893; Paris, April 18, 1894. First London production May 19, 1894, under the management of Sir Augustus Harris. First North American production at the Metropolitan Opera House, New York, February 4, 1895, with Eames, Maurel, Scalchi, de Lussan and Campanari, under the direction of Maurice Grau. Given several performances in 1896, after which it was not heard again at the Metropolitan for fourteen years. Campanari was the only member of the original cast to appear in the revival, the new cast including Scotti, Destinn, Alda, Gay and Ranzenberg.

BACHMANN AS FALSTAFF

Characters and Original Metropolitan Cast

SIR JOHN FALSTAFF...........Baritone......Maurel
FENTON, a young gentleman........Tenor....Russitano
FORD, a wealthy burgher........Baritone...Campanari
DR. CAIUS, a physician............Tenor ......Vanni
BARDOLFO, }followers of Falstaff...{Tenor....Rinaldini
PISTOLA,   {Bass .....Nicolini
MRS. ALICE FORD..............Soprano......Eames
NANETTA, her daughter.........Soprano...de Lussan
MRS. QUICKLEY ....Contralto......Scalchi
MRS. MEG PAGE.........Mezzo-Soprano....de Vigne

It was the youthful dream of the great composer, Verdi, to write a comic opera, but it was not until he was nearing eighty years of age that his dream was realized. The music of *Falstaff* denotes in all things almost the antithesis of the style and methods and ideals of Verdi's early operas. The music is vivacious and sparkling, being interspersed with delightful fragments of melody.

Sir John Falstaff is a merry rogue, so conceited as to believe himself irresistible to all womankind. His egotism leads him to think he has fascinated both *Mistress Page* and *Mistress Alice Ford,* and he writes each of the ladies a love letter identical in contents. The two women compare the notes and plan to punish the Knight for presuming to address them in such terms of affection.

Ford learns of *Falstaff's* advances to his wife and flies into a jealous rage. *Mistress Ford* sends *Dame Quickley* to *Sir John* with an invitation to call, which he is quick to accept. Scarcely does he arrive at *Ford's* house than *Dame Quickley* reports the coming of *Mistress*

118

Page, and *Falstaff* is compelled to hide behind a screen. Then the angry *Ford* appears with his friends, determined to capture *Falstaff,* but the latter takes refuge in a clothes basket. *Mistress Ford* has the basket thrown into the ditch, and the unlucky suitor receives a good shaking-up before the jeering crowd.

Falstaff, undaunted by his basket experience, arranges to meet *Lady Ford* again, the trysting place this time being at Herne's Oak, in Windsor Park. *Ford* and his men, including *Pistola* and *Bardolfo,* who have turned against *Falstaff* because of his bad treatment of them, overhear the arrangements and plan to be there also. Now, *Ford's* daughter, *Nanetta,* is in love with *Fenton,* but her father de-

BYRON

FALSTAFF GETS IN THE BASKET—ACT II

mands that she marry *Dr. Caius. Ford* tells the doctor that this is a good time for him to secure *Nanetta,* and promises to aid him. *Dame Quickley,* however, learns of this, and the women plan to have *Fenton* spoil the designs of the physician.

Falstaff's love scene with *Mistress Ford* is interrupted by *Ford's* friends, disguised as elves and fairies, who thrash the fat knight soundly. In the confusion *Dr. Caius* mistakes *Bardolfo* for *Nanetta, Ford* is finally won over, and his daughter and *Fenton* are happily married.

The Victor offers a very fine record of one of the best known airs from the opera: the *Quand' ero paggio,* sung by *Falstaff* to *Mistress Alice Ford* in Act II.

GERLACH

SCOTTI AS FALSTAFF

JADLOWKER AS FENTON

Falstaff here boasts of the days when he was a dashing gallant, slender of form, handsome as a picture, and hints that much of this charm still remains, after which he attempts to make love to *Alice.*

Quand' ero paggio (When I Was Page)

By Antonio Scotti, Baritone   *(In Italian)* 88194 12-inch, $3.00

Faust, the Aged Philosopher, Wearies of Life

FAUST
(Fowst)

OPERA IN FIVE ACTS

Words by Barbier and Carre, founded upon Goethe's tragedy. Music by Charles Gounod. First produced at the *Théâtre Lyrique*, Paris, March 19, 1859. First performance in Berlin at the Royal Opera, January 1863. First performance in London June 11, 1863; in New York November 26, 1863, at the Academy of Music, with Kellogg, Mazzoleni, Biachi and Yppolito. In New Orleans November 12, 1866.

Some famous American productions were in 1883, with Nilsson, Scalchi, and Campanini; and the same year with Nordica (début) as *Marguerite*; in 1892 with Eames, the de Reszkes and Lasalle; and recently with Caruso and Farrar.

Characters

FAUST (*Fowst*) ....Tenor
MEPHISTOPHELES (*Mef-iss-tof'-el-leez*) Bass
VALENTINE (*Val'-en-teen*) ....Baritone
BRANDER, or WAGNER ......Baritone
SIEBEL (*See'-bel*) ....Mezzo-Soprano
MARGUERITE (*Mahr-guer-eet'*) ....Soprano
MARTHA ....Contralto

Students, Soldiers, Villagers,
Sorcerers, Spirits.

The action takes place in Germany.

FAUST

TH. IMPERIAL DE L'OPERA
Les bureaux seront ouverts à 7 heures   On commencera à 7 heures 1/2.
35.   Aujourd'hui MERCREDI 3 Mars 1869.
PREMIÈRE REPRÉSENTATION

FAUST

Opéra en CINQ actes de *MM. J. Barbier et M. Carré.*
Musique de M. CH. GOUNOD
D. vertissement de M. JUSTAMANT.—Décors de MM. DESPLECHIN, CAMBON,
RUBÉ, CHAPERON et LAVASTRE.

Marguerite	Méphistophélès	Faust
Mme NILSSON	M. FAURE	M. COLIN
	Siebel	Valentin	Wagner
Mme MAUDUIT	M. DEVOYOD	M. GASPARD
	Marthe,	Mme DESBORDES

Mrs PONSARD, MICHELABRE, FRERET, KŒNIG, MÉRMANN, WISSERE
DELAHAYE, DE SOMOS.
Au 3me acte, LES CHŒURS augmentés de 1/   ts.

DANSE
Mlle FIORETTI, FONTA E FIOCI
MARQUET BARATTE MERAN
Mmes MORANDO, STOIKOFF, CARABIN, LAMY,
BLANCHE, NINI, SALABA, GOSSI, HAIRIVEAU, A
PALLIER, FATOU, LAURENT, MORIS BELLMAR, M

VENDREDI 5 et LUNDI 8   FAUST

Le Bureau de location, rue Drouot, au coin de la rue Rossini.
PRIX, DES PLACES :

PROGRAM OF A FAMOUS REVIVAL (1869)

Fifty-six years have elapsed since the first production of this masterpiece by Gounod; and it is to-day sung throughout the world more than any other five operas combined. At the Paris Opéra alone it has been given more than 1500 times, and the new setting recently provided for it there cost not less than 150,000 francs, a sum which would not be risked on any other opera whatever. During the decade 1901-1910 Faust had nearly three thousand performances in German opera houses.

It seems strange now, in view of the overwhelming success of Faust, to recall that it was received with indifference in Paris, and all but failed in Milan. The London production, however, with Titiens, Giuglini, Trebelli, Gassier and Santley, was quite successful; and in the following June Patti sang *Marguerite* for the first time, the opera receiving a tremendous ovation.

The story is familiar to almost every one and will be but briefly sketched here. The libretto by Barbier and Carre does not attempt to follow the Goethe drama, but merely makes use of the *Faust-Marguerite* incident. This is sufficient, however, to provide an intensely interesting subject for Gounod's lovely music.

Prélude to Faust

By L'Orchestre Symphonique, Paris   58016 12-inch, $1.00

The prelude to Faust is a short one, merely giving a clue to the drama which is to follow. The fateful single note of the full orchestra with which it opens and the mysterious chromatic chords stealing in from the strings form a fitting introduction to a drama of such unusual portent.

The tempo is then accelerated and a passage suggesting *Faust's* mental struggles leads to the lovely melody in F major (*Dio possente*). The prelude closes with sustained chords, solemn and impressive.

ACT I—The Compact

The first act reveals the studio of *Faust*, an aged philosopher and alchemist, who is seen surrounded by musty parchment rolls and the rude scientific apparatus of the fifteenth century. The fitful light of an expiring lamp is a symbol of the despair in the heart of the aged *Faust*, as after a lifetime spent in the pursuit of learning, he realizes that he knows but little of true knowledge. Tired of the struggle, he resolves to end it with a poisonous draught, and raises the goblet to his lips; but pauses as the songs of some happy peasants float through the open window. He goes to the window, and filled with rage at the sight of human happiness, he curses all earthly things and calls on Satan to aid him. This scene is given in a most impressive record by De Tura and La Scala Chorus.

La vaga pupilla (Rise, Slumb'ring Maiden)

By Gennaro De Tura and La Scala Chorus (In Italian) 76019 12-inch, $2.00

CHORUS OF PEASANT GIRLS (*passing without the window*):

Ah! careless, idle maiden,
Wherefore dreaming still?
Day with roses laden
Cometh o'er the hill.
Brooks and bees and flowers
Warble to the grove,
Who has time for sadness?
Awake to love!

FAUST:
Foolish echoes of human gladness,
Go by, pass on your way!
(*His hand trembles.*)
Goblet so often drained by my father's hand
so steady,
Why now dost thou tremble in mine?

CHORUS OF REAPERS (*without*):
Cometh forth, ye reapers, young and hoary!
The earth is proud with harvest glory!
Rejoice and pray.

FAUST:
If I pray there is none to hear—
To give me back my love,
Its believing and its glow.
Accurst be all ye thoughts of earthly pleasure!
Fond dreams of hope! ambitions high,
And their fulfillment so rare!
Accurst, my vaunted learning,
And forgiveness and prayer!
Infernal king, appear!

(*Mephistopheles appears.*)

PLANÇON AS MEPHISTOPHELES

Mephistopheles, attired in the dress of a gallant, promptly appears in response to the call and proposes that the good Doctor shall enter into a compact with him. In return for riches, glory, power, anything he desires, *Faust* shall merely give up his soul! The aged philosopher, spurning gold or power, cries out for youth, only youth!

Io voglio il piacer (The Pleasures of Youth)

By Gaetano Pini-Corsi, Tenor;
Aristodemo Sillich, Bass
(*In Italian*) *63174 10-in., $0.75

The bargain is soon agreed upon and *Faust* is about to pledge his soul in return for youth and love, but as he still hesitates, *Mephisto* says, "See how fair youth invites you! Look!"

O merveille (Heavenly Vision)

By Enrico Caruso, Tenor;
Marcel Journet, Bass
(*In French*) 89039 12-in., $4.00

KRELING   FAUST DREAMS OF YOUTH AND BEAUTY

Then follows the delicate passage for strings which accompanies the vision. *Faust*, gazing rapturously on the beautiful *Marguerite*, sings:

The scroll is signed in letters of fire, *Faust* drains the magic potion and is transformed into a youth. The spirited duet which follows, ends the first act.

*Double-Faced Record—See page 144.

123

KERMESSE SCENE (PARIS OPÉRA)

ACT II—The Fair

(The scene shows a fair in progress in the public square of a German town)

A motley crowd of students, soldiers, old men, young women and matrons are disporting themselves—drinking, talking, flirting, quarreling; and this animated chorus, with which the Kermesse Scene begins, graphically pictures the whole.

Kermesse Scene

By New York Grand Opera Chorus	*(In French)*	74213	12-inch, $1.50
By La Scala Chorus	*(In Italian)*	*68160	12-inch, 1.25

Each group delivers its quota in distinctive fashion, the soldiers' sturdy declaration contrasting with the laughing, chattering passages allotted to the women; the high-pitched falsetto of the gossiping old men always proving a favorite portion of this number. At the close the different groups combine into a chorus of six parts. This wonderful piece of choral writing is reproduced in a striking manner, and gives a most realistic picture of the Kermesse.

SOLDIERS:
Red and white liquor, coarse or fine,
What can it matter, so we have wine?
OLD MEN:
Each new feast-day brings the old story,
Danger gone by, how we enjoy it!
While to-day each hot-headed boy
Fights for to-day's little glory!

GIRLS:
Only look how they do eye us,
Yonder fellows gay!
Howsoever they defy us,
Never run away!
STUDENTS:
How those merry girls do eye us
We know what it means—
To despise us, to decoy us,
Like so many queens!

Double-Faced Record—See page 144.

MATRONS:
Only see the brazen creatures
With the men at play;
Had the latter choice in features,
They would turn this way!

SOLDIERS:
Long live the soldier,
The soldier gay!
Be it ancient city, be it maiden pretty,
Both must fall our prey!

Here *Valentine*, the brother of *Marguerite*, is found among the crowd of soldiers just about to depart for the war, and he sings the noble *Dio possente*, a farewell to his sister and his home.

Dio possente (Even the Bravest Heart)

By Antonio Scotti, Baritone	(*In Italian*)	88203	12-inch,	$3.00
By Emilio de Gogorza, Baritone	(*In Italian*)	88174	12-inch,	3.00
By Titta Ruffo, Baritone	(*In Italian*)	92043	12-inch,	3.00
By Francesco Cigada (*Double-faced—See page 144*)	(*Italian*)	68275	12-inch,	1.25

In the preceding recitative he speaks of his fears in leaving his sister *Marguerite* alone, and contemplates with affection the amulet she has given him to bring good fortune.

VALENTINE:
Dear gift of my sister,
Made more holy by her pray'r.
However great the danger,
There's naught can do me harm,
Protected by this charm!

The familiar "Cavatina" then follows:

Even bravest heart may swell,
In the moment of farewell,
Loving smile of sister kind,
Quiet home I leave behind;
Oft shall I think of you,
Whene'er the wine-cup passes 'round,
When alone my watch I keep
And my comrades lie asleep

Upon the tented battleground.
But when danger to glory shall call me,
I still will be first in the fray,
As blithe as a knight in his bridal array,
Careless what fate may befall me,
When danger shall call me.
Oft shall I sadly think of you
When far away, far away.

COPY'T DUPONT
JOURNET AS MEPHISTO

This *Dio possente* was not in the original production of the opera, but was written by Gounod especially for Santley in the English production at Her Majesty's Theatre, 1864.

The Victor offers a wide choice to buyers of this fine "Cavatina." Scotti's *Valentine* is always a revelation in dramatic possibilities. This rôle, too often allotted to a mediocre artist, is filled by him with dignity; and he makes a serious and soldierly *Valentine*, singing the music with admirable richness of tone and beauty of expression.

Although Mr. de Gogorza has not sung the number in opera, it is frequently seen on his concert programs, and he sings it superbly. Other fine renditions in Italian are the ones by Ruffo, the famous Italian baritone, who has made such a success in this country, and Cigada, a well-known European baritone, who has not yet visited America.

Le veau d'or (The Calf of Gold)

By Pol Plançon, Bass	(*In French*)	81038	10-inch,	$2.00
By Marcel Journet, Bass	(*In French*)	64036	10-inch,	1.00

We are now in the full bustle of the Fair Scene, where in front of an inn a crowd of drinkers are listening to one of their number, *Wagner*, singing a somewhat coarse ditty concerning a rat. *Mephistopheles* breaks in upon the revelers, and offers to sing a song of his own, "The Song of the Golden Calf." After the diabolically suggestive introduction by the orchestra, with its semi-quavers and descending chromatics, we hear the bold opening passage of this anthem in praise of Mammon, of which the calf is symbolic.

KRELING   MEPHISTOPHELES AND FAUST VIEW THE WORLD

MEPHISTOPHELES:
Calf of Gold! aye in all the world
To your mightiness they proffer,
Incense at your fane they offer
From end to end of all the world.
And in honor of the idol
Kings and peoples everywhere
To the sound of jingling coins
Dance with zeal in festive circle,
Round about the pedestal,
Satan, he conducts the ball!
Calf of Gold, strongest god below!
To his temple overflowing
Crowds before his vile shape bowing,
As they strive in abject toil,
As with souls debased they circle
Round about the pedestal,
Satan, he conducts the ball!

Two renditions of this effective bass
song are offered by the Victor. Plançon's rendition is a spirited one, the
number always being sung by him with
a full appreciation of its caustic raillery.
Journet's record is also a splendid one,
and shows the magnificent voice of this
artist to great advantage.

Mephistopheles now proceeds to as-
tonish the company by his feats of magic,
first reading their palms and then drawing wine from the barrel of Bacchus—
the inn sign perched up aloft—each man
drawing the wine he likes the best. The
scene which follows, a most dramatic
one, is effectively given by Amato,
Journet and the Metropolitan Chorus.

Faust—Scene les Epées (Scene of the Swords)

**By Pasquale Amato, Baritone; Marcel Journet, Bass; and
Metropolitan Opera Chorus**   (Giulio Setti, Director)
(In French) 89055 12-inch, $4.00

The record begins with the invocation to Bacchus.

MEPHISTOPHELES:
I drink to you all!
(*Throwing it out with a wry face.*)
Bah! what rubbishy wine.
Let me see if I cannot find you better!
(*Striking the image of Bacchus with his
sword.*)
What ho, Bacchus! up there! some liquors!
Come while you can,
And each one drink the wine he likes the best!

He then affronts *Valentine* by proposing the health of *Marguerite,*
and the soldier draws his sword, only to find that some unforeseen
force has made it powerless in his hand.

COPY'T MISHKIN

SAMMARCO AS VALENTINE
ACT II

MEPHISTOPHELES:
I propose the health of the
dearest of all dears,
Our Margarita!
VALENTINE:
Enough!
Bridle thy tongue, or thou
diest by my hand!

MEPHISTOPHELES:
Come on! (*Both draw*)
CHORUS:
Come on!
MEPHISTOPHELES (*mocking*):
So soon afraid, who so lately
defied me?
VALENTINE:
My sword! O disgrace! In
my hand is powerless!

Valentine, however, turns the handle upwards, thus making the Sign of the Cross, the soldiers doing likewise, and they now face the Tempter with confidence.

VALENTINE AND SOLDIERS:
'Gainst the powers of evil our arms assailing,
Strongest earthly might must be unavailing.
VALENTINE:
But know thou art powerless to harm us!
VALENTINE:
Look hither!
(*Holds up his sword to form a cross.*)

SOLDIERS (*imitating him*):
Look hither!
ALL:
Whilst this blest sign we wear
Thou canst not harm us!
Whilst this blest sign we wear
Thou canst not harm us!

Mephistopheles is discomfited, and cowers in terror as the soldiers sing the choral, with its striking unison passage for male voices, alternated with bursts of harmony.

This is a remarkably fine reproduction, the men's voices being rich and sonorous, and the dramatic feeling intense.

The delightful waltz, which has been a model of its kind ever since the first performance of Faust, now begins.

PHOTO BYRON
MEETING OF MARGUERITE AND FAUST—ACT II

Waltz from Kermesse Scene
By Pryor's Band (*Double-Faced—See page 144*) 16552 10-inch, $0.75

This favorite number is played by the band with the absolute precision and daintiness which are indispensable to its proper performance.

Faust now observes *Marguerite* and approaching her, greets her respectfully, offering his escort.

FAUST:
High-born and lovely maid,
Forgive my humble duty,
Let me, your willing slave,
Attend you home to-day?

She modestly declines, saying:

MARGUERITE:
No, my lord, not a lady am I,
Nor yet a beauty;
And do not need an arm,
To help me on my way.

FAUST (*gazing after her*):
By my youth! what a charm!
She knows not of her beauty.
Oh! darling child, I love thee!

The waltz now re-commences and the act ends in a wild and exciting dance, in which all join—students, soldiers and women.

PAUL BOYER & BERT   SETTING FOR GARDEN SCENE AT PARIS OPÉRA

ACT III—The Garden Scene

The Garden Scene of Faust is undoubtedly Gounod's finest inspiration; and the sensuous beauty of the music with which the composer has surrounded the story of *Marguerite's* innocence and trust betrayed, has held many millions in rapt attention during the fifty years since it was first heard.

Flower Song—Le parlate d'amor (In the Language of Love)

By Louise Homer, Contralto   (*In Italian*)   87075   10-inch, \$2.00
By Corinne Morgan, Contralto   (*In English*) *35086   12-inch,   1.25
By Emma Zaccaria, Mezzo-Soprano   (*In Italian*) *62085   10-inch,   .75

This fresh and dainty song of *Siebel* ushers in the act. The gentle boy enters *Marguerite's* garden, thinking of the dark prophecy of *Mephistopheles*, who had told him (in Act II):

> "Each flower that you touch,
> Every beauty you dote on
> Shall rot and shall wither!"

Siebel now thinks to put this curse to a test, and prepares to send a message of love to *Marguerite* by means of a flower, singing

> "In the language of love, oh gentle flow'r,
> Say to her I adore her."

Then gath-
ering a blos-
som he ex-
claims, as
he sees it
fade:

Son viz-zi, ahi-mè lo stre-go ma-le det-to mel di-ce-va or   or. . . .
'Tis with-er'd! A-las! that dark stran-ger fore-told me What my fate must   be. . . .

---

*Double-Faced Record—See page 144.

But the happy thought occurs to him to dip his fingers in the font of holy water by the side of the cottage. He does so, and is delighted to find the spell broken. The first strain then reappears, closing the aria.

This popular number is offered in Italian by Homer and Zaccaria and in English by Miss Morgan.

Salut demeure (All Hail, Thou Dwelling)

By Enrico Caruso	(In French)	88003	12-inch, $3.00
By John McCormack	(In Italian)	74220	12-inch, 1 50
By George Hamlin	(In English)	74139	12-inch, 1.50
By Charles Harrison	(In English)	*35354	12-inch, 1.25

Mephistopheles and *Faust*, who have been secretly watching *Siebel*, now appear; the Tempter being in high spirits at the apparent success of his schemes, while *Faust* gazes in rapture at the garden where his beloved one is wont to walk, and sings his lovely *cavatina*. He thus rhapsodizes the modest dwelling of *Marguerite*:

All hail, thou dwelling pure and lowly!
Home of an angel fair and holy,
What wealth is here, what wealth outbidding gold,
Of peace and love, and innocence untold!
Bounteous Nature!
'Twas here by day thy love was taught her,
Here thou didst with care overshadow thy daughter
In her dream of the night!
Here, waving tree and flower
Made her an Eden-bower of beauty and delight.

COPY'T BURR M'INTOSH

CARUSO AS FAUST

KRELING FAUST AND MEPHISTOPHELES ENTERING
MARGUERITE'S GARDEN

Double-Faced Record—See page 144.

The Caruso record of this number, which the tenor sings in French, is one of the finest in his entire list; while the rendition in Italian by McCormack is a splendid one. Two noteworthy renditions in English are also offered by Hamlin and Harrison.

While *Faust* is singing his apostrophe to *Marguerite's* dwelling, *Mephistopheles*, with an eye to more practical things, has replaced *Siebel's* humble nosegay with a splendid bouquet, a more fitting accompaniment to the casket of jewels with which *Marguerite* is to be tempted.

Marguerite enters the garden, pensively dreaming of the handsome stranger she had met in the market place. Her entrance is announced on the clarinets and violins in a lovely strain suggesting the coming song.

She seats herself at the spinning wheel and murmurs dreamily:

I wish I could but know who was he that
addressed me;
If he was noble—or at least what his
name is. . . .

Le Roi de Thule (Ballad of the King of Thulé)

By Geraldine Farrar, Soprano
(*French*) 88229 12-in., $3.00

Then rebuking herself for her idle fancies, she applies herself to her spinning and begins this plaintive *chanson* :

"Once there was a king in Thulé
Who was until death always faithful,
And in memory of his loved one
Caused a cup of gold to be made."

Then her thoughts return to *Faust*, and breaking off the song, she sings as if to herself:

Il a-vait bon-ne grà ce, à ce-qu'il me sem-blé
He was so gen-tle in bear - ing his voice was so kind.

Again impatient with her wandering mind, she finishes the ballad.

Miss Farrar sings this beautiful folk-song with surpassing loveliness of voice, and in the dreamy sentimental style which it requires.

Finding herself in no humor to spin, *Marguerite* moves toward the house and sees the flowers, which she stops to admire, thinking them from *Siebel*. The box of jewels then catches her eye, and after some misgivings she opens it. Then follows the bright and sparkling "Jewel Song," or *Air des bijoux*, in which childish glee and virginal coquettishness are so happily expressed.

"Oh Heav'n! what brilliant gems!
Can they be real?
Oh never in my sleep did I dream of aught so lovely!"

exclaims the delighted *Marguerite*.

Air des Bijoux (Jewel Song)

By Nellie Melba, Soprano
(*In French*) **88066** 12-inch, **$3.00**
By Marcella Sembrich, Soprano
(*In French*) **88024** 12-inch, 3.00

PATTI AS MARGUERITE, 1875

FARRAR AS MARGUERITE

By Geraldine Farrar, Soprano
(*In French*) **88147** 12-inch, **$3.00**

By Giuseppina Huguet
(*Double-faced—See page 144*)
(*In Italian*) **68160** 12-inch, 1.25

No less than four fine records of this well-known and popular air are presented for the choice of Victor opera lovers.

Melba's rendition is a most delightful one, her voice exhibiting the most entrancing smoothness; in its loveliness, flexibility and brilliancy it seems absolutely without a flaw.

Sembrich's *Marguerite* was always a fine impersonation, and her delivery of the number is exceedingly artistic, being one of the cleanest and most finished bits of coloratura singing ever heard in opera.

Miss Farrar's brilliant *Marguerite* has been much admired during the past few seasons, and this number shows well the loveliness and flexibility of her voice. A fine record in the black label class is contributed by Mme. Huguet, doubled with the Kermesse record described in Act II.

Quartet—Seigneur Dieu! (Saints Above, What Lovely Gems!)

By Geraldine Farrar, Soprano ; Enrico Caruso, Tenor ;
Marcel Journet, Bass ; and Mme. Gilibert, Mezzo-Soprano

(*In French*)   95204   12-inch, $5.00

A FAMOUS CAST OF 1863—PATTI, FAURE
AND DI CANDIA

The first of the great quartet records begins with the entrance of *Martha*, a susceptible matron who is companion to the motherless girl. The duenna is struck with astonishment at the sight of the jewels, and begins to question *Marguerite*, when she is interrupted by *Mephistopheles*, who appears with *Faust;* and to excuse his entrance tells *Martha* that her husband is dead. This announcement is received with cries of grief and sympathy from the women, and the impressive pause which ensues is followed by the beautiful quartet, in which Gounod expresses the various emotions of the characters.

Mephistopheles then begins to flatter the vain matron and pay her mock attentions, so that *Faust* may have an opportunity to plead his cause without interruption. This dialogue with the susceptible duenna furnishes the only touch of comedy in the opera.

MEPHISTOPHELES:
Happy will be the man
Whom you choose for your next!
I trust he may be worthy!
MARTHA:
But there's naught more doleful in nature
Than is an old, unmarried creature!
MEPHISTOPHELES:
Such a creature, old and alone,
I confess, has often made me shiver.
MARTHA:
You may escape the chance forever
And should do so ere you turn to stone!

Faust urges the timid girl to take his arm, at which she demurs, while the crafty Tempter continues his flattering attentions to *Martha*. The second quartet bit then follows, closing the record.

Quartet—Eh quoi toujours seule ? (But Why So Lonely ?)

By Geraldine Farrar, Soprano ; Enrico Caruso, Tenor ;
Marcel Journet, Bass ; and Mme. Gilibert, Mezzo-Soprano

(*In French*)   95205   12-inch, $5.00

The second part of the scene begins with the beautiful dialogue between *Marguerite* and *Faust*. She confides to him her loneliness, and in an exquisite passage speaks of her dead sister.

MARGUERITE:
My mother is gone;
At the war is my brother;
One dear little sister I had,
But the darling, too, is dead!
The angel! the angel!
Loved me, and loved me only;
I waited on her night and day.
How I worked for her! oh, so dearly!

But those to whom we cling most nearly
Are the first to be called away.
Sure as ever morning came,
Came her call, and I must be there!
Since she could speak, she called me mother.
Oh, my bird! ne'er for another
Half so truly my heart will care!

Faust is tender and sympathic, and the impressionable girl's heart turns more and more toward the handsome stranger, who seems all that a lover should be.

FAUST:
If a second angel, made by Heaven,
Could so pure, could so perfect be,

She was an angel!
An angel, sister to thee.

The record closes with the final quartet passage, by far the most effective bit of concerted writing in the opera.

Marguerite's Surrender

Mephistopheles has succeeded in getting rid of *Martha,* who vainly looks for him in the garden, and he now watches with satisfaction the lovers, who are wandering among the trees in the moonlight.

MARGUERITE (*alarmed*):
I pray you go, the night comes on!
FAUST (*protesting*):
Dear angel!
MARGUERITE (*running off*):
Pray you leave me!
FAUST (*following*):
Ah! unkind one! to deny me!
MEPHISTOPHELES:
'Ere the scene becomes too moving
'Twere best to fly! (*He hides.*)

MARTHA (*aside*):
Now be most civil!
Methinks—why he has gone!
My lord! my dear lord!
(*She goes in search of Marguerite.*)

MEPHISTOPHELES (*reappearing*):
Yes! So let her run! Ouff!
Yonder jolly matron loving,
Was longing, upon my word,
Tenderly to wed the devil!

The Tempter now sings the famous Incantation, in which he calls upon night and the flowers to aid him in his diabolical plot against the soul of *Marguerite.*

Invocation Mephistopheles (Oh Night, Draw Thy Curtain!)

By Marcel Journet, Bass   (*In French*)   64119   10-inch, $1.00

Stretching out his arms, he invokes the powers of Night, that its mysterious scents and seductive charms may aid him in his work of the lovers' undoing. In this stately passage the singer drops for a time the satirical vein of the previous quartet, and gives the invocation with befitting solemnity and grandeur.

MEPHISTOPHELES:
It was high time—
See, 'neath the balmy linden,
Our lovers devoted approaching; 'tis well!
Better leave them alone,
With the flow'rs and the moon.

O night! draw around them thy curtain!
Let naught waken alarm, or misgivings ever!
Ye flowers, aid the enchanting charm,
Her senses to bewilder; till she knows not
Whether she be not already in Heaven!

This is the most impressive passage in the whole part of *Mephistopheles,* and it is magnificently sung by Journet.

The lovers appear again, and *Mephistopheles* discreetly retires from view. The first part of the exquisite duet then follows.

Tardi si fa ! (The Hour is Late !)

By Geraldine Farrar, Soprano,
and Enrico Caruso, Tenor
(*In French*)   89032   12-inch, $4.00

By Giuseppina Huguet, Soprano,
and Fernando de Lucia, Tenor
Piano Acc. (*In Italian*)   92053   12-inch,   3.00

Marguerite, finding herself alone with *Faust,* looks in vain for *Martha,* and not seeing her, endeavors to bid farewell to her lover.

MARGUERITE:
The hour is late!   Farewell!
FAUST:
Oh, never leave me, now, I
pray thee!
Why not enjoy this lovely
night a little longer?
Let me gaze on the form be-
fore me!
While from yonder ether blue
Look how the star of eve,

Bright and tender, lingers o'er
me!
To love thy beauty too!
MARGUERITE:
Oh! how strange, like a spell,
Does the evening bind me!
And a deep languid charm
I feel without alarm,
With its melody enwind me,
And all my heart subdue!

FARRAR AS MARGUERITE

The second part of the duet begins with the lovely *Sempre amar,* in which *Marguerite* and *Faust* pledge their love.

Dammi ancor (Let Me Gaze on Thy Beauty)

By Alice Nielsen, Soprano, and Florencio Constantino, Tenor
(*In Italian*)   74076   12-inch, $1.50

(This record is in part the same as 89032, one exception being that the recitative, "The Hour is Late," between *Marguerite* and *Faust,* is omitted.)

Eternelle (Forever Thine)

By Geraldine Farrar, Soprano, and Enrico Caruso, Tenor
(In French) 89031 12-inch, $4.00

And now the lovers plight their troth in the fateful word "Eternelle," which, with the solemn chords in the wood wind, sounds like a true lover's sigh.

Faust, in an exquisite strain, calls on Heaven, the moon and stars to witness that his love is true.

FAUST:
O tender moon, O starry Heav'n
Silent above thee where angels are enthron'd.
Hear me swear how dearly do I love thee!
(Struck with a sudden fear, the timid girl begs Faust to depart):

MARGUERITE:
Ah! begone! I dare not hear!
Ah! how I falter! I faint with fear!
Pity, and spare the heart of one so lonely!

FAUST *(tenderly protesting):*
Oh, dear one, let me remain and cheer thee,
Nor drive me hence with brow severe!
Marguerite, I implore thee!

MARGUERITE:
By that tender vow that we have sworn,
By that secret torn from me,
I entreat you only in mercy to be gone!

FAUST:
Oh, fair and tender child!
Angel, so holy, thou shalt control me.
I obey—but at morn?

MARGUERITE *(eagerly):*
Yes, at morn, very early!
At morn, all day!

FAUST:
One word at parting! Thou lov'st me?
(She hastens toward the house, but stops at the door and wafts a kiss to Faust) I love thee!

FAUST *(in rapture):*
Were it already morn! Now away!

Elle ouvre sa fenêtre (See! She Opens the Window!)

By Geraldine Farrar, Soprano, and Marcel Journet, Bass
(In French) 89040 12-inch, $4.00

Hurrying away full of thoughts of the morrow, when he will see his *Marguerite* again, *Faust* is confronted by the sneering *Mephistopheles,* who bars his way.

COPY'T MISHKIN

CONSTANTINO AS FAUST

MEPHISTOPHELES *(contemptuously):*
Thou dreamer!

FAUST:
Thou hast overheard?

MEPHISTOPHELES:
I have—your parting with its modest word!
Go back, on the spot, to your school again!

FAUST:
Let me pass!

MEPHISTOPHELES:
Not a step; you shall stay and overhear
That which she telleth the stars!
See! She opens the window!

Marguerite had entered the house, but returns to the window, looks out at the night and stars, and pours forth her soul in song.

MARGUERITE *(leaning out in the moonlight):*
He loves me! He loves me!
Repeat it again, bird that callest!
Soft wind that fallest!
He loves me! Ah, our world is glorious,
And more than Heaven above! The air is balmy
With the very breath of love!
How the boughs embrace and murmur!
Ah, speed, thou night, away!

One of the most original and beautiful of the Faust melodies, this makes a fitting termination of the exquisitely beautiful Garden Scene. A lovely melody in 9⁄8 time, divided between flute and clarionet, forms the basis of the movement, and in this the soprano joins in short dreamy phrases.

Her longing for the passing of night and the return of *Faust,* expressed in the last ecstatic phrase, is answered by the cry of her lover, and *Mephistopheles,* who has been holding *Faust* back, now releases him.

FAUST *(rushing to the window):*
Marguerite!

MARGUERITE:
Ah! *(she faints in his arms).*

MEPHISTOPHELES *(with sardonic laughter):*
There! Ha, ha, ha! ha!
(The curtain slowly falls.)

KRELING MARGUERITE LONGS FOR FAUST'S RETURN

Fantasie from Garden Scene
By Mischa Elman,
Violinist (*Piano acc.*)
64122 10-inch, $1.00

For those who wish to enjoy some of the exquisite melodies of this act in an instrumental form only, the *potpourri* by Elman is included here.

In this record the young artist does not show us feats of execution, but brings out all the sensuous beauty of the music which Gounod composed for this immortal scene. It is one of the loveliest bits of violin playing imaginable.

ACT IV—The Desertion

Quando a te lieta (When All Was Young)
By Louise Homer,
Contralto (*In Italian*)
88200 12-inch, $3.00

The opening of the fourth scene shows the unhappy *Marguerite* seated at her spinning wheel, brooding over the sorrows which have overtaken her young life. *Siebel*, her faithful friend, enters and talks of vengeance against the absent *Faust*, but *Marguerite* defends him and sadly goes into the house. Left alone, *Siebel*, with gentle melancholy, sings this exquisite romance, beginning:

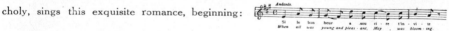

This song has long been a favorite number with many famous contraltos, and its lovely

SOLDIERS' CHORUS—ACT IV

melody is frequently used in our churches as a setting to "Come Unto Me," and other sacred words.

SIEBEL:
When all was young and pleasant May was blooming,
I, thy poor friend, took part with thee in play;
Now that the cloud of Autumn dark is glooming,
Now is for me, too, mournful the day!

Hope and delight have pass'd from life away!
We were not born with true love to trifle!
Nor born to part because the wind blows cold:
What tho' storm the summer garden rifle,
O Marguerite! Still on the bough is left a leaf of gold!

From Ditson libretto, copy't 1896.

The scene abruptly changes to the square in front of the cathedral, with the house of *Marguerite* shown at one side. The victorious soldiers, just returned from the war, enter, accompanied by delighted wives and sweethearts, and sing their famous Soldiers' Chorus, a jubilant inspiring number, and one of the finest marches ever composed.

Deponiam il brando (Soldiers' Chorus)

By New York Grand Opera Chorus	(*In French*)	74214	12-inch, $1.50
By Pryor's Band (*Double-Faced—See page 144*)		16502	10-inch, .75
By La Scala Chorus (*Double-Faced—See page 144*) (*Italian*)		62624	10-inch, .75
By Mountain Ash Party of Wales	(*In English*)	5689	10-inch, .60

This number was written for a previous opera by Gounod, but was taken bodily and added to Faust, a happy thought which added another splendid touch to a successful work.

Several renditions of this great chorus are offered, both vocal and instrumental, and a complete translation of the words is given.

DUEL SCENE—ACT IV

(English)   (Italian)   (French)

The Soldiers' Chorus—Deponiam il brando—Déposons les armes

Fold the flag, my brothers,
Fold the flag, my brothers,
Lay by the spear!
We come from the battle once more;
Our pale praying mothers,
Our wives and sisters dear,
Our loss need not deplore,
Yes! 'tis a joy for men victorious,
To the children by the fire, trembling in our arms,
To old age of old time glorious,
To talk of war's alarms!

Glory and love to the men of old,
Their sons may copy their virtues bold,
Courage in heart and sword in hand,
Ready to fight or ready to die, for Fatherland!
Who needs bidding to dare, by a trumpet blown?

Who lacks pity to spare, when the field is won?
Who would fly from a foe, if alone, or last?
And boast he was true, as cowards might do
When peril is past?
Glory and love to the men of old, etc.

Now to home again we come,
The long and fiery strife of battle over;
Rest is pleasant after toil as hard as ours
Beneath a stranger sun.
Many a maiden fair is waiting here
To greet her truant soldier lover,
And many a heart will fail and brow grow pale,
To hear the tale of peril he has run!
Glory and love to the men of old, etc.

The unhappy *Marguerite*, shunned by her companions and deserted by all save the faithful *Siebel*, is brooding within the cottage, fearing to meet her brother, who has just returned from the war. *Mephistopheles*, not content with the evil he has already wrought, returns to taunt the maiden with her fault, and sings this insulting and literally infernal song, each verse of which ends with a mocking laugh.

Serenade — Mephistopheles (Catarina, While You Play at Sleeping)

By Pol Plançon, Bass	(*In French*) 81040	10-inch, $2.00
By Marcel Journet, Bass	(*In French*) 74036	12-inch, 1.50

After the second verse occurs this famous passage—

Ha! ha! ha! ha! ha! ha! ha! ha! ha! ha! ha! ha! ha! ha! ha! ha! ha! ha! ha!

with its beginning on a high G and its octave jumps to the low G, concluding with a peal of Mephistophelean laughter.

Two versions, by two famous exponents of the part of *Mephistopheles*, are offered for a choice.

MEPHISTOPHELES:
Thou who here art soundly sleeping,
Close not thus thy heart,
Close not thus thy heart!
Caterina! wake thee! wake thee!
Caterina! wake! 'tis thy lover near!
Hearken to my love-lorn pleading;
Let thy heart be interceding,
Awake, love, and hear!
Ha, ha, ha, ha! ha! ha! ha! had ha! ha!
Don't come down until, my dear,
The nuptial ring appear
On thy finger sparkling clearly—
The wedding-ring—the ring shineth clear.
Ha! ha! ha! ha! etc.

Caterina! cruel, cruel!
Cruel to deny to him who loves thee—
And for thee doth mourn and sigh—
A single kiss from thy rosy lips.
Thus to slight a faithful lover,
Who so long hath been a rover,
Too bad, I declare!
Ha, ha, ha, ha, ha!
Not a single kiss, my dear,
Unless the ring appear!
Ha, ha, ha, ha! etc.

SAMMARCO AS VALENTINE

MELBA AS MARGUERITE—
CHURCH SCENE

PAINTED BY KRELING

The Death of Valentine

Plancon's *Mephistopheles* was invariably a finished performance—witty, elegant, debonaire and sonorous. It was a polished Devil that he pictured; yet beneath the polish we could see the sinister Satan ever present. In his record of this mocking serenade he is at his best, and the number is sung with the brilliancy and vocal finish to be expected of this fine artist.

Journet's impersonation is always highly praised, and he sings the music superbly. This famous serenade is given here with much spirit.

Que voulez-vous, messieurs? (What is Your Will?) (Duel Scene)

By Enrico Caruso, Tenor; Antonio Scotti, Baritone; and Marcel
Journet, Bass   *(In French)* 95206 12-inch, $5.00

By Van Hoose, Journet and de Gogorza   *(In French)* 74004 12-inch, 1.50

Valentine, smarting with shame of his sister's disgrace, comes from the house and exclaims, "What is your will with me?" *Mephistopheles* replies in his most mocking voice that their "serenade" was not meant for him. "For my sister, then!" cries *Valentine* in a rage, and draws his sword. The great trio then follows, leading up to a splendid climax, and is closely followed by the duel, in which *Valentine* is wounded.

KRELING   MARGUERITE AT THE SHRINE

Morte di Valentino (Death of Valentine)

By Antonio Scotti, Baritone, and Grand Opera Chorus
(In French) 88282 12-inch, $3.00

Leaving the wounded *Valentine* on the ground, the assailants rapidly depart, and a crowd of soldiers and women assemble around the dying soldier, the chorus here crying out in accents of pity, in which *Marguerite* joins. *Valentine,* seeing his sister, utters curses upon her, the solemnity of the scene enhanced by the sustained trumpet tones in the accompaniment.

VALENTINE:
  Too late! too late!
  There's no need, good friends, to bewail me!
  Too often have I looked on death to be afraid,
  Now that he is near.
MARGUERITE *(entering)*:
  Valentine! Valentine!
VALENTINE:
  Marguerite, my sister,
  What brings thee here? Begone!
MARGUERITE:
  Mercy!
VALENTINE *(sternly)*:
  Thy shame hath slain me!
  (To the soldiers)
  Her fine betrayer's sword
  Hath sent her brother home!

The throng endeavor to mitigate the dying man's anger, and *Marguerite* begs forgiveness, but *Valentine* dies with the curse upon his lips.

This dramatic scene is vividly pictured in the wonderful painting by Kreling, presented on the opposite page. These Kreling paintings, some ten in number, are reproduced in this work through the courtesy of Mme. Sofia Romani, who has loaned the Editor her collection, perhaps the only one in America.

Scene de L'Eglise (I) (Church Scene, Part I)

By Geraldine Farrar and Marcel Journet   *(In French)* 89035 12-inch, $4.00

We now come to the impressive and almost terrible scene outside the church.

Marguerite, cursed by her dying brother, abandoned by all but the faithful *Siebel,* is kneeling at a small altar. Fearing to enter, and endeavoring to seek consolation in prayer, she supplicates Heaven to accept her repentance.

MARGUERITE:
Oh, Thou who on Thy throne
Giv'st an ear for repentance!
Here, before Thy feet, let me pray!

MEPHISTOPHELES (*invisible*):
No! thou shalt pray no more!
Let her know ere she prayeth,
Demons of ill, what is in store!

CHORUS OF DEMONS:
Marguerite!

MARGUERITE (*faintly*):
Who calls me?

DEMONS:
Marguerite!

MARGUERITE (*terrified*):
I falter—afraid!
Oh! save me from myself!
Has even now the hour of torture begun!

MEPHISTOPHELES (*taunting her*):
Recollect the old time, when the angels, caressing,
Did teach thee to pray.
Recollect how thou camest to ask for a blessing
At the dawn of the day!
When thy feet did fall back, and thy breath it did falter
As though to ask for aid;
Recollect thou wast then of the rite and the altar
In thine innocence afraid!
And now be glad and hear
Thy playmates do claim thee from below, to their home!
The worm to welcome thee, the fire to warm thee,
Wait but till thou shalt come!

As this terrible prophecy is heard from the invisible Evil Spirit, *Marguerite* is overcome with terror and sinks down almost fainting.

Scene de L'Eglise (II) (Church Scene, Part II)

By Geraldine Farrar, Soprano; Marcel Journet, Bass; and Metropolitan Opera Chorus   (*In French*) 89037 12-inch, $4.00

PAINTED BY KRELING
MARGUERITE AND THE TEMPTER

The unhappy girl, beside herself with terror, cries out wildly:

Ah! what sound in the gloom,
Is beneath me, around me?
Angels of wrath? is this your sentence of cruel doom?

Then as the chorale is heard from within the church, she endeavors to break the encircling Satanic spell and kneels again in prayer.

CHOIR (*within the church*):
When the book shall be unsealed,
When the future be revealed,
What frail mortal shall not yield?

MARGUERITE:
And I, the frailest of the frail,
Have most need of Thy forgiveness!

MEPHISTOPHELES:
No! Let them pray, let them weep!
But thy sin is deep, too deep,
To hope forgiveness! No!

CHOIR:
Where shall human sinner be,
How lie hid in earth and sea,
To escape eternity?

MARGUERITE (*wildly*):
Ah, the hymn is around and above me,
It bindeth a cord 'round my brow!

MEPHISTOPHELES:
Farewell, thy friends who love thee!
And thy guardians above thee!
The past is done! the payment now!

MARGUERITE AND CHOIR:
O Thou! on Thy throne, who dost hear me,
Let a tear of mercy fall near me,
To pity and save!

MEPHISTOPHELES:
Marguerite! Mine art thou!

MARGUERITE: Ah!

Tormented beyond further endurance, the unhappy girl's reason gives way, and with a terrible cry she falls lifeless before the church.

Words are pitiful things in describing such a scene as this, given as these two artists render it. The conflict in the soul of *Marguerite*, the taunting apostrophe of *Mephistopheles* as he strives to prevent his victim from praying, while the sombre strains of the *Dies irae* issue from the church, form a musical picture which cannot be adequately described.

THE WALPURGIS NIGHT

At the period of the first production of Faust, a ballet was an absolutely essential part of an opera, if it were to be given at the Paris Opera, though to-day it is seldom performed.

Gounod placed his ballet between the death of *Valentine* and the Prison Scene; called it a Walpurgis Night, set it in a mountain fastness amid ruins, and called to the scene the classic queens, *Helen, Phryne* and *Cleopatra,* who danced to weird and distorted versions of melodies from the opera.

Ballet Music (Part I—Valse, "Les Nubiennes")

By L'Orchestre Symphonique, Paris   58015   12-inch, $1.00
By Vessella's Italian Band   *17284   10-inch,   .75

The first part, which in the opera accompanies the dance of the Nubian Slaves, is a most striking portion, beginning with introductory chords, followed by the violins in this delicious melody: afterward repeated with bassoon obbligato.

Ballet Music No. 2—Adagio (Cleopatra and the Golden Cup)

By L'Orchestre Symphonique, Paris   58018   12-inch, $1.00

The second part is the *adagio* movement accompanying the scene in which the Nubian Slaves drink from golden cups the poisons of *Cleopatra,* who herself moistens her lips from a vase in which she has dissolved her most precious pearls.

Ballet Music Nos. 5 and 6 (Les Troyennes et Variation)

By L'Orchestre Symphonique, Paris   58020   12-inch, $1.00
By Vessella's Italian Band   *17284   10-inch,   .75

These two parts are heard during the appearance of the goddess *Phryne,* who rises, a veiled apparition, and commands the dance to recommence.

Ballet Music—Finale, "Danse de Phryne"

By L'Orchestre Symphonique, Paris   58021   12-inch, $1.00

The finale is brisk in movement, rising to a wild climax and ending suddenly with a crashing chord. It is a most effective and exciting bit of ballet composition, and accompanies the dance of *Phryne,* who surpasses all her rivals and wins the favor of *Faust,* arousing the anger and jealousy of the courtesans—*Helen, Cleopatra, Aspasia* and *Lais*—and the dance develops into a bacchanalian frenzy, graphically pictured in Gounod's music.

ACT V

SCENE—*The Prison Cell of Marguerite*

The short final act of Faust is truly one of the grandest of operatic compositions, Goethe's story giving Gounod ample opportunity for some most dramatic writing. *Marguerite's* reason is gone—grief and remorse have driven her insane, and in a frenzy she has destroyed her child. Condemned to death, she lies in prison, into which *Mephistopheles* and *Faust,* defying bolts and bars, have entered.

"Mon coeur est pénétré d'épouvante!" (My Heart is Torn)

By Geraldine Farrar and Enrico Caruso   (*In French*)   89033   12-inch, $4.00

Gazing at the unhappy girl, who is sleeping on a pallet of straw, *Faust* cries:

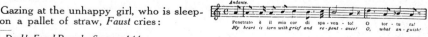

* *Double-Faced Record—See page 144.*

141

KRELING   The Redemption of Marguerite

and, as the full measure of his own guilt comes to him, continues:

FAUST:
Oh, what anguish! She lies there at my feet
A young and lovely being, imprisoned here
As if herself, not I, were guilty!
No wonder that her fright has reason ta'en
away!
Marguerite! Marguerite!

MARGUERITE (*awaking*):
Ah, do I hear once again, the song of time
gone by—
'Twas not the cry of the demons—
'Tis his own voice I hear!

She forgets all but that her loved one is before her, and sings in a transport of love

MARGUERITE:
Ah! I love thee only!
Since thou cam'st to find me
No tears more shall blind me!
Take me up to Heaven,
To Heaven by thy aid!

FAUST (*supporting her tenderly*):
Yes, I love thee only!
Let who will, now goad
Or mock me, or upbraid.
Earth will grow as Heaven.
By thy beauty made!

Attends! voici la rue (This is the Fair)

By Geraldine Farrar and Enrico Caruso   (*In French*) 89034 12-inch, $4.00

Marguerite's mind wandering, she sings dreamily of the Fair, where first *Faust* appeared to her:
'Tis the Fair!
Where I was seen by you, in happy days
gone by,
The day your eye did not dare
To meet my eye!

Marguerite now rehearses the first meeting with *Faust,* his respectful greeting, and her modest and dignified reply:

"High born and lovely maid, forgive my humble duty;
Let me your willing slave, attend you home to-day?"
"No my lord! not a lady am I, nor yet a beauty,
Not a lady, not a beauty,
And do not need an arm to help me on my way!"
FAUST (*in despair*):
Come away! If thou lov'st me!
MARGUERITE (*dreamily, her thoughts in the past*):
How my garden is fresh and fair!

Every flower is incense breathing,
And through the still evening air
A cloud of dew, with perfume wreathing;
Hark! how the nightingale above
To every glowing crimson rose
Fondly murmurs thy love!
FAUST (*urging her*):
Yes! but come! They shall not harm thee!
Come away!
There is yet time to save thee!
Marguerite! Thou shalt not perish!
MARGUERITE (*listlessly*):
'Tis all too late! Here let me die!
Farewell! My memory live to cherish!

The impassioned duet then follows, *Faust* endeavoring to persuade her to escape; but the poor weak mind cannot grasp the idea of safety. The duet is interrupted by the impatient *Mephistopheles*, whose brutal "*Alerte*" begins the final trio.

Trio—Alerte! ou vous êtes perdus! (Then Leave Her!)

By Geraldine Farrar, Enrico Caruso and Marcel Journet
(*In French*) 95203 12-inch, $5.00
By Victor Opera Trio   (*In English*) 60097 10-inch, .75
By Giuseppina Huguet, Pietro Lara and Torres de Luna
(*In Italian*) *62085 10-inch, .75

Mephistopheles, fearing the coming of the jailers, and uncertain of his own power, cries out:

Then leave her, then leave her, or remain to your shame;
If it please you to stay, mine is no more the game!
MARGUERITE (*in horror, recognizing the Evil One, the cause of all her woes*):
Who is there! Who is there!
Dost thou see, there in the shadow;

What does he here! He who forbade me to pray!
MEPHISTOPHELES (*to Faust*):
Let us go, ere with dawn
Doth justice come on;
Hark! the horses panting in the courtyard below,
To bear us away!
Come, ere 'tis day!

As he sings, the tramping and neighing of horses are heard in the accompaniment.

MARGUERITE (*with fresh courage, defying him*):
Away, for I will pray! (*in rapture*)
Holy Angels, in Heaven bless'd
My spirit longs with thee to rest!
FAUST: Come, ere 'tis too late to save thee!

* *Double-Faced Record—See page 144.*

The inspiring trio, perhaps the most thrilling and moving of all operatic compositions, then commences; *Marguerite* continuing her prayer, *Faust* urging her to follow him, while *Mephistopheles,* in desperation, repeats his warning to *Faust.*

MEPHISTOPHELES:
Let us leave her!
Come away! the dawn is grey,
Come, ere they claim thee!
FAUST:
Lean on my breast.
O come! I'm here to save thee!

MARGUERITE:
Holy angels, in Heaven bless'd,
My spirit longs with thee to rest!
Great Heaven, pardon grant, I implore thee,
For soon shall I appear before thee!
(*She dies.*)

At the close of the trio, *Mephistopheles* is about to triumph over the soul of his victim, when a company of angels appear and announce that *Marguerite* is saved. The Evil One, dragging *Faust* with him, disappears in a fiery abyss.

DOUBLE-FACED AND MISCELLANEOUS FAUST RECORDS

Gems from Faust
" Kermesse Waltz "—" Flower Song "—" Jewel Song "—" Garden Scene "—" Prison
Scene "—" Soldiers' Chorus "
By Victor Opera Co.   31879   12-inch, $1.00

Selection from Faust   By Sousa's Band 31104   12-inch   1.00
Introduction to Kermesse Scene, Act I—Flower Song, Act II—Kermesse Waltz, Act I—
Soldiers' Chorus, Act IV

Selection from Faust   By Victor Band
Introduction to Act III—Flower Song—Waltz and Ballet
from Finale, Act II   } 35016   12-inch,   1.25
Crown Diamonds Overture   By Victor Band

Flower Song   By Corinne Morgan   (*In English*)
Drink To Me Only With Thine Eyes   By Harry Macdonough } 35086   12-inch,   1.25

All Hail Thou Dwelling Lowly
By Charles Harrison   (*In English*)
Elixir of Love   (*Elisir d'Amore*)   A Furtive Tear
By Charles Harrison   (*In English*) } 35354   12-inch,   1.25

Aria dei gioielli (Jewel Song)
By Giuseppina Huguet, Soprano   (*In Italian*)
La Kermesse (Kermesse Scene) By La Scala Chorus (*In Italian*) } 68160   12-inch,   1.25

Dio possente   (Even the Bravest Heart)
By Francesco Cigada   (*In Italian*)
Favorita—Quando le soglie   By Mileri and Minolfi   (*In Italian*) } 68275   12-inch,   1.25

Alerte! ou vous êtes perdus!   (Then Leave Her!)
Huguet, Lara and De Luna
Le parlate d'amor (Flower Song)   By Emma Zaccaria } 62085   10-inch,   .75

Deponiam il brando (Soldiers' Chorus)   By La Scala Cho
Don Pasquale—Sogno soave e casto   By Acerbi, Tenor   (*In Italian*) } 62624   10-inch,   .75

Io voglio il piacer   (The Pleasures of Youth)
By Pini-Corsi and Sillich   (*In Italian*)
Forza del Destino—Solenne in quest' ora   Colazza and Caronna } 63174   10-inch,   .75

Soldiers' Chorus   Pryor's Band
Devil's March   (*von Suppe*)   Pryor's Band } 16502   10-inch,   .75

Waltz from Kermesse Scene   Pryor's Band
In Happy Moments   (*from Maritana*)   Alan Turner } 16552   10-inch,   .75

Ballet Music "Dance of Nubian Slaves"   Vessella's Band
Ballet Music ("Dance of the Trojan Maidens" and
"Mirror Dance")   By Vessella's Italian Band } 17284   10-inch,   .75

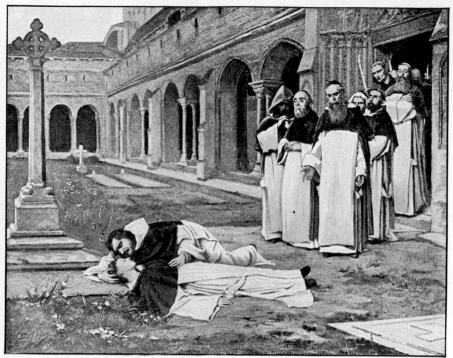

THE DEATH OF LEONORA

(German)
DIE FAVORITIN
(*Dee Fah-voh-ree'-tin*)

(Italian)
LA FAVORITA
(*Lah Fah-voh-ree'-tah*)

(English)
THE FAVORITE

OPERA IN FOUR ACTS

Text by Alphonse Royer and Gustave Waez, adapted from a drama of Baculard-Darnaud, "*Le Comte de Comminges.*" Music by Gaetano Donizetti. In its present form it was first produced at the *Académie*, Paris, December 2, 1840. First London production in English, 1843; in Italian February 16, 1847. First New Orleans production February 9, 1843. English version at the Park Theatre, New York, October 4, 1848. Some later American productions were in 1895-96, with Manelli, Cremonini, Ancona and Plançon; and in 1898, at Wallack's Theatre by the Royal Italian Opera Company, and in 1905 at the Metropolitan.

Cast

ALPHONSO XI, King of Castile...................................Baritone
FERDINAND, a young novice of the Convent of St. James of Compostella,
    afterwards an officer.....................................Tenor
DON GASPAR, the King's Minister..........................Tenor
BALTHAZAR, Superior of the Convent of St. James..................Bass
LEONORA DI GUSMANN, the King's favorite...................Soprano
INEZ, her confidante......................................Soprano

Courtiers, Guards, Monks, Attendants, etc.

Scene and Period: The action is supposed to take place in Castile, about the year 1340.

ACT 1
SCENE—*The Monastery of St. James*

The rise of the curtain discloses a Spanish cloister with its secluded garden and weather-stained wall, while in the distance is a glimpse of the tiled roofs of the city. *Ferdinand,* a novice in the monastery, confesses to the Prior, *Balthazar,* that he has seen a beautiful woman and has fallen in love with her. He describes his meeting with the fair one in a lovely song, *Una vergine.*

Una vergine (Like An Angel)
By Florencio Constantino, Tenor   (In Italian)   64090   10-inch, $1.00
The good Prior is horrified and urges him to confess and repent.

Non sai tu che d'un giusto (Know'st Thou)
By Gino Martinez-Patti, Tenor, and Cesare Preve, Bass
(In Italian)   *62635   10-inch, $0.75

BALTHAZAR:
Ah, my son, my life's latest solace,
May thy innocence rescue thee still!
Thou, thou who shouldst be my successor,
And all my solemn duties fill.
FERDINAND:
Ah, father, I love her!
BALTHAZAR:
This woman, wretched one! oh, knowest thou
Who has lur'd thee thus to shame?
Knowest thou her, for whom thy holiest vow
Is forfeit? Her rank—her name?
FERDINAND:
I know her not; but I love her!
BALTHAZAR:
Begone! too profane! Fly these cloisters
Far, far from hence!—avoid my sight.

FERDINAND (*in rapture*):
Yes, ador'd one! this heart's dearest idol!
For thee I will break ev'ry tie!
To thee all my soul I surrender—
At thy dear feet content to die!
Forgive me! Father, I go!
BALTHAZAR:
Hence, audacious! away in madness!
I'll not curse thee! no—depart!
If Heaven spare thee, soon in sadness,
Thou'lt hither bring a broken heart!
FERDINAND:
Ah, dear Idol! this heart so enchaining,
In vain thy spell I strive to break!
To thee only my truth maintaining,
My cloister I forsake!

The Prior's pleading fails to restore *Ferdinand* to his duty, and he leaves the convent to search for the beautiful unknown. As he goes he turns and stretches out his arms toward *Balthazar,* who averts his head.

The scene changes to the Island of Leon, where *Inez,* an attendant of *Leonora,* and a chorus of maidens are gathering flowers. They sing a melodious chorus,

Bei raggi lucenti (Ye Beams of Gold)
By Ida Roselli, Soprano, and La Scala Chorus
(In Italian)   *62635   10-inch, $0.75

which tells of the love which their mistress feels for a handsome youth whom she has seen but once, and who is now on his way to the Isle at *Leonora's* request.

Ferdinand, who, shortly after his departure from the monastery, had received a note bidding him come to the Isle of Leon, now arrives in a boat, blindfolded, is assisted to land by the maidens, and the bandage removed. He gazes around him wonderingly, and asks *Inez* the name of the unknown lady who has sent for him. She smilingly refuses, and tells him only her mistress may reveal the secret. *Leonora* now appears, and the maidens depart. A tender love scene follows, but the Favorite is anxious, fearing that *Ferdinand* will learn that she is the King's mistress. She shows him a parchment which she says will insure his future, and then bids him leave her forever.

Fia vero! lasciarti! (Fly From Thee!)
By Clotilde Esposito and Sig. Martinez-Patti   *68309   12-inch, $1.25
Ferdinand, beginning the duet, indignantly refuses, saying:

FERDINAND:
Fly from thee! Oh, never!
'Twere madness to try
From thee to sever;
'Twere better to die!
LEONORA:
Farewell! Go; forget me!

Thy vows and thy love!
No longer regret me—
Mine image remove.
The rose tho' she fair be,
A canker that wears,
Can never restor'd be
By anguish or tears!

Inez enters and whispers to *Leonora* that the King has arrived at the villa. *Leonora* gives *Ferdinand* the parchment and bids him again to depart, then exits hastily. *Ferdinand* reads it and is delighted to find that it is a captain's commission, and declares that he will win great honors to lay at the feet of his love.

* Double-Faced Record—See page 149.

ACT II
SCENE—*Gardens of the Alcazar Palace*

The King enters and admires the beauty of the palace, which he has just acquired from the Moors by the victory of his army, led by the young captain, *Ferdinand*. A message comes from *Balthazar,* the King's father-in-law, who is at the head of the powerful Church party, and *Alfonso* is threatened with the wrath of the Church if he does not give up *Leonora*. In a fine air he declares he will not submit.

Vien Leonora (Leonora, Thou Alone)
By Francesco Cigada, Baritone   (*In Italian*)   *68061   12-inch, $1.25

Leonora enters and the King tenderly asks the cause of her melancholy. She tells him her position is intolerable, and asks that she be allowed to leave the Court. She begins the duet, *Quando le soglie.*

Quando le soglie (From My Father's Halls)
By Lina Mileri and Renzo Minolfi   (*In Italian*)   *68275   12-inch, $1.25

Ah! l'alto ardor (Oh, Love!)
By Margarete Matzenauer and Pasquale Amato   89062   12-inch, $4.00

Leonora recalls the circumstances connected with her departure from her father's home.

MLLE. BAILAC AS FAVORITA

LEONORA:
When from my father's halls you bore me,
A poor simple maiden, betray'd, deceived,
Alas! within these walls I hop'd, fulfilled
Would be those vows so sworn!
KING (*with remorse*): No more!
LEONORA:
Silent and alone, shunned by the world,
Live I in the dark: the mistress of the King.
Vainly glitter these jewels,
Vainly bloom these flowers around me.
The lip may smile, but the heart is weeping!
KING:
But tell me the cause of your grief.
LEONORA:
Ah! ask not to know it.
Permit me, sir, to leave this court!
KING:
No man can love thee more than I!
LEONORA:
I dare not look so high as thee.
KING (*aside*):
Oh, love! soft love! her bosom filling,
With sweet response each fibre thrilling,
Inspire her heart!
LEONORA (*aside*):
Oh, love, alas! this bosom filling,
With secret woe each fibre thrilling!
KING:
Disperse this gloom; enjoy the feasts
Spread 'round thee by my tender love!

They are interrupted by the entrance of *Balthazar,* who brings the mandate from the Pope. The King defies him, saying:

KING:
My will is sacred! On my brow
Rests the royal diadem!

This lady I shall wed, and whoever
Doubts my right shall feel
The anger of a monarch!

Balthazar then begins the finale, one of the most impressive of the concerted numbers. He threatens the King with the wrath of God and denounces *Leonora* as an abandoned woman.

Ah! paventa il furor (The Wrath of Heaven)
By Amelia Codolini, Francesco Cigada, Aristodemo Sillich and La Scala Chorus
(*In Italian*)   *16536   10-inch, $0.75

The curtain falls on a dramatic tableau,—*Leonora* weeping with shame, the King hesitating between love and ambition, while the terrible *Balthazar* thunders the papal curse down upon the guilty pair.

Double-Faced Record—See page 149.

ACT III
SCENE—*A Room in the Palace*

Ferdinand, who has won distinction in the wars, is received by the King, who asks him to name his own reward. The young captain asks for the hand of a noble lady to whom he owes all his renown, and when the King asks her name he points to *Leonora*. *Alfonso* gazes at her coldly and sternly and sings his ironical air.

A tanto amor (Thou Flow'r Beloved)

By Mario Ancona, Baritone	(*In Italian*)	88063	12-inch, $3.00
By Mattia Battistini, Baritone	(*In Italian*)	92045	12-inch, 3.00
By Francesco Cigada, Baritone	(*In Italian*)	*16536	10-inch, .75

ALFONSO:
Thou flow'r belov'd,
And in hope's garden cherish'd,
With sighs and tears refresh'd,
Both night and morn;
Fad'st from my breast,
Thine ev'ry beauty perished,
And in thy stead alone have left a thorn!

He consents to the marriage, however, and announcing that they must prepare to wed in an hour, goes out with *Ferdinand*. *Leonora*, left alone, decides to sacrifice her own feeling and renounce *Ferdinand*. She gives expression to her mingled joy and despair in a noble air:

O mio Fernando (Oh, My Ferdinand)

By Margarete Matzenauer, Contralto   (*In Italian*)   88363   12-inch, $3.00

LEONORA:
Oh, my Ferdinand, were mine this earth's whole treasure—
Mine, too, each star of yon blue heav'n:
To purchase thee one pleasure,
All, all at once by this fond hand were giv'n!
All should be thine, save my poor name degraded;
And thine should be, too, my life's latest sigh!
Ah! But ere I give to thee a name thus clouded,
And thou deceive, I'll die!

Her resolution is no sooner taken, however, than she resolves to tell him all and throw herself on his mercy. She calls *Inez*, and bidding her seek out *Ferdinand* and reveal all, goes to her apartments to prepare for the wedding. *Inez* prepares to obey, but on her way is arrested by the order of the King.

The King enters with *Ferdinand*, to whom he gives the title of *Count of Zamora*. *Leonora* appears and is overjoyed to see *Ferdinand* still looking at her lovingly, not knowing that *Inez* has failed in her mission, and that he is yet ignorant of her secret.

The ceremony is performed and the pair are presented to the Court, but are met with cold and averted looks. *Ferdinand*, although not aware of the cause, resents this and is about to draw his sword when *Balthazar* enters and demands peace.

When he learns of the wedding he is horrified, and tells *Ferdinand* he has married the King's mistress. *Ferdinand* is furious and denounces the King, who, seized with sudden remorse, begins the great finale to Act III.

Orsù, Fernando (Stay! Hear Me, Ferdinand!)

By Maria Cappiello, Mezzo-Soprano; Giuseppe Acerbi, Tenor;
Francesco Cigada, Baritone   (*In Italian*)   *62659   10-inch, $0.75

Ferdinand hurls at the King's feet his badge of honor and his broken sword and leaves the Court, followed by *Balthazar*. *Leonora* faints as the curtain falls.

ACT IV
SCENE—*The Cloisters of the Monastery*

The opening number in this act is the impressive *Splendon piu belle*, considered by many critics to be the finest of the Favorita numbers. The scene represents the cloister at the Convent of St. James of Compostella, illumined by the rays of the rising sun. The monks have assembled to welcome back the prodigal *Ferdinand*, who, heartbroken at the falseness of *Leonora*, is returning to renew his vows. The ceremonies are conducted by *Balthazar*, who begins this great number.

Splendon più belle in ciel le stelle (In Heavenly Splendor)

By Marcel Journet and Opera Chorus	(*In Italian*)	74273	12-in., $1.50
By Torres de Luna, Bass, and La Scala Chorus	(*In Italian*)	*68061	12-in., 1.25
By Perello de Segurola, Bass, and La Scala Chorus	(*Italian*)	*16551	10-in., .75

Balthazar entreats him to lift his eyes from earthly things and contemplate the stars, which typify a forgiving Heaven.

Double-Faced Record—See page 149.

The monks now go into the chapel to prepare for the final rites, and *Ferdinand,* left alone, casts a look behind him to the world he has left forever, and sings his lovely *Spirto gentil.*

Spirto gentil (Spirit So Fair)

By Enrico Caruso, Tenor (*In Italian*) 88004 12-inch, $3.00
By Gennaro de Tura, Tenor (*In Italian*) 76012 12-inch, 2.00
By Evan Williams, Tenor (*In English*) 74141 12-inch, 1.50

FERDINAND:
Spirit so fair, brightly descending,
Then like a dream all sadly ending,
Hence from my heart, vision deceiving,
Phantom of love, grief only leaving,

In thee delighting, all else scorning,
A father's warning, my country, my fame!
Ah, faithless dame, a passion inviting,
Fair honor blighting, branding my name,
Grief alone thou leav'st, phantom of love!

The monks now lead *Ferdinand* to the chapel. *Leonora,* who has come hither disguised as a novice to entreat forgiveness of her lover, hears him take the final vows and despairingly falls at the altar. *Ferdinand* comes from the chapel, and seeing a poor novice, assists him to rise. He is at first horrified to recognize *Leonora,* and bids her begone, but she pleads for mercy.

LEONORA:
Ah, heavenlike, thy mercy showing,
Turn not thy heart away from me!
FERDINAND (*his love returning*):
From tears thy words persuasion borrow,
Like a spell their softness impart,
Those sighs, the hope of some bright morrow

Waken once more in my heart!
(*Impetuously.*)
I love thee!
Come, ah, come, 'tis vain restraining
Passion's torrent onward that dashes,
O'er my bosom still art thou reigning
And we together will live and die!

Pietoso al par d'un Nume (As Merciful as God)

By Esposito and Martinez-Patti (*In Italian*) *62659 10-inch, $0.75

Again gently reminding him of his vows, she falls from weakness and privation.

LEONORA: 'Tis Heaven calls thee!
FERDINAND (*recklessly*):
Yet more power hath love;
Come, could I possess thee
There's naught I would not brave!

LEONORA (*feebly*):
Heav'n forgive me, now I'm dying,
We shall hereafter meet no more to be parted,
Farewell, now, farewell!
(*She dies.*)

DOUBLE-FACED AND MISCELLANEOUS FAVORITA RECORDS

Quando le soglie (From My Father's Halls) By Lina Mileri, Contralto, and Renzo Minolfi, Baritone (*Italian*) Faust—Dio possente (Gounod) By Francesco Cigada (*In Italian*)	68275	12-inch, $1.25
Fia vero! lasciarti! (Fly From Thee!) Clotilde Esposito, Soprano, and Sig. Martinez-Patti, Tenor (*In Italian*) Norma—In mia mano alfin tu sei Giacomelli and Martinez-Patti	68309	12-inch, 1.25
Vien Leonora (Leonora, Thou Alone) F. Cigada (*Italian*) Splendon più belle in ciel (In Heavenly Splendor) By Torres de Luna, Bass, and La Scala Chorus (*In Italian*)	68061	12-inch, 1.25
A tanto amor (Flow'r Beloved) By Cigada (*In Italian*) Ah! paventa il furor Codolini, Cigada and Sillich (*In Italian*)	16536	10-inch, .75
Non sai tu che d'un giusto (Know'st Thou) By Gino Martinez-Patti, Tenor, and Cesare Preve, Bass (*Italian*) Bei raggi lucenti (Beams of Gold) Roselli and Cho. (*Italian*)	62635	10-inch, .75
Orsù, Fernando (Stay! Hear Me, Fernando!) By Cappiello, Acerbi and Cigada (*In Italian*) Pietoso al par d'un Nume (As Merciful as God) By Esposito and Martinez-Patti (*In Italian*)	62659	10-inch, .75
Splendon più belle in ciel le stelle (In Heavenly Splendor) By Perello de Segurola, Bass, and Chorus (*In Italian*) Manon—Et je sais votre nom By Korsoff and Beyle (*In French*)	16551	10-inch, .75

*Double-Faced Record—See above list.

(German)

FIDELIO
(Fee-deh'-lee-oh)

or, CONJUGAL LOVE

GRAND OPERA IN TWO ACTS

Words adapted by Joseph Sonnleithner from Bouilly's *Léonore, ou l'Amour Conjugal.* Music by Ludwig von Beethoven. First produced at the *Theatre an der Wein,* Vienna, November 20, 1805. A revised version was given in 1806 and a third production in 1814. Produced in London, at the King's Theatre, May 18, 1832. In English at Covent Garden, June 12, 1835. In Italian at Her Majesty's, May 20, 1851. In Paris at the Théâtre Lyrique, translated by Barbier and Carré, and in three acts, May 5, 1860. First American performance in New York, September 9, 1839, with Giubilei, Manvers and Poole. Other notable productions were in 1857, with Johannsen, Weinlich and Oehrlein; in 1858, with Mme. Caradori and Karl Formes; in 1868, with Mme. Rotter, Habelmann and Formes; at the New Orleans Opera, in Italian, December 11, 1877; the Damrosch production of 1884, with Mme. Brandt, Mlle. Belz and Herr Koegel; the Metropolitan revival of 1901, with Ternina as *Léonore*; and the revival of 1913.

BEETHOVEN (1770-1827)

Characters

DON FERNANDO, Minister	Baritone
DON PIZARRO, Governor of the State Prison	Baritone
FLORESTAN, a prisoner	Tenor
LÉONORE, his wife, known as Fidelio	Soprano
ROCCO, jailor	Bass
MARZELLINE, his daughter	Soprano
JAQUINO, gatekeeper	Tenor

Soldiers, Prisoners, People, etc.

Place: A Spanish State prison in the vicinity of Seville.

150

PHOTO WHITE

SECOND ACT SCENE AT THE METROPOLITAN

Fidelio must ever be regarded with great interest as being the only opera written by one of the greatest composers. Originally given as *Fidelio*, it was rewritten and condensed into two acts by Breuning, still a third revision being made in 1814 by Treitschke. At the time of the second production in 1806 the title was changed to *Leonore*, Beethoven writing a new overture, now known as *Leonore No. 3*. The complete overture is given in three parts by the Victor Concert Orchestra.

PHOTO WHITE
FLORESTAN AND HIS FAITHFUL WIFE

Leonore Overture No. 3
By Victor Concert Orchestra
(Parts I and II) 35268 12-in., $1.25

Part III Victor Concert Or. *Adagio from 4th Symphony (Beethoven)* Vessella's Band	35269 12-in., 1.25

The action of the opera occurs in a fortress near Seville. *Don Florestan*, a Spanish nobleman, has been imprisoned here for life, and to make his fate certain his mortal enemy, *Don Pizarro*, Governor of the prison, has announced his death, meanwhile putting the unfortunate man in the lowest dungeon, where he is expected to die by gradual starvation, thus rendering unnecessary a resort to violent means.

Ha, welch ein Augenblick (Fateful Moment)
By Otto Goritz, Baritone *(In German)* 64165 10-in., $1.00

In this air the wicked Governor unfolds his hatred and his malignant intentions toward *Florestan*.

GOVERNOR:
Fateful moment! My revenge is near!
Long I've waited for this hour,
Fearful lest he should escape me!
Over my enemy I triumph;
He who would my life have taken!
Oh, fateful moment!
Ah, what a day is this!
My vengeance shall be sated,
And thou, thy doom is fated.
Once in the dust I trembled
Beneath thy conquering steel,
But fortune's wheel is turning
In torments thou art burning
The victim of my hate!

An extremely pleasant and agreeable person this Spanish Governor must have been! Goritz sings this striking air in a highly effective manner, fairly exuding the spirit of revenge.

Don Florestan, however, has a devoted wife who refuses to believe the report of his death. Disguising herself as a servant, and assuming the name of *Fidelio* she secures employment with *Rocco*, the head jailor. *Rocco's* daughter falls in love with the supposed handsome youth, and he is soon in such high favor that he is permitted to accompany *Rocco* on his visits to the prisoner.

ORIGINAL PROGRAM OF FIDELIO—
VIENNA

Hearing that the Minister of the Interior is coming to the prison to investigate the supposed death of *Florestan*, the Governor decides to murder him, and asks *Rocco's* help. *Fidelio* overhears the conversation and gets *Rocco* to allow her to dig the grave. Just as *Don Pizarro* is about to strike the fatal blow, *Fidelio* rushes forward, proclaims herself the wife of the prisoner and shields him. The Governor is astonished for a moment, but recovers himself and is about to sacrifice both, when a flourish of trumpets announces the coming of the Minister, and *Don Pizarro* is soon disgraced, while *Florestan* is pardoned and given back to his faithful wife.

REMBRANDT

SCENE FROM FIDELIO (BERLIN OPERA)

(German)   (English)
DIE FLEDERMAUS   THE BAT

COMIC OPERA IN THREE ACTS

Text by C. Haffner and Richard Genée. Music by Johann Strauss. First production, Vienna, April 5, 1847, at the Theatre an der Wein. Produced at Berlin, July, 1874. Given in Paris under the title of *La Chauve Souris* and *La Tsigane;* and in Italy as *Il Pipistrello.* First London production in 1895, at the Coburg Court Theatre. Given in English by the Beecham Opera Company in 1910, at His Majesty's Theatre. Produced at the Casino, New York, March 16, 1885, with De Wolf Hopper in the cast. Given several performances at the German Theatre, and revived at the Metropolitan Opera House by Mr. Amberg's Company, March 6, 1890. A notable revival occurred at the Metropolitan February 15, 1905, with a cast including Caruso, Sembrich, Walker, Alten, Reiss and Goritz. In 1912 an adaptation by Gladys Unger, called "The Night Birds," was given in London, and later in New York, under the title "The Merry Countess," with new lyrics by Arthur Anderson.

Characters

VON EISENSTEIN, a banker.....................................Tenor
ROSALIND, his wife.......................................Soprano
PRINCE ORLOFSKY ....Tenor
FRANK, the prison director ....Tenor
DR. FALKE, a notary.....................................Tenor
DR. BLIND, a lawyer.....................................Tenor
ALFRED, Prince Orlofsky's musician........................Tenor
ADELE, Rosalind's maid..................................Soprano

An American, a Spaniard, a distinguished Egyptian, members of the Ballet, etc.

Time and Place: Germany; the last century.

GERMAN POSTER ANNOUNCING FLEDERMAUS RECORDS

There are six composers by the name of Strauss, but this comic opera is by the well-known writer of the "Blue Danube." The music is in the popular Viennese style, and was the pioneer of the Viennese operetta. In dramatic effect it is French, the libretto being an adaptation of Meilhac and Halévy's *Le Réveillon.*

Baron *von Eisenstein,* who has been sentenced to prison for eight days for insulting an official, is persuaded by *Notary Falke* to postpone for one day the beginning of his sentence and to attend a ball at the residence of *Prince Orlofsky. Falke,* it appears has an old score to settle with *von Eisenstein.* The previous winter, attending a ball dressed as a bat, the baron had compelled him to walk to his home in his bird dress, to the amusement of the people. He now hopes to find an opportunity for revenge, and when *von Eisenstein* takes a mournful farewell of his wife, telling her he is going to prison, *Falke* invites *Rosalind* and her maid, *Adele,* to attend the ball.

After the departure of her husband *Rosalind* is visited by an old admirer, *Alfred,* and when *Frank,* the governor of the prison, comes to take *von Eisenstein* to jail, he mistakes *Alfred* for his prisoner, and carries him off. *Rosalind* goes to the ball masked in order to better observe her husband. *Falke* introduces her as a Hungarian Countess, and she so enchants her unsuspecting husband that he presents her with his treasured watch, which the lady keeps to be used as evidence the next day. *Frank* attends the ball and makes love to *Adele.*

When the festivities are over *Frank* returns to the prison, where *Eisenstein* later appears to give himself up. He is surprised to learn that *"Eisenstein"* has already been arrested on the previous evening, but keeps his own counsel, and later learns that *Alfred* had called on his wife the night before. When *Rosalind* appears at the jail, he accuses the pair, but she produces the watch as evidence that her husband also has something to confess. The Prince arrives, and *Dr. Falke* explains that he ("Old Dr. Bat") has contrived the whole scheme, *Rosalind* forgives her husband and all ends happily.

The Victor offers a fine medley from this delightful opera, famous for its entrancing

PHOTO WHITE SCENE FROM THE MERRY COUNTESS

melodies, its gaiety and the delicate beauty of the score. In the recent revival under the title "Merry Countess," the plot was revised, and tells of a count who is arrested after an auto accident and sentenced to five days in jail. This jail is the liveliest spot in town for that period of time, and matters come to a climax when the warden arrives, finds a ball in progress, and is himself arrested and locked up.

The Victor Opera Company gives an extremely brilliant presentation of this version containing portions of eight of the principal numbers.

Gems from "Merry Countess"

Chorus, "The Hours Fly By"—Duet, "So, My Pet, Don't Fret"—Solo and Chorus, "Well I Never"—Trio, "Married Life"—Solo, "King Champagne" —Trio, "Faithless One"—Chorus, "Oh, What a Night"—Chorus, "Darling, Do"

By the Victor Opera Company   31875 12-inch, $1.00

SCENE FROM THE RECENT AMERICAN PRODUCTION

THE PHANTOM SHIP

(German)

DER FLIEGENDE HOLLÄNDER

(Dehr Flee'-gen-deh Hol'-lan-der)

(English)

THE FLYING DUTCHMAN

A ROMANTIC OPERA IN THREE ACTS

Text and score by Richard Wagner. First produced at the Royal Opera in Dresden, January 2, 1843, with a Paris production the following year under the title of *Le Vaisseau Fantôme*. Produced in Berlin in 1844; Zurich, 1852; Weimar, 1853; Vienna, 1860; Munich, 1864. First London production July 23, 1870, under the title *L'Olandese Dannato*, the book being translated into Italian by Marchesi; and in English by Carl Rosa October 3, 1876. Another Italian version was given at Covent Garden, this time called *Il Vascello Fantasma*, June, 1877. First American production at Philadelphia, November 8, 1876, by the Pappenheim Opera Company, in Italian; first New York production, in English, January 26, 1877; in German, March 12, 1877. First New Orleans production November 29, 1877.

Cast

DALAND, a Norwegian sea captain . . . . Bass
SENTA, his daughter . . . . Soprano
ERIC, a huntsman . . . . Tenor
MARY, Senta's nurse . . . . Contralto
DALAND'S STEERSMAN . . . . Tenor
THE DUTCHMAN . . . . Baritone
Sailors, Maidens, Hunters, etc.

Place : On the coast of Norway

155

FERD. LEEKE

DALAND:
Farewell! To-day thou shalt my daughter see!
(Flying Dutchman, Act I.)

THE STORY

One of the most melodious of Wagner's operas, and the most popular in Germany to-day, *Fliegende Holländer* is also the one which was most promptly condemned by the critics after its production. Its present vogue is a notable example of the change in musical taste since 1843.

Wagner was led to write the *Flying Dutchman* after reading Heine's legend of the unhappy mariner, who, after trying long in vain to pass the Cape of Good Hope, had sworn that he would not desist if he had to sail on the ocean to eternity. To punish his blasphemy he is condemned to the fate of the Wandering Jew, his only hope of salvation lying in his release through the devotion unto death of a woman; and to find such a maiden he is allowed every seven years to go on shore.

Flying Dutchman Overture

By Pryor's Band   31787   12-inch, $1.00

The overture is a complete miniature drama, em-bodying the events of the opera to follow. Driven by the gale, the Phantom Ship approaches the shore, while amid the fury of the tempest is heard the theme of *The Curse:*

The storm increases and reaches its height in a won-derful piece of writing. No composer ever succeeded in portraying a raging storm with such vivid effect. Amid a lull in the tempest, we hear the melancholy complaint of the *Dutchman* from the great air in the first act, *"Wie oft . . . Mein Grab, es schloss sich nicht?"*

(*My grave I find it not!*) A gleam of hope appears in the Redemption theme, and a joyous strain is heard from the sailors of *Daland's* ship, which is safe in the harbor.

Thus the various events of the drama are presented in miniature; and the overture is in fact a complete *résumé* of the opera, summarizing the leading *motifs.* It is superbly played by Mr. Pryor's fine organization.

ACT I

SCENE—*The Coast of Norway*

The curtain rises showing a rocky sea coast in Norway, with the ship of *Daland* anchored near the shore. As the crew furl the sails, *Daland* goes ashore, and climbing the cliff, sees that he is only seven miles from home, but as he must wait for a change in the wind, bids the crew go below and rest.

The *Steersman* remains on watch, and to keep awake sings a sailor ballad:

STEERSMAN:
Through thunder and wars of distant seas,
     My maiden, come I near!
Over towering waves, with southern breeze,
     My maiden, am I here!
My maiden, were there no south wind,
     I never could come to thee;
O fair south wind, to me be kind!
     My maiden, she longs for me!
          Ho-yo-ho! Hallo-ho!
From the shores of the south, in far-off lands,
     I oft on thee have thought;
Through thunder and waves from Moorish
     strands,
     A gift I thee have brought.
My maiden, praise the sweet south wind—
     I bring thee a golden ring.
O fair south wind, to me be kind!
     My maiden doth spin and sing.
          Ho-yo-ho! Hallo-ho!

DALAND

157

BYRON

Senta and the Maidens   (Mme. Gadski on the Right)

He soon falls asleep, however, and fails to see the *Flying Dutchman,* which now appears, with blood-red sails and black masts, for one of her periodical visits.

The spectral crew furl the sails and drop the rusty anchor. The *Dutchman* stands on the deck, and delivers his great soliloquy.

Wie oft in Meeres tiefsten Schlund (In Ocean's Deepest Wave)

By Otto Goritz, Baritone
(In German) 74230 12-inch, $1.50

Gloomily gazing at the land, he sings his preliminary recitative:

The term is past and once again are ended the
　　seven long years;
The weary sea casts me upon the land.
Ha! haughty ocean!
A little while and thou again wilt bear me!
Though thou art changeful, unchanging is my
　　doom!
Release, which on the land I seek for,
Never shall I meet with!

　　An introduction in 6-8 *allegro molto* leads to the aria:

BERGER   RENAUD AS THE DUTCHMAN

DUTCHMAN:
　　Engulf'd in ocean's deepest wave,
　　Oft have I long'd to find a grave;
　　But ah! a grave, I found it not!
　　I oft have blindly rushed along,
　　To find my death sharp rocks among;
　　But ah! my death, I found it not.
　　And oft, the pirate boldly daring,
　　My death I've courted from the sword,
　　Here, cried I, work thy deeds unsparing,
　　My ship with gold is richly stor'd!
　　Alas, the sea's rapacious son,
　　But sign'd the cross, and straight was gone

Nowhere a grave, no way of death!
Mine is a curse of living breath.
Thee do I pray
Bright angel sent from Heaven.
Was there a fruitless hope to mock me given,
When thou didst tell me how to gain release?
A single hope with me remaineth,
A single hope still standeth fast;
When all the dead are raised again,
Destruction then I shall attain.
Ye worlds, your curse continue not!
Endless destruction be my lot!

Daland comes on deck and is astonished to see the strange ship. He wakes the *Steersman* and they hail the stranger, who asks *Daland* to give him shelter in his home, offering him treasure.

THE DUTCHMAN:
　　Oh, grant to me a little while
　　　　thy home,
　　And of thy friendship thou
　　　　wilt not repent;
　　With treasure brought from
　　　　every clime and country
　　My ship is richly laden: wilt
　　　　thou bargain?

On hearing that *Daland* has a daughter he proposes marriage. The simple Norwegian is dazzled by such an honor from a man apparently so wealthy, and freely consents, provided his daughter is pleased with the stranger.

FIRST ACT SETTING USED IN MUNICH

The wind changes and *Daland* sails for his home, the *Dutchman* promising to follow at once.

ACT II

SCENE—*A Room in Daland's Home*

The maidens are busily spinning—all but *Senta, Daland's* daughter, who is idly dreaming, with her eyes fixed on the fanciful portrait of the *Flying Dutchman* which hangs on the wall.

The legend of the unhappy *Hollander* has made a strong impression on the young girl, and he seems almost a reality to her. The maidens ridicule her, saying that her lover, *Eric,* will be jealous of the *Dutchman. Senta* rouses herself and commences the ballad, which begins with the motive of *The Curse.*

Traft ihr das Schiff (Senta's Ballad)

By Johanna Gadski, Soprano

(In German) 88116 12-inch, $3.00

With growing enthusiasm she goes on, describing the unhappy lot of the man condemned to sail forever on the sea unless redeemed by the love of a woman. Then with emotion she cries:

VAN ROOY AS THE DUTCHMAN

Doch kann dem blei-chen Man-ne Er lö-sung ein-stens noch wer-den,
Yet this the spec-tral man from his life-long curse may de-liv-er.

This is the theme of *Redemption by Woman's Love,* and as *Senta* sings the beautifully tender and melodious phrase, she runs toward the portrait with outstretched arms, hardly conscious of the now alarmed maidens.

SENTA:
Yo-ho-hoe! Yo-ho-hoe! Yo-ho-hoe! Yo-ho-hoe!
Saw ye the ship on the raging deep
Blood-red the canvas, black the mast?
On board unceasing watch doth keep
The vessel's master pale and ghast!
Hui! How roars the wind! Yo-ho-hoe! Yo-ho-hoe!
Hui! How bends the mast! Yo-ho-hoe! Yo-ho-hoe!
Hui! Like an arrow she flies
Without aim, without goal, without rest!
(*She gazes at the portrait with growing excitement*)
Yet can the spectre seaman
Be freed from the curse infernal,
Find he a woman on earth
Who'll pledge him her love eternal.

The maidens are so alarmed at *Senta's* outburst of passion that they run out and

DUPONT GADSKI AS SENTA

call *Eric,* who meets them at the door with news of the *Dutchman's* arrival. They run to the shore while *Eric* remains and reproaches *Senta.* She refuses to listen and the distracted lover runs out.

Suddenly the door opens and the *Dutchman* appears. *Senta* is transfixed with surprise as she involuntarily compares the portrait with the living man. A long silence follows. The *Dutchman,* his eyes fixed on the glowing face of the maiden, advances toward her. *Daland,* well satisfied with the apparent understanding between the stranger and his daughter, leaves them together.

The *Hollander* sees in *Senta* the angel of whom he had dreamed and who is to banish the curse, and she sees the original of the portrait on which the sympathy of her girlish and romantic heart had been lavished. The *Dutchman* asks *Senta* if she agrees with her father's choice of a husband. She gladly consents, and a long love duet follows, the final theme of which is "faith above all."

Wie aus der Ferne (Like a Vision)

By Otto Goritz, Baritone

(In German) 74322 12-inch, $1.50

DESTINN AS SENTA

THE DREAM—SENTA AND ERIC

Versank ich jetzt (Do I Dream?)

By Johanna Gadski, Soprano,
and Otto Goritz, Baritone
(*In German*) 88370 12-inch, $3.00

Wohl kenn' ich Weibes (Woman's Holy Duties)

By Johanna Gadski, Soprano,
and Otto Goritz, Baritone
(*German*) 88371 12-inch, $3.00

At the close of the duet, the *Dutchman* and *Senta* rejoice at his deliverance from the spell:

THE DUTCHMAN:
    A healing balm for all my sorrows
    From out her plighted word doth flow.
SENTA:
    'Twas surely wrought by pow'r of magic
    That I should his deliv'rer be.
THE DUTCHMAN:
    Hear this! Release at last is granted!
    Hear this, ye mighty:
    Your power is now laid low!
SENTA:
    Here may a home at last be granted,
    Here may he rest, from danger free!
    What is the power within me working?
    What is the task it bids me do?
    Almighty, now that high Thou hast raised me,
    Grant me Thy strength, that I be true!

Daland re-enters and is delighted to find such a complete understanding between the two. He invites the *Dutchman* to the fête that evening in celebration of the safe arrival of the

CLICHE BRAND

THE BAYREUTH SETTING OF ACT III

Norwegian ship. *Senta* repeats her vow unto death, and a magnificent trio closes the act.

ACT III
SCENE—*Daland's Harbor*

This scene shows the ships anchored in the bay near *Daland's* home. *Daland's* vessel is gay with lanterns, in contrast to the gloom and silence which marks the *Dutchman's* ship. A gay Norwegian chorus is followed by a spirited hornpipe with a most peculiar rhythm. Bits of these numbers are to be heard in the Pryor's Band records of the Overture and Fantasia.

The maidens now appear with baskets of eatables, and are joyfully received by the sailors. Having supplied the wants of their own countrymen, they approach the *Dutchman's* ship and call to the sailors, but only a ghostly silence rewards them. Piqued at this neglect, they turn their remaining baskets over to the Norwegian sailors and return home.

Suddenly the sea around the *Dutchman* begins to rise, and a weird glow lights the ship. The crew appear and begin a sepulchral chant, which causes the gay Norwegians to cease singing, cross themselves in terror, and finally go below. With mocking laughter, the crew of the *Dutchman* also disappear and the ship is in darkness.

HUFFERT, BERLIN

SCHUMANN-HEINK AS MARY

Senta and *Eric* appear and a stormy scene ensues. He has heard of her engagement to the strange captain, and is beside himself. He kneels and begs her to have pity on him. Suddenly the *Hollander* comes upon the scene and is horror-stricken at the tableau. Believing *Senta* to be false, he cries, "All is lost; *Senta,* farewell!"

The crews of both ships appear and the townsmen rush to the scene. The *Dutchman* reveals his identity and declares himself cursed forever. He springs upon his ship—the crimson sails expand as if by magic and the ship departs, with the crew chanting their weird refrain.

Senta, in wild exaltation, rushes to the shore calling toward the departing vessel:

FROM AN OLD PRINT   SENTA IS FAITHFUL UNTO DEATH

"I am faithful unto death," and throws herself into the sea. The *Flying Dutchman* sinks beneath the water, and rising from the wreck can be seen the forms of *Senta* and the *Dutchman* clasped in each other's arms. The curse has been banished—true love has triumphed!

{Flying Dutchman Fantasia	By Pryor's Band }	35158 12-inch, $1.25
{ *Pagliacci—Prologue*	*By Pryor's Band* }	

This brilliant selection contains some of the finest music of this wonderful masterpiece, in which Wagner has portrayed the story of the *Dutchman* condemned to sail forever on the stormy sea unless redeemed by the love of a woman.

Two variations of the exquisite theme representing *Redemption by Woman's Love* are given. We first hear the magnificent strain played by the orchestra in Act III when *Senta* plunges into the sea, after the *Dutchman,* believing her false, has sailed away; then follows the theme first heard in *Senta's* ballad, one of the finest numbers in the opera. Then appears the second of the two principal themes: the *Flying Dutchman* motive:

a weird melody representing the restless wanderer. In strong contrast comes the rollicking chorus of *Daland's* sailors, "Steersman, Leave the Watch," and the fantastic dance which follows:

CLICHE VAN DER WEYDE

THE LATE SIR HENRY IRVING
AS VANDERDECKEN

The Fantasia is brought to an effective close with a portion of the great duet between *Senta* and the *Dutchman,* leading up to a splendid climax.

FINAL SCENE OF THE "FLYING DUTCHMAN" AT THE LYCEUM THEATRE, LONDON
(FROM AN OLD PRINT)

LA FORZA DEL DESTINO

(Lah Fort'-zah del Des-tee'-noh)

(English)

THE FORCE OF DESTINY

OPERA IN FOUR ACTS

Book by Piave; music by Giuseppe Verdi. First produced at St. Petersburg, November 11, 1862; in London June 22, 1867; in Milan 1869; Paris, 1876; Berlin, 1878. First New York production February 2, 1865, with Carozzi-Zucchi, Massimilliani and Bellini. It was not heard again for fifteen years, when it was produced at the Academy of Music, with the last act rewritten by the composer, the cast including Annie Louise Cary, Campanini, Galassi and Del Puente.

The only production in North America subsequent to that time was that of the Lombardi Opera Company in San Francisco several years ago.

CHARACTERS

MARQUIS OF CALATRAVA, *(Kal-ah-trah'-vah)*	Bass
DONNA LEONORA, } his children	Soprano
DON CARLO, }	Baritone
DON ALVARO, *(Ahl-vah'-roh)*	Tenor
ABBOT OF THE FRANCISCAN FRIARS	Bass
MELITONE, a friar	Baritone
CURRA, Leonora's maid	
TRABUCO, muleteer, afterwards a peddler	Tenor
A SPANISH MILITARY SURGEON	Tenor
AN ALCADE	Bass

Muleteers, Spanish and Italian Peasants and Soldiers,
Friars of the Order of St. Francis, etc.

Scene and Period : Spain and Italy ; about the middle of the eighteenth century.

Verdi's opera of *La Forza del Destino* was never a great success; its story, which is taken from a drama of the Duke of Rivas, entitled *Don Alvaro o la Fuerzer del Sino,* being doleful and so crowded with horrors that not even the beautiful music could atone for the gloomy plot.

The overture is a most interesting and rather elaborate one.

Overture   *(Double-faced—See page 168)*   Pryor's Band   35215   12-inch, $1.25
{Overture, Part I   La Scala Orchestra} 68009   12-inch,   1.25
{Overture, Part II   La Scala Orchestra}

It opens with a trumpet blast which sufficiently foreshadows the tragic character of the opera, this being followed by an air in the minor, leading up to a striking theme which steals in softly from the strings.

This is the beautiful subject of the *Madre Pietosa,* afterwards heard with such magnificent effect in the opera.

Part II opens with a light and pretty pastoral melody quite in the Italian vein. A notably brilliant passage for strings brings us again to the *Madre Pietosa* melody, this time delivered in a triumphant *fortissimo,* after which the overture works up to a truly animated and powerful finale.

ACT I

SCENE—*Drawing Room in the House of the Marquis of Calatrava*

Don Alvaro, a noble youth from India, becomes enamored with *Donna Leonora*, the daughter of the *Marquis of Calatrava*, who is strongly opposed to the alliance. *Leonora*, knowing her father's aversion, determines to make her escape with *Alvaro*, aided by *Curra*, her confidant.

She is in the act of eloping when her father appears, and is accidentally slain by her lover. *Leonora*, horror-stricken, rushes to her father, who curses her with his dying breath.

ACT II

SCENE I—*An Inn at Hornacuelos*

The second act begins in a village inn, where *Don Carlo*, son of the murdered *Marquis*, is disguised as a student in order to better avenge his father. *Leonora*, who is traveling in male attire, arrives at the inn, and is horror-stricken at seeing her brother, who has sworn to kill her lover *Alvaro* and herself. She flees to the convent of Hornacuelos, arriving at night.

SCENE II—*The Convent of Hornacuelos*

Kneeling in the moonlight, she prays to the Virgin to protect her. This beautiful prayer is splendidly sung here by Mme. Boninsegna, accompanied by the chorus of La Scala.

Madre, pietosa Vergine (Holy Mother, Have Mercy)

By Celestina Boninsegna, Soprano, and La Scala Chorus

(*In Italian*)   92031   12-inch, $3.00

The effect produced by the solo voice with the background of male voices singing the *Venite* in the chapel is powerful and thrilling, and forms one of the finest of the Victor reproductions of Verdi's scenes.

LEONORA:
Oh, Holy Virgin,
Have mercy on my sins!
Send help from Heaven
To erase from my heart
That ungrateful one.
(*The friars are heard in their morning hymn.*)
THE FRIARS:
Venite, adoremus et procelamus
An te Deum, ploremus, ploremus
Coram Domino, coram Domino qui fecit nos.

LEONORA:
O sublime song,
Which like incense,
Ascends heavenward.
It gives faith, comfort,
And quiet to my soul.
I will go to the holy sanctuary.
The pious father cannot refuse to receive me.
O Lord! Have mercy on me,
Nor abandon me.
(*She rings the bell of the convent.*)

Leonora is admitted to the convent by the *Abbot*, to whom she confesses. He procures her a nun's robe and directs her to a cave, assuring her that a curse will rest upon anyone who seeks to know her name or to enter her abode. In her gratitude she sings the second great air.

La Vergine degli angeli (May Angels Guard Thee)

By Celestina Boninsegna, Soprano, and La Scala Chorus

(*In Italian*)   91075   10-inch, $2.00

Again we have the effect of the solemn chant of the priests blending with the prayer of *Leonora*.

THE FRIARS:
La Vergine degli Angeli
Vi copra del suo manto,
E voi protegga vigile
Di Dio l'Angelo santo.
(*Leonora kisses the hand of the Abbot and goes to her retreat. The monks return to the church.*)

LEONORA:
Let the Holy Virgin
Cover you with her mantle,
And the angels of God
Watch over you!

ACT III

SCENE—*A Military Camp near Velletri*

In Act III we are transported to Italy, where we meet *Alvaro*, who has enlisted in the Spanish army. In a sad but beautiful air he recounts his misfortunes, and appeals to heaven for pity.

O tu che in seno agli Angeli (Thou Heavenly One)

By Enrico Caruso, Tenor

(*In Italian*)   88207   12-inch, $3.00

ALVARO:
Life is a misery . . . In vain I seek death. . . . Seville! . . . Leonora! . . . . Oh, memories! Oh, night! Thou hast taken from me all my happiness! I shall ever be unhappy. . . . So it is written. . . . My father tried to make his country free, and to wear a crown by marrying the only daughter of Ineas. He was foiled in his design. . . . I was born in prison. . . . The desert educated me; unknown is my royal descent! My ancestors aspired to a throne. Alas! They were beheaded! Oh, when will my misfortune cease? Thou who hast ascended in heaven, all beautiful and pure from mortal sins, do not forget to look on me, a poor sufferer, who without hope fights eagerly for death against destiny! Leonora, help me and have mercy on my sufferings!

In the next scene he saves the life of *Don Carlo,* whose wanderings in search of vengeance have led him to this region. Both having assumed fictitious names, they do not know each other, and swear eternal friendship. Shortly afterward, during an engagement, *Don Alvaro,* wounded, is brought in on a stretcher by his soldiers. Thinking himself dying, he sends away the soldiers and requests that he be left alone with *Don Carlo.* The great duet, the finest number in the opera, then occurs.

Solenne in quest'ora (Swear in This Hour)

By Enrico Caruso, Tenor, and Antonio Scotti, Baritone
(*In Italian*)   89001   12-inch, $4.00

By Lambert Murphy and Reinald Werrenrath
(*In Italian*)   70103   12-inch,   1.25

By Carlo Barrera and Giuseppe Maggi   (*In Italian*)   *68213   12-inch,   1.25

By Luigi Colazza and Ernesto Caronna   (*In Italian*)   *63174   10-inch,   .75

The wounded man confides a case of letters to his friend *Don Carlo* to be destroyed, making him swear that he will not look at the contents. *Carlo* swears, and the friends bid each other a last farewell.

ALVARO:
My friend . . . swear that you will grant my last wish.
CARLO: I swear! ALVARO: Look at my breast.
CARLO: A key!
ALVARO:
Open this case and you will find a sealed parcel. . . . I trust it to your honor. . . . It contains a mystery which must die with me . . . when I am dead destroy the letters.
CARLO:
So be it.
ALVARO (*feebly*):
Now I die happy . . . . let me embrace you . . . . farewell!
CARLO: Put thy trust in heaven! BOTH: Adieu!

The Caruso and Scotti rendition of this number is considered by many to be one of the most perfect and beautiful of all the Red Seal Records. It is certainly the most wonderfully lifelike reproduction of these two great voices which could be imagined. The Purple Label Record by Mr. Murphy and Mr. Werrenrath is an excellent one, exhibiting the fine voices of these two young singers to great advantage.

Just at this point it may be well to settle a controversy which has been raging ever since the issue of the Caruso-Scotti record in 1906. This argument concerns the identity of the voices in the opening measures, and is the natural result of a remarkable similarity between Caruso's lower register and the medium tones of Scotti's voice. The Victor Catalogue Editor now appoints himself a court of final appeal, and declares that contrary to the usual impression it is Caruso, not Scotti, who begins the record! Here are the opening measures just as sung by the artists:

DON ALVARO (CARUSO).

So - len - ne   in quest' ora   giu - rar - mi   do - ve - te   Far
Swear   in   this   hour   *my   last   wish   to   grant   me,   So*

DON CARLOS (SCOTTI).   DON ALVARO (CARUSO).

pa - go un mio voto   Lo giu - ro   lo giu - ro,   Sul co - re cer - ca - te
do   not   re - fuse me,   *I   swear,   I   swear,*   *Up - on   my   heart   you'll find*

Alvaro, however, does not die, and in the next scene his identity becomes known to *Don Carlo,* who challenges him. They fight, and *Alvaro,* thinking he has killed his enemy, resolves to end his days in a monastery.

ACT IV
SCENE—*Same as Act II, Scene II*

Five years have now elapsed and the last act reveals again the cloister of Hornacuelos, where *Alvaro,* now *Father Raphael,* is discovered by *Don Carlo,* who with a persistence rivaling that of a Kentucky mountaineer, revives the feud and tries to force him to renew the combat. *Alvaro* finally consents, and they agree to fight in a deserted spot near by. This agreement is expressed in a fiery duet.

Invano Alvaro! (In Vain, Alvaro!)
By Enrico Caruso, Tenor, and Pasquale Amato, Baritone
(*In Italian*) 89052 12-inch, $4.00

The host of Victor opera-lovers who are familiar with the wonderful duet from Act III, by Caruso and Scotti, will note with delight the issue of another famous duet from this opera, sung by Caruso and Amato.

This great scene has been recorded in two parts. *Carlo* demands that *Alvaro* renew the feud, but the priest refuses, saying that vengeance is with God. *Don Carlo* taunts him with a terrible persistence, until the monk, goaded past endurance, consents to fight to the death.

CARLOS:
In vain, Alvaro,
Thou hast hid from the world,
And concealed thy coward heart
With the habit of a monk!
My hate and desire for vengeance
Have enabled me to persist
Until I have discovered your retreat!
In this lonely spot
We shall not be disturbed,
And your blood shall wipe out
The stain upon my honor;
That I swear before God!
ALVARO *(recognizing him)*:
Don Carlos! Thou livest!

CARLOS:
Yes! and for long years
I have sought and now find thee.
By thy hand I fell,
But God restored my strength
That I may avenge thy crimes!
Here are two swords,
Thy choice now make!
ALVARO:
Leave me! By this holy habit
Thou may'st see my repentance!
CARLOS *(in fury)*:
Coward!
Thou shalt not hide behind thy robes!
ALVARO *(agitated)*:
Coward! Oh, God
Give me strength to forgive thee!

Le minaccie, i fieri accenti (Thy Menaces Wild!)
By Enrico Caruso, Tenor, and Pasquale Amato, Baritone
(*In Italian*) 89053 12-inch, $4.00
By Titta Ruffo, Baritone, and Emanuele Ischierdo, Tenor
(*In Italian*) 92504 12-inch, 4.00
By Carlo Barrera, Tenor, and Giuseppe Maggi, Baritone
(*Double-faced—See page 168*) (*In Italian*) 68213 12-inch, 1.25

Alvaro recovers his poise and endeavors to appeal to the reason of his enemy, showing him the futility of reopening the feud. Part II begins as follows:

ALVARO *(firmly)*:
Thy menaces wild
Be heard only by the winds,
I cannot listen!
Brother, let us submit to fate
And the will of God!
CARLOS:
Thou hast left me
A sister deserted and dishonored!
ALVARO:
No! I swear it!
I adore her with a holy love.
CARLOS *(furiously)*:
Thy cowardly pleadings
Cannot move me to pity.
Take thy sword and fight!
ALVARO:
Brother, let me kneel to thee.
(He kneels.)
CARLOS:
Ah, by such an act
Thou showest thy base origin!

ALVARO *(rising, unable to control himself)*:
My lineage is brighter than a jewel—
CARLOS *(sneeringly)*:
A jewel flaw'd and discolored!
ALVARO *(in fury)*:
Thou liest!
Give me a sword. Lead on!
CARLOS:
At last!
ALVARO *(recovering himself)*:
No, Satan shall not thus triumph.
(Throws down his sword.)
CARLOS:
Then coward, I brand thee with dishonor!
(Strikes him.)
ALVARO:
Oh, God, no more!
(To Don Carlos)
Defend thyself!
BOTH:
We both must die,
Our hatred will be appeased
And Satan will claim us for his own!

ACT V

SCENE—*A Wild Spot Near Hornacuelos*

The scene changes to the vicinity of *Leonora's* cave. Pale and worn, the unhappy woman comes from the cave, and in another great air implores Heaven to let her die, as she is unable to forget her lover.

Pace, mio Dio (Mercy, O My Lord)

By Luisa Tetrazzini, Soprano		(*In Italian*)	88502	12-inch, $3.00
By Celestina Boninsegna, Soprano		(*In Italian*)	92027	12-inch, 3.00

> LEONORA:
> Mercy, oh Lord!
> My sorrows are too great to bear.
> This fatal love has been my undoing,
> But still do I love him,
> Nor can I blot his image from my heart;
> Yet 'tis Heaven's decree that I shall see him
> no more!
> Oh Lord, let me die,
> Since death alone can give me peace!

A storm now breaks, and *Leonora* retires within the cave just as *Alvaro* and *Carlo* appear for the final combat. *Alvaro* recognizes the spot as an accursed one, but declares that it is a fitting place for the ending of so deadly a feud.

Don Carlo falls mortally wounded, and desiring to repent his sins asks *Alvaro*, who is known as *Father Raphael*, to confess him, but the monk is under the curse of the cave and cannot. He goes to call the friar who dwells in the cave; *Leonora* rushes forth, sees her brother wounded and embraces him, but true to his vow he makes a dying effort and stabs her to the heart.

This dramatic scene has been put by Verdi into the form of a trio.

Non imprecare, umiliati (Swear Not, Be Humble)

By Ida Giacomelli, Soprano; Gino Martinez-Patti, Tenor; Cesare Preve,
Bass (*Double-faced—See below*)   (*In Italian*) 68026 12-inch, $1.25

Don Alvaro then completes the catalogue of horrors by throwing himself from a cliff just as the monks arrive singing the *Miserere*. The curtain then falls, evidently because, as one critic has said, every member of the cast being dead, there seems to be no reasonable excuse for keeping it up any longer!

DOUBLE-FACED FORZA DEL DESTINO RECORDS

{ Overture	By Arthur Pryor's Band }	35215	12-inch,	$1.25
{ Orpheus in Hades Overture (*Offenbach*)	By Arthur Pryor's Band }			
{ Overture, Part I	By La Scala Orchestra }	68009	12-inch,	1.25
{ Overture, Part II	By La Scala Orchestra }			
{ Le minaccie, i fieri accenti (Let Your Menaces)				
By Carlo Barrera, Tenor, and Giuseppe Maggi, Baritone				
	(*In Italian*)	68213	12-inch,	1.25
{ Solenne in quest'ora (Swear in This Hour)	By Carlo			
Barrera, Tenor, and Giuseppe Maggi, Baritone	(*In Italian*)			
{ Non imprecare, umiliati	By Ida Giacomelli, Soprano;			
Gino Martinez-Patti, Tenor; Cesare Preve, Bass				
	(*In Italian*)	68026	12-inch,	1.25
{ Ballo in Maschera—Ah! qual soave brivido (*Thy Words, Like Dew*)				
By Ida Giacomelli, Soprano, and Gino Martinez-Patti, Tenor				
	(*In Italian*)			
{ Solenne in quest'ora (Swear in This Hour) By Luigi				
Colazza, Tenor, and Ernesto Caronna, Baritone (*Italian*)		63174	10-inch,	.75
Faust—Io voglio il piacer (*The Pleasures of Youth*) By				
G. Pini-Corsi, Tenor, and Aristodemo Sillich, Baritone (*Italian*)				

FRA DIAVOLO—ACT III

FRA DIAVOLO

(Frah Deeah'-voh-loh)

COMIC OPERA IN THREE ACTS

AUBER

Libretto by Scribe, devised from the story of Lesueur's earlier opera, *La Caverne*. Music by Daniel François Esprit Auber. First production at the *Opéra Comique*, Paris, January 28, 1830. Presented in Vienna, 1830. London, at the Drury Lane Theatre, in English, November 3, 1831; in Italian, at the Lyceum Theatre, 1857. First American production at the Old Park Theatre, New York, in English, June 20, 1833. Produced in New Orleans in 1836. It was not until 1864 that it was given in Italian in New York, at the Academy of Music, with Clara Louise Kellogg. Colonel Mapleson gave three performances of the opera at the Academy of Music in 1885. Zelie de Lussan made her début here in the part with the Boston Ideals in 1888. Recently revived at the Manhattan Opera and afterwards at the New Theatre by the Metropolitan forces.

Characters

FRA DIAVOLO, calling himself "Marquis of San Marco"............Tenor
LORD ROCBURG (Lord Allcash), an English traveler.................Tenor
LADY PAMELA (Lady Allcash), his wife........................Soprano
LORENZO, Chief of the Carabiniers...............................Tenor
MATTEO, the innkeeper.......................................Bass
ZERLINA, his daughter......................................Soprano
GIACOMO and BEPPO, companions of Fra Diavolo.............Bass-Tenor

The Scene: Italy, in the neighborhood of Terracina.

SANTLEY AS FRA DIAVOLO

The story of *Fra Diavolo* is melodramatic in the highest degree. *Lorenzo*, in command of the Roman Dragoons, is leaving *Matteo's* inn to capture *Diavolo* and his brigands, just as *Lord Rocburg* and his wife, *Pamela*, who are traveling under the names of *Lord* and *Lady Allcash*, arrive, lamenting their misfortunes, having been robbed on the road. Another traveler, calling himself *Marquis of San Marco*, who is no other than *Fra Diavolo*, appears soon after and is also welcomed by the innkeeper, *Matteo*, and his daughter, *Zerlina*. *Lorenzo* is in love with *Zerlina*, but she has been promised by her father to a rich peasant. The *Marquis* openly courts *Lady Allcash* and at the same time manages to relieve her of her jewels.

Giacomo and *Beppo*, two of *Diavolo's* companions, appear on the scene, and when all are asleep, are admitted through the window by the bandit. All three conceal themselves in *Zerlina's* room, and after she has retired they proceed to again rob *Lord* and *Lady Allcash*. *Lorenzo* now returns, having killed most of the band of robbers and recovered the Englishman's property.

He expects to receive the proffered reward of ten thousand piastres, and his hopes of winning *Zerlina* seem brighter.

The soldiers arrive at the inn in time to discover the robbery, but *Diavolo* covers the retreat of his fellow-bandits by pretending to have a rendezvous with some lady, arousing the jealousy of both the Englishman and *Lorenzo*, the latter challenging him to a duel.

The last act of the opera shows the forest where the duel is to take place. As *Lorenzo* sadly watches the marriage procession of *Zerlina* and the peasant *Francisco* approach, he recognizes in the crowd *Giacomo* and *Beppo*. Both are arrested by the young captain, who through them hopes to capture the chief, *Fra Diavolo*. The two brigands are forced to betray *Diavolo* and lure him into a trap, where he is ensnared and shot. As a fitting climax, the happy *Lorenzo* wins *Matteo's* daughter for his bride.

Those who hear these records of Auber's melodious opera will be charmed by the brilliant and fluent measures, varied here and there with pretty bits of sentiment, which go hand in hand with the romantic story of the Italian bandit.

The Victor offers a fine record of the *Agnese la zitella*, the popular Italian melody which *Diavolo* sings in Act II, to warn his companions, *Beppo* and *Giacomo*, that all is quiet in the house and they may now carry out their scheme to again rob *Lord Rocburg* and *Lady Pamela*.

COPY'T DUPONT   FARRAR AS ZERLINA

Records of the Overture and principal selections from the opera by two famous bands are also offered, while the brilliant opera aggregation has given a tuneful presentation of some of the gems of Auber's work.

Gems from Fra Diavolo

Chorus, "Victoria"—Solo, "On Yonder Rock Reclining"—Easter Chorus, "Hail, Blessed Morn"—Chorus, "Bless'd Powers That Still the Good Protect"—Solo, "Friend Beppo, See"—Finale, "Victoria."

By the Victor Opera Company   31829   12-inch, $1.00

LORD AND LADY ALLCASH

The medley opens with the chorus of greeting to the soldiers:

Victoria! Victoria! Joy now reigns around.

Then comes a bit of *Zerlina's* ballad about the dread *Fra Diavolo*, "On Yonder Rock Reclining," followed by the Easter Chorus. The prayer in Act III, "Blest Powers That Still the Good Protect,"next occurs.

DIAVOLO AND ZERLINA

The remaining numbers are the boast of *Diavolo* as he sees victory for all his schemes: "The lord's gold and his wife all are mine!" and the chorus of thanksgiving at the final capture and death of the bandit, sung to the melody of *Diavolo's* air in Act I.

Overture to Fra Diavolo	By Pryor's Band			
Marriage of Figaro Overture (*Mozart*)	By Pryor's Band	35109	12-inch,	$1.25
Fra Diavolo Selection	By Vessella's Italian Band			
Daughter of the Regiment Selection (*Donizetti*)	By Vessella's Italian Band	35191	12-inch,	1.25
Agnese, la zitella (Agnes, Beautiful Flower)	By Pietro Lara, Tenor (*In Italian*)			
Barbiere—Guarda Don Bartolo	By Huguet, Corsi, Pini-Corsi and Badini	63171	10-inch,	.75

ZERLINA'S ROOM—ACT II

THE WOLF'S GLEN SCENE

(German)   (English)

DER FREISCHÜTZ   THE FREESHOOTER

(Der Fry´-sheutz)

ROMANTIC OPERA IN THREE ACTS

Words by Friedrich Kind; music by Carl Maria von Weber; completed as *Die Jägarsbraut,* May 13, 1820.   Produced at Berlin, June 18, 1821; in Paris (as *Robin des Bois,* with new libretto by Blaze and Sauvage, and many changes), at the Odéon, December 7, 1824.   Another version, with translation by Pacini, and recitatives by Berlioz, at the Académie Royale, June 7, 1841, under the title of *Le Franc Archer.*   In London as *Der Freischutz* or *The Seventh Bullet,* with many ballads inserted, July 23, 1824; in German, at King's Theatre, May 9, 1832; in Italian, as *Il Franco Arciero,* at Covent Garden, March 16, 1850 (recitatives by Costa). First New York production, in English, March 2, 1825.   This was followed by other versions, Charles E. Horn appearing as *Caspar* in 1827.   German performances were given at the old Broadway Theatre, 1856, and by other German companies in the sixties.   Produced at the Metropolitan under Dr. Damrosch in 1884, and at the Academy of Music in 1896.   Recently revived at the Metropolitan, with Gadski, Jadlowker and Goritz.

Cast

PRINCE OTTOKAR, Duke of Bohemia........Baritone
CUNO, head ranger...........................Bass
MAX, ⎱ two young foresters...............⎰Tenor
CASPAR, ⎰   ⎱ Bass
KILIAN, a rich peasant......................Tenor
A HERMIT...................................Bass
ZAMIEL, the fiend huntsman...................
AGNES, Cuno's daughter...................Soprano
ANNIE, her cousin.........................Soprano

Chorus of Hunters, Peasants and Spirits.

Scene and Period: Bohemia, about 1750.

PRINCE OTTOKAR

CLAIRE DUX AS AGATHA

The word *freischutz*, probably better translated as "free marksman," means a *Schütz* or marksman who uses charmed bullets which do not depend on the aim of the shooter.

Overture to Freischutz

By Sousa's Band   *35000   12-inch, $1.25
By La Scala Orchestra
  *62636   10-inch,   .75

The overture presents the story of the opera in a condensed form. An introduction with a tender horn passage leads us into the forest. Night is falling and mysterious sounds are heard. The *allegro*, representing the doubts of the good but vacillating young hunter, begins, and the sound of the magic bullets can be heard as they drop in the melting pot. Next a beautiful melody, portraying love and happiness, appears, but this in turn is succeeded by another mood of distress. At length the triumphant strain indicative of the final victory is sounded, leading up to a splendid climax.

Sousa's Band has given a stirring performance of this brilliant overture, while the rendition by La Scala Orchestra will please those who prefer orchestral music.

The story of the opera is founded on a German tradition, told among huntsmen, that whoever will sell his soul to *Zamiel*, the Demon Hunter, may receive seven magic bullets, which will always hit the mark. For each victim whom he succeeds in securing for the Demon, his own life is extended, and he receives a fresh supply of the charmed missiles.

Cuno, head ranger to *Ottakar*, a Bohemian prince, has two assistants, *Max* and *Caspar*, both excellent marksmen. *Max* is in love with *Agnes*, *Cuno's* daughter, who has promised to be his bride only on condition that he proves himself the best shot at a forthcoming contest. This contest, however, is won by *Kilian*, a peasant. *Max*, in a dramatic air, bewails his bad luck.

Durch die Walder (Thro' the Forest)

By Daniel Beddoe, Tenor
  (*In English*)   74244   12-inch, $1.50

He believes he is cursed by an evil spirit which causes his hand to fail.

MAX:
O, I can bear my fate no longer!
  E'en hope is banished from my soul!
What unknown grief thus haunts my spirit,
  And o'er me works its dark control?
Thro' the forests, thro' the meadows,
  Joy was wont with me to stray,
While my rifle, never failing,
  Made each bird and beast my prey.
When at length from chase returning,
  Ere home rose before my sight,
Agnes, smiling met me,
  Cloth'd in beauty's heavenly light.
But now am I by Heaven forsaken.

Caspar, who has already put himself in the power of *Zamiel*, sees here an opportunity to ex-

A FRENCH ARTIST'S WEIRD CONCEPTION OF THE BULLET-CASTING SCENE

Double-Faced Record—See page 175.

MAX

tend his own days of grace, and advises *Max* to seek the magician and secure some of the magic bullets.

He finally induces *Max* to meet him in the Wolf's Glen in order to receive the magic bullets, which he declares will always hit the mark. *Max* departs and *Caspar* gives vent to a fierce joy in a florid and dramatic number.

In the meantime *Agnes* is anxiously awaiting her lover and is much alarmed at his non-appearance. *Annie,* her cousin, endeavors to cheer her by singing a gay air.

Annie's Air, "Comes a Gallant Youth "

By Marie A. Michailowa, Soprano
(*In Russian*) 61134 10-inch, $1.00

She describes playfully the attitude a shy maiden should assume when the right young man happens along.

ANNIE:
Comes a gallant youth towards me,
Be he golden hair'd or dark,
Eyes that flash as he regards me,
Him my captive I will mark!

Eyes bent down to earth for shyness,
As befits a modest maid,
With a stolen look of slyness
Yet may ev'rything he said!

And if swift emotion rushes,
Shot from answ'ring lip and eye,
Nothing worse than maiden blushes
Need the gallant stranger spy!

CASPAR

Annie begs *Agnes* to retire, but the young girl says she will wait for her lover. Left alone, she draws the curtains aside, revealing a starlight night. She exclaims at the beauty of the night, and folding her hands in prayer, she prays for the safety of her lover, and asks Heaven to watch over them both.

PHOTO BOYER   AGATHA AND ANNA

Preghiera (Agatha's Prayer)

By Emilia Corsi *62636 10-inch, $0.75

Max arrives, followed by *Annie,* but seems embarrassed and says he must go to bring in a stag he has shot near the Wolf's Glen. *Agnes* begs him not to go near that haunted spot, but he disregards her warning and goes out.

The scene changes to the Wolf's Glen, where *Max* meets *Caspar,* and the magic bullets are cast amid scenes of horror, while the demon *Zamiel* hovers near awaiting his prey. *Max* is returning with his prize when he meets the Prince, who asks him to shoot a dove. The hunter complies, just missing *Agnes,* who has come to the wood in search of her lover. *Caspar* is wounded by the very bullet which he had intended should slay *Agnes* at the hands of *Max. Zamiel* carries off his victim, while *Max* is forgiven and all ends happily.

Double-Faced Record—See page 175.

PRINCE OTTOKAR PARDONS MAX—FINAL SCENE OF THE OPERA

DOUBLE-FACED FREISCHUTZ RECORDS

{Overture to Freischütz { Carmen Selection	By Sousa's Band} By Sousa's Band}	35000 12-inch, $1.25
{Overture to Freischütz {Preghiera (Agatha's Prayer)	By La Scala Orchestra} Emilia Corsi, Soprano (Italian)}	62636 10-inch, .75
{Prayer from Freischütz { Venetian Love Song (Canzone Amorosa)	By Victor Brass Quartet} By Victor Orchestra}	16320 10-inch, .75

LANDE   THE BATTLEFIELD OF LEIPZIG—ACT III (CARUSO, DESTINN AND AMATO)

(Italian)

GERMANIA

(Jaer-mah'-nee-ah)

A Lyric Drama in a Prologue, Two Scenes and Epilogue

Text by Luigi Illica. Music by Alberto Franchetti. First production at the Teatro Dal Verme, Milan, in 1902. The opera was given thirty performances at La Scala in two seasons, and has since been heard in Spain, Portugal, Russia and South America. First American production, New York, January 22, 1910, with Caruso, Destinn and Amato.

Cast of Characters

GIOVANNI FILIPPO PALM..Bass
FEDERICO LŒWE ⎫..⎰ Tenor
CARLO WORMS ⎬Students...⎨Baritone
CRISOGONO ⎭..⎱Baritone
RICKE ....Soprano
JANE, her sister...Mezzo-Soprano
LENE ARMUTH, an aged beggar-woman....................Mezzo-Soprano
JEBBEL, her nephew..Soprano
STAPPS, Protestant Priest..Bass
LUIGI ADOLFO GUGLIELMO LÜTZOW ....Bass
CARLO TEODORO KÖRNER..Tenor
SIGNORA HEDVIGE ....Mezzo-Soprano
PETERS, a herdsman ....Bass
Chief of German Police...Bass

Historical Personages, Students, Soldiers, Police Officers, Members and
Associates of the "Tugendbund," "Louise-Bund"
and "Black Knights"; Forest Girls.

Time: 1813.

  The opera is the work of an Italian nobleman, who, although a very wealthy man, is ambitious and makes the writing of operas his hobby. *Germania* is a picturesque and interesting opera, full of local color, describing the Germany of the time of Napoleon, with its many conspiracies; and for this the Baron has written much effective and agreeable music. The action takes place in 1813, at the time of the battle of Leipzig.

PROLOGUE

SCENE—*An Abandoned Mill near Nuremberg*

A company of students, under the leadership of *Giovanni Palm,* have occupied an old mill, and are shipping sacks of grain, which really contain political documents intended to rouse the people to revolt. Prominent among the students is *Worms,* who previously had a love affair with *Ricke,* a young girl who is now betrothed to *Loewe,* the poet and warm friend of *Worms.*

Loewe is expected to arrive at any moment, and *Ricke* dreads his coming, as she has made up her mind to tell him her guilty secret. *Worms,* however, divines her purpose and bids her keep silent, as in the duel which was sure to occur *Loewe* would likely be the one to die.

Loewe arrives and is joyfully greeted by the conspirators. He encourages them to fresh efforts in his noble aria.

Studenti, udite! (Students, Hear Me!)

By Enrico Caruso, Tenor   *(In Italian)*   87053   10-inch, $2.00

Caruso delivers this inspiring number with splendid effect, showing well the beauty and power of his marvelous voice.

LANDE

CARUSO AS FEDERICO

The enthusiasm which follows *Loewe's* great address is rudely interrupted by the arrival of the police, who seize *Palm* and take him away to his death.

ACT I

SCENE—*A Cottage in the Black Forest*

Seven years have elapsed. Hither *Loewe* has come after the disastrous campaign of 1806, which followed the plotting in the old mill. He lives in this hut with his aged mother and the two girls, *Ricke* and her sister *Jane.* *Worms* has disappeared and is supposed to be dead.

Loewe is about to be married to *Ricke,* and the bridesmaids now arrive to deck the cottage with flowers. *Ricke,* thinking of her past, is melancholy, but the marriage ceremony is performed and the bride and bridegroom are left alone. *Federico* clasps her in his arms and sings his beautiful air to the eyes of his bride.

Non chiuder gli occhi vaghi (Close Not Those Dreamy Eyes)

By Enrico Caruso, Tenor

(In Italian) 87054 10-inch, $2.00

Forgetting the past, *Ricke* yields herself to the joy of the moment and tenderly kisses him, when suddenly from the forest is heard a familiar voice singing an old student song. "*Worms!*" joyfully cries *Federico,* and runs out to meet his old friend, who is wasted and battle-scarred.

Worms, in a dramatic aria, tells his friend how he has literally come back from the dead. He relates his thrilling escape from prison, his delight in his new-found liberty, and his earnest desire for vengeance.

Worms is astonished to see *Ricke,* who has been listening half hidden behind the folds of a curtain. She looks coldly at him and he uneasily says he must be on his way. *Federico*

FRANCHETTI PLAYING HIS SCORE TO D'ANNUNZIO

protests, but *Worms* insists and departs. *Ricke*, overcome by this reminder of her past misfortune, resolves to leave her husband, and writes him a note and flees into the forest. *Federico* returns, reads the note, and wrongfully concludes that she has fled with *Worms*.

ACT II
SCENE—*A Cellar in Konigsberg*

In this underground retreat *Worms* is again plotting against *Napoleon*. A meeting of the Council is in progress, when *Federico* appears and demands that *Worms* shall fight with him to the death, but *Worms*, kneeling, asks *Federico* to kill him. *Federico* replies with a violent blow in the face, at which *Worms* decides to fight him, and preparations for the duel are begun. They are interrupted by the entrance of *Queen Louise*, who suggests that such brave men had better be using their swords for their country. Fired with enthusiasm, the enemies embrace each other and swear to die for Germany.

EPILOGUE
SCENE—*The Battlefield of Leipzig*

The awful three days' conflict is over and the field is a mass of ruins, battered wheels and dead and wounded men. *Ricke* searches for the body of *Federico* that she may look upon his face once more. She finds him dying, but he recognizes her, and telling her that the body of *Worms* is nearby, asks her to forgive him as he himself has done. *Ricke* looks on the face of the man who had ruined her life and forgives him.

She returns to her husband and when he dies in her arms waits beside his body for her own death, which she feels approaching. As the sun sets the defeated *Napoleon* with the shattered remains of his army is seen retreating.

CELLAR SCENE—ACT II

(Italian)

LA GIOCONDA

(Lah Joh-kon'-dah)

OPERA IN FOUR ACTS

Libretto by Arrigo Boïto; an adaptation of Victor Hugo's drama, "Angelo." Music by Amilcare Ponchielli. First presented at La Scala, Milan, April 8, 1876. Rewritten by Boïto and given at Genoa, December, 1876, and the following February at La Scala. First London production, June 7, 1883. Given in Petrograd, January 30, 1883; in Vienna, April 28, 1883; in France, at Nice, December 29, 1886. First New York production, December 20, 1883, with Nilsson, Scalchi, Fursch-Madi, del Puente and Novara. Revived at the Metropolitan Opera House, New York, December 25, 1913.

Characters

LA GIOCONDA, a ballad singer..................Soprano
LA CIECA, *(See-ay'-kah)* her blind mother........Contralto
ALVISE, *(Al-vee'-zeh)* one of the heads of State Inquisition..Bass
LAURA, his wife......................Mezzo-Soprano
ENZO GRIMALDO, a Genoese noble..............Tenor
BARNABA, a spy of the Inquisition.............Baritone
ZUANE, a boatman.........................Bass
ISEPO, public letter-writer......................Tenor
A PILOT.................................Bass

Monks, Senators, Sailors, Shipwrights, Ladies, Gentlemen, Populace, Masquers, etc.

The action takes place in Venice, in the seventeenth century.

Gioconda is a work of great beauty, full of wonderful arias, duets and ensembles, with fine choral effects, and a magnificent ballet. The book is founded on Hugo's "Tyrant of Padua," and tells a most dramatic story, which, however, cannot be called inviting, as the librettist has crowded into it nearly all the crimes he could think of!

But the average audience does not concern itself much with these horrors, being engaged in listening to the beautiful music, and admiring the splendid scenes and colorful action.

ACT I

SCENE—*Street near the Adriatic Shore, Venice*

Gioconda, a ballad singer who is in love with *Enzo,* a Genoese noble and captain of a ship now in the harbor, supports her blind mother, *La Cieca,* by singing in the streets of Venice. She has attracted the attention of *Barnaba,* an influential police spy, and he plans to gain her affections.

This is the situation at the rise of the curtain. The stage is filled with people: peasants, sailors, masquers, all in holiday attire. *Barnaba* is leaning against a pillar, watching the gay scene. The chorus sings the opening number, *Sports and Feasting.*

COPY'T MISHKIN   DESTINN AS GIOCONDA

179

LANDE   SCENE—ACT I

Feste! pane! (Sports and Feasting!)

By La Scala Chorus   (*In Italian*) *45010 10-inch, $1.00

At the close of this number, *Barnaba* advances and announces the commencement of the Regatta. All hasten to the shore, while *Barnaba* remains to soliloquize on his plot to secure the lovely *Gioconda*. *Gioconda* enters, leading her mother, *La Cieca,* by the hand, and *Barnaba* hastily hides behind a column to watch them. *La Cieca* sings a beautiful air, blessing her daughter for her tender care, and this leads to a trio.

Figlia che reggi tremulo pié (Daughter, My Faltering Steps)

**By A. Rossi Murino, Soprano; López Nunes, Soprano;
Ernesto Badini, Baritone**   (*In Italian*) *55017 12-inch, $1.50

LA CIECA:
Daughter, in thee my faltering steps
Find guidance and protection;
I gratefully bless my loss of sight,
That heightens thy affection!
While thou unto mankind thy songs are sing-
ing,
To Heav'n my ceaseless pray'rs their flight are
winging,
For thee I pray and render thanks to Fate
That left me sightless,—but not desolate!

GIOCONDA (*tenderly*):
Place thy dear hand once more in mine
Thy steps I'm safely guiding;
Here recommence thy daily life,
In calm contentment gliding.
BARNABA (*aside*):
With fiercest joy my heart would be enrap-
tured
If in my net she were securely captured!
The wildest ecstasies within me waken!
Beware thee, moth, if in my net thou'rt taken!

Gioconda leaves to seek *Enzo,* but *Barnaba* stops her and boldly declares that he loves her. She shudders with an instinctive aversion, and bids him stand aside. He attempts to seize her, but she eludes him and makes her escape, leaving the spy furious and planning revenge.

The people now return from the Regatta, bearing the victor on their shoulders. *Barnaba,* seeing the defeated combatant, *Zuane,* conceives a plan to deprive *Gioconda* of her mother, thus leaving him free to carry out his plans. He takes *Zuane* aside and tells him that the blind *La Cieca* is a witch who has cast a spell over him, causing his defeat. The old woman is being roughly handled by *Zuane* and his friends when *Enzo* suddenly appears and protects her, holding the mob at bay.

* *Double-Faced Record—See page 187.*

Alvise, Chief of the Council, enters with his wife *Laura*, formerly betrothed to *Enzo*. *Laura* pleads for *Cieca*, and she is protected by *Alvise*. The blind woman voices her gratitude in this lovely song, which is familiar to most concert-goers.

Voce di donna (Angelic Voice)

By Louise Homer, Contralto (*In Italian*) 85104 12-inch, $3.00
By Margarete Ober, Contralto
(*In Italian*) 64443 10-inch, 1.00

This beautiful air of the blind mother is considered the finest single number in Ponchielli's work, and is undoubtedly one of the loveliest gems in this or any other opera.

Certain it is that no *Ciecas* of present memory have ever delivered this romance with such richness of voice and such touching pathos. This beautiful passage—

A te que sto ro . sa . rio che le pre . ghie . re a . du . na,
This ro . sa . ry I give thee, Round it my heart-felt prayers cling.

which is sung as *La Cieca* presents the rosary, is perhaps the most effective part of the aria.

The singing of this *Voce di donna* by these artists makes these records the gems of the Victor's fine production of *La Gioconda*, and one or both of them should be in every opera collection.

COPY'T DUPONT

HOMER AS LAURA

LA CIECA:
  Thanks unto thee, angelic voice,
  My fetters asunder are broken;
  I cannot see the face of her
  By whom those words were spoken.
  (*Takes the rosary from her belt.*)

This rosary I offer thee—no richer boon possessing—
  Deign to accept the humble gift, 'twill bring to thee a blessing,
  And on thy head may bliss descend; I'll ever pray for thee!

All go into the church except *Enzo*, who stands gazing after *Laura*, having recognized his former love. *Barnaba* approaches him and tells him that *Laura* plans to visit the Genoese noble's ship that night. *Enzo*, whose love for *Laura* has revived at the sight of her, is delighted at this news, and forgetting *Gioconda*, he returns to his ship.

This scene has been put by Verdi into the form of a dramatic duet, sung here by Conti and Badini, of the La Scala forces.

Enzo Grimaldo (Duet Enzo and Barnaba)

By F. Conti, Tenor, and E. Badini, Baritone
(*In Italian*) *45033 10-inch, $1.00

BARNABA (*approaching Enzo*):
  Enzo Grimaldo,
  Prince of Santa Fior, thou art pensive.
ENZO (*aside*):
  I am discovered!
BARNABA:
  What magic stupor steals away thy senses?
  'Tis of the Lady Laura, Alvise's wife, thou'rt thinking.
ENZO (*astonished*):
  Who art thou?
BARNABA (*impressively*):
  I know all;
  Can penetrate thy thoughts, however secret.
  Thy birthplace was Genoa!
ENZO:
  Prince I am not, but sailor. Yonder's my ship.
  I am Dalmatian, Enzo Giordan.

COPY'T MISHKIN

CARUSO AS ENZO

* *Double-Faced Record—See page 187.*

BARNABA:
  For others, but not for me. Proscribed thou
    wert by Venice,
  Yet hither thou art led, by chainless impulse,
  Thy life to peril. Thou didst love a maiden
  Yonder, in thine own Genoa, but she another's
    bride became.

ENZO:
  I have pledged my faith to Gioconda.

BARNABA:
  Poor wand'ring ballad-singer!
  Her thou dost love as sister, but Laura as thy
    mistress.
  Thou hadst all hope abandoned, dreamed not
    to see her features,
  But here, under her velvet mask, thy beau-
    teous angel saw thee
  And recognized thee.

ENZO (joyfully):
  Oh, happiness!

BARNABA:
  Love sees through disguises,
  All this night will her husband stay at the
    Doge's palace,
  With the Great Council. Laura shall be on
    board thy vessel.
  Love's sweetest consolations await thee!

ENZO:
  Ah, with what joy my heart is filled,
  Fortune at last is kind!
  But who art thou, oh, gloomy messenger of
    joy?

BARNABA:
  I hate thee! I am the demon-in-chief
  Of the Council of Ten. Read this. Beware
    thee!
  (Opens his dress and shows the letters "C. X."
  (Council of Ten) embroidered in silver on
  his vest.)

ENZO (starting back):
  Oh, horror!

BARNABA (fiercely):
  To thy doom at once I could bring thee, but
    I spare thee.
  Gioconda loves thee, hates me fiercely;
  I have sworn to crush her heart,
  Enzo's death would little serve me;
  She must learn how false thou art.

ENZO (aside):
  Kind Heaven, to her thy mercy show,
  Save her from grief and pain;

COPY'T MISHKIN

MARTIN AS ENZO

But ah, sweet Laura, my adored,
Bring to my arms again!

BARNABA (to Enzo):
  Go! not a moment lose,
  Spread thy white sails to the skies,
  (Aside)
  I can my triumph read
  In each glad glance of thine eyes!

ENZO (going):
  When the dark night falls,
  On board my ship I shall await my Laura.

BARNABA (sneeringly):
  Good luck attend you!
  (Exit.)

Barnaba then writes to *Alvise* that his wife plans to elope with *Enzo*. He speaks the words aloud as he writes, and is heard by *Gioconda*, who is overcome at this evidence of her lover's faithlessness; and, heartbroken, enters the church with her mother. *Barnaba* sings the famous Soliloquy to the Doge's Palace, given here in splendid style by Ruffo.

Oh Monumento! (Oh, Mighty Monument)
  By Titta Ruffo, Baritone   (In Italian) 88396 12-inch, $3.00

The act closes with a famous dance, the *Furlana*, played here by the famous Orchestra Sinfonica of La Scala.

Furlana (Finale, Act I)
  By Italian Orchestra   *45033 10-inch, $1.00

ACT II

SCENE—*A Lagoon near Venice—it is night. Enzo's ship is shown at anchor,
with sailors grouped on deck, resting*

Barnaba, disguised as a fisherman, appears in his boat, hails the sailors, and sings them a merry ballad, *Ah, pescator!*

Ah, pescator affonda l'esca (Fisher Boy, Thy Bait Be Throwing!)
  By Titta Ruffo, Baritone   (In Italian) 88394 12-inch, $3.00
  By Pasquale Amato and Opera Chorus (In Italian) 87093 10-inch, 2.00
  By Ernesto Badini, Baritone, and Chorus (In Italian) *45010 10-inch, 1.00

* Double-Faced Record—See page 187.

LANDE

ENZO'S VESSEL.—ACT II

This is one of the most popular numbers in the opera, its beautiful melody and rhythmical swing being a welcome relief in the midst of so much that is gloomy.

After taking careful note of the strength of the crew, *Barnaba* sends his aide for the police galleys and leaves in his boat.

Enzo now appears, and is greeted by his men with enthusiasm. He is in a gay humor, thinking of *Laura's* expected visit, and bids the sailors go below while he keeps the watch.

Left alone, he gives expression to his joy in this great aria, one of the most beautiful in the whole range of opera. Caruso sings the number with exquisite purity of tone and a lavish outpouring of voice.

Cielo e mar (Heaven and Ocean)

By Enrico Caruso, Tenor	(*In Italian*)	88246	12-inch, $3.00
By Giovanni Martinelli, Tenor	(*In Italian*)	64409	10-inch, 1.00
By Florencio Constantino, Tenor	(*In Italian*)	64070	10-inch, 1.00
By Franco de Gregorio, Tenor	(*In Italian*)	*45027	10-inch, 1.00

Especially noticeable is this fine passage—

vie - ni al ba - cio Del - la vi - ta e del - l'a - mo - re, del l'a mor!
come to the kiss - es That would make thee all, would make thee all t my own!

which the tenor delivers in splendid style, fairly thrilling his hearers.

Other fine records of this effective number, by Martinelli, Constantino and de Gregorio, are also offered.

ENZO:

Heaven and ocean! yon ethereal veil
Is radiant as a holy altar,
My angel, will she come from heaven?
My angel, will she come o'er ocean?
Here I await her, I breathe with rapture
The soft zephyrs fill'd with love.
Mortals oft, when fondly sighing,

Find ye a torment, O golden, golden dreams.
Come then, dearest, here I'm waiting;
Wildly panting is my heart.
Come, then, dearest! oh come, my dearest!
Oh come, taste the kisses that magic bliss impart!
Oh come! Oh come! Oh come!

* *Double-Faced Record—See page 187.*

CONSTANTINO AS ENZO

Laura now appears, and after a rapturous embrace, the lovers plan to set sail when the wind rises. *Enzo* goes below to rouse the men, after saying:

ENZO:
For flight now prepare thee. O my beloved,
Rest here awhile.

Laura, alone, exclaims: "My heart is full of happy tears," then kneels at the foot of the altar and prays for forgiveness.

Stella del marinar (Star of the Mariner)
By Margarete Ober, Mezzo-Soprano
(*In Italian*) 64442 10-inch, $1.00

LAURA:
Star of the mariner, Virgin most holy!
Be my defender in this hour of trial!
Thou seest by how much ardor, by how much faith,
I am led to adventure this audacious step!
Under thy mantle, kneeling sinners shelt'ring,
Find refuge for one who is praying and trembling.
Send down, in answer to my fervent prayer,
Upon my head, O Virgin, full of mercy,
A blessing from on high!

Mme. Ober, whose *Laura* is one of her most successful rôles, and who made a pronounced impression in the revival of Ponchielli's opera at the Metropolitan, sings this lovely prayer in a manner which brings out in a marked degree the beauty of her voice.

Gioconda, disguised, enters and denounces *Laura.* They sing a splendid dramatic duet in which each declares her love for *Enzo* and defies the other.

L'amo come il fulgor del creato! (I Adore Him!)
By Elena Ruszcowska, Soprano, and Bianca Lavin de Casas, Mezzo-Soprano
(*In Italian*) 88271 12-inch, $3.00

Gioconda is about to stab her rival, when the sight of a rosary worn by her intended victim causes her to repent, and she aids *Laura* to escape just as her husband, summoned by *Barnaba,* is approaching.

Enzo appears and is greeted with reproaches by *Gioconda,* who tells him that the war galleys, led by *Barnaba,* are coming to capture the ship. *Enzo,* stung by *Gioconda's* scorn, and heartbroken at the loss of *Laura,* fires his ship to prevent it falling into the hands of *Barnaba.*

ACT III
SCENE—*A Room in the Palace of Alvise. Night*

Alvise is discovered alone, in violent agitation, planning the death of *Laura* because of her attempted elopement with *Enzo.*

He sings a dramatic air, picturing his fearful revenge.

Sì! morir ella de'! (To Die is Her Doom!)
By Amleto Galli, Bass
(*In Italian*) *55019 12-inch, $1.50

ALVISE (*in violent agitation*):
Yes, to die is her doom! My name, my honor,
Shall not with impunity be disgraced.
From Badoers, when betrayed,
Pity 't were vain to hope.
Though yesterday upon the fatal isle
She 'scaped this vengeful hand,
She shall not escape a fearful expiation.
Last night a sharp poniard should have pierced her bosom;
This night no poniard I'll use; she dies by poison!
(*Pointing to the adjoining room.*)
While there the dancers sing and laugh,
In giddy movements flying,
Their mirthful tones shall blend with groans,

Breath'd by a sinner dying.
Shades of my honored forefathers!
Soon shall your blushes disappear;
Soon shall a deadly vengeance prove
Honor to me is dear.
While dance the giddy crowd,
In mirthful movements flying,
Here shall be heard the bitter groans,
The sinner breathes in dying.
Yonder, the nobles of the nation
Are gathered at my invitation;
Here, an insulted husband
For signal vengeance cries!
Exult, in dances and in songs,
While here a faithless one dies!

---

* *Double-Faced Record—See page 187.*

The guilty woman now enters at his summons and is denounced by him. He orders her to take poison, and leaves her. She is about to obey, when *Gioconda*, who has been concealed in the room, appears, takes the poison from her and gives her a narcotic, which will produce a death-like trance. *Laura* drinks this and *Gioconda* exits just as *Alvise* appears. Seeing the empty phial on the table he believes *Laura* has obeyed his will.

The second scene shows a magnificent hall in the palace, where *Alvise* is giving a masked ball. The famous *Dance of the Hours* is given for the entertainment of the guests.

Dance of the Hours

By Victor Herbert's Orch.	*55044	12-inch,	$1.50
By Victor Herbert's Orch.	70070	12-inch,	1.25
By Victor Orchestra	*35087	12-inch,	1.25
By Victor Orchestra	31443	12-inch,	1.00
By Wm. H. Reitz (*Xylophone*)	*17147	10-inch,	.75

This is one of the most beautiful of ballets and symbolizes, like many other modern Italian ballets, the struggle between the conflicting powers of light and darkness, progress and ignorance. The music is fascinating in the extreme.

Enzo is present among the maskers, and when *Barnaba* whispers in his ear that *Laura* is dead, he unmasks and denounces *Alvise*, who causes his arrest. The great finale begins with *Enzo's* solo:

Già ti veggo (I Behold Thee)

By Lotti, de Gregorio, Badini and Chorus
(*In Italian*) *55019 12-inch, $1.50

The emotions of the various characters may be understood by the quotations below.

ENZO (*aside*):
I behold thee motionless, pallid,
Shrouded in thy snowy veil!
Thou art dead, love! thou art dead, love!
Ah, my darling, hopeless I wail.
The sharp axe for me is waiting,
Opens wide a dark abyss;
But to thee shall torture guide me,
Soon we'll share celestial bliss!

GIOCONDA:
Sadly fall the tear-drops,
In the silence of despair;
Break, oh heart! sad eyes, rain torrents!
Fate, thy sharpest doom prepare!

BARNABA (*aside to Gioconda*):
Yield thee, yield thee! all around thee
See what pow'r I have for ill!

GIOCONDA (*aside to Barnaba*):
Do thou save him, bring him safe out there,
Close by the Redentor, and then
Myself I will surrender
To thee, fearfulest of men.

BARNABA (*to Gioconda*):
Though despair may prompt thy offer,
I accept it for my part.

LA CIECA:
Thou art weeping, O Gioconda,
Let me fold thee to my breast.
Never love, like love maternal,
Can encounter every test.

ALVISE:
'Mid the splendor this fête surrounding,
Thou art unwelcome, cavalier;
But, ere long, new scenes of horror
Shall from thee attention claim.
Thou shalt soon see if I am watchful
Of the honor of my name!

COPY'T M'SHKIN

ANCONA AS BARNABA

To complete his revenge, *Alvise* now draws aside a curtain and shows the guests the body of *Laura*, acknowledging that he took her life. Horror and indignation are expressed by those present, and *Enzo* attempts to kill *Alvise*. He fails, is seized by the guards, and is led away to prison as the curtain falls.

ACT IV

SCENE—*A ruined palace on an island in the Adriatic. Venice visible in the distance.*

To this desolate island *Gioconda* has managed to bring the unconscious *Laura*, in an endeavor to save her. As the curtain rises two men are carrying the insensible form into the ruin. *Gioconda* asks the men to seek out her mother, whom she fears never to see again. Left alone, she approaches the table, looks fixedly at a flask of poison, and begins her terrible song, one of the most dramatic of the numbers in Ponchielli's work.

* *Double-Faced Record—See page 187.*

THE RUINED PALACE—ACT IV

Suicidio (Suicide Only Remains)
By Emmy Destinn, Soprano   (*In Italian*)   88478   12-inch, $3.00
By Elda Cavalieri   (*Double-Faced—See page 187*)   (*In Italian*)   55015   12-inch, 1.50

COPY'T MISHKIN   OBER AS LAURA

Mme. Destinn's *Gioconda* is one of the greatest impersonations of the rôle over witnessed in America. She delivers this great final air of the opera with dramatic power, singing it, as she always does the music of Ponchielli's work, with superb effect.

For a moment the unhappy girl is tempted to complete *Alvise's* work by giving the poison to *Laura,* but banishes the temptation and throws herself down in a passion of weeping. *Gioconda* has secured the release of *Enzo,* and has sent for him to come to the ruined palace, intending, with splendid generosity, to restore the lovers to each other.

Enzo now arrives, thinking that he is only to visit the grave of *Laura,* and during a bitter scene with Gioconda, he hears the voice of *Laura,* who has revived and now calls feebly. *Enzo* rushes forward in a transport of joy, while *Gioconda* makes further preparations for their escape. The lovers express their gratitude and depart, while *Gioconda* prepares for the end. She is about to swallow the poison when *Barnaba* appears, and in terrible accents demands why she has broken her word to him. She pretends to yield to him.

> GIOCONDA (*at first terrified, recovers her courage, and retains it to the end*):
> Yes, I keep to my compact; we both swore to keep it,
> And ne'er will Gioconda be false to her oath.
> May Heaven in mercy withhold condemnation,
> And pardon us both!

Barnaba is overjoyed and begins the final duet, the most dramatic scene in the opera.

Vo' farmi più gaia (Thou'rt Mine Now!)
By A. Rossi Murino and E. Badini   (*In Italian*)   55017   12-inch, $1.50

BARNABA:
Thou'rt mine now! and swift from this deso-
late heart,
Expelled by love's rays, sombre shadows de-
part.
GIOCONDA (*to Barnaba, who is approaching her*):
Restrain awhile thy ardent passion!
Thou soon shalt in splendor Gioconda behold!
For thee I am braiding my clustering tresses
With purple and gold!
(*Concealing her terror, she adorns herself.*)
With glittering jewels, the gay tinsel worn
nightly
By madcaps theatrical, cover'd I'll be:
Now list to the song that this ardent young siren
Will sing unto thee!
I keep to my compact, no false oath was mine;
(*Changing her tone.*)
Thou claimest Gioconda? Well, demon accursed,
Gioconda is thine!
(*She stabs herself to the heart with the dagger
that she had secreted while adorning herself,
and falls dead at his feet.*)
BARNABA (*in horror*):
Ah, stay thee! 'Tis a jest!
(*With fiendish joy.*)
Well, then, thou shalt hear this,
And die ever damned!
(*Bending over the corpse of Gioconda, and
screaming furiously into her ear.*)
LAST NIGHT THY MOTHER DID OFFEND ME:
I HAVE STRANGLED HER!
(*Wildly.*) She hears me not!
(*With a cry of half-choked rage he rushes
from the ruin. The curtain falls.*)

COPY'T MISHKIN
AMATO AS BARNABA

DOUBLE-FACED AND MISCELLANEOUS LA GIOCONDA RECORDS

Figlia che reggi tremulo pié (Daughter, My Faltering Steps)
  By Murino, Nunes and Badini (*In Italian*)
Vo' farmi più gaia (Thou'rt Mine Now)
  By A. Rossi Murino, Soprano; E. Badini, Baritone   55017 12-inch, $1.50

Già ti vedi (I Behold Thee)   By F. Lotti, Soprano;
  de Gregorio, Tenor; E. Badini, Baritone (*In Italian*)
Sì! morir ella de'!   By Amleto Galli, Bass (*In Italian*)   55019 12-inch, 1.50

Suicidio! (Suicide Only Remains)   By Elda Cavalieri
  Mefistofele—L'altra notte   By Elda Cavalieri   55015 12-inch, 1.50

Dance of the Hours   By Herbert's Orchestra
  Kamennoi-Ostrow (Rubinstein)   By Herbert's Orchestra   55044 12-inch, 1.50

Dance of the Hours   By Victor Orchestra
  Sweet Longings (Violin-Flute)   By Rattay and Lyons   35087 12-inch, 1.25

Opening Chorus—"Feste! pane!"   La Scala Chorus
  Barcarola—"Pescator affonda l'esca"   By E. Badini   45010 10-inch, 1.00

Enzo Grimaldo   By Conti and Badini (*In Italian*)
  Furlana (Finale, Act I)   By Italian Orchestra   45033 10-inch, 1.00

Cielo e mar!   By Franco de Gregorio (*In Italian*)
  Manon Lescaut—Ah, Manon! mi tradisce By de Gregorio (*Italian*)   45027 10-inch, 1.00

Dance of the Hours (Xylophone)   By Wm. H. Reitz
  Maurice Tango (Banjo)   By Fred Van Eps   17147 10-inch, .75

SIEGFRIED TAKES THE MAGIC DRINK—ACT I

(German)

GÖTTERDÄMMERUNG

(*Goet'-ter-daem'-mer-oonk*)

(English)

THE DUSK OF THE GODS

MUSIC DRAMA IN THREE ACTS AND A PRELUDE

Words and music by Richard Wagner. Wagner began composition of the music at Lucerne in 1870 and it was completed November 21, 1874. First produced at Bayreuth, August 17, 1876, with Materna and Unger. First American production at New York, January 25, 1888, with Lehmann, Seidl-Krauss, Traubman, Niemann and Fischer. Many notable American productions have been made at the Metropolitan, the latest being February, 1914, with Kurt, Ober, Fornia, Berger, Weil, Goritz and Braun.

Characters

SIEGFRIED...	Tenor
GUNTHER (*Goon'-ter*)	Bass
HAGEN (*Hah'-gen*)	Bass
BRÜNNHILDE..	Soprano
GUTRUNE (*Goot-troon'-eh*)	Soprano
WOGLINDA,	Soprano
WELLGUNDA, }Rhine-Nymphs	Soprano
FLOSSHILDE,	Contralto

PRELUDE

SCENE—*The Walkure's Rock*

The Dusk of the Gods, the last part of the tetralogy, consists of three acts and a prelude. In the prelude we once more see *Brünnhilde* on the rock, where she had lain during her magic sleep, and where *Siegfried* had found her and taken her as his bride. The hero, after a brief period of domestic happiness in a cave near by, decides to leave his bride for awhile and go in search of adventures, giving her the Nibelung's Ring as a pledge of faith. This ring he had obtained when he slew the dragon *Fafner*, and as the opera progresses it will be seen that he is doomed to suffer the consequences of the fatal curse, invoked on every possessor of the Ring by *Alberich*, from whom it was forcibly taken by *Wotan*.

GUTRUNE: Welcome, O guest, to Gibich's house!
From its daughter take thou the drink.

PROLOGUE

As the curtain rises *Brünnhilde* and *Siegfried* come out of the cave, *Siegfried* in full armor and the *Valkyrie* leading her horse by the bridle. She begins her tender address of farewell:

Zu neuen Thaten (Did I Not Send Thee?)

By Johanna Gadski
(*German*) 87098 10-in., $2.00

Did I not send thee, sweetest hero, to fresh exploits, frail were my love. But one misgiving fights against it, for fear not wholly thy heart I hold. I gave to thee all that gods had taught; heavenly runes, the richest hoard; but my restoreless maidenhood's strength snatch'd thou from me, who but seek to serve thee. My wisdom fails, but good will remains; so full of love, but failing in strength, thou wilt despise perchance the poor one, who having giv'n all, can grant thee no more!

This lovely air is delivered by Mme. Gadski with tenderness and feeling, and the record is an unusually fine example of the perfect recording of a beautiful soprano voice.

ACT I

SCENE—*Castle of King Gunther*

Siegfried joyously sets out on his journey and soon comes to the Court of *King Gunther* on the Rhine, where dwells also *Gunther's* sister *Gutrune,* and their half-brother *Hagen,* who is a son of *Alberich,* the dwarf. *Hagen* knows the history of the Ring and is anxious to restore it to his father, so he artfully tries to win the help of *Gunther.* Knowing that the hero is approaching the castle, he outlines this scheme, which is to give *Siegfried* a drink which will make him forget *Brünnhilde* and fall in love with *Gutrune,* after which *Gunther* can win the peerless *Brünnhilde* for himself. *Gunther* is tempted, and when *Siegfried's* horn announces his approach he consents.

Siegfried greets them as friends, and when offered the magic drink he accepts and immediately loses all recollection of *Brünnhilde.* Seeing the lovely *Gutrune,* who stands with lowered eyes, he exclaims:

SIEGFRIED (*gazing on Gutrune with a kindling eye*):
Thou fair one, whose beams
My breast have enflamed,
Why fall thus thine eyes before mine?
(*Gutrune looks up at him, blushing.*)
Ha! sweetest maid!
Screen those bright beams!
The heart in my breast
Burns with their strength.

Gutrune, trembling with emotion, leaves the Hall, and *Siegfried,* gazing after her, asks *Gunther* if he has a wife. The King, prompted by *Hagen,* replies that he knows of one he would wed, but that she is surrounded by a magic

GUNTHER

fire which he cannot pass. *Siegfried* seems trying to remember his past, but fails, looks confused, then suddenly says:

> SIEGFRIED (*with a sudden start*):
> I—fear not the fire,
> And thy bride fain will I fetch;
> For thy own am I
> And my arm is thine:
> If Gutrune for wife I may gain!

In order that *Brünnhilde* may think that it is *Gunther* who has won her, it is agreed that *Siegfried* shall, by means of the Tarnhelm, change himself into *Gunther's* form. Thinking only of his reward, *Siegfried* eagerly departs.

Hier sitz' ich zur wacht (Here I Wait)

By Marcel Journet, Bass
(*In German*)
74276 12-inch, $1.50

Hagen, left alone, outlines his coming triumph, when he shall possess the Ring, and avenge its theft from his father, *Alberich.*

EDOUARD DE RESZKE
AS HAGEN

> HAGEN:
> Here I sit and wait, watching the hall,
> Warding the house from all foes.
> Gibich's son is wafted by winds;
> A-wooing forth is he gone.
> And fleetly steereth a stalwart man,
> Whose force all perils can stem.
> His own bride he brings down the Rhine;
> But he will bring *me* the Ring.
> Ye gallant partners, gleeful companions,
> Push ye then merrily hence!
> Slight though your natures,
> Ye still may serve the Nibelung's son!

DALMORES AS SIEGFRIED

SCENE II—*The Walkure's Rock*

The scene changes to the Valkyrie Rock again, where *Brünnhilde* awaits *Siegfried's* return. She is astonished and alarmed when she sees a stranger approaching, not understanding how he has penetrated the fiery barrier. It is *Siegfried* in the form of *Gunther.* He announces that he is *Gunther* come to win her for his wife. *Brünnhilde,* in horror and despair, holds up the Ring, exclaiming:

> BRÜNNHILDE:
> Stand back! bow to this token!
> No shame can touch me from thee
> While yet this Ring is my shield.

Siegfried attempts to take it from her and after a struggle, succeeds. As he draws the helpless and despairing *Brünnhilde* into the cave the curtain falls.

ACT II

SCENE—*The Rhine near Gunther's Castle*

Hagen and *Alberich* discuss the progress of the plot to regain the Ring. *Hagen* swears to accomplish it, and *Alberich* vanishes. *Siegfried,* in his own form, but wearing the Tarnhelm, arrives, greets him cheerily and says he has gained *Gunther's* wife for him, but that they are re-

HAGEN AND ALBERICH

CLICHE HANS BRAND

SETTING OF ACT II AT BAYREUTH

turning home more slowly. *Gutrune* comes to meet *Siegfried*, and they go to the Hall. *Hagen* sounds his horn to summon the vassals and bids them prepare for a feast, as *Gunther* has taken a bride.

Gunther now arrives in his boat, leading *Brünnhilde*, who is pale and downcast. *Siegfried* and *Gutrune* come out to meet them and *Brünnhilde* sees *Siegfried* in his rightful form. She recoils in horror at seeing him with another woman, and regarding her as a stranger. She then perceives the Ring on *Siegfried's* finger and demands to know where he obtained it. He seems confused and regards the Ring with a puzzled air. *Brünnhilde*, beginning to comprehend what has occurred, denounces him, and *Gunther,* beginning to doubt whether *Siegfried* had kept his oath to respect *Brünnhilde* as a brother's bride, looks threateningly at him. *Siegfried,* eager to set himself right, swears the oath of the spear.

The vassals make a ring round *Siegfried* and *Hagen*. *Hagen* holds out his spear; *Siegfried* lays two fingers of his right hand on its point.

SIEGFRIED:
Haft of war, hallowed weapon!
Hold thou my oath from dishonor!
On this spotless spear-head
I speak the oath:
Spear-point, aid thou my speech!
Where steel e'er can strike me,
Strike thou at me:
Wher'er death can be dealt me
Deal it to me,
If she is really wronged,—
If I have injured my friend!

Brünnhilde, unable to contain herself at this evidence of *Siegfried's* baseness, repeats his oath and denounces him.

COPY'T DUPONT

GADSKI AS BRÜNNHILDE

191

FERD. LEEKE

Siegfried:
    If you threaten my life,
    Hardly you'll win from my hand the ring!

Helle Wehr! Heilige Waffe! (Haft of War! Hallowed Weapon)

By Johanna Gadski, Soprano   (*In German*)   87052   10-inch, $2.00

Siegfried looks at her in pity, thinking her mad, and goes to the Hall with *Gutrune*. *Brünnhilde, Hagen* and *Gunther* remain behind, the latter in deep depression. *Hagen* tells *Brünnhilde* that he will avenge her wrongs. "Thou?" says *Brünnhilde*, contemptuously, and tells him that only in his back is *Siegfried* vulnerable, and that no magic protection was placed there because she knew that never would he retreat. *Gunther* now rouses himself and the three decide that *Siegfried* must die for his treachery.

ACT III

SCENE I—*A Wild Valley near the Rhine*

The Rhine nymphs rise to the surface of the water and sing of the Rhinegold. They spy *Siegfried* and ask him to give up the Ring, but he refuses, and they warn him that he shall die that very day. He laughs at the prophecy, and as he watches them swim away, says lightly:

> SIEGFRIED:
> Alike on land and water,
> Woman's ways I've learnt to know.
> The man who resists their smiles
> They seek by threats to frighten.
> And when these both are scorned
> They bait him with bitter words.
> And yet were Gutrune not my wife,
> I must have promptly captured
> One of those pretty maids!

Hunting horns are heard and *Siegfried* gayly answers with his own. *Gunther, Hagen* and the hunters descend from the hill and greet him. They camp and begin to eat and drink. *Siegfried* tells them of his adventure with *Mime* and the Dragon. *Hagen* gives him a magic drink which brings back his memory and he goes on to tell of the forest bird and his quest of the lovely *Brünnhilde*. *Gunther* begins to listen attentively, but when *Siegfried* reaches this part of his narrative, *Hagen* plunges his spear in *Siegfried's* back and he falls. *Gunther*, in pity for the dying man, leans over him, and *Seigfried* faintly says:

> SIEGFRIED:
> Brünnhilde! Heavenly bride!—
> Look up! Open thine eyelids!
> What hath sunk thee once more in sleep?
> Who drowns thee in slumber so drear?
> The wak'ner came, his kiss awoke;—
> Again now the bride's bonds he has broken;—
> Enchant him Brünnhilde's charms!
> Ah! now forever open her eyelids!
> Ah! and what od'rous breeze is her breath!
> Thrice blessed ending—
> Thrill that dismays not—
> Brünnhilde beckons to me! (*He dies.*)

SCENE II—*Hall in Gunther's Palace*

Siegfried's Funeral March   Vessella's Italian Band   *35369   12-inch, $1.25

Siegfried's Funeral March is the wonderful symphonic piece—a funeral oration over the last descendant of the gods, and a farewell to the slain hero—which occurs in the last act of *Götterdämmerung*. The first motive is solemnly tragic, and pictures the cold wing of death flying over the procession. Then the heroic motive of the *Volsungs* follows; and from this moment, with the rhythm of the Funeral March, all the motives, passionate, dramatic or tragic, which have already been developed separately in the course of the tetralogy, are heard one by one. Thus is heard the love motive, while from the deep tone of the double-basses and 'cellos the funeral theme of the *Volsungs* rises, which gradually

* Double-Faced Record—See page 195.

SIEGFRIED'S DEATH—ACT III

develops and gains in strength, preparing for the entrance of the heroic motive of the sword (*Valkyrie*). Then comes the fatal motive of *Siegfried's* prophecy, increasing in force until it bursts into *Siegfried's* motive, an heroic paraphrase of the joyful shout of the child of the forest.

We next hear the complaint of the Rhine maidens, the motive of *Brünnhilde's* captivity, and the curse-motive (*Rhinegold*), while in fancy we picture the funeral procession disappearing among the mountains into the silence of the night, only a pale beam of moonlight tragically enlightening the imposing scene.

Siegfried's body is borne mournfully to the Hall, where the weeping *Gutrune* meets them and clasps her husband's lifeless form. *Hagen* now demands the Ring as his booty, but *Gunther* refuses to yield it and they draw their swords, *Gunther* being killed by *Hagen*.

Hagen now attempts to withdraw the Ring from *Siegfried's* finger, but as he approaches the arm of the dead hero is raised threateningly, and all recoil in terror.

Brünnhilde now approaches and gazes long and sadly at *Siegfried's* face, then orders a funeral pyre erected to burn the hero's body. The vassals obey and build a huge pyre on the bank of the Rhine, on which the body is laid. *Brünnhilde* summons two ravens from the rocks, and begins her great *Immolation Scene*.

Fliegt heim (Immolation Scene)

By Johanna Gadski, Soprano   (*In German*)   88185 12-inch, $3.00

She bids the ravens fly to *Loki*, god of fire, that he may complete the downfall of the gods by burning Valhalla.

> BRÜNNHILDE: Draweth near in gloom
> The Dusk of the gods.
> Thus, casting my torch,
> I kindle Valhalla's tow'rs!

She kindles the pile, which burns rapidly, and the two ravens disappear in the distance. *Brünnhilde's* horse is brought in, and she takes off the bridle.

BRÜNNHILDE (*to the horse*):
Grani, my horse, greet thee again!
Wouldst thou know dear friend,
What journey we follow?
By flame illumined lies there thy lord,
Siegfried, the star of my life.
To meet with thy master neighest thou
    merrily?
Lo! how the flame
Doth leap and allure thee!
Feel how my breast too hotly doth burn;
Sparkling fureflame my spirit enfolds.
O, but to clasp him—
Recline in his arms!
In madd'ning emotion
Once more to be his!
Heiajaho! Grani! Greet we our hero!
Siegfried! Siegfried! see!
Sweetly greets thee thy wife!

She swings herself on the steed
and rides straight into the burning pile,
which flames up mightily, half consuming the Hall itself. The Rhine then rises
and puts out the flames, and on the
surface are seen the Rhine daughters,
who seize the Ring from the embers.
Hagen, who has been anxiously watching, now rushes into the waters, crying:
"The Ring is mine!" The nymphs
seize him and drag him down in the
flood. An increasing red glow is seen
in the sky, and *Valhalla* appears in
flames, with the gods and heroes calmly
awaiting their doom. As the flames
envelop all, the curtain falls.

THE RHINE MAIDENS WARNING SIEGFRIED

DOUBLE-FACED GÖTTERDÄMMERUNG RECORDS

{ **Fantasia from the Opera**   **By Arthur Pryor's Band**
      Siegfried and Brunnhilde, Act I—Finale, Scene I, " Siegfried's
      Horn Call "—Finale of Opera.   } 35315   12-inch, $1.25

{ *Rhinegold Selection* (*Wagner*)   *By Conway's Band*
{ **Siegfried's Funeral March**   **By Vessella's Italian Band**
{ *Walkure—Ride of the Valkyries*   *By Vessella's Italian Band* } 35369   12-inch, 1.25

FROM THE PAINTING BY MAKART   THE RHINE MAIDENS RECOVER THE RHINEGOLD

THE MARQUIS LEAVES FOR THE WARS—ACT I

GRISÉLIDIS

OPERATIC MIRACLE PLAY IN THREE ACTS AND A PROLOGUE

Poem by Armand Sylvester and Eugene Morand. Music by Massenet. First production, *Opéra Comique*, Paris, November 20, 1901, with Mme. Lucienne Breval. Produced at Brussels, March 18, 1902, and Milan, November 25, 1902. First production in America at the Manhattan Opera House, New York, January 19, 1910.

Characters

GRISÉLIDIS, wife of the Marquis .... Soprano
FIAMINA, the Devil's wife .... Soprano
BERTRADE .... Soprano
THE MARQUIS DE SALUCES .... Baritone
ALAIN, a shepherd .... Tenor
THE DEVIL .... Baritone
THE PRIOR .... Baritone

Scene and Period : Provence, France ; the thirteenth century.

Grisélidis is based on a modern "mystery" which was produced by Armand Sylvester and Eugene Morand at the *Comedie Français* in 1891. In this play the author gave a much changed version of a legend, *Patient Grisel*, which has had a place in European literature since the eleventh century. It is one of the stories that Boccaccio tells in his *Decameron*, and the same tale has been used by Chaucer in his *Canterbury Tales*.

The plot of *Grisélidis* is quite refreshing in contrast to most grand opera plots, its principal theme being true love and faithfulness. The opera opens with a *Prologue*, occurring in the forest of Provence. The *Marquis de Saluces*, lord of the region, while walking along the forest edge, meets the young and beautiful *Grisélidis*. He falls deeply in love with her and asks her to be his wife, whereupon she replies that she is his slave and must obey his will. Together they depart for the chateau of the *Marquis*, leaving the poor shepherd, *Alain*, who is also in love with *Grisélidis*, bewailing the fate which has robbed him of his sweetheart.

A year elapses, and in Act I we see the *Marquis* about to depart for the war against the Saracens. The scene shows the inside of the Chateau; in the background a triptych open, with an image of St. Agnes holding in her arms a white lamb, and at her feet an image of the *Devil*. The *Marquis* expresses his great love for his wife, and says that he would be willing to swear in the presence of the *Devil* himself that she would always be faithful and true. Suddenly the stone image of the *Devil* comes to life, bounds on the stage and offers to wager the *Marquis* that during his absence at the wars *Grisélidis* will break her vows of faithfulness. At first the *Marquis* spurns the wager, but finally accepts and gives the *Devil* his wedding ring to show his absolute trust in *Grisélidis*. The latter is left alone with her little son, *Loys*, as her husband departs for the war.

DIABLE AND FIAMINA—ACT II

Act II shows the terrace of the Castle. The *Devil* induces his wife, *Fiamina*, to join him in his wicked plans to tempt *Grisélidis*, and they appear at the Castle disguised as a Levantine merchant and a Moorish slave. The merchant (*Devil*) tells *Grisélidis* that her husband bought the slave from him in the Orient, being greatly attracted by her charms, and tells her that her husband commands that the slave be installed as mistress of the Chateau. As proof of the truth of his statement he shows *Grisélidis* the *Marquis'* wedding ring, and she submissively declares that she will obey her husband's orders. This acquiescence is contrary to the *Devil's* expectations, and in consternation he now has his *Evil Spirits* bring *Alain* to the Castle, hoping to tempt *Grisélidis* to fly with the shepherd, who still loves her; but little *Loys* appears just in time to save his mother when her resistance is weakening. As *Alain* rushes away, in despair, the *Devil* suddenly appears, seizes *Loys* and disappears, and the act ends with a wild search for the child.

The third act shows the interior of the Chateau with the triptych as in Act I. The *Devil* again appears to *Grisélidis*, this time disguised as an old man. He tells her that *Loys* has been kidnapped by a pirate, who demands a kiss from *Grisélidis* in return for surrendering her child. Mother love forces her to yield, and she starts for the harbor. The *Marquis* comes home from the wars and the *Devil* tells him *Grisélidis* has gone to keep a rendezvous with her lover, but the *Marquis* refuses to believe these accusations against his wife. *Grisélidis* returns and tells the *Marquis* of the kidnapping of little *Loys*, and they pray that help may be given them to fight the powers of evil. Whereupon the cross on the altar is turned into a flaming sword, and when *Grisélidis* prays to St. Agnes that her son be restored to her, there is a flash of lightning, a clap of thunder and the triptych opens, revealing the image of St. Agnes holding in her arms, not the white lamb, but the child *Loys*. A glad pealing of bells can be heard as the *Marquis* and *Grisélidis*, with their child between them, are happily reunited.

The Victor offers here a very fine record of the air *Ouvres-vous sur mon front*, which occurs at the beginning of the opera. It is the song of the shepherd *Alain*, telling of his love for the maiden, *Grisélidis*.

Ouvres-vous sur mon front, portes du Paradise! (Open Now to My Eyes, Portals of Paradise!)

By Charles Dalmores, Tenor   (*In French*) 88397 12-inch, $3.00

FROM THE PAINTING BY CZACKORSKI HAMLET AND THE ACTORS—ACT II

HAMLET

OPERA IN FIVE ACTS

Book by Barbier and Carré, based on Shakespeare's play. Music by Ambroise Thomas. First production March 9, 1868, at the Paris *Académie*, with Christine Nilsson and Faure. First London production June 19, 1869, in Italian. Produced at the Academy of Music, New York, April 20, 1872, with Nilsson, Cary, Brignoli, Barre and Jamet; in 1882, with Gerster and Ciappini; and in 1892, with La Salle and Marie Van Zandt. Revived recently by the Chicago Opera Company for Ruffo.

Cast

HAMLET	Baritone
CLAUDIUS, King of Denmark	Bass
LAERTES, Polonius' son	Tenor
Ghost of the dead King	Bass
POLONIUS, Chancellor	Bass
GERTRUDE, Hamlet's mother, Queen of Denmark	Mezzo-Soprano
OPHELIA, daughter of Polonius	Soprano

Lords, Ladies, Officers, Pages, Peasants, etc.

Scene: Elsinore, in Denmark.

The story of *Hamlet, Prince of Denmark*, is so well known that it would seem hardly necessary to describe the plot at any length. However, for operatic purposes the librettists were obliged to modify and reconstruct certain portions of the tragedy, and the revised version will be briefly sketched here.

The present King of Denmark, *Claudius*, has seized the throne, after having murdered the late King, *Hamlet's* father. At the opening of the opera *Hamlet* knows nothing of the murder, but is highly incensed at his mother for having married *Claudius* before she had been two months a widow.

ACT I

SCENE I—*A Room of State in the Palace*

The new Queen is being presented to the Court at a public reception. She is annoyed because *Hamlet* shows his displeasure by absenting himself from the ceremony. After the presentation is over, *Hamlet* enters slowly, in a melancholy mood.

HAMLET: Ah! vain indeed is grief!
Affection, too, doth seem short lived indeed.
My much-loved father but two months dead;
And yet, unto another wedlock, my mother hath consented;
"Frailty, thy name is woman."

His bitter musing is interrupted by the entrance of *Ophelia,* his betrothed. She has heard that *Hamlet* intends to leave the kingdom and asks if he has ceased to love her. In the beautiful love duet he reassures her, and tells her why the palace has become intolerable to him.

Nega se puoi la luce (Love Duet)

By Maria Galvany, Soprano, and Titta
Ruffo, Baritone   *(In Italian)*   92500   12-inch, $4.00

HAMLET:
Celestial maiden, 'tis not thee I chide,
The purity of thy mind doth speak through
    those sweet eyes!
"Doubt that the stars are fire,
Doubt that the sun doth move,
Doubt truth to be a liar;
But never doubt my love."

OPHELIA:
It may be so, but such excess of love
Hath no enduring power;
Thou couldst not leave me to my sorrow,
Did thy heart know such love as mine!
Ye heavenly powers,—celestial choir,
That aye surround the eternal throne,
From your bright homes above,
Bear witness to my truthful love.

HAMLET:
Beloved Ophelia!

OPHELIA:
Ah! never will we part!

SCENE II—*Esplanade of the Palace. It is Night*

Horatio and *Marcellus* are discovered excitedly discussing the appearance of the spectre of the murdered King. They greet *Hamlet* and tell him of the ghostly visitor, which appeared just at midnight. *Hamlet* is much affected, and suggests that as it is nearly twelve the ghost may come again.

The clock strikes, and the figure of the murdered King appears.

Hamlet speaks to the spectre:

HAMLET:
Thou spirit dread, thou shade revered,
Hear thou thy hapless son's lament.
In pity answer,—speak to me!
Tell me why the sepulchre,
Wherein we saw thee peacefully en-
    tombed,
Hath op'd his ponderous and marble
    jaws,
To cast thee forth again?

The ghost motions *Horatio* and *Marcellus* to withdraw, and when they are gone he tells *Hamlet* of the murder and bids him become the avenger, but asks him to leave his mother's punishment to God. *Hamlet* is much affected and exclaims:

HAMLET:
Yes! Shade revered! Thy bidding
    shall be done.
O light, O sun, O glory, O love to me
    so dear,
Farewell! Farewell!

The ghost, before disappearing, pauses at the back of the stage, and stands with one hand extended toward *Hamlet;* at this moment *Horatio* and *Marcellus* re-enter, and appear terror-stricken at the spectacle before them. Trumpets and joyous music are heard without as the curtain falls.

PHOTO DU GUY
RENAUD AS HAMLET

PLAY PICTORIAL   HAMLET AND THE GHOST

ACT II
SCENE—*Garden of the Palace*

Ophelia enters and is much disturbed because *Hamlet* seems to avoid her. The Queen finds her weeping, and after questioning her says that *Hamlet* has also acted strangely toward his mother and fears his reason is affected.

Hamlet, seeking to entrap the King in some manner into betraying himself, has engaged a troupe of players to present a play which shall enact a similar crime. The King and Queen are delighted that he seems to seek amusement, and gladly accept his invitation to witness the play.

PLAY PICTORIAL   THE KING REVEALS HIS GUILT—ACT II

When the royal pair have departed, the players come on and are instructed by *Hamlet* in the plot he has conceived. The Prince then calls for wine and bids the players be merry, offering to sing them a drinking song.

O vin, discaccia la tristezza (Brindisi) (Wine, This Gloom Dispel)
By Titta Ruffo, Baritone, and La Scala Chorus   (*Italian*)   92037   12-inch, $3.00
By Francesco Cigada, Baritone, and La Scala Chorus   *16572   10-inch,   .75

HAMLET:
O wine! the gloom dispel,
That o'er my heart now weighs;
Come grant me thine intoxicating joy;
The careless laugh—the mocking jest!
O wine! Thou potent sorcerer,
Grant thou oblivion to my heart!
Yes, life is short, death's near at hand,

We'll laugh and drink while yet we may.
Each, alas, his burthen bears.
Sad thoughts have all;—grim thoughts and sorrows;
But care avaunt, let folly reign,
The only wise man he,
Who wisdom's precepts ne'er obeys!
(*The curtain falls on a scene of merriment.*)

SCENE II—*The Palace Hall.*   *On one side a stage has been erected*

The court assembles and the play begins, *Hamlet* placing himself where he can watch the King closely. As the action proceeds the guilty man shows unmistakable evidence of agitation, and finally in a rage he orders the players away. *Hamlet* rushes forward and denounces the murderer, but the Court believes his accusation to be the ravings of a madman, and all leave the room as he faints in *Horatio's* arms.

ACT III
SCENE—*The Queen's Apartments*

Hamlet enters and sings his farewell soliloquy.

Monologo (Soliloquy)
By Titta Ruffo, Baritone   (*In Italian*)   92042   12-inch, $3.00

This is Thomas' splendid setting of the well-known soliloquy and one of the most conspicuous numbers in the opera. Although the librettists took many liberties with Shakespeare's drama, they did not venture to alter such a well-known excerpt as this.

* *Double-Faced Record—See page 201.*

HAMLET: To be, or not to be, that is the question.
To die, to sleep; perchance to dream;
Ah! were it allowed me to sever
The tie that binds me to mortality,
And seek "the undiscovered country
From whose bourne no traveler returns!"
"Ay! to be, or not to be?
To die, to sleep; perchance to dream."

The Queen and *Ophelia* enter and plead with *Hamlet* to banish his wild imaginings. He sternly rebukes them, advises *Ophelia* to retire to a convent, and accuses his mother of being an accomplice. The ghost again appears, visible only to *Hamlet*, bids him spare his mother, and slowly disappears. The Prince conducts the Queen to the door, urging her to pray and repent.

ACT IV

A rural scene near a lake. Willows line the shore

Ophelia, driven insane by *Hamlet's* desertion of her, has wandered to the lake. She plays with a garland of flowers, and sings her wonderful aria, usually known as the *Mad Scene*, one of the most difficult of all florid compositions.

Ballata d'Ofelia (Mad Scene)

By Nellie Melba   (*In French*)   88251   12-inch, $3.00
By Giuseppina Huguet (*Italian*) *35180   12-inch, 1.25

An exquisite introduction by the orchestra is heard as *Ophelia* enters—a strange, wild figure, with flowing hair and torn white dress. She speaks to the wondering peasants and tells them childishly of the lark which she heard at dawn, fol-

PHOTO ERMINI
RUFFO AS HAMLET

lowing with a brilliant display of bird-like trills and staccatos. *Ophelia* then turns to the shepherds and asks them to listen to her song, a strange, sad melody, which is interrupted at intervals by wild laughter and weeping. Presently she seems to forget, and placidly plays with her flowers, until the magical siren's song is heard luring her to the water's edge, and she plunges in and floats away, singing of *Hamlet's* vow of love.

ACT V— *The Churchyard*

Hamlet comes hither to attend the funeral of *Ophelia*. He sings his beautiful song to her memory and resolves to take his own life upon her grave.

Come il romito fior (As a Lovely Flower)

By Titta Ruffo, Baritone, and La Scala Chorus
(*In Italian*)   92064   12-inch, $3.00

By Enrico Pignataro, Baritone
(*In Italian*) *63424   10-inch,   .75

COPY'T DUPONT
CALVÉ AS OPHELIA

When the cortege has arrived, the ghost again appears and looks reproachfully on *Hamlet*, who stabs the King, and as the curtain falls the people, now convinced of their monarch's guilt, acclaim *Hamlet* as his successor.

DOUBLE-FACED HAMLET RECORDS

Ballata d'Ofelia (Mad Scene)	By Huguet, Soprano	(*Italian*)	35180	12-inch, $1.25
Dinorah—Si, carina caprettina	By Giuseppina Huguet, Soprano			
Brindisi	By Francesco Cigada and Chorus	(*In Italian*)	16572	10-inch, .75
Ernani—Festa da ballo	By La Scala Chorus	(*In Italian*)		
Come il romito fior	By Enrico Pignataro	(*In Italian*)	63424	10-inch, .75
Pallide Mammole—Romanza	By Lavin de Casas	(*In Italian*)		

THE FOREST—ACT II

HÄNSEL UND GRETEL
(Haen'-zel oondt Gray'-tel)

(Italian) (English)
NINO E RITA   HANSEL AND GRETEL
(Neen-yo ay Ree'-tah)   *(Han-sel and Gray'-tel)*
(or HANS AND GRETCHEN)

A FAIRY OPERA IN THREE ACTS

Text by Adelheid Wette. Music by Engelbert Humperdinck. First produced December 23, 1893, at Weimar, under the direction of Richard Strauss. Milan, April 6, 1897. The work was soon given in every opera house in Germany, and its popularity spread throughout Europe. First American performance at Daly's Theatre, New York, October 8, 1895, under the direction of Augustus Harris; New Orleans, December 25, 1909. First performance at the Metropolitan Opera House, 1905, with Homer, Alten, Abarbanell and Goritz, and it has remained a strong favorite ever since. Recently revived by the Chicago Opera Company.

MUSICAL AMERICA

HUMPERDINCK

Cast

PETER, a broom-maker...............................Baritone
GERTRUDE, his wife...........................Mezzo-Soprano
HÄNSEL, } their children .... { Mezzo-Soprano
GRETEL, }   { Soprano
THE WITCH who eats children.................Mezzo-Soprano
SANDMAN, the Sleep Fairy...........................Soprano
DEWMAN, the Dawn Fairy...........................Soprano

202

PHOTO WHITE

THE GOLDEN STAIRCASE

It is now some seventeen years since Humperdinck's lovely fairy opera was brought out in America by Augustin Daly, and it has since been firmly established in the repertoire of every producer of grand opera.

GOSSIN

THE CHILDREN AT HOME

Hänsel and Gretel has been called the Peter Pan of grand opera; the audiences who witness it being invariably delighted with the childish joyousness and fairy charm of Humperdinck's work.

This delightful opera is built upon the simple Grimm tale of *Babes in the Woods,* and first suggested itself to the composer to amuse his sister's children. It was afterward elaborated into a complete opera, which has become one of the most important and interesting of modern German works.

Two German peasant children, *Hans* and *Gretchen,* are sent to the woods for strawberries and get lost. The *Sandman* finds the babes and sings them to sleep, while angels and fairies watch over them. They are awakened by the *Dew Man,* and go for breakfast to the house of the *Witch,* who plans to eat them; but when she opens the oven to see if it is hot enough to cook *Hans,* she herself is pushed in by *Gretchen.*

Several numbers from this interesting opera are presented here.

ACT I

The scene is laid in the house of *Peter*, where the two children are busily working—*Hänsel* making brooms and *Gretel* knitting a stocking. *Gretel* begins the old German folk-song, "Susie, What is the News?" with its nonsense about the geese going barefoot because of their lack of shoes. *Hänsel*, thinking more of his stomach than of the feet of the geese, asks when they are likely to have something to eat. Little *Gretel* reproves him for making a fuss about something which cannot be helped.

Suse, liebe Suse (Little Susie!)

By Alma Gluck, Soprano, and Louise Homer, Contralto (*In German*)
88418 12-inch, $3.00

Peter now returns to his cottage and finds the children gone after strawberries.

THE CHILDREN IN THE WOOD

In this air he frightens his wife by telling of the witch who lives in a honey-cake house, and who after enticing little children into it, bakes them into gingerbread in her oven.

Eine Hex' steinalt (The Old Witch)

By Otto Goritz, Baritone   (*In German*)   64164 10-inch, $1.00

Mr. Goritz's admirable character study as *Peter*, the tipsy, kind-hearted and superstitious father, was one of the features of the Metropolitan revival, and this odd number is given by him with much effectiveness.

BOYER   HÄNSEL AND GRETEL KNOCKING AT THE WITCH'S DOOR

ACT II

This scene shows the depths of the forest, into which the children have wandered. *Hänsel* picks berries while *Gretel* weaves garlands of flowers. Darkness soon comes, and the children are frightened and cling together. A little gray man, the *Sandman*, or *Sleep Fairy*, strews sand in their eyes as he sings his air.

Der kleine Sandmann bin ich (I Am the Sleep Fairy)

By Gluck and Homer (*In German*)
88419 12-inch, $3.00

The children slumber, and as the curtain falls angels are seen keeping guard over them.

PHOTO WHITE

THE HOME OF THE WITCH

ACT III

The curtain rises, showing *Hänsel* and *Gretel* still asleep in the wood. The *Dawn Fairy* shakes dewdrops on the children and wakes them just as the mist clears away, revealing the house of the *Witch*.

The children approach cautiously and begin to nibble at the gingerbread fence, when the *Witch* comes out and casts a spell over them.

Hexenritt und Knusperwalzer (Witch's Dance)

By Alma Gluck and Louise Homer   (*In German*)   87131   10-inch, $2.00

She makes a good fire in the stove for the purpose of roasting the babes, and in her joy she rides wildly around the room on a broomstick, singing this unique *Hexenritt*.

The duet begins with the soliloquy of the *Witch* as she sees *Gretel* peeping into the oven, and prepares to push her in to be baked into magic gingerbread.

The second part of the duet is the portion called the "Witch's Waltz," and is sung and danced by *Hänsel* and *Gretel* after the wicked *Witch* has been pushed into the oven. They dance around the room, wild with joy, and then prepare to eat their fill of the good things stored in the *Witch's* house.

After the death of the *Witch* the gingerbread children come to life and thank the children for releasing them from the spell. The father and mother of *Hänsel* and *Gretel* now arrive and embrace the children as the curtain falls.

LARCHER

THE CHAMBER OF HEROD

(French)

HÉRODIADE

(*Ay-rohd-yadd'*)

OPERA IN FIVE ACTS

Words by Paul Milliet and Henri Grémont, based on Gustave Flaubert's novelette, *Herodias*. Music by Jules Massenet. First production December 19, 1881, at the *Théâtre de la Monnaie*, Brussels. Produced in Paris at the *Théâtre Italien*, February 1, 1884, with Jean and Eduard de Reszke, Maurel, Tremelli and Devriès. Revived at the *Théâtre de la Gaîté* in 1903, with Calvé and Renaud. First German production in Hamburg, 1883, with Sucher, Krauss and Winkelmann. First London production 1904, under the title *Salome*, with Calvé, Kirkby Lunn, Dalmores and Renaud, and with the locale changed to Ethiopia by the British censor's orders. First American production at the New Orleans Opera in 1892. Produced by Oscar Hammerstein at the Manhattan Opera House, New York, November 8, 1909, with Cavalieri, Gerville-Réache, Duchêne, Dalmores and Renaud. Revived February, 1914, by the Philadelphia-Chicago Opera Company.

COPY'T MISHKIN

DALMORES AS HEROD

CAST

JOHN THE PROPHET......................Tenor
HEROD, King of Galilee................Baritone
PHANUEL, a young Jew..................Bass
VITELLIUS, a Roman proconsul..........Baritone
THE HIGH PRIEST.......................Baritone
A VOICE IN THE TEMPLE.................Bass
SALOME................................Soprano
HERODIAS..............................Contralto
A YOUNG BABYLONIAN WOMAN...............

Merchants, Soldiers, Priests, Levites, Seamen, Scribes,
Pharisees, Galileans, Samaritans, Ethiopians,
Nubians, Arabs, Romans.

The action takes place in Jerusalem—Time, about 30 A. D.

206

CAUTIN & BERGER

CALVÉ AS SALOME

The first Paris production of this opera was especially interesting because of the first appearance of Jean de Reszke as a tenor (he was formerly a baritone). It was not until 1904, however, that the opera was brought out in London (under the title of Salome) with Mme. Calvé, Dalmores and Renaud in the leading rôles. Mr. Hammerstein's production of this work during a recent season at the Manhattan Opera is well remembered by opera goers as a most brilliant one.

The opera contains much of the best music Massenet has written; and the plot, while based on the well-known Scriptural story, does not follow the Bible or tradition very closely, differing quite largely from Salome.

ACT I

SCENE—*Court of Herod's Palace at Jerusalem*

Salome enters and is greeted by *Phanuel*, a young Jew, who is astonished that she should be in the Palace, and wonders if she can be ignorant of the fact that *Herodias* is her mother. *Salome* tells him she is seeking *John the Prophet*, and in this air she describes how he had saved her from the desert when a child, and how good and kind he is.

Il est doux, il est bon (He is Kind, He is Good) By Emma Calvé (*French*) 88130 12-in., $3.00

Salome goes out just as *Herod* enters searching for her. *Herodias* rushes in and demands *John's* head, saying that he had insulted her. *John* appears, denounces them both and drives them out, terrified. *Salome* enters and tells *John* of her love for him, but he bids her turn to God.

ACT II

SCENE—*Herod's Chamber*

Herod lies on his luxurious couch, while attendants sing to him. He can think of no one but *Salome*, and bids the slaves dance to distract his mind. A love potion is given him by a slave, who says it will make him see the face of the one he loves.

He then sings the famous *Vision fugitive*, considered the most beautiful of the airs in the opera.

Vision fugitive (Fleeting Vision)
By Emilio de Gogorza, Baritone
(*In French*) 88153 12-inch, $3.00

COPY'T MISHKIN

GERVILLE-RÉACHE AS HERODIAS

Herod describes the vision of *Salome* which haunts him night and day, and declares that to possess her he would gladly surrender his soul. He drinks the love potion, and falls on the couch in a delirious sleep.

SCENE II—*Public Square at Jerusalem*

The scene shows *Herod* receiving messages from the allies, and denouncing Rome. *Herodias* enters and announces that the

CAUTIN & BERGER

RENAUD AS HEROD

PUBLIC SQUARE IN JERUSALEM—ACT III

Roman general, *Vitellius,* is approaching. The people are terrified, but *Vitellius* declares that Rome desires the favor of the Jews and will give back the Temple of Israel.

John and *Salome* enter and *Vitellius* is surprised at the honor paid to the *Prophet.* *Herod* gazes with eyes of love at *Salome,* while *Herodias* watches her jealously. *John* denounces *Vitellius* as the curtain falls.

ACT III
SCENE I—*Phanuel's House*

Phanuel is disclosed gazing at the city, which lies silent under a starry sky, and prophesying the fate which is to overwhelm it.

Air de Phanuel (Oh, Shining Stars)
By Marcel Journet, Bass   (*In French*)   74152   12-inch, $1.50

He calls upon the stars to tell him what manner of man is this *John,* who speaks with such authority. "Is he a man or a god?" he cries. *Herodias* enters, much agitated. *Phanuel* inquires what has brought the Queen to his house, and she cries, "Vengeance on the woman who has stolen *Herod's* love!" He reads her fate by the stars, and sees nothing but blood in the horoscope. She asks him about her child, lost so long ago, and he takes her to the window and shows her *Salome,* who is just entering the Temple. Horrified, *Herodias* cries, "My daughter? Never! That is my rival!"

SCENE II—*Inner Court of the Temple*

The second scene shows the entrance of the Temple. *Salome* enters half fainting, having heard that *John* has been cast in prison, and falls exhausted at the prison entrance. *Herod* enters, and seeing *Salome,* breaks out into a mad declaration of his love, but she repulses him with horror, and tells him she loves another. He declares he will find this lover and kill him, and goes out as the people enter the Temple.

John is brought in and denounced by the priests, but prays for them as they demand

INNER COURT OF THE TEMPLE—ACT III

his death. *Salome* runs to *John* and falls at his feet, wishing to die with him. *Herod*, seeing that it is *John* whom *Salome* loves, orders them both put to death, and they are seized and borne out by guards as the curtain falls.

COPY'T MISHKIN

DUFRANNE AS PHANUEL

ACT IV

SCENE I—*Prison Cell in the Temple*

John and *Salome* are here seen in prison. *John* admits that he loves the young girl, and urges her to fly and save her life, but she refuses, declaring she will die with him. Priests appear and order *John* to death, and command *Salome* to be taken to the Palace by *Herod's* commands. She resists desperately, but is dragged away.

SCENE II—*Great Hall in the Temple*

The great festival in honor of the Roman Empire is in progress. *Salome* is brought in and again entreats to be allowed to die with *John*. She appeals to the Queen, saying, "If thou wert ever a mother, pity me." *Herodias* trembles at the word, and gazing on her daughter, seems about to yield, when the executioner appears at the back with a dripping sword and cries, "The *Prophet* is dead." *Salome* gives a terrible cry and tries to kill the Queen, who screams: "Mercy! I am thy mother!" *Salome* recoils in horror, curses her mother and stabs herself.

(*Curtain*)

LONDON OPERA HOUSE

COVENT GARDEN, LONDON

FAMOUS OPERA HOUSES OF EUROPE

THE GREAT BANQUET SCENE IN ACT I

(French)
LES HUGUENOTS
(Layz Yoogn'-noh)

(German)
DIE HUGENOTTEN
(Dee Hoo-gen-ott'-en)

(Italian)
GLI UGONOTTI
(Glee Oo-goh-not'-tih)

(English)
THE HUGUENOTS
(Hew'-gen-ahts)

OPERA IN FIVE ACTS

Libretto by Scribe and Deschamps. Score by Meyerbeer. First presented at the *Académie* in Paris, February 29, 1836. First given in Italy at *Tetro della Pergola,* Florence, December 26, 1841, under the title of *Gli Anglicani.* First London production in German in 1842; in Italian, July 20, 1848. First New Orleans performance April 29, 1839 (first in America). Some notable New York productions were in 1858, with La Grange, Siedenburg, Tiberini and Formes; in 1872, with Parepa-Rosa, Wachtel and Santley; in 1873, with Nilsson, Cary, Campanini and del Puente; in 1892, with Montariol, de Reszke, Lasalle, Albani and Scalchi; in 1901, with Melba, Nordica, de Reszke and Plançon; in 1905, with Sembrich, Caruso, Walker, Plançon, Scotti and Journet; in 1907, with Nordica, Nielsen, Constantino and de Segurola; at the Manhattan in 1908, with Pinkert, Russ, Bassi and Ancona; and at the Metropolitan in 1914, with Caruso, Destinn, Hempel, Matzenauer, Braun and Scotti.

Cast

COUNT OF ST. BRIS, *(Sah Bree')* ⎫ Catholic noblemen .... ⎰ Baritone
COUNT OF NEVERS, *(Nev-airz')* ⎬ .... ⎱ Baritone
RAOUL DE NANGIS, *(Rah-ool' day Non-zhee')* a Protestant gentleman ......Tenor
MARCEL, *(Mahr-chel')* a Huguenot soldier and servant to Raoul ....Bass
MARGARET OF VALOIS, *(Val-ooah')* betrothed to Henry IV..........Soprano
VALENTINE, daughter of St. Bris.................................Soprano
URBANO, *(Ur-bah'-noh)* page to Queen Margaret ....Mezzo-Soprano
Ladies and Gentlemen of the Court, Pages, Citizens, Soldiers, Students, etc.

Scene and Period: Touraine and Paris; during the month of August, 1572.

211

This opera is considered the composer's masterpiece, and is indeed a wonderfully imposing work, with its splendid scenes, beautiful arias and concerted numbers, and its thrilling dramatic situations. The romance as well as the fanaticism of the period are faithfully pictured, and the whole presented on a magnificent scale. The opera is undeniably too long for a single evening's performance, requiring almost five hours when given entire. The Victor, however, has been merciful, and has selected only the gems of the work.

The story relates to one of the most dramatic periods in French history, and tells of the massacre of Huguenots in 1572, and of the efforts of *Margaret of Valois*, the betrothed of *Henry IV*, to reconcile the disputes between the Protestants and the Catholics.

ACT I

SCENE I—*House of the Count of Nevers*

The overture is a short one and consists mainly of the Lutheran chorale, which occurs several times in various portions of the opera. The curtain rises, disclosing a magnificent salon in the house of *Nevers*, where a gay party of Catholic noblemen are feasting. The Count explains that he expects another guest, a Huguenot, whom he hopes they will treat with courtesy. *Raoul* arrives and makes a favorable impression on the guests. *Nevers* toasts the ladies, proposing that each relate an adventure with some fair one; *Raoul*, being the latest arrival, is called upon first, and describes his rescue of an unknown beauty (who proves afterward to be *Valentine, St. Bris'* daughter) from some drunken revelers. In this air he tells of her beauty and the deep impression she made on him.

Più bianca—Romanza (Fairer Than the Lily)

By Enrico Caruso, Tenor	(*In Italian*) 88210 12-inch, $3.00
By M. Gautier, Tenor	(*In French*) *45007 10-inch, 1.00

Caruso sings the music allotted to *Raoul* charmingly, especially this delicate Romanza, in which he describes the vision of the unknown with whom he has fallen in love. In dreamy tones he sings the recitative, after which a short introduction brings us to the romanza, beginning

RAOUL:
Fairer far e'en than fairest lily,
Than spring morn more pure and more lovely
    and bright,
An angel of Heaven born beauty
Burst upon my ravish'd sight.
Sweetly she smiled as I stood by her side,
Sighing the love which e'en her tongue to
    speak denied;
And in her eyes the love-light gleamed,
Bidding me hope her love to gain.
Oh! she was charming past all expression!
And as before her form divine I bent my
    knee,
I falter'd forth. "Fair angel, that cometh
    from Heav'n above,
For evermore shall I love none but thee!"

The applause which greets this recital is interrupted by the entrance of *Marcel*, who makes no secret of his displeasure at seeing his master dining with Romanists. *Raoul* apologizes, begging indulgence for an old soldier and faithful servant who loves him, and the guests call on *Marcel* for a song. The grim soldier offers to sing an old Huguenot song of warning both against Rome and the wiles of woman.

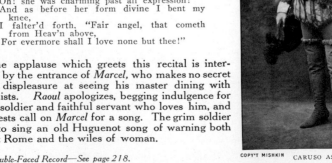

COPY'T MISHKIN   CARUSO AS RAOUL

Double-Faced Record—See page 218.

MARCEL:
Sirs, I will; an old Huguenot song against the snares of Rome and the dark wiles of woman. You, sirs, should know it well—it is our battle song: you heard it at Rochelle, for there 'twas sung, 'mid the din of drums and trumpets; with a full accompaniment—piff, paff, piff, paff,— of bullets from our ranks, thus out it rang:

COPY'T DUPONT PLANCON AS ST. BRIS

Piff! Paff! (Marcel's Air)
By Marcel Journet, Bass
(In French)   **74156**   12-inch, $1.50

MARCEL:
Old Rome and her revelries,
Her pride and her lust, boys,
The monks and their devilries,
We'll grind them to dust, boys!
Deliver to fire and sword
Their temples of Hell,
Till of the black demons
None live to tell!
Woe to all defilers fair!
I ne'er heed their shrieking—
Woe to the Dalilahs fair,
Who men's souls are seeking!
Deliver to fire and sword
Those children of Hell,
Till of the black demons
None live to tell!

Refrain
Piff, paff, piff; slay them all,
Piff, paff, piff, ev'ry soul!
Piff, paff, piff; paff; piff; piff, paff, piff, paff!
All vainly for aid or for mercy they call;
No pity for them! No they die—slay all!
No, no, no, no, no, no, no; slay all!

Journet's portrayal of the grim, stubborn old servant is a very fine one, and his rendition of the *Piff, Paff* is remarkable in its rugged force and stern simplicity.

A servant of *Nevers* announces a veiled lady to see him and he retires to an adjoining room. *Raoul* catches sight of the lady through the window as she lifts her veil, and is astonished and grieved to recognize the beauty he had saved from the ruffians.

A young page now enters, and in a lovely air, familiarly called the *Page Song,* announces that she has a message for one of the cavaliers present.

Nobil Signori salute! (Noble Sirs, I Salute You)
By Louise Homer, Contralto
(In Italian)   **85107**   12-inch, $3.00

This gay and brilliant cavatina is considered one of the most difficult of contralto numbers. It begins with a long and very ornamental cadenza, followed by this graceful melody:

worked up with much spirit and reintroduced after a striking series of vocal figures sung on the word "no." Mme. Homer's execution of this florid air exhibits well the great flexibility of her fine voice.

Meyerbeer intended this part for soprano, but it is usually transposed and sung by a contralto.

URBANO:
A most charming noble lady,
Whom with envy kings might view,
With a message here has charged me,
Cavaliers, cavaliers, to one of you.
I do not name him; but honor be
Unto the good knight, whoe'er be he!
And until now, sirs, there ne'er hath been
Mortal so favor'd by beauty's queen!

PHOTO WHITE THE CASTLE OF CHENONCEAUX—ACT II

The note proves to be for *Raoul*, and bids him consent to come blindfolded in a carriage, without question, to wherever his guide will take him. The young man is puzzled but decides to obey, and shows the note to the others. They recognize the seal of *Margaret of Valois*, and cast looks of envy at him as he follows the page.

ACT II

SCENE—*Castle and Gardens of Chenonceaux*

The Queen is seated on a kind of throne surrounded by her maids, who, with *Urbano*, are assisting in her toilet. She rises and sings her great air in praise of fair Touraine.

O, vago suol della Turenna (Fair Land of Touraine)

By Maria Galvany, Soprano
　　　(*In Italian*)　88234　12-inch, $3.00
By Frieda Hempel, Soprano
　　　(*In French*)　88382　12-inch,　3.00
By Giuseppina Huguet, Soprano
　　　(*In Italian*)　*35123　12-inch,　1.25

QUEEN:
　Oh, lovely land of fair Touraine!
　Thy vine-clad hills, thy sparkling fountains,
　Thy green banks and thy murm'ring zephyrs,
　All fill my soul with peace and love!
　Yet, for a difference in belief,
　This fair scene may by war be stain'd!
　Oh, that men would observe the moral,
　To love and fear the all-powerful Being!
　But hence with sorrow!
　Care we will banish;
　Quick, let it vanish, far, far away!
　In the land where I reign,
　From the mount to the main,
　All re-echo the strain
　That's devoted to love!

COPY'T DUPONT HOMER AS THE PAGE

Double-Faced Record—See page 218.

The maids disperse, and *Valentine* enters and tells the Queen that she has seen the *Count de Nevers*, who has promised to release her from the engagement which had been arranged. *Margaret* informs her that she has another cavalier in mind—meaning *Raoul*, who is now conducted to the ladies and his mask removed. He is much astonished to find that it is the Queen who has sent for him, and pledges his honor and his sword to her service. He does not, however, perceive *Valentine*, who has retired at the moment of his entrance.

COPY'T MISHKIN   SCOTTI AS NEVERS

The nobles of the Court, Protestant and Catholic, now enter, having been sent for by *Margaret*. She announces that she is planning a marriage which shall reconcile all their differences, and asks them to swear to live in peace with each other. Raoul, Nevers, St. Bris and the nobles gather around the Queen and take the oath.

SCALCHI AS THE PAGE

Valentine is now led in by her father and presented to *Raoul*. He starts in astonishment, having recognized the lady he had rescued, and whom he had seen meeting *Nevers*.

RAOUL (*in a stifled voice*):
  Great Heaven! what do I see?
MARGARET:
  Why this astonishment?
RAOUL:
  What! is this the bride you would
    offer to me?
MARGARET:
  Yes, to marry and to love.
RAOUL:
  What perfidy! what treachery!
  I her husband! Never, never!

A terrible scene follows, *St. Bris* challenging *Raoul*, who is ordered under arrest by the Queen. *Valentine* is overcome with shame, and the Catholics are furious. *Marcel* is delighted that his master has escaped marriage with a Catholic, and the curtain falls as the Lutheran chorale is again heard in the orchestra.

ACT III

SCENE—*A Square in Paris*

Catholic students are seated outside an inn on the left while opposite some Huguenot soldiers are drinking and playing dice. The soldiers sing their famous Rat-a-plan.

COPY'T MISHKIN
DALMORES AS RAOUL

Coro di Soldati (Soldiers' Chorus, "Rataplan")

By Metropolitan Opera Chorus   (*In Italian*) *45051 10-inch, $1.00

A wedding procession passes on its way to the church; it is for *Valentine*, who has been persuaded to wed *Nevers*. *Valentine* asks that she be permitted to spend the day in the

NILSSON AS VALENTINE

chapel in prayer. While there she overhears a plot to assassinate *Raoul*, and at once goes in search of *Marcel* to inform him of the plan. She meets him in the square and tells him of the plot.

Nella notte io sol qui veglio (Here By Night Alone I Wander)

By Maria Grisi, Soprano, and Perello De Segurola, Bass *(In Italian)*
*63404 10-inch, $0.75

Marcel thanks her for the warning and goes with his friends to the rescue. A general conflict is threatened but is prevented by the Queen, who appears just in time. She tells *Raoul* that *Valentine* is innocent of wrong, having merely gone to *Nevers'* house to ask him to release her. *Raoul* is overcome with remorse, but the knowledge comes too late, as *Valentine* is already the wife of *Nevers*.

COPY'T MISHKIN
CONSTANTINO AS RAOUL

A richly decorated boat approaches, occupied by the nuptial suite. *Nevers* leads *Valentine* to it, and as all salute the bridal couple the boat moves away, while *Raoul*, overcome by grief, is supported by *Marcel*. The curtain falls.

ACT IV

SCENE—*A Room in Nevers' Castle*

Valentine, alone, broods over her sorrows, confessing to herself that although wedded to another, she still loves *Raoul*. She is astounded to see her lover appear, he having braved death and entered the castle to see her again. *Valentine* hears her father's voice, and hastily conceals *Raoul* behind the tapestry. The Catholic nobles enter to discuss the plot outlined by *St. Bris*. They finally agree to his fiendish proposal, and swear to slaughter the Huguenots. *Nevers* is horrified at the bloody scheme to exterminate all Protestants, and refusing to become an assassin, he breaks his sword, and is led away by the guards.

The conference closes with the famous *Benediction of the Swords*, perhaps the greatest and most thrilling of all operatic scenes.

Benediction of the Swords

By Marcel Journet, Bass, and Metropolitan Opera Chorus
(In Italian) 74275 12-inch, $1.50

The number begins with the strain sung by *St. Bris* in his recital of the plan.

Vo - le - te yoi, in - sieme a me, col - pi - re i tra - di - tor? Eb - ben!
Will ye all join with me the trai - tors to de - stroy? *'Tis well!*

This is followed by the noble strain of the *Benediction*, one of the best known passages in Meyerbeer's work—

D'un sa - cro zel l'ar do - re cie - le - vie scal - di l'al - ma
On Heav'n's just cause re - ly - ing, This im - pious race de - fy - ing

─────────

Double-Faced Record—See page 218.

ST. BRIS:
Do you wish our dear country to save?

MONKS AND NOBLES:
It is our wish! our hearts' desire!

ST. BRIS:
To serve our noble King,
Will ye the traitors destroy?

MONKS AND NOBLES:
The King's commands, we will obey!

ST. BRIS:
'Tis well! now hear the King's decree:
These Huguenots, whose vile detested race we
hate,
Shall from this day by the sword disappear!

ST. BRIS:
On Heaven's just cause relying,
This impious race defying,
'Mid thousands round thee dying,
Now swear that no mercy thou'lt show!
To compass Heav'n's desiring,
Now for vengeance we go!

COPY'T DUPONT

JEAN DE RESZKE AS RAOUL

Then comes the furious and fanatical chorus of priests
and lords, one of the most difficult of ensembles.

ALL:
Strike them down, men and children, all!
And let no mercy ever be shown!
By the sword they shall perish,
And their temples be o'erthrown!

ST. BRIS:
Be silent, my friends, and breathe not e'en a
murmur
To wake our slumb'ring foe!

ALL:
Whisper low, not a word,
Not a breath or sign revealing, while we,
silent stealing,
Strike the impious foe!
(With fury.)
Now for vengeance! we will go!

The number closes with the famous passage for the basses which finishes on a low E
natural, sung very pianissimo, as the company disperses.

The nobles having gone, *Raoul* comes out, horrified at what he has heard, and wishes to
warn his friends, when *Valentine,* thinking to save his life, urges him to remain, telling him
that she loves him. In a transport of delight he begins the great duet.

VALENTINE: Raoul, they will kill thee; ah, in pity stay! (Act IV.)

CIPOLLA   THE FINAL TRAGEDY

Dillo ancor (Speak Those Words Again!)
By Giacomelli and Martinez-Patti   (*In Italian*)   *35123 12-inch, $1.25

RAOUL:

Ah! say again thou lov'st me!
From darkness drear I have
  awakened to bliss!
Forever now we're united,

Thou hast link'd thy fate to
  mine—
Forever, forever, forever!
Say once again thou lov'st me!

The great bell of St. Germain, the signal to prepare for the slaughter, is heard tolling, and *Raoul* makes a fresh effort to go to the aid of his people. *Valentine* clings to him, but he rushes to the window, and shows her that the massacre has already begun; then tears himself from her arms and leaps from the window, while she falls fainting.

In American productions, because of the great length of Meyerbeer's work, the opera has ended with the shooting of *Raoul* by the mob as he leaps from the window; but in the original version a fifth act occurs, in which *Nevers* is killed, and *Valentine*, renouncing her faith, is united by *Marcel* to *Raoul*. *St. Bris* and his party enter the street, and not recognizing *Valentine*, fire upon the three and kill them. The curtain falls as *St. Bris* discovers that he has murdered his daughter.

DOUBLE-FACED HUGUENOTS RECORDS

{O vago suol della Turenna (Fair Land of Touraine) Huguet {Dillo ancor By Giacomelli and Martinez-Patti	35123	12-inch,	$1.25
{Plus blanche (Fairer Than the Lily) M. Gautier (*In French*) { Guillaume Tell—Asile Hereditaire—M. Gautier, Tenor (*In French*)	45007	10-inch,	1.00
{Coro di Soldati By Metropolitan Opera Chorus (*In Italian*) { Magic Flute—O Isis By Metropolitan Opera Chorus (*In German*)	45051	10-inch,	1.00
{Nella notte io sol By Grisi and Segurola (*In Italian*) { Lucrezia Borgia—Vieni la mia vendetta By Giulio Rossi, Bass	63404	10-inch,	.75

* *Double-Faced Record—See above list.*

IRIS' FATHER CURSES HER

IRIS
(Eê-ris)

OPERA IN THREE ACTS

Text by Luigi Illica; music by Pietro Mascagni. First production, Costanzi Theatre, Rome, November 22, 1898. Revised by the composer and produced at La Scala, Milan, January, 1899. First American production, Philadelphia, October 14, 1902, during the tour of Mascagni's own company. Two days later New York heard the same organization give the opera, but the production by the Metropolitan Opera Company did not occur until 1908, with a cast including Caruso, Eames, Scotti and Journet. Revived April 3, 1915, with Bori, Scotti and Botta.

Characters

CIECO, the blind man...Bass
IRIS, his daughter ....Soprano
OSAKA..Tenor
KYOTO, a takiomati ....Baritone

Ragpickers, Shopkeeper, Geishas, Mousmé (laundry girls), Citizens, Strolling Players.

In Greek mythology *Iris* (literally "Rainbow") was the Goddess of the Rainbow, and and as such was the Messenger of Peace to all the inhabitants of the earth.

Illica has named his Japanese heroine after this Greek goddess, and the story is enacted by Japanese characters under the shadow of the Fujiyama, the Wisteria Mountain, to which all Japanese bow. The story is somewhat symbolical in character, and through the rather simple plot runs a sort of weird Japanese philosophy.

COPY'T WHITE

IRIS IN HER GARDEN (MME. BORI)

ACT I

SCENE—*The Home of Iris near the City*

Iris is a young and innocent country girl who lives with her blind father, *Cieco*, on the outskirts of the town, and spends her days worshipping the Sun and playing with her dolls. *Osaka*, a rich and dissolute nobleman, sees the lovely girl in her garden and contrives with *Kyoto*, a *takiomati* or dive keeper, to obtain possession of her. It is not easy to lead *Iris* away from her old blind father, to whom she is devoted, but by means of a doll show they arouse her curiosity, and as she approaches nearer and nearer to the puppets, three Geisha dancers surround her and quietly carry her off, while *Osaka* leaves money to pay the old man for her, thereby making the abduction legal. *Cieco* returns and is led to believe that his daughter has gone to the Yoshiwara (a questionable street) of her own accord, and in a rage goes in search of her, securing two peddlers to help him.

ACT II

SCENE—*Interior of a house in the Yoshiwara*

In the second act the bewildered *Iris* wakes up in a luxurious mansion in the Yoshiwara. *Osaka* appears and wooes her, but the young girl only answers his entreaties by appealing to be sent back to her little cottage, her father and her garden. *Osaka* is angry at her unresponsiveness and calls *Kyoto* to take her away, whereupon the *takiomati* resolves to make money by exhibiting her with his puppet show. While thus on exhibition, *Osaka* repents his hasty decision, and decides to buy her back from *Kyoto*. *Iris* suddenly hears her father's voice in the crowd, but the old man has only come to bitterly curse her, and overwhelmed with shame, she jumps from the window to the sewer below and is lost.

ACT III

SCENE—*A waste space outside the City*

In the third act some ragpickers, who are searching the river for débris from the sewers, discover *Iris*, who is still alive but only partly conscious. The men flee as she is reviving, and she reflects dreamily on the world and fate. The rising Sun soothes her, and believing that she is entering into a new life, she dies contentedly. The Sun sheds its warm rays upon her, and flowers finally cover the body.

The somewhat sordid story was made interesting at the recent revival by the artistic work of Mme. Bori, whose impersonation of Iris was a real delight. This singer has given the Victor two of the most effective arias in Mascagni's work—the *In pure stille,* the joyous song of *Iris* in Act I, in which she sings to the flowers in her little garden, while the *Mousmé* form picturesque groups by the riverside with their rush baskets piled high with snowy garments; and the *Un di al tempio* from the scene in the palace in Act II, in which *Iris* relates to *Osaka* a vision of pleasure and death she had one day in the Temple when she was a child.

In pure stille (Life is Gaily Passing)
By Lucrezia Bori, Soprano   (*In Italian*) 87219 10-inch, $2.00

Un di al tempio (One Day at the Temple)
By Lucrezia Bori, Soprano   (*In Italian*) 88524 12-inch, $3.00

SCENE FROM JEWELS OF THE MADONNA

(Italian)
I GIOJELLI DELLA MADONNA
(German)
DER SCHMUCK DER MADONNA
(English)
THE JEWELS OF THE MADONNA

OPERA IN THREE ACTS

Libretto by C. Zangarini and E. Golisciani; music by Ermanno Wolf-Ferrari. First performed as *Der Schmuck der Madonna* at the Kurfuersten Oper, Berlin, December 23, 1911. First American production at the Auditorium Theatre, Chicago, January 16, 1912. First Philadelphia performance February 14, 1912. First New York performance March 5, 1912. Later included in the repertoire of the Century Opera Company, and given with much success.

PHOTO BECI

SETTING OF ACT I

Characters

GENNARO, in love with
    Maliella............Tenor
MALIELLA, in love with
    Rafaele ....Soprano
RAFAELE, leader of the
    Cammorists.......Baritone
CARMELA ....Soprano
BIASO ....Tenor
CICCILLO.............Tenor
STELLA.............Soprano
CONCETTA......... Soprano
SERENA ....Soprano
GRAZIA .... Dancer
TOTONNO ....
ROCCO.................Bass
Vendors, Monks, People of the
    Streets, etc.

Time and Place: *The scene is laid in Naples, at the present time.*

Few operas of recent years have met with the unqualified success which has been accorded Wolf-Ferrari's vivid melodrama of Neapolitan life. The story of the opera is the composer's own idea, based on actual happenings in the squalid, superstitious life of the people of Naples, feverish with its reckless gayety, and mingled with sadness and gloom. The wild doings of the Cammorists, the preparations for the celebration in honor of the Virgin, the pageantry of the Catholic ceremonial and the wild tumult of Neapolitan revelries form the background and atmosphere for this realistic music-drama.

SCENE—ACT II

The plot may be summed up as follows: *Maliella*, a wayward Neapolitan beauty, is loved by her foster brother, *Gennaro*, a simple, honest lad, but the girl is infatuated with the dashing *Rafaele*, leader of the Cammorists. *Rafaele* proudly boasts that he would stop at nothing to prove his love for *Maliella*, declaring he would even steal for her the jewels which deck the image of the Virgin. The young girl, annoyed by *Gennaro*'s attentions, taunts him with not daring to do for her what *Rafaele* had offered. Almost in the hope of winning her favor the poor fellow steals to the church at night, secures the jewels, and lays them at *Maliella's* feet. At first she is fascinated by the brilliancy of the gems, but as she realizes the awful sacrilege *Gennaro* has committed she flies to *Rafaele*, whom she finds in the inn of the Cammorists.

He, in a frenzy of jealousy, spurns her, declaring she has sold herself for the jewels. The unhappy girl drowns herself, and *Gennaro*, in an abandon of remorse and despair, places the jewels on an altar, prays for mercy, and drives a dagger into his heart. As the people, bent on vengeance, burst into the room, they see the body of the unfortunate youth lying before the Madonna.

The two *intermezzi* from Jewels of the Madonna are delightful examples of the exquisite music which Wolf-Ferrari has written for this work. One is the beautiful waltz intermezzo between the second and third acts, and the other, an effective number mainly for harp, flute and strings, is played before Act II. These are given in delightful fashion by Vessella's Band and by the Victor's fine organization, under Mr. Rogers' direction.

DOVER ST. STUDIOS

SAMMARCO AS RAFAELE

MATZENE

HAMLIN AS GENNARO

GENNARO AND MALIELLA

JEWELS OF THE MADONNA RECORDS

Intermezzo (Second Entr'acte) Vessella's Band / Lucia Sextette (Donizetti) Vessella's Band	35356	12-inch, $1.25
Intermezzo (Second Entr'acte) Victor Orchestra / Merry Wives of Windsor Overture (Nicolai) New Symphony Orchestra of London	35270	12-inch, 1.25
First Entr'acte (Intermezzo between Acts I and II) Victor Orchestra / Danse Macabre (Saint-Saëns, Op. 40) Vessella's Italian Band	35381	12-inch, 1.25

Rafaele's Serenade (Act II)
By Pasquale Amato, Baritone
  (with Metropolitan Opera Chorus)
    (In Italian) 87193 10-inch, 2.00

  This beautiful Serenade occurs in the second act of the opera. The scene is the garden of *Maliella's* house. It is evening, and from the distance are heard the strains of an old Neapolitan folk ballad, sung by a chorus afloat on the bay. This is succeeded by the tinkling of mandolins and guitars behind the wall of *Maliella's* garden. *Rafaele* and his companions appear, and he sings his Serenade, which begins: "Aprila bella la fenestrella."

SCENE—ACT III

THE JUGGLER TRYING TO AMUSE THE CROWD—ACT I

(French)

LE JONGLEUR DE NOTRE DAME

(English)

THE JUGGLER OF NOTRE DAME

MIRACLE PLAY IN THREE ACTS

Text by Maurice Lena, from a mediæval miracle play, *Etui de Nacre*, by Anatole France. Music by Jules Massenet. First production at Monte Carlo, February 18, 1902, with Renaud. First Paris production at the Opéra Comique, May, 1904, and afterward given in all the principal cities of Europe. First American production, Manhattan Opera House, New York, November 27, 1908, with Mary Garden, Renaud and Dufranne.

Characters

JEAN, a Juggler...........................Tenor
BONIFACE, cook of the Abbey............Baritone
PRIOR OF THE MONASTERY.................Bass
MUSICIAN MONK.........................Baritone
SCULPTOR MONK.........................Bass
POET MONK.............................Tenor
PAINTER MONK..........................Baritone

Two Angels, Apparition of the Virgin, Monks, Cavaliers, Citizens

Time and Place: Cluny, near Paris; sixteenth century

The story of Le Jongleur de Notre Dame is adapted from a "miracle tale" by Anatole France, and the events occur in Cluny in the Middle Ages. The legend tells of a poor juggler who tried to show his devotion to the Holy Virgin, and though his method appeared

THE JUGGLER

grotesque and even sacrilegious to the priests, the Virgin accepted his homage and glorified his death. Maurice Lena amplified France's story and made an admirable play of it, and for this beautiful legend Massenet has provided some highly effective and reverential music.

At the beginning of the opera, *Jean*, a poor juggler, haggard and worn, joins the merry-making crowd of villagers in the square in front of the monastery. It is May Day, and the people want to be amused, but when poor *Jean* tries to earn a few sous by his wornout tricks, they laugh and jeer at him. Suddenly the *Prior* of the Abbey appears and drives away the crowd, threatening *Jean* with the torments of the after-life if he does not mend his ways. He charges the boy to forsake his juggler's life and enter the monastery, and the poor, hungry lad, after one look at a cart of provisions which arrives for the monks, consents and goes into the monastery with the *Prior*.

The second act opens in the monastery study, where the monks are arguing among themselves over the relative importance of the arts they represent. The *Prior* orders them off to the chapel, while *Jean* laments to *Boniface*, the cook, his inability to do anything that can please the Virgin. The kindly *Boniface* relates to the despondent lad a fable, "The Legend of the Sagebrush," which shows that the humblest offering is acceptable to the Virgin if tendered in a sincere and reverent spirit. The tale makes a strong impression on *Jean*, and he resolves to serve the Church in his own humble way.

In Act III, the youthful monk enters the chapel, lays aside his monk's dress, and in his old juggler's clothes takes his place in front of the altar, singing his old street songs and performing the old tricks. The *Prior* and monks presently appear and are shocked at what they consider acts of sacrilege. They try to seize *Jean* and throw him out, but *Boniface* protects him, and, as he holds the monks back, the face of the Virgin in the picture above the altar becomes illuminated. She extends her hands in benediction over the now crouching *Jean*, as the monks draw back in awe, and the lad, radiant, falls dying in the arms of the wondering *Prior*, while a choir of angels is heard chanting "Glory to Jean."

Mr. Journet gives an admirable rendition of the effective Legend.

Legende de la Sauge   (Legend of the Sagebrush)
By Marcel Journet, Bass   (*In French*)   74123   12-inch, $1.50

PHOTO MANUEL   INTERIOR OF MONASTERY—ACT II

THE OPENING SCENE OF KÖNIGSKINDER—FARRAR AND THE GEESE

(German)   (English)

KÖNIGSKINDER   THE KING'S CHILDREN
(*Koenigs'-kin-der*)

FAIRY OPERA IN THREE ACTS

Book by Ernst Rosmer (Elsa Bernstein). Music by Engelbert Humperdinck. First production in any country December 28, 1910, at the Metropolitan Opera House, New York, with Farrar, Homer, Jadlowker and Goritz in the cast, and under the personal direction of the composer, who then made his first visit to America. The opera has since been given in London and throughout Europe—in Milan in 1912 as "Figlia di Re."

FARRAR AS THE GOOSE GIRL

Characters

THE GOOSE GIRL...................Soprano
THE KING'S SON....................Tenor
THE WITCH........................Contralto
THE FIDDLER.......................Baritone
THE WOODCUTTER....................Bass
THE BROOMMAKER....................Tenor
INNKEEPER........................Bass
INNKEEPER'S DAUGHTER.........Mezzo-Soprano

Tailor, Stable-maid, Gate-keepers, Citizens,
Councillors, Musicians, Children, etc.

The opera of *Königskinder* is based on a three-act play by Ernst Rosmer (in private life Elsa Bernstein), with incidental music by Humperdinck, which was first produced at Munich, January 23, 1897. The following year it was given at Irving Place Theatre, New York, and four years later in English as *Children of the King*.

Humperdinck composed the music for the play in 1895-96. The introductions to Acts II and III were produced at a concert of the Bach Society in Heidelberg, June 2, 1896, the composer conducting. These excerpts were also given at Frankfort,

THE BERLIN CAST WITH THE COMPOSER

Berlin and Leipsic before the play was produced. Introduction to Act II was played at the Montauk Theatre, Brooklyn, November 22, 1896, at a concert of the Brooklyn Saengerbund, and in December both introductions were given in Boston by the Boston Symphony Orchestra.

The opera is allegorical in character, illustrating the stupidity of mankind in failing to recognize true loyalty when it appears to them in disguise. It is a human little story, full of pathos, humor and tenderness, and no one could have given it the gentle, sympathetic touch better than Humperdinck.

The story tells of a *Goose Girl* who lives with an old *Witch* in the hills above the town of Hellabrunn. A poorly-dressed youth comes out of the woods and tells the *Goose Girl* of his wanderings. He is in reality the *King's Son*, but the girl does not know this. The boy falls in love with the beautiful maiden, and asks her to go maying with him through the summer land. The girl longs to run off with him, but finds her feet glued to the ground. The *King's Son*, believing her afraid to go, tells her she is unworthy to be a king's mate, and leaves her, vowing she shall never see him again till a star has fallen into a lily which is blooming nearby.

The *Witch* returns and scolds the *Goose Girl* for wast-

WHITE

THE GOOSE GIRL FEEDING HER FLOCK
(GERALDINE FARRAR)

GORITZ AS THE FIDDLER

HEMPEL AS THE GOOSE GIRL

FARRAR AND JADLOWKER

RETURN TO THE HUT—ACT III

ing her time on a man. The *Fiddler* enters, followed by the *Woodcutter* and *Broommaker* from the town, who come to ask the *Witch* if she had seen the *King's Son,* as the King is dead and the people want the son to rule in his place. The *Witch* tells them that the first person who enters the city gate next day at noon, no matter what his seeming social condition may be, will be crowned King. The *Woodcutter* and *Broommaker* depart, but the *Fiddler* lingers, hoping to get a glimpse of the *Goose Girl,* who is in the hut. She appears and tells him her sorrows, and he assures her she shall wed the *King's Son.* The girl prays that his words may come true, and as she kneels a shooting star falls into the heart of the lily. She runs off into the woods with her flock in search of her lover.

In Act II we see the town of Hellabrunn in an uproar, awaiting the new ruler. At the inn near the town gates is the *King's Son,* still in rags. Musicians enter and a dance begins. The *Gatekeeper* refuses to allow the people to crowd in the gateway, keeping it clear for the entry of the *King.* The *Woodcutter* is invited to relate his adventures in the woods, and he says that on the stroke of twelve the *King's Son* will enter the gates. The people scoff at the suggestion that their new King might come in rags, but as the clock strikes twelve, the crowd rushes toward the gates and beholds the *King's Son* in his rags, and the *Goose Girl,* escorted by her flock, entering the city. The people, with the exception of the *Fiddler,* who recognizes the *King's Son,* mock the couple and drive them out with sticks.

In Act III the *Fiddler,* who has been cast out of the town for his defense of the *King's Son* and the *Goose Girl,* is seen at the *Witch's* hut, feeding the doves the girl has left behind her. He lives here alone, the *Witch* having been burned at the stake by the people,

PHOTO WHITE   DEATH OF THE KING'S CHILDREN

who declared she had deceived them in her promise of a new ruler. A troop of children come to beg the *Fiddler* to lead them in a search for the lost *King's Son* and his sweetheart, and he gladly consents. The *Woodcutter* and the *Broommaker* arrive and go into the hut, and hardly has the sound of the searching party died away than the *King's Son* and *Goose Girl* appear. They are half famished and beg of the *Woodcutter* something to eat, and he finally gives them some poisoned pastry which he finds in the hut. The outcasts eat it and die, and when the *Fiddler* and the children return from their useless search they can only mournfully bear away to the hills for burial the bodies of the poor *Kingly Children.*

KÖNIGSKINDER RECORDS (In German)

Lieber Spielmann (Dearest Fiddler)

Geraldine Farrar, Soprano   88405 12-inch, $3.00

The song of the *Broommaker's* child, who is spokesman for the throng of children who come to the hut in Act III to beg the *Fiddler* to lead them in a search for the outcasts.

O du liebheilige Einfalt du! (Thou Innocent One)

By Otto Goritz, Baritone   64184 10-inch, $1.00

This is the *Fiddler's* answer to the appeal of the children that he go with them in their search for the *Royal Pair.*

Ihr Kindlein sie sind gefunden (Children, We Have Found Them)

By Otto Goritz, Baritone   74287 12-inch, $1.50

Sung by the *Fiddler* as the searching party return to the hut and discover the bodies of the *Children.*

GROUP OF CHILDREN—ACT III

LAKMÉ

(Lak-may)

OPERA IN THREE ACTS

Book by Goudinet and Gille, taken from the story, *Le Mariage de Loti*. Music by Léo Delibes (*Deh-leeb'*). First production Paris, April 14, 1883. First London production at the Gaiety Theatre, June 6, 1885. First American performance in 1883, by the Emma Abbot Opera Company, a version that can hardly be taken seriously. First adequate production March 1, 1886, at the Academy of Music, by the American Opera Company, under Theodore Thomas, with Pauline L'Allemand in the title rôle. Produced at the Metropolitan Opera House, April 2, 1890, with Patti; and again on April 22, 1892, with Marie van Zandt and de Reszke. Revived in 1911 by the Chicago Opera Company for Tetrazzini.

Characters

GERALD, } officers of the British army in India.............. { Tenor
FREDERIC, } { Baritone
NILAKANTHA, a Brahman priest...............................Bass
HADJI, a Hindoo slave.......................................Tenor
LAKMÉ, daughter of Nilakantha............................Soprano
ELLEN, daughter of the Governor...........................Soprano
ROSE, her friend..Soprano
MRS. BENSON, governess of the young ladies............... Mezzo-Soprano
MALLIKA, slave of Lakmé........................... Mezzo-Soprano
A FORTUNE TELLER...
A CHINESE MERCHANT...
A SEPOY...

Hindoos, Men and Women, English Officers and Ladies, Sailors, Bayaderes, Chinamen, Musicians, Brahman, etc.

Scene and Period: India, at the present time.

The music of Delibes' opera is wholly beautiful, and the principal numbers are exquisite compositions—lovely in idea and execution.

The story resembles in some points both Aida and Africaine; all three are more or less Oriental; *Lakmé,* like *Aida,* loves her country's enemy; *Nilakantha* and *Nelusko* possess similar traits; while *Lakmé* and *Selika* both poison themselves botanically.

The Oriental atmosphere is somewhat spoiled by the introduction of the modern and rather commonplace English characters, but the romantic ending atones for any shortcomings.

ACT I

SCENE—*A Garden in India*

Nilakantha, Lakmé's father, hates the English invaders and resists their presence in India. *Gerald* and *Frederic,* English officers, while sauntering with some English ladies, venture on sacred ground near *Nilakantha's* temple, and when rebuked they all depart but *Gerald,* who remains to sketch some Oriental jewels which *Lakmé* had left in the garden. He takes up the trinkets and sings his charming air, *Idle Fancies.*

SYBIL SANDERSON AS LAKMÉ

Fantaisie aux divins mensonges (Idle Fancies)

By M. Rocca, Tenor   (*In French*)   *16573   10-inch, $0.75

He is struck with the daintiness and beauty of the gems and tries to picture the unknown beauty to whom they belong.

GERALD:

Idle fancy, cradled by delusion,
  You mislead me now as of old.
Go to dreamland, turn back in confusion,
  Fair dove fantastic, with wings of gold.
(*Taking up a bracelet.*)
  Of some fair maid round her arm folding,
  This bracelet rich must oft entwine.
Ah! what delight would be the holding,
  The hand that passes there, in mine.
(*Taking up a ring.*)
  This ring of gold, my dream supposes,
  Oft has followed, wand'ring for hours,
The small foot, that but reposes
  On mossy banks or beds of flowers.

This necklace, too, with her own perfume scented,
  Embalm'd as yet with sweets from her lips that came,
Has felt the true heart, beating, glad, contented,
  Trembling with joy at the one well-loved name.
Away, fly, fond illusions,
  Swift'ly passing visions that my reason disturb!
Idle fancy, cradled by delusion, etc.

(From the Ditson Edition.)

This beautiful air has been sung for the Victor by a brilliant and accomplished young tenor, M. Rocca, of the *Opera Comique*.

Hearing some one approaching, *Gerald* hides himself in the shrubbery. *Lakmé* enters and lays flowers at the feet of an idol. She is about to go when she pauses and tries to analyze a strange feeling which has come over her, saying:

LAKMÉ:

In my heart now I feel there's a murmur so strange,
The flow'rs are more lovely appearing,
And Heaven's more radiant now.
From woods a new song I am hearing,
Fond zephyrs caress my brow.
And a fragrance that's here is filling,
All my senses with a rapture so thrilling!

She then sings her first lovely song,

Pourquoi dans les grands bois (Why Love I Thus to Stray?)

By Alice Verlet, Soprano
(*In French*)   *45006   10-inch, $1.00

and asks herself why she loves to wander in the forest and why she is both sad and glad.

BERGER   VALLANDRI AS LAKMÉ

LAKMÉ:

Why love I thus to stray,
In woods here, day by day,
While tears have sway?
Why doth the dove's note sadden,
And fill my heart with sighing;
As doth a fading flow'ret,
Or a leaf eastward flying?
Yet are these tears most sweet to me,
Tho' sad they be!
And my heart is gladsome,
Tho' I'm sighing, I'm gladsome.

Ah! why?
Why look for reasons here, in the song of the stream,
Where roses dream?
In leaves that fall around?
In my heart soft reposes, like a lily at rest,
Sweeter balm than yield roses, by gentle winds caressed,
Or by loving lips pressed. Tho' I sigh, I'm gladsome,
Ah, why?

She suddenly sees *Gerald* among the trees and utters a cry of fear. Her attendants run in, but some intuition tells her not to reveal *Gerald's* presence, and she sends them away. Going to his hiding place she denounces him for trespassing on sacred ground, and bids him begone. He begs her for a few moments' conversation, and tells her of the impression she has made on his heart.

GERALD: Ah! linger, go not yet, so thoughtful, sweet, unchiding!
    Let blushing charms that mine eyes now have met,
    O'ermantle thy cheek,
    Its lily pallor hiding!

* *Double-Faced Record—See page 233.*

Lakmé looks on the handsome youth with interest, but tells him she fears the return of her father, who would surely seek vengeance for the Englishman's desecration of holy ground. *Gerald* departs just as *Nilakantha,* summoned by *Lakmé's* attendants, enters, and seeing traces of a trespasser, declares that he must die. They go in pursuit of *Gerald,* leaving *Lakmé* motionless with fear.

ACT II

SCENE—*A Street in an Indian City*

Act II shows a public square, lined with Chinese and Indian shops and bazaars. English visitors are strolling about, viewing the scenes with interest. *Nilakantha,* disguised as a beggar, is seeking traces of the intruder, whom he has sworn to kill. *Lakmé* is with him, wearing the dress of a dancing girl. He orders his daughter to sing, hoping that the Englishman will recognize her voice and betray himself. She sings the famous *Bell Song.*

Où va la jeune Hindoue (Bell Song)
By Luisa Tetrazzini, Soprano
(*In Italian*)   88297   12-inch, $3.00
By Bessie Abott, Soprano
(*In French*)   88084   12-inch,   3.00
By Maria Galvany, Soprano
(*In Italian*)   88219   12-inch,   3.00
By Ellen Beach Yaw, Soprano
(*In French*)   74090   12-inch,   1.50

PHOTO FELIX

MARCHAL AS LAKMÉ

Delibes has ingeniously used bells to give character to this number, which is a most intricate one, especially in the refrain, where voice, woodwind and bells blend with many charming touches.

PHOTO REUTLINGER

ABOTT AS LAKMÉ

LAKMÉ:
Down there, where shades more deep are glooming,
What trav'ler's that, alone, astray?
Around him flame bright eyes, dark depths illuming,
But on he journeys, as by chance, on the way!
The wolves in their wild joy are howling,
As if for their prey they were prowling;
The young girl forward runs, and doth their fury dare.
A ring in her grasp she holds tightly,
Whence tinkles a bell, sharply, lightly,
A bell that tinkles lightly, that charmers wear!
(*She imitates the bell.*)
Ah! Ah! Ah! Ah!
While the stranger regards her
Stands she dazed, flush'd and glowing,
More handsome than the Rajahs, he!
*   *   *   *   *   *
And to heaven she soars in his holding,
It was Vishnu, great Brahma's son!
And since the day in that dark wood,
The trav'ler hears, where Vishnu stood,
The sound of a little bell ringing,
The legend back to him bringing,
A small bell ringing like those the charmers wear!

As *Nilakantha* had planned, *Gerald* recognizes *Lakmé* and betrays himself. The Brahman goes to collect his Hindoos, intending to kill the Englishman, while *Lakmé* finds *Gerald,* warns him of the plot, and tells him of a hut in the forest where he may be free from pursuit.

LAKMÉ: In the forest near at hand,
A hut of bamboo is hiding,
'Neath a shading tree doth stand,
This roof of my providing.
Like a nest of timid birds,
In leafy silence abiding,
From all eyes secret it lies,
And waits it there a happy pair!

Far away from prying sight,
Without there's naught to reveal it,
Silent woods by day and night,
Ever jealously conceal it;
Thither shalt thou follow me!
When dawn earth is greeting,
Thee with smiles I shall be meeting.
For 'tis there thy home shall be.

Gerald at first refuses thus to hide, declaring it unworthy of a British officer, but *Lakmé* pleads with him and he consents; but as he attempts to follow her he is stabbed by *Nilakantha,* who then escapes. *Lakmé* runs to *Gerald,* and overjoyed to find his wound is not serious, she prepares, with the help of her faithful attendant *Hadji,* to bear him to the forest retreat.

ACT III
SCENE—*An Indian Forest*

Act III shows the hut in the tropical forest. *Gerald* is lying on a bed of leaves while *Lakmé* watches over him, singing soothing melodies. He opens his eyes and greets her with rapture, singing his beautiful *In Forest Depths.*

Vieni al contento profondo
(In Forest Depths)
By John McCormack, Tenor
(*In Italian*)   64171   10-inch, $1.00

This lovely *cantilena* is given in delightful style by Mr. McCormack.

THIERY AS LAKMÉ

GERALD:
I too recall,—still mute, inanimate,—
I saw you bent o'er my lips; while thus lying,
My soul upon your look was attracted and
  fastened;
'Neath your breath life awoke and recovery
  hastened.
O my charming Lakmé;
Through forest depths secluded,
Love's wing above us has passed;
Earth-cares have not been intruded,
And heaven on us falls at last.
These flow'ring vines, with blooms capricious,
Bear o'er our pathway scents delicious;
Which soft hearts, with raptures beset,
While all else we forget!

As the days pass and *Gerald* recovers his strength, he seems to forget all else but his love for the Brahman maiden, but one day, while she is absent, his friend *Frederic* finds him and urges him to return to his duty, telling him his regiment is ordered off at once to suppress an outbreak among the Hindoos. *Gerald* promises to be at his post in time, but asks for a few moments in which to say good-bye to *Lakmé*. *Frederic* leaves with his promise, and when *Lakmé* comes back she finds *Gerald* changed. She asks the reason, but before he can answer the distant sound of bugles calling the regiment together is heard. She sees by his face that he means to go back to his friends, and in despair she eats some flowers of the deadly stramonium tree and dies in his arms, just as her father and friends arrive upon the scene.

REUTLINGER   CHARPANTIER AS LAKMÉ

DOUBLE-FACED AND MISCELLANEOUS LAKMÉ RECORDS

Pourquoi dans les grands bois (Why Love I Thus to Stray?)	By Alice Verlet, Soprano	(*In French*)	45006 10-inch, $1.00
Mignon—Polonaise	By Mlle. Korsoff, Soprano	(*In French*)	
Fantaisie aux divins mensonges (Idle Fancies)	By M. Rocca, Tenor	(*In French*)	16573 10-inch, .75
Rigoletto—Cortigiani, vil razza dannata—Renzo Minolfi		(*Italian*)	

NOTE—Quotations are from the Ditson libretto, by permission—Copy't 1890, Oliver Ditson Co.

LINDA DI CHAMOUNIX

OPERA IN THREE ACTS

Words by Rossi; music by Donizetti. First production in Vienna, May 19, 1842; in Paris, November 17, 1842; in London, June, 1843; in New York, at Palmo's Theatre, January 4, 1847, with Clotilda Barili. Given at the Academy of Music, March 9, 1861, with Clara Louise Kellogg. Revived April 23, 1890, with Patti, at the Metropolitan.

Cast

MARQUIS OF BOISFLEURY ....Baritone
CHARLES DE SIRVAL, his son ....Tenor
THE PARISH PRIEST ....Bass
ANTONIO LOUSTOLOT, a farmer ....Bass
MADELINE, his wife ....Mezzo-Soprano
LINDA, their daughter ....Soprano

Time and Place :   Chamounix and Paris, 1760, during the reign of Louis XV.

The story tells of an aged couple, *Loustolot* and *Madeline*, and their only daughter *Linda*, who dwell in the valley of the Chamounix (in the French Alps). *Linda* loves a young painter, *Charles,* who has come to the valley to paint the mountains. The *Marquis de Sirval*, who holds a mortgage on *Loustolot's* farm, visits the old couple and assures them that he will not press the mortgage; but at the same time he is secretly plotting to effect the ruin of *Linda*.

Linda enters and speaks of her love for *Charles*. She then sings the gem of the first act, a favorite with colorature sopranos for more than seventy years.

O luce di quest' anima (Guiding Star of Love!)

By Luisa Tetrazzini, Soprano   (*In Italian*)   88506   12-inch, $3.00
By Giuseppina Huguet, Soprano (*Double-Face*) (*In Italian*)   62090   10-inch,   .75

LINDA:
Poor are we both in worldly state;
On love we live,—on hope we dream!
A painter yet unknown, is he,
Yet by his genius he will rise,
And I his happy wife shall be! Oh, what joy!

Oh! star that guidest my fervent love,
Thou'rt life and light to me;
On earth, in Heav'n above,
Entwin'd our hearts will be.
Oh, come, then, come, my best belov'd!

This air, while primarily intended as a vehicle for vocal display, is so spontaneous in its gaiety, and so genial in melody, as to possess exceptional captivating charm for a song of this type. In this performance we hear Tetrazzini at her best. The lightness and joy of the opening phrases, the golden notes, the piquant delivery, together constitute a triumph of the true Italian vocal art—the real *bel canto*.

Charles enters, and the lovers sing their charming duet.

A consolarmi affrettati (Oh, That the Blessed Day Were Come)

By Emma Trentini, Soprano, and Alberto Caffo, Tenor   62090   10-inch, $0.75

The worthy parish priest having warned *Linda's* parents of the dishonorable intention of the *Marquis*, they decide to remove *Linda* from the danger, and send her to Paris. The *Marquis* pursues her to the city and renews his attentions, while *Charles* (who is in reality the son of the *Marquis*) is compelled by his father to transfer his attentions to another. *Linda's* father comes to Paris in disguise, and discovers his daughter. Believing her to be an abandoned woman, he curses her, and she becomes insane through grief.

The last act again shows the little farm at Chamounix. The demented *Linda* has made her way back to her parents, and is found by *Charles,* who has escaped the unwelcome marriage and now brings the release of the farm from debt. The sight of her lover causes *Linda* to fall in a death-like swoon, but when she recovers her reason has returned, and the lovers are united.

LOBETANZ PLAYING FOR THE PRINCESS—ACT I

(German)   (English)
LOBETANZ   MERRYDANCE

MUSICAL PLAY IN THREE ACTS

Text by Otto Julius Bierbaum ; music by Ludwig Thuille. First production at Mann-heim, Germany, 1898. First production in America November 18, 1911, with Gadski, Jadlowker, Witherspoon and Murphy.

GADSKI AS THE PRINCESS

Cast

LOBETANZ......................................Tenor
THE PRINCESS............................Mezzo-Soprano
THE KING...Bass
THE FORESTER, ⎫
THE HANGMAN, ⎬........................Speaking Parts
THE JUDGE, ⎭
  Girls, musicians, prisoners, two heralds, the people.

Time and Place : Germany in the Middle Ages.

The story of *Lobetanz* resembles an old fairy tale in its simplicity, the Prince Charming in this instance being a wander-ing musician, and the ending, as in all good fairy stories, being of the " lived-happy-ever-after " variety.

The curtain rises on a rose fête, which young girls are pre-paring in anticipation of the arrival of the *King* and his daugh-ter. The *Princess* is ill, and the *King* has appointed a day of festivity in the hope that it will revive her. *Lobetanz*, a wandering musician, strolls into the *King's* rose garden, where the preparations are being made, and stays to watch the royal

235

WHITE   THE GALLOWS SCENE

procession, which is accompanied by poets and singers. The musicians play and sing to the *Princess*, but all their efforts fail to please her. Suddenly a violin is heard from an arbor in the rear of the garden. The *Princess* is immediately fascinated with the music, and *Lobetanz* comes forward, his instrument on his shoulder. The pathos of his playing so affects the *Princess* that she swoons, and *Lobetanz* barely escapes from the wrath of the people.

In the second act the strolling minstrel meets the *Princess* in a wood and tells her of his love for her. The lovers are interrupted by the arrival of the *King* and the royal hunting party, and *Lobetanz* is seized by the pikemen and dragged away, while the *Princess* falls in a swoon.

The third act shows the unfortunate lover in prison, charged with witchcraft, and sentenced to be hanged. As preparations are being made to place the noose about his neck, the funeral procession of the *Princess* approaches. *Lobetanz* begs to be allowed to play upon his violin once more, declaring he can revive her. The *King* promises him his daughter's hand if he can bring her back to life again. As *Lobetanz* plays, the flush of life appears upon the cheeks of the young girl, and she slowly revives and is clasped in her lover's arms. The act closes with a merry dance, in which every one joins, and we are left to suppose that the lovers "live happy ever after."

The air which Mme. Gadski has sung for the Victor occurs in Act I, in the scene representing the rose garden of the *King*, where the rose festival is to be celebrated. The *Princess*, at the bidding of the *King*, offers a greeting to Spring and the roses.

An allen Zweigen (Lovely Blossoms of Spring)
By Johanna Gadski, Soprano   (*In German*)   88362   12-inch, $3.00

WHITE, N. Y.   THE FLOWER FESTIVAL—ACT I

LOHENGRIN

(Loh'-en-grin)

OPERA IN THREE ACTS

Words and music by Richard Wagner. First produced at Weimar, Germany, August 28, 1850, under the direction of Liszt. Produced at Weisbaden, 1853; Munich and Vienna, 1858; Berlin, 1859. First London production, 1875, and also, in Italian, at Covent Garden the same year. First production in English at Her Majesty's, in 1880. St. Petersburg, 1875; Paris, 1887. First American production at Stadt Theatre, in New York, April 3, 1871; in New York, in Italian, March 23, 1874, with Nilsson, Cary, Campanini and Del Puente; in German, in 1885, with Brandt, Krauss, Fischer and Stritt—this being Anton Seidl's American début as a conductor. First New Orleans production, in Italian, December 3, 1877; in French, March 4, 1889.

Lohengrin is the second of all operas in popularity in Germany (*Carmen* taking the lead), and during the decade, 1901-1910, had 3,458 performances.

PROGRAM OF ORIGINAL
PRODUCTION

Characters

HENRI THE FOWLER, King of Germany . . . . Bass
LOHENGRIN . . . . Tenor
ELSA OF BRABANT . . . . Soprano
DUKE GODFREY, her brother . . . . Mute Personage
FREDERICK OF TELRAMUND, Count of Brabant . . Baritone
ORTRUD, his wife . . . . Mezzo-Soprano
THE KING'S HERALD . . . . Bass

Saxon, Thuringian and Brabantian Counts and Nobles, Ladies of Honor, Pages, Attendants.

Scene and Period: Antwerp, first half of the tenth century.

Most of us are familiar with the story of the Knight *Lohengrin*, who comes in his boat, drawn by a swan, to defend *Elsa* from the charge (preferred by *Telramund* and *Ortrud*, who covet *Elsa's* estates) of having murdered her young brother, *Godfrey.*

Telramund is vanquished and disgraced by *Lohengrin*, who wins *Elsa* as his bride. One condition he exacts from her—that she shall never ask who he is or whence he came. By the influence of *Ortrud*, however, she rashly questions him, and in fulfillment of his vow, but in deep grief, he leaves her and departs in his boat drawn by a dove. The ethereal Grail harmonies, the lovely *Swan Motive*, the noble *Prayer of the King* and the *Bridal Chorus* make this one of the most melodious of all the master's operas.

Prelude

By La Scala Orchestra   31779   12-inch, $1.00

The prelude, one of the most beautiful of all Wagner's compositions, symbolizes the descent from Heaven of a group of angels bearing the Holy Grail. The number begins with soft A major chords in the highest register of the violin. The motive of the Grail is then announced:

GADSKI AS ELSA

237

GEGRÜSST DU GOTTGESANDTER HELD! SEI GEGRÜSST!

KING AND PEOPLE: "Hail, thou hero from on high!"

WITHERSPOON AS THE KING

Coming nearer and nearer, the light of the Grail is seen in the sky, while the air is filled with the blessings dispensed by the holy cup. As the sounds grow louder, the senses are overwhelmed, until at the tremendous climax thundered out by the full orchestra the mystic light of the Grail is seen in all its glory.

The mysterious Grail motive then fades away, being played at the end by muted strings; and the number ends with the same A major chords *pianissimo*.

ACT I

SCENE—*Banks of the Scheldt, near Antwerp*

King Henry of Germany arrives at Antwerp and finds Brabant in almost a state of anarchy. He summons the counts and nobles of Saxony and Brabant to meet under the Oak of Justice, and calls on *Frederick of Telramund* for an explanation, saying:

GORITZ AS TELRAMUND

KING:
Here, to my grief, I meet with naught but strife,
All in disunion, from your chiefs estranged!
Confusion, civil warfare meet we here.
On thee I call, Frederick of Telramund!
I know thee for a knight as brave as true,
I charge thee, let me know this trouble's cause.

Frederick now advances and begins his narrative, boldly accusing *Elsa* of the murder of her brother.

FREDERICK:
Thanks, gracious King, that thou to judge art come!
The truth I'll tell thee, falsehood I disdain.
When death was closing round our valiant Duke,
'Twas me he chose as guardian of his children,
Elsa the maiden, and Gottfried her brother;
Whose dawning with tender care I guarded,
Whose welfare I have treasured as my honor.
My sov'reign, mark now, if I'm aggrieved.

When of my honor's treasure I am robbed!
One day, when Elsa had with her brother wandered forth,
Without the boy, trembling, she returned,
With feign'd lamenting, questioned of his safety,

ELSA RELATING HER DREAM

MLLE. DUBEL (PARIS OPÉRA)

MLLE. ACKTE (HELSINGFORS)

LUISE PETZL (HAMBURG OPERA)

MLLE. KAISER (THÉATRE NATIONAL)

Famous European Singers in the Rôle of "Elsa"

BANKS OF THE SCHELDT—ACT I

ELSA AND LOHENGRIN

Pretending she had been from him divided,
And in vain his traces she had sought,
Fruitless was every search we made to find him;
And when I questioned her with words severe,
Her pallor and her falt'ring tongue betray'd her,
Her crime in its guilty blackness stood confess'd!
A horror fell upon me of the maid;
The claim upon her hand her father had conferr'd
With willing heart, I straight resigned,
And chose a wife full pleasant to my sense,
Ortrud, daughter of Radbod, true in death.
I here arraign her, Princess Elsa of Brabant;
Of fratricide be she charged!
I claim dominion o'er this land by right;
My nearest kinsman was the valiant Duke,
My wife descended of the race
That gave this land their rulers thro' long ages past.
O King, give judgment! All now thou hast heard!

The *King* is much disturbed, and asks that *Elsa* be sent for. When she enters timidly, with downcast eyes, he says kindly: "Speak, *Elsa*, in thy King thou may'st confide!"

The young girl seems bewildered and dreamily sings the lovely *Traum*, telling of her vision of a splendid Knight who came to be her defender.

Elsa's Traum (Elsa's Dream)

By Johanna Gadski, Soprano
By Emma Juch, Soprano (*Piano acc.*)

(*In German*) 88038 12-inch, $3.00
(*In German*) 74014 12-inch, 1.50

241

FERD. LEEKE

LOHENGRIN:
Thy life I spare:
May'st thou in peace repent!
(Lohengrin, Act I.)

ARRIVAL OF LOHENGRIN

ELSA: Oft when the hours were lonely,
I unto Heav'n have pray'd,
One boon I ask'd for only,
To send the orphans aid;
Away my words were wafted,
I dreamt not help was nigh,
But One on high vouchsaf'd it,
While I in sleep did lie.
(with *growing enthusiasm*)
I saw in splendor shining,
A knight of glorious mien,
On me his eyes inclining,
With tranquil gaze serene.
A horn of gold beside him,
He leant upon his sword,
His words so low and tender,
Brought life renew'd to me.
(with *rapture*)
My guardian, my defender,
Thou shalt my champion be.

The *King* is much moved, and calls for a judgment of God after the fashion of the time. The trumpeters blow the summons to the four points of the compass, and the Herald calls:

Who will do battle here for Elsa of Brabant!
Let him appear!

At first there comes no response, and *Elsa* is in despair, but after a second call a knight in shining armor is seen approaching in a boat drawn by a swan.

Nun sei bedankt, mein lieber Schwan! (Thanks, My Trusty Swan!)

By Fernando de Lucia,
Tenor (*In Italian*)
76002   12-inch, $2.00
By Leo Slezak, Tenor
(*In German*)
61203   10-inch,   1.00

Lohengrin steps out, then turning and caressing the swan, sings:

LOHENGRIN:
I give thee thanks, my faithful swan!
Turn thee again and breast the tide,
Return unto that land of dawn
Where joyous we did long abide,
Well thy appointed task is done!
Farewell! farewell! my trusty swan!
(*to the King*)
Hail, gracious sov'reign!
Victory and honor be thy valor's
meed!
Thy glorious name shall from the
land
That chose thee ruler, ne'er depart.

The knight now announces that he has come to defend the maiden, who is unjustly accused by her enemy.

LOHENGRIN:
Ye knights, nobles and freemen of
this land,
Guiltless and true is Elsa of Brabant!
Thy tale was falsehood, Count Tel-
ramund,
By Heav'n's assistance all thou shalt
recant!

PANEL BY HUGO BRAUNE

THE FIGHT BETWEEN LOHENGRIN AND TELRAMUND—ACT I

THE PLOT—ACT II

The *King* bids the nobles prepare to fight, and in this noble *Gebet* calls upon Heaven to judge between the combatants.

Mein Herr und Gott —Koenig's Gebet (King's Prayer)
By Marcel Journet, Bass (*In German*)
64013 10-inch, $1.00

KING HENRY:
O King of kings, on Thee I call;
Look down on us in this dread hour!
Let him in this ordeal fall
Whom Thou know'st guilty, Lord of pow'r!
To stainless knight give strength and might,
With craven heart the false one smite;
Do Thou, O Lord, to hear us deign,
For all our wisdom is but vain!

ELSA AND LOHENGRIN:
Now, Lord, make known Thy just decree,
I have no fear, I trust in Thee!
ORTRUD:
In his strong arm I trust alone,
That nor defeat nor fear hath known.
FREDERICK:
I here await thy just decree!
Great Lord, let not my honor tarnished be!

Frederick is soon stricken to the earth by *Lohengrin*, who is proclaimed a hero. *Elsa* is pronounced innocent, plights her troth to her brave defender, and the curtain falls amid general rejoicing.

ACT II
SCENE—*Court of the Palace*

This scene shows the inner court of the palace at Antwerp. It is night. *Frederick* and *Ortrud*, disgraced and dressed in sombre garments, are seated on the church steps. They upbraid each other, *Frederick* accusing *Ortrud* of inventing the story of *Elsa's* crime. A long duet follows, ending in a terrible plot for vengeance.

Elsa appears on the balcony of the palace, all unconscious of the wretched and disgraced *Telramund* and *Ortrud*, who are hidden in the shadow. In a blissful reverie, the young girl sings to the soft breezes of the knightly *Lohengrin*, to whom she is now betrothed.

FROM AN OLD PRINT   ORTRUD KNEELING TO ELSA

Euch Lüften, die mein Klagen (Ye Wandering Breezes)
By Johanna Gadski, Soprano
(*In German*) 88377 12-inch, $3.00

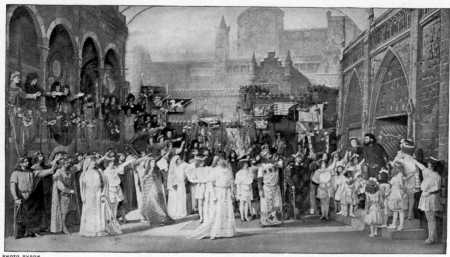

THE KING DENOUNCING TELRAMUND—ACT II

ELSA:
  Ye wand'ring breezes heard me,
    When grief was all I knew;
  Now that delight hath stirred me,
    My joy I'll breathe to you!

TELRAMUND AND ORTRUD:
  'Tis she! Be near, ye powers of
    darkness!

ELSA (continuing dreamily):
  Thro' heaven's azure ye bore him,
    Ye wafted him to me;
  'Mid stormy waves watched o'er him,
    My guide, my love to be!
  Where'er thy pinion rusheth,
    The mourner's tears are dried;
  My cheek that burns and flusheth
    With love, oh cool and hide!

Du Aermste (Thou Unhappy One)

By Emma Eames and Louise Homer   (In German)   89021   12-inch, $4.00

Elsa, who has finished her rapturous soliloquy to the wandering breeze, still lingers on the balcony, enjoying the balmy night and dreaming of her betrothal on the morrow. *Ortrud,* pursuing the plot agreed upon with *Frederick,* appears and calls to *Elsa,* who hearing her name, cries:

  Who calls? How strangely
  My name resoundeth thro' the night!

Ortrud feigns repentance, and *Elsa,* in her new-found happiness, forgives her, saying:

  Unhappy one, that thy heart could know
    the treasure
  Of love that knows not fear or doubt!
  No child of earth that bliss can measure
  Who doth not dwell in faith devout!
  Rest thee with me!

Ortrud warns *Elsa* against trusting her husband too blindly, hinting of the mystery in his life, and thus plants a seed of suspicion in the young girl's heart. The duet then follows:

  ELSA:
    Oh, let me teach thee
    How trust doth hallow joy and love.
    Turn, then, to our faith, I beseech thee,
    Oh, turn unto our faith divine,
    For God is love!
  ORTRUD (aside—with fierce joy):
    Oh! pride of heart, I yet will teach thee,
    That an illusion is this love,
    The gods of vengeance soon shall reach
      thee,
    Their wrath-destroying thou shalt prove!

Elsa enters the palace and *Telramund* renews his vow of imprecation.

EAMES AS ELSA

245

Day breaks, and the Herald appears and announces the banishment of *Telramund. Elsa,* attended by her ladies, passes on her way to the minster but is suddenly confronted by *Ortrud,* who has arrayed herself again in splendid garments. She taunts *Elsa* with the fact that her knight has no name.

COPY'T DUPONT

SCHUMANN-HEINK AS ORTRUD

> ORTRUD:
>> Your stranger, say, as what doth thou
>>> proclaim him?
>> If I have heard aright, thou canst not
>>> name him!
>
> ELSA (*indignantly*):
>> Thou slanderer, taunt me no more,
>> Let my reply all doubts assure—
>> So pure and noble is his nature,
>> As none can match in high renown.
>> Oh, can there live so vile a creature
>> As to asperse all honor's crown?

The *King* and *Lohengrin* now enter and *Elsa,* astonished and grieved, goes to *Lohengrin,* saying:

> ELSA:
>> My champion! shelter me against her
>>> wrath!
>> Blame me, if I obey'd not thy command;
>> I heard her weeping sore by yonder
>>> portal,

>> And in compassion harbor'd her this
>>> night,
>> And now with harsh and bitter words of
>>> hatred
>> She taunts me for my boundless trust
>>> in thee!

ACT III

SCENE I—*The Bridal Chamber in the Palace*

The act opens with the *Wedding March,* played by the orchestra.

Prelude to Act III—The Wedding March

By Herbert's Orchestra   *55048   12-inch, $1.50
By La Scala Orchestra   *62693   10-inch, .75

This is followed by the beautiful *Bridal Chorus,* one of the loveliest numbers in the opera. As the curtain rises, showing the bridal chamber, the strains of the march continue, but in a softer mood. The great doors at the back open, and the bridal party enters,—the ladies leading *Elsa* and the King and nobles conducting *Lohengrin,*—they come to the front and the chorus begins:

> CHORUS:
>> Faithful and true, we lead thee forth
>> Where Love, triumphant, shall crown ye with joy!
>> Star of renown, flow'r of the earth,
>> Blest be ye both far from all life's annoy!
>> Champion victorious, go thou before!
>> Maid bright and glorious, go thou before!
>> Mirth's noisy revel ye've forsaken,
>> Tender delights for you now awaken;
>> Fragrant abode enshrine ye in bliss;
>> Splendor and state in joy ye dismiss!
>
> EIGHT LADIES (*passing around the bridal pair*):
>> As solemn vows unite ye
>> We hallow ye to joy!
>> This hour shall still requite ye,
>> When bliss hath known alloy!

After a striking and effective modulation the first strain is repeated by the full chorus.

> Faithful and true, now rest you here.
> Where Love, triumphant, etc.

PHOTO GERLACH   OBER AS ORTRUD

* *Double-Faced Record—See page 250.*

The party goes slowly out, leaving the bridal pair alone, while the strains of the nuptial air die away in the distance.

The full strength of the Victor organization has been used for the vocal rendition, and the result is a record of surpassing beauty. An instrumental record of this number is also offered.

Bridal Chorus

By Victor Opera Chorus
(*In English*) 31846 12-inch, $1.00
By Arthur Pryor's Band
31227 12-inch, 1.00
By La Scala Chorus
(*In Italian*) *16537 10-inch, .75

The bridal pair are left alone and a long duet occurs, part of which is recorded here by two famous artists of La Scala.

Cessero i canti alfin (The Song Has Died Away)

By Giuseppina Huguet, Soprano;
Fernando de Lucia, Tenor
(*In Italian*) 92055 12-inch, $3.00

The beautiful air which *Lohengrin* sings in the duet, *Dost Thou Breathe the Incense,* is also given here by Dalmores.

FRAGMENT OF THE BRIDAL CHORUS IN WAGNER'S OWN HANDWRITING

Athmest du nicht mit mir die süssen Düfte ? (Dost Thou Breathe the Incense Sweet ?)

By Charles Dalmores, Tenor   (*In German*) 87088 10-inch, $2.00

This duet is scarcely over when the poison instilled in *Elsa's* mind by *Ortrud* causes her, in violation of her promise, to question *Lohengrin* as to his name and origin. He remonstrates with her, at first gently and then with authority, reminding her that she has promised not to ask his name. She becomes more and more agitated, saying :

HOMER AS ORTRUD

ELSA:
No, thou shalt not compel me to trust by words of blame—
No, not unless thou tell me thy country and thy name!

LOHENGRIN:
Elsa, oh, I conjure thee!

ELSA:
What fatal spell is thine?
In vain wouldst thou assure me—
Declare thy race and name!

They are interrupted by the entrance of *Frederick* and four associates, who break in with drawn swords. *Elsa* shrieks and hands *Lohengrin* his sword, with which he strikes *Frederick* dead. The nobles surrender, and *Elsa* falls senseless in *Lohengrin's* arms. After a long silence, *Lohengrin* orders the body into the Judgment Hall, and gives *Elsa* in charge of her ladies.

SCENE II—*Same as Act I*

A quick change of scene shows again the banks of the Scheldt at Antwerp, as in Act I. The *King* and his nobles await the coming of *Lohengrin,* who is to accompany them to battle. They are startled by the entrance of the nobles bearing the body

* *Double-Faced Record—See page 250.*

of *Telramund. Lohengrin* enters and is greeted by the King with warmth:

KING:

> Hail, heav'n-sent hero, welcome here!
> Thy loyal vassals all are near,
> Waiting for thee to give the word,
> And fight by thy all-conq'ring sword.

All are surprised when the knight announces that he is forced to decline the command of the expedition, and tells of the attempt on his life.

LOHENGRIN:

> My gracious sov'reign, bear me blame-
> less,
> Reasons have I that must be nameless,
> The destin'd campaign I suspend!
> To lead ye forth to battle here I came
> not;
> But judge me, for your leniency I claim
> not.
> Then, firstly, do ye hold that I am guilty?
> Your just decree to me is due.
> He sought my life despite honor and
> fealty—
> Say, did I right when him I slew?

The King declares *Telramund* to be justly slain, and *Lohengrin* now reveals with reluctance that *Elsa* has broken her promise.

LOHENGRIN:

> And further, I declare in face of Heav'n,
> Though bitter grief to me it bode,
> That from her fair allegiance hath been
> driven
> The wife that Heav'n on me bestow'd.

PANEL BY BRAUNE

TELRAMUND INTERRUPTING THE BRIDAL PROCESSION—
ACT II

MEN:

> Elsa! say, oh, what hast thou done?
> Sentence so stern how hast thou
> won?

LADIES:

> Woe is thine, Elsa!

LOHENGRIN:

> Ye all have heard her give her word
> in token
> That she my name and country ne'er
> would ask:
> That promise her impatient heart
> hath broken—
> Vainly I hop'd she would fulfill her
> task!
> Now mark me well, I will no more
> withhold it,
> Nor have I cause to shrink from
> any test;
> When I my name and lineage have
> unfolded
> Ye'll know that I am noble as the
> best!

Then follows the great narrative of *Lohengrin,* one of the most dramatic declamations in all opera.

COPY'T MISKIN

DALMORES AS LOHENGRIN

KRAUS AS LOHENGRIN

Lohengrin's Narrative—In fernem Land (In Distant Lands)

By Herman Jadlowker, Tenor   (*In German*)   76026   12-inch, $2.00
By Evan Williams, Tenor   (*In English*)   74130   12-inch, 1.50

LOHENGRIN:

In distant land, by ways remote
and hidden,
There stands a mount that men
call Monsalvat;
It holds a shrine, to the profane
forbidden:
More precious there is nought on
earth than that,
And thron'd in light it holds a
cup immortal,
That whoso sees from earthly
sin is cleans'd;
'Twas borne by angels thro' the
heav'nly portal—
Its coming hath a holy reign
commenc'd.
Once every year a dove from
Heav'n descendeth,
To strengthen it anew for
works of grace;
'Tis called the Grail, the pow'r
of Heav'n attendeth
The faithful knights who guard
that sacred place.
He whom the Grail to be its
servant chooses
Is armed henceforth by high in-
vincible might;
All evil craft its power before
him loses,
The spirits of darkness where
he dwells take flight.
Nor will he lose the awful charm
it blendeth,
Although he should be called to
distant lands,
When the high cause of virtue
he defendeth:
While he's unknown, its spell he
still commands.
By perils dread the holy Grail
is girded,

ELSA AND LOHENGRIN

No eye rash or profane its light may see;
Its champion knight from doubtings shall be warded,
If known to man, he must depart and flee.
Now mark, craft or disguise my soul disdaineth,
The Grail sent me to right yon lady's name;
My father, Percival, gloriously reigneth,
His knight am I, and Lohengrin my name!

After this amazing narrative, which causes a great
stir among the people, the swan appears to conduct
Lohengrin away.

LADIES AND MEN:
While I hear him the wondrous tale revealing,
The holy tears adown my cheek are stealing!
ELSA:
'Tis dark around me! Give me air!
Oh, help, help! oh, me, most wretched!
LADIES AND MEN (*in great excitement*):
The swan! the swan! the swan!
The stream he floateth down.
The swan! ah, he comes!
ELSA (*half-fainting*):
Oh, horror! ah, the swan!

MORENA AS ELSA

LOHENGRIN:
Too long I stay—I must obey the Grail!
My trusty swan! O that this summons ne'er
  had been!
Oh, that this day I ne'er had seen!
I thought the year would soon be o'er
When thy probation would have pass'd;
Then by the Grail's transcendent pow'r,

In thy true shape we'd meet at last!
Oh, Elsa, think what joys thy doubts have
  ended!
Couldst thou not trust in me for one short
  year?
Then thy dear brother, whom the Grail
  defended,
In life and honor thou had'st welcomed here!

Ortrud, in triumph, now reveals the fact that the swan is really *Elsa's* brother, whom she had transformed by magic. *Lohengrin* kneels in prayer, and as the dove of the Grail is seen descending, the swan sinks, and *Gottfried*, the young Duke, arises, restored to human form. *Lohengrin's* boat is drawn away by the dove as *Elsa* faints in her brother's arms.

DOUBLE-FACED AND MISCELLANEOUS LOHENGRIN RECORDS

Introduction to Act III (Bridal March)	By Herbert's Orchestra	55048	12-inch,	$1.50
Wedding March (Mendelssohn)	*By Herbert's Orchestra*			
Lohengrin Fantasie	By Rosario Bourdon, 'Cellist	35399	12-inch,	1.25
Souvenir (Drdla)	*By Maximilian Pilzer, Violinist*			
Selection, No. 1	By Sousa's Band	35114	12-inch,	1.25
Flower Song (Blumenlied)	*By Rosario Bourdon, 'Cellist*			
Selection, No. 2	By Pryor's Band	35147	12-inch,	1.25
Quintet from Act I—Elsa's Aria—Finale, Act I				
Meditation from Thais—Intermezzo Religieuse	*By Howard Rattay, Violinist*			
Prelude, Act III	By La Scala Orchestra	62693	10-inch,	.75
Walküre—Cavalcata	*By La Scala Orchestra*			
Coro delle nozze (Bridal Chorus)	By La Scala Chorus	16537	10-inch,	.75
Tannhauser—Pilgrims' Chorus	*By Pryor's Band*			

PHOTO GIGI BASSANI

THE ARRIVAL OF LOHENGRIN

I LOMBARDI   THE LOMBARDS
(Ee Lohm-bar-dih)

OPERA IN FOUR ACTS

Words by Solera. Music by Verdi. First produced at La Scala, Milan, February 11, 1843, a year after the production of Verdi's Nabucco. Produced in Berlin, September, 1843; London, at Her Majesty's Theatre, March 3, 1846; Paris, *Théâtre Italien*, January 10, 1863. First New York production March 3, 1847, by an Italian Opera Company, under the management of Signor Sanguinico Patti (father of Adelina Patti), and Signor Pogliani. In the spring of 1914 Lombardi was given in Florence by the Scolopian Fathers of San Giovannino. Each year it is their custom to celebrate the last three evenings of the carnival season with a musical performance in their little church in Via Martelli, and last year, as a tribute to Verdi, his story of the Lombards in the Crusades was chosen.

Characters

PAGANO, a bandit, brother to Arvino...............................Bass
ARVINO, a nobleman of Lombardy................................Tenor
PIRRO, an accomplice of Pagano.....................................Bass
ACCIANUS, King of Antioch...Tenor
ORONTES, son of Accianus...Tenor
VICLINDA, wife of Arvino...Soprano
GISELDA, her daughter...Soprano
SOPHIA, mother of Orontes......................................Contralto

---

Time and Place: Lombardy and Antioch, in the Holy Land, in the eleventh century.

Much of the music of Lombardi was afterward used by Verdi in his *Jerusalem*, brought out at the *Académie*, Paris, November 26, 1847, this being the last appearance of the famous tenor Duprez.

The action of the opera takes place at the time of the first crusade against the Saracens. Previous to the events of Act I, *Pagano* and *Arvino*, sons of *Folco* the Lombard, Prince of Rhodes, both fall in love with *Viclinda*, who prefers *Arvino* and marries him. *Pagano*, filled with jealousy, tries to take his brother's life, but is unsuccessful and flees his country, becoming a brigand.

The opera opens in the square in front of the Cathedral Church of St. Ambrose at Antioch. *Pagano* has returned, repentant and forgiven, but when he sees the happiness of his brother and the woman he still loves, the old feeling of revenge returns. With the assistance of *Pirro*, armor-bearer to *Arvino*, he again makes an attempt upon his brother's life, but by mistake stabs his father, *Folco*. In despair at his crime he flies to the deserts of Palestine, and becoming a hermit, repents and lives a holy life.

The scenes of the second act are laid in and about Antioch. *Giselda*, daughter of *Arvino*, grown to womanhood, has been taken prisoner by the Saracens, and during her captivity falls in love with *Orontes*, a Saracen prince, in whose harem she is a prisoner, and whose mother, *Sophia*, befriends her. *Arvino*, meanwhile, at the call of *Peter* the hermit—who is, unknown to him, his brother *Pagano*—has crossed the water with knights and warriors to the first crusade; he seeks the hermit to inquire about his daughter, who promises that he shall soon meet her. *Pirro*, his old accomplice, having also repented of his crime, has promised to open the gates of Antioch to the Christian soldiers.

The next scene is in the harem of *Orontes* in Antioch, where *Giselda* is prisoner. On the entrance of her father and *Peter* the hermit, she, believing them to have slain her lover, gives them but a cold welcome, which greatly incenses her father. *Orontes*, meanwhile, having escaped, dressed as a Lombard, persuades *Giselda* to fly with him, but being pursued, he is mortally wounded and dies in the hermitage of *Peter*, having first become a convert to Christianity.

The last act opens with *Giselda* having a vision of her lover in heaven. *Pagano*, or *Peter* the hermit, leads the Crusaders to the siege of Jerusalem, and, in protecting his brother, is mortally wounded. He then reveals his identity and dies embracing *Arvino*.

Qual volutta (With Sacred Joy)

By Frances Alda, Soprano; Enrico Caruso, Tenor and
Marcel Journet, Bass   (*In Italian*)   95211   12-inch $5.00

This great trio, one of the most famous of all the numbers from the older Italian operas, occurs in Act III, in the scene representing the Valley of Jehosophat, near Jerusalem. *Giselda,* a Christian maiden, who has been held a prisoner in Antioch, falls in love with a Saracen enemy, *Orontes,* and when Antioch is captured by the Christians, the lovers are forced to flee the wrath of *Giselda's* father, who is in command of the conquering army.

In the pursuit *Orontes* is wounded, but the lovers are protected by a hermit, who takes them to his cavern.   The trio begins at the moment when *Orontes* renounces his Saracen faith and becomes a Christian for *Giselda's* sake.

Caruso opens in his purest tones with *Orontes'* sympathetic melody—

and this is followed by duet passages between *Giselda* and the priest, and later between the tenor and soprano.   The terzetto grows more intense and moving as it proceeds, and the three voices, which combine in dramatic fashion, conclude the trio with a splendid triumphant note.

ROOM IN MILAN IN WHICH VERDI DIED

LOUISE

OPERA IN FOUR ACTS

Words and music by Gustave Charpentier. First presented at the *Opéra Comique,* Paris, February 2, 1900. First American production at the Manhattan Opera, 1908.

Characters

LOUISE . . . . Soprano
HER MOTHER . . . . Contralto
HER FATHER . . . . Baritone
JULIEN, an artist . . . . Tenor
Girls at the Dressmaking Establishment, Street Peddlers, People, etc.

Scene and Period : Paris ; the present time.

Charpentier's first opera, *Louise,* is a romance of bohemian Paris. The story tells of *Louise,* a beautiful young girl engaged in a dressmaking establishment. *Julien,* a romantic artist, falls in love with the maiden, and soon finds his love returned. The mother and father of *Louise* disapprove of the gay young artist, but *Julien* will not give up his sweetheart, and implores her to leave her hard work and go with him to a little home. *Louise* at first steadily refuses, knowing how her parents would grieve, but *Julien* persists, tempts her with visions of a bright future with him, and at last, unable to resist, the young girl consents. Here she falls in with a merry company of true Parisian bohemians, who crown her as the Queen of Revels. In the midst of a gay party her mother appears, begging the young girl to return to her father, who is ill. *Louise* is filled with remorse and returns to her home, trying all the while to forget the gay, happy life she has left at Montmartre. Her father reproaches her for her conduct, and *Louise,* remembering only the kindness and tenderness of *Julien,* rushes out into the night and hastens back to the protection of her lover.

The Victor offers three fine records of the lovely *Depuis le jour,* sung by *Louise* in the garden at Montmartre in Act III. The young girl tells *Julien* how happy she has been since they came to the cottage, comparing her life with him to the dreary one she had left.

Depuis le jour (Ever Since the Day)

By Nellie Melba, Soprano	(*In French*)	88477	12-inch,	$3.00
By Alma Gluck, Soprano	(*In French*)	74252	12-inch,	1.50
By Florence Hinkle, Soprano	(*In French*)	70085	12-inch,	1.25

(Italian)

LUCIA DI LAMMERMOOR
(Loo-chee'-ah dee Lah-mair-moor')

(English)

LUCY OF LAMMERMOOR

OPERA IN THREE ACTS

Text by Salvator Cammerano, derived from Scott's novel, "The Bride of Lammermoor." Music by Gaetano Donizetti. First production at Naples, September 26, 1835. Performed in London, at Her Majesty's, April 5, 1838; Paris, 1839; New Orleans, December 28, 1841; New York, in English, at the Park Theatre, November 17, 1845; and in Italian, November 14, 1849. Notable revivals occurred April 7, 1890, at the Metropolitan, with Patti; April 26, 1894, at the Metropolitan, with Melba; November 20, 1900, American Theatre, w th Yvonne de Treville.

PATTI AS LUCIA IN 1860

Characters

HENRY ASHTON, of Lammermoor........Baritone
LUCY, his sister ....Soprano
SIR EDGAR, of Ravenswood ....Tenor
LORD ARTHUR BUCKLAW ....Tenor
RAYMOND, chaplain to Lord Ashton ....Tenor
ALICE, companion to Lucy ....Mezzo-Soprano
NORMAN, Captain of the Guard at Ravenswood..Tenor

Ladies and Knights related to the Ashtons; Pages, Soldiery, and Domestics in the Ashton family.

Scene and Period: The action takes place in Scotland, close of the sixteenth century.

The prolific Donizetti (1797-1848) wrote no fewer than sixty-three operas, the most popular of these being, of course, Lucia di Lammermoor. It has long been the custom with a certain class of critics to run down the old Italian school of opera represented by Lucia, and talk about the artificiality of the music, thinness of the orchestration, etc. But the public in general pays very little attention to these opinions, because they love the music of Lucia, as their grandfathers did, and realize that throughout the whole work there runs a current of tenderness and passion, expressed in simple melody that will ever appeal to the heart.

Let us now forget the critics and tell the simple and sorrowful story, and listen to the melodious airs which have given pleasure to many millions in the eighty years since its production.

The plot of Lucia is founded on Sir Walter Scott's novel, "The Bride of Lammermoor." *Lord Henry Ashton, Lucy's* brother, knowing nothing of her attachment to his enemy, *Edgar of Ravenswood,* has arranged a marriage between *Lucy* and the wealthy *Lord Arthur,* in order to retrieve his fallen fortunes. Learning that *Lucy* is in love with *Edgar,* he intercepts her lover's letters and executes a forged paper, which convinces *Lucy* that *Edgar* is false to her. Convinced of her lover's perfidy, and urged by the necessities of her brother, she unwillingly consents to wed *Sir Arthur.*

The guests are assembled for the ceremony, and *Lucy* has just signed the contract, when *Edgar* appears and denounces *Lucy* for her fickleness. *Edgar* is driven from the castle, and the shock being too much for the gentle mind of *Lucy,* she becomes insane, kills her husband and dies. *Edgar,* overcome by these tragic happenings, visits the churchyard of Ravenswood and stabs himself among the tombs of his ancestors.

PHOTO ERMINI

CONSTANTINO AS EDGAR

ACT I

SCENE I—*A Forest near Lammermoor*

The curtain rises, disclosing *Norman,* and followers of *Sir Henry. Norman* tells the retainers to watch carefully and ascertain who is secretly meeting *Lucy.* In the opening chorus they promise to watch with diligence.

Opening Chorus, Act I

La Scala Chorus (*Italian*) *62106 10-inch, $0.75

Sir Henry enters and talks with *Norman* of his suspicion that *Lucy* has formed an attachment for some unknown knight. *Norman* suggests that it may be *Edgar. Henry* is furious and declares he will have a deadly vengeance.

SCENE II—*A Park near the Castle*

Lucy enters, accompanied by her faithful attendant, *Alice.* She has come from the castle to meet her lover, *Edgar;* and while waiting for him, tells *Alice* of the legend of the fountain, which relates how a Ravenswood lover once slew a maiden on this spot.

Regnava nel silenzio (Silence O'er All)

By Tetrazzini (*In Italian*) 88303 12-inch, $3.00
By Giuseppina Huguet, Soprano
(*In Italian*) *16539 10-inch, .75

Lucy shudderingly relates how she once saw the spectre of the murdered girl, and fears it is an omen of the future.

LUCIA:

Silence o'er all was reigning,	Threat'ning it did uprear,
Dark was the night and low'ring,	Stood for a moment immovable,
And o'er yon fountain her pallid ray	Then vanish'd from my view!
Yon pale moon was pouring,	(*Despondently.*)
Faintly a sharp but stifled sigh	Oh, what horrid omen is this?
Fell on my startled ear,	I ought to banish from my heart this love,
And straightway upon the fountain's brink,	But I cannot; it is my life,
The spectre did appear!	And comfort to my suff'ring soul!
But slow on high its skeleton hand,	

This graceful number is given by Mme. Tetrazzini with rare charm and pathos; the concluding ornamental passages being sung with especial delicacy. The black label rendition by Mme. Huguet is also a very attractive one.

This is followed by the second part,—the beautiful

Quando rapita in estasi (Swift as Thought)

Graziella Pareto
(*In Italian*) 76009 12-inch, $2.00
Giuseppina Huguet *63172 10-inch, .75

an animated melody admirably given here by Mme. Huguet and Mme. Pareto.

Edgar appears and tells *Lucy* that he has been summoned to France, and proposes that he seek out *Henry* and endeavor to end the mortal feud which exists between the families. *Lucy,* knowing her brother only too well, entreats him to keep their love secret or they will be forever parted. *Edgar,* roused to fury by this evidence of *Henry's* mortal hate, renews his vow of vengeance, beginning a dramatic duet.

MATZENE, CHICAGO

SAMMARCO AS SIR HENRY

* *Double-Faced Record—See page 261.*

The Bride of Lammermoor

Sulla tomba che rinserra (By My Father's Tomb)

By Emma Trentini, Soprano, and Gino Martinez-Patti, Tenor

(*In Italian*) *16574 10-inch, $0.75

EDGAR:
By the lone tomb, o'er the cold grave
Where my father's bones lie moulding,
With thy kindred eternal warfare
To the death I swore to wage!
Ah! when I saw thee my heart relented:
Of my dark vow I half repented,
But my oath remains unbroken,
Still I've power to redeem my gage!

LUCY:
Ah! pray calm thee, ah, restrain thee;
Think what misery will soon enthral me;
I can scarce from fear sustain me;
Would'st thou have me die from terror?
Yield thee, yield thee to the dictates of affection,
'Tis a nobler, purer passion,
Let that thought thy rage assuage!

Edgar now says that he must go, and in a tender duet, which closes the act, the lovers bid each other farewell.

Verranno a te sull' aura (Borne on the Sighing Breeze)

By Alice Nielsen, Soprano, and Florencio Constantino, Tenor

(*In Italian*) 74064 12-inch, $1.50

By Emma Trentini, Soprano, and Martinez-Patti, Tenor

(*In Italian*) *62106 10-inch, .75

EDGAR:
My sighs shall on the balmy breeze
That hither wafts thee, be borne, love;
Each murm'ring wave shall echo make.
How I thy absence do mourn, love!
Ah! think of me when far away,
With nought my heart to cheer;
I shall bedew each thought of thee
With many a bitter tear!

LUCY:
The balmy breeze that bears thy sigh,
Will waft one back from me, love;
The murm'ring waves re-echoing still
I'm ever constant to thee, love!
Ah! think of me when far away,
With nought my heart to cheer;
I shall bedew each thought of thee
With many a bitter tear!
Ah! thou wilt not fail to write me,
Many a lonely hour 'twill cheer;

EDGAR:
Fear not! Have no fear, thou shalt hear!

BOTH:
My sighs shall on the balmy breeze
That hither wafts thee be borne, love; etc.

COPY'T FOLEY

MCCORMACK AS EDGAR

Edgar tears himself from her arms and departs, leaving the half-fainting *Lucy* to be consoled by her faithful *Alice*.

ACT II

SCENE I—*An Ante-room in the Castle*

Sir Henry and his retainer *Norman* are discussing the approaching marriage of *Lucy* to *Arthur*. The events which have occurred since Act I are indicated by this extract from the text:

HENRY:
Should Lucy still persist
In opposing me—

NORMAN:
Have no fear! The long absence
Of him she mourneth, the letters
We've intercepted, and the false news thou'lt tell her,
Will quench all hope that yet may linger.
Believing Edgar faithless, from her bosom
love will vanish!

HENRY:
See, she approaches! Thou hast that forged letter,
Give it me. Now haste thee to the northern entrance,
There keep watch and await
The approach of Arthur, and with all speed, on his arrival
Conduct him hither!

(*Exit Norman.*)

Lucy enters, pale and listless, and to her brother's greeting:

HENRY:
Draw nearer, my Lucy.
On this fair day accept a brother's greeting!
May this glad day, sacred to Love and Hymen,

Auspicious prove to thee. Thou hear'st me?
Thou'rt silent!

she answers with a last appeal to him to release her from this hated marriage.

* *Double-Faced Record—See page 261.*

Il pallor funesto (If My Cheek is Pale)

By Linda Brambilla and Francesco Cigada   (*In Italian*)   *16574   10-inch, $0.75

LUCY:
See these cheeks so pale and haggard,
See these features so worn with sadness!
Do not they betray too plainly
All my anguish, all my despair?
Pardon may'st thou from Heaven
Not vainly ask for this thy inhuman constraint.
HENRY:
Cease this wild recrimination,
Of the past be thou but silent!
Flown has my anger! Banish thy dejection!
Buried be all that thine honor could taint.
A noble husband, thou wilt have.

LUCY:
Cease to urge me!
To another true faith have I sworn!
HENRY:
'Tis well!
By this letter thou may'st see
How he keeps his faith with thee!
Read it.
(*Hands her a letter.*)
LUCY:
How beats my flutt'ring heart!
(*Reads*):
Ah! great Heaven!

Henry, in desperation, now tells her that unless she consents to wed *Arthur* he will be disgraced and ruined.   This begins another duet, the *Se tradirme*.

Se tradirmi, tu potrai (I'm Thy Guardian)

By Huguet, Soprano ; Cigada, Baritone   (*In Italian*)   *62089   10-inch, $0.75

HENRY:
I'm thy guardian, dar'st thou brave me?
I'm thy brother—wilt thou save me?
From the hands of thee, my sister,
Must I meet a traitor's doom?
See the axe, by one thread hanging;
Hark! the deep toned deathbell clanging.
Hath affection lost all power?
Wilt consign me unto the tomb?

LUCY:
I'm thy sister, dost thou love me!
I am dying, will that move thee!
From the hands of thee, my brother,
Must I meet now this dreadful doom!
Hopeless misery all surrounding,
E'en while the marriage bell is sounding:
Fear and hate will be my dower;
Better had I wed the tomb!

However, convinced of *Edgar's* falseness, she half consents to the sacrifice, and retires to prepare for the ceremony.

SCENE II—*The Great Hall of the Castle*

The knights and ladies sing a chorus of congratulation to the bride and bridegroom, while *Sir Henry* greets the guests and asks them to pardon *Lucy's* agitated bearing, as she is still mourning for her mother.

Lucy enters and is escorted to the table where the notary is preparing the marriage papers. Believing her lover false, she cares little what becomes of her, and passively signs the contract. Pale as death and almost fainting, she is being supported by her faithful maid and her family adviser, *Raymond*, when suddenly a terrible silence ensues, as *Edgar*, the lover of *Lucy* and the deadly enemy of her brother, appears at the back of the room dressed in a sombre suit of black. The wedding guests are dumb with amazement at the daring of the young noble in thus presenting himself unbidden at the house of his enemy. The great sextette, the most dramatic and thrilling number in the entire range of opera, now begins.

Unlike many operatic ensembles, this sextette is not merely a most remarkable bit of concerted writing, but is so well fitted to the scene in which it occurs that even the enemies of Donizetti, who call Lucia merely a string of melodies, are compelled to admit its extreme beauty and powerful dramatic qualities.

Sextette—Chi mi frena (What Restrains Me)

By Marcella Sembrich, Enrico Caruso, Antonio Scotti, Marcel Journet,
    Mme. Severina and Francesco Daddi   (*In Italian*)   96200   12-inch, $7.00
By Tetrazzini, Caruso, Amato, Journet, Jacoby and Bada
                        (*In Italian*)   96201   12-inch,   7.00
By Victor Opera Sextette   (*In Italian*)   70036   12-inch,   1.25
By Vessella's Italian Band   *35356   12-inch,   1.25
By Pryor's Band   31460   12-inch,   1.00
Transcription by Ferdinand Himmelreich   (*Pianoforte*) *35223   12-inch,   1.25

Edgar remains standing, with his eyes steadily fixed on the unhappy *Lucy*, who is unable to meet his glance. This dramatic silence is broken by the commencement of the sextette, as *Edgar* and *Sir Henry*, with suppressed emotion, sing their short duet:

* *Double-Faced Record—See page 261.*

HENRY AND EDGAR:
    Instant vengeance, what restraineth,
    What thus stays my sword in scabbard?
EDGAR:
    Yet, ungrateful one, I love thee still!
HENRY:
    And remorse my breast doth fill!
LUCY (despairingly):
    I had hop'd that death had found me,

And in his drear fetters bound me,
But he comes not to relieve me!
Ah! of life will none bereave me?
RAYMOND AND ALICE:
    Ah! like a rose that withers on the stem,
    She now is hovering 'twixt death and life!
ARTHUR:
    Hence, thou traitor, hence betake thee,
    Ere our rage shall o'erwhelm thee!

One by one the characters in the scene take up their portions of the sextette until the great climax, one of the most dramatic moments in opera, is reached.

Henry and Edgar, who have drawn their swords, are separated by Raymond, who commands them in Heaven's name to sheath their weapons. Henry asks Edgar why he has come, and exhibits the signed contract, but Edgar refuses to believe the evidence of his eyes and asks Lucy if she had signed it. With her eyes fixed on him she tremblingly nods her head in assent. Edgar, in a furious rage, tears the contract in pieces, flings it at the fainting maiden, and rushes from the castle as the curtain falls.

ACT III

SCENE I—The Tower of Ravenswood Castle

Edgar is brooding on his misfortunes when a horseman rides up, dismounts and enters the tower. It proves to be Sir Henry, who has come to challenge Edgar to a duel to the death. They agree to fight the following morning, and in this duet ask the night to hasten away, that their vengeance may be consummated.

O sole più rapido (Haste, Crimson Morning)

By Giuseppe Acerbi and Renzo Minolfi   (In Italian)   *62644   10-inch, $0.75

SCENE II—Hall in Lammermoor Castle

The peasants and domestics of the castle are making merry at their feast in honor of the marriage when Raymond enters, greatly agitated, bearing the fearful news that Lucy has become insane and has killed her husband.

RAYMOND ANNOUNCING THE TRAGEDY—ACT III

* Double-Faced Record—See page 261.

O qual funesto avvenimento (Oh! Dire Misfortune)
By Aristodemo Sillich, Bass, and Chorus (*Double-Faced—see page 261*)
(*In Italian*) *62644 10-inch, $0.75

Raymond's tidings have scarcely been spoken when Lucy enters, pale and lovely, and all unconscious of the horrified servants, begins her famous so-called Mad Scene.

Mad Scene (With Flute Obbligato)

By Luisa Tetrazzini, Soprano	(*In Italian*)	88299	12-inch, $3.00
By Marcella Sembrich, Soprano	(*In Italian*)	88021	12-inch, 3.00
By Nellie Melba, Soprano	(*In Italian*)	88071	12-inch, 3.00
By Maria Galvany, Soprano	(*In Italian*)	88221	12-inch, 3.00
By Graziella Pareto, Soprano	(*In Italian*)	76006	12-inch, 2.00
By Olive Kline (*Double-Faced—see page 261*)	(*In Italian*)	55047	12-inch, 1.50

By Edith Helena, Soprano (*Double-Faced—see page 261*)
(*In English*) 35214 12-inch, 1.25
By Marie Michailowa, Soprano (*In Russian*) 61129 10-inch, 1.00

Forgetting her marriage, the demented maiden speaks one moment of the happy day when she will be Edgar's wife, and next is terrified by a vague feeling that something has come between them.

This famous number must be judged solely as a brilliant piece of vocalism; it can hardly be considered dramatically, because when the prima donna loses her reason in this style of opera, it only means that the scales become more rapid and the roulades more difficult! The unfortunate Lucy in her agony seems inclined and able to sing the most difficult and florid music conceivable, and venture without hesitation on passages at which a sane person would stand aghast! In short, Donizetti forgot his dramatic mission temporarily in his efforts to write a show piece of musical execution.

LUCY:
I hear the breathing of his tender voice,
That voice beloved sounds in my heart forever.
My Edgar, why were we parted?
Let me not mourn thee;
See, for thy sake, I've all forsaken!
What shudder do I feel thro' my veins?
My heart is trembling, my senses fail!
(*She forgets her trouble and smiles.*)
Come to the fountain;
There let us rest together,
Ah me! see where yon spectre arises,
Standing between us! Alas! Dear Edgar!

See yon phantom rise to part us!
(*Her mood again changes.*)
Yet shall we meet, dear Edgar, before the altar.
Hark to those strains celestial!
Ah! 'Tis the hymn for our nuptials!
For us they are singing!
The altar for us is deck'd thus,
Oh, joy unbounded!
'Round us the brilliant tapers are shining,
The priest awaits us.
Oh! day of gladness!
Thine am I ever, thou mine forever!
(*She falls fainting into the arms of Raymond.*)

TETRAZZINI AS THE
DEMENTED LUCY

Donizetti's scene seems especially set apart for the display of such a coloratura as Melba possesses, and she sings this florid music with such brilliancy and graceful fluency that the listener is dazzled.

The rôle of the unhappy Lucy is also admirably fitted to Tetrazzini's peculiar talents, and as the heroine of Donizetti's lovely opera she has made quite the greatest success of her career. When she reaches this florid and difficult Mad Scene, the listeners are absolutely electrified, and such a torrent of enthusiasm bursts forth that the diva is usually compelled to repeat a portion of the aria.

Mme. Sembrich's rendition proves that the compass of her voice is all but phenomenal, and she sings the difficult music with delightful flexibility.

Other renditions of this well-known scene are given by Mme. Galvany and Mme. Pareto, the famous Italian prima donnas, and by Michailowa, the famous Russian singer. Although none of these artists has yet visited America, their beautiful voices are heard in thousands of homes in which the Victor is a welcome entertainer. The Blue Label and Black Label classes are also adequately represented in the records by Miss Kline and Miss Helena.

The unhappy Lucy, after having in this scene again enacted the terrible events of the previous day, falls insensible and is carried to her room by Alice and Raymond.

SCENE II—*The Tombs of the Ravenswoods*

Edgar, weary of life, has come to the rendezvous arranged with *Henry*, intending to throw himself on his enemy's sword, the last of a doomed race. But he waits in vain, for *Henry*, filled with remorse at the consequences of his schemes, has left England, never to return. *Edgar* sings the first of the two beautiful airs written by Donizetti for this scene.

Fra poco a me ricovero (Farewell to Earth)

By John McCormack, Tenor (*In Italian*) 74223 12-inch $1.50

His attention is now attracted by a train of mourners coming from the castle, accompanied by *Raymond*, who reveals to the unhappy man that *Lucy* is dying, and even while they converse the castle bell is heard tolling, a signal that the unhappy maiden is no more.

The grief-stricken lover then depicts his emotion in the second air, a lovely number with sadness in every tone.

Tu che a Dio spiegasti l'ali (Thou Hast Spread Thy Wings to Heaven) (O bell' alma innamorata)

By John McCormack, Tenor (*In Italian*) 74224 12-inch, $1.50
By Florencio Constantino, Tenor (*In Italian*) 74066 12-inch, 1.50
By Gino Martinez-Patti (*Double-Faced—see below*) (*Italian*) 62089 10-inch, .75

The dramatic interest deepens as the air proceeds, until the finale, when *Edgar*, in an excess of penitence, prays that not even the spirit of the wronged *Lucy* may approach so accursed a tomb as that of Ravenswood.

EDGAR:
Tho' from earth thou'st flown before me,   I'll follow thee above.
My ador'd, my only treasure;   Tho' the world frown'd on our union,
Tho' from these fond arms they tore thee,   Tho' in this life they did part us,
Soon, soon, I'll follow thee,   Yet on high, in fond communion,
   Shall our hearts be turned to love!

Breaking from *Raymond*, who endeavors to prevent the fatal act, *Edgar* stabs himself, and supported in the good man's arms, he repeats in broken phrases the lovely *O bell' alma innamorata*, and lifting his hands to Heaven, as if to greet the spirit of *Lucy*, he expires.

DOUBLE-FACED AND MISCELLANEOUS LUCIA RECORDS

{ Mad Scene By Olive Kline, Soprano (*In Italian*)
{ Dinorah—Shadow Song By Olive Kline, Soprano (*In Italian*) } 55047 12-inch, $1.50

{ Mad Scene By Edith Helena, Soprano (*In English*)
{ Trovatore—Peaceful Was the Night By Edith Helena (*In English*) } 35214 12-inch, 1.25

{ Sextette (Transcription) Pianoforte By Himmelreich
{ Caprice Español (Moszkowski) Pianoforte By Charles G. Spross } 35223 12-inch, 1.25

{ Sextette Vessella's Italian Band
{ Jewels of the Madonna—Intermezzo Vessella's Band } 35356 12-inch, 1.25

{ Regnava nel silenzio Giuseppina Huguet, Soprano (*Italian*)
{ Norma—Casta Diva By Giuseppina Huguet, Soprano (*In Italian*) } 16539 10-inch, .75

{ Il pallor funesto (If My Cheek is Pale)
{   By Linda Brambilla and Francesco Cigada (*In Italian*)
{ Sulla tomba che rinserra (By My Father's Tomb)
{   By Emma Trentini and Martinez-Patti (*In Italian*) } 16574 10-inch, .75

{ Se tradirmi tu potrai (I'm Thy Guardian)
{   By Giuseppina Huguet, and Francesco Cigada, (*In Italian*)
{ Tu che a Dio spiegasti l'ali (Thou Hast Spread Thy Wings)
{   (O bell' alma innamorata) By Martinez-Patti (*In Italian*) } 62089 10-inch, .75

{ O qual funesto avvenimento Sillich and Chorus (*In Italian*)
{ O sole più rapido By Acerbi and Minolfi (*In Italian*) } 62644 10-inch, .75

{ Opening Chorus By La Scala Chorus (*In Italian*)
{ Verranno a te sull' aura (Borne on Sighing Breeze)
{   By Trentini and Martinez-Patti (*In Italian*) } 62106 10-inch, .75

{ Quando rapita in estasi (Swift as Thought)
{   By Giuseppina Huguet, Soprano (*In Italian*)
{ Lucrezia Borgia—Rischiarata è la finestra—La Scala Cho (*Italian*) } 63172 10-inch, .75

LUCREZIA AND THE SLEEPING GENNARO——ACT I

(Italian)

LUCREZIA BORGIA

(Loo-krez'-yah Bor'jah)

OPERA IN THREE ACTS

Text by Felice Romani, taken from a work of the same name by Victor Hugo. Music by Gaetano Donizetti. First presented to the public at La Scala, Milan, in 1834; given at the *Théâtre Italien,* Paris, October 27, 1840. First London production, June 6, 1839; in English, December 30, 1843. Produced in New Orleans, April 27, 1844. Produced in New York at the Astor Place Opera House, 1847, and September 5, 1854, with Maria Grisi; in 1876, with Tiefjens and Brignoli, and not again until Colonel Mapleson gave a production at the Academy of Music, October 30, 1882. In February, 1892, it was announced at the Metropolitan with Lehmann, Kalisch and de Reszke, but abandoned owing to the illness of Mme. Lehmann. The next production did not occur until 1902, with Caruso, de Macchi, and Scotti.

Characters

LUCREZIA BORGIA . . . . Soprano
MAFFIO ORSINI *(Maf'-fee-oh Or-see'-nee)* . . . . Contralto
GENNARO, *(Jen-nah'-roh)* ⎱ ⎰ Tenor
LIVEROTTO, ⎱ Tenor
VITELLOZZO, ⎰ Young noblemen in the service of the Venetian Tenor
PETRUCCI, ⎱ Republic Bass
GAZELLA, ⎰ Bass
IL DUCA ALFONSO . . . . Baritone

Scene and Period: Italy; the beginning of the sixteenth century.

262

THE PLOT

The plot of Donizetti's opera cannot be called a cheerful one—it is, in fact, crowded with horrors. However, it was a great favorite with American audiences for many years, being one of the stock operas of Emma Abott during nearly her whole career. The opera was revived in 1904 for Caruso, but failed to score, and it is quite likely that those who admire its few fine airs must depend on their Victors if they wish to hear them.

COPY'T DUPONT

DE MOSCHI AS LUCREZIA

Lucrezia, the heroine, was a conspicuous member of the notorious patrician family—the *Borgias*—celebrated for their diabolical success as poisoners.

Lucrezia Borgia married as her second husband *Don Alfonso, Duke of Ferrara*. By her former marriage she had a son named *Gennaro*, of whose existence the *Duke* is ignorant. This son had, at birth, been placed in the care of a fisherman who brought him up as his own child.

ACT I

At the opening of the story *Lucrezia*, who in spite of her criminal practices has still the mother's yearning towards her own child, goes in disguise to Venice to visit him.

She finds her son in the company of some gay Venetian gallants. She watches them, and presently *Gennaro*, wearied by the mirth of his companions, draws apart and falls asleep on a seat. *Lucrezia* draws near, and gazing on his youthful beauty, she forgets everything except that she is his mother. She gently presses a kiss on his brow and prepares to depart, when he awakes and asks who she is. She evades the question, and leads him to talk about his mother, whom he says he has never seen. Feeling drawn toward the beautiful stranger, he tells his story, in the fine *Di pescatore*.

Di pescatore ignobile (In a Fisher's Lowly Cot)
By Francesco Marconi, Tenor   (*In Italian*)   76004   12-inch, $2.00

She bids him farewell, and is about to take her leave when *Orsini* appears, recognizes her, and after brutally reciting her crimes one by one, tells the horror-stricken *Gennaro* that it is the *Borgia*. All turn from her in horror, and *Lucrezia* falls fainting.

ACT II

Gennaro afterwards shows his hatred and contempt for the *Borgias* by tearing down *Lucrezia's* coat of arms from her palace gates, and is imprisoned by the *Duke's* orders. *Lucrezia*, ignorant of the identity of the individual who has insulted her, complains to the *Duke*, who promises that the perpetrator shall be immediately punished. He gives vent to his feelings in his air, *Vieni la mia vendetta*.

Vieni, la mia vendetta (Haste Thee, for Vengeance)
By Giulio Rossi, Bass   (*In Italian*)   *63404   10-inch, $0.75

Gennaro is sent for and *Lucrezia* at once recognizes him. Full of horror, she turns to the *Duke* and begs him to overlook the offense. The *Duke* is relentless and compels *Lucrezia* herself to hand a poisoned cup to her son. She obeys, but afterward contrives to give the youth an antidote. He suspects her of treachery, but she pleads so tearfully with him that he trusts her and drinks the remedy.

ACT III

This act opens with a chorus of bravos, who have been set to watch the dwelling of *Gennaro*.

Rischiarata è la finestra (Yonder Light is the Guiding Beacon)
By La Scala Chorus   (*In Italian*)   *63172   10-inch, $0.75

Gennaro, whose life has been saved by the antidote *Lucrezia* had given him, instead of escaping from the city as she had advised him, accompanies *Orsini* to a banquet which has been secretly arranged by *Lucrezia*, and to which have been invited the young men who had recognized and denounced her in Venice.

In this scene occurs the famous *Brindisi*, or drinking song.

Double-Faced Record—See page 264.

Brindisi (It is Better to Laugh)

By Ernestine Schumann-Heink, Contralto   (*In German*)   88188   12-inch, $3.00
By Sophie Braslau, Contralto   (*In Italian*)   64468   10-inch,   1.00

This air is a very well known one, and has been frequently sung, but Mme. Schumann-Heink puts such brilliant spirit into it, and sings it with such wealth of gayety, such astonishing range and such agility, that the rendition amazes the listener. It is certain that no music-lover of the present generation has ever heard it sung so brilliantly. The high notes are taken with the ease of a soprano, and altogether this familiar drinking song has never been so well delivered.

The rôle of *Maffio Orsini* was always one of Mme. Schumann-Heink's favorites, and she makes a gallant figure as the gay Roman youth. This gay and fascinating air is also brilliantly sung by Miss Braslau, the high notes being taken with ease, beauty of tone and fine execution.

The words are well suited to the gayety of the music, and have been translated as follows:

Brindisi

It is better to laugh than be sighing.
When we think how life's moments are flying;
For each sorrow Fate ever is bringing,
There's a pleasure in store for us springing.
Tho' our joys, like to waves in the sunshine,
  Gleam awhile, then are lost to the sight,
Yet, for each sparkling ray
That so passes away,
Comes another as brilliant and light.

In the world we some beings discover,
Far too frigid for friend or for lover;
Souls unblest, and forever repining,
Tho' good fortune around them be shining.
It were well, if such hearts we could banish
  To some planet far distant from ours;
They're the dark spots we trace,
On this earth's favored space;
They are weeds that choke up the fair flow'rs!

Then 'tis better to laugh than be sighing;
They are wise who resolve to be gay;
When we think how life's moments are flying,
Enjoy Pleasure's gifts while we may!

In the midst of the feast the door opens, the *Borgia* appears and tells them that they are doomed, as the wine has been poisoned by her.

<small>PHOTO BERT</small>

LUCREZIA DISCOVERS SHE HAS POISONED HER SON

To her horror she sees *Gennaro* among the guests. He, too, has drunk of the fatal wine. She again offers him an antidote, which he refuses, because the amount is insufficient to save the lives of his friends. *Lucrezia* confesses the relationship between them, but *Gennaro* spurns her and dies. The *Duke* now appears, intending to share in *Lucrezia's* hideous triumph, but finds his wife surrounded by her victims—some dead, others dying. *Lucrezia*, a witness to the horrible result of her crime, suffers the keenest remorse, drinks some of her own poison and herself expires.

DOUBLE-FACED LUCREZIA BORGIA RECORDS

Vieni, la mia vendetta   By Giulio Rossi, Bass   (*In Italian*)
   Gli Ugonotti—Duetto Valentina Marcello   } 63404   10-inch, $0.75
         By Maria Grisi, Soprano, and Perello De Segurola, Bass

Rischiarata è la finestra (Yonder Light is the Guiding
   Beacon)   By La Scala Chorus   (*In Italian*)
   Lucia di Lammermoor—Quando rapita in estasi   } 63172   10-inch,   .75
         By Giuseppina Huguet, Soprano

THE MARRIAGE SCENE—ACT I

(Italian)

MADAMA BUTTERFLY
(Mah-dah'-mah)

(English)

MADAME BUTTERFLY

OPERA IN TWO ACTS

A Japanese lyric tragedy, founded on the book of John Luther Long and the drama by David Belasco, with Italian libretto by Illica and Giacosa. Music by Giacomo Puccini. First produced at La Scala, Milan, in 1904, it proved a failure. Revived the following year in slightly changed form with much success. First American presentation (in English) occurred in October, 1906, in Washington, D. C., by Savage Opera Company. Produced in English at the New Orleans Opera, January 9, 1907, and in French January 6, 1912. First representation in Italian at Metropolitan Opera House, February 11, 1907, with Farrar, Caruso, Homer and Scotti.

Characters

MADAME BUTTERFLY (Cho-Cho-San) ....Soprano
SUZUKI, *(Soo-zu'-key)* Cho-Cho-San's servant....................Mezzo-Soprano
B. F. PINKERTON, Lieutenant in the United States Navy...............Tenor
KATE PINKERTON, his American wife....................Mezzo-Soprano
SHARPLESS, United States Consul at Nagasaki......................Baritone
GORO, a marriage broker..Tenor
PRINCE YAMADORI, suitor for Cho-Cho-San.......................Baritone
THE BONZE, Cho-Cho-San's uncle...........................Bass
CHO-CHO-SAN'S MOTHER...............................Mezzo-Soprano
THE AUNT..Mezzo-Soprano
THE COUSIN..Soprano
TROUBLE, Cho-Cho-San's child

Cho-Cho-San's relations and friends—Servants.

At Nagasaki, Japan—Time, the present.

HOMER

FARRAR

The Story

Puccini's opera, which from the first aroused the keenest interest among opera-goers, has become an enduring success. The original Metropolitan production in Italian was under the personal direction of Puccini himself, who refined and beautified it according to his own ideas into one of the most finished operatic productions ever seen here.

The story of the drama is familiar to all through John Luther Long's narrative and the Belasco dramatic version. The tale is the old one of the passing fancy of a man for a woman, and her faithfulness even unto death, which comes by her own hand when she finds herself abandoned.

Puccini has completely identified his music with the sentiments and sorrows of the characters in John Luther Long's drama, and has accompanied the pictorial beauty of the various scenes with a setting of incomparable loveliness. Rarely has picturesque action been more completely wedded to beautiful music.

ACT I

SCENE—*Exterior of Pinkerton's house at Nagasaki*

At the rise of the curtain *Goro,* the marriage broker who has secured *Pinkerton* his bride, is showing the Lieutenant over the house he has chosen for his honeymoon. *Sharpless,* the American Consul and friend of *Pinkerton,* now arrives, having been bidden to the marriage. Then occurs the fine duet, which Caruso and Scotti have sung here in splendid style.

Amore o grillo (Love or Fancy ?)

By Enrico Caruso, Tenor, and Antonio Scotti, Baritone

(In Italian) 89043 12-inch, $4.00

COPY'T MISHKIN

MARTIN AS PINKERTON

Pinkerton, joyous in the prospect of his marriage with the dainty Japanese girl, and quite careless of the consequences which may result from such a union, describes his bride to the Consul, who gives the young lieutenant some good advice, bidding him be careful, that he may not break the trusting heart of the *Butterfly* who loves him too well.

The number closes with a splendid climax, as *Pinkerton* recklessly pledges the "real American wife" whom he hopes to meet some day; while the Consul gazes at his young friend with some sadness, as if already in the shadow of the tragedy which is to come.

Now is heard in the distance the voice of *Butterfly,* who is coming up the hill with her girl friends; and she sings a lovely song, full of the freshness of youth and the dawning of love.

Entrance of Cio-Cio San

By Geraldine Farrar, Soprano
(In Italian) 87004 10-inch, $2.00
By Frances Alda, Soprano
(In Italian) 64334 10-inch, 1.00
By Edith Helena, Soprano
(In English) *17346 10-inch, .75

The friends and family having been duly introduced to *Pinkerton,* they go to the refreshment table, while *Butterfly* timidly confides to *Pinkerton,* in this touching number, that she has for his sake renounced her religion, and will in future bow before the God of her husband.

Ieri son salita (Hear Me)

By Geraldine Farrar, Soprano   (*In Italian*) 87031 10-inch, $2.00

The contract is signed and the guests are dispersing when *Butterfly's* uncle rushes in and denounces her, having discovered that she has been to the Mission, renounced her religion, and adopted that of her husband.

Double-Faced Record—See page 271.

She is cast off by the family, who flee from the scene in horror. *Butterfly* at first weeps, but is comforted by the Lieutenant, who tells her he cares nothing for her family, but loves her alone.

Then occurs the incomparably beautiful duet which closes the first act, and which is beyond all question the finest of the melodious numbers which Puccini has composed for the opera; and the effect of this exquisite music, given on a darkened stage amid the flashing of fireflies, is wholly beautiful.

O quanti occhi fisi (Oh Kindly Heavens)

By Geraldine Farrar
and Enrico Caruso
(*In Italian*) 89017   12-in., $4.00
By Olive Kline and
Paul Althouse
(*In Italian*) *55058   12-in.,   1.50

Miss Farrar sings all of Puccini's music fluently and gracefully, but is always at her best in this exquisite love duet, while the number is Caruso's finest opportunity in the opera, and he makes the most of it. The blending of the voices of the artists is remarkably effective, and the ecstatic climax at the end is splendidly given, both singers ending on a high C sharp.

BUTTERFLY'S UNCLE DENOUNCING HER—ACT I

An excellent record in the Blue Label class, by Miss Kline and Mr. Althouse, is also presented to lovers of this opera.

ACT II

SCENE—Interior of Butterfly's Home—at the back a Garden with Cherries in Bloom

Three years have now elapsed, and *Butterfly,* with her child and faithful maid, *Suzuki,* are awaiting the return of *Pinkerton.* *Suzuki* begins to lose courage, but *Butterfly* rebukes her and declares her faith to be unshaken.

Un bel di vedremo (Some Day He'll Come)

By Geraldine Farrar, Soprano	(*In Italian*)	88113	12-inch,	$3.00
By Emmy Destinn, Soprano	(*In Italian*)	88468	12-inch,	3.00
By Frances Alda, Soprano	(*In Italian*)	74335	12-inch,	1.50
By Agnes Kimball, Soprano	(*In English*)	70054	12-inch,	1.25
By Mlle. Heilbronner, Soprano	(*In French*)	*35409	12-inch,	1.25

This highly dramatic number is sung after *Butterfly* has reproached *Suzuki* for her doubts, and in it she proudly declares confidence in her husband. In the English version this is called the "Vision Song," as it describes her vision of the arrival of *Pinkerton's* ship.

Ora a noi! (Letter Duet)

By Geraldine Farrar, Soprano,
and Antonio Scotti, Baritone
(*In Italian*) 89014   12-inch, $4.00

COPY'T DUPONT

THE LETTER FROM PINKERTON—ACT II
(GERALDINE FARRAR)

Double-Faced Record—See page 271.

Butterfly is visited by *Sharpless,* who has received a letter from *Pinkerton,* and has accepted the unpleasant task of informing *Butterfly* that the Lieutenant has deserted her. He finds his task a difficult one, for when he attempts to read *Pinkerton's* letter to her, she misunderstands its purport and continually interrupts the Consul with little bursts of joyful anticipation, thinking that *Pinkerton* will soon come to her. Finally realizing something of his message, she runs to bring her child to prove to *Sharpless* the certainty of her husband's home-coming.

BUTTERFLY AND "TROUBLE"

Sai cos' ebbe cuore (Do You Know, My Sweet One)
By Geraldine Farrar, Soprano
(*In Italian*) 87055 10-in., $2.00
By Emmy Destinn, Soprano
(*In Italian*) 91084 10-in., 2.00

In this pitiful air she asks little "*Trouble*" not to listen to the bad man (*Sharpless*), who is saying that *Pinkerton* has deserted them.

Shocked at the sight of the child, which he knew nothing about, *Sharpless* gives up in despair the idea of further undeceiving her, knowing that she will soon learn the truth, and leaves *Butterfly*, who refuses to doubt *Pinkerton*, in an exalted state of rapture over the idea of her husband's return.

Throughout the duet may be heard the mournfully sweet "waiting motive" played softly by the horns, and accompanied by strings *pizzicati*. This is beautifully given here, and the record is a most impressive one.

The sound of a cannon is heard, and with aid of a glass the two women see *Pinkerton's* ship, the *Abraham Lincoln,* entering the harbor.

Duet of the Flowers
By Geraldine Farrar, Soprano,
and Louise Homer, Contralto
(*In Italian*) 89008 12-in., $4.00

Greatly excited, *Butterfly* bids the maid strew the room with flowers, and they scatter the cherry blossoms everywhere, singing all the while weird harmonies which are hauntingly beautiful.

Miss Farrar's impressive *Cio-Cio-San*, childish and piquant in its lighter aspects and pitifully tragic in its final scenes, and Mme. Homer's *Suzuki*, the patient handmaiden, who loves and protects her mistress through all the weary years of waiting, are two most powerful impersonations. Of the music written for these two rôles, this exquisite duet is especially attractive.

Night is falling, and not expecting *Pinkerton* until morning, *Butterfly, Suzuki* and the child take their places at the window to watch for his coming. As the vigil begins, in the orchestra can be heard the "Waiting Motive," with its accompaniment by distant voices of the sailors in the harbor, producing an effect which is indescribably beautiful.

FARRAR AND HOMER IN ACT II

SCENE II—Same as the Preceding

The curtain rises on the same scene. It is daybreak. *Suzuki,* exhausted, is sleeping, but *Butterfly* still watches the path leading up the hill. *Suzuki* awakes and insists on *Butterfly* taking some rest, promising to call her when the Lieutenant arrives.

Sharpless and *Pinkerton* now enter, and question *Suzuki,* the Lieutenant being deeply touched to find that *Butterfly* has been faithful to him, and that a child has been born.

Suzuki, seeing a lady in the garden, demands to know who she is, and *Sharpless* tells her it is the wife of *Pinkerton,* he having married in America.

The introduction by Puccini's librettist of this character has been severely criticised, many considering it of doubtful taste, and forming a jarring note in the opera. So strong is this feeling in France, that the part of *Kate* has been eliminated from the cast.

The faithful maid is horrified, and dreads the effect of this news on her mistress. Weeping bitterly, she goes into *Butterfly's* chamber, while the friends are left to bitter reflections, expressed by Puccini in a powerful duet.

Ve lo dissi? (Did I Not Tell You?)

By Enrico Caruso and Antonio Scotti
(*In Italian*)   89047   12-inch, $4.00

Pinkerton realizes for the first time the baseness of his conduct, while the Consul reminds him of the warning he had given him in Act I,—to beware lest the tender heart of *Butterfly* be broken.

With the re-entrance of *Suzuki* occurs the trio for *Pinkerton, Sharpless* and *Suzuki*.

Lo so che alle sue pene (Naught Can Console Her)

By Martin, Fornia and Scotti
(*In Italian*)   87503   10-inch, $3.00

This trio is dramatically given by Martin, Fornia and Scotti, who have made great successes in the several rôles of *Pinkerton, Suzuki* and *Sharpless*.

COPY'T MISHKIN

DESTINN AS BUTTERFLY

Finale Ultimo (Butterfly's Death Scene)

By Geraldine Farrar, Soprano		(*In Italian*)	87030	10-inch,	$2.00
By Emmy Destinn, Soprano		(*In Italian*)	91086	10-inch,	2.00
By Edith Helena	(*Double-faced—See page 271*)	(*In English*)	17346	10-inch,	.75

Now comes the pathetic death scene at the close of the opera. *Butterfly,* convinced that *Pinkerton* has renounced her, blindfolds her child that he may not witness her suicide,

PHOTO HALL   THE DEATH OF BUTTERFLY

takes down the dagger with which her father committed *hari-kari,* and after reading the inscription on the handle, "To die with honor when one can no longer live with honor," she stabs herself.

In her death struggle she gropes her way to the innocent babe, who, blindfolded and waving his little flag, takes it all in the spirit of play. The tragic intensity of this scene always moves many to tears.

Pinkerton enters to ask *Butterfly's* forgiveness and bid her farewell, and is horrified to find her dying. He lifts her up in an agony of remorse.

In the orchestra, strangely mingling with the American motive, the tragic death motive may be heard as the curtain slowly falls.

DOUBLE-FACED AND MISCELLANEOUS MADAME BUTTERFLY RECORDS

Madame Butterfly Selection   By Victor Orchestra   31631   12-inch, $1.00
Introduction—Pinkerton's Song, Act I—Duet, Finale of Act I—Duet, Butterfly and
Suzuki, from Act II—Finale of Act II.

This selection begins with the entrance music of *Pinkerton*, accompanied by the
American theme for which Puccini has utilized the "Star Spangled Banner."
Then in succession are heard the gay air of the thoughtless Lieutenant (as a cornet
solo) in which he describes the characteristics of his countrymen; the principal strain of the
love duet with which the act closes; the exquisitely poetical "Duet of the Flowers," part
of which is given on the orchestra bells; and the beginning of the supremely beautiful scene
where *Butterfly*, her maid and little son, take their places at the window to watch until
morning for the husband's coming, while in the distance can be heard the faint voices of
singers in the night, producing a mournful and indescribable effect.

Then from the last scene we hear the return of *Pinkerton* announced just as *Butterfly* has
taken her life; the American *motif* strangely contrasting with the tragic music of the death
scene; and a few measures of the final curtain music, with its ancient Japanese melody.

Madame Butterfly Fantasie—By Victor Herbert's Orch   70055   12-inch, $1.25
Opening of the Opera—"Waiting Music," Act II—Duet, Act I—"Entrance of Butterfly"—"Love Duet"— Finale, Act I.

Madame Butterfly Selection, No. 1	By Pryor's Band	35148	12-inch,	1.25
Bartered Bride Overture	*By Pryor's Band*			
Madame Butterfly Selection, No. 2	By Pryor's Band	35331	12-inch,	1.25
Tannhauser Selection	*By Pryor's Band*			
Sur la mer calmée (Some Day He'll Come) By Mlle. Heilbronner, Soprano (*In French*)		35409	12-inch,	1.25
Daughter of the Regiment—Salut à la France) By Mlle. Heilbronner, Soprano (In French)				
Madame Butterfly Selection	By Pryor's Band	31697	12-inch,	1.00
Madame Butterfly Fantasie	By Victor Sorlin 'Cello	31696	12-inch,	1.00
What a Sky, What a Sea (Entrance of Butterfly, Act I) By Edith Helena, Soprano (*In English*)		17346	10-inch,	.75
Beloved Idol (Butterfly's Death Scene, Act II) By Edith Helena, Soprano (*In English*)				

BUTTERFLY AND SUZUKI IN THE GARDEN

THE GREAT INVOCATION SCENE

(French)

LA FLÛTE ENCHANTÉE

(*Lah Fleut Ahn-shan-tay'*)

(German)

DIE ZAUBERFLÖTE

(*Dee Tsow-ber-floh'-teh*)

(English)

THE MAGIC FLUTE

(Italian)

IL FLAUTO MAGICO

(*Eel Flau'-toh Maj'-ee-koh*)

OPERA IN TWO ACTS

Libretto by Schickaneder, adapted from a tale by Wieland, "Lulu, or the Magic Flute." Music by Wolfgang Amadeus Mozart. First produced in Vienna, September 30, 1791, Mozart directing. First Paris production as "*Les Mystères d'Isis*," August 20, 1801. First London production, in Italian, in 1811; in German, 1833; in English, 1838. First New York production April 17, 1833, at the Park Theatre, in English, and not again until November 21, 1859, when it was given at the German Theatre in Italian. Later productions included that of 1876, with Carlotta Patti; at the Grand Opera House, with di Murska, Lucca and Ronconi; and at the Academy with Gerster.

The latest revival was at the Metropolitan in 1912, with Destinn, Parks, Homer, Goritz, Slezak, Lambert Murphy, and afterwards with Hempel in the cast.

Characters

SARASTRO, (*Sahr-ass'-troh*) High Priest of Isis........................Bass
TAMINO, (*Tah-mee'-noh*) an Egyptian Prince........................Tenor
PAPAGENO, (*Pap-ah-gay'-noh*) a bird-catcher.....................Baritone
THE QUEEN OF NIGHT....................................Soprano
PAMINA, (*Pam-ee'-nah*) her daughter............................Soprano
MONOSTATOS, (*Moh-noh-stat'-oss*) a Moor, chief slave of the Temple.....Baritone
PAPAGENA, (*Pap-ah-gay-nah*)....................................Soprano

Three Lady Attendants of the Queen of Night; Three Boys belonging to
the Temple, and fulfilling the designs of Sarastro; Priests and
Priestesses of the Temple of Isis; Male and Female
Slaves; Warriors of the Temple, Attendants, etc.

The action occurs at the Temple of Isis at Memphis, about the time of Ramses I.

"A fantastic fable was the groundwork; supernatural apparitions and a good dose of comic element were to serve as garnish. But what did Mozart build on this preposterous foundation? What godlike magic breathes throughout this work, from the most popular ballad to the noblest hymn! What many-sidedness, what marvelous variety! The quintessence of every noblest bloom of art seems here to blend in one unequaled flower."—*Richard Wagner.*

Strictly speaking, the Magic Flute is not an opera, but rather a fairy extravaganza accompanied by some of the most delightful music imaginable. To fully appreciate Mozart's work it should be heard in some German town on a Sunday evening, where middle-class families and sweethearts find much enjoyment in the mixture of mystery, sentiment, comedy and delightful music which make up the opera. The libretto is, of course, utterly absurd, describing as it does the magic of the pipes of *Tamino* which

PHOTO BERT

PAPAGENA AND PAPAGENO

had the power to control men, animals, birds, reptiles and even the elements, and as the flute is continually playing throughout the work, the results may be imagined.

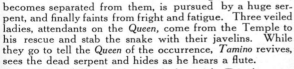

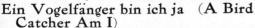

THE THREE LADIES OF THE QUEEN

Overture

By La Scala Orchestra *68207 12-inch, $1.25

The overture is not only one of the greatest of its kind, but one of the most generally appreciated. Its wonderful fugue, "in which Mozart sports with fugal counterpoint as though it were mere child's play," is played by the orchestra in a striking manner. This fugue is announced first by the clarinets and a few bars later the cornets take up the theme, followed by every instrument in the marvelous finale.

ACT I

The scene shows a rocky landscape with the Temple of the *Queen of the Night* visible in the background. *Tamino,* an Egyptian prince who is traveling with his friends, becomes separated from them, is pursued by a huge serpent, and finally faints from fright and fatigue. Three veiled ladies, attendants on the *Queen,* come from the Temple to his rescue and stab the snake with their javelins. While they go to tell the *Queen* of the occurrence, *Tamino* revives, sees the dead serpent and hides as he hears a flute.

Ein Vogelfänger bin ich ja (A Bird Catcher Am I)

By Otto Goritz (German) 64163 10-inch, $1.00

Papageno, a bird catcher, admirer of damsels, and all-around rogue, enters and sings a merry lay, piping at every pause. In his song the fowler describes his occupation of snaring birds, but says he would like catching women better!

PHOTO WILLINGER

PAPAGENO

Double-Faced Record—See page 277.

PAPAGENO:
> The fowler comes, in spite of rain,
> And sings his song in merry strain;
> This merry fowler, too, is known
> By young and old, from zone to zone.
> Knows how to whistle every sound
> That birds may sing the whole year round.
> Oh, none can be more blithe than I,
> With these sweet warblers of the sky.
>
> The fowler comes, in spite of rain,
> And sings his song in merry strain;
> This merry fowler, too, is known
> By young and old, from zone to zone.
> A net for maidens I should like
> Would catch the pretty dears by dozens,
> I'd shut them safely up at home,
> And never let them forth to roam.

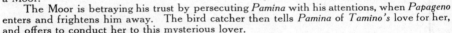

In the part of *Papageno* Mr. Goritz has few rivals, and his impersonation was one of the great features of the recent revival at the Metropolitan.

Tamino now comes forward and gives *Papageno* credit for having killed the serpent, an honor which he promptly accepts. The three ladies now return, rebuke *Papageno* and show *Tamino* a photograph of the *Queen of Night's* daughter, the lovely *Pamina*, who has been taken from her mother by *Sarastro*, the *Priest of Isis*, to save her from evil influences. *Tamino* falls in love with the picture and offers to rescue the maiden. He is given an all-powerful magic flute, and accompanied by *Papageno* sets out for *Sarastro's* palace.

The scene changes to a room in the palace of the High Priest, where *Pamina* is discovered in charge of *Monostatos*, a Moor.

TAMINO AND PAMINA

The Moor is betraying his trust by persecuting *Pamina* with his attentions, when *Papageno* enters and frightens him away. The bird catcher then tells *Pamina* of *Tamino's* love for her, and offers to conduct her to this mysterious lover.

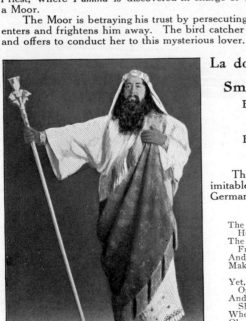

SARASTRO

(*Italian*) (*German*)
La dove prende—Bei Männern—
(*English*)
Smiles and Tears

By Emma Eames, Soprano, and
Emilio de Gogorza, Baritone
(*In Italian*) 89003 12-inch $4.00

By Johanna Gadski, Soprano, and
Otto Goritz, Baritone
(*In German*) 88369 12-inch. 3.00

This charming duet, with its grace and inimitable gaiety, introduces the melody of an old German song, *Bei Männern*

Smiles and Tears

The smile, that on the lip is playing,
  How oft 'twill hide a heart's deep woe!
The tear, that down the cheek is straying,
  From purest springs of joy may flow.
And smiles and tears, so legends say,
Make up the sum of Life's brief day.

Yet, whilst that smile the brow is wreathing,
  One word shall change it to a tear,
And one soft sigh's impassion'd breathing
  Shall bid the tear-drop disappear,
When each alike misleads in turn,
Oh, who the heart's deep lore shall learn!

After many adventures *Tamino* and *Pamina* meet, and by means of the magic flute they are about to escape, but are interrupted by *Sarastro*,

PHOTO WHITE   THE HIGH PRIEST BLESSING THE LOVERS

who agrees to unite the lovers if they will remain and be purified by the sacred rites ; and as the priest separates them and covers their heads with veils, the curtain falls.

ACT II

The first scene shows a noble forest and the *Temple of Wisdom*. The priests assemble, a n d *Sarastro* orders the lovers brought before him. He then sings this superb Invocation, one of the most impressive numbers in the opera.

Invocation (Great Isis)
By Pol Plançon, Bass
(*Piano acc.*) (*In Italian*)
85042 12-inch, $3.00
By Marcel Journet, Bass
(*French*) 64235 10-inch, 1.00
By Metropolitan Opera
Chorus (*In German*)
*45051 10-inch, 1.00

In the Invocation, *Sarastro* calls on the gods Isis and Osiris to give *Tamino* and *Papageno* strength to bear the trial now at hand.

Great Isis, great Osiris!
  Strengthen with wisdom's strength this lyre pair;
Ye who guide steps where deserts lengthen,
  Brace theirs with nerve, your proof to bear!
Grant them probation's fruit all living;
  Yet, should they find a grave while striving,
Think on their virtues, gracious gods,
  Take them elect to your abodes!

In the noble rôle of *Sarastro* Plançon is especially effective, and his dignified impersonation of the benignant High Priest, who smooths out all the fantastic tangles in the situations which occur in Mozart's opera, is always singularly impressive.

The lovers are admitted to the Temple and begin their probation.

In the next scene *Pamina* is discovered asleep in a bower of roses. The *Queen* suddenly rises from the earth and gives *Pamina* a dagger, telling her to kill *Sarastro* or *Tamino* can never be hers. *Pamina* hesitates, and her mother, in a terrifying and dramatic song, threatens vengeance on all concerned.

Aria della Regina (The Queen's Air)
By Bessie Abott, Soprano
(*In Italian*) 88051 12-inch, $3.00
By Maria Galvany, Soprano
(*In Italian*) 87059 10-inch, 2.00

The Queen of Night, *Astriflammante*, is one of the most striking characters in Mozart's opera, and the few numbers allotted to her are difficult and florid ones. This great aria

PHOTO REMBRANDT   TAMINO

Double-Faced Record—See page 277.

PHOTO BECKER & MAAS

QUEEN OF THE NIGHT

is one which the most experienced of sopranos always approaches with misgiving, because of its excessive demands on the vocal powers. Miss Abott and Mme. Galvany completely meet these demands, both singing the air gracefully and with superb execution.

ASTRIFLAMMANTE:
The pangs of hell are raging in my bosom,
Death and destruction wildly flame around!
Go forth and bear my vengeance to Sarastro,
Or as my daughter thou shalt be disown'd!
I cast thee off forever,
I spurn thee and renounce thee,
If thou dar'st to brave my wrath;
Through thee Sarastro is to perish!
Hear, gods of vengeance!
Hear a mother's vow! (*She disappears.*)

Sarastro enters and soothes *Pamina,* saying that he will take a righteous revenge on the *Queen* by obtaining the happiness of her daughter. He then sings the noble Cavatina, considered one of the greatest of bass arias.

Qui sdegno non s'accende (Within These Sacred Walls)
By Pol Plançon, Bass (*Piano acc.*)
(*In Italian*) 85077 12-inch, $3.00
By Marcel Journet, Bass
(*In French*) 74266 12-inch, 1.50

In this number Plançon is at his best, and the noble strains are delivered in the broad, sonorous style which the music requires, while a splendid rendition by Journet in French is also offered.

SARASTRO: Within this hallowed dwelling
Revenge and sorrow cease;
Here troubled doubt dispelling,
The weary heart hath peace.
If thou hast stray'd, a brother's hand
Shall guide thee t'ward the better land.
This hallow'd fane protects thee
From falsehood, guile and fear;
A brother's love directs thee,
To him thy woes are dear.

The probationary trials of the lovers continue through many strange scenes, in one of which *Pamina* meets *Tamino,* and not knowing that he has been forbidden to speak to any woman, cries out that he no longer loves her. She then sings this pathetic little air, which Mme. Destinn has interpreted here so beautifully.

Ach ich frühl's, es ist verschwunden (My Happiness Has Flown)
By Emmy Destinn, Soprano (*In German*)
88510 12-inch, $3.00

The music of this master demands singers of great understanding and feeling, who must possess not only voice but intelligence and taste.

That Destinn possesses these qualifications in ample measure is fully apparent to all who listen to her superb Mozart reproductions. Almost poignant in the intensity of its beauty is the artist's singing, which reaches an unforgettable climax in "Ach! ich fühl's."

PAMINA: Wretch that I am, too well I know
Naught is left me but to mourn,
Condemn'd to drain the cup of woe,
Joy to me will ne'er return.
Oh, Tamino, if for thee,
My sighs and bitter tears are vain,
Come, kind death, in pity free
My weary bosom from its pain!

Pamina, thinking *Tamino* has deserted her, wishes to die, and tries to stab herself with the dagger her mother

COPY'T DUPONT

GADSKI AS PAMINA

has given her, but is prevented by the three boys, or *genii* (under instructions from *Sarastro*), who assure her that *Tamino* is still true and promise to conduct her to him.

Du also bist mein Braütigam ? (Thou Art My Bridegroom!)

By Johanna Gadski, Soprano, and Mmes. Sparks, Case and Mattfeld

(In German) 88441 12-inch, $3.00

Mme. Gadski gives the strains of *Pamina* in her usual finished style, while the music of the three "boys" is sung by Mmes. Sparks, Case and Mattfeld, with voices of clear, youthful timbre which exhibit well the grace and brightness of Mozart's music.

PAMINA:
Oh dagger! thou are my bridegroom!
By thee alone I'll end my care.

THE BOYS:
Oh woe! what said Pamina there?
And see, she is to madness near.

PAMINA:
I wish to die, since the man,
Whom I ne'er can hate,
This faithful heart will thus desert.
(Tries to stab herself.)

THE BOYS:
Hold, unhappy one! and hear!
Could Tamino see thee thus,
He with sorrow would expire,
For he fondly loveth thee.

PAMINA *(recovers herself)*:
What! did he feel responding love,
And yet concealed his feelings?

FRESCO IN THE VIENNA OPERA

TAMINO AND PAMINA

THE BOYS:
This, alas, we must not tell,
But we will show him now to thee;
And with wonder thou wilt see,
That his heart is thine alone!

PAMINA:
Lead me forth! I wish to see him!

ALL:
Come, wu him forthwith will seek.
Two hearts that truly love,
Can human weakness never part.

Papageno finally becomes discouraged and tries to hang himself, but the three *genii* enter and suggest that he try the magic bells. This proves effective and *Papagena* makes her appearance. They then sing their joyous and amusing duet.

Papagena, Papageno!

By Johanna Gadski, Soprano, and Otto Goritz, Baritone

(In German) 87510 10-inch, $3.00

PAPAGENO:
Pa-Pa-Papagena!
PAPAGENA:
Pa-Pa-Papageno!
PAPAGENO:
Art thou, then, quite given to me?
PAPAGENA:
Yes, I am quite given to thee.
PAPAGENO:
Well, then, be my dear little wife.
PAPAGENA:
Well, then, my husband, my life.
BOTH:
What a joy shall we not feel,

When the gods their gifts reveal!
Little boys and girls galore,
All we want and many more.

PAPAGENO:
First a little Papageno!
PAPAGENA:
Then a little Papagena!
BOTH:
What can with such joys compare,
When many, many, many, many.
Papa-pa-pagenos,
Papa-pa-pagenas,
The blessings of glad parents are?

The trials being finally completed, the lovers are united in the sacred Temple. The *Queen* and her accomplices attempt to prevent the ceremony, but the scene suddenly changes to the Temple of the Sun, where *Sarastro* is seen on his throne with *Tamino* and *Pamina* beside him, while the baffled *Queen* and her train sink into the earth.

DOUBLE-FACED MAGIC FLUTE RECORDS

Magic Flute Overture	La Scala Orchestra	68207 12-inch, $1.25
Meistersinger Prelude	La Scala Orchestra	
O Isis und Isiris (Great Isis)		
By Metropolitan Opera Chorus *(In German)*		45051 10-inch, 1.00
Huguenots—Coro di Soldati (Soldiers' Chorus)		
By Metropolitan Opera Chorus *(In Italian)*		

FARRAR AS MANON

SETTING OF ACT I

(French)

MANON
(Man-on')

OPERA IN FOUR ACTS

Words by Meilhac and Gille, after the novel of Abbé Prévost. Music by Jules Massenet. First production at the *Opéra-Comique*, Paris, January 19, 1884; at Brussels, March 15, 1884. First London production May 7, 1885; in English by the Carl Rosa Company, at Liverpool, January 17, 1885. In French at Covent Garden, May 19, 1891; in Italy at Milan, October 19, 1893. First American production at New York, December 23, 1885, at the Academy of Music, with Minnie Hauk, Giannini and Del Puente. First New Orleans production January 4, 1894. Some notable revivals were in 1895 with Sybil Sanderson and Jean de Reszke; in 1896, with Melba and de Reszke; in 1899 with Saville, Van Dyk, Dufriche and Plançon; in 1909, at the Metropolitan, with Caruso, Farrar, Scotti and Note; and in 1912, with Caruso, Farrar, Gilly and Reiss.

Cast

CHEVALIER DES GRIEUX (*Shev-al-yay' d'h Gree-ay'*) ....Tenor
COUNT DES GRIEUX, his father ....Bass
LESCAUT, (*Les-koh'*) Manon's cousin, one of the Royal Guard ....Baritone
GUILLOT MORFONTEIN, a roué, Minister of France....................Bass
DE BRÉTIGNY, (*Bray-tee-ynee'*) a nobleman ....Baritone
MANON, a school girl ....Soprano
People, Actresses and Students

Time and place: 1721; Amiens, Paris, Havre.

The story of *Manon* is, of course, taken by Massenet's librettists from the famous novel of the Abbé Prévost, but for operatic purposes several changes have been made, notably in the events of the fourth act, which takes place in France instead of America.

Manon is a country girl, gay, pretty and thoughtless, who meets a handsome young cavalier, *des Grieux,* while on her way to a convent to complete her education. He falls in love with her and she with him as far as her nature will allow, and when he tells her of the gaieties and pleasures of Paris, she needs little persuasion to induce her to elope with him to the Capital, to the chagrin of *Guillot*, whose carriage the lovers coolly appropriate.

Soon tiring of love in a cottage, however, the young girl encourages the attentions of a rich nobleman, *de Brétigny*, and when *des Grieux* is taken away forcibly by his father, she seizes the opportunity and leaves with her new lover.

In Act III she learns that *des Grieux*, despondent because of her faithlessness, has resolved to enter a monastery. Her fickle affections turn again to him, and she visits him at the Seminary of St. Sulpice. He at first repulses her, saying his love is dead, but is unable to resist her, and they depart together.

The next act occurs in a gambling house, where *des Grieux* is endeavoring to win money to support *Manon* in the luxury she demands. *Guillot*, in revenge for the trick played on him in Act I, causes their arrest, *des Grieux* for cheating and *Manon* as a dissolute woman.

The last scene occurs on the road to Havre, where *des Grieux* and *Lescaut*, *Manon's* cousin, plan to rescue *Manon* as she is being taken to the ship, en route to the prison colony in Louisiana. The soldiers appear, but it is a dying *Manon* they escort, and the unfortunate girl, after repenting and asking forgiveness of *des Grieux*, dies in his arms.

ACT I
SCENE I—*Courtyard of an Inn at Amiens*

As the curtain rises the crowd of villagers, including *Lescaut*, are waiting the coming of the coach, which presently arrives and discharges *Manon*. The young girl regards the animated scene with much interest, and soon espies *Lescaut*, her cousin, who was to meet her at this point and escort her to the convent school. He greets her and compliments her on her charming appearance. She blushes and then artlessly tells him of her impressions during the journey from her country home. The scene from this point has been recorded by the Scala singers.

Restate qui (Wait a Moment)
By Elisa Tromben, Soprano; Federico Federici, Tenor; G. Pini-Corsi,
Tenor; Riccardo Tegani, Baritone   (*In Italian*) *55000 12-inch, $1.50

Lescaut asks *Manon* to excuse him for a while as he must go to see after her luggage.

> LESCAUT (*to Manon*):
> Wait a moment.
> Be prudent; I am going to find your luggage.

He goes out, and the townspeople desert the square, leaving *Manon* alone. The *roué, Guillot,* appears on the balcony of the hotel, crying: "Miserable landlord! Are we never to have any wine?"

He sees *Manon,* and his evil eyes light up at this vision of youth and beauty.

> GUILLOT:
> Heavens! What do I see? Young lady!
> Ahem! Ahem! Young lady!
> (*Aside*)
> Really, my head is turning round!
>
> MANON (*aside and laughing*):
> What a funny man!
>
> GUILLOT:
> Young lady, I am Guillot de Morfontaine. I
> am rich and would give a good deal to hear
> a word of love from you. Now, what do
> you say to that?
>
> MANON:
> That I should be ashamed, if I were not more
> disposed to laugh.
>
> DE BRETIGNY:
> Now then, Guillot, what's the game? We are
> waiting for you.
>
> GUILLOT:
> Oh, go to the Devil.
>
> POUSETTE (*to Guillot*):
> Are you not ashamed? At your age!

COPY'T DUPONT   ALDA AS MANON

*Double-Faced Record—See page 286.

DE BRETIGNY:
 This time I swear the dog has by chance found a prize.
 Never did sweeter look light up a woman's face!
 Now then, Guillot, let the girl alone and come in. We are calling you.
GUILLOT:
 Ay, ay, in a moment.
 (To Manon):
 My little one, give me a word.
DE BRETIGNY:
 Guillot, let the girl alone.

GUILLOT (softly to Manon):
 A postillion is coming directly; when you see him, understand that a carriage is at your service. Take it, and afterwards you shall know more.
LESCAUT (who has just entered):
 What do you say?
GUILLOT (confused):
 Oh, sir! nothing, sir!
LESCAUT (boisterously):
 Oh, sir! Did you say—
GUILLOT (returning to the pavilion):
 Nothing, sir, I said.

Guillot is frightened by the gruff soldier, to the amusement of the bystanders, who laugh at the baffled libertine until he flees in confusion.

Lescaut now warns *Manon* to beware of the men she may meet.

LESCAUT (to Manon):
 He spoke to you, Manon.
MANON (lightly):
 Well, can you say 'twas my fault?
LESCAUT:
 That's true; and in my eyes you are so good that I won't trouble myself.
 (The two guardsmen enter.)
FIRST GUARDSMAN (to Lescaut):
 How now! Thou comest not!

SECOND GUARDSMAN:
 Both cards and dice are waiting your pleasure below.
LESCAUT:
 I come; but first to this young lady, with your leave, good sirs,
 I must speak some words of counsel full of wisdom.
GUARDSMEN (in mock resignation):
 To his wisdom we'll listen.

Mi raccomando (Wait for Me)

By Elisa Tromben, Soprano; Federico Federici, Tenor; Chorus
(*In Italian*) *55000   12-inch, $1.50

The young girl promises to be prudent and *Lescaut* leaves with the guardsmen.

LESCAUT (to Manon):
 Give good heed to what I say—
 Duty calls me now away,
 To consult these comrades here
 Upon a point that's not quite clear.
 Wait for me, Manon, just a moment, no more.
 Make no mistake, but prudent be,
 And if, forsooth, some silly man

 Should whisper folly in your ear,
 Behave as though you did not hear.
 For safety's sake adopt that plan.
 (To the Guardsmen, aside)
 Now let us go and see on which of us the goddess of the game will look with loving eyes.
 (They go out.)

Des Grieux now enters, and seeing *Manon*, is much impressed with her beauty and modest bearing. He addresses her respectfully, beginning the lovely duet, *Et je sais votre nom.*

Et je sais votre nom (If I Knew But Your Name)

By Mlle. Korsoff, Soprano, and Léon Beyle, Tenor   (*In French*) *16551   10-inch, $0.75

The young girl answers simply, but feels herself strangely drawn to the young student. The transition from strangers to lovers is a quick one, as will be seen by the translation.

DES GRIEUX:
 If I knew but your name—
MANON (with simplicity):
 I am called Manon.
DES GRIEUX (with emotion):
 Manon!
MANON (aside):
 How tender are his looks,
 How delightful his voice to my soul!
DES GRIEUX:
 All my fond foolish words,
 I pray you forgive!
MANON (naively):
 How condemn your words when they charm my heart;
 To my ears they are music!
 Would to Heav'n such language were mine,
 You fit answer to make.

CLEMENT AS DES GRIEUX

*Double-Faced Record—See page 286.

DES GRIEUX (*in a transport of joy*):
Lovely enchantress, all-conquering beauty,
Manon, from henceforth thou art mistress of
my heart!
MANON:
Oh! what joy!
I'm henceforth the mistress of his heart!
DES GRIEUX:
Ah, speak to me!
MANON:
I am only a simple maiden.
(*Smiling*)
Believe me, I'm not wicked,
But I often am told by those at home,
That I love pleasures too well;
(*Sadly*)
I am now on my way to a convent,
That, sir, is the story of Manon,
(*With simplicity*)
Of Manon Lescaut!
DES GRIEUX (*with ardor*):
No, I will not believe that fate can be so
hard!
That one so young and so fair can be destined
to dwell in a living tomb.

MANON:
But 'tis, alas! the sovereign will of Heaven,
To whose service I'm devoted,
And no one from this fate can deliver me.
DES GRIEUX (*firmly*):
No, no! Not from you, Manon, shall hope
and joy be torn.
MANON (*joyfully*):
Oh, Heaven!
DES GRIEUX:
For on my will and power you can safely
depend.
MANON (*with energy*):
Ah! to you I owe far more, far more than life.
DES GRIEUX (*passionately*):
Ah! Manon, you shall never leave me now!
Since I would gladly roam thro' all the world,
Seeking for you, love, an unknown retreat,
And carry you there in my arms.
MANON:
To you, my life and my soul!
To you I give my life for evermore!
DES GRIEUX:
Light of my soul! Manon,
The mistress of my heart for evermore!

Manon now observes the carriage of *Guillot*, which had been offered her, and suggests that they take it and fly together. *Des Grieux* joyfully agrees and they sing their second duet.

Nous vivrons à Paris (We Will Go to Paris)

By Lucette Korsoff, Soprano, and Léon Beyle, Tenor
(*In French*) *45009 10-inch, $1.00

MANON AND DES GRIEUX:
We to Paris will go. Heart to heart!
And, though fortune may frown, never part!

Evermore bliss is ours,
And with love's sweetest flow'rs
Will we crown the bright hours!

Hearing *Lescaut's* voice from within the hotel, where he has been gambling, the lovers hastily enter the carriage and drive off, while *Guillot* swears revenge and *Lescaut* bewails his double loss of money and cousin.

ACT II

SCENE—*Apartment of Des Grieux and Manon in Paris*

Des Grieux is writing at a desk, while *Manon* is play-fully looking over his shoulder. He tells her he is writing to his father:

DES GRIEUX:
This letter's for my father, and I tremble lest
he should read in anger what I write from
my heart.
MANON:
You are afraid?
DES GRIEUX:
Yes, Manon, I'm afraid.
MANON:
Ah, well, then we'll read it together.
DES GRIEUX:
Yes, that's the way. Together we'll read.

On l'appelle Manon (She is Called Manon)

By Farrar, Soprano, and Caruso, Tenor
(*In French*) 89059 12-inch, $4.00

By Mlle. Korsoff, Soprano; Beyle, Tenor
(*In French*) *45009 10-inch, 1.00

Continuing this charming scene, she takes the letter from him and reads with simplicity:

COPY'T MISHKIN

DE SEGUROLA AS LESCAUT

Double-Faced Record—See page 286.

MANON:
"She is called Manon, and is young and fair. In her all charms unite. She has grace, radiant youth and beauty; music flows in a stream from her lips; in her eyes shines the tender light of love."

DES GRIEUX (ardently):
In her eyes shines the tender light of love.

MANON:
Is this true? Ah, I knew it not. (Tenderly) But I know how much I am loved.

DES GRIEUX (with passion):
Thou art loved! Manon, I adore thee!

MANON:
Come, come, good sir, there's more to read yet.

DES GRIEUX:
"Like a bird that through all lands follows the spring, so her young soul to life is ever open. Her lips, like flowers, smile and speak to the zephyrs that kiss them in passing."

MANON (repeating):
"To the zephyrs that kiss them in passing." (Pensively) Do you think your father will give his consent?

DES GRIEUX:
Yes; he will never in such a matter as this oppose me.

MANON:
Dost thou desire it?

DES GRIEUX:
I desire it, with all my soul!

MANON:
Then embrace me, Chevalier. (They embrace.) And now, go;—send thy letter.

Des Grieux starts to go, but seeing some beautiful flowers on the table asks who sent them. Manon replies evasively, and asks if he does not trust her and if he is jealous. He assures her of his perfect confidence.

A noise is heard outside, and Lescaut, accompanied by de Brétigny, a French nobleman, enters, the former loudly demanding satisfaction from des Grieux for the abduction of his cousin. Des Grieux at first defies him, but remembering that he is a member of Manon's family, shows him the letter he had written to his father asking her hand in marriage. Lescaut engages him in conversation, thus giving de Brétigny an opportunity to speak to Manon aside. He tells her that des Grieux is to be carried off by his father that night, and urges her to fly with him. Tempted by the thoughts of wealth the young girl hesitates. Lescaut now loudly expresses satisfaction with the attitude of des Grieux, and departs with de Brétigny.

Des Grieux goes out to post the letter and Manon struggles with the temptation which has come to her; the pathetic air, Adieu notre petite table, indicating that she is yielding.

Adieu notre petite table (Farewell, Our Little Table)

By Geraldine Farrar, Soprano   (In French)   88146   12-inch, $3.00
By Mme. Vallandri, Soprano, and Léon Beyle, Tenor
                                      (In French) *45008   10-inch,   1.00

NOTE.—In record 45008 Mme. Vallandri sings a portion of the "Farewell" solo and this is followed by the short duet which precedes the "Dream."

She regards the little table at which they had served their simple meals.

MANON:
Farewell, our pretty little table! So small and yet so large for us. Side by side so often there we've sat. (With a sad smile.) I smile as now I call to mind what narrow space we lovers filled. A single glass served both of us, and each, in drinking, sought upon its margin where dear lips had been. Ah! best of friends, how thou hast loved!

Hearing des Grieux approaching, she hastily tries to conceal her tears. He observes them, however, and tries to soothe her by relating a dream he has had.

(Italian)   (English)   (French)

Il sogno—The Dream—Le Rêve

By Enrico Caruso, Tenor   (In Italian)   81031   10-inch, $2.00
By Edmond Clement, Tenor,   (In French)   74258   12-inch,   1.50
By Fernando de Lucia, Tenor   (Piano acc.)   (In Italian)   66001   10-inch,   1.50
By John McCormack, Tenor   (In Italian)   64312   10-inch,   1.00
By Léon Beyle, Tenor   (In French)   *45008   10-inch,   1.00

"Listen, Manon," he cries, "On my way I dreamed a lovely dream."

DES GRIEUX:
With fancy's eye I saw, Manon, A sweet and lowly cot, Its white walls, deck'd with flowers fair, Gleam'd thro' the wood! Beneath whose peaceful shadows Ran clear the babbling brook; Overhead, 'mid verdant leaves Sang so sweet and full the joyous birds,

'Tis paradise! Ah, no, All is sad, so sad and dreary, For, O my only love, thou art not there.

MANON (softly):
'Tis a vision, 'tis but a fancy!

DES GRIEUX:
No! for thus we'll pass our life, If but thou wilt, O Manon!

*Double-Faced Record—See page 286.

LANDE ANTEROOM OF ST. SULPICE—METROPOLITAN OPERA SETTING

A knock is heard and *Manon* exclaims, aside, "Oh, Heaven, already they have come for him!" She tries to prevent him from opening the door, but he insists, and is seized and carried away, while *Manon,* suddenly repenting, is overcome with grief.

FARRAR AS MANON—ACT III

ACT III

SCENE—*A Street in Paris on a Fête Day*

Manon enters, accompanied by *de Brétigny* and several gallants. She is in a gay mood and extols youth and love in a fine vocal gavotte.

Gavotte—Obéissons quand leur voix appelle (Hear the Voice of Youth)

By Geraldine Farrar, Soprano
(*In French*) 87023 10-inch, $2.00
By Giuseppina Huguet, Soprano
(*In Italian*) *45028 10-inch, 1.00

MANON:
List to the voice of youth when it calleth,
It bids ye to love for aye!
And ere the pride of beauty falleth,
Love then while you may.
Profit then by the time of youth,
And do not stay to count the days,
Remember well this adage—be merry and gay
  always!
The heart, alas, to love is e'er willing,
And ever willing to forget,
So while its pulse is thrilling,
Love, ere its day hath set!

Manon, seeing *des Grieux's* father, timidly approaches him and asks if *des Grieux* has forgotten her. She learns that the young man has forgiven her, buried his love, and is planning to enter a monastery. When the Count has departed, the capricious girl resolves to go to St. Sulpice and see for herself if she has been so easily forgotten; and as the curtain falls she is calling to *Lescaut* to conduct her thither.

Double-Faced Record—See page 286.

SCENE II—*Reception Room at St. Sulpice*

At the beginning of this scene the Count pleads with his son not to retire from the world, but *des Grieux* says he is resolved, and his father takes a sorrowful leave. Left alone, *des Grieux* sings his lovely song of renunciation, declaring he will now seek the peace of mind which only faith in Heaven can give.

(French)   (Italian)   (English)

Ah! fuyez, douce image!—Dispar, vision!—Depart, Fair Vision!

By Enrico Caruso, Tenor	(*In French*)	88348	12-inch, $3.00
By Gino Giovannelli, Tenor	(*In Italian*) *55001	12-inch,	1.50
By M. Rocca, Tenor	(*In French*) *16575	10-inch,	.75

He goes slowly out and *Manon* enters, shuddering at the gloomy walls and wondering if her lover has quite forgotten her. *Des Grieux* soon returns and is astounded to see *Manon*, bidding her begone, saying his love is dead. She cannot believe it, and cries: "These eyes that oft thou hast kissed with ardor, do they shine no more? Am I not Manon?"

Des Grieux is deeply moved, but asks Heaven for strength to resist her. Her pleadings finally have their effect, and he cries: "Ah! Manon! No longer will I struggle against myself!" and they depart together.

ACT IV

SCENE—*A Gambling Room in Paris*

Des Grieux has been persuaded by *Manon* to come to this place in the hope of winning money to satisfy her desire for luxury. He plays for high stakes and wins large sums from *Guillot*, who leaves in a rage. As *des Grieux* is showing *Manon* the gold he has won, a loud knocking is heard and the police enter with *Guillot*, who denounces *des Grieux* as a swindler and *Manon* as his accomplice. They are arrested and taken to prison, but *des Grieux* is afterward released through his father's influence, while *Manon* is ordered to be deported to America by way of Havre.

Concertato finale—O dolor

By Aristodemo Giorgini, A. Santoro, S. Nicolicchia and Chorus

(*In Italian*) 87083 10-inch, $2.00

THE GAMBLING SCENE—ACT IV

---

* *Double-Faced Record—See page 286.*

ON THE HAVRE ROAD—ACT V

ACT V

SCENE—*On the Road to Havre*

Des Grieux and *Lescaut* are on the Havre road, waiting for the soldiers who are escorting the prisoners to the ship bound for America, *des Grieux* having conceived the mad idea of rescuing *Manon*. Beginning the duet he sings his sad and remorseful air, *Manon in Chains!*

Manon, la catena (Manon in Chains!)

By Remo Andreini, Tenor; Riccardo Tegani, Baritone; and Chorus (*Double-Faced, see list below*) (*In Italian*)
55001 12-inch, $1.50

DES GRIEUX (*discovered seated by the wayside*):
Manon, poor Manon! Must I see thee herded with these wretched beings and be powerless to aid? O Heaven! Merciless Heaven! Must I then despair! (*He sees Lescaut approaching.*) He comes! (*Advancing impetuously to Lescaut.*) Thy fellows now make ready; the soldiers will soon reach this place. Thy men are fully armed; they will rescue Manon and give her back to me! What! can it not be done? Are all my fond hopes vain? Oh! why dost thou keep silence?

The voices of the soldiers are now heard in the distance singing as they ride. *Des Grieux* and *Lescaut* listen attentively, and the former, realizing that they are almost at hand, madly tries to rush forward. *Lescaut* dissuades him, saying he has a better plan, as he is well acquainted with the officer in command. When the escort arrives, *Manon* is found to be very ill and is left behind by the officer at *Lescaut's* suggestion. During a heart-rending scene *Manon* asks and receives the forgiveness of *des Grieux*, repents her sins and dies in his arms.

DOUBLE-FACED AND MISCELLANEOUS MANON RECORDS

Restate qui (Wait a Moment) By Elisa Tromben, Federico Federici, G. Pini-Corsi, Riccardo Tegani (*Italian*) Mi raccomando (Wait for Me) By Tromben, Federici and La Scala Chorus (*In Italian*)	55000 12-inch,	$1.50
Io son solo (Alone at Last) By Gino Giovannelli (*Italian*) Manon, la catena (Manon in Chains!) By Remo Andreini, Riccardo Tegani and Chorus (*In Italian*)	55001 12-inch,	1.50
Nous vivrons à Paris (We Will Go to Paris) By Mlle. Korsoff, Soprano; Léon Beyle, Tenor On l'appelle Manon (She is Called Manon) By Mlle. Korsoff, Soprano ; Léon Beyle, Tenor (*In French*)	45009 10-inch,	1.00
Adieu notre petite table (Farewell, Our Little Table) By Mme. Vallandri and Léon Beyle (*In French*) Le Rêve (The Dream) By Léon Beyle, Tenor (*In French*)	45008 10-inch,	1.00

Gavotte—Obéissons quand leur voix apelle
    By Giuseppina Huguet, Soprano (*In Italian*)
  Traviata—Non sapete   *By Battaglioli and Badini* (*In Italian*)
	45028 10-inch,	1.00

Et je sais votre nom (If I Knew But Your Name)
    By Mlle. Korsoff, Soprano; Léon Beyle (*In French*)
  Favorita—Splendon piu belle in ciel le stelle (In Heav'nly Splendor)   *By de Segurola and La Scala Chorus* (*In Italian*)
	16551 10-inch,	.75

Ah! fuyez, douce image ! (Depart, Fair Vision)
    By M. Rocca, Tenor (*In French*)
  Carmen Selection (Bizet)   *By Pryor's Band*
	16575 10-inch,	.75

(Italian)

MANON LESCAUT

(*Man-on' Les-koh'*)

OPERA IN FOUR ACTS

Music by Giacomo Puccini, the libretto (founded on Abbé Prévost's novel) being mainly the work of the composer and a committee of friends. English version by Mowbray Marras. First presented at Turin, February 1, 1893, with Cremonini, Ferrani and Moro. Produced at Covent Garden, May 14, 1894; at Trieste, June 10, 1893; at Hamburg, November 7, 1893. First performance in France at Nice, March 19, 1906, at Marseilles (not given at Paris until 1910); at Madrid, November 4, 1893. First performance in America at Buenos Aires, June 9, 1893; in the United States at Grand Opera House, Philadelphia, in English, August 29, 1894, with Selma, Kronold and Montegriffo. Given in French by a small traveling company at Wallack's Theatre, May 27, 1898, and at the Tivoli Opera House, San Francisco, in 1905. Produced at Wallack's Theatre, New York, May 27, 1898, by the Royal Italian Grand Opera Company. First important New York production, January 18, 1907, with Caruso, Cavalieri and Scotti, under the direction of the composer, who then visited America for the first time.

Characters

MANON LESCAUT..Soprano
LESCAUT, sergeant of the King's Guards.........................Baritone
CHEVALIER DES GRIEUX (*d'h Gree-ay'*) ....Tenor
GERONTE DE RAVOIR, Treasurer-General...........................Bass
EDMUND, a student..Tenor

An Innkeeper, a Dancing-master, a Sergeant, a Captain. Singers, Beaux and Abbés, Girls, Citizens, Students, People, Courtezans, Sailors.

Scene and Period: Paris and vicinity; second half of the eighteenth century.

THE STORY

The Abbé Prévost romance has been treated operatically by several composers, the first being Halévy, who wrote a ballet on the subject in 1830. Other settings followed—by Balfe, 1836; Auber in 1856 and Massenet in 1884.

Puccini's version consists of four detached scenes selected from the novel, and the hearer should possess some knowledge of the story to fully understand the action of the opera.

The first act shows the courtyard of an inn at Amiens. *Manon's* brother, *Lescaut*, a dissolute soldier, is escorting his pretty little sister to the convent where she is to complete her education. While *Lescaut* is carousing with some chance companions, *Manon* meets a handsome gallant, *des Grieux*, who chances to be dining at the inn, dressed as a student. The prospect of school not appealing strongly to the young girl, she readily agrees to elope with *des Grieux*, thereby spoiling the plans of the old *roué*, *Geronte*, who had planned to abduct the pretty school girl. *Manon* soon tires of *des Grieux* and his poverty, and leaves him for the wealthy *Geronte*; but even this luxury fails to bring her happiness, and when *des Grieux* appears again she runs away with him.

FARRAR AS MANON

Geronte is furious and denounces *Manon* to the police as an abandoned woman. She is condemned to be deported to the French possessions in Louisiana. *Des Grieux* and *Lescaut* try to rescue her, but the attempt fails, and in desperation the former begs the commandant to permit him to accompany her to America.

In the final scene the lovers are shown in a desert near New Orleans. (The Abbé Prévost's knowledge of American geography was evidently limited, as was that of the French artist who drew the scene on page 290, with its lofty mountains!) *Des Grieux* leaves *Manon* to search for water, and returns just in time to see her die in his arms, after a most affecting scene.

ACT I

SCENE—*A Street in front of an Inn at Amiens*

Des Grieux, dressed as a student, strolling among the crowd, meets *Edmund* and a party of students, who warmly greet him. He is in a gay mood and in this charming air asks if there is one among the girls who will take pity on his lonely condition.

Tra voi belle brune (Now Among You)

By Franco de Gregorio, Tenor   (*In Italian*) *45015   10-inch, $1.00

A diligence now arrives, and *Manon* and her brother and *Geronte*, a chance traveling companion, alight. *Des Grieux* is struck with the beauty of the young girl, and when *Lescaut* and *Geronte* have gone into the inn to arrange for quarters, he questions her respectfully. She tells him that she is bound for a convent, but does not wish to go. *Lescaut* now calls to his sister, and she enters the inn after promising to meet *des Grieux* later in the evening.

The young man gazes after her, and says to himself, in a fine air, that never has he seen so lovely a picture of youth and innocence.

Donna non vidi mai (Never Did I Behold)

By Enrico Caruso, Tenor   (*In Italian*) 87135   10-inch, $2.00
By Giovanni Martinelli, Tenor   (*In Italian*) 64410   10-inch, 1.00
By Egidio Cunego, Tenor   (*In Italian*) *45016   10-inch, 1.00

The students now gather round, bantering *des Grieux* on his new conquest, but he is in no mood for joking and goes into the inn. *Lescaut* now joins a crowd of soldiers who are gambling, and soon becomes absorbed in the game. *Geronte*, seeing the brother thus engaged, seeks the landlord and plots to abduct *Manon*. *Edmund* overhears the scheme and informs *des Grieux*, who finds *Manon* and induces her to elope with him. They take

*Double-Faced Record—See page 290.

the carriage which *Geronte* had ordered and make their escape, leaving him furious. However, he finds *Lescaut* and suggests that they go to Paris in search of the runaways. *Lescaut*, who has been drinking, consents, delicately hinting that if *Geronte* will admit him into the family group, he will use his influence to induce *Manon* to desert *des Grieux* for the older but wealthier suitor.

ACT II

SCENE—*An Apartment in Geronte's House in Paris*

Manon, who has left *des Grieux* for the wealthier *Geronte*, is seen surrounded by the utmost luxury, attended by her hairdresser, dancing master, etc. *Lescaut* enters, evidently much at home, and congratulates her on her change of fortune, taking to himself all the credit. She says she is happy, but asks *Lescaut* if he has heard any news of *des Grieux*. *Lescaut* tells her that the young man is disconsolate, and is gambling in order to get wealth to win her back to him.

Manon gazes pensively at the rich hangings, and in a fine air expresses her longing for the humble cottage she has left.

In quelle trine morbide (In Those Silken Curtains)
By Frances Alda, Soprano   (*In Italian*)   87106   10-inch, $2.00

They are interrupted by the entrance of a company of Madrigal singers who have been sent by *Geronte* to amuse *Manon*, and they sing a beautiful Madrigal.

Madrigale—Sulla vetta del monte (Speed O'er Summit)
By Lopez-Nunes, Soprano, and Chorus   (*In Italian*) *45015 10-inch, $1.00

When the singers have departed, the dancing master appears to teach *Manon* the minuet. She takes her lesson, while *Geronte* and several friends watch her admiringly.

Des Grieux now enters and reproaches *Manon* bitterly. At the sight of him her love returns, and she begs him to take her away from all this luxury. They sing a passionate duet, followed by a lovely solo for *des Grieux*, who reproaches *Manon* for her fickleness.

Ah! Manon, mi tradisce (Manon, Kind and Gentle)
By Franco de Gregorio, Tenor   (*In Italian*) *45027 10-inch, $1.00
By Giorgio Malesci, Tenor   (*In Italian*) *63421 10-inch,   .75

Geronte surprises them, but controls his rage, and sarcastically wishing them a pleasant *tête-à-tête*, goes out. *Lescaut* shortly afterward rushes in and announces that *Geronte* has sent for the police. *Des Grieux* begs *Manon* to escape at once, but she insists on collecting her jewels first. This delay is fatal, and she is arrested and taken to prison, charged with being an abandoned woman.

WHITE

THE HAVRE HARBOR—ACT III

* *Double-Faced Record—See page 290.*

ACT III

SCENE—*The Harbor at Havre*

Manon has been banished from France, and is now embarking on the ship for the French colony in Louisiana. *Des Grieux,* unable to secure her release, entreats the officers to permit him to go on board. The captain, touched by the grief of the unhappy lovers, consents, and with a cry of joy *Des Grieux* embarks just as the ship is sailing.

ACT IV

SCENE—*A Desolate Spot in Louisiana*

This act is merely a long duet in which the sad, but very human, tragedy is ended. The music portrays the failing strength of *Manon,* the despair of *Des Grieux* when he is powerless to aid her, the last farewell of the lovers, and the bitter grief of the unhappy young man when *Manon* dies. As she expires, unable to bear more, he falls senseless on her body.

COPY'T MISHKIN

CARUSO AS DES GRIEUX

DOUBLE-FACED AND MISCELLANEOUS MANON LESCAUT RECORDS

Tra voi belle brune Franco de Gregorio, Tenor (*In Italian*) Madrigale—Sulla vetta del monte (Speed O'er Summit) By Lopez-Nunes, Soprano, and Chorus (*In Italian*)	45015 10-inch,	$1.00
Donna non vidi mai Egidio Cunego, Tenor (*In Italian*) Tosca—*Gia mi struggea* By Ernesto Badini, Baritone (*In Italian*)	45016 10-inch,	1.00
Ah! Manon, mi tradisce Franco de Gregorio (*In Italian*) Gioconda—*Cielo e mar!* (Heaven and Ocean) By de Gregorio	45027 10-inch,	1.00
Ah! Manon, mi tradisce By Giorgio Malesci (*In Italian*) Ernani—*Infelice e tu credevi* Aristodemo Sillich, Bass (*In Italian*)	63421 10-inch,	.75

THE BURIAL OF MANON—ACT V

MARITANA
ROMANTIC OPERA IN THREE ACTS

Libretto by Edward Fitzball. Music by William Vincent Wallace. First produced at Drury Lane, London, November 15, 1845. First American production in Philadelphia, May 4, 1848, by the Seguins. Other notable productions: In 1854 at the old Broadway Theatre, New York, with Louise Pyne and Sims Reeves; in 1857 by the Pyne and Harrison Opera Company, with the composer conducting; in 1865 by the Harrison English Opera Company, at Niblo's, with Theodore Thomas conducting; in 1868 by the Caroline Richings Opera Troupe, and in 1870 by the Parepa-Rosa English Opera Company. More recent revivals by the Metropolitan English Opera Company, Gustave Hinrich and Henry W. Savage.

Characters

CHARLES II, King of Spain...................................Bass
DON JOSE DE SANTAREM, his Minister.........................Baritone
DON CAESAR DE BAZAN.......................................Tenor
MARQUIS DE MONTEFIORI.....................................Bass
LAZARILLO..Mezzo-Soprano
MARITANA, a gypsy singer..................................Soprano
MARCHIONESS DE MONTEFIORI.................................Soprano

Time and Place: The scene is laid in Madrid, at the time of Charles II.

Wallace's lovely opera of old Madrid is still beloved for its tunefulness and its sentimental music. The ideal of opera fifty years ago was that of quiet, unaffected sweetness, and the composer in his Maritana achieved that quality to perfection. The story of the opera is founded upon that well-known play, *Don Caesar de Bazan*.

ACT I
SCENE—*A Public Place in Madrid*

The opening scene shows a band of gypsies singing in the streets. The young king, *Charles*, listens and is fascinated by the beauty of *Maritana*, one of the gypsies. The crafty *Don Jose*, the *King's* Minister, extols her charms to His Majesty, hoping that the *King* will compromise himself so that he (*Don Jose*) can inform the *Queen* and further his own designs on Her Majesty. *Don Caesar*, a jovial cavalier and a former friend of *Don Jose's*, appears in a slightly exhilarated condition, and in befriending a forlorn lad, *Lazarillo*, involves himself in a duel with *Lazarillo's* master. This leads to his arrest for dueling in Holy Week, and he is sentenced to die, to the grief of *Maritana*, who has taken a fancy to the gay cavalier.

ACT II
SCENE—*Interior of a Fortress*

Don Caesar sleeps in his cell, with the faithful *Lazarillo*, who has accompanied his benefactor, by his side. The Minister enters, and *Caesar*, in a famous solo, "Let Me Like a Soldier Fall," begs to be allowed to die like a soldier instead of being hanged. He is assured that it can be arranged if, in the meantime, he will consent to be married. Anxious to avoid such an ignominious death, *Don Caesar* consents without inquiring who the bride is to be. The wedding banquet is being served when *Lazarillo* arrives with a pardon, which *Jose* secures and hides, his scheme being to have *Don Caesar* shot and then induce *Maritana* to go to the palace by pretending that her husband is there, and then compromise the *King*. Here, *Don Jose*, thinking of his affection for the *Queen*, sings a beautiful ballad.

In Happy Moments
By Alan Turner, Baritone

(*In English*) *16552 10-inch, $0.75

DON JOSÉ:
In happy moments day by day,
The sands of life may pass,
In swift but tranquil tide away
From time's unerring glass.
Yet hopes we used as bright to deem,
Remembrance will recall;
Whose pure and whose unfading beam
Is dearer than them all.

Though anxious eyes upon us gaze,
And hearts with fondness beat,
Whose smile upon each feature plays
With truthfulness replete.
Some thoughts none other can replace,
Remembrance will recall,
Which in the flight of years we trace,
Is dearer than them all.

* *Double-Faced Record—See page 292.*

Maritana, who has been promised a glorious future if she will consent to wed *Don Caesar*, enters, heavily veiled, and the marriage takes place, after which the guards enter for the execution. *Lazarillo*, however, has drawn the bullets from the guns, and when the soldiers fire, *Caesar* is unharmed, but pretends death, and later escapes to a ball at the Montefiori palace.

SCENE II—*An Apartment in the Montefiori Palace*

Under instructions from *Don Jose*, the *Marquis* introduces *Maritana* as his niece. *Caesar* reaches the palace and demands his bride. In despair he exclaims:

DON CAESAR: I seek my wife in vain, for like some phantom she eludes me. Thus ever are they fading, the fondest hopes I've cherished. For me now nought remaineth but dreamy memories.

There is a Flower
By John McCormack, Tenor

(*In English*) 64307 10-inch, $1.00

There is a flow'r that bloometh,
When autumn leaves are shed,
With the silent moon it weepeth,
The spring and summer fled.
The early frost of winter
Scarce its brow hath overcast.
Oh, pluck it ere it wither
'Tis the mem'ry of the past.

It wafteth perfume o'er us
Which few can e'er forget,
Of the bright scenes gone before us,
Of sweet though sad regret!
Let no heart brave its power,
By guilty thoughts o'ercast,
For them a poison'd flower
Is the mem'ry of the past.

Don Jose arranges that *Don Caesar* shall be presented to the *Marchioness*, who is closely veiled. The scheme does not work, however, as *Caesar* hears *Maritana's* voice and tries to claim her, but she is quickly spirited away.

ACT III
SCENE—*Apartment in the Palace of the King*

In the last act *Maritana* is in the palace, wondering what is to become of her amid all the conflicting scenes and counter schemes. She sings her plaintive ballad.

MARITANA:
Scenes that are brightest
May charm awhile
Hearts which are lightest,
And eyes that smile;
Yet o'er them above us,
Tho' nature beam
With none to love us
How sad they seem.

Words cannot scatter
The thoughts we fear,
For tho' they flatter,
They mock the ear.
Hopes will still deceive us
With tearful cost,
And when they leave us,
The heart is lost.

The scheming Minister introduces the *King* as *Maritana's* husband, but *Caesar* suddenly appears and now boldly demands his bride, but *Don Jose* demands his arrest as an escaped prisoner. Before explanations can be made the *King* is summoned by the *Queen*, while *Don Caesar* and *Maritana* consult together, finally deciding to appeal to the *Queen*. While waiting for her in the palace gardens, *Caesar* overhears *Jose* telling Her Majesty that the *King* has a rendezvous with *Maritana* that evening. *Caesar* appears, denounces him as a traitor, and slays him. When the *King* hears of *Caesar's* loyalty, he repents of his designs on *Maritana* and gives her to the hero, besides making him Governor of Valencia.

The Victor offers several splendid records from this melodious opera, including six numbers blended into a most appropriate medley by the Victor Opera Company; a Victor Band record of the tuneful *Overture;* the song of *Don Caesar* in Act II, *There is a Flower,* given by Mr. McCormack; and a violin record of the favorite *Scenes That Are Brightest,* from Act III, and the fine *In Happy Moments,* sung by Turner.

{Overture to Maritana	By the Victor Band}	35071 12-inch, $1.25
{ Manila Waltz	*By United States Marine Band*}	
There is a Flower	By John McCormack, Tenor	64307 10-inch, 1.00
{Scenes That Are Brightest	By Charles D'Almaine, Violinist}	16093 10-inch, .75
{ Waltz from Faust	*By Charles D'Almaine, Violinist*}	
{In Happy Moments	By Alan Turner, Baritone}	16552 10-inch, .75
{ Faust—Waltz from Kermesse Scene	(Gounod) By Pryor's Band}	

Gems from Maritana

Chorus, "Angelus"—Solo, "Scenes That Are Brightest"—Solo, "Let Me Like a Soldier Fall"—Trio, "What Mystery"—Chorus, "Oh, What Pleasure"—Finale, "Viva Maritana"
By Victor Light Opera Co.

31804 12-inch, $1.00

PAINTED BY BECKER

MARRIAGE OF FIGARO AND SUSANNA

(Italian) (French)

NOZZE DI FIGARO   MARIAGE DE FIGARO
(Not'-zeh dee Fee'-gar-oh)   (Mah-ree-ahzh' deh Fee'-gah-row)

(English)

THE MARRIAGE OF FIGARO

OPERA IN FOUR ACTS

Text by Lorenza da Ponte, founded on a comedy by Beaumarchais of the same name. Music by Mozart. First production at the National Theatre, Vienna, May 1, 1786, with Mozart conducting. In Paris as *Le Mariage de Figaro*, in five acts, with Beaumarchais' spoken dialogue, at the Academie, March 20, 1793; at the Theatre Lyrique, as *Les Noces de Figaro*, by Barbier and Carré, in four acts, May 8, 1858. In London, in Italian, at the King's Theatre, June 18, 1812. First American production April 8, 1835, in English. Some notable revivals were—in the 70's, with Hersee, Sequin and Parepa-Rosa; in 1889, with Nordica, Eames, de Reszke, Ancona and Arnoldson; in 1902, with Sembrich, Eames, Fritzi Scheff, de Reszke and Campanari; and in 1909, with Sembrich, Eames, Farrar and Scotti.

Cast

FIGARO, (*Fee'-gah-roh*) the Barber, valet to the Count....................Bass
COUNT ALMAVIVA, (*Al-mah-vee'-vah*) a Spanish noble...............Baritone
COUNTESS ALMAVIVA, his wife ....Soprano
SUSANNA, maid of the Countess, betrothed to Figaro...............Soprano
CHERUBINO, (*Chay-rue-bee'-noh*) page to the Countess.................Soprano
MARCELLINA, (*Mar-chel-lee'-nah*) servant to Bartolo ....Contralto
BARTOLO, a rejected lover of Susanna ....Bass
BASILIO, (*Bah-zee'-lee-oh*) a busybody...................................Tenor
DON CURZIO ....Tenor
ANTONIO, gardener to the Count....................................Bass
Servants, Country People, Guards.

Scene and Period: Seville; the seventeenth century. The action is a direct continuation of the Barber of Seville.

293

CHERUBINO'S BALLAD

Mozart's Marriage of Figaro, with its merry plot and music, is one of the most delightful of musical comedies, and regret must be expressed for the all too infrequent performance of this ever-young and lovely opera, in which the complications of the story, the quick changes of mood, and the sparkling humor are all so well reflected in the music. In no single opera, perhaps, is there such a succession of musical gems as in Figaro. Each is perfect in its way and each seems to enhance the beauty of the others.

This comedy by Beaumarchais, on which the plot is founded, has been utilized by many composers, Mozart's version being written in 1785.

Those who have read the story of *Barber of Seville* will find themselves again making the acquaintance of *Bartolo, Almaviva* and *Figaro,* some time after the marriage of the dashing *Count* to *Bartolo's* ward. The *Count* has settled down quietly on his estates, while *Figaro,* as a reward for his services as a matchmaker, has been appointed major-domo of the castle. *Figaro* is in love with the *Countess'* maid *Susanna,* and expects to marry her soon, but unfortunately for his plans, had also promised to wed *Marcellina,* the ex-housekeeper of *Bartolo,* on the very same day. Further complications are promised by the fact that the *Count,* already wearying of his wife, is making love to *Susanna* himself.

ACT I

SCENE I—*A Room in the Count's Chateau*

Overture

By Arthur Pryor's Band
*35109   12-inch, $1.25

The overture is a most delightful one, written in true Mozartian style, and Mr. Pryor has given a brilliant reading of it, bringing out all its beauties.

Se vuol ballare, Signor Continor (Will You Dance?)

By Herbert Witherspoon, Bass
(*In Italian*)   64473   10-inch, $1.00

At the opening of the opera *Susanna* tells *Figaro* that the *Count* is trying to flirt with her, and *Figaro* plans revenge. *Marcellina* has confided in *Dr. Bartolo,* and as the portly doctor still harbors a grudge against *Figaro* for robbing him of his ward, he consents to help her. The *Countess,* who seems to be the only one in the castle not engaged in intrigue of some kind, thinks only of her husband, and how to bring him back to her side.

COPY'T DUPONT

CALVÉ AS CHERUBINO

* *Double-Faced Record—See page 299.*

THE GREAT HALL OF BARTOLO'S PALACE—ACT I, SCENE II

ACT II

SCENE I—*Apartment of the Countess*

At the beginning of Scene II, the *Countess* sings her lovely appeal to Cupid.

Porgi amor (Love, Thou Holy Impulse)

By Teresa Arkel, Soprano (*Italian*)
*63419 10-inch, $0.75

Susanna enters and tells the *Countess* of her husband's fickleness and they consult *Figaro*, who plans to make the *Count* jealous by telling him that the *Countess* is to meet a lover that evening in the garden. It is planned to send *Marcellina* in the *Countess'* place, and *Cherubino*, dressed as a young girl, to meet the *Count* in *Susanna's* place.

Figaro departs, and *Cherubino* enters. Seeing his mistress, he begins to heave deep sighs, but *Susanna* mocks him and tells the *Countess* he has written a song about his lady love. The *Countess* bids him sing it, and he takes his guitar and describes the delights and torments caused by Cupid's arrow.

Voi che sapete (What is This Feeling?)

By Nellie Melba, Soprano (*In Italian*)
88067 12-inch, $3.00

The song is in ballad form, to suit the situation, the voice giving out the clear, lovely melody, while the stringed instruments carry on a simple accompaniment *pizzicato*, to imitate the guitar; and this delicate outline is shaded and animated by solo wind instruments.

It is difficult to say which to admire most—the gracefulness of the melodies, the delicacy of disposition of the parts, the charm of the tone-coloring, or the tenderness of expression—the whole is of entrancing beauty.

GADSKI AND RIEGELMAN AS COUNTESS AND CHERUBINO

* *Double-Faced Record—See page 299.*

CHERUBINO:
What is this feeling makes me so sad?
What is this feeling makes me so glad?
Pain that delights me,—How can it be?
Pleasure that pains me!—
Fetter'd though free!
Whence, too, these yearnings,
Strange to myself?
Tell me their meaning, spirit or elf!
Why am I burning? Why do I freeze?
Restless forever, never at ease.
All is so altered, nothing's at rest,
Or are these changes but in my breast?
Gentler the breezes, day is more bright;
Fairer the moonbeams shine on the night:
Greener the forest, greener the hill,
Soft, too, the music flows from each rill.

BLANCHE'S PAINTING OF THE
LOVE-SICK PAGE

The women now dress up the page to represent *Susanna*, and have no sooner finished when the *Count* knocks, and *Cherubino* hides in the closet. The *Count* observes his wife's confusion, and hearing noises in the closet, becomes jealous. He demands that she open the closet door, and when she refuses he goes for a crowbar. The moment he is out *Cherubino*, aided by *Susanna*, slips out and escapes through the window, and *Susanna* enters the closet in his place. When the *Count* returns and opens the door, the maid comes out and the husband is forced to apologize for his suspicions.

Marcellina now enters with her lawyer and demands that *Figaro* shall keep his promise to marry her. The *Count* promises to look into the matter.

ACT III
SCENE I—*A Cabinet in the Count's Residence*

The third act opens with a scene between *Susanna* and the *Count*. He plans to force her to accept his attentions by threatening to make *Figaro* wed the ancient *Marcellina*, while *Susanna* endeavors to gain time. This scene is continued in a charming and graceful duet.

ACT III AT THE MUNICH OPERA

PHOTO BERT

THE COUNT IS JEALOUS—ACT II

Crudel perchè finora (Too Long You Have Deceived Me)

By Geraldine Farrar, Soprano, and Antonio Scotti, Baritone

(*In Italian*) 89027 12-inch, $4.00

Susanna pretends to encourage the attentions of the *Count,* in furtherance of the plot conceived by the *Countess;* while at the same time she deftly repels his advances. Finally she promises to meet him in the arbor and the *Count* is in ecstasies.

COUNT:
Too long you have deceived me;
Hope, weary, bids farewell.
SUSANNA:
What passes in her bosom
A maiden dreads to tell.
COUNT: You'll meet me in the grove, then?
SUSANNA: When sunset's on the lea.
COUNT: And do not mean it falsely?
SUSANNA: Oh, no; rely on me!
COUNT (*aside*):
What transport now is flying
Thro' this enraptured breast!
SUSANNA (*aside*):
Oh, may the scheme I'm trying,
Bring all to peace and rest!
COUNT: Then, by the garden bower?
SUSANNA: At twilight I will be.
COUNT: You'll not forget the hour?
SUSANNA: Oh, no, depend on me.
COUNT: In the garden?
SUSANNA: Yes!
COUNT: You'll not forget?
SUSANNA: No! No! No! Oh, no, depend on me!
COUNT (*retiring*): I have won her!
SUSANNA (*aside*): Well, cunning as you are, sir,
This time you've met your match!

Of the seven duets in which *Susanna* takes part in the opera, the *Crudel perche* is the most effective, and Miss Farrar and Mr. Scotti, both accomplished Mozart singers, deliver it delightfully.

The two now separate, each satisfied with the interview,—the *Count* believing she has yielded, and *Susanna* convinced that she has him in a trap.

Marcellina, with her lawyer, *Bartolo* and *Figaro* now enter, and *Figaro* is informed that he must wed *Marcellina* or pay damages; but the discovery of a birthmark proves him to be the long lost son of *Marcellina*. He embraces his mother just as *Susanna* comes in, and she, seeing *Figaro* with his arms around the woman he was lately trying to avoid, decides that he has changed his mind. Matters are explained, however, and preparations for the wedding are begun.

Susanna now seeks the *Countess* and tells her mistress that the *Count* wishes to meet her (*Susanna*) in the garden. The *Countess* then dictates a letter in which *Susanna* is to appoint a time and place for the meeting. The writing of this letter is portrayed in a delicate duet.

Che soave zeffiretto (Letter Duet—Song to the Zephyr)

By Marcella Sembrich, Soprano, and Emma Eames, Contralto   *(In Italian)*   95202   12-inch, $5.00

This number is always greatly enjoyed in representations of the opera, being a fine example of the Mozartian style and full of beauties, not only in the vocal parts, but in the masterly orchestration.

SCENE II—*Hall in the Chateau*

In this scene *Figaro* and *Susanna* are married, and in the course of the festivities *Susanna* contrives to slip the note to the *Count*, who is overjoyed.

HEMPEL AS SUSANNA

ACT IV

SCENE—*The Garden of the Chateau*

The last setting shows the garden where the most delightful of the comedy scenes takes place. *Figaro* enters and soliloquizes on the fickleness of woman. After his air he hides, just as *Susanna*, disguised as the *Countess*, and the *Countess* disguised as *Susanna*, enter. The mistress conceals herself, while *Susanna*, awaiting the *Count*, and knowing that *Figaro* is listening, sings her famous soliloquy.

Deh vieni non tardar (Oh, Come, My Heart's Delight)

By Marcella Sembrich, Soprano   *(In Italian)*   88020   12-inch, $3.00
By Frieda Hempel, Soprano   *(In Italian)*   88450   12-inch, 3.00

She pours out her whole soul in this address to the imaginary lover, in order to increase the jealousy of *Figaro*, who is hidden near by. This is one of the most exquisite numbers in the opera.

SUSANNA:
Ah, why so long delay? speed, speed thee hither!
While thou'rt away, all nature seems to wither.
Tho' bright the moon, and bright the stars are glowing,
Deeper around the wood its shade is throwing.
In ev'ry gentle murmur of the river,
In the rustling reeds that near it quiver,
A voice to love invites, the bosom filling
With love alone, all other passions stilling;—
Come then, my dearest,—the hours are quickly flying!
Let me with roses bind now thy head!

THE GARDEN—ACT IV

COPY'T DUPONT

DE LUSSAN AS CHERUBINO

Cherubino, having an appointment with the maid *Barbarina,* now enters, and seeing the *Countess,* thinks it is *Susanna* and kisses her. The *Countess* struggles, and the little rascal says:

> CHERUBINO:
> Why to me a kiss deny?
> With the Count you are not shy!
> Come, come, give o'er, then,
> And strive no more, then;
> One kiss to your little friend!
> COUNTESS (*struggling*):
> Hence, or I will call for assistance!
> CHERUBINO:
> One kiss only—no resistance!

The *Count* arrives just in time to see this, and giving *Cherubino* a box on the ear, sends him flying. He then makes love to the supposed *Susanna,* the *Countess* disguising her voice and encouraging him. *Figaro* now sees *Susanna,* whom he of course takes to be the *Countess,* and tells her that her husband and *Susanna* are together. *Susanna* reveals herself and *Figaro* embraces her. The *Count* sees this embrace and his jealousy making him forget his new conquest, he seizes *Figaro* and calls for help. The plot is now revealed, and the *Count,* confessing he is conquered, begs the *Countess'* forgiveness and promises to be a model husband. As the curtain falls the three happy couples are entering the house to continue the marriage festivities.

DOUBLE-FACED MARRIAGE OF FIGARO RECORDS

{Overture	By Arthur Pryor's Band}	35109	12-inch,	$1.25
{ Fra Diavolo Overture	By Arthur Pryor's Band}			

{Porgi amor	By Teresa Arkel, Soprano (*In Italian*)}	63419	10-inch,	.75
{ Toglietemi la vita ancor—Romanza	By Teresa Arkel (*In Italian*)}			

(Italian)
MARTA
(*Mahr'-tah*)

(English)
MARTHA
(*Mahr'-thah*)

OPERA IN FOUR ACTS

Libretto by St. George and Friedrich.　Music by Friedrich von Flotow.　The opera is an elaboration of "Lady Henrietta, or the Servant of Greenwich," a ballet-pantomime, with text by St. George and music by Flotow, Burgmuller and Deldevez, which was suggested by an actual incident and presented in Paris in 1844.　*Martha* was first produced at the Court Opera, Vienna, November 25, 1847, with Anna Kerr and Carl Formes.　First London production July 1, 1858, at Covent Garden, in Italian, and at Drury Lane in English.　First Paris production 1858.　In Italy, at Milan, April 25, 1859.　Given in 1865 at the *Théâtre Lyrique,* with Patti.　First American production 1852, in German.　First New Orleans production January 27, 1860, with Mlle. Dalmont.　A notable New York production occurred in 1887 with Patti, Guille, Del Puente and Scalchi.　Later Metropolitan performances were in 1896 ; 1897 (sadly memorable because of the death of Castelmary on the stage in the second act) ; 1900, in English ; and the brilliant revival in 1906, with Caruso, Sembrich, Homer and Plançon.

Characters of the Drama

LADY HARRIET DURHAM, Maid-of-honor to Queen Anne . . . . Soprano
NANCY, her friend . . . . Mezzo-Soprano
SIR TRISTAN MICKLEFORD, Lady Harriet's cousin . . . . Bass
PLUNKETT, a wealthy farmer . . . . Bass
LIONEL, his foster-brother, afterwards Earl of Derby . . . . Tenor
THE SHERIFF OF RICHMOND . . . . Bass
THREE SERVANTS OF LADY HARRIET, ... Tenor and Two Basses
THREE MAIDSERVANTS, ... Soprano and Mezzo-Soprano

Chorus of Ladies, Servants, Farmers, Hunters and Huntresses, Pages, etc.

The scene is laid, at first, in the Castle of Lady Harriet, then in Richmond
and environs, during the reign of Queen Anne.

Flotow's melodious opera has always been a most popular one, with its spirited Fair Scene, its beautiful duets and quartet, the famous third act finale and the beloved "Last Rose of Summer."

The composer was of noble birth, a son of Baron von Flotow of Mecklenburg, and was born in 1812.　His father destined him for a diplomat, but the boy loved music, and went to Paris to study.　His first attempt at opera was *Pierre et Catharine,* followed by *Stradella* and others.

Many great *prima donne* have sung the rôle of *Martha*—Patti, Nilsson, Kellogg, Gerster, Richings, Parepa Rosa ; and in the present day Sembrich, have charmed their audiences with Flotow's beautiful strains.

The fine overture, which contains many of the best known melodies, is splendidly played here by the band.

Overture

By Pryor's Band　*35133　12-inch, $1.25
By Pryor's Band　31478　12-inch, 1.00

* Double-Faced Record—See page 307.

LIONEL AND PLUNKETT—ACT 1

ACT I

SCENE I—*Boudoir of Lady Harriet*

Lady Harriet, maid-of-honor to Queen Anne, is weary of the monotony of court life. She is bored by her admirers, and jewels and flowers pall upon her. "Why do you weep?" says her faithful maid, *Nancy.* "I do not know," exclaims *Harriet.*

Mesta ognor (Ah, These Tears)
By Louise Homer and Bessie Abott (*In Italian*) 89009 12-inch, $4.00

NANCY:
Of the knights so brave and charming
Who surround our gracious queen,
And themselves with wit are arming,
Some one has so lucky been
Your cold and haughty heart to win!
Is there aught in this alarming?
LADY HARRIET:
Vain belief! How can rejoice me
Such insipid, idle love?
For to please and interest me
Flattery is not enough!
NANCY:
This is really too distressing;
Her's is called a brilliant lot!
If love does not work a wonder,

This flower fades and blossoms not!
Balls and tournaments are giving,
And your colors win the prize,
Proudly from the banners waving,
While the victor vainly sighs
For a smile from your fair eyes,
Which his armor penetrated!
LADY HARRIET:
All my glowing ardent wishes
Please me not when they're fulfill'd!
NANCY:
Then, from ennui to save you,
Nothing is for you remaining
But to let your heart be conquer'd,
Not a particle retaining!

Tristan, Harriet's cousin, a gay but rather ancient beau, is now announced and proposes a long list of diversions for *Harriet's* amusement. She declines them all and teases him unmercifully. The song of the servant maids, on their way to the Richmond Fair, now floats in through the window; and hearing these strains of the happy peasants, *Harriet* conceives a madcap desire to accompany them. *Nancy* and *Tristan* protest, but she orders them to go with her. Dresses are procured and they start for the fair, the ladies in the disguise of servant girls, and *Tristan* garbed as a farmer.

SCENE II—*The Fair at Richmond*

The scene changes to the Richmond Fair, where a motley crowd of men and maidens are looking for positions. Two young farmers, *Plunkett* and *Lionel,* now enter, the latter

THE FAIR SCENE

being an orphan and adopted brother of *Plunkett.* *Lionel's* father, on his deathbed, had given *Plunkett* a ring, which was to be presented to the *Queen* should the son ever be involved in difficulties.

In this fine duet the friends speak of *Lionel's* father and the incident of the ring.

Solo, profugo (Lost, Proscrib'd)

By Enrico Caruso and Marcel Journet
(*In Italian*) 89036 12-inch, $4.00
By Van Hoose and de Gogorza
(*In Italian*) 74005 12-inch, 1.50

Lionel tells the story of his adoption by *Plunkett's* family in the fine aria beginning—

So - lo, pro - fu - go, re jet - to, Di mia vi - ta `sul mat - ti.
Lost, pro - scrib'd, a friend-less pil - grim, Sink ing at your cot tage door.

This air is universally popular and has been used for many poems, including several hymns. *Plunkett* then sings—

Ne gram-mar sa - per po - tem - mo chi foss' ei, don - de ve - nia
We have nev - er learn'd your sta - tion, nev - er knew your fa ther's rank

and tells of the great love he has for his adopted brother.

The duet, which is a very beautiful one, then follows:

PLUNKETT:
  We have never learnt his station,
  Never knew your father's rank;
  All he left to tell the secret
  Was the jewel on your hand.
  "If your fate should ever darken,"
  Quoth he, "Show it to the Queen;
  She will save you, she will guard you
  When no other help is seen."
LIONEL:
  Here in peace and sweet contentment
  Have I passed my life with you;

"LOST, PROSCRIBED"

Stronger, daily, grew a friendship
  That forever lasts, when true.
BOTH: Brother, think not wealth and splendor,
  If perchance they e'er be mine,
  Can as happy this heart render
  As the friendship fix'd in thine.

The disguised ladies now appear, accompanied by the unwilling and disgusted *Tristan*, who considers the whole affair a joke in very bad taste. The two young farmers spy the girls, and being much taken with their looks, offer to hire them. The ladies, carrying further their mad prank, accept the money which is offered them, not knowing that they are legally bound thereby to serve their new masters for a year. *Tristan* loudly protests, but is hooted off the grounds, and the frightened girls are taken away by the farmers.

THE SPINNING WHEEL QUARTETTE

ACT II

SCENE—*A Farmhouse*

As the curtain rises the farmers enter, dragging with them the unwilling and terrified maidens.

Siam giunti, o giovinette   (This is Your Future Dwelling)

By Frances Alda, Soprano; Josephine Jacoby, Contralto; Enrico Caruso, Tenor; Marcel Journet, Bass   (*In Italian*) 95207 12-inch, $5.00

The farmers address the maidens as follows:

LIONEL AND PLUNKETT:
  This is your future dwelling;
  And traveling has an end.
HARRIET AND NANCY:
  We're reaping for our folly,
  Full measur'd punishment!
LIONEL AND PLUNKETT (*cordially*):
  Our house and home are yours now,
  Their comfort you will share.
HARRIET AND NANCY (*ironically*):
  Their house and home are ours now,
  O we unhappy pair!

LIONEL AND PLUNKETT:
  At dawn of day and morn's first glimpse
  Be up and stir about!
HARRIET AND NANCY:
  What vulgar ways they make us take!
  Before the sun is out!
  More monstrous things they'll next command
  That we never heard about!
LIONEL:
  And extra crowns your purse may see
  Before the year is out!

The quartet passage with which this record ends is one of the most beautiful in Flotow's opera.

Che vuol dir cio (Surprised and Astounded!)

By Frances Alda, Soprano; Josephine Jacoby, Contralto; Enrico Caruso, Tenor; Marcel Journet, Bass   (*In Italian*)   95208   12-inch, $5.00

When the ladies have recovered their breath and begin to realize that they are in no immediate danger, the temptation to plague their employers is irresistible, and when the young men endeavor to instruct the new servants in their duties the fun commences.

At the close of the first quartet passage, *Plunkett* shows the girls the door of their room. Anxious to escape from the scene and have an opportunity to discuss their predicament, they start toward their room, but *Plunkett,* thinking of his appetite, stops them.

COPY'T DUPONT

SEMBRICH AS MARTHA—ACT I

    PLUNKETT (*interposing*):
      Not quite so fast—
      First prepare a light repast!
    HARRIET AND NANCY:
      Kitchen work! O these barbarians!
    LIONEL:
      Why not excuse them? They are tired!
    PLUNKETT (*firmly*):
      Too much kindness will not do.

However, even the gruff farmer has realized by this time that these are servant girls of a most unusual kind, and hesitates to scold them.

PLUNKETT:
  What names bear you?
HARRIET AND NANCY:
  We?
LIONEL:
  Yes. you!
PLUNKETT:
  Yes, of course!
HARRIET:
  Martha is mine.
LIONEL: Martha?

HARRIET:
  Yes!
PLUNKETT (*to Nancy*):
  Well, and yours?
NANCY (*aside to Harriet*):
  (What shall I tell him?)
PLUNKETT:
  Well, don't you know it?
NANCY (*hesitatingly*):
  Ju-ju-julia!

PLUNKETT (*mimicking her*):
  Ju-oo-olia! You're proudly nam'd girl!
  (*With exaggerated courtesy.*)
  Julia! Be kind enough—
  If your ladyship so please it—
  (*Gruffly*)
  To hang my hat and mantle up!
NANCY (*indignantly*):
  Do it yourself!

PLUNKETT (*taken aback*):
  Bold! by the prophets!
LIONEL (*to Plunkett*):
  Not so bluntly give your orders,
  Rather wishes breathe, like me:
  (*Very politely*)
  Martha, take these things, prithee!
  (*Harriet takes them, but promptly throws them
    on the floor.*)

Astonished at such revolutionary conduct from servants, the young men exclaim:

LIONEL AND PLUNKETT:
  Surpris'd I am and astounded,
  And I can say no more;
  Such impudence unbounded,
  Was never seen before!

HARRIET AND NANCY:
  Surpris'd they are and confounded,
  And sorely puzzled is their brain;
  This blow has smartly sounded,
  May be they'll never try again!

The maidens determine to lead their captors a strenuous life, and when they are ordered to get supper they promptly refuse.

LANDE

METROPOLITAN SETTING OF ACT II

Presto, presto (Spinning Wheel Quartet)

By Frances Alda, Soprano; Josephine Jacoby, Contralto; Enrico Caruso,
Tenor; Marcel Journet, Bass   (*In Italian*)   95209   12-inch, $5.00
By Victor Opera Quartet   (*In English*)   70052   12-inch, 1.25

Lionel and *Plunkett*, astonished at such signs of insubordination, unheard of in servants of the seventeenth century, decide to learn what accomplishments these strange domestics do possess, and request them to show their skill at spinning.

PLUNKETT:
Quick now, fetch the spinning-wheels
From out the corner!
HARRIET AND NANCY:
Do you want us then to spin?
LIONEL:
Yes, most surely.
PLUNKETT:
Do you think
That for talking we engag'd you?
HARRIET AND NANCY:
Ha, ha, ha! To see us spinning!
PLUNKETT (*angrily*):
"Ha, ha, ha! To see us spinning!"
If you want your wages paid
You must earn them first, my maid.
Come and make then a beginning.
Fetch the wheels now!
HARRIET AND NANCY (*with mock humility*):
We obey, sir!
LIONEL (*to Plunkett*):
Not so harsh, you frighten them.

(*The ladies bring the wheels and place them in the foreground.*)
PLUNKETT:
Begin now, I command it.
HARRIET AND NANCY:
We cannot!
LIONEL AND PLUNKETT (*astonished*):
How? What?
Sit down now!
GIRLS:
We're seated. (*Taking seats behind the wheels.*)
PLUNKETT:
Turn the wheel! brr, brr, brr!
(*Imitating the noise of the wheel.*)
GIRLS:
It will not turn!
LIONEL:
With your thumb and your first finger
Draw a thread and twist it round.
GIRLS (*in mock despair*):
But the stubborn wheel won't move, sir!

When it is plainly seen that they are ignorant of the art the young men offer to teach them.

LIONEL AND PLUNKETT (*spinning*):
When the foot the wheel turns lightly
Let the hand the thread entwine;
Draw and twist it, neatly, tightly,
Then 'twill be both strong and fine!

HARRIET AND NANCY (*sitting down at the wheels*):
What a charming occupation
Thus to make the thread entwine;
Gently guided, drawn and twisted,
It becomes both strong and fine!

At the close of the quartet *Nancy* maliciously overturns the wheel and runs out, pursued by *Plunkett*, and leads him a merry chase, causing him to lose his temper, while

Lionel finds himself falling in love with the beautiful *Martha*. She laughs at him, but is nevertheless impressed with his good looks and manly bearing; so much so that when he asks her to sing she consents, and taking the rose from her bosom she sings the exquisite "Last Rose of Summer."

Last Rose of Summer

By Adelina Patti, Soprano	(*In English*)	95030	12-inch,	$5.00
By Luisa Tetrazzini, Soprano	(*In English*)	88308	12-inch,	3.00
By Marcella Sembrich, Soprano	(*In English*)	88102	12-inch,	3.00
By Alice Nielsen, Soprano	(*In English*)	74121	12-inch,	1.50
By Lucy Marsh, Soprano	(*In English*)	60126	10-inch,	.75
By Elizabeth Wheeler, Soprano (*Double-Faced*)	(*In English*)	16813	10-inch,	.75

As is generally known, this air is not by Flotow, but is an old Irish tune, to which Moore fitted his poem. In fact, Martha undoubtedly owes much of its vogue to this ancient Irish air, which was called "The Groves of Blarney." Moore wrote the words about 1813, and they have become the most popular of all his verses.

'Tis the last rose of summer,
Left blooming alone;
All her lovely companions
Are faded and gone;
No flower of her kindred,
No rosebud is nigh
To reflect back her blushes,
Or give sigh for sigh!

I'll not leave thee, thou lov'd one,
To pine on the stem;
Since the lovely are sleeping,
Go sleep thou with them.
Thus kindly I scatter
Thy leaves o'er the bed—
Where thy mates of the garden
Lie scentless and dead!

Nancy now returns, still pursued by the exasperated *Plunkett*.

PLUNKETT:
Don't you try this game again, girl!
Where do you suppose she was?
In the kitchen was the vixen
Breaking bottles, glasses, dishes,
And a good deal have I suffer'd,
Till at last I caught the lass!
NANCY:
Let me go! Don't make me mad, sir,
Or some scratching you will see!

PLUNKETT (*releasing her*):
By the prophets! she has spirit!
I confess, that pleases me!
NANCY (*plaintively*):
Martha!
PLUNKETT:
Pooh! What's wrong with you now?
Standing as if thunder-struck!
Get yourselves to bed, ye idlers!
Off with you, my saucy Puck!
(*The clock strikes twelve.*)

The farmers, somewhat subdued by the knowledge that they have engaged two most spirited and insubordinate damsels, now bid their new-found servants good night in this beautiful number, one of the gems of Flotow's opera.

Quartetto notturno (Good Night Quartet)

By Frances Alda, Soprano; Josephine Jacoby, Contralto; Enrico Caruso,
   Tenor; Marcel Journet, Bass   (*In Italian*)   95210   12-inch, $5.00
   By Lyric Quartet   (*Double-faced—See page 307*)   (*In English*)   17226   10-inch,   .75

PLUNKETT AND LIONEL:
Midnight sounds!
LADY AND NANCY:
Midnight sounds!
LIONEL (*to Martha*):
Cruel one, may dreams transport thee
To a future rich and blest!
And tomorrow, gently yielding,
Smile upon me! sweetly rest!
PLUNKETT (*to Nancy*):
Sleep thee well, and may thy temper
Sweeter in my service grow;

Still your sauciness is rather
To my liking—do you know?
MARTHA AND NANCY:
Yes, good-night! such night as never
We have lived to see before;
Were I but away, I'd never
Play the peasant any more!
ALL:
Good-night!
(*Harriet and Nancy retire to their chamber,
and Plunkett and Lionel leave by the large
door, locking it after them.*)

The maidens now peep out from their room, and seeing no one, come out, and are excitedly discussing their chances of escape, when *Tristan's* voice is heard outside softly calling to them. Overjoyed, they make their escape through the window, and return to their home in the carriage provided by *Tristan*.

LANDE

THE QUEEN'S HUNTING PARK—ACT III

ACT III

SCENE—*A Hunting Park in Richmond Forest*

Act III represents the Forest of Richmond, where the *Queen* is hunting with her attendants. The young farmers, who have sought vainly for their late servants, have come hither to witness the hunting and forget the two maidens who have wrought such havoc with their affections.

The act opens with the spirited apostrophe to porter beer, sung by *Plunkett*.

Canzone del porter (Porter Song)

By Marcel Journet, Bass   (*In Italian*)   64014   10-inch, $1.00
By Carlos Francisco (*Double-faced, see page 307*)   (*In Italian*)   16812   10-inch,   .75

This most famous of old English beverages is highly praised by the jovial *Plunkett*, who gives it credit for much of Britain's vigorous life.

PLUNKETT:

I want to ask you, can you not tell me,   And that explaineth where'er it reigneth
What to our land the British strand   Is joy and mirth! At ev'ry hearth
Gives life and power? say!   Resounds a joyous song!
It is old porter, brown and stout,   Look at its goodly color here!
We may of it be justly proud,   Where else can find you such good beer?
It guides John Bull, where'er he be,   So brown and stout and healthy, too!
Through fogs and mists, through land and sea!   The porter's health I drink to you!

Yes, hurrah! the hops, and hurrah! the malt,
They are life's flavor and life's salt.
Hurrah! Tra, la, la, la, la, la, la, la!

The farmers disperse, leaving *Lionel* alone, and he sings his famous "M'appari," the melodious air of the broken-hearted lover, in which he tells of his hopeless passion for the fair *Lady Harriet,* whom he knows only as *Martha.*

M'appari (Like a Dream)

By Enrico Caruso, Tenor   (*In Italian*)   88001   12-inch, $3.00
By Evan Williams, Tenor   (*In English*)   74128   12-inch,   1.50

LIONEL:

Like a dream bright and fair,   Oh! return happy hours, fraught with hope
Chasing ev'ry thought of care,   so bright;
Those sweet hours pass'd with thee   Come again, sunny days,
Made the world all joy for me.   Sunny days of pure delight.
But, alas! thou art gone,   Fleeting vision cloth'd in brightness,
    And that dream of bliss is o'er.   Wherefore thus, so soon depart;
Ah! I hear now the tone   O'er my pathway shed thy lightness
    Of thy gentle voice no more;   Once again, and cheer my heart.

Lionel suddenly encounters *Lady Harriet,* and although amazed at seeing her in the dress of a lady, warmly pleads his love.

LIONEL:
Yes, 'tis thee!
Once more I do behold thee!
Praised be God; it is no dream!
HARRIET (*aside*):
My heart!
LIONEL:
Lookest down so proudly;
Yet my heart knew thee at once.
HARRIET (*with dignity*):
Knew me? You're mistaken!
LIONEL:
I've hoarded thy fair image
Deep in my breast—No—

This dress does not deceive me—
'Tis thee, thee! Be Heaven blest!
HARRIET:
Madman, you dream!
LIONEL:
Ah! If but a dream,
This, a creation, of my brain,
Then, oh Martha, let me enjoy
This delusion while it lasts!
(*He attempts to seize her hand.*)
HARRIET:
Hold! presumptuous man!
No further! thou hast rav'd too long uncheck'd!

COURT BUFORD
CARUSO AS LIONEL

Lady Harriet is forced to call the hunters, to whom she declares that *Lionel* must be mad. He is distracted, while *Plunkett* endeavors to console him. The great finale, a part of which closes the Opera Medley (see below), then occurs. It is a magnificent piece of concerted music.

ACT IV

SCENE I—*Plunkett's Farm House*

Plunkett is discovered alone, musing on the unhappy plight of his foster brother, who, since his rejection by *Harriet,* is inconsolable.

Nancy enters, and she and *Plunkett* soon come to an understanding. They decide to present *Lionel's* ring to the *Queen,* hoping thus to clear up the mystery of his birth.

SCENE II—*A Representation of the Richmond Fair*

Lionel's ring has been shown to the *Queen,* who discovers that the young man is really the son of the banished *Earl of Derby.* However, he refuses to accept his rightful rank and continues to brood over the insult offered him in the forest. As a last resort a complete reproduction of the Fair Scene of Act II is arranged, with booths and the crowd of servants all represented. *Harriet, Nancy* and *Plunkett* are dressed in the costumes worn at their first meeting.

Lionel is led in by *Plunkett,* and when he sees *Harriet* in the dress of a servant, the cloud seems to pass from his mind and he embraces her tenderly. The two couples pledge their troth and all ends happily.

DOUBLE-FACED AND MISCELLANEOUS MARTHA RECORDS.

Overture to Martha By Pryor's Band Nocturne in E♭ (*Opus 9*) (*Chopin*) By Victor Sorlin, 'Cellist (*Piano acc.*)	35133	12-inch,	$1.25
Last Rose of Summer By Elizabeth Wheeler, Soprano (*In English*) Tannhauser—The Evening Star By Victor Sorlin, 'Cellist	16813	10-inch,	.75
Good Night Quartet By Lyric Quartet Madrigal from "The Mikado" (*Brightly Dawns our Wedding Day*) (*Gilbert-Sullivan*) By Lyric Quartet	17226	10-inch,	.75
Canzone del porter (*Porter Song*) By Carlos Francisco, Baritone (*In Italian*) Trovatore—Il balen del suo sorriso (*The Tempest of the Heart*) By Francesco Cigada, Baritone (*In Italian*)	16812	10-inch,	.75

Gems from Martha

Chorus of Servants—Quartet, "Swains So Shy"—"Last Rose of Summer"—"Good Night Quartet"—"May Dreams Transport Thee"—Finale, "Ah, May Heaven Forgive Thee."

By the Victor Opera Company (*In English*) 31797 12-inch, $1.00

(Italian)
BALLO IN MASCHERA
(Bah'-loh een Mahs'-keh-rah)

(French)
BAL MASQUÉ
(Bahl Mahs-kay')

(English)
MASKED BALL

OPERA IN THREE ACTS

Text by M. Somma, music by Verdi. First produced in Rome at the *Teatro Apollo*, February 17, 1859; at Paris, *Théâtre des Italiens*, January 13, 1861. First London production June 15, 1861. First New York production February 11, 1861. Some notable revivals occurred in 1903 with de Reszke; February 6, 1905, with Caruso, Eames, Homer, Scotti, Plançon and Journet; and November 22, 1913, with Caruso, Destinn, Matzenauer, Hempel and Amato.

Characters

RICHARD, Count of Warwick and Governor of Boston.................Tenor
REINHART, his secretary...Baritone
AMELIA, wife of Reinhart..Soprano
ULRICA, a negress astrologer....................................Contralto
OSCAR, a page...Soprano
SAMUEL,⎱ enemies of the Count ....⎰Bass
TOM, ⎰   ⎱Bass

Scene and Period: In and near Boston, end of the seventeenth century.

The opera was composed for the San Carlo, Naples, and first called Gustavo III (after an assassinated Italian monarch), but after the announcement had almost created a riot in Naples, Verdi was forced to change the scene from Stockholm to Boston, and the name to Ballo in Maschera. Finally it was thought best to abandon the Naples premiére altogether, and the opera was taken to Rome.

There are many, of course, who consider this work old-fashioned—and so it is, not pretending at all to be a great music drama; but there are many far more ambitious works with certainly less real music. The familiar *Eri tu* and *Saper vorreste* and the fine concerted numbers in Acts II and III are well worth hearing. The Victor has assembled a very fine collection of the best music in the opera, and presents it with the belief that this revival is the best heard in recent years.

Richard, Count of Warwick and Governor of Boston, falls in love with *Amelia,* the wife of *Reinhart,* his secretary and intimate friend. This love is returned, but the wife's conscience troubles her, and she consults *Ulrica,* a black sorceress, hoping to secure a drug that will cause her to forget *Richard. Ulrica* sends her to gather a certain herb which will prove effective. *Richard,* who had also gone to consult the astrologer, overhears the conversation, and follows *Amelia* to the magic spot. *Amelia's* husband, who has come in search of *Richard* to warn him of a conspiracy to assassinate him, now appears, and *Richard* makes his escape, after requesting *Reinhart* to escort the veiled lady to her home without attempting to learn her identity. On the way, however, they are surrounded by the conspirators and *Amelia* is revealed. *Reinhart* swears vengeance on his false friend and joins the plotters.

At the Masked Ball, *Richard* is stabbed by *Reinhart,* but the dying man declares the innocence of *Amelia* and forgives his murderer.

ACT I

SCENE I—*A Hall in the Governor's House*

The hall is filled with people—officers, deputies, gentlemen, etc.—waiting for the appearance of the Governor. He enters, is warmly greeted by those assembled, receives their petitions and inspects a list of the guests invited to the masked ball. The famous *La rivedrà,* the quartet from the first act, then occurs.

La rivedrà nell'estasi   (I Shall Behold Her)

**By Enrico Caruso, Tenor; Frieda Hempel, Soprano; Leon Rothier, Bass;
A. Perello de Segurola, Bass; and Chorus** (*In Italian*) **89077   12-inch, $4.00**

This number, although usually taking its title from the famous solo of *Richard, La rivedrà*, actually begins with his greeting of the people who have assembled for the *Governor's* morning audience:

RICHARD (*saluting the assembly*):
  My friends, soldiers, and
  You beloved companions so dear to me,
  My duty bids me watch o'er my faithful sub-
    jects,
  And protect them.
  Justice requires it—
  The only charm in power
  Is to dry their tears and crown
  Good deeds with glory.

OSCAR (*addressing the Governor*):
  Here is the list of guests invited to the ball.

RICHARD:
  Hast thou forgotten the name of any fair one?

OSCAR:
  The list is complete.

RICHARD (*seeing Amelia's name*):
  Amelia—dear sweet name!
  Its mere sound fills my heart with joy!
  Her beauteous, charming image
  Inspires my soul with love.
  Here soon I shall behold her
  In all her tender charms.
  No matter what the splendor
  Of night's most brilliant stars,
  I swear none is so brilliant
  As my love's dazzling eyes!

COPY'T DUPONT

CARUSO AS RICHARD

The people now join in a chorus of praise, while the conspirators, headed by *Samuel* and *Tom*, decide to select a more auspicious moment to consummate their plots against the *Governor*.

SAMUEL, TOM AND CONSPIRATORS (*aside*):
  The hour is not propitious
  The carry out our mission.
  From this unsafe position
  'Tis better to retire.

THE PEOPLE:
  All selfish thoughts discarding,
  With generous affection
  Our welfare and protection
  Are still his sole desire.

Caruso is especially happy in this remarkably melodious and graceful solo and in the dialogue with *Oscar* (Mme. Hempel), the ensuing ensemble being admirably given by Hempel, Caruso, Segurola and the Metropolitan Chorus.

Reinhart enters and tells the Governor of a plot against his life.

Alla vita che t'arride   (On the Life Thou Now Dost Cherish)

By Mattia Battistini, Baritone   (*In Italian*) **88232   12-inch, $3.00**
By Titta Ruffo, Baritone   (*In Italian*) **87113   10-inch, 2.00**

In this fine air he enthusiastically praises *Richard's* noble acts, and tells him his friends and faithful subjects will defeat the plans of the conspirators.

A negro woman, *Ulrica*, is now brought in and accused of being a witch. *Richard* laughs at the accusation and dismisses the woman. He calls his courtiers around him, and suggests that for a lark they go disguised to the hut of the sorceress and consult her. The friends agree, and the plotters, headed by *Samuel* and *Tom*, see a chance to further their plans.

SCENE II—*The Hut of Ulrica*

The hut is crowded with people who have come to have their fortunes told. The sorceress stands over her magic cauldron and sings her incantation.

Re dell' abisso (King of the Shades)

By Carolina Pietracewska, Contralto   *(In Italian)*   76005   12-inch, $2.00

She calls on the abyssmal king to appear and aid in her mystic rites.

ULRICA (*as if inspired*):
Hasten, O King of the Abyss!
Fly through the ambient air
And enter my abode.
Three times has been heard screeching,

The ominous lapwing.
Three times, too, has been hissing
The venomous red dragon,
And three times have been groaning
The spirits from the graves!

The Governor now arrives, dressed as a sailor, and accompanied by his companions. They are conversing with the witch when a knock is heard, and all leave the hut by *Ulrica's* orders except *Richard,* who conceals himself in a corner.

Amelia enters and asks the sorceress to give her peace of mind by banishing a love which she cannot control. The witch promises speedy relief if *Amelia* will gather a certain herb from which can be brewed a magic liquor.

Della città all'occaso (Hard by the Western Portal)

By Ida Giacomelli, Soprano; Lina Mileri, Contralto; Gino Martinez-Patti, Tenor   *(In Italian)*   *68143   12-inch, $1.25

Amelia asks for directions, and the witch proceeds:

ULRICA:
Then pause and listen.
Go from the city eastward,
To where by gloom engirted
Fall the pale moonbeams on the field,

Accurs'd, abhor'd, deserted,
And cull the flowers lowly
From those black rocks unholy,
Where crimes have dark atonement made
With life's departing sigh!

The frightened girl consents to go that very night, and takes her departure. *Ulrica* now admits the people again, and *Richard*, in the character of the sailor, asks her to tell his fortune. His inquiry of the prophetess takes the form of a barcarolle—the favorite measure of a sea-song—and the ballad, vigorous and tuneful, has all the swing of a rollicking song of the sea.

Di' tu se fedele (The Waves Will Bear Me)

By Enrico Caruso, Tenor, and Metropolitan Opera Chorus
(In Italian)   87091   10-inch, $2.00

GORITZ AS REINHART

This attractive ballad is full of humor, the *staccato* passages toward the close indicating the Governor's impatience to learn the future. In a gay mood he banters the woman, asking her to tell him if he will meet with storms on his next voyage.

RICHARD:
Declare if the waves will faithfully bear me;
If weeping the lov'd one from whom I now
tear me,
Farewell, to me saying, my love is betraying.
With sails rent asunder, with soul in com-
motion,
I go now to steer thro' the dark waves of
ocean,
The anger of Heav'n and Hell to defy!
Then haste with thy magic, the future
exploring,
No power have the thunder or angry winds
roaring,
Or death, or affection my path to deny!

This famous *Barcarolle* has been a favorite with many great tenors, but no one has ever sung it as Caruso has given it here.

Ulrica rebukes him, and examining his palm, tells him he is soon to die by the sword of that friend who shall next shake his hand.

Quintetto, "È scherzo, od è folia" (Your Prophecy Absurd!)

By Enrico Caruso, Tenor; Frieda Hempel, Soprano; Mme. Duchene, Mezzo-Soprano; Leon Rothier, Bass; A. Perellode Segurola, Bass; and Metropolitan Opera Chorus   *(In Italian)*   89076   12-inch, $4.00

* *Double-Faced Record—See page 314.*

The quintette, although it takes its title from the commencement of *Richard's* laughing "È scherzo," really begins with the comment of the horror-stricken courtiers:

OSCAR AND COURTIERS:
Dreadful thought!

ULRICA (*impressively*):
Thus 'tis written on high!

RICHARD (*airily*):
But food for mirth and mocking,
This prophecy so shocking,
I' faith perforce it makes me laugh,
Their woeful looks to note.

ULRICA (*meaningly, to Samuel and Tom*):
And you, my lords, no jesting
You deem my dark forecasting,
You find not in your hearts to laugh;
Dark scenes before you float!

SAMUEL AND TOM (*alarmed*):
Her tongue like sharp arrows smites me,
Her lightning glance affrights me!
A confidante of Satan,
She can dive into your soul.

OSCAR AND CHORUS:
Can he thus be fated,
To die assassinated?
The very thought is agony
And harrows up my soul!

COPY'T MISHKIN
CARUSO AS RICCARDO

COPY'T MISHKIN
HEMPEL AS OSCAR

The Victor record of the quintette is made with the identical cast of the recent Metropolitan revival, which was an ideal one. Caruso was most happy in the rôle of *Richard*, singing the lighter music with gaiety and abandon, and the more dramatic parts with thrilling power. Frieda Hempel sang *Oscar* beautifully, and was a perfect picture in her boy's costume. Mlle. Duchene's dramatic *Ulrica* brought her many favorable notices, while de Segurola and Rothier as the two arch conspirators were admirable.

The conspirators, *Samuel* and *Tom,* are uneasy, thinking themselves suspected, but the Governor laughs and asks who will grasp his hand to prove the prophecy false. No one dares to grant his request.

RICHARD:
Which one will prove
The prophecy false?
(*Offers his hand, but all refuse it.*)

Reinhart, who has become anxious about his chief and has come in search of him, now enters, and seeing the Governor, shakes him by the hand, calling him by name, to the astonishment of all those not in the secret. *Sir Richard* tells the witch she is a false prophet, as this is his most faithful friend.

RICHARD:
The oracle has lied!
That man who grasped my hand
Is my most faithful friend!

COPY'T MISHKIN
ROTHIER AS TOMASO

COPY'T MISHKIN
DE SEGUROLA AS SAMUEL

All the people greet the Governor with cheers, and kneeling, sing the hymn:

O figlio d'Inghilterra (Oh, Son of Glorious England)

By Giuseppina Huguet, Ines Salvador, Francesco Cigada, Aristodemo Sillich, and La Scala Chorus (*In Italian*) *63173 10-inch, $0.75

This noble concerted number, which closes the first act, is sung in a splendid manner by Huguet, Salvador, Cigada and Sillich of La Scala forces, assisted by the famous chorus of that opera house.

ACT II

SCENE I—*A Field near Boston—on one side a Gallows*

Amelia, much frightened by her lonely surroundings, enters in search of the magic herb. She sings her dramatic air, *Yonder Plant Enchanted.*

Ma dall'arido stelo divulsa (Yonder Plant Enchanted)

By Johanna Gadski, Soprano (*In Italian*) 88496 12-inch, $3.00
By Lucia Crestani, Soprano (*In Italian*) *68143 12-inch, 1.25

COPY'T DUPONT

EAMES AS AMELIA

AMELIA:
When at last from its stem I shall sever
Yonder weed of dread virtue enchanted,
From my tempest-torn bosom forever
When that image so ethereal shall perish,
What remains to thee then, oh, my heart!
Ah, tears blind me!
The weight of my sorrow
Chains my steps on their desolate journey!
Heart, have courage;
From these rocks their hardness borrow!
Come, oh, Death, let thy merciful dart,
Still forever my poor throbbing heart!
(*A distant clock strikes.*)
Hark! 'tis midnight! Ah, yon vision!
Moving, breathing, lo! a figure,
All mist-like upward wreathing!
Ha! in those orbits baleful anger is seething;
Fix'd on me they angrily burn!
Deign, oh, Heaven, Thy strength to impart
To this fainting, fear-stricken heart.

The vision resolves itself into *Richard*, who now approaches. The unhappy girl confesses that she loves him, but begs him to leave her. They sing a fine duet.

Ah! qual soave brivido (Like Dew Thy Words Fall)

By Ida Giacomelli and Gino Martinez-Patti (*In Italian*) *68026 12-inch, $1.25

RICHARD:
Like dew thy words fall on my heart,
Aglow with love's fond passion!
Ah, murmur with compassion those gentle
words again!
Bright star that bidst all gloom depart,
My hallow'd love enshrining;
While thus on me thou'rt shining,
Ah, let night forever reign!

AMELIA:
From out the cypress bower,
Where I had thought it laid in death,
Returns with giant power, the love my heart
doth fear!
Ah, would by Heaven 'twere granted,
To sigh for him my latest breath,
Or in death's sleep enchanted rest my weary
spirit here!

RICHARD:
Amelia! thou lov'st me!
AMELIA:
I love thee,
But thy noble heart will protect me from
mine own!

They are interrupted by the appearance of *Reinhart*, who comes to warn *Richard* that his enemies are lying in wait to murder him. *Richard*, unwilling to leave *Amelia*, is forced to ask *Reinhart* to escort the veiled lady to the city without seeking to discover her identity. *Reinhart* swears to obey, and *Richard* makes his escape. The couple start for Boston, but are surrounded by the conspirators, who take *Reinhart* to be the Governor. Disappointed in their prey, they tear the veil from the unknown lady and *Reinhart* is astounded to see that it is his wife. The great finale to Act II now occurs.

* *Double-Faced Record—See page 314.*

Ve' se di notte qui con la sposa (Ah! Here by Moonlight)

By Giacomelli, Minolfi, Preve and Chorus   (*Italian*) *35179 12-inch, $1.25

Amelia is overcome with shame, but protests her innocence. *Reinhart* bitterly upbraids her and denounces his false friend *Richard,* while the conspirators depart, anticipating the sensation which the city will enjoy on the morrow.

Reinhart, now bent on revenge, decides to cast his lot with the plotters, and the act closes as he says to *Amelia* with deep meaning:

REINHART (*alone with Amelia*):
I shall fulfill my promise
To take thee to the city!

AMELIA (*aside*):
His voice like a death warrant
Doth sound in my ear!

ACT III

SCENE I—*A Room in Reinhart's House*

Reinhart is denouncing *Amelia* for her supposed crime, and finally decides to kill her. She begs to be allowed to embrace her child once more, and her husband consenting, she goes out.

Morrò ma prima in grazia (I Die, Yet First Implore Thee)

By Johanna Gadski   (*In Italian*) 88497 12-inch, $3.00

Left alone, the unhappy man repents his resolution, and resolves to spare the guilty woman's life. In the greatest of the airs allotted to *Reinhart* he swears to avenge his wrongs.

Eri tu che macchiavi quell'anima (Is It Thou?)

By Emilio de Gogorza	(*In Italian*)	88324	12-inch,	$3.00
By Pasquale Amato	(*In Italian*)	88464	12-inch,	3.00
By Titta Ruffo	(*In Italian*)	88544	12-inch,	3.00
By Mattia Battistini	(*In Italian*)	92044	12-inch,	3.00
By Francesco Cigada	(*In Italian*)	*35179	12-inch,	1.25
By Giuseppe de Luca	(*In Italian*)	*62086	10-inch,	.75

Samuel and *Tom* enter and *Reinhart* tells them he knows of their plots, and will assist them, as he desires the Governor's death. They draw lots, and *Reinhart* is chosen to be the assassin. *Amelia* enters in time to realize the state of affairs, and is about to plead for the Governor's life, when *Oscar,* the page, enters bearing an invitation to the Masked Ball. The page, beginning an effective quartet, tells of the brilliancy of the occasion, and at the close of the number the conspirators go out, after agreeing on the password "Death!"

SAMMARCO AS REINHART COPY'T MISHKIN

Di che fulgor (What Dazzling Light)

By Giuseppina Huguet, Francesco Cigada, Carlo Ottoboni and Maria Grisi
(*In Italian*) *62086 10-inch, $0.75

SCENE II—*The Governor's Private Office*

Richard, alone, resolves to tear the unworthy love from his heart and send *Amelia* and *Reinhart* to England.

Ma se m'é forza perderti—Romanza (Forever to Lose Thee!)

By Enrico Caruso, Tenor
(*In Italian*) 88346 12-inch, $3.00

COPY'T MISHKIN
ZEROLA AS RICHARD

The recitative indicates this decision:

RICHARD:
Haply I have decided, finding peace of mind
Reinhart will return to his country,
His wife, submissive, will follow him.
Farewells unspoken, the broad ocean will divide us.

* *Double-Faced Record—See page 314.*

He summons courage and writes the order for the departure of *Reinhart*. Concealing it in his bosom, he gives expression once more to his love for the fair *Amelia* :

RICHARD:

If compelled to lose thee now	Within my inmost heart.
To part from thee forever:	And now, what dark forebodings
My burning thoughts will fly to thee,	Around my soul are thronging?
Though fate our lot may sever.	When, once more to behold thee,
Thy memory still enshrined shall be	Seems like a fatal longing!

Caruso sings this lovely air with that wonderful ease of delivery and golden voice which have made him the greatest of tenors.

A page brings a note to the Governor from an unknown lady who warns him of the plot, but *Richard* resolves to brave his enemies and attend the ball.

SCENE III—*Grand Ballroom in the Governor's House*

LUNDT, BERLIN

THE PAGE

Reinhart, mingling with the guests, meets the page *Oscar,* and attemps to learn how the Governor is dressed. The page teases him, singing his gay air, *Saper vorreste.*

Saper vorreste—Canzone (You Would be Hearing)

By Luisa Tetrazzini (*In Italian*) 88304 12-inch, $3.00

In reply to *Reinhart's* questions the merry page tauntingly sings :

OSCAR:

You'd fain be hearing, what dress he's wearing
When he has bidden, the fact be hidden?
I know right well but may not tell
　　Tra la la la, la la la!
Of love my heart feels all the smart,
Yet watchful ever, my secret never
Rank nor bright eyes shall e'er surprise!
　　Tra la la la, la la la!

The page finally reveals to *Reinhart* that the Governor is dressed in black, with a red ribbon on his breast.

Amelia meets the Governor and warns him against the plotters. He bids her farewell and is about to go, when *Reinhart* stabs him. The dying Governor, supported in the arms of his friends, tells *Reinhart* that his wife is guiltless, and that to remove her from temptation he had planned to send *Reinhart* to England to fill an honored post.

The secretary is overcome with remorse, and *Richard* dies, after declaring that *Reinhart* must not be punished.

DOUBLE-FACED MASKED BALL RECORDS

Della città all'occaso (Hard by the Western Portal) 　　By Giacomelli, Mileri and Martinez-Patti (*In Italian*) Ma dall'arido stelo divulsa (Yonder Plant Enchanted) 　　By Lucia Crestani, Soprano (*In Italian*)	68143	12-inch, $1.25
Ve' se di notte qui con la sposa (Here By Moonlight) 　　By Giacomelli, Minolfi, Preve and Chorus (*In Italian*) Eri tu (Is it Thou ?)　　By Francesco Cigada (*In Italian*)	35179	12-inch, 1.25
Ah! qual soave brivido (Like Dew Thy Words Fall on 　My Heart)　　By Giacomelli and Martinez-Patti *Forza del Destino—Non imprecare umiliati—By Ida Giacomelli,* *Gino Martinez-Patti and Cesare Preve*　　(*In Italian*)	68026	12-inch, 1.25
O figlio d'Inghilterra (Oh, Son of Glorious England) 　　By Huguet, Salvador, Cigada, Sillich and Chorus (*In Italian*) *Ernani—Ernani involami*　　*By Maria Grisi, Soprano* (*In Italian*)	63173	10-inch, .75
Eri tu (Is it Thou ?)　　By Giuseppe de Luca (*In Italian*) Di che fulgor (What Dazzling Light) 　　By Huguet, Cigada, Ottoboni and Grisi (*In Italian*)	62086	10-inch, .75

SCENE FROM MEFISTOFELE—ACT III

(French)
MEFISTOFELE
(May-phee-stoh'-feh-leh)

(English)
MEPHISTOPHELES
(Mef-iss-tof'-e-leez)

OPERA IN FOUR ACTS

Text and music by Arrigo Boïto; a paraphrase of both parts of Goethe's "Faust." The first production at La Scala, Milan, 1868, was a failure. Rewritten and given in 1875 with success. First London production July 6, 1880. First American production at the Academy of Music, November 24, 1880, with Campanini, Cary and Novara. First New Orleans production January 19, 1881, in Italian, and February 17, 1894, in French. Other New York productions were in 1896, with Calvé; in 1889 in German, with Lehmann; and in 1901 with McIntyre, Homer and Plançon; in 1904 with Caruso and Eames; at the Metropolitan, in 1907, for Chaliapine; in 1906 at the Manhattan Opera; the Chicago opera revival for Ruffo; and the recent Metropolitan production with Caruso, Destinn, Hempel and Amato.

Characters

MEFISTOFELE . . . . Bass
FAUST . . . . Tenor
MARGARET . . . . Soprano
MARTHA . . . . Contralto
WAGNER . . . . Tenor
HELEN . . . . Soprano
PANTALIS . . . . Contralto
NEREUS . . . . Tenor

Celestial Phalanxes, Mystic Choir, Cherubs, Penitents, Wayfarers, Men-at-arms, Huntsmen, Students, Citizens, Populace, Townsmen, Witches, Wizards, Greek Chorus, Sirens, Naiads, Dancers, Warriors.

FAUST LEAVING HIS STUDIO—ACT I

315

Arrigo Boïto well deserves a conspicuous place among the great modern composers. His Mefistofele ranks with the masterpieces of modern Italy, and contains scenes of great beauty, notably the Garden Scene, with its lovely music, and the Prison Scene, in which the pathos of the demented *Margaret's* wanderings, the beautiful duet and the frenzy of the finale are pictured by a master hand.

Boïto is not only a composer, but a poet of ability and a clever librettist. Notable among his writings are the librettos of Verdi's *Otello* and *Falstaff*, which should rather be called dramas set to music, for it is unfair to class them with the old-fashioned Italian librettos.

The story of Boïto's opera is directly drawn from Goethe's *Faust,* but the composer has chosen episodes from the whole of Goethe's story, not confining himself to the tale of *Gretchen,* but including the episode of *Helen of Troy.* In his *Mefistofele* Boïto has followed the great poet's work more closely than did Gounod's librettist, and the work is a deeper one in many respects.

PROLOGUE

SCENE—*The Regions of Space*

The prologue to Boïto's opera is a most impressive scene, which takes place in the indefinite regions of space. Invisible angels and cherubim, supported by the celestial trumpets, sing in praise of the Ruler of the Universe.

Mefistofele is represented hovering between Hell and Earth, denying the power of God. He addresses the Almighty in his *Hail, Great Lord!*

Ave Signor (Hail, Sovereign Lord)

By Marcel Journet, Bass   (*In Italian*) 64126 10-inch, $1.00

The Devil contends that man is but a weakling, easily cheated of his salvation. Standing on a cloud *Mefistofele* mockingly addresses the Creator:

Hail, Sovereign Lord,
Forgive me if my bawling
Somewhat behind is falling
Those sublime anthems sung
In heavenly places!
Forgive me if my face is
Now wanting the radiance
That, as with a garland,
The cherub legion graces!
Forgive me if in speaking,
Some risk I'm taking of ir-
rev'rent outbreaking!
The puny king of puny
earth's dominions
Erreth through wrong opin-
ions
And like a cricket, with a
long leap rushing,
'Mid stars his nose is push-
ing,
Then with superb fatuity
tenacious,
Trills with pride contuma-
cious!
Vain, glorious atom!
Proud 'mid confusion!
Phantom of man's delusion!
Ah! in such deep degrada-
tion
Is fallen the master,
Lord of the whole creation,
No more have I the will,
While in that station,
Him to tempt to ill!

From the Ditson Edition
Copy't 1880, Oliver Ditson Co.

PHOTO BERT
CHALIAPINE AS MEFISTOFELE

JOURNET AS MEFISTOFELE

Then, discussing *Faust* with the Mystic Chorus, *Mefistofele* wagers that he can entice the philosopher from the path of virtue. The challenge is accepted, and *Mefistofele* disappears to begin his plots against the soul of *Faust.*

Journet sings this great number splendidly, and it has been pronounced one of the most striking features of his Victor list.

ACT I

SCENE I—*A Square in Frankfort—Easter Sunday*

The aged philosopher, *Faust*, and his pupil *Wagner*, while mingling with the crowd, observe a grey *Friar* who seems to be shadowing their movements. *Faust* is alarmed and says to *Wagner*:

FAUST: Observe him closely. Tell me, who is he?
WAGNER: Some lowly Friar, who begs alms from those he passes.
FAUST: Look more closely. He moves slowly on in lessening circles; and with each spiral, comes ever nearer and nearer. Oh! as I gaze, I see his footprints marked in fire!
WAGNER: No, master, 'tis some idle fancy that thy brain deceives thee; I only see there a poor grey friar. Timidly he ventures to approach us, and we are to him but two passing strangers.
FAUST: Now he seems as though he wove nets about our path. His circles grow smaller! He draweth close! Ah!
WAGNER (*carelessly*): Look calmly. 'Tis a grey friar, and not a specter. Muttering his prayers, he tells his beads as he journeys. Come hence, good master.

As they leave the square, followed by the *Friar*, the scene changes to *Faust's* laboratory.

SCENE II—*The Studio of Faust. It is Night*

Faust enters, not observing that the *Friar* slips in behind him, and conceals himself in an alcove. The aged philosopher delivers his soliloquy, *Dai campi*.

Dai campi, dai prati (From the Green Fields)

By John McCormack, Tenor   (*In Italian*) 64303 10-inch, $1.00
By Alberto Amadi, Tenor (*Double-Faced*) (*In Italian*) 63313 10-inch, .75

He speaks of his deep contentment, his love for God and his fellow-man.

FAUST:
From the meadows, from the valleys, which lie bathed in moonlight,
And where paths silent sleep, I come returning; my soul filled
With calmness, mysterious and deep,
The passions, the heart rudely trying,
In quiet oblivion are lying;
My spirit knows only its love for its fellows;

Its love for its God!
Ah! From the meadows, from the valleys,
I come to read the blest Evangels;
Who delight me, and fill me with holy fire!
(*Opens a Bible placed upon a high reading desk. As he begins to meditate he is startled by a cry from the Friar in the alcove.*)

This is one of the most beautiful of all Italian operatic airs, and is sung by Mr. McCormack with a loveliness of tone which makes every note a delight, while a black label rendition, and an excellent one, is furnished by Mr. Amadi.

The *Friar* appears, and throwing off his disguise, reveals himself as the Devil, offering to be *Faust's* servant if he will accompany him. "What is the price?" asks the philosopher. "Up here I will obey thee," says *Mefistofele*, "but below our places will be reversed." *Faust* says he cares nothing for the future, and if *Mefistofele* can give him but one hour of happiness, for that one hour he would sell his soul.

FAUST:
About the future, not a thought do I give.
If thou dost bring me one hour
Of peace and quiet, in which may rest my spirit;
If thou wilt myself and the world unveil before me;

If I should haply say to the moment flying:
"Stay thee, for thou art blissful!"
Ah! let me die then,
And let hell there engulf me!

The bargain is made and they set forth on their adventures.

ACT II

SCENE—*The Garden of Margaret*

Faust (now a handsome young man known as *Henry*) is strolling in the garden with *Margaret*, while *Mefistofele*, as in Gounod's version, makes sarcastic love to *Martha*, whom Boïto has pictured as *Margaret's* mother. *Faust* pleads for a meeting alone with the maiden, but she dares not consent because her mother sleeps lightly. He gives her a sleeping draught, assuring her that it will not harm her mother, but merely cause her to sleep soundly. The four then sing a fine quartet, and the scene suddenly changes to the Brocken.

NOTE—Mefistofele quotations are from the Ditson libretto, by permission. (Copy't 1880, Oliver Ditson Company)

SCENE II—*The Summit of the Brocken*

This scene shows a wild spot in the Brocken mountains by moonlight. The wind is whistling in weird gusts. *Mefistofele* is helping *Faust* to climb the jagged rocks, from which flames now and then dart forth. Will-o'-the-wisps flutter to and fro, and *Faust* welcomes them, grateful for the light they give.

Folletto, folletto (Sprites of Hades)

By de Tura, Mansueto, and Chorus
(*In Italian*) 87067 10-inch, $2.00

Mefistofele echoes him, ever urging him to climb onward.

MEFISTOFELE:
Come up higher, and higher, and higher,
Farther yet 'tis more dreary the road
That will lead us to Satan's abode!
Dark the sky is, the ascent grows steeper,
Come up higher, and higher!
FAUST:
Ah! wild-fire, pallid light,
Now so dim, now so bright,
Flash o'er us thy ray, to illumine our way.
Come nigher, come nigher,
For dark is the ascent as higher and higher.
Come flame wildly dancing,
Come nigher, and nigher!

FARRAR AND MARTIN IN ACT II

Arriving at the summit, *Mefistofele* summons the infernal host—demons, witches, wizards, goblins, imps—and presides over the satanic orgies as King. All pay him homage and dance in wildest joy as he breaks into fragments a glass globe, typifying the earth, crying: "On its surface vile races dwell, degraded, toilsome, quarreling among themselves. They laugh at me, but I can laugh also!"

Faust now sees a vision of *Margaret*, on her way to prison for the murder of her mother and her babe. A red stain on her neck horrifies him, but *Mefistofele* laughs and says, "Turn away your eyes." The act closes in a riotous orgy, the demons whirling and dancing in a mad revelry. This wild scene is graphically pictured in Kreling's painting.

KRELING   THE VISION OF MARGARET

ACT III

SCENE—*The Prison of Margaret*

The demented girl is lying on a straw bed. She rouses herself and sings her sad ballad, *L'altra notte*.

L'altra notte (Last Night in the Deep Sea)

By Geraldine Farrar, Soprano
(*Italian*) 88114 12-inch, $3.00
By Elda Cavalieri, Soprano
(*Italian*) 55015 12-inch, 1.50

She raves of the cruel jailors, whom she says threw her babe into the ocean and now accuse her of the crime.

MARGARET:
To the sea, O night of sadness!
They my babe took and in it threw him!
Now to drive me on to madnèss,
They declare 'twas I that slew him!
Cold the air is, the dark cell narrow,
And my spirit broken to-day,
Like the timid woodland sparrow,
Longs to fly; ah, to fly off, far, far away,
Father, pity me!
In a deathly slumber falling,
Died my mother, no aid could save her;
And to crown the woe appalling,
They declare I poison gave her!

Mefistofele now enters, followed by *Faust,* who begs the demon to save *Margaret.* The fiend reminds *Faust* that it is his own fault, but promises to try, and goes out.

Faust goes to *Margaret,* who does not know him and is frightened, thinking her jailers have come for her. He urges her to fly with him, and they sing a tender duet, *Far Away.*

Lontano, lontano (Away From All Strife)

By Geraldine Farrar, Soprano, and Edmond Clement, Tenor (*Italian*) 88422 12-in., $3.00

MELBA AS HELEN

By Giuseppina Huguet, Soprano, and Gennaro de Tura, Tenor
(*In Italian*)
87056 10-inch, $2.00

MARGARET AND FAUST:
Away, far from strife and commotion,
O'er waves of a wide-spreading ocean,
'Mid perfumes exhaled by the sea,
'Mid palm trees and flow'rs in profusion,
The portal of peace and seclusion,
The blue isle seems waiting for me.
There, skies in their beauty transcendent,
Seem girt with a rainbow resplendent,
Reflecting the sun's loving smile.
The flight of all hearts that are loving,
And hopeful and moving and roving,
Is turned towards that life-giving island.
Away to that island far distant!

The return of *Mefistofele* drives *Margaret* into a frenzy, and she refuses to leave the prison, finally falling into *Faust's* arms in her death agony. Her senses returning for a brief period, she forgives him and dies, while a chorus of celestial beings announce that her soul is saved. *Faust* and *Mefistofele* disappear just as the headsman and jailers come to conduct *Margaret* to execution.

ACT IV

The Night of the Classical Sabbath

We are now transported to distant Greece, where *Mefistofele* has resurrected

KRELING   MARGARET GOING TO EXECUTION

the beautiful *Helen of Troy* for the further temptation of *Faust*. The scene shows an enchanting spot on the banks of the Peneus, with the moon shedding a golden light upon *Helen*, *Pantalis* and groups of Sirens. *Helen* begins her enchanting ode to the moon, followed by the trio.

Scena della Grecia—La luna immobile (Moon Immovable!)

By N. Ardoni, Soprano; Lavin de Casas, Mezzo-Soprano; Gaetano
Pini-Corsi, Tenor   (*In Italian*)   87068   10-inch, $2.00

Faust and *Mefistofele* enter and the former soon forgets all else in the love of the fair Grecian. *Mefistofele*, however, feels out of place in this classic neighborhood, and leaving *Faust* in the arms of *Helen*, returns to the Brocken, where he amuses himself with his satanic crew.

DEATH OF FAUST

EPILOGUE
SCENE—*Faust's Studio*

Faust has returned to his studio, again old and feeble and full of remorse for his past life. He has tasted the pleasures of earth and found them empty. He sings his famous epilogue:

Giunto sul passo (Nearing the End of Life)

By Alberto Amadi, Tenor   (*In Italian*)   63313   10-inch, $0.75

FAUST:
Nearing the utmost limit of life's extremest goal,
In a vision delightful did wander forth my soul.
King of some placid region, unknown to care and striving,
I found a faithful people and fain would aid their living.
Ah! would then that this fair vision could but be my last dream!
Look you—the crowds now come within my observation!
Lo, the crowds turn t'wards cities, Heav'nward turn the nation!
Holy songs now I hear.
Now I bathe in the radiant splendor of Heaven's glorious morning!
Ideal bliss upon my soul is already dawning!

Mefistofele enters for his final triumph, but *Faust* turns to the Bible and seeks salvation *Mefistofele*, in desperation, summons the Sirens to his aid, but *Faust*, leaning on the sacred book, prays for forgiveness, and the defeated *Mefistofele* sinks into the ground. A shower of roses, a token of *Faust's* salvation, falls on the dying man as the curtain descends.

DIE MEISTERSINGER   THE MASTERSINGERS
(Dee My'-ster-zinger)

OPERA IN THREE ACTS

Both text and music of *Die Meistersinger von Nürnberg* are by Wagner. The idea of the opera was suggested to the composer in boyhood, as was Tannhäuser, by the reading of one of Hoffmann's novels, and was planned as a kind of burlesque of the *Minnesinger* contest in Tannhäuser. First production in Munich, June 21, 1868, with Franz Nachbaur, under the direction of Von Bülow. Vienna first heard the opera in 1870; Berlin the same year; Leipsic in 1872, and Milan 1890.

The first performance in England took place under Richter, at Drury Lane, May 30, 1882; an Italian version was given at Covent Garden, July 13, 1889, and an English production by the Carl Rosa Company at Manchester, April 16, 1896.

In 1888 it was given for the first time at Bayreuth; and the first American production took place at the Metropolitan Opera House, New York, January 4, 1886, with Fischer, Staudigl, Kemlitz, Krämer, Aguste Krauss and Marianne Brandt. Some notable American performances occurred in 1901, with de Reszke, Gadski, Schumann-Heink, Dippel and Bispham; in 1905, with Van Rooy, Mme. Aino Acte and Burgstaller.

Characters

Character		Voice
HANS SACHS, cobbler,		Bass
POGNER, goldsmith,		Bass
VOGELGESANG, furrier,		Tenor
NACHTIGAL, buckle maker,		Bass
BECKMESSER, town clerk,		Bass
KOTHNER, baker,	Master-Singers...	Bass
ZORN, pewterer,		Tenor
EISSLINGER, grocer,		Tenor
MOSER, tailor,		Tenor
ORTEL, soap boiler,		Bass
SCHWARZ, stocking weaver,		Bass
FOLZ, coppersmith,		Bass
SIR WALTER VON STOLZING, a young Franconian knight		Tenor
DAVID, apprentice to Hans Sachs		Tenor
EVA, Pogner's daughter		Soprano
MAGDALENA, Eva's nurse		Soprano
A NIGHT WATCHMAN		Bass

FIRST PROGRAM OF MEISTER-SINGER, MUNICH, 1868

Burghers of all Guilds, Journeymen, Apprentices, Girls and People.

Scene: Nüremberg in the middle of the sixteenth century.

OTTO GORITZ
AS HANS SACHS

To the opera-going public in general Meistersinger is the most entertaining of all the Wagner operas. Its gaiety and tunefulness are charming, and its story easily understood by an audience, which cannot be said of most of the works by the master.

The humor is essentially German,—an intermingling of playfulness, satire, practical jokes, and underneath all something of seriousness and even sadness, while the romantic element, provided by the lovers, *Eva* and *Walter*, is not lacking.

The opera is a satire on the musical methods of the days of the Reformation, the mediæval burgher's life in Nuremberg being pictured with a master hand. The loves of *Walter* and *Eva*; the noble philosophy of *Sachs*, the cobbler-poet; the envy of the ridicu-

Eva Bestows the Wreath of Victory

WALTER'S TRIAL—ACT I

lous *Beckmesser;* and the youthful frolics of *David*—all are surrounded by some of the most glorious music imaginable.

The first act opens in St. Catherine's Church at Nuremberg, where *Eva,* daughter of the wealthy goldsmith *Pogner,* and *Walter,* a young knight, meet and fall in love. When *Walter* learns that *Eva's* hand has been promised by her father to the winner of the song contest, he resolves to compete, and remains for the examination before the meeting of Mastersingers. *Beckmesser,* who also wishes to marry *Eva,* is chosen marker, and under the rigid rules of the order gives *Walter* so many bad marks that he is rejected in spite of the influence of *Hans Sachs* in his favor.

Act II shows a street, with the houses of *Hans Sachs* and *Pogner* on opposite sides. The apprentices, who are putting up the shutters, plague *David* on his affection for *Magdalena, Eva's* nurse. *Sachs* drives them away and sends *David* to bed, then sits down in his doorway and soliloquizes. He cannot forget the song which *Walter* delivered before the Mastersingers,—its beauty haunts him.

SACHS:
    The elder's scent is waxing
    So mild, so full and strong!
    Its charm my limbs relaxing:
    Words unto my lips would throng.
    But I'd better stick to my leather
    And let all this poetry be!
    (*He tries again to work.*)
    And yet—it haunts me still.
    I feel, but comprehend ill;
    Cannot forget it,—and yet cannot grasp
        it;
    I measure it not, e'en when I clasp it.
    It seemed so old, yet new in its chime,—
    Like songs of birds in sweet May-time:—
    Spring's command
    And gentle hand
    His soul with this did entrust:
    He sang because he must!

Eva now learns of *Walter's* rejection and is so indignant that she promises to elope with him. The lovers are interrupted and forced to hide by *Beckmesser,* who comes beneath *Eva's* window for the double purpose of serenading her and rehearsing the song he is to sing for the prize on the morrow. *Hans Sachs,* hearing the tinkling of the lute, peeps out, and just as *Beckmesser* begins to sing *Sachs* breaks out into a jolly folk-song.

DAVID: "Forgive me, Master, and pardon the slip!"

SACHS:
    Tooral looral!
    Tiddy fol de rol!
    Oho! Tralala! Oho!

When mother Eve from Paradise
Was by the Almighty driven,
Her naked feet so small and nice,
By stones were sorely riven!

Beckmesser is greatly annoyed and says *Sachs* must be drunk. After a long altercation with the cobbler, *Beckmesser* finally starts his song, but as *Sachs* continues to hammer on his shoe at each mistake or wrong accent, *Beckmesser* gets badly mixed, and delivers himself of this doggerel:

BECKMESSER:
I see the dawning daylight,
With great plea*sure* I do;
For now my heart takes a right
Cour*age* both fresh and new.
I do not think of dying,
Rather of trying
A young mai*den* to win.
Oh, where*fore* doth the weather
Then *to*-day so excel?
I *to* all say together

'Tis *be*cause a dam*sel*
By her loved father,
At *his* wish rather,
To *be* wed *doth* go in.
The bold man who
Would come and view,
May see the maiden there so true,
On whom my hopes I firmly glue,
There*fore* is the sky *so* bright blue,
As I said to begin.

BERT DAVID AND HANS SACHS

The neighbors now begin to put their heads out the windows and inquire who is bawling there so late. *Magdalena* opens *Eva's* window and signals to *Beckmesser* to go away; but *David,* thinking she is waving her hand at the marker, becomes jealous and attacks *Beckmesser.* The noise brings everyone into the street, and the curtain falls on something resembling a riot.

Act III opens in *Sachs'* workshop. *Walter,* who had spent the night with *Sachs,* comes in and tells the cobbler of a wonderful melody which had come to him in a dream. They write it down and leave it on the table. *Walter* goes out and *Beckmesser* enters, sees the song, and questions *Sachs* about it. *Sachs* makes him believe it is his own and offers to give it to him, having conceived a plan to force the Mastersingers to consent to the appearance of *Walter. Beckmesser* is overjoyed and runs out to learn the song. *Eva* enters to get a shoe fitted, and then occurs the great scene in which the famous quintet is sung. The young girl, who has just had fully revealed to her the noble character of *Hans Sachs,* turns to the good shoemaker, and with a grateful heart sings—

EVA:
Through thee life's treasure
I control,
Through thee I measure
First my soul.

And were my choice but free,
'Tis you would please my eyes;
My husband you should be,
None else should win the prize!

Sachs then alludes to the fate of *King Mark* in Tristan, who married *Isolde* only to find too late that she loved another, and says:

SACHS:
To find the man before too late
I sought, or else that had been my fate!

He calls in *Magdalena* and *David,* who are dressed for the festival, and tells them he wishes them for witnesses for a christening. All look amazed, and *Sachs* explains that he wishes to christen *Sir Walter's* Master Song. As no apprentice can be a witness, *Sachs* surprises *David* by creating him a journeyman. *Eva* then commences the *Quintette of Baptism* with a short solo, beginning:

EVA AND SACHS—ACT II

LANDE

SCENE OF ACT II

EVA.

Se - - lig, wie die Son - - ne mei - nes Glü - ckes lacht,
Bright - ly as the sun up - on my for - tune breaks.

BECKMESSER'S SERENADE

In the rapture of her new-found love she sings of the Prize Song:

EVA:
In this sweet and holy strain
Lies a secret hidden;
Stilling all the welcome pain
That fills my heart unbidden;

MAGDALENA AND DAVID (*bewildered*):
Am I awake or dreaming still?

WALTER (*tenderly to Eva*):
Is it still the morning dream?
Dare I try to rede its theme?
But this strain, tho' whispered here,
Will greet thine ear loud and clear,
'Mid the Master's guild shall rise,
There to win the highest prize!

HANS SACHS (*with deep emotion*):
To the maid I fain would sing
Of my secret hidden;
But to tell my heart's sweet pain,
Now it is forbidden!

SCENE II—*A Field on the Shores of the River Pegnitz*

The scene suddenly changes to an open meadow on the banks of the Pegnitz, where the contest is to be held. The spectacle is a brilliant one, with gaily decorated boats discharging the various Guilds, with the wives and families of the members. It is in this scene that the famous March of the Guilds is played. A fine rendition of this number has been given by Sousa's Band.

March of the Guilds

By Sousa's Band   (*Double-faced, see page 328*)   35044 12-inch, $1.25

The Mastersingers now arrange their procession and march to take their places on the platform.

WALTER:
The maid Elysian
I saw in vision,
She whom my heart doth choose!
(Meistersinger, Act III.)

When all are assembled, *Sachs* rises, and in a noble address states the terms of the contest.

A Master, noble, rich and wise,
Will prove you this with pleasure:
His only child, the highest prize
With all his wealth and treasure,
He offers as inducement strong
To him who in the art of song
Before the people here
As victor shall appear.
This crown's of worth infinite,
And ne'er in recent days or olden,
By any hand so highly holden,
As by this maiden tender:
Good fortune may it lend her!
(*Great stir among all present. Sachs goes up to Pogner, who presses his hand, deeply moved.*)

COPY'T DUPONT GADSKI AS EVA

Beckmesser, who is in an awful state with his efforts to commit *Walter's* song to memory, wipes his heated brow and begins. He confuses his old melody with the new one, loses his place, mixes his lines, and is forced by the laughter of the people to stop. In a towering rage he accuses *Sachs* of plotting his defeat, then flings down the song and rushes off. *Sachs* calmly picks up the scroll and remarks that the song is a very fine one, but that it must be rendered properly. The Mastersingers accuse him of joking, but he declares:

SACHS: I tell you, sirs, the work is fine;
But it is easy to divine
That Beckmesser has sung it wrong.
I swear, though, you will like the song
When someone rehearses
The rightful tune and verses.
And he who does will thus make known
That he composed them, clearly;
A Master's name, too, he should own
Were he but judged sincerely.
I am accused and must defend:
A witness let me bid attend!
Is there one here who knows I'm right,
Let him appear before our sight.
(*Walter advances amid a general stir.*)
THE MASTERS: Ah, Sachs! You're very sly indeed!—
But you may for this once proceed.
SACHS: It shows our rules are of excellence rare
If now and then exceptions they'll bear.

PEOPLE: A noble witness proud and bold!
Methinks he should some good unfold.

COPY'T DUPONT
HOMER AS MAGDALENA

SACHS: Masters and people all agree
To give my witness liberty.
Sir Walter von Stolzing, sing the song!
You, Masters, see if he goes wrong.

The Mastersingers agree that *Walter* may attempt the air, and he mounts the platform and sings the noble *Prize Song.*

Preislied (Prize Song)

By Evan Williams
(*In English*) 74115 12-inch, $1.50
By Mischa Elman, Violinist
74186 12-inch, 1.50
By Lambert Murphy, Tenor
(*In German*) 70080 12-inch, 1.25
By Sousa's Band (*Double-faced, see page 328*)
35044 12-inch, 1.25
By Victor Sorlin, 'Cellist (*Double-faced, see page 328*)
35111 12-inch, 1.25

COPY'T DUPONT
FISCHER AS SACHS IN FIRST AMERICAN PRODUCTION, 1886

WALTER (*who has ascended to the platform with firm and proud steps*):

Morning was gleaming with roseate light,
The air was filled
With scent distilled
Where, beauty-beaming,
Past all dreaming,
A garden did invite.

(*The Masters here, absorbed, let fall the scroll they are watching to prove that Walter knows the song; he notices it without seeming to do so, and now proceeds in a freer style.*)

Wherein, beneath a wondrous tree
With fruit superbly laden,
In blissful love-dream I could see
The rare and tender maiden,
Whose charms beyond all price,
Entranced my heart—
Eva, in Paradise!

THE PEOPLE (*softly to one another*):
That is quite different! Who would surmise
That so much in performance lies?

WALTER:
Evening fell and night closed around;
By rugged way
My feet did stray
Towards a mountain,
Where a fountain
Enslaved me with its sound;

And there beneath a laurel tree,
With starlight glinting under,
In waking vision greeted me
A sweet and solemn wonder;
She dropped on me the fountain's dews,
That woman fair—
Parnassus's glorious Muse.

(*With great exaltation*):
Thrice happy day,
To which my poet's trance gave place!
That Paradise of which I dreamed,
In radiance before my face
Glorified lay.
To point the path the brooklet streamed:
She stood beside me,
Who shall my bride be,
The fairest sight earth ever gave,
My Muse, to whom I bow,
So angel—sweet and grave.
I woo her boldly now,
Before the world remaining,
By might of music gaining
Parnassus and Paradise.

PEOPLE (*accompanying the close, very softly*):
I feel as in a lovely dream,
Hearing but grasping not the theme!
Give him the prize!

MASTERS:
Yes, glorious singer! Victor, rise!
Your song has won the Master-prize!

Eva, who has listened with rapt attention, now advances to the edge of the platform and places on the head of *Walter,* who kneels on the steps, a wreath of myrtle and laurel, t h e n leads him to her father, before whom they both kneel. *Pogner* extends his hands in benediction over them. *Walter* and *Eva* lean against *Sachs,* one on each side, while *Pogner* sinks on his knee before him as if in h o m a g e. The Mastersingers point to *Sachs,* with outstretched hands, as to their chief, while the 'prentices clap hands and shout and the people wave hats and kerchiefs in enthusiasm.

COPY'T MISHKIN

WITHERSPOON AS POGNER

HALL

GORITZ AS BECKMESSER

DOUBLE-FACED MEISTERSINGER RECORDS

{Prize Song	By Sousa's Band}	35044	12-inch, $1.25
{Meistersinger March	By Sousa's Band}		
{Prize Song	By Victor Sorlin, 'Cellist}	35111	12-inch, 1.25
{ Ernani Selection	By Pryor's Band}		
{Prelude	By La Scala Orchestra}	68207	12-inch, 1.25
{ Magic Flute Overture	By La Scala Orchestra}		

(French)

MIGNON

(Meen-yohn')

OPERA IN THREE ACTS

Text by Barbier and Carre, based upon Goethe's *Wilhelm Meister*. Music by Ambroise Thomas. First production at the *Opéra Comique*, Paris, November 17, 1866. In London at Drury Lane, 1870. First New York production November 22, 1872, with Nilsson, Duval and Capoul. Revived at the Metropolitan in 1900, with de Lussan, Adams, Selignac and Plançon; by Oscar Hammerstein in 1907, with Bressler-Gianoli, Pinkert, Bonci and Arimondi, and at the Metropolitan in 1908, with Farrar, Jacoby, Abott, Plançon and Bonci. Thomas' work is among the most popular of all operas in Germany, and during the decade 1901-1910 was given nearly three thousand presentations.

Characters of the Drama

MIGNON, a young girl stolen by gypsies . . . . Mezzo-Soprano
FILINA, (*Fil-lee'-nah*) an actress . . . . Soprano
FREDERICK, a young nobleman . . . . Contralto
WILHELM MEISTER, a student . . . . Tenor
LAERTES, (*Layr'-teez*) an actor . . . . Tenor
LOTHARIO, (*Loh-thah'-ree-oh*) an Italian nobleman . . . . Basso Cantante
GIARNO, (*Jahr'-noh*) a gypsy . . . . Bass
Townsfolk, Peasants, Gypsies, Actors and Actresses.

The scene of Acts I and II is laid in Germany; of Act III in Italy.

Overture to Mignon

{Part I }
{Part II}   By La Scala Orchestra}68025   12-inch, $1.25
By Pryor's Band   (*Condensed*)   31336   12-inch,   1.00

The overture is full of the grace and delicacy for which Thomas' music is celebrated, and contains the principal themes, notably *Filina's* dashing "Polonaise." The Pryor record is a fine example of the perfection attained in the playing of this organization.   Every detail of the wonderful instrumentation which Thomas has written, and especially the passages for the wood-wind, is clearly brought out.   A fine orchestral rendition by the La Scala players, in two parts, is also offered.

COPY'T DUPONT

FARRAR AS MIGNON

ACT I

SCENE—*Courtyard of a German Inn*

Mignon, a daughter of noble parents, was stolen when a child by gypsies, and as the act opens is a girl of seventeen, forced to dance in the public streets by the brutal *Giarno,* chief of the gypsy band.

The first scene shows the courtyard of a German inn, where townspeople and travelers are drinking. After the vigorous opening chorus, sung here by the La Scala forces, *Lothario,* a wandering minstrel, enters and sings, accompanying himself on his harp.

Opening Chorus and Solo, " Fuggitivo e tremante" (A Lonely Wanderer)

By Perelló de Segurola, Bass,
and La Scala Chorus
(*In Italian*) *55004 12-inch, $1.50

* *Double-Faced Record—See page 335.*

329

TETRAZZINI AS FILINA

Fuggitivo e tremante (A Lonely Wanderer)

By Cesare Preve, Bass (*In Italian*) *62650 10-inch, $0.75

The minstrel is in reality *Mignon's* father, whose mind was affected by his daughter's abduction, and he wanders about seeking her.

> LOTHARIO: A lonely wanderer am I! I stray from door to door,
> As fate doth guide, or as the storm doth hurry me.
> Far, far I'll roam in search of *her!*

The gypsy band appears and *Mignon* is ordered to dance by *Giarno,* who threatens her with his stick when she wearily refuses. *Wilhelm,* a young student, protects her from the gypsy and questions her about her parents. She remembers but little, but tells him of her impression of home in this lovely *Connais-tu le pays,* full of tender beauty.

(French) (English)
Connais-tu le pays ? (Knowest Thou the Land ?)
(German) (Italian)
Kennst du das Land ? Non conosci il bel suol ?

By Marcella Sembrich, Soprano	(*In French*)	88098	12-inch,	$3.00
By Ernestine Schumann-Heink, Contralto	(*In German*)	88090	12-inch,	3.00
By Geraldine Farrar and Fritz Kreisler	(*In French*)	88538	12-inch,	3.00
By Geraldine Farrar, Soprano	(*In French*)	88211	12-inch,	3.00
By Emmy Destinn, Soprano	(*In German*)	88467	12-inch,	3.00
By Emmy Destinn, Soprano	(*In German*)	91083	10-inch,	2.00
By Giuseppina Huguet, Soprano	(*In Italian*)	*35178	12-inch,	1.25

Seven records of this beautiful air, by five famous singers, are listed here.

This air is one of the happiest inspirations of the composer. It is said that much of its charm comes from Thomas' intimate study of Scheffer's painting, "Mignon." At any rate he has caught the inner sense of Goethe's poem and has expressed it in exquisite tones. The opening passage:

Andantino (♩ = 120.) dolce.

Con - nais - tu le - pa - ys ou fleu rit l'o - ran gu?
Know , est thou yon der land where the or - ange grows!

gives us an idea of the melody, one of the most beautiful in the entire range of opera. The passionate longing of the orphan child for her childhood home is effectively expressed in this superb climax:

MIGNON.
c'est là...... c'est là que je vou - drais vi - vre,
'Tis there!.. 'Tis there! my heart's love o - bey - ing

in which *Mignon* seems to pour forth her whole heart in a flood of emotion. The words are most beautiful ones.

Knowest Thou the Land ?

MIGNON:
Knowest thou yonder land where the orange grows,
Where the fruit is of gold, and so fair the rose?
Where the breeze gently wafts the song of birds,
Where the season round is mild as lover's words?
Where so calm and so soft, like Heaven's blessing true,
Spring eternally reigns, with the skies ever blue?
Alas, why afar am I straying, why ever linger here?
'Tis with thee I would fly!
'Tis there! 'Tis there! my heart's love obeying,
'Twere bliss to live and die!
'Tis there my heart's love obeying,
I'd live, I would die!

Wilhelm, full of pity for the helpless girl, offers *Giarno* a sum of money to release her, and goes into the inn to complete the bargain. *Lothario* comes to *Mignon* to bid her farewell, saying he must go south, following the swallows.
Then occurs the beautiful "Swallow Duet," one of the gems of the opera.

Les Hirondelles (Song of the Swallows)

By Geraldine Farrar, Soprano; Marcel Journet,
Bass (*In French*) 89038 12-inch, $4.00

COPY'T DUPONT ABOTT AS FILINA

* *Double-Faced Record—See page 335.*

BY HANS PRINTZ

MIGNON AND LOTHARIO

MIGNON: (*accompanying herself on the harp*):
 Oh swallows gay and blithe,
 Ye joy of every land,
 Unfold your gentle wings,
 Speed quickly on your way!
LOTHARIO:
 The harp, touched by her gentle hand
 A melancholy sound mysteriously gives forth.
MIGNON:
 Ye blithe and gentle swallows,
 Unfold your nimble wings;
 Quick, hasten to the land
 Where winter never reigns.
 Thrice happy bird, thrice happy bird,
 Who first the wished-for good
 Right joyously shall reach.

The effectiveness of Thomas' exquisite score depends very much on the perfection of its rendering; and this is especially true of the first act music—the *Connais-tu, Lothario's* song, and this serene and beautiful duet, given so charmingly here.

Very little need be said about Miss Farrar's familiar impersonation of *Mignon*. It is always delightful, both to eye and ear. Journet sings the music of *Lothario* with dignity and beauty of voice; while Farrar's every note is exquisite in its loveliness.

Wilhelm is now invited to go to the Castle of *Prince Tieffenbach* with the troupe of players, headed by the lovely *Filina,* who has observed the handsome student with an appreciative eye. He hesitates, thinking of *Mignon,* but she begs to be allowed to accompany him disguised as a servant.

MIGNON:
 Stranger! thou didst purchase me—
 Dispose of me, henceforth, e'en as thou wilt.
WILHELM:
 In this very town, to which Fate hath brought
  thee,
 There lives an aged relative of mine,
 Who, to her home, will gladly welcome thee.
MIGNON:
 Must I then part from thee?
WILHELM:
 My child, thou can'st *not* dwell with me;
 Ill could I the part perform,
 Of father!
MIGNON:
 Could I not disguise myself,
 And as thy servant, travel with thee?
WILHELM (*taking her hands*):
 And what couldst thou do then?
MIGNON:
 With love and gratitude,
 My heart is filled.
 To follow thee, O master mine,
 Indeed were happiness to me!
WILHELM:
 Would'st thou anew thy liberty renounce,
 And be a slave once more?
MIGNON (*sadly*):
 Well since my prayers thou wilt not hear,
 (*pointing to Lothario, who approaches*)
 I'll e'en depart with *him!*
LOTHARIO (*rushing to Mignon, and encircling
  her with his arms*):
 Come! my footsteps follow;
 Through by-paths lone and wild!
 (*Attempts to draw Mignon with him.*)

Wilhelm finally yields a reluctant consent, not knowing what else to do, and the act ends with the departure of the players.

PHOTO MANUEL

FARRAR AS MIGNON—ACT II

ACT II

SCENE I—*A Boudoir in Tieffenbach Castle*

Act II represents a room in the Prince's castle. *Filina* is seated in front of her toilet table, musing on the handsome *Wilhelm*, who has made a deep impression on her somewhat volatile affections. *Wilhelm* enters with *Mignon*, who meets with a cool reception from the gay actress. *Wilhelm* makes love to *Filina* while *Mignon* watches them with a sad heart, as she has learned to love her new master. When left alone, she tries by the aid of *Filina's* rouge to make her complexion as beautiful as that of the actress who has dazzled her master, and, noting the effect in the glass, sings a gay song with an odd refrain, called by the composer "Styrienne."

Styrienne, "Je connais" (I Know a Poor Maiden)

By Geraldine Farrar, Soprano   (*In French*) 88152   12-inch, $3.00

MIGNON:
Well I know a poor young child,
A sad young child of Bohemia,
On whose pale sunken cheeks joy ne'er rested,
Ah! ah! ah! ah! what a dull story!
I cannot leave the glass,
So much improved I'm seeming,
Am I the same, or dreaming?
Ah! la la.
(*Looking in the glass*):
Am I still Mignon?
Can it be Mignon that I see?
One fine day, the child in play,
A stratagem boldly trying,
To the master's good pleasure applying,
Ah! ah! ah! what a foolish story!

I fain would turn away,
But so improved am seeming,
Am I the same, or dreaming?
Ah! Ah! la la
Am I still Mignon?
No! no! 'tis I no longer!
But then! 'tis not she either!
Some other secrets she must have her charms to heighten.
(*Opens the door of the dressing room*):
Is it not there she keeps her gayest dresses?
Yes! alas! were I Filina, would he love me as well?
What idle folly!   (*From the Ditson score.*
'Tis a demon now tempts me!   Copy't 1880.)

Mignon now goes into the closet, and after *Wilhelm* has returned makes her appearance in one of *Filina's* dresses. He tells her in a beautiful air that he must leave her.

Addio, Mignon (Farewell, Mignon)

By M. Régis, Tenor   (*In French*)   *45023   10-inch, $1.00
By Emilio Perea, Tenor   (*Piano acc.*)   (*In Italian*)   *63420   10-inch,   .75

Mignon utters a cry of grief and begins to weep, while *Wilhelm* tenderly says:

WILHELM:
Farewell, Mignon, take heart!
Thy tears restrain!
In the bright years of youth no grief doth linger long.
Weep not, Mignon!
O'er thee just Heaven will watch with fost'-ring care.
Oh, may'st thou thy dear native land once more regain!
May fortune on thy fate henceforth benignly smile!
It pains me much to leave thee: my stricken heart
With thy lone destiny will ever sympathize!
Farewell, Mignon, take heart!
Then dry thy tears.

Mignon refuses money which he offers her, and is about to bid him farewell when *Filina* enters, and seeing *Mignon* in one of her own dresses, eyes her with sarcastic amusement, which puts *Mignon* into a jealous rage and she rushes into the cabinet, tears off the borrowed finery and puts on her gypsy garments.

SCENE II—*The Gardens of the Castle*

The scene changes to the park of the castle. *Mignon*, in despair, attempts to throw herself into the lake, but is prevented

VAN ENDERT AS MIGNON

* *Double-Faced Record—See page 335.*

by *Lothario,* who consoles her. In a fit of jealousy she wishes that fire would consume the castle in which *Filina* had won her master's affections. *Lothario* is puzzled by this and goes off muttering to himself.

The actors and guests now issue from the castle proclaiming the beauty and talent of *Filina.* In the flush of her triumph she sings the brilliant *Polonese* or *polacca* (French, *Polonaise*), one of the most difficult and showy of all soprano airs.

Polonese, " Io son Titania" (I'm Fair Titania !)

By Luisa Tetrazzini, Soprano
              (*In Italian*)   88296   12-inch, $3.00

By Giuseppina Huguet, Soprano
              (*In Italian*)   *35178   12-inch,   1.25

By Lucette Korsoff, Soprano
              (*In French*)   *45006   10-inch,   1.00

Io son Titania
(Behold Titania!)

CHORUS:
She is truly divine, Filina!
At her feet we lay our hearts and our flowers!
What charms, what beauties are hers!
Ah! what success! Bravo! Honor to Titania!

THE LATE BRESSLER-GIANOLA
AS MIGNON

FILINA:
Yes; for to-night I am queen of the fairies!
Observe ye here, my sceptre bright,
(*Raising the wand which she holds in her hand.*)
And behold my num'rous trophies!
(*Pointing to the wreath which has been presented to her.*)
I'm fair Titania, glad and gay,
Thro' the world unfetter'd I blithely stray.
With jocund heart and happy mien,
I cheerily dance the hours away,

Like the bird that freely wings its flight.
Fairies dance around me,
Elfin sprites on nimble toe around me gaily dance.
For I'm fair Titania!
Both night and day. My attendants ever sing,
The achievements of the god of Love!
On the wave's white foam,
'Mid the twilight grey, 'mid hedges, 'mid flowers,
I blithely do dance!
Behold Titania, glad and gay!

Wilhelm now sees *Mignon* and is about to speak to her when *Filina* interposes and asks her to go to the castle on some errand. The young girl, glad to escape meeting *Wilhelm,* obeys, but has no sooner gone than the castle is discovered to be in flames, the half-witted *Lothario* having set fire to it after having heard *Mignon's* jealous wish.

Wilhelm rushes into the burning castle and soon reappears with the unconscious form of *Mignon,* while the curtain falls on a magnificent tableau.

ACT III

SCENE—*Count Lothario's Castle in Italy*

This act takes place in the castle of *Lothario,* to which the old man has instinctively returned with *Mignon,* followed by *Wilhelm,* who now realizes that he loves his youthful ward. The young girl is recovering from a dangerous illness, and as *Lothario* watches outside her sick room, he sings a beautiful lullaby or *berceuse,*

Berceuse (Lullaby) (Ninna nanna)

By Pol Plancon, Bass	(*In Italian*)	85126	12-inch,	$3.00
By Marcel Journet, Bass	(*In Italian*)	74270	12-inch,	1.50
By Gaudio Mansueto, Bass	(*In Italian*)	*55004	12-inch,	1.50
By Cesare Preve, Bass	(*In Italian*)	*62650	10-inch,	.75

* Double-Faced Record—See page 335.

LOTHARIO:

I've soothed the throbbing of her aching heart,
And to her lips the smile I have restored.
Her weary eyes at last have closed
In gentle slumber;

By day and night some heav'nly spirit
The maiden doth protect;
On wings celestial, it doth hover round
Protecting her from harm!

Wilhelm takes *Lothario's* place as watcher, and tells of his new-found affection in a beautiful air.

Elle ne croyait pas (Pure as a Flower)
By M. Regis, Tenor
(In French) *45023 10-inch, $1.00

WILHELM:

In soothing yon poor, hapless maiden
At last I have discovered her secret;
From her sweet lips my name escaped!
Ah! little thought the maid,
In innocence arrayed,
What she in her breast had nurtured,
Would ardent love become,

And thus pervert the peaceful current
Of her peaceful life.
Oh balmy April,
Who to the wither'd flowers restoreth their
colors,
Kiss her fair cheek,
And a grateful sigh of love cause to escape!

Mignon now comes with feeble step on the balcony, and seeing *Wilhelm,* is much agitated. He endeavors to soothe her, but she insists that only *Lothario* loves her. *Lothario* now enters, and announces that he is the *Count Lothario,* having been restored to his right mind by the familiar scenes of his ancestral home. He shows them the jewels and prayer book of his lost daughter, and tells them her name was *Sperata. Mignon* starts at the name and murmurs:

Ah, that sweet name to my ear is familiar,
A memory of my childhood
It may be, that's gone forever!

She then begins to read from the book a little prayer, but soon drops the book and continues from memory, her hands clasped and her eyes raised to Heaven. *Lothario* is much agitated and when she has finished, recognizes her as his lost daughter. Father and daughter are reunited, while a blessing is bestowed on the young people by the happy *Lothario.*

DOUBLE-FACED AND MISCELLANEOUS MIGNON RECORDS

Gems from Mignon By the Victor Light Opera Co "Away Ye Friends"—"Polonaise"—Barcarolle, "Now On We Sail"—"Pure as a Flower"—"Dost Thou Know"—"Finale" Gems from Tales of Hoffman By Victor Light Opera Co	35337	12-inch, $1.25
Opening Chorus and Solo, " Fuggitivo e tremante " By Andrea Perelló de Segurola, Bass, and La Scala Chorus Ninna nanna By Gaudio Mansueto, Bass	55004	12-inch, 1.50
Preludio, Parte 1a (Overture, Part 1) La Scala Orchestra Preludio, Parte 2a (Overture, Part 2) La Scala Orchestra	68025	12-inch, 1.25
Polonese—Io son Titania! (I'm Fair Titania!) By Giuseppina Huguet, Soprano (In Italian) Non conosci il bel suol? (Dost Thou Know That Fair Land?) By Giuseppina Huguet, Soprano (In Italian)	35178	12-inch, 1.25
Polonaise—Io son Titania! By Mlle. Korsoff, Soprano (In French) Lakmé—Pourquoi dans les grands bois By Alice Verlet, Soprano (In French)	45006	10-inch, 1.00
Adieu, Mignon, Courage (Farewell, Mignon) By M. Regis, Tenor (In French) Elle ne croyait pas (Pure as a Flower) By M. Regis, Tenor (In French)	45023	10-inch, 1.00
Fuggitivo e tremante (A Lonely Wanderer) By Cesare Preve, Bass Ninna nanna (Cradle Song) By Cesare Preve, Bass	62650	10-inch, .75
Gavotte By Maud Powell, Violinist	64454	10-inch, 1.00
Gavotte By Victor String Quartet Norma Selection (Bellini) By Pryor's Band	16323	10-inch, .75
Addio, Mignon (Farewell, Mignon) By Emilio Perea, Tenor (In Italian) Stelle d'Oro—Romanza By Silvano Isalberti, Tenor (In Italian)	63420	10-inch, .75

* *Double-Faced Record—See above list.*

WHITE

SCENE FROM MIKADO

THE MIKADO

OR

THE TOWN OF TITIPU

COMIC OPERA IN TWO ACTS

Text by W. S. Gilbert; music by Sir Arthur Sullivan. First produced at the Savoy Theatre, London, March 14, 1885. First American production at the Museum, Chicago, July 6, 1885, followed by the production at the Union Square Theatre, New York, July 20, 1885. All star revival by Messrs. Shubert and William A. Brady at the Casino Theatre, May 30, 1910. Revived at the Majestic Theatre by the Gilbert and Sullivan Festival Company, 1913.

Characters

MIKADO of Japan..Baritone
NANKI-POO, his son, disguised as a minstrel, in love with Yum-Yum....Tenor
KO-KO, Lord High Executioner of Titipu ....Comedian
POOH-BAH, Lord High Everything Else.............................Bass
PISH-TUSH, a noble lord.....................................Baritone
YUM-YUM ⎤   Soprano
PITTI-SING ⎬ Three sisters, wards of Ko-Ko ....⎨ Mezzo-Soprano
PEEP-BO ⎦   Soprano
KATISHA, an elderly lady, in love with Nanki-Poo ....Contralto
Schoolgirls, nobles, guards and coolies.

Time and Place: The scene is laid in Japan; present time.

It is beginning to be recognized that the Gilbert and Sullivan operas are pure English classics—not in the sense of being dull—but because they are national, and possess those qualities which will cause them in the future to be valued equally with the Comedies of Shakespeare. The *Mikado* is undoubtedly the greatest of these, and curiously enough it was this opera which first anticipated the rise of Modern Japan, although the characters portrayed are by no means Japs, but ourselves —in a very thin disguise.

GILBERT

SULLIVAN

This charming travesty of Japan has been the greatest popular favorite of all comic operas since its original production in the eighties. The story is so generally known that a brief outline of the plot is all that is necessary here.

Nanki-Poo is in love with *Yum-Yum,* who is betrothed to her guardian, *Ko-Ko,* Lord High Executioner. *Poo-Bah,* "retailer of state secrets at a low figure," tells *Nanki-Poo* of his sweetheart's betrothal to another, but the young man secures an interview with *Yum-Yum* and confesses he is the *Mikado's* son, disguised in the hope of escaping punishment for his

POOH BAH, PITTI-SING, KO-KO, MIKADO AND KATISHA

refusal to marry *Katisha.* *Ko-Ko* receives a message from the *Mikado,* telling him he must see that some one in Titipu is beheaded within the month or he will lose his position, which message interferes with the Lord High Executioner's matrimonial arrangements. *Nanki-Poo* agrees to sacrifice himself if he may marry *Yum-Yum* and have her with him during the intervening month. This is agreed to and the wedding plans are made.

At the opening of the second act *Yum-Yum* is preparing for the ceremony. While talking with *Nanki-Poo* she is interrupted by *Ko-Ko,* who tells her that according to the law, when a married man is executed his wife is burned alive. This news cools *Yum-Yum's* ardor, but *Nanki-Poo,* to save her, swears that he will that day perform the Happy Dispatch or hari-kari. As this would be dangerous for *Ko-Ko,* he promises in alarm to swear falsely to the execution of *Nanki-Poo.*

The *Mikado* now arrives and *Ko-Ko* tells him the execution has taken place, but the *Mikado,* on learning who the victim is, flies into a rage and says he has beheaded the heir to the throne, and must himself suffer torture for his act. However, *Nanki-Poo* opportunely appears and *Ko-Ko* gains his pardon by marrying *Katisha,* while *Yum-Yum* and *Nanki-Poo* are happily united.

Two splendid records by the Victor opera forces are offered, containing no less than thirteen of the favorite numbers, admirably sung and grouped in a most attractive manner. The Lyric Quartet has given the dainty *Brightly Dawns Our Wedding Day*, one of the most beautiful examples of the *Madrigale* in existence, and Miss Romaine the charming song of *Yum-Yum, The Moon and I*, which she sings exquisitely.

DOUBLE-FACED AND MISCELLANEOUS MIKADO RECORDS

Gems from " Mikado "—Part I

"Behold the Lord High Executioner "—" The Flowers that Bloom in the Spring "—" Three Little Maids "—" Tit Willow "—" He's Gone and Married Yum-Yum "—" With Joyous Shout "

By the Victor Light Opera Company 31789 12-inch, $1.00

Gems from " Mikado "—Part II

"Gentlemen of Japan "—" A Song of the Sea "—" Three Little Maids from School "—" Moon Song "—" Emperor of Japan "—" My Object all Sublime "—Finale

By the Victor Light Opera Company 31881 12-inch, 1.00

Yum-Yum's Song—The Moon and I (Act III)
By Margaret Romaine, Soprano 60122 10-inch, .75

{ Madrigale—Brightly Dawns Our Wedding Day
By the Lyric Quartet } 17226 10-inch, .75
{ *Martha—Good Night Quartet* *By the Lyric Quartet* }

{ Mikado Waltzes By Pryor's Band } 35124 12-inch, 1.25
{ *Belle of New York Selection* *By Pryor's Band* }

SCENE FROM MIKADO

SCENE FROM MIREILLE

(French)
MIREILLE
(*Mih-ray'-yeh*)

(English)
MIRELLA
(*Mih-rel'-lah*)

OPERA IN FIVE ACTS

Words by M. Carré, from *Mirèio*, Provençal poem by Mistral; music by Gounod. First version given at Saint Rémy-de-Provence, under the direction of the composer, in 1863. Produced in Paris March 19, 1864. Reduced to three acts, with the addition of the waltz, and reproduced December 15, 1864. In London, in Italian, in five acts, as Mirella, July 5, 1864. The first performance in America of which the editor has a record was at New Orleans, January 29, 1885, in Italian. April 23, 1885, given at the Academy of Music, New York, with Patti in the cast.

Cast

RAMON, a rich farmer...Bass
MIRELLA, his daughter.......................................Soprano
AMBROISE...Bass
VINCENT, ⎫ his children............................... ⎧ Tenor
VINCENETTE, ⎭ ....⎩Mezzo-Soprano
TAVENA, a fortune-teller....................................Contralto
OURRIAS, a bull tamer.......................................Baritone

Peasants and People; Pilgrims.

Mirella, which came later than *Faust* in order of production, is an example of the more delicate art of Gounod, and the story of the faithfulness of the heroine for her peasant lover is reflected in the music with true Provençal warmth and color.

The librettist took for his subject the pastoral poem *Mirèio*, by the beloved poet of Provence, Frederic Mistral, and Gounod has given it a tuneful setting with much local color, including many folk-songs.

The first scene opens in a mulberry grove, where *Mirella* is teased by the village girls about her attachment for *Vincent*, the basket-maker. *Tavena*, the fortune-teller, warns the young girl that *Ramon*, *Mirella's* father, will never consent to the union. *Mirella* meets *Vincent* and the warning of *Tavena* is soon forgotten. The lovers renew their pledges and agree to meet soon at the Chapel of the Virgin.

The young girl is also informed by the fortune-teller that *Vincent* has a rival, a wild herdsman, who has asked *Mirella's* father for her hand and obtained his consent. When the herdsman appears *Mirella* repulses him, declaring

MIREILLE—ACT I

her irrevocable attachment for *Vincent*. She then starts on the long journey across the desert to meet her lover at the chapel, and on the way meets *Tavena*, who assures her that *Vincent* will be waiting for her. The journey proves almost too much for the young girl's strength, and when she finally arrives at the chapel she is completely exhausted, and faints on the threshold. *Vincent* soon appears and ministers to his fainting love. *Ramon,* who has followed his daughter, soon appears, and moved to pity by her sad condition, gives his consent to the union of the lovers, and all ends happily.

This delightful *Valse* occurs in the first act, where *Mirella* fancifully appeals to the swallows to bring her tidings of her lover. Miss Abott's lovely and flexible voice is shown to great advantage in this brilliant number.

Valse, Act I
By Bessie Abott, Soprano
(*In French*) 88129 12-inch, $3.00

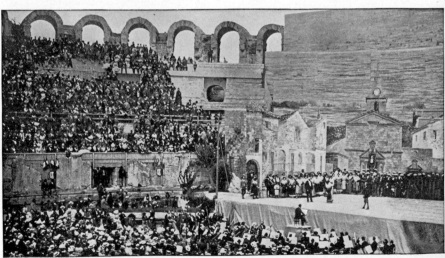

AN OPEN AIR PRODUCTION OF MIREILLE AT ARLES

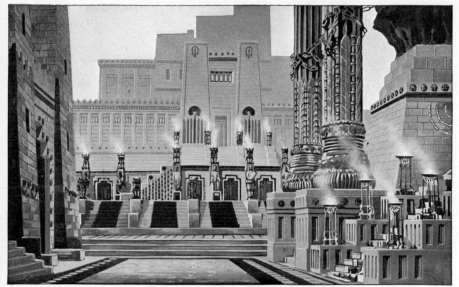

THE TEMPLE SCENE (LA SCALA REVIVAL OF 1913)

NABUCCO, or NABUCODONOSOR

OPERA IN FOUR ACTS

Text by Solera; music by Giuseppe Verdi. First production at La Scala, Milan, March 9, 1842, was a great success and broke all Scala records by reaching sixty-five performances in one season. Produced at Vienna, April 4, 1843; Berlin, 1844; Paris, October 16, 1845; London, in English, as "Nino," at Her Majesty's Theatre, March 3, 1846. In 1900, a year before Verdi's death, the opera was revived in Rome and met with great success. First American production, New York, April 4, 1848. "Nabucco" was the opera selected to open the 1913 season at La Scala, being presented with a sumptuous setting October 1st, two months in advance of the usual time, in honor of the Verdi centenary.

Characters

NABUCCO, Assyrian king..Baritone
FENENA, his daughter ....Contralto
ABIGAIL, an Amazon...Soprano
OROTASPES, Babylonian priest ....Bass
HYDASPES...Tenor
Priests, Couriers, Soldiers and Townspeople

Time and Place: Babylon; sixth century B. C.

"Nabucco" (a revision of the original title, "Nabucodonosor") was the third of Verdi's works, and the one which established his reputation in France.

Verdi, in his reminiscences tells interestingly of the writing of this opera. It was at a time when the young composer, discouraged by poverty, illness, and the failure of his first attempts at opera, had resolved to write no more. Merelli, the manager of La Scala, who had agreed to accept all new operas written by Verdi, came to see him and talked kindly to him, saying:

"Listen, Verdi, I cannot oblige you to work by force; still, my confidence in you is undiminished. Who knows but some day you will decide to take up your pen? In that case, it will only be necessary to give me notice two months before the beginning of an operatic season, and I promise you that whatever opera you bring me shall be represented."

These words, however, did not persuade Verdi, but Merelli went on to speak of a new libretto he had just received from Solera.

"'Imagine,' said Merelli, 'one of Solera's librettos, superb, magnificent, extraordinary; the most grandi, ose dramatic situations, full of interest, with such beautiful verses, and that beast Nicolai will listen to nothing of it. He declares that the story is impossible, and so on. '"Here!' he cried, 'here! look at this; it is Solera's libretto—such a grand subject, and to refuse it! Here you are; take it, and read it.' I refused, but he placed the book in my hands; it was a big pamphlet written in big characters, as was the style in those days. I rolled it up, and saying ' good-bye' to Merelli, wended my way homewards. I reëntered my house, and with an almost violent gesture threw the manuscript on the table. In falling on the table it had opened itself, and my eyes fell upon the open page before me, precisely upon this verse,

'Va pensiero, sull' ali dorate.'
(Fly away, thought, on golden wings.)

"I then read a fragment, I read two fragments, but strong in my resolution to compose no more, I gained command over my feelings, shut up my book, and went to bed. But Nabucco kept running in my head, and sleep did not visit my eyelids. I arose, read the libretto not once or twice, but three times, and so carefully that the next morning I knew Solera's poem by heart. In spite of this I did not feel disposed to change my mind about composing, and during the day I went back to the theatre to give Merelli his manuscript. However, he refused to take it, seized me by the shoulder, and not only briskly put me outside his study, but actually shut the door and locked it in my face.

"What was to be done? Nothing but to go home, which I did. I went back with Nabucco in my pocket.

"One day one verse, one day another verse, here a note and there a phrase, and little by little the opera was written. We were then in the autumn of '41, and remembering my promise to Merelli, I went to him to announce that Nabucco was finished, and that in consequence he could have it performed the forthcoming carnival and Lenten season at La Scala. So, near the end of February, '42, the Nabucco rehearsals began, and twelve days after the piano rehearsal, on the 9th of March, the first representation took place.

"It is with this work my artistic career commenced, and even if I had to struggle against innumerable difficulties, it is likewise certain that Nabucco was born under a happy star; even the very things which might have been hurtful to its success by some chance were the very things which happened to be favourable. To begin with, I had written a villainous letter to the manager, from which it was highly probable that the said manager would have sent the young composer to the devil; but just the contrary happened. The old and patched-up costumes, rearranged with taste, became simply splendid. The old worn-out scenery, touched up and readjusted by the painter, Perrani, produced extraordinary effect; especially on the first representation, the scene of the temple caused such an overwhelming enthusiasm, that the public applauded certainly not less than ten minutes. At the last rehearsal we did not even know whether the military band was to come on, or where, and the leader, Tutsch, had been very much embarrassed. I indicated a measure to him at rehearsal, and on the first night the music came on the stage with such precision in the crescendo that the public burst out into the wildest storm of applause I had yet heard." Verdi concludes: "You see, it is not always well to confide in benevolent stars, and experience has proven to me the justice of our proverb: "Fidarsi è bene, ma non fidarsi è meglio" (To trust oneself is well, but to distrust oneself is better.)

The opera was a triumph, and from that day we see Verdi on the road to success.

Abigail, the principal character in this four-act opera, is an ambitious Amazon who has risen to a high place among the Assyrians through her influence over the King. The first scene reveals a group of frightened townspeople in Babylon, as their ancient enemies, the Assyrians, led by *King Nabucco*, are besieging the walls. The besiegers finally scale the walls and when the gates are open *Nubucco, Abigail* and the Assyrians enter. *Orotaspes*, the High Priest and real leader of the Babylonians, hopes to arrange terms of peace with *Nabucco* through the old King's daughter, *Fenena*, who the Babylonians are holding captive. *Hydaspes*, a prince of Babylon, has fallen deeply in love with *Fenena*, and when he hears *Orotaspes* threaten the girl's life if her father persists in his intention to subjugate the Babylonians, he traitorously disarms *Orotaspes*, leaving him at the mercy of *Nabucco*. The Assyrians thereupon promptly destroy the Temple.

Abigail discovers that *Nabucco* has only used her to bring about his own success, and that *Fenena*, and not she, is to be sent back to Assyria to rule in the King's absence. This, together with the fact that she is in love with *Hydaspes*, whose love for *Fenena* leaves him blind to the Amazon's passion, stirs her anger and jealousy, and she resolves upon revenge.

A report is circulated that *Nabucco* is dead, and immediately *Abigail* assumes command of the Assyrians. The King, however, reappears, and in his anger at *Abigail*, defies his own gods and those of the Babylonians. For this rash act he is suddenly stricken insane. *Abigail* seizes the royal crown and proclaims herself sovereign. An idol is set up which the Babylonians are compelled to worship. The ambitious usurper secures *Nabucco's* signature to a decree sentencing all the Babylonians to be slaughtered, and as *Fenena* has embraced the religion of *Hydaspes* and hence become a Babylonian, her death warrant is issued. Fortunately, *Nabucco* is made to realize the situation, is converted to the religion of the Babylonians, and his reason is restored. He assumes again his royal position and rescues *Fenena* before the death decree can be executed, while poison puts an effective end to the high ambitions of *Abigail*.

Tremin gl' insani del mio   (They Shall Tremble Before Me)

By Titta Ruffo, Baritone   (*In Italian*)   87194   10-inch, $2.00

This famous air of *Nabucco* is from the great Temple Scene in Act I. Mr. Ruffo sings it magnificently here.

SCENE—ACT I

NATOMA

(Nah-toh'-mah)

(The Maid from the Mountains)

OPERA IN THREE ACTS

Text by Joseph D. Redding; music by Victor Herbert. First produced by the Philadel-phia-Chicago Opera Company, at the Metropolitan Opera House, Philadelphia, February 25, 1911. First New York production February 28, 1911.

Characters

(With the Cast of the First Performance)

DON FRANCISCO DE LA GUERRA, a noble Spaniard of the old régime
Bass (Huberdeau)
BARBARA, his daughter.............................Soprano (Grenville)
NATOMA, an Indian girl................................Soprano (Garden)
PAUL MERRILL, Lieutenant of the U. S. Brig "Liberty"..Tenor (McCormack)
JUAN ALVARADO, a young Spaniard................Baritone (Sammarco)
JOSÉ CASTRO, a half-breed...........................Baritone (Preisch)
FATHER PERALTA, Padre of the Mission Church.........Bass (Dufranne)
PICO, ⎫ Comrades of Castro.......................⎧Tenor (Crabbé)
KAGAMA,⎭   ⎩Bass (Nicolay)

Chiquita, a dancing girl; Two American Officers; Nuns; Convent Girls;
Friars; Soldiers; Spanish Dancers, etc.

Scene and Period: California, under the Spanish régime, 1820.

Victor Herbert's Natoma treats of one of the most romantic periods of American his-tory, the scene being laid in California in the days of Spanish rule. The opera takes its title from its Indian heroine, and the characters comprise Indians, Spaniards and pioneer Americans. The story centres around *Natoma,* an Indian girl; *Barbara,* the lovely daughter of *Don Francisco de la Guerra,* a noble Spaniard of the old régime; and *Lieut. Paul Merrill,* of the U. S. Navy, who is loved by both *Natoma* and *Barbara.*

ACT I

SCENE—*Hacienda of Don Francisco on the Island of Santa Cruz*

At the opening of Act I *Don Francisco* is gazing over the waters of the Santa Barbara channel waiting the coming of his daughter *Barbara,* who is leaving the convent at the close of her school days. *Alvarado,* a hot-headed young Spaniard and *Barbara's* cousin, who is anxious to marry the young girl and thus gain control of the vast estates left her by her

343

MATZENE   HAMLIN AS LIEUT. PAUL MERRILL

mother, is also anxiously waiting her arrival. *Natoma* has met *Lieutenant Paul* and there is already a bond of sympathy between the handsome Indian maiden and the young officer. The two are now seen approaching, the Indian girl innocently telling the young officer that her mistress, *Barbara,* is very beautiful. Suddenly realizing that *Paul* may forget her when he sees *Barbara,* she begs him to let her be his slave. When *Barbara* arrives and meets *Paul* it is a case of love at first sight, and later, when *Alvarado* urges his suit, the young girl haughtily refuses him. In a rage he plots with *Castro,* the half-breed, to carry *Barbara* off to the mountains the next day, when the celebrations in honor of her coming of age are at their height. This plot is overheard by *Natoma,* who is concealed in the arbor. All the guests take their departure, and *Barbara,* alone on the porch in the moonlight, declares her love for *Paul.* The young lieutenant appears and they sing an impassioned love duet. When a light is seen in the hacienda, the young girl, thinking it is her father, urges *Paul* to take his departure, and goes into the hacienda. As the curtain falls *Natoma,* who realizes that her mistress is now her rival, is seen seated alone in the window, gazing out into the night.

ACT II
SCENE—*Plaza in Front of the Mission Church, Santa Barbara*

In the dim light of early morning *Natoma* is singing her "song of fate," and as dawn begins to break the Spanish soldiers appear, the flag of Spain is raised, and trumpeters

WHITE   THE DAGGER DANCE—ACT II

and drummers play the national salute. The vaqueros and rancheros arrive, singing of their life on the plains, while the dancing girls join in the revelry. *Pico* sings his stirring *Vaquero's Song*, which in performances of the opera always arouses great enthusiasm, and which is vigorously sung here by Mr. Cartwright, while the melodious chorus is splendidly rendered by the Opera forces.

PHOTO WHITE

MC CORMACK AS PAUL

Vaquero's Song
By Earl Cartwright, Baritone, and Chorus
(In English)   5871   10-inch, $0.60

Don Francisco and his daughter appear on horseback, with *Natoma* walking by their side. The guests assemble, and after the Castilian custom, *Don Francisco* places on his daughter's brow a woof of royal lace, signifying that she succeeds to title and estate. *Barbara* sings a brilliant song of happiness, love and springtime, with an exquisite accompaniment, in which Mr. Herbert has woven the songs of birds, the rustling of leaves and the breezes of spring with marvelous skill. Mme. Gluck in this rendition quite surpasses anything she has yet done for the Victor, and pours out her vocal resources lavishly and with evident enjoyment.

Spring Song (I List the Trill of Golden Throat)
By Alma Gluck, Soprano
(In English)   74274   12-inch, $1.50

The sailors from the U. S. S. *Liberty* appear, and with them is *Lieutenant Paul*, who extends his compliments on behalf of his commander in the form of a spirited address.

Paul's Address (No Country Can My Own Outvie)
By John McCormack, Tenor   *(In English)*   74295   12-inch, $1.50

The Panuelo, or "dance of declaration," follows, in which each man places his hat on the head of the girl he loves. *Barbara* infuriates *Alvarado* by gaily tossing his hat into the crowd when he places it on her head, but before he can speak *Castro* appears and dares any one to dance with him the ancient Dagger Dance of California. *Natoma* accepts the challenge, and they dance to the wild and barbaric rhythm. This old dance is, like other characteristic numbers in the opera, based on Indian melodies which Mr. Herbert has been collecting for some years.

As the scene becomes more absorbing, *Alvarado* and *Pico* slip close to *Barbara,* and, throwing a serape over her head, attempt to carry her off. *Natoma,* who has been watching *Alvarado,* rushes wildly past *Castro* and plunges her dagger into the Spaniard, who falls lifeless. The crowd rushes at *Natoma* to avenge the death of *Alvarado* and *Paul* draws his sword to protect her. Suddenly the Mission door opens, and *Father Peralta* slowly advances, holding aloft the cross. The people kneel, and the Indian girl, dropping her dagger, approaches the priest and falls at his feet. They go into the church as the curtain falls.

ACT III
SCENE—*Interior of the Mission Church*

As the curtain rises *Natoma* is kneeling on the steps of the altar, crooning an Indian cradle song. She invokes the Great Spirit to give her strength to join her people, and seek vengeance for her misfortunes. The old priest seeks to calm her, and finally strikes the one responsive chord in her heart—her love for her mistress. He recalls to her mind her happy childhood days with *Barbara,* and she realizes that she can yet make her mistress happy, and that fate has decreed the union between *Natoma* and *Paul*.

The church now fills with the people, who respond to the words of *Father Peralta*. *Paul* and *Barbara* sit near the altar in opposite pews, and at a sign from the priest the Indian girl walks down the aisle to where they are seated. Under her spell they kneel, facing the altar, and *Natoma,* lifting the amulet she wears around her neck, bestows it as a blessing on her beloved mistress. Turning, she walks toward the convent garden, and as the priest in the pulpit raises his hands in benediction, the doors of the cloister close upon her.

THE OPÉRA, PARIS

THE MARIENSKOI OPERA, ST PETERSBURG

FAMOUS OPERA HOUSES OF EUROPE

NORMA (*proudly*): Then fulfill thy fate, and follow him! (Act I.)

NORMA
(*Nor'-mah*)

OPERA IN TWO ACTS

Book by Felice Romani, founded on an old French story. Score by Vincenzo Bellini. First production December 26, 1831, at Milan. First London production at King's Theatre, in Italian, June 20, 1833. In English at Drury Lane, June 24, 1837. First Paris production Théâtre des Italiens, 1833. First Vienna production, 1833; in Berlin, 1834. First New York production February 25, 1841, at the Park Theatre. Produced at the New Orleans Opera, December 31, 1842. Other American productions: September 20, 1843, with Corsini and Perozzi; October 2, 1854, with Grisi, Mario and Susini, at the opening of the Academy of Music; and December 19, 1891, at the Metropolitan, with Lehmann. Recently revived by the Boston Opera Company.

Characters

NORMA, High Priestess of the Temple of Esus ....Soprano
ADALGISA, a Virgin of the Temple.............................Soprano
CLOTILDE, attendant on Norma ....Soprano
POLLIONE, a Roman proconsul commanding the legions of Gaul ...... Tenor
FLAVIO, his lieutenant ....Tenor
OROVESO, the Arch-Druid, father of Norma.......................Bass

Priests and Officers of the Temple, Gallic Warriors, Priestesses and Virgins of the Temple, two children of Norma and Pollione

Scene and Period : The scene is laid in Gaul, shortly after the Roman conquest

Norma, although an opera of the old school and seldom performed nowadays, contains some of the loveliest of the writings of Bellini. Its beauties are of the old-fashioned kind which our forefathers delighted in, and which are an occasional welcome relief from the abundance of "music dramas" with which we are surrounded of late. Especially charming is the spirited overture, always a favorite on band programs.

NORMA: Now, for your judgment, a new victim is offered—I am guilty! (Act II, Scene III.)

Overture to Norma

By Arthur Pryor's Band   *35166 12-inch, $1.25

The briskness and sparkle of this fine overture and its inspiring climax are well preserved in Mr. Pryor's vigorous rendering.

The scene is laid among the Druids at the time of the Roman invasion. *Norma,* the
High Priestess, though sworn to bring about the expulsion of Rome, is secretly married to
a Roman proconsul, *Pollione,* by whom she has two children. She rebukes the Druids for
wishing to declare war, and after the ceremony of cutting the mistletoe, she invokes peace
from the moon in the exquisite prayer, *Casta Diva.*

Casta Diva (Queen of Heaven)

By Marcella Sembrich, Soprano	(*In Italian*)	88104	12-inch, $3.00
By Celestina Boninsegna, Soprano	(*In Italian*)	92025	12-inch, 3.00
By Giuseppina Huguet, Soprano	(*In Italian*)	*16539	10-inch, .75

This lovely air still holds a high place in popular favor, its beauty and tenderness making it well worthy of a place among modern airs. As evidence of the great popularity of
this number, three famous prima donnas have selected it for their Victor lists.

NORMA:
Queen of Heaven, while thou art reigning
Love upon us is still remaining,
Clad in pureness, alone disdaining
Grosser earth's nocturnal veil.
Queen of Heaven, hallow'd by thy presence,
Let its holier, sweeter essence,
Quelling ev'ry lawless license,
As above, so here prevail!

In the next scene *Norma* discovers that her husband loves *Adalgisa,* and in her rage she
contemplates killing her children; but her mother's heart conquers, and she resolves to

* *Double-Faced Record—See page 349.*

yield her husband and children to *Adalgisa* and expiate her offences on the funeral pyre. *Adalgisa* pleads with her, urging her to abandon her purpose, and offers to send *Pollione* back to her.

This scene is expressed in the *Hear Me, Norma,* familiar to every music-lover.

GRISI AS NORMA

Mira o Norma (Hear Me, Norma)

By Ida Giacomelli, Soprano,
and Lina Mileri, Contralto

(*In Italian*) *62101 10-inch, $0.75
By Arthur Pryor's Band *16323 10-inch, .75

The lovely strains of this melodious number have delighted countless hearers in the eighty years since it was written.

ADALGISA:
Dearest Norma, before thee kneeling,
View these darlings, thy precious treasures;
Let that sunbeam, a mother's feeling,
Break the night around thy soul.

NORMA:
Wouldst win that soul, by this entreating
Back to earth's delusive pleasures,
From the phantoms, far more fleeting,
Which in death's deep ocean shoal?

Pollione refuses to return to *Norma* and attempts to seize *Adalgisa* against her will. *Norma* foils this attempt and reasons with him, telling him he must give up his guilty love or die. This is expressed in a dramatic duet.

In mia mano (In My Grasp)

By Ida Giacomelli, Soprano, and Gino Martinez-Patti, Tenor

(*In Italian*) *68309 12-inch, $1.25

NORMA:
In my grasp although I have thee,
Yet with kind intent I bear me:
And can free ye. Hear me:
Swear by the babes that prove me woman.

Swear by the gods that guide the Roman,
Adalgisa to relinquish
And this heinous love extinguish;
Then to Hades thy soul I send not!

Pollione still refuses, and *Norma* strikes the sacred shield to summon the Druids. She declares war on Rome and denounces *Pollione,* but offers to save his life if he will leave the country. He refuses, and she is about to put him to death, when love overcomes justice and the Priestess denounces herself to save *Pollione.* *Norma's* noble sacrifice causes his love to return and they ascend the funeral pyre together. As the flames mount about them they are declared purified of all sin.

DOUBLE-FACED AND MISCELLANEOUS NORMA RECORDS

Overture By Arthur Pryor's Band Oberon Overture (*Weber*) *By Arthur Pryor's Band*	35166	12-inch, $1.25
In mia mano alfin tu sei (In My Grasp) By Ida Giacomelli, Soprano, and Gino Martinez-Patti, Tenor (*In Italian*) Favorita—Fia vero lasciarti (*Shall I Leave Thee ?*) By Clotilde Esposito, Soprano, and Gino Martinez-Patti, Tenor (*In Italian*)	68309	12-inch, 1.25
Norma Selection (Hear Me, Norma!) By Pryor's Band Mignon—Gavotte *By Victor String Quartet*	16323	10-inch, .75
Casta Diva (Queen of Heaven) By Giuseppina Huguet, Soprano (*In Italian*) Lucia—Regnava nel silenzio (*Silence O'er All*) By Giuseppina Huguet, Soprano (*In Italian*)	16539	10-inch, .75
Mira o Norma (Hear Me, Norma) By Ida Giacomelli, Soprano, and Lina Mileri, Contralto (*In Italian*) Carmen—Preludio, Act IV *By La Scala Orchestra*	62101	10-inch, .75

* *Double-Faced Record—See above list.*

THE ENCHANTED FOREST—ACT I

OBERON
or
THE ELF-KING'S OATH

ROMANTIC FAIRY OPERA IN THREE ACTS

Text by James Robinson Planché; music by Carl Maria von Weber. First produced at Covent Garden, London, April 12, 1826, in English, under the personal direction of the composer. Translated into German by Theodor Hell, and given in Leipsic, December, 1826; Vienna, March 20, 1827; Berlin, July 2, 1828. First Paris production, in German, in 1830, was a comparative failure. Revived at the Théâtre Lyrique, translation by Nuitter, Beaumont and Chazot, with success, February 27, 1857. Revived in London, December 7, 1878. First American production, Academy of Music, New York, March 29, 1870, in English, with Parepa-Rosa and Mrs. Seguin. The opera was first sung in Italian at Her Majesty's, London, July 3, 1860, with recitatives by Sir Julius Benedict, and this version was given in Philadelphia in 1870. Revived in New York in 1912.

Characters

SIR HUON DE BORDEAUX...Tenor
SHERASMIN, his Squire...Baritone
OBERON, King of the Fairies...................................Tenor
REZIA, daughter of Haroun.....................................Soprano
FATIMA, her attendant...Mezzo-Soprano
PUCK..Mezzo-Soprano
TWO MERMAIDS..Mezzo-Soprani

Acting Characters

HAROUN EL RASCHID, Caliph of Bagdad...........................
BABEKAN, a Saracen Prince.....................................
ALMANZOR, Emir of Tunis.......................................
ABDALLAH, a Corsair...
ROSHANA, wife of Almanzor.....................................
Chorus of Fairies, Ladies, Knights, etc.

M. PLAMONDON AS OBERON

After the successful production of the English version of Weber's Der Freischutz in 1824, Weber was requested to write a new opera especially for Covent Garden. The composer, really the creator of the German romantic opera, had a great love for romantic subjects, and his choice of Wieland's beautiful poem was a most fortunate one. It was written in 1825-26, and is the composer's last dramatic work, having its first production less than two months before his death. At the first Oberon performance Weber received a tremendous ovation, and after the London production the opera was translated and produced at several German theatres; but in spite of the beautiful music it soon lost its hold on the public and disappeared for many years. A notable revival occurred some years ago at Wiesbaden, and was such a great success that a gala performance is now given annually in the presence of a distinguished audience.

THE OVERTURE

Weber's great overtures show his genius better, perhaps, than any of his writings. Preeminent among them is, of course, this immortal "Oberon," with its wonderful instrumental coloring, breathing the very atmosphere of Elfland. The chief elements of the story of the opera are outlined in the overture. After an introduction, the horn of *Oberon* is heard, with the tip-toeing of the fairies represented by the clarinets. Throughout the whole work are interwoven the exquisite melodies of Fairyland, and at the close is heard a portion of *Rezia's* air, "Ocean, Thou Mighty Monster."

⎰Oberon Overture	Pryor's Band⎱ 35166 12-inch, $1.25
⎱ *Norma Overture* (*Bellini*)	*Pryor's Band*⎰

THE STORY

The story of "Oberon" originally appeared in a famous collection of French romances, "La Bibliothèque Bleue," under the title "Huon of Bordeaux." The German poet Wieland adopted the principal incidents of the story as the basis of his poem, and Sotheby's translation of it was used in preparation of the text.

The opening scene of the opera occurs in Fairyland, where the fairies are dancing around the sleeping *Oberon*, the Elfin-King. *Oberon* has quarreled with his fairy partner, *Titania*, who vows never to be reconciled to her King until he shall find two lovers constant to each other through trial and temptation. The King's "tricksy spirit," *Puck*, hears of the plight of *Sir Huon* of Bordeaux, a young knight, who has killed the son of Charlemagne, and who is for this condemned to travel to Bagdad and slay the person who sits at *Haroun's* left hand, and claim *Haroun's* daughter, *Rezia*, as his wife. *Oberon* determines to use *Sir Huon* and *Rezia* to bring about his reunion with *Titania*. *Puck* brings

LOFFITTE AS HUON

Sir Huon to the Elfin-King, who shows him a vision of *Haroun's* daughter, *Rezia*. *Huon* falls in love with her and on waking, *Oberon* promises him that he shall possess the maiden, giving him a magic horn which will summon the Elfin-King at *Huon's* need. *Huon* is transported to Bagdad and carries *Rezia* away, but a storm is raised by *Oberon* and they are shipwrecked on a desert island.

PHOTO ORICELLY   BORGO AS REZIA

Rezia is captured by pirates and sold to the *Emir of Tunis,* while *Huon,* believed to be dead, is left on the beach.

Huon, however, is transported by the fairies across the sea, and enters the harem in search of *Rezia,* but is captured by the *Emir* and condemned to be burned alive with *Rezia.* At this crisis *Oberon,* hearing the fairy horn, appears with *Titania,* saves the lovers, and bears them to the Court of Charlemagne, where *Huon* is pardoned, and *Oberon* and *Titania,* influenced by the constancy of *Huon* and *Rezia,* are reunited.

The air which is listed here belongs to the scene wherein the lovers are shipwrecked. It is sung by *Rezia,* the opening recitative describing the terrors of the sea.

This celebrated example of dramatic writing is given in an impassioned manner by Mme. Gadski. The dignity of the opening phrases, the alternate hope and fear aroused at the sight of the approaching sail, and the tumultuous joy of rescue are all finely expressed by this celebrated artist, the final high C being admirably taken.

Ozean! Du Ungeheuer (Ocean, Thou Mighty Monster)

By Johanna Gadski, Soprano   (*In German*) 88495 12-inch, $3.00

REZIA:

Ocean! thou mighty monster,
That liest curl'd
Like a green monster round about the world!
To musing eye thou art an awful sight,
When calmly sleeping in the morning light;
But when thou risest in thy wrath, as now,
And fling'st thy folds around some fated prow,
Crushing the strong ribb'd bark as 'twere a shell,
Then, Ocean, thy pow'r is fierce and fell!
Still I see thy billows flashing,
Through the gloom their white foam flinging,
And the breakers' sullen dashing
In mine ear hope's knell is ringing!

But lo! methinks a light is breaking
Slowly o'er the distant deep,
Like a second morn awaking
Pale and wan from its sleep.
And now the sun bursts forth,
The wind is lulling fast,
And the broad wave but pants from fury past.
Cloudless o'er the blushing water,
Now the setting sun is burning,
Like a victor, red with slaughter,
To his tent in triumph turning.
Ah, perchance these eyes may never
Look upon its light again.
Fare thee well, bright orb, forever,
Thou for me wilt rise in vain!

But what gleams so white and fair,
Heaving with the heaving billow?
'Tis a seabird, wheeling there
O'er some wretch'd wat'ry pillow.
No, it is no bird I mark,
Joy! it is a boat! a sail!
And yonder rides a gallant bark,
Unimpair'd by the gale!
Oh, transport! my Huon, haste down to the shore!
Quick, quick, for a signal, this scarf shall be wav'd,
They see me, they answer!
They ply the strong oar!
Huon, Huon my husband, my love,
We are saved!

ELYSIUM—ACT II

(Italian)

ORFEO ED EURIDICE

(Or-feh'-oh ayd Ay-oo-ree-dee'-cheh)

(English)

ORPHEUS AND EURYDICE

(Or'-fee-us and U-ri-dee'-chee)

OPERA IN FOUR ACTS

Book by Ramieri De Calzabigi; music by Christoph Willibald von Gluck. First production in Vienna, October 5, 1762, Gluck conducting. First Paris production, 1778, when the rôle of *Orpheus* was transposed for high tenor. First London production at Covent Garden, June 26, 1770. Some notable revivals were during the Winter Garden season of 1863; in 1885 (in German), by the Metropolitan Opera under Walter Damrosch; the English production in 1886 by the National Opera Company; the Abbey revival in Italian in 1892; and the Metropolitan production of 1910, with Homer, Gadski and Gluck.

Cast

ORPHEUS . . . . Contralto
EURIDICE . . . . Soprano
LOVE . . . . Soprano
A HAPPY SHADE . . . . Soprano

Shepherds and Shepherdesses, Furies and Demons, Heroes and
Heroines in Hades.

This opera, which has been called "Gluck's incomparable masterpiece," and of which the great Fétis wrote, "it is one of the most beautiful productions of genius," may be properly termed a purely classical music drama. The music is exquisite in its delicacy and

353

HOMER AND GADSKI AS ORPHEUS AND
EURYDICE

grace, while the story is an interesting and affecting one. Orpheus may be called the grandfather of grand opera, it being the oldest work of its kind to hold its place on the stage, the first representation occurring one hundred and fifty years ago.

The opera has had only one adequate American production previous to the recent Metropolitan revival, and that was during the American Opera Company season of 1886—the Abbey revival of 1892 meeting with but indifferent success. Such has been the interest aroused by the recent performances, that it is likely to be heard quite frequently in the future.

The story concerns the Greek poet *Orpheus,* who grieves deeply over the death of his wife *Euridice,* and finally declares he will enter the realms of *Pluto* and search for her among the spirits of the departed. The goddess *Love* appears and promises to aid him, on condition that when he has found *Euridice* he will return to earth without once looking at her.

Orpheus journeys to the Gates of Erebus, and so softens the hearts of the Demon guards by his grief and his exquisite playing of his lyre, that he is permitted to enter. He finds *Euridice,* and without looking at her, takes her by the hand and bids her follow him. She obeys, but failing to understand his averted gaze, upbraids him for his apparent coldness and asks that he shall look at her.

Su e con me vieni cara (On My Faith Relying)
By Johanna Gadski, Soprano; Louise Homer, Contralto
(*In Italian*) 89041 12-inch, $4.00

Orpheus, knowing that to cast a single look at his loved one means death to her, keeps his face averted. The dialogue portrays the emotions of the characters, while Gluck's music suggests the present perplexity and the tragedy which is to follow.

Unable to endure longer the reproaches of his wife, he clasps her in his arms, only to see her sink down lifeless.

(German) (Italian)
Ach, ich habe sie verloren—Che faro senza Euridice
(English)
I Have Lost My Eurydice
By Mme. Schumann-Heink
(*In German*) 88091 12-inch, $3.00
By Louise Homer (*In Italian*) 88285 12-inch, 3.00

"Malheureux! qu'ai-je fait? Et dans quel précipice m'a plongé mon funeste amour!" ("Wretched one, what have I done! Into what gulf has my fatal love cast me?") cries the hapless youth, and breaks into his lovely and pathetic lamentation.

ORPHEUS: "I have lost my Eurydice
My misfortune is without its like.
Cruel fate! I shall die of my sorrow.
Eurydice, Eurydice, answer me!
It is your faithful husband.
Hear my voice, which calls you.
Silence of death! vain hope!
What suffering, what torment, wrings my heart!"

COPY'T DUPONT
HOMER AS ORPHEUS

354

LANDE

THE GATES OF HELL—ACT IV

Of the many beautiful numbers in Gluck's drama this lovely aria of mourning (best known by the Italian title *Che faro senza Euridice*) is the most familiar.

Orpheus is about to kill himself when *Love* appears and cries:

LOVE:
  Hold, Orpheus!
ORPHEUS (*despairingly*):
  What would you with me?
LOVE:
  Thine anguish well doth prove
  Thy constancy and truth.
  'Tis time that the trial be ended!

Eurydice! revive!
  To embrace the fond youth
  Who dared so much for thee!
ORPHEUS:
  My Eurydice!
EURYDICE (*reviving*):
  My Orpheus! (*They embrace.*)

(*Curtain*)

MISCELLANEOUS ORFEO RECORDS

Melodie (from "Ballet Music")   By Maud Powell, Violinist   64075   10-inch, $1.00
Melodie (from "Ballet Music")   By Fritz Kreisler, Violinist   64313   10-inch,   1.00

MAIRET

EURYDICE RESTORED TO ORPHEUS—ACT III

FROM THE PAINTING BY BECKER   OTELLO AND DESDEMONA

(Italian)

OTELLO
(*Oh-tel'-loh*)

(English)

OTHELLO
(*Oth-thel'-loh*)

OPERA IN FOUR ACTS

Text by Arrigo Boito, after the drama of Shakespeare. Music by Giuseppe Verdi. First production February 5, 1887, at La Scala, Milan, with Tamagno as *Otello*. First London production May 18, 1889. First performance in English given by the Carl Rosa Opera Company, at Manchester, 1893. First American production April 16, 1888, with Campanini as *Otello*. Some notable revivals occurred in 1894, with Tamagno and Maurel; in 1902, with Eames, Alvarez and Scotti; and in 1908 at the Manhattan, with Melba, Zenatello and Sammarco. First New Orleans production January 22, 1905, in English.

Characters

OTELLO, a Moor, general in the Venetian army.....................Tenor
IAGO, (*Ee-ah'-goh*) his ensign......................................Baritone
CASSIO, (*Cass'-ee-oh*) his lieutenant...............................Tenor
RODERIGO, (*Roh-der-ee'-goh*) a Venetian gentleman...................Tenor
LODOVICO, (*Loh-doh-vee'-koh*) ambassador of the Venetian Republic.......Bass
MONTANO, predecessor of Othello in the government of Cyprus........Bass
DESDEMONA, wife of Othello...............................Soprano
EMILIA, (*Ay-mee'-lee-ah*) wife of Iago.........................Mezzo-Soprano

Soldiers and Sailors of the Republic; Venetians; Cyprians; Greek, Dalmatian and Albanian Soldiers; an Innkeeper.

Scene and Period: End of the fifteenth century; a seaport in Cyprus.

MAIRET

VERDI AND MAUREL AT FIRST
PERFORMANCE OF OTELLO

After having given the world his splendid *Aida*, Verdi rested on his laurels and was silent for sixteen years; then, at the age of seventy-four, he suddenly astonished the world with his magnificent Otello, a masterly music-drama which alone would suffice to make him famous.

The change from the Verdi of 1853 and Il Trovatore, to the Verdi of 1887 and Otello, is amazing. Each opera produced by him shows a steady advance, until something approximating perfection is reached in Otello, the writing of which was an astonishing feat for a man of nearly eighty years of age.

The text, by that accomplished scholar and master librettist, Boito, follows closely the tragedy of Shakespeare.

ACT I

SCENE—*Otello's Castle in Cyprus. A Storm is Raging and the Angry Sea is visible in the Background*

Venetians, soldiers, including *Iago, Roderigo* and *Cassio*, are awaiting the return of *Otello*. His vessel arrives safely, and amid much rejoicing the Moor announces that the war is over, the enemy's ships having all been sunk. He goes into the castle, and *Iago* and *Roderigo* plan the conspiracy against *Cassio* and *Otello*, by which *Roderigo* hopes to secure *Desdemona* for himself and *Iago* to be revenged on *Otello*.

They join the soldiers and try to induce *Cassio* to drink. He refuses, but when *Iago* toasts *Desdemona*, he is compelled to join. *Iago* sings the rousing *Brindisi* :

Brindisi—Inaffia l'ugola (Drinking Song —Clink the Wine Cup)

By Pasquale Amato, Baritone, and Chorus
    (*In Italian*) 88338 12-inch, $3.00
By Antonio Scotti, Baritone
    (*In Italian*) 88082 12-inch, 3.00
By Antonio Scotti, Baritone
    (*In Italian*) 87040 10-inch, 2.00

during which he continues to fill *Cassio's* glass. When the latter is quite drunk they pick a quarrel with him, and he draws his sword, wounding *Montano*, while *Iago* and *Cassio* rouse a cry of "riot," which brings *Otello* from the castle. He disgraces *Cassio* and orders all to disperse, remaining alone with *Desdemona* for a long love scene. Part of this scene has been recorded here by Mme. Lotti and M. Conti, of Milan. The curtain falls as husband and wife go slowly into the castle.

Quando narravi (When Thou Speakest)

By F. Lotti, Soprano; F. Conti, Tenor
    (*In Italian*) *55023 12-inch, $1.50

COPY'T MISHKIN

SLEZAK AS OTELLO

ACT II

SCENE —*A Room in the Castle*

The crafty *Iago* is advising *Cassio* how to regain the favor of *Otello*, telling him that he must induce *Desdemona* to intercede for him. *Cassio* eagerly goes in search of *Desdemona*, while *Iago* gazes after him, satisfied with the progress of his schemes, and then sings the superb *Credo*.

*Double-Faced Record—See page 360.

Credo (Iago's Creed)

By Pasquale Amato, Baritone (In Italian) 88328 12-inch, $3.00
By Titta Ruffo, Baritone (In Italian) 88466 12-inch, 3.00
By Ernesto Badini, Baritone
(In Italian) *55023 12-inch, $1.50

This is a free adaptation of *Iago's* last speech with *Cassio* in Shakespeare, Act II. In his setting Verdi has expressed fully the character of the perfidious *Iago*: cynical, vain, weak and subtle. He declares that he was fashioned by a cruel God who intended him for evil, and that he cares naught for the consequences, as after death there is nothing.

Iago sees *Desdemona* approach and *Cassio* greet her, and as soon as the young officer is earnestly pleading with her to intercede for him, *Iago* runs in search of *Otello,* and sows the first seeds of jealousy in the heart of the Moor, bidding him watch his wife well. *Otello,* much troubled, seeks *Desdemona* and questions her. She begins to intercede for *Cassio,* but the Moor repulses her, and when she would wipe his perspiring brow, roughly throws down the handkerchief, which is picked up by *Iago.*

Left alone with *Iago, Otello* gives way to despair, and expresses his feelings in the bitter *Ora e per sempre.*

Ora e per sempre addio (And Now, Forever Farewell)

By Francesco Tamagno, Tenor
(In Italian) 95003 10-inch, $5.00
By Enrico Caruso 87071 10-inch, 2.00

Now finally convinced that *Desdemona* is deceiving him, he bids farewell to peace of mind, ambition and the glory of

PHOTO BERT
AMATO AS IAGO

conquest. *Iago* further says that he has seen *Desdemona's* handkerchief in *Cassio's* room, at which news *Otello* is beside himself with rage. The act closes with the great scene in which *Iago* offers to help *Otello* secure his revenge, and they swear an awful oath never to pause until the guilty shall be punished.

Si pel ciel (We Swear by Heaven and Earth)

By Enrico Caruso, Tenor ; Titta Ruffo, Baritone
(In Italian) 89075 12-inch, $4.00

The rendition of this duet, one of the most striking numbers in Verdi's opera, is a wonderful one, and holds the listeners spellbound. The issue of this record by the great tenor and baritone is counted by the Victor as one of its most notable achievements.

ACT III

SCENE—*The Great Hall of the Castle*

Otello now seeks *Desdemona* and contrives an excuse to borrow her handkerchief. She offers it, but he says it is not the one, and asks for the one with the peculiar pattern which he had given her. She says it is in her room and offers to bring it, but he at once denounces her, and sends her away astonished and grieved at the sudden jealousy which she cannot understand. He remains looking after her in the deepest dejection, then sings his sorrowful soliloquy, *Dio mi potevi.*

Dio mi potevi scagliare (Had it Pleased Heaven)

By Antonio Paoli, Tenor
(In Italian) 88240 12-inch, $3.00
(In Italian) *55009 12-inch, 1.50

LE THÉÂTRE ALDA AS DESDEMONA

By Carlo Barrera, Tenor

Double-Faced Record—See page 360.

Iago now tells Otello how he had slept in Cassio's room lately and had heard Cassio talking in his sleep, bemoaning the fate which had robbed him of Desdemona and given her to the Moor.

Cassio enters, and Iago, bidding Otello watch behind a pillar, goes to the young officer, and with fiendish ingenuity induces him to talk of his sweetheart Bianca. Otello, listening, thinks that it is of Desdemona that Cassio speaks, as Cassio produces the fatal handkerchief, telling Iago he had found it in his room, and wondering to whom it can belong. Otello, seeing the handkerchief and not hearing the conversation, has no further doubt of Desdemona's guilt, and when Cassio departs he asks Iago how best can he murder them both. The villain suggests that Desdemona be strangled in her bed, and says he will himself kill Cassio.

In a highly dramatic duet, given here by Barrera and Badini, they swear a solemn oath of vengeance.

Ah! mille vite (A Thousand Lives!)
By Barrera and Badini   *55009   12-inch $1.50

COPY'T MISHKIN

SCOTTI AS IAGO

Messengers now arrive from the Senate bearing orders for Otello, who has been recalled to Venice, and Cassio appointed Governor of Cyprus in his stead. He announces his departure on the morrow, and then unable to control his rage and jealousy he publicly insults Desdemona and flings her to the ground. As she is being led away by her maids he falls in a fit. The people, considering the summons to Venice an additional honor for the Moor, rush in, shouting "Hail to Otello," when Iago, pointing with fiendish triumph to the prostrate body, cries, "Behold your Lion of Venice!"

SCOTTI, WICKHAM, ALDA AND SLEZAK IN OTELLO

ACT IV
SCENE—Desdemona's Bedroom

The heartbroken Desdemona is preparing to retire, assisted by her maid, Emilia. She tells Emilia that an old song of her childhood keeps coming into her mind. Then she sings the sad and beautiful Willow Song. This is an old melody which has been definitely traced to the sixteenth century, and which is supposed to be much older.

Salce, salce (Willow Song)
By Nellie Melba, Soprano   (In Italian) 88148 12-inch, $3.00

This plaintive song seems like the lamentation of a broken heart, its last words being prophetic of the coming tragedy.

The faithful Emilia leaves her, and she kneels before the image of the Madonna and sings the noble Ave, one of the most inspired portions of the wonderful fourth act.

Ave Maria (Hail, Mary)
By Nellie Melba, Soprano   (In Italian) 88149 12-inch, $3.00
By Frances Alda, Soprano   (In Italian) 88213 12-inch, 3.00

*Double-Faced Record—See page 360.

LANDE
THE MURDER OF DESDEMONA (ALDA AND SLEZAK)

The "Ave Maria" is introduced by a characteristic monotone for the voice, accompanied by some organ-like harmonies which steal in with exquisite effect from the strings of the orchestra.

The portrayal of the mingled apprehension and resignation of *Desdemona* in this scene through the medium of the voice is worthy to rank with Melba's most celebrated operatic creations—her *Marguerita*—her *Juliet*—her *Mimi*. The purity and youthfulness of the feeling imparted, apart from the freshness and delicate perfection of the tones themselves is amazing, filling the mind with wonder at the perpetual miracle of the singer's perfect art. Mme. Alda, whose *Desdemona* has been one of the finest of her impersonations at the Metropolitan, sings the number beautifully.

At the close of the air *Desdemona* remains kneeling and prays in broken accents, her voice being almost inaudible.

Otello enters and rushes toward the bed, but stops and gazes at his sleeping wife a long time, then approaches and kisses her. She wakes and speaks his name. He accuses her again of an intrigue with *Cassio,* but she swears that it is false. He disregards her cries for mercy and strangles her. *Emilia* knocks at the door and is admitted by *Otello,* who hardly realizes what he has done. Seeing *Desdemona* lifeless, she accuses him of the crime and calls loudly for help. All rush in and *Emilia,* seeing *Iago,* denounces him as the author of the plot, and tells *Otello* that *Desdemona* was innocent. The Moor is torn with remorse, and tenderly gazing on his dead wife, sings his last air.

Morte d'Otello (Death of Otello)

By Francesco Tamagno, Tenor
(*In Italian*) 95002 10-inch, $5.00
By Nicola Zerola, Tenor 74217 12-inch, 1.50

He then draws a dagger and stabs himself, and with a final effort to embrace the *Desdemona* he has so cruelly wronged, he dies.

ALVAREZ AS OTHELLO

DOUBLE-FACED OTELLO RECORDS

Dio mi potevi scagliare (Had It Pleased Heaven) By Carlo Barrera, Tenor (*In Italian*) Giuramento—Ah! mille vite (A Thousand Lives) By Carlo Barrera and Ernesto Badini (*In Italian*)	55009	12-inch, $1.50
Quando narravi (When Thou Speakest) By F. Lotti, Soprano; F. Conti, Tenor (*In Italian*) Credo (Otello's Creed) By Ernesto Badini (*In Italian*)	55023	12-inch, 1.50
Brindisi, Act I and Morte d'Otello, Act IV Vessella's Italian Band Gioconda—Prelude, Act I *Vessella's Italian Band*	35459	12-inch, 1.25

I PAGLIACCI   THE PLAYERS

(Ee Pahl-yat'-chee)

Drama in Two Acts. Words and Music by R. Leoncavallo

The English version quoted from is by Henry Grafton Chapman

Quotations from text and music (except the Prologue) by kind permission of G. Schirmer. (Copy't 1906)

LEONCAVALLO

Ruggiero Leoncavallo was born at Naples, March 8, 1858, and was the son of a magistrate, the Chevalier Vincont, president of the tribunal of Potenza. His mother was a daughter of the celebrated artist, Raffaele d'Auria, famous for his decorations in the royal palace at Naples. He took up the pianoforte at an early age with Simonetti, a well-known teacher of Naples, and entered the Neapolitan Conservatoire, where he studied under Cesi, Ruta and Rossi. At sixteen he made a concert tour as a pianist with some success. Leaving the Conservatoire at eighteen he promptly showed his leaning toward operatic composition by beginning to write an opera, the libretto based on de Vigny's well-known drama, Chatterton. Finding an *impresario*, the production of this opera was promised, but at the last moment he was deserted by his manager and the young composer was reduced to poverty. He did not despair, however, and abandoning for a time his operatic pretensions, set to work at anything which would give him a living. He gave lessons and played accompaniments at café concerts, finally becoming a concert pianist, the latter occupation taking him to many countries—England, France, Holland, Germany and Egypt. Returning to Italy after several years of these wanderings, he proved that he had not been idle by submitting to the house of Ricordi the first part of a tremendous trilogy based on the subject of the Renaissance in Italy.

This monumental work he entitled *Crepusculum* (Twilight), and the three parts were called: I—*Medici*; II—*Girolamo Savonarola*; III—*Cezare Borgia*. This Ricordi accepted, agreeing to produce the first part, and Leoncavallo spent a year in its completion. Three years passed by and the production was not made. In despair he went to the rival firm of Sonzogno, which encouraged him to write the opera which was to make him famous. The young composer went to work and in the space of five months completed his opera, basing the plot on an actual occurrence in the court where his father was presiding as judge.

The production of Pagliacci was made on May 21, 1892, at the Teatro dal Verme, Milan. Its success was overwhelming, and the name of Leoncavallo was heard throughout the world. His fame led to the production, in 1893, of the first section of the great trilogy, *Medici*; but it was not well received. Other operas by Leoncavallo which have been produced with more or less success are: Chatterton (produced 1896); Bohême (1897); Zaza (1900); and finally Roland, written at the request of the German Emperor (1904). He has written also a symphonic poem, *Serafita*; a ballet (*La Vita d'una Marionetta*) and several comic operas.

But it is Pagliacci which will keep the name of Leoncavallo remembered. Its masterfully constructed libretto; its compelling and moving story; the orchestration, written with extraordinary skill; and finally, its moving and intensely dramatic plot, which always holds an audience in rapt attention.

It is indeed a matter for congratulation that the Victor is able to offer such a fine production of this master work.

ANNOUNCEMENT

The Victor Company takes pleasure in announcing Leoncavallo's famous two-act musical drama, recorded especially for the Victor under the personal direction of the composer. The records in the series were made in the presence of Signor Leoncavallo, and the music conducted by him, a feature which should make this collection ever valuable and unique. Any question arising in future concerning the composer's intentions in regard to the opera may be decided by reference to this performance as he himself conducted it. This advantage would have been priceless with regard to many well-known operas of the past, as it would have settled many controversies. But now, by means of the Victor, the composer's ideas may be imperishably recorded.

The artists selected by Signor Leoncavallo to interpret his great work are well known and most competent ones. Mme. Huguet, one of Italy's most beloved *prima donne*, has a voice of ample range and power, and sings the music of *Nedda* most beautifully. Cigada's *Tonio* is a remarkable performance, the richness and beauty of his voice being especially noticeable in the Prologue and the duet with *Nedda*. As *Canio* a choice of tenors is offered, the more delicate voice of Barbaini being contrasted with the splendid fire and intensity of Paoli's singing. Badini as *Silvio* is fully adequate, while the smaller parts are well filled. Nothing need be said about the orchestra and chorus of La Scala, as their reputation is world wide.

Leoncavallo's beautiful opera is admirably suited for reproduction on the Victor, and while listening to the singing of the artists who have rendered these dramatic scenes, no great imagination is required to picture the various situations.

In addition to the La Scala series, which was made under the composer's direction, many other Pagliacci records are listed in their proper places.

THE ARGUMENT

During the orchestral introduction *Tonio,* in his clown costume, suddenly appears in front of the curtain and begs permission to revive the ancient Greek prologue. He then comes forward as Prologue and explains that the subject of the play is taken from real life; reminds the audience that actors are but men, with passions like their own, and that the author has endeavored to express the real feelings and sentiments of the characters he will introduce. He then orders up the curtain.

The first act shows the entrance to an Italian village. *Canio* and his troupe of strolling players, or *pagliacci,* having paraded through the village, return to their traveling theatre, followed by a noisy crowd of villagers. *Canio* announces a performance for that evening at seven, then goes with *Peppe* into the tavern. *Tonio,* the clown, remains behind ostensibly to care for the donkey, but takes advantage of his master's absence to make love to *Nedda, Canio's* wife. She repulses him scornfully, striking him with her whip, and he swears to be revenged. *Silvio,* a rich young villager, in love with *Nedda,* now joins her and begs her to fly with him. She refuses, but admits that she loves him, her confession, being overheard by *Tonio,* who hurries in search of his master. *Canio* returns too late to see *Silvio,* but hears *Nedda's* parting words, "Forever I am thine!" Mad with jealousy, he demands the lover's name, and when *Nedda* refuses, tries to kill her, but is restrained by the others. *Nedda* goes to dress and *Canio* is in despair at the thought of being obliged to play while his heart is breaking.

Act II: The curtain rises on the same scene and the play is about to begin. This proves to be the usual farce in which the Clown makes love to Columbine during the absence of her husband, Punchinello, but is laughed at and resigns his pretensions, finally consenting to act as a lookout while Columbine and her accepted lover, Harlequin, dine together.

Strangely enough, this conventional farce is very like the situation in the real lives of the players, and when Punchinello (*Canio*) arrives and surprises the lovers, as the play demands, he loses his head when he hears Columbine repeat in the farce the very words he overheard her say to her real lover earlier in the day. Mad with rage, he again demands her lover's name. *Nedda* tries to save the situation by continuing the play, while the audience is delighted by such realistic acting until the intensity of *Canio's* passion begins to terrify them. The other players endeavor to silence him, but in vain. Finally, stung by his taunts, *Nedda* defies him and is stabbed, *Canio* hoping that in her death agony she will reveal the name of her lover. She falls, calling upon *Silvio,* who rushes from the crowd only to receive in turn the dagger of the outraged husband. As *Canio* is disarmed by the peasants he cries as if in a dream, *"La commedia e finita"*—(The comedy is ended).

LE THÉÂTRE   ARRIVAL OF THE PLAYERS—ACT I

(Italian)   (English)
I PAGLIACCI   THE PLAYERS
(*Ee Pahl-yat'-chee*)

(German)   (French)
DIE BAJAZZI   PAILLASSE
(*Dee Bah-yot'-si*)   (*Pah-yahss*)

DRAMATIC OPERA IN TWO ACTS

Libretto and music by Ruggiero Leoncavallo. First performed at the Teatro dal Verme, Milan, on May 21, 1892; in Vienna, September 17, 1892; in London, May 19, 1893; Dresden, January 23, 1893; Paris, in French, December 17, 1902. First New York production June 15, 1894, with Kronold, Montegriffo and Campanari. Some famous casts of recent years at the Metropolitan and the Manhattan opera: Caruso, Farrar, Stracciari—Alvarez, Scheff, Scotti—Farrar, Bars, Scotti—Cavalieri, Rousseliere, Scotti—Deveyne, Martin, Campanari, etc.

Characters in the Drama

NEDDA (*Ned'-dah*) (in the play "*Columbine*"), a strolling player,
  wife of Canio. . . . . .Soprano
CANIO (*Kah'-nee-oh*) (in the play "*Pagliaccio*" [*Punchinello*]),
  master of the troupe. . . . . .Tenor
TONIO (*Toh'-nee-oh*) (in the play "*Taddeo*"), the clown. . . . . .Baritone
PEPPE (*Pep'-pay*) (in the play "*Harlequin*"). .Tenor
SILVIO, (*Sil'-vee-oh*) a villager. . . . . .Baritone

Villagers and Peasants

The scene is laid in Calabria, near Montalto, on the Feast of the Assumption.
Period, between 1865 and 1870.

THE PROLOGUE

Leoncavallo chose to introduce his characters in a novel manner, and wrote this number in the midst of the orchestral prelude, when *Tonio* comes forward, like the prologue of ancient Greek tragedy, and explains that the subject of the play is taken from real life, and that the composer has devoted himself to expressing the sentiment, good or bad, but always human, of the characters he introduces.

Prologo (Prologue)

By Pasquale Amato, Baritone	(*In Italian*)	88326	12-inch,	$3.00
By Antonio Scotti, Baritone	(*In Italian*)	88029	12-inch,	3.00
By Antonio Scotti, Baritone	(*In Italian*)	81021	10-inch,	2.00
By Emilio de Gogórza, Baritone	(*In Italian*)	88176	12-inch,	3.00
By Titta Ruffo, Baritone	(*In Italian*)	92040	12-inch,	3.00
By Pryor's Band		*35158	12-inch,	1.25

Prologo (Prologue) (Complete in two parts)

Part I—Si puo? (A Word)
By Titta Ruffo, Baritone (*In Italian*) 88392 12-inch, $3.00

Part II—Un nido di memorie (A Song of Tender Memories)
By Titta Ruffo, Baritone (*In Italian*) 88393 12-inch, 3.00

{ (a) Part I—Si puo? (A Word)
By Francesco Cigada, Baritone (*In Italian*)
(b) Part II—Un nido di memorie (A Song of Tender *35171 12-inch, 1.25
Memories)
By Francesco Cigada, Baritone (*In Italian*) }

The first part of the Prologue is in itself a miniature overture, containing the three representative themes associated with the main events of the drama to be unfolded.

The first is the motive which always accompanies the appearance of the players or *pagliacci*:
The second theme represents *Canio's* jealousy and is a sombre strain suggestive of revenge:
The third represents the guilty love of *Nedda* and *Silvio*:

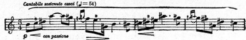

and appears frequently throughout the opera, not only in the love duet, but in the last act, when *Nedda* refuses to betray her lover even with death awaiting her.

The presentation of these themes is followed by the appearance of *Tonio*, the clown, who peeps through the curtain and says:

> Ladies and gentlemen!
> Pardon me if alone I appear.
> I am the Prologue!

He then comes in front of the curtain and explains the author's purpose, which is to present a drama from real life, showing that the actors have genuine tragedies as well as mimic ones.

Our author loves the custom of a prologue to his story,
And as he would revive for you the ancient glory,
He sends me to speak before ye!
But not to prate, as once of old,
That the tears of the actor are false, unreal,
That his sighs and the pain that is told,
He has no heart to feel!
No! our author to-night a chapter will borrow
From life with its laughter and sorrow!
Is not the actor a man with a heart like you?
So 'tis for men that our author has written,
And the story he tells you is true!

---

* *Double-Faced Record—See page 375.*

He then goes on to speak of the author's inspiration, and says:

A song of tender mem'ries
Deep in his list'ning heart one day was ringing;
And then with a trembling hand he wrote it,
And he marked the time with sighs and tears.
Come, then;
Here on the stage you shall behold us in human fashion,
And see the sad fruits of love and passion.
Hearts that weep and languish, cries of rage and anguish,
And bitter laughter!

The beautiful *andante* which follows is the most admired portion of the aria, and is indeed a noble strain.

Ah, think then, sweet people, when ye look on us,
Clad in our motley and tinsel,
For ours are human hearts, beating with passion,
We are but men like you, for gladness or sorrow,
'Tis the same broad Heaven above us,
The same wide, lonely world before us!
Will ye hear, then, the story,
As it unfolds itself surely and certain!
Come, then! Ring up the curtain!

The curtain now rises, as the *pagliacci motive* reappears in the orchestra.

Opening Chorus—" Son qua! " (They're Here!)
By La Scala Chorus (*In Italian*) *16814 10-inch, $0.75

COPY'T MISHKIN

SAMMARCO AS TONIO

The first scene, representing the edge of a small village in Calabria, is now revealed to the audience. The people are engaged in celebrating the Feast of the Assumption, and among the attractions offered to the crowds who have flocked to the village is the troupe of strolling players headed by *Canio*. These wandering mountebanks are common in the rural districts of Italy and are known as *pagliacci*. They take with them a small tent (usually carried in a cart drawn by a donkey), which they set up in the market places of the small villages, or anywhere that they see a prospect for the earning of a modest living.

A number of the townspeople have assembled in front of the little theatre and are awaiting the return of the clowns, who have been parading through the village to announce their arrival, as is the custom. As the curtain rises, the sound of a drum and trumpet is heard from a distance, and the villagers are full of joy at the prospect of a comedy performance. They express their excitement in a vigorous opening chorus. This is a clever bit of writing, but so difficult that it is seldom well given. The famous chorus of La Scala, however, under the leadership of Maestro Sabaino, have given this stirring number in splendid style. This oft-recurring phrase:

Ev - vi - va! il prin - ci - pe.. ... se' dei pa-glia - ci!
Long life to him, the prince. .. of all pa-glia - cios!

which is presented with many odd modulations, produces a peculiar and novel effect.

BOYS: Hi! They're here!
They're coming back!
Pagliaccio's there
The grown-up folks and boys
All follow after!
Their jokes and laughter
They all applaud.

WOMEN: See, there's the wagon!
My, what a fiendish din!
The Lord have mercy on us!
ALL: Welcome Pagliaccio;
Long life to him,
The prince of all pagliaccios;
You drive our cares away
With fun and laughter!

The little troupe has now come into view and the noise is redoubled. *Canio* appears at the head of his company, his wife, *Nedda,* riding in the cart drawn by a donkey, while *Tonio* and *Peppe* make hideous noises on the bass drum and cracked trumpet, which constitute the orchestra of the players. *Canio* is dressed in the traditional garb of the clown, his face smeared with flour and his cheeks adorned with patches of red. He tries to

Double-Faced Record—See page 375.

address the crowd, but the noise is tremendous. *Tonio* beats the drum furiously to silence the voices, but it is not until *Canio* has raised his hand to command attention that he is allowed to speak.

Un grande spettacolo! (A Wond'rous Performance!)

By Antonio Paoli, Tenor; Francesco Cigada, Baritone; Gaetano Pini-Corsi, Tenor; and Sig. Rosci, Baritone
(*In Italian*) 92009 12-inch, $3.00

He begins to address the peasants in this fashion:

> CANIO:
> A wondrous performance
> I say will be given,
> By your humble servants
> This evening at seven.
> The wrath of Pagliaccio
> Will there be presented—
> What vengeance he took,
> And the trap he invented!
> You'll witness the carcass of Tonio tremble,
> And see him dissemble and pile up the plot!
> So honor us by coming this even;
> Come all, then, at seven!

The crowd boisterously express their joy at the prospect of an evening's entertainment. *Canio* now turns to assist *Nedda* to alight from

ARRIVAL OF THE PLAYERS

the cart, but finds *Tonio*, the Fool, there before him. Giving him a cuff on the ear, he bids him be off, and *Tonio* slinks away muttering. The boys in the crowd jeer him, saying:

> Does that suit you, Mr. Lover?

Tonio threatens the boys, who run away. He goes grumbling into the theatre, saying, aside:

> He'll pay for this ere it's over!

One of the peasants invites the players to the wine shop for a friendly glass. They accept, and *Canio* calls to *Tonio* to join them, but he replies from within: "I'm rubbing down the donkey," which causes a villager to remark, jestingly:

> A PEASANT: Careful, Pagliaccio!
> He only stays behind there
> For making love to Nedda!

Canio smiles, but knits his brow and is evidently impressed by the thought.

> CANIO: Eh! What?
> You think so?

(*He becomes serious, and signing to the peasants to come round him, he begins to address them.*)

COPY'T MISHKIN   CARUSO AS CANIO

Un tal gioco (Such a Game!)

By Nicola Zerola, Tenor   (*In Italian*) 64206 10-inch, $1.00

The first trace of *Canio's* jealous nature is now shown, as he takes with apparent seriousness the idle joke of the peasant, and begins to warn the spectators as follows:

CANIO: Such a game, I'd have you know,
'Twere better not to play, my neighbors!
To Tonio, aye, to you all I say it!
For the stage there and life, they are different altogether!

* * * * * * * * * *

If up there, (*pointing to the theatre*)
Pagliaccio his lady should discover
With some fine fellow in her room,
He'd give the two a rating . . . or resign himself,
And take a jolly beating!

(*With a sudden change of tone*)

But if Nedda I really should surprise so,
What came after were a far different story!

Nedda, who is listening, is surprised and says aside: "What does he mean?" The villagers, rather puzzled at his earnestness, ask him if he is serious. With an effort he rouses himself from his gloomy mood and says lightly:

Not I—I love my wife most dearly!

(*He approaches Nedda and kisses her on the forehead.*)

The sound of bagpipes (oboe) is heard in the distance, telling of the merrymaking in the village, and the church bells begin to toll the call to vespers. The people commence to disperse, and *Canio* again repeats his melodious strain of invitation:

Ma poi ri-cor-da- - te-vi! A ven-ti trè o - - - rel
But then, you will not. . for-get! This eve-ning at sev - - enl

(*He goes with several peasants into the inn.*)

Coro della campane (Chorus of the Bells)

By La Scala Chorus

(*In Italian*) *35172 12-inch, $1.25

This is the famous Bell Chorus, or "Ding Dong" Chorus, one of the most remarkable numbers in the opera. It is sung with spirit, and the chiming bells are introduced in a most effective manner. The people go off singing and the measures die away in the distance.

Ballatella, "Che volo d'augelli!" (Ye Birds Without Number!)

By Lucrezia Bori, Soprano (*In Italian*) 88398 12-inch, $3.00
By Alma Gluck, Soprano (*In Italian*) 74238 12-inch, 1.50
By Giuseppina Huguet, Soprano (*In Italian*) *35172 12-inch, 1.25

Nedda, left alone, is troubled by her remembrance of *Canio's* manner and wonders if he suspects her.

But shaking off her depression, she becomes once more alive to the brightness of the day, which fills her with a strange delight. A gay tremolo in the strings announces the theme of the birds, and *Nedda* speaks of her mother, who could understand their language.

NEDDA: Ah, ye birds without number!
What countless voices!
What ask ye? Who knows?
My mother, she that was skillful at telling one's fortune,
Understood what they're singing,
And in my childhood, thus would she sing me.

Then follows the brilliant *Balatella* or Bird Song, beginning:

Stri - do - no las - sù,. li - be - ra - men - to
There on high they cry, In free-dom fly - ing,

COPY'T DUPONT
FARRAR AS NEDDA

It is a most beautiful number with an exquisite accompaniment, mainly of strings. Two splendid celebrity records are offered, while a very fine rendition by Mme. Huguet is given as part of a double-faced record.

COPY'T MISHKIN

GLUCK AS NEDDA

So ben che deforme (I Know That You Hate Me)

By Giuseppina Huguet, Soprano, and Francesco Cigada, Baritone

(*In Italian*) *35173 12-inch, $1.25

At the close of her song *Nedda* finds that the hideous *Tonio* has been listening, and now seeing the handsome Columbine alone, begins to make love to her; but she scornfully orders him away. He persists, but his protestations are greeted with mocking laughter, and *Nedda* says insolently:

NEDDA:
There's time, if you like,
Once more to tell me this evening
When you will be acting the fool!
*   *   *   *   *   *   *
Just now, it is painful.

In a furious rage, *Tonio* swears she must listen to her and cries:

TONIO:
You mock me? Wretched creature!
By the cross of the Savior
You shall pay for this, and dearly!

NEDDA:
A threat, eh? Come, or I'll be calling Canio!
TONIO:
But not until I've kissed you!
(*Rushing toward her.*)

Nulla scordai! (Naught I Forget!)

By Giuseppina Huguet, Francesco Cigada, and Ernesto Badini

(*Doubled with above duet*)   (*In Italian*) *35173 12-inch, $1.25

Tonio, driven almost to madness by *Nedda's* scorn and ridicule, seizes and tries to kiss her. She strikes him across the face with her whip, crying:

Oh, you would, you cur!

TONIO (*screaming*): By the Blessed Virgin of Assumption,
Nedda, I swear it,
You shall pay me for it! (*Rushes off.*)
NEDDA (*watching him*): Scorpion! at last you've shown your nature!
Tonio, the clown,
The heart of you is just as crooked as your body!

SILVIO

The young villager, *Silvio*, whom *Nedda* has secretly met on previous visits to the town, now jumps over the wall. *Nedda*, alarmed, cries:

NEDDA: Silvio! In the daytime? What folly!
SILVIO (*smiling*): I fancy it's no great risk I'm taking!
Canio I spied from afar with Peppe yonder.
Ay! at the tavern I saw them!

She tells him of *Tonio's* behavior and bids him beware, as the clown is to be feared. Her lover cheers her and laughs at her fears, and they sing the beautiful love duet, in which *Silvio* urges her to fly with him; but she is afraid and begs him not to tempt her. He persists, and reproaches her for her coldness, until finally in a passion of abandonment she yields, singing the beautiful passage which begins the record:

Then together they sing the lovely duet:

NEDDA (Overcome and yielding)
perdutamente con passione
Più mosso

Nul - la scor - dai ... scon - vol ta e tur - ba - ta........
Naught I for - get, ... but see with a - mo - tion......

BOTH: All, all forgot!
NEDDA: Look into my eyes, love,
All is forgotten!
Then kiss me, dear!

SILVIO: Thou'lt come?
NEDDA (*passionately*):
Aye! kiss me once more!
BOTH: I love thee!

* *Double-Faced Record—See page 375.*

CANIO SURPRISES THE LOVERS—ACT II

The lovers, who have cast aside all prudence and see only each other, fail to observe *Canio*, who has been warned by *Tonio* and has hurried from the tavern.

> TONIO (*holding Canio back*): Now just step softly,
> And you will catch them now!
> SILVIO (*disappearing over the wall*):
> To-night at midnight,
> I'll be there below!
> NEDDA: 'Till to-night then,
> And forever I'll be thine!

(*She sees Canio and gives a cry of fear.*)

Aitalo Signor! (May Heaven Protect Him!)

By Antonio Paoli Tenor; Giuseppina Huguet,
Soprano; Francesco Cigada, Baritone; Gaetano
Pini-Corsi, Tenor (*In Italian*) 92011 12-inch, $3.00

Canio, who has not seen *Silvio*, but has heard *Nedda's* part-ing words, now rushes toward the wall. *Nedda* bars his way. The record begins with the melodramatic music written by Leonca-vallo for this exciting struggle, during which *Canio* pushes her aside and runs in pursuit of *Silvio*.

SILVIO AND NEDDA

> NEDDA (*listening anxiously*): May Heaven protect him now!
> CANIO (*from behind*): Scoundrel! Where hidest thou?
> TONIO (*laughing cynically*): Ha! Ha! Ha!
> NEDDA (*turning to Tonio with loathing*): Bravo! Well done, Tonio!
> TONIO (*with fiendish satisfaction*): I hope in the future to do better!

Canio re-enters, out of breath and com-pletely exhausted. As he turns to *Nedda* with suppressed rage we hear again in the accom-paniment that dismal theme of revenge:

CARUSO SINGING "VESTI LA GIUBBA"

CANIO:
No one!
That shows how well he knows that path.
But no matter!
(*Furiously*):
Because right now you'll tell me his name!
NEDDA (*indifferently*):
Me?
CANIO (*in frenzy*):
You! By God in Heaven!
And if up to this moment I have not cut your throat,
* * * * * * * * * * *
'Tis because I'd have you name him!
Speak now!

Nedda proudly refuses. Filled with joy because of *Silvio's* escape, she cares not what may be her own fate. *Canio,* beside himself, rushes on her with the knife, but *Peppe* holds him back and takes away his weapon. *Tonio* comes to *Peppe's* assistance, saying:

Restrain yourself, good master,
'Tis best to sham awhile.
The fellow will come back,
You take my word for it!

They finally persuade him to restrain himself, and beg him to make ready for the play, as the audience is already assembling.

Nedda goes into the theatre and *Canio* remains alone, his head bowed with shame and baffled revenge in his soul.

Vesti la giubba (On With the Play)

By Enrico Caruso, Tenor		(*In Italian*)	88061	12-inch, $3.00
By Nicola Zerola, Tenor		(*In Italian*)	64169	10-inch, 1.00
By Giovanni Martinelli, Tenor		(*In Italian*)	64484	10-inch, 1.00
By Paul Althouse, Tenor	(*Double-Faced*)	(*In Italian*)	45055	10-inch, 1.00

We now come to the most famous of the numbers in Leoncavallo's opera, the great Lament of Pagliaccio. Its heart-breaking pathos never fails to touch the listener, when sung by such artists as the Victor offers.

The unhappy *Canio,* left alone after the exciting scene with *Nedda,* wrings his hands and cries:

CANIO:
To play! When my head's whirling with madness,
Not knowing what I'm saying or
what I'm doing!

Yet I must force myself!
I am not a man,
I'm but a Pagliaccio!

The great aria now follows, in which the unfortunate Pagliaccio describes how he must paint his face and make merry for the public while his heart is torn with jealousy.

CANIO:
The people pay you, and they must have
their fun!
If Harlequin your Columbine takes from
you,
Laugh loud, Pagliaccio!
And all will shout, well done!
* * * * * *
Laugh, Pagliaccio, for the love that is ended!
(*Sobbing*):
Laugh for the pain that is gnawing your
heart!

CANIO

(*He moves slowly toward the theatre, weeping; he stops at the entrance and hesitates. Seized by a new fit of sobbing, he buries his face in his hands; then as the curtain slowly falls, rushes into the tent.*)

Caruso's *Canio* is still the great feature of Pagliacci, and his magnificent singing of this famous lament cannot be described—it must be heard. In all that this artist has done there is no piece of dramatic singing to equal in emotional force his delivery of the reproaches of the clown, which he pours out not only on his faithless wife, but on himself and the occupation that bids him be merry when his heart is breaking. Sometimes Caruso's voice merely delights the ear—here he searches the heart; and is not merely the greatest of tenors, but is the clown himself, full of the most tragic emotion.

ACT II

SCENE—Same as Act I

La Commedia (The Play) Part I, Serenata d'Arlecchino (Harlequin's Serenade)

By Giuseppina Huguet and Gaetano Pini-Corsi
(*In Italian*) *35174 12-inch, $1.25

Passing over the preparations for the play and the quarreling chorus of the peasants as they fight for the best seats, which is not interesting without the action, we come to the commencement of the comedy. The curtain is drawn aside, disclosing a small room with two side doors and a window at the back. *Nedda* as Columbine is discovered walking about anxiously. The tripping minuet movement which runs throughout the action of the comedy now begins.

Columbine rises and looks out of the window, saying:

> Pagliaccio, my husband, till late this evening
> Will not be at home.

The sound of a guitar, cleverly imitated by the violins, *pizzicato,* causes Columbine to utter a cry of joy, and the voice of Harlequin is heard outside in the Serenade, beginning:

NEDDA AS COLUMBINE

HARLEQUIN (Peppe, behind scene)

> O...... Co - lom - bi - na, il te - ne - ..o fi - do Ar-leo chin
> O........ Col - um-bine, your Har - le - quin is here with you,

in which he extravagantly rhapsodizes his sweetheart.

La Commedia (The Play) Part II, E dessa! (Behold Her!)

By Giuseppina Huguet, Soprano; Francesco Cigada, Baritone; and Gaetano Pini-Corsi, Tenor
(*In Italian*) *35174 12-inch, $1.25

Tonio as Taddeo, with his basket, now peeps through the door and says exaggeratedly, with a comical cadenza:

Moderato e sostenuto (lifting his hands and the basket upwards)
[In mock-tragic style]

> È des - sa! Dei, co-me è bel · · · · la!
> Be - hold her! Is - n't she love · · · · ly!

The audience laughs in delight as *Tonio* tries to express his love by a long, exaggerated sigh. Columbine tries to suppress him by inquiring about the chicken he had been sent for, but *Tonio* kneels, and holding up the fowl says:

> See, we are *both* before thee kneeling!

His pretensions are cut short by Harlequin, who enters and leads him out by the ear. As he goes he gives the lovers a mock benediction, singing:

> Then I my claim surrender. Bless you, my children!

Versa il filtro nella tazza sua! (Pour the Potion in His Wine, Love!)

By Augusto Barbaini, Tenor; Giuseppina Huguet, Soprano; Francesco Cigada, Baritone; and Gaetano Pini-Corsi, Tenor
(*In Italian*) *35175 12-inch, $1.25

AMATO AS TONIO

*Double-Faced Record—See page 375.

371

The lovers now partake of their feast and make merry together. Harlequin takes from his pocket a little vial, which he gives to Columbine, saying:

HARLEQUIN:
Take this little sleeping draught,
'Tis for Pagliaccio!
Give it him at bedtime,
And then away we'll fly.

COLUMBINE (*eagerly*):
Yes, give me!

Upon the scene suddenly bursts *Tonio,* in mock alarm, bawling loudly

Be careful! Pagliaccio is here!
Trembling all over, he seeks for weapons!
He has caught you, and I shall fly to cover!

The lovers simulate the greatest alarm, at which the excited spectators are highly pleased, and applaud lustily. Harlequin leaps from the window, and *Nedda* continues the scene by repeating Columbine's next lines, which by a strange chance are the very words she had spoken to *Silvio* earlier in the day:

Larghetto affettuoso ($\quad = 88$)
COLUM. (at the window)

A sta - not - te   E per sem - pre   io   sa   rò   tua!
Till to - night, then!   And for ev - er   I   shall be thine!

Canio, dressed as Punchinello, now enters from the door on the right.

CANIO (*with suppressed rage*):
Hell and damnation!
And the very same words, too!
(*Recovering himself*):
But, courage!

(*Taking up his part*):
You had a man with you!

COLUMBINE (*lightly*):
What nonsense! You are tipsy!

PAGLIACCIO (*restraining himself with difficulty*):
Ah, if thou wast alone here
Why these places for two?

COLUMBINE:
Taddeo was supping with me.

TADDEO (*from within*):
Believe her, sir! She is faithful!
(*Sneering*):
Ah, they could never lie, those lips
so truthful!

The audience laughs loudly, which enrages the unhappy man, and forgetting his part he turns to *Nedda* and fiercely demands the name of her lover:

CANIO:
Woman, 'tis thy lover's name I want,
The wretched scoundrel from whose
arms thou comest!
Oh, shameless woman!

NEDDA (*faintly*: *much alarmed*):
Pagliaccio! Pagliaccio!

Throwing off entirely the mask of the player, *Canio* becomes again the jealous husband, and sings this great aria, which is second only to the *Vesti la giubba* in dramatic power.

No, Pagliaccio non son! (No, Punchinello No More!)

By Enrico Caruso, Tenor
(*Italian*) 88279 12-inch, $3.00
By Nicola Zerola, Tenor
(*Italian*) 74247 12-inch, 1.50
By Augusto Barbaini, Tenor
(*Italian*) *35175 12-inch, 1.25

Double-Faced Record—See page 375.

FROM "THE GREAT OPERAS" BY J. CUTHBERT HADDEN

COLUMBINE AND HARLEQUIN AT SUPPER

CANIO:

No, Pagliaccio, I'm not!
If my face be white,
'Tis shame that pales it
And vengeance twists my fea-
tures!

*   *   *   *   *   *

I am that foolish man
Who in poverty found and
tried to save thee!
He gave a name to thee,
A burning love that was mad-
ness!
(*Falls in a chair, over-
whelmed.*)

The people, while a little puzzled by such intensity, loudly applaud what they think is a piece of superb acting.

CANIO (*recovering himself*):

All my life to thee I sacrificed with
gladness!

Full of hope and believing far less
in God than thee!

*   *   *   *   *   *

Go! Thou'rt not worth my grief,
O thou abandoned creature!
And now, with my contempt,
I'll crush thee under heel!

Caruso's rendering of this great scene is a magnificent one. The opening passage is delivered with tremendous power, as *Canio* pleads his defense, saying that he is no longer a player, but a man, and protests as a man against the wrong inflicted upon him. His passion gives place to a softer strain as he speaks of his love for *Nedda*, his faithfulness and his sacrifices for her. At the close is the intense climax, with its splendid high B flat. Other fine renditions of the air are by Zerola and Barbaini.

Finale to the Opera

**By Antonio Paoli, Tenor; Giuseppina Huguet, Soprano; Francesco
Cigada, Baritone; Gaetano Pini-Corsi, Tenor; Ernesto Badini,
Tenor; and Chorus**   (*In Italian*)   **92013**   **12-inch, $3.00**

The close of *Canio's* great air, "No, Pagliaccio No More!" is greeted with loud cries of "bravo" from the excited audience.

Nedda is now thoroughly alarmed, but courageously faces her husband with outward calm.

    THE PLAY—ACT II

NEDDA (*coldly but seriously*):

'Tis well!
If thou think'st me vile,
Send me off, then,
Before this moment's over!

CANIO (*laughing loudly*):

Ha! Ha!
Oh, nothing better would'st
thou ask,
Than to be let run to meet
thy lover!
No! by Heaven, for here thou
stayest,
Until thy paramour's vile
name thou sayest!

Nedda, in desperation, tries to continue the play, and as the little gavotte movement is resumed in the accompaniment, she sings:

NEDDA:

Oh dear, I never knew that
you
Were such a fearful man, sir!
The man who's been to sup
with me
And caused you all this bother
Was only Harlequin, you see.
Poor Harlequin, no other!

CANIO: Name him, or else I'll kill you! (Act II.)

The crowd begins to laugh, but is checked by *Canio's* appearance, which is alarming.

CANIO (*violently*): Ah, you defy me!
* * * * * * * *
You'll name him, or else I'll kill you!
(*Shouting*): Who was it?
NEDDA (*throwing off her mask defiantly*):
No, by my mother,
I'm faithless, or whatever you choose to call me;
(*Proudly*): But cowardly, no, never!
* * * * * * * *
I will not speak!
No, not even if you kill me.

As she sings we hear triumphantly appearing above her voice the love motive:

telling of her passion for *Silvio*, which is to endure even unto death. *Canio* now rushes toward her, but is restrained by *Tonio* and *Peppe*. *Nedda* tries to escape, but *Canio* breaks away and stabs her, crying:

CANIO: Take that!
Perhaps in death's last agony,
You will speak!

Nedda falls, and with a last faint effort calls:

"Oh, help me, Silvio."

Silvio, who has drawn his dagger, rushes to her, when *Canio* cries:

Ah, 'twas you! 'Tis well! (*Stabs him.*)

CANIO (*as if stupefied, letting fall his knife*):
The comedy is ended!

Then once more is heard the tragic motive of jealousy and death, now thundered out by the orchestra as if rejoicing at its final triumph.

Curtain.

CANIO

DOUBLE-FACED AND MISCELLANEOUS PAGLIACCI RECORDS

{Prologue, Part I By Francesco Cigada, Baritone (*In Italian*)			
{Prologue, Part II By Francesco Cigada, Baritone (*In Italian*)	35171	12-inch, $1.25	
{Prologue By Pryor's Band			
{ *Flying Dutchman Fantasia* By Pryor's Band	35158	12-inch, 1.25	
{Coro della campane By La Scala Chorus (*In Italian*)			
{Che volo d'augelli By Giuseppina Huguet, Soprano (*Italian*)	35172	12-inch, 1.25	
{So ben che deforme By Huguet and Cigada (*In Italian*)			
{Nulla scordai! By Huguet, Cigada and Badini (*In Italian*)	35173	12-inch, 1.25	
{La Commedia—Part I By Huguet and Pini-Corsi			
{La Commedia—Part II By Giuseppina Huguet, Soprano;	35174	12-inch, 1.25	
{ Francesco Cigada, Baritone; Gaetano Pini-Corsi, Tenor			
{Versa il filtro nella tazza sua!			
{ By Barbaini, Huguet, Cigada and Pini-Corsi (*In Italian*)	35175	12-inch, 1.25	
{No, Pagliaccio non son! By Augusto Barbaini (*In Italian*)			
{Opening Chorus,"Son qua" By La Scala Chorus (*In Italian*)			
{ *Trovatore—Per me ora fatale*—Ernesto Caronna and Chorus (*Italian*)	16814	10-inch, .75	
{Gems from Pagliacci			
{ Chorus—"Ding Dong"—"This Evening at Seven"—			
{ Bird Song, "Ye Birds Without Number"—"Pagliaccio's			
{ Lament" (Vesti la giubba)—Duet, The Comedy, "Just	35343	12-inch, 1.25	
{ Look, My Love"—Chorus, "See, They Come"			
{ By Victor Opera Company (*In English*)			
{ *Gems from Cavalleria Rusticana*			
{ By Victor Opera Company (*In English*)			

This interesting *potpourri* opens with the famous Bell Chorus, in which chiming bells are introduced in a most effective manner.

Then comes *Canio's* address to the peasants, telling them about the play, followed by *Nedda's* beautiful song to the birds, with its exquisite accompaniment.

Next we have the great lament of *Pagliaccio*, a bit of the comedy duet between *Columbine* and *Harlequin,* and the record concludes with the rousing chorus of villagers which greets the coming of the players at the beginning of the opera.

LE THÉÂTRE

THE COMEDY IS ENDED!

PANEL BY BRAUNE

TEMPLE OF THE GRAIL

PARSIFAL

A FESTIVAL DRAMA IN THREE ACTS

Music and libretto by Richard Wagner; based on the famous Grail Legend.   First produced at Bayreuth, July 28, 1882, not elsewhere until 1903, when the work was given at
the Metropolitan Opera House, in spite of the determined opposition of Mme. Wagner.   A
production in English was afterward given by Henry W. Savage.   The copyright expired
in 1913 and productions at Berlin, Paris, Rome, Bologna, Madrid and Barcelona followed.

Characters

TITUREL, a Holy Knight . . . . .Bass
AMFORTAS, his son. . . . . .Baritone
GURNEMANZ, a veteran Knight of the Grail. . . . . .Bass
PARSIFAL, a "guileless fool" . . . . .Tenor
KLINGSOR, an evil magician . . . . .Bass
KUNDRY . . . . .Soprano

Knights of the Grail; Klingsor's Fairy Maidens.

THE STORY

The story of the Grail is perhaps the most beautiful in legendary lore. Wagner's version, which was inspired by a mediæval epic written about 1300 by Wolfram von Eschenbach, of Thuringia, whom Wagner has already introduced to us in Tannhauser, tells of the Holy Grail, the cup from which Christ drank at the Last Supper with His disciples, and into which was placed the blood which flowed from the wounds of the Saviour.

This sacred cup, together with the lance which caused these wounds, was in danger of profanation from infidel hands, and was therefore sent by holy messengers to a pure Knight, *Titurel,* who built a splendid sanctuary on an inaccessible rock in the Pyrenees and gathered together a company of Knights of unimpeachable honor, who are devoting their lives to the guarding of the Grail. Once each year a dove descends from Heaven to renew the sacred powers of the Grail and its guardians. Such a subject as this, mystic, symbolic and poetic, so inspired Wagner that in *Parsifal* he reached his highest sphere as a composer. By no other writer or composer has this most beautiful of legends been so reverently treated, or given such a wonderful significance.

The events which are supposed to occur before the opening of the opera must be understood before a clear idea of the action of Wagner's work can be gained. *Titurel,* finding himself growing old, appoints his son, *Amfortas,* as his successor. Near the Castle of Monsalvat there lives *Klingsor,* a Knight, who, feeling himself growing old and wishing to atone for his sins, vainly tries to join the Order of the Grail, but without avail. In revenge, he consults an Evil Spirit and plots to bring about the downfall of the Knights. To this end he invokes the aid of a company of sirens, half women and half flowers, called flower girls, who dwell in a magic garden. One by one the Knights have fallen from grace because of the allurements of the flower maidens, until *Amfortas,* seeking to end these fatal enchantments, resolves to go himself, carrying the sacred Lance, which he is confident will be proof against the magic of the sirens. But, alas! he is not only defeated, but is wounded by the sacred Lance, which his enemy seizes and turns against him, making a wound which nothing can heal. The unhappy *Amfortas* returns to the Castle weighted with an eternal remorse and a perpetual agony from his wound, but is forced as head priest to continue to celebrate the Holy Rites, all the while feeling himself unworthy. In vain he seeks far and wide for a remedy for his wound and forgiveness for his sin, until one day in a vision he hears an invisible voice proclaim that only a guileless fool (*i. e.,* one who is ignorant of sin and who can resist temptation), and whom heavenly messengers will guide to Monsalvat, will be able to bring him relief.

Amfortas' downfall was brought about by a strange being, *Kundry,* who seems to have two natures. She appears alternately as a devoted servant of the Grail, and, when under the magic influence of *Klingsor,* as a woman of terrible beauty, who lures to their ruin all Knights who come within her power. This cursed existence is a punishment for a crime committed in a previous existence, when as *Herodias* she mocked at Christ on the cross.

ORIGINAL PROGRAM OF PARSIFAL
(BAYREUTH, 1882)

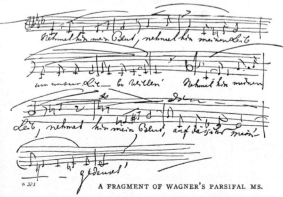

A FRAGMENT OF WAGNER'S PARSIFAL MS.

GURNEMANZ AND THE NOVICES—ACT I

ACT I

SCENE—*A Forest Near Monsalvat*

The rise of the curtain shows *Gurnemanz,* a veteran Knight, with two novices, asleep. Trumpet calls from the Castle awaken them, and they join in prayer, afterward preparing the bath with which *Amfortas* seeks to heal his wound. Messengers from the Castle report that the latest balm which he had tried failed to bring relief. *Gurnemanz* is much grieved, and sinks down in dejection, until he is roused by the approach of *Kundry,* who comes in hurriedly, dressed in sombre garments and in her normal mind, but exhausted with fatigue. She brings a new remedy which she had sought in distant Arabia. When *Amfortas* arrives with his train for a bath in the sacred lake, the new balm is offered to him. He accepts and thanks the strange-looking woman for her kindness. When the procession departs the novices attack *Kundry,* calling her a sorceress, but she is defended by *Gurnemanz,* who says she is devoted to the King but is subject to strange spells, during which she vanishes for long periods.

GURNEMANZ:
  Yea, under a curse she may have been:
  Here now's her home,—
  Renewed become,
  That of her sins she may be shriven
  From former life yet unforgiven,
  Seeking her shrift by such good actions
  As advantage all our knightly factions.
  Sure she does well in working thus:
  Serves herself and also us.

NOVICE:
  Then it is not surely her fault
  So much distress hath come to us?

GURNEMANZ:
  True, when she often stayed afar from us
  Then broke misfortune ever in.
  I long have known her now;
  But Titurel knew her yet longer:
  When he yon castle consecrated,
  He found her sleeping in this wood,
  All stiff, rigid, like death.
  Thus I myself did find her lately,
  Just when the trouble came on us
  Which yonder miscreant beyond the mountain
  So shamefully did bring about.

PANEL BY STASSEN

PANEL BY BRAUNE

PARSIFAL AND THE SWAN

GURNEMANZ:
Could'st thou do murder
Here in holy forest?
Why harmed thee that goodly Swan?

Suddenly a wild swan falls wounded at the feet of *Gurnemanz*, and two Knights appear dragging the innocent *Parsifal*, who had shot it, not knowing it was under the King's protection. He is reproached by *Gurnemanz* and questioned, but can tell little of himself. He remembers that his mother was called *Herzeleid* and lived in a forest. *Kundry*, whose attention is attracted, explains that the youth's father was *Gamuret*, and after his death in battle his mother took him away from the haunts of men lest he meet the same fate. She is now dead, and *Parsifal* is a wanderer.

The train of *Amfortas* again approaches, returning from the lake. *Gurnemanz* invites *Parsifal* to accompany them to the Castle, the thought having occurred to him that this strange youth may be the "guileless fool" who is to be the means of *Amfortas'* regeneration.

GURNEMANZ CONDUCTING PARSIFAL TO MONSALVAT—ACT I

GURNEMANZ:
>From bathing comes the King again;
High stands the sun now:
Let me to the holy Feast then conduct thee;
For—an thou'rt pure,
Surely the Grail will feed and refresh thee.
*(He has gently laid Parsifal's arm on his own
neck, and, supporting his body with his arm,
leads him slowly along.)*

PARSIFAL: What is the Grail?

GURNEMANZ: I may not say:
But if to serve it thou be bidden,
Knowledge of it will not be hidden.
And lo!
Methinks I know thee now indeed:
No earthly road to it doth lead,
By no one can it be detected
Who by itself is not elected.

PARSIFAL: I scarcely move,—
Yet swiftly seem to run.

GURNEMANZ:
My son, thou seest
Here time and space are one.

The change to the Castle Hall is here effected by a moving scene behind *Gurnemanz* and *Parsifal,* so that they seem to be walking slowly along, at first through the forest, then into a covered gallery which ascends to the Castle. This effective device was first used at Bayreuth, and afterward in the American representations.

THE TEMPLE OF THE GRAIL

SCENE II—*The Castle Hall*

The two suddenly find themselves in a vast hall, filled with a strange light, while invisible bells are pealing. *Parsifal* is dazzled and fascinated by the wonderful sight, while he is carefully watched by *Gurnemanz,* who hopes to see signs of an awakening knowledge of his mission.

In the hall the Knights are preparing for the daily rites which occur before the Holy Grail. Then one of the most impressive scenes in the opera takes place. The unfortunate *Amfortas* is brought in on a couch and prepares to preside at the ceremony. In agony of mind and body, he endeavors to postpone the rites, but the voice of his aged father, *Titurel,* is heard from the dark chapel commanding him to proceed. *Amfortas,* in a heart-breaking plea, begs Heaven to permit him to die, to end his intolerable sufferings.

AMFORTAS:

No! Leave it unrevealed!
May no one, no one know the anguish dire
Awaked in me by that which raptures ye!
What is the wound and all its torture wild,
'Gainst the distress, the pangs of Hell,
In this high post—accurst to dwell!—
Woeful inheritance on me pressed,
I, only sinner 'mid the blessed,
The holy house to guard for others
And pray for blessings upon my purer brothers!
Oh, chast'ning—chast'ning dire! descended
From the Almighty One offended.
For grace and for compassion yearning
My panting heart is riven.
The hot and sinful blood doth surge,

SEIG IM GLAUBEN! SELIG

NEHMET HIN MEIN BLUT
NEHMET HIN MEINEN LEIB
AUF DASS IHR MEIN GEDENKT

PANEL BY BRAUNE   PARSIFAL WATCHING THE RITES—ACT I

Ever renewed from my yearnings' fountain,
Which no expiation yet can purge
Have mercy! Have mercy!
God of pity, oh! have mercy!

Titurel's voice is again heard, urging *Amfortas* to proceed, and the pain-racked priest raises himself from the couch and offers the prayer of consecration. As he speaks a blinding ray of light streams down from the vault above and falls on the Grail, which glows with a great luster. The Cup is covered and all partake of the bread and wine, after which they file slowly out. During the ceremony *Parsifal* has stood fascinated, but with impassive face. *Gurnemanz,* finally out of patience, comes up and thrusts him out, saying:

GURNEMANZ:
Thou art, then, nothing but a fool!
(*He opens a small side door.*)
Come away, on thy road be gone
And put my rede to use:
Leave all our swans for the future alone
And seek thyself, gander, a goose!
(*He pushes Parsifal out and slams the door
angrily on him as the curtain falls.*)

COURT OF KLINGSOR'S CASTLE

ACT II

SCENE—*Klingsor's Magic Castle*

In the inner keep of a tower open above; stone steps lead up to the battlemented summit and down into darkness below the stage, which represents the rampart. Magical implements and necromatic appliances are seen. *Klingsor* is discovered sitting at one side on a rampart before a metal mirror.

KLINGSOR:
The time has come!

Lo! how my magic tow'r entices
Yon fool who neareth, shouting like a child!

He lights incense, which immediately fills part of the background with a bluish vapor. He then reseats himself and calls toward the depth with mysterious gestures:

KLINGSOR:
Arise! Draw near to me!
Thy master calls thee, nameless woman:
She-Lucifer! Rose of Hades!

Herodias wert thou, and what else?
Gundryggia there, Kundry here:
Approach! Approach then, Kundry!
Thy master calls—appear!

In the bluish light arises the form of *Kundry.* She is heard to utter a dreadful cry, as if half awakened from a deep sleep. She tries to resist him, but *Klingsor's* power over her finally prevails. He tells her she must tempt *Parsifal,* who is now approaching the Castle of *Klingsor.*

KLINGSOR (*wrathfully*):
Have a care!
One his contempt and scorn hath repented;
The stern one, strong in holiness,
By whom I once was spurned
His stock I've ruined:
Unredeemed shall the Relics' curator soon languish;
And soon—I feel it—
I shall possess the Grail.
Ha! ha!
How suited thy taste Amfortas the brave,
Whom to thee in rapture I gave?

KUNDRY: Oh!—Mis'ry—Mis'ry!
Weak e'en he! Weak—all men!
By my curse and with me
All of them perish!
Oh, unending sleep,
Only release,
When—when shall I win thee?
KLINGSOR:
Ha! He who spurns thee setteth thee free;
So try't with yon boy who draws near!
KUNDRY: Oh woe's me! woe's me!
Awakened I for this?
Must I—must?

With a last cry of protest and anguish she vanishes in a bluish mist. The tower sinks beneath the earth, while a magic garden filled with wonderful flowers and plants rises to take its place. On the wall stands *Parsifal*, looking down on the garden in astonishment. From all sides, from the garden and from the palace, rush in mazy courses lovely damsels, first singly and then in numbers; their dress is hastily thrown about them, as if they had been suddenly startled from sleep. They have discovered that several of their lovers have been slain by an unknown foe, and seeing *Parsifal*, they accuse him of the deed. *Parsifal* comes nearer, saying innocently:

PARSIFAL (*in great astonishment*):
  Lovely maidens, had I not to slay them,
  When they endeavored to check approach to your charms?
DAMSELS: To us camest thou?
PARSIFAL:
  I've seen nowhere yet beings so bright:
  If I said fair, would it seem right?
DAMSELS (*with merriment*):
  Then wilt thou not treat us badly?
PARSIFAL (*smiling*):
  I could not so.
DAMSELS:
  But sadly
  What thou hast done has annoyed us;
  Our playmates thou hast destroyed us:
  Who'll sport with us now?
PARSIFAL:
  Then well will I.

KLINGSOR COMMANDING KUNDRY TO LURE PARSIFAL

HALL   PARSIFAL AND THE FLOWER MAIDENS   (HENRY W. SAVAGE PRODUCTION)

"But Parsifal
Shunned their circle of entwining arms
With gentle gestures."—*Act II.*

DAMSELS (*laughing*):
   If thou art friendly come more nigh.
   Let kindness be accorded,
   And thou shalt be rewarded:
   For gold we do not play
   But only for love's sweet pay.
   Wouldst thou console us rightly
   Then win it from us, and lightly.

Some have gone into the groves and now return in flower dresses, appearing like flowers themselves. They playfully quarrel for possession of *Parsifal*, who stands looking about him in quiet enjoyment of the scene. He finally gently repulses them, saying:

PARSIFAL:
   Ye wild-crowd of beautiful flowers,
   If I am to play, ye must widen youɪ
   bowers.

As they push closer to him he becomes angry and tries to flee, but his attention is suddenly arrested as *Kundry* calls, "Parsifal, tarry!" He stops in astonishment, saying:

PARSIFAL:
   Parsifal . . .?
   So once, when dreaming, my mother
      called me.
KUNDRY'S VOICE:
   Here bide thee, Parsifal!
   Where joy and gladness on thee shall
      fall.
   Ye frivolous wantons, leave him in
      peace:
   Flow'rs soon to be faded,
   He came not here for your delight!
   Go home, tend the wounded:
   Lonely awaits you many a knight.

Gently laughing, they disappear into the Castle. The form of *Kundry* now becomes visible as a woman of exquisite beauty, reclining on a flowery couch.

PARSIFAL:
   What callest thou me, who am nameless?
KUNDRY:
   I named thee, foolish pure one, "Fal parsi,"—

Thou, guileless fool, art "Parsifal."
So cried, when in Arabia's land he expired,
Thy father, Gamuret, unto his son.

Ich sah das Kind (I Saw the Child)
By Margarete Matzenauer, Contralto   *In German* 88364 12-inch, $3.00

Tenderly gazing at the now attentive youth, she begins, softly:

KUNDRY:
   I saw the child upon its mother's breast;
   Its infant lisping laughs yet in my ear:
      Though filled with sadness,
   How laughed then even Heart's Affliction,
      When, shouting gladness,
   It gave her sorrow's contradiction!
   In beds of moss 'twas softly nested,
   She kissed it till in sleep it rested:
      With care and sorrow
   The timid mother watched it sleeping;
      It waked the morrow
   Beneath the dew of mother's weeping.
   All tears was she, encased in anguish,
   Caused by thy father's death and love:

   That through like hap thou shouldst not lan-
      guish,
   Became her care all else above.
   Afar from arms, from mortal strife and riot,
   Sought she to hide away with thee in quiet.
   All care was she, alas! and fearing:
   Never should aught of knowledge reach thy
      hearing.
   Hear'st thou not still her lamenting voice,
   When far and late thou didst roam?
      For days and nights she waited,
      And then her cries abated;
   Her pain was dulled of its smart,
   And gently ebbed life's tide;
   The anguish broke her heart,
   And—Heart's Affliction—died.

Mme. Matzenauer, whose *Kundry* is one of her greatest impersonations, sings this number with exquisite tenderness and great beauty of voice.

Parsifal is greatly affected and sinks at *Kundry's* feet, distressed. She embraces him tenderly and tries to comfort him, while he seems to imagine that it is again his mother whose gentle embraces he is receiving. As she gives him the kiss which is to complete his subjection he awakes to a knowledge of his mission, realizes *Kundry's* evil purpose and repulses her with scorn. She pleads with him, playing on his sympathies:

KUNDRY:
 Let me upon thy breast lie sobbing,
 But for one hour together throbbing;
 Though forced from God and man to flee,
 Be yet redeemed and pardoned by thee!

PARSIFAL:
 Eternally should I be damned with thee,
 If for one hour I forgot my holy mission,
 Within thy arm's embracing!—
 To thy help also am I sent,
 If of thy cravings thou repent.
 The solace, which shall end thy sorrow,
 Yields not that spring from which it flows:
 Salvation canst thou never borrow,
 Till that same spring in thee shall close.

Finally, enraged by his refusal, she calls for help. Fearing that he will escape, *Klingsor* and the flower maidens rush out of the Castle.

COPY'T MISHKIN
MATZENAUER AS KUNDRY

KLINGSOR (*poising a lance*):
 Halt there! I'll ban thee with befitting gear:
 The Fool shall perish by his Master's spear!

He flings the spear at *Parsifal*, but an invisible force stops it and it remains floating over his head. *Parsifal* grasps it with his hand and brandishes it with a gesture of exalted rapture, making the sign of the Cross with it.

PARSIFAL:
 This sign I make, and ban thy cursed magic:
 As the wound shall be closed,
 Which thou with this once clovest,—
 To wrack and to ruin
 Falls thy unreal display!

BRAUNE
PARSIFAL CAPTURING THE
SACRED SPEAR

As with an earthquake the Castle falls to ruins, the garden withers up to a desert, the damsels become shriveled flowers strewn around on the ground.

Kundry sinks down at *Parsifal's* feet, while the hero, gazing at her with compassion, and referring to the Holy Grail, where true salvation can alone be found, cries:

PARSIFAL:
 Thou know'st—
 Where only we shall meet again!

(*He disappears, and the curtain falls quickly.*)

HALL
KLINGSOR HURLING THE SACRED LANCE

GURNEMANZ'S HERMITAGE—ACT III

ACT III

SCENE—*A spring landscape in the grounds of Monsalvat. At the back a small hermitage*

Gurnemanz, now an aged man, in hermit's dress but still wearing the tunic of a Knight of the Grail, comes out of the hut and listens. He then goes to a thicket and finds *Kundry* apparently lifeless, but she revives under his ministrations. She is dressed as in Act I, and soon arises and goes immediately, like a serving maid, to work. She enters the hut, procures a water jug which she fills at the spring. *Gurnemanz* watches her carefully, seeing signs of a change in her. *Parsifal* now enters from the wood in complete armor and seats himself. *Gurnemanz,* not recognizing him, reminds him that no armed knight is allowed in the sacred premises, and especially on this day, Good Friday. Without saying a word, *Parsifal* rises, removes his helmet, and kneels down in silent prayer. *Gurnemanz* in surprise, says softly to *Kundry:*

GURNEMANZ:
Dost know who 'tis? . . .
He who long since laid low the swan.
(*Kundry confirms him by a slight nod.*)
For sure 'tis he!
The fool whom in anger I dismissed.

Ha! by what path aye came he?
That Spear—I recognize!
(*In great emotion.*)
Oh!—holiest day,
To which my happy soul awakes!
(*Kundry has turned away her face.*)

Parsifal rises slowly from his prayer, gazes calmly around, recognizes *Gurnemanz,* and stretches out his hand to him in greeting.

PARSIFAL:
Thank Heaven that I again have found thee!

Gurnemanz questions him and is confirmed in his belief that this is the one who is to redeem the sins of the Grail brotherhood. He tells *Parsifal* of the sad state of affairs at the Castle.

GURNEMANZ:

Here art thou, in the Grail's domain;
Here waits for thee the knightly band.
Ah, how they need the blessing,
The blessing that thou bring'st!—
Since that first day in which thou camest here,
The mourning which thou heardest then—
The anguish—sorely has increased.
Amfortas, struggling with his torture,
With the wound that tore his spirit,
Desired with reckless daring then his death:
No pray'rs, no sorrow of his comrades
Could move him to fulfill his holy office.
Pale, dejected stays around
The crushed and leader-lacking band of knights.
Here on the woodside lone I hid myself,
For death with calmness waiting,

To which my old commander has succumbed;
For Titurel, my cherished chief,
When he no more beheld the Grail's refulgence,
Expired,—a man like others!

PARSIFAL (*flinging up his arms in intense grief*):
And I—I 'tis,
Who all this woe have wrought!
Ha! what a grievous,
What a heinous guilt
Must then my foolish head
Forever be oppressed with!
If no atonement, expiation
My blindness e'er can banish!
I, who to save men was selected,
Must wander undirected;
All paths of safety from me vanish!

He is on the point of falling, helplessly. *Gurnemanz* supports him and allows him to sink down on the grassy knoll. *Kundry* has brought a basin of water with which to sprinkle *Parsifal,* but *Gurnemanz* waves her away, saying that holy water alone must be used for his anointment.
Parsifal asks to be guided to *Amfortas,* and *Gurnemanz* and *Kundry* busy themselves in preparing him for the ordeal. *Kundry* bathes his feet and dries them on her hair. *Parsifal* asks *Gurnemanz,* who by his pure life has become worthy of this office, to anoint him with the water of purification and the contents of the golden vial which *Kundry* produces from her bosom. *Gurnemanz* consents, and bestows on *Parsifal* the title of Prince and King of the Grail. *Parsifal* now looks at *Kundry* with deep compassion, and taking up some water sprinkles her head, saying:

PARSIFAL:
I first fulfill my duty thus:—
Be thou baptized,
And trust in the Redeemer!
(*Kundry bows her head to the earth
and appears to weep bitterly.*)

PARSIFAL (*turns round and gazes with gentle
rapture on the woods and meadows*):
How fair the woods and meadows seem to-day!
Many a magic flow'r I've seen,
Which sought to clasp me in its baneful twinings;
But none I've seen so sweet as here,
These tendrils bursting with blossom,
Whose scent recalls my childhood's days
And speaks of loving trust to me.

DEN HEIL'GEN SPEER—
ICH BRING IHN EUCH ZURÜCK—
PANEL BY BRAUNE

PARSIFAL BEARING THE LANCE TO THE CASTLE

GURNEMANZ:
That is Good Friday's spell, my lord!

PARSIFAL:
Alas, that day of agony!
Now surely everything that thrives,
That breathes and lives and lives again,
Should only mourn and sorrow?

Gurnemanz explains that this beauty of the woods and fields is caused by the spell of Good Friday, and that the flowers and trees, watered by the tears of repentant sinners, express by their luxuriousness the redemption of man.

COPY'T PACH BROS.   PARSIFAL, KUNDRY AND GURNEMANZ ENTERING THE CASTLE—ACT III

COPY'T MISHKIN

WITHERSPOON AS GURNEMANZ

Char-Freitags Zauber (Good Friday Spell)

By Herbert Witherspoon, Bass
In German   74144   12-inch, $1.50

GURNEMANZ: Thou see'st, that is not so.
The sad repentant tears of sinners
Have here with holy rain
Besprinkled field and plain,
And made them glow with beauty.
All earthly creatures in delight
At the Redeemer's trace so bright
Uplift their pray'rs of duty.
To see Him on the Cross they have no power:
And so they smile upon redeemed man,
Who, feeling freed, with dread no more doth
    cower,
Through God's love-sacrifice made clean and
    pure:
And now perceives each blade and meadow-
    flower
That mortal foot to-day it need not dread;
For, as the Lord in pity man did spare,
And in His mercy for him bled,
All men will keep, with pious care,
To-day a tender tread.
Then thanks the whole creation makes,
With all that flow'rs and fast goes hence
That trespass-pardoned Nature wakes
Now to her day of Innocence.

389

WHITEHILL AS AMFORTAS

Kundry has slowly raised her head again, and gazes with moist eyes, earnestly and calmly beseeching *Parsifal*.

PARSIFAL:
I saw my scornful mockers wither:
Now look they for forgiveness hither?—
Like blessed sweet dew a tear from thee too floweth:
Thou weepest—see! the landscape gloweth.
(*He kisses her softly on the brow.*)

Distant bells are heard pealing, very gradually swelling.

GURNEMANZ:
Mid-day.
The hour has come:—
Permit, my lord, thy servant hence to lead
thee!

Gurnemanz has brought out a coat-of-mail and mantle of the Knights of the Grail, which he and *Kundry* put on *Parsifal*. The landscape changes very gradually, as in the first act. *Parsifal* solemnly grasps the Spear, and, with *Kundry*, follows the conducting *Gurnemanz*. When the wood has disappeared and rocky entrances have presented themselves in which the three become invisible, processions of Knights in mourning garb are perceived in the arched passages, the pealing of bells ever increasing. At last the whole immense hall becomes visible, just as in the first act, only without the tables. There is a faint light. The doors open again, and from one side the Knights bear in *Titurel's* corpse in a coffin. From the other *Amfortas* is carried on in his litter, preceded by the covered shrine of the Grail. The bier is erected in the middle; behind it the throne with canopy where *Amfortas* is set down.

FIRST TRAIN (*with the Grail and Amfortas*):
To sacred place in sheltering shrine
The Holy Grail do we carry.

SECOND TRAIN (*with Titurel's coffin*):
A hero lies in this dismal shrine
With all this Heavenly strength,
To whom all things once God did entrust:
Titurel hither we bear.

Amfortas' Gebet, "Mein Vater!" (Amfortas' Prayer, "My Father")

By Whitehill, Baritone
In German
74406 12-inch, $1.50

AMFORTAS (*raising himself on his couch*).
My father!
Highest venerated hero!
Thou purest, to whom once e'en the angels bended!
Oh! thou who now in Heavenly heights
Dost behold the Saviour's self,
Implore Him to grant that His hallowed blood,
He pour upon these brothers.
To them new life while giving,
To me may offer—but Death!
My father! I—call thee.
Cry thou my words to Him:
"Redeemer, give to my son release!"

SEVERAL KNIGHTS (*pressing forward*):
Uncover the shrine!
Do thou thine office!

AMFORTAS (*in a paroxysm of despair*):
No!—No more!
I bid ye to slay me!

ETCHING BY EQUSQUIZA   AMFORTAS

(*Tears open his dress.*)
Behold me!—the open wound behold!
Here is my poison—my streaming blood.
Take up your weapons!
Kill both the sinner and all his pain:
The Grail's delight will ye then regain!

PARSIFAL HEALING AMFORTAS—ACT III

All have shrunk back in awe and *Amfortas* stands alone in fearful ecstasy. *Parsifal,* accompanied by *Gurnemanz* and *Kundry,* has entered unperceived, and now advancing, stretches out the Spear, touching *Amfortas'* side with the point.

PARSIFAL:
One weapon only serves:—
The one that struck
Can staunch thy wounded side.

Amfortas' countenance shines with holy rapture, and he totters with emotion, *Gurnemanz* supporting him.

PARSIFAL:
Be whole, unsullied and absolved!
For I now govern in thy place.
Oh, blessed by thy sorrows,
For Pity's potent might
And Knowledge's purest power
They taught a timid Fool.
The holy Spear—
Once more behold in this.

All gaze with intense rapture on the Spear which *Parsifal* holds aloft, while he looks steadfastly at its point and continues:

Oh, mighty miracle of bliss!—
This that through me thy wound restoreth.
With holy blood behold it poureth.

Which yearns to join the fountain glowing.
Whose pure tide in the Grail is flowing!
Hid be no more that shape divine:
Uncover the Grail! Open the shrine!

The boys open the shrine and *Parsifal* takes from it the Grail and kneels, absorbed in its contemplation, silently praying. The Grail glows with light, and a halo of glory pours down over all. *Titurel,* for the moment reanimated, raises himself in benediction in his coffin. From the dome descends a white dove and hovers over *Parsifal's* head. He waves the Grail gently to and fro before the upgazing Knights. *Kundry,* looking up at *Parsifal,* sinks slowly to the ground, dead. *Amfortas* and *Gurnemanz* do homage on their knees to *Parsifal.*

ALL (*with voices from the middle and extreme heights, so soft as to be scarcely audible*):
Wond'rous work of mercy:
Salvation to the Saviour!

(*The curtain falls.*)

MISCELLANEOUS PARSIFAL RECORDS

Processional of the Knights of the Holy Grail
By Arthur Pryor's Band   31735   12-inch, $1.00

Parsifal Fantasia (including the following *motives*)
"The Eucharist"—"The Flower Maidens"—"The Grail"
By Arthur Pryor's Band   31242   12-inch, $1.00

"Then suddenly the heavenly splendor fell
And flamed and glowed within the sacred cup."

SCENE FROM PATIENCE

PATIENCE, OR BUNTHORNE'S BRIDE

COMIC OPERA IN TWO ACTS

Libretto by W. S. Gilbert; music by Sir Arthur Sullivan. First produced at the Opéra Comique, London, April 23, 1881. First American production at the Standard Theatre, New York, September 23, 1881. It was revived at the Herald Square Theatre, July 10, 1896; at the American Theatre, in March, 1900, by the Castle Square Opera Company; and recently at the Lyric Theatre in New York.

Characters

With the Original American Cast

REGINALD BUNTHORNE, a fleshly poet........................Wm. White
ARCHIBALD GROSVENOR, an idyllic poet...................James B. Key
LADY ANGELA, ⎫
LADY SAPHIR, ⎪ ⎧ Alice Burville
LADY SAPHIR, ⎬ Rapturous maidens .... ⎨ Rose Chapelle
LADY ELLA, ⎪ ⎪ Jennie Stone
LADY JANE, ⎭ ⎩ Augusta Roche
PATIENCE, a dairy maid...............................Carrie Burton
COLONEL CALVERLY, ⎫ ⎧ Wm. T. Carleton
MAJOR MURGATROYD, ⎬ Officers of the Dragoon Guards ⎨ Arthur Wilkinson
LIEUTENANT DUNSTABLE, ⎭ ⎩ A. Cadwallader

Guards, Esthetic Maidens.

Time and Place: Castle Bunthorne; the last century.

Patience is Gilbert's famous satire on the esthetic craze of the early 80's, set to some of the most delightful of all Sullivan's music. This absurd school of estheticism, represented by Oscar Wilde and his imitators, did not long survive the witty ridicule which Gilbert aimed at it, and soon disappeared. The opera was one of the most successful of the Gilbert and Sullivan series, and well deserved its great vogue.

In the first act twenty love-sick maidens are sighing, and singing plaintively of their love for *Bunthorne*. *Patience*, a buxom milkmaid, appears and ridicules them, telling them the

Dragoon Guards are expected shortly; but though the maidens doted upon the *Dragoons* a year ago they scorn them now. The *Guards* arrive, also *Bunthorne,* followed by the fair twenty, who pay no attention whatever to the *Dragoons* but follow the poet, listening to his latest creation, whereupon the *Dragoons* leave in a rage. When alone *Bunthorne* confesses to himself that he is a sham. *Patience* appears, and the poet immediately makes love to her, but she is frightened and runs to *Lady Angela,* who tells her it is her duty to love some one. *Patience* thereupon declares she will not allow the day to go by without falling in love.

Grosvenor, the idyllic poet, and an old playmate of *Patience,* enters, and she promptly falls in love with him, but he remains indifferent. *Bunthorne,* twined with garlands, enters, led by the maidens, and, unable to decide between them, puts himself up as the prize in a lottery, but *Patience* interrupts the drawing and announces that she will be his wife. She is promptly accepted, whereupon the fickle maidens transfer their affections to *Grosvenor.* This does not please *Bunthorne,* and he predicts that his rival shall "meet a horrible doom."

In the opening of the second act we see a rather ancient damsel, *Jane,* mourning because of the maidens' desertion of *Bunthorne,* who is content with a milkmaid. *Grosvenor* enters, followed by *Patience,* who tells him that she still loves him but that her duty is toward *Bunthorne.* *Bunthorne* enters with *Jane* clinging to him in spite of all his efforts to get rid of her. Finally, in a jealous rage at *Patience's* regard for the fleshly poet, he exits with *Jane.* Now the maidens are beginning to make advances to the *Dragoons,* and the poets begin to quarrel with each other. *Bunthorne* asks *Grosvenor* how to make himself less attractive, and is told to dress himself in a more commonplace manner. When the maidens find he has given up esthetics they declare they will do likewise. *Patience* deserts *Bunthorne* for *Grosvenor,* the maidens find suitors among the *Dragoons,* and *Jane* goes over to the *Duke,* leaving *Bunthorne* lonely and disconsolate.

The Opera Company has given us a splendid medley of the airs of this delightful opera, no less than six of the most interesting numbers, in abbreviated form, being included.

Gems from Patience

Chorus, "Twenty Love-Sick Maidens We"—Male Chorus, "The Soldiers of Our Queen"—Solo, "Love is a Plaintive Song"—Solo and Chorus, "A Most Intense Young Man"—Sextet, "I Hear the Soft Note"—Finale, "Oh, List, While We Our Love Confess."

By the Victor Light Opera Company   31816   12-inch, $1.00

PHOTO WHITE

BUNTHORNE AND THE LOVE-SICK MAIDENS

PESCATORI DI PERLE

PEARL FISHERS

(Pes-kah-toh'-ree dee Pear'-leh)

OPERA IN THREE ACTS

Text by Carré and Cormon. Music by Georges Bizet. First production at the Théâtre Lyrique, Paris, September 29, 1863. First London production, entitled "Leila," at Covent Garden, April 22, 1887; and as *Pescatori di Perle*, May 18, 1889. Recently revived at Covent Garden for Tetrazzini. First New York production January 11, 1896, at the Metropolitan Opera House, with Calvé.

Characters

LEILA, a priestess...Soprano
NADIR, a pearl fisher ....Tenor
ZURGA, a chief ....Baritone
NOURABAD, high priest..Bass

Priests, Priestesses, Pearl Fishers, Women, etc.

Scene and Period : Ceylon ; barbaric period.

Les Pêcheurs de Perles, one of Bizet's earlier operas and the first one to achieve success, is a work dealing with an Oriental subject, and contains much music of charm and originality, showing traces of that dramatic force which reached its full development in *Carmen.* The character of the music, less passionate and highly colored than *Carmen,* is yet equally original and of even more striking beauty.

The story tells of the love of two Cingalese pearl fishers for the priestess *Leila,* and of the generosity of the unsuccessful rival, who helps the lovers to escape at the cost of his own life.

THE PRELUDE

The prelude is a most beautiful number, and considered one of the finest of Bizet's instrumental writings.

Preludio (Prelude)

By La Scala Orchestra   *62100 10-inch, $0.75

ACT I

SCENE—*The Coast of Ceylon*

The rise of the curtain discloses a company of Cingalese pearl fishers, who, after choosing one of their number, *Zurga,* to be their chief, are enjoying themselves with games and dances. *Nadir* appears and *Zurga* recognizes him as a friend of his youth. They greet each other and speak of the days when they were rivals for the hand of a beautiful woman. *Nadir,* beginning the duet, recalls the moment when the friends first beheld the lovely *Leila.*

DUFRANNE AS ZURGA

Del tempio al limitar (Au fond du têmple saint)

(English)

(In the Depths of the Temple)

By Enrico Caruso, Tenor, and Mario Ancona, Baritone

	(In Italian)	89007	12-inch, $4.00
By Giorgini and Federici	*(In Italian)*	88319	12-inch, 3.00
By Clement, Tenor, and Journet, Bass	*(In French)*	76022	12-inch, 2.00
By John McCormack and G. Mario Sammarco	*(Italian)*	87082	10-inch, 2.00
By Giuseppe Acerbi and Renzo Minolfi	*(In Italian)*	*68063	12-inch, 1.25

Double-Faced Record—See page 398.

In an impressive strain he describes the scene within the Temple of Brahma:

NADIR:
In the depths of the temple
A lovely form we beheld,
That form I still can see!

ZURGA:
'Twas a vision of beauty!

NADIR:
The kneeling worshipers, astonished,
Now murmur, "The goddess comes!"

ZURGA:
She descends from the altar
And, moving near to us

Lifts her veil, revealing
A face that haunts me still
With its beauty ethereal!

NADIR:
But now her veil she drops
And, passing through the wandering crowd
She disappears.
Now a strange emotion overpowers me,
I fear to touch thy hand.

ZURGA:
A fatal love both our souls possess.

They speak of their sudden realization of the fact that they had both fallen in love at sight with the priestess, and fearing their friendship was in danger, they swore never to see her again. The comrades, now pronouncing themselves entirely cured of their infatuation, pledge anew their friendship and swear to be brothers to the end.

A fisherman now enters and announces the arrival of the mysterious veiled lady who comes once a year to pray for the success of the fisheries, and whom the Ceylonese have adopted as their guardian saint. She enters and begins her prayer. *Nadir* recognizes her voice and realizes that it is the priestess *Leila*. The pearl fishers sing a chorus of appeal to *Brahma* for a blessing, in which *Leila* joins.

Brahma gran Dio (Divine Brahma!)
By Linda Brambilla, Soprano, and La Scala Chorus

(*In Italian*) *68062 12-inch, $1.25

This is a most impressive record, the lovely voice of Mme. Brambilla showing to great advantage above the choral background.

Leila goes into the temple and the people disperse. *Nadir*, left alone, is agitated by his discovery, realizing that he still loves the maiden. He recalls the memories of his first sight of her in a lovely song.

Mi par d'udire ancora (I Hear as in a Dream)
**By Florencio Constantino,
Tenor**   (*In Italian*)
74067 12-inch, $1.50

Leila reappears and the act closes with her prayer to Brahma for the good fortune of the fishermen. Just as the curtain falls she recognizes *Nadir*, and contrives to let him know that she loves him.

ACT II
SCENE—*A Ruined Temple*

As the curtain rises *Leila* and *Nourabad*, the high priest, are seen, they having sought shelter in the ruins of an ancient temple. The high priest, in a fine air, reminds *Leila* of her oath to renounce love and marriage and devote herself to the welfare of the people. She says that she will keep her promise and tells him of a vow she made when a child to a fugitive who implored her to save his life. Although his pursuers held a dagger to her breast she refused to betray him and he escaped to safety.

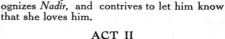

PHOTO REUTLINGER

MME. MENDÈS AS LEILA

Double-Faced Record—See page 398.

Siccome un di caduto (A Fugitive, One Day)
By Giuseppina Piccoletti, Soprano (*Piano acc.*) (*Italian*) *68307 12-inch, $1.25

The high priest sternly recites the punishment which will overtake her should she prove false to her vow. "Shame and death be thy portion!" cries the stern priest. Left alone, the miserable woman broods over her unhappy plight. Bound by an oath which she now regrets, and conscious of her love for *Nadir,* which may mean death for them both, she sinks down in an agony of despair. *Nadir* enters and asks her to fly with him, defying Brahma and the priests. She at first repulses him, but love is finally triumphant and the lovers rapturously embrace, while a fearful storm rages, unheeded, without the ruins.

This scene is expressed by a splendid duet, two records of which are given here for a choice.

Non hai compreso un cor fedel (You Have Not Understood)
By Giuseppina Huguet, Soprano, and Fernando de Lucia,
Tenor   (*In Italian*) 92054 12-inch, $3.00
By Giuseppina Piccoletti, Soprano, and Ivo Zaccari,
Tenor   (*In Italian*) *68062 12-inch, 1.25

The lovers are surprised by *Nourabad,* and *Nadir* flees, closely pursued by the priests. He is captured and brought back, while *Zurga* is summoned to pronounce sentence on the guilty lovers. His friendship for *Nadir* moves him to mercy, and he spares their lives and bids them fly the country. As they go, however, the high priest tears the veil from *Leila,* and when *Zurga* realizes that it is the woman *Nadir* has sworn never to see, he is enraged and sentences them both to death.

ACT III
SCENE I—*The Camp of Zurga*

Zurga is discovered alone, brooding over the impending death of his friend and the woman he loves. His mood of despair is interrupted by *Leila,* who appears at the entrance to his tent and asks him to dismiss the guards and speak with her alone. She asks mercy for *Nadir* in a dramatic aria.

Temer non so per me (I Fear Not)
By Emilia Corsi, Soprano
(*In Italian*) *63394 10-inch, $0.75

She proudly refuses to plead for her own life, but begs that he spare the friend whom she loves. *Zurga* refuses and summons the guards to conduct her to execution.

SCENE II—*The Place of Execution*
The scene shows the wild spot where the funeral pile has been erected. *Leila* and *Nadir* are led in, and are about to mount the pyre when a red glow is seen in the sky, and *Zurga* enters crying that the camp is on fire, and bids the people fly to save their children and effects:

ZURGA:
    The fire of Heaven has fallen,
    The flame invades and destroys!
    Run ye, there is yet time
    To save your children from death.
       (*The Indians run out in disorder.*)

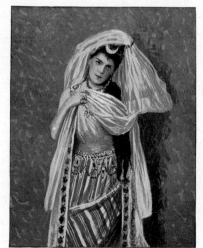

DUPONT

MME. DE NUOVINA AS LEILA

Double-Faced Record—See page 398.

All run out except *Leila, Nadir* and *Zurga,* and the high priest, who, suspecting a plot, hides to hear what *Zurga* will say. The latter confesses that he kindled the fire in order to save the lovers. Unfastening their chains, he bids them escape, while *Nourabad* runs to warn the Indians, and *Leila* and *Nadir,* beginning the great trio, voice their gratitude.

Terzetto finale—Fascino etereo

By Linda Brambilla, Soprano; Giuseppe Acerbi, Tenor; Francesco
Cigada, Baritone   (*In Italian*) *68063 12-inch, $1.25

BIZET

The lovers praise the generosity and greatness of *Zurga,* who for the sake of friendship has committed an act which may cost him his own life. He bids them fly at once, and they go as the voices of the enraged Indians are heard returning for vengeance. *Nourabad* denounces *Zurga* for the escape of the victims and for the destruction of the camp.

> NOURABAD (*pointing to Zurga*):
> 'Tis the traitor who aided their escape,
> His hand started the devouring fire.
> What say the people?
> THE PEOPLE:
> Death to the traitor!

Zurga is forced to mount the funeral pyre, and as the flames mount about him he cries:

> ZURGA:
> Farewell, my friend!
> Farewell, my Leila!
> On me may their rage at last be satisfied,
> For thee I give my life!

As *Zurga* dies a fiery glow reveals that the forest is ablaze, and all prostrate themselves, fearing the displeasure of Brahma. The curtain falls as the flames envelop the stage.

DOUBLE-FACED AND MISCELLANEOUS PEARL FISHERS SELECTIONS

Del tempio al limitar (In the Depths of the Temple)
    By Giuseppe Acerbi and Renzo Minolfi (*In Italian*)
Terzetto finale—Fascino etereo
    By Linda Brambilla, Soprano; Giuseppe Acerbi,
        Tenor; Francesco Cigada, Baritone (*In Italian*)
	68063	12-inch, $1.25

Non hai compreso un cor fedel (You Have Not Under-
    stood)   By Giuseppina Piccoletti, Soprano, and
                 Ivo Zaccari, Tenor (*In Italian*)
Brahma gran Dio (Divine Brahma!) By Lina Brambilla,
        Soprano, and La Scala Chorus (*In Italian*)
	68062	12-inch, 1.25

Siccome un di (A Fugitive, One Day)
        By Giuseppina Piccoletti, Soprano (*In Italian*)
    Hermes—S'io t'amo   By Melis and Taccani (*In Italian*)
	68307	12-inch, 1.25

Preludio (Prelude)   By La Scala Orchestra
    Ebrea—Rachele allor che Iddio
        By Gino Martinez-Patti, Tenor (*In Italian*)
	62100	10-inch, .75

Temer non so per me (I Fear Not)
        By Emilia Corsi, Soprano (*In Italian*)
    Jana—Si dannato morro   By Taccani (*In Italian*)
	63394	10-inch, .75

*Double-Faced Record—See above list.

(French)
LA PERLE DU BRESIL
(Pairl du Breh-zeel')

(English)
THE PEARL OF BRAZIL

LYRICAL DRAMA IN THREE ACTS

Words by Gabriel and Sylvain Saint Étienne; music by Félicien David.   First produced at the Théâtre Lyrique, Paris, November 22, 1851.   Revived at the same theatre March, 1858, with Mme. Miolan-Carvalho; and at the Opéra Comique, 1883, with Emma Nevada as *Zora.*

Characters
(With the Original Cast)

ZORA...Mlle. Duez
LORENZ, her lover...Soyer
ADMIRAL SALVADOR.......................................Bouché

Sailors, Brazilians, etc.

The Pearl of Brazil was David's first dramatic work, and is the story of *Zora,* a young girl whom *Admiral Salvador* found in Brazil, and whom he intends to educate and eventually to marry.   They set sail from South America, but *Salvador* soon discovers that *Zora* has a lover, *Lorenz,* a young lieutenant, who has disguised himself as a sailor and is on board in order to be near his sweetheart.   A storm arises and the ship is compelled to seek shelter in a harbor of Brazil.   The natives attack the ship and almost overpower the sailors, when *Zora* chants a hymn to the Great Spirit, and the Brazilians, recognizing their compatriot, make peace.   In gratitude for the young girl's act, which saved the lives of all on board, the *Admiral* gives his consent to her marriage with *Lorenz.*

The *Charmant oiseau* is the most beautiful number in David's opera, and is offered here by three celebrated sopranos.   This is one of the most famous of colorature airs, and one of which coloorature sopranos are very fond, as it exhibits to perfection the skill of the singers, showing to rare advantage the flexibility of the voice, especially in the duet with the flute, with its difficult runs.

Charmant oiseau (Thou Charming Bird) *With flute obbligato*

By Luisa Tetrazzini, Soprano	*(In French)*	88318	12-inch,	$3.00
By Emma Calvé, Soprano	*(In French)*	88087	12-inch,	3.00
By Marie Michailowa, Soprano	*(In Russian)*	61130	10-inch,	1.00

Delightful bird of plumage glowing
With sapphire and with ruby dyes,
'Mid the shade his rare beauty showing
Before our wonderstricken eyes;
When on the branch with blossoms trembling,
He poises swinging gay and bright,
His checkered pinions' gleams resembling
A many-colored prism of light.
How sweet is he, the Mysoli!

When day appears his joyful singing
Awakes the dawn's enchanted rest;
When evening falls his notes are ringing,
While fiery day fades from the west.
A-down the grove the silence doubles,
As now his plaintive dulcet lay,
That breathes of love's ecstatic troubles,
From out the tulip tree dies away.
How sweet is he, the Mysoli!

From Ditson edition—Copy't Oliver Ditson Co.

WHITE, N.Y.   SCENE FROM PINAFORE

H. M. S. PINAFORE
OR
THE LASS THAT LOVED A SAILOR
COMIC OPERA IN TWO ACTS

Text by W. S. Gilbert; music by Sir Arthur Sullivan. First produced at the Opéra Comique, London, May 28, 1878. First American production occurred in New York in 1878, but was unauthorized, and was followed by the first important production at the Boston Museum, in November, 1879. Successfully revived in New York in 1911 and again in 1912.

Characters

RT. HON. SIR JOSEPH PORTER, K. C. B., First Lord of the Admiralty . . Baritone
CAPTAIN CORCORAN, Commanding "H. M. S. Pinafore" . . . . Baritone
RALPH RACKSTRAW, able seaman . . . . Tenor
DICK DEADEYE, able seaman . . . . Bass
BILLY BOBSTAY, boatswain's mate . . . . Bass
BOB BECKET, carpenter's man . . . .
TOM TUCKER, midshipmite . . . .
SERGEANT OF MARINES . . . .
JOSEPHINE, the Captain's daughter . . . . Soprano
HEBE, Sir Joseph's first cousin . . . . Mezzo-Soprano
LITTLE BUTTERCUP, a bumboat woman . . . . Contralto

First Lord's Sisters, his Cousins and Aunts, Sailors, Marines.

Time and Place: The scene is laid on the quarterdeck of "H. M. S. Pinafore"; time, the present.

The production of this little opera marked the temporary retirement of *opera bouffe* in America; its dainty music and the sparkling wit of its dialogue being grateful to a public which was becoming satiated by the productions of German and French composers. Gilbert's satire was keen, but the wit was always delicate without a single touch of the coarseness which frequently marred the *opera bouffe* translations.

Pinafore has an inexhaustible fund of this Gilbertian wit, and never fails to please an audience. When first presented in London, however, so little interest was shown that the management decided to withdraw the piece, but its ultimate success was quite phenomenal.

DE WOLF HOPPER AS DEADEYE

ACT I

The story of Pinafore is so generally known that it is like repeating an old, familiar tale to outline the plot. The rise of the curtain shows the deck of His Majesty's Ship *Pinafore*. The *Captain* is in a mournful mood because his daughter does not favor his plan to marry her to *Sir Joseph Porter*, and confesses that she loves an ordinary sailor. Soon after she meets *Ralph*, who tells her of his love, but is haughtily repulsed. In desperation he threatens to shoot himself, and *Josephine* then confesses that she cares for him. Their plans to get ashore and be married are overheard by *Dick Deadeye*, a sort of comedy villain, who threatens to prevent their elopement.

ACT II

In the second act *Little Buttercup* naively reveals her affection for the *Captain*, but he tells her he can only be her friend. This angers her, and she prophesies a change in his fortunes. *Sir Joseph* enters and complains to the *Captain* that *Josephine* has disappointed him. *Corcoran* tells him his daughter is probably dazzled by the exalted station of her suitor, and suggests that he plead his cause on the ground that love levels all rank. *Sir Joseph* accepts his suggestion, but only succeeds in strengthening his rival's cause, as *Josephine* becomes even more firmly resolved to wed *Ralph*. *Dick Deadeye* now reveals the planned elopement, and the *Captain* stops the couple as they are stealing away, demanding where they are going. *Ralph* confesses his love, which so angers *Corcoran* that he swears. *Sir Joseph* overhears him and orders him to his cabin, but on being told the cause of the excitement, orders *Ralph* also to be confined. *Little Buttercup*, interrupting, reveals her secret and tells how the *Captain* and *Ralph* were accidentally exchanged when both were infants. Whereupon *Sir Joseph*, revealing the crowning absurdity of Gilbert's plot, sends for the seaman, gives him command of the ship and nobly consents to his marriage with *Josephine*. The *Captain*, who now automatically becomes a common sailor, marries the happy *Little Buttercup*.

The Victor's fine singing organization has given two splendid medleys from this melodious nautical opera, and these attractive records contain, in condensed form, thirteen of the most popular numbers from the production. Mr. Mac Farlane, whose Captain Corcoran was one of the features of the recent revival, sings the melodious serenade from Act II most effectively.

{Gems from "H. M. S. Pinafore," Part I   Victor Light Opera Co.} 35386   12-in., $1.25
{Gems from "H. M. S. Pinafore," Part II Victor Light Opera Co.}

Gems from " H. M. S. Pinafore," Part I

Opening Chorus, "We Sail the Ocean Blue"—Air, Ralph and Chorus, "A Maiden Fair to See"—Song, "Captain, I Am the Monarch of the Sea"—"I'm Called Little Buttercup"—"Captain of the Pinafore"—Finale, Act I, "His Foot Should Stamp."
By the Victor Light Opera Company   31782   12-in.,   1.00

Gems from " H. M. S. Pinafore," Part II

"The Gallant Captain of the Pinafore"—"When I Was a Lad"—"The Merry Maiden and the Tar"—"Carefully on Tip-toe Stealing"—"Baby Farming"—"Farewell, My Own"—"For He is an Englishman."
By the Victor Light Opera Company   31835   12-in.,   1.00

PIQUE DAME
(*Peek Dahm*)
OR
THE QUEEN OF SPADES
OPERA IN THREE ACTS

Text by Modeste Tschaikowsky, the composer's brother, taken from Puschkin's novel of the same name. Music by Peter Iltitsch Tschaikowsky. First production at St. Petersburg, December, 1890; in Vienna, under Gustav Mahler, 1902; at La Scala, Milan, 1905-6; Berlin, 1907, with Destinn, Goetz, Griswold and Grüning. First American production at the Metropolitan Opera House, New York, March 5, 1910, in German, under Mahler, with Destinn, Slezak and Alma Gluck. This was the first production in America of any of Tschaikowsky's operas, an odd fact in view of the great popularity of the composer's concert music, although "Eugen Onegin" had previously been given in concert form.

Characters

THE COUNTESS (Pique Dame)..........................Mezzo-Soprano
LISA, her granddaughter.......................................Soprano
PAULINE...Contralto
HERMANN, a young officer ....Tenor
TOMSKY, his friend...Tenor
PRINCE JELETSKI, betrothed to Lisa..........................Baritone

---

Time and Place : St. Petersburg ; eighteenth century.

The story of "Pique Dame" is a melodramatic one, full of superstition and tragedy. The *Queen of Spades* (*Pique Dame*), is an elderly countess who possesses the secret of the three fateful cards which bring luck at the gaming table. Her granddaughter, *Lisa*, betrothed to *Prince Jeletski*, is deeply in love with *Hermann*, a young officer, who is seeking a way to make a fortune that he may marry the young girl. *Lisa* gives her lover the key to her grandmother's rooms, where he goes at night in an effort to extract from the old Countess the secret of the three cards. The Countess will not listen to his pleadings and orders him from her apartment, but when he draws his pistol in an effort to compel her to reveal to him the names of the cards, she falls dead from terror.

The next scene shows *Hermann* in his barrack room. As the funeral of the *Countess* passes the barracks, a gust of wind blows the window open, and the ghost of the *Queen of Spades* appears, declaring, "Your fate is sealed! These are the cards—ace, seven, three." She vanishes, and the officer goes out to meet *Lisa,* who is waiting for him on the banks of the Neva. The young girl fails in her effort to prevent *Hermann* from carrying out his determination to go to the gambling house, and as he leaves her she throws herself into the Neva. In the last act *Hermann* is gambling madly with the Prince. He has won on the first two cards, but when the third card, the queen of spades, turns up, he loses all. The spectre of the *Countess* appears, and *Hermann*, imagining she has come for his life, stabs himself.

Tschaikowsky has written much beautiful music for this work, but the gem of the opera is probably the delightful duet for *Lisa* and *Pauline* in the second scene of Act I. It reminds one somewhat of the lovely Tales of Hoffman "Barcarolle," and the record, because of the beauty of the music and its charming rendition by Mmes. Destinn and Duchêne, is likely to become one of the most popular of Victor duet records.

Es dämmert (It is Evening) Act I, Scene II
By Emmy Destinn and Maria Duchêne *(In German)* 88520 12-inch, $3.00
By Marie Michailowa and Mme. Tugarinoff *(Russian)* 61136 10-inch, 1.00

LISA AND PAULINE:

It is evening. The beaming rays
Are sinking; the gloom of night is near,
In the sky a last pale streak
Seems like a distant shore.
From the hills a cooling breeze is wafted,

Laden with the sweet scent of roses,
And gently wave the boughs of the linden.
In peace rests the valley, with mist overhung,
No sound disturbs the wond'rous peace!
The birds scarcely stir in their soft nests,
And only the crickets' song is heard.

WHITE   SCENE FROM PIRATES OF PENZANCE

THE PIRATES OF PENZANCE

OR

THE SLAVE OF DUTY

COMIC OPERA IN TWO ACTS

Text by Sir W. S. Gilbert; music by Sir Arthur Sullivan. The first performance on any stage took place in New York, December 31, 1879, under the immediate supervision of Mr. Sullivan and Mr. Gilbert, the cast including J. H. Ryley, Signor Brocolini, Hugh Talbot, Frederic Clifton, Blanche Roosevelt and Alice Barnett. Produced at the Opéra Comique, London, April 3, 1880. Revived June 3, 1912, by Messrs. Shubert and W. A. Brady, with Eugene Cowles, Arthur Aldridge, George MacFarlane, De Wolf Hopper, Blanche Duffield and Josephine Jacoby.

Characters

MAJOR-GENERAL STANLEY.....................................Baritone
PIRATE KING..Bass
SAMUEL, his lieutenant...Tenor
FREDERIC, the pirate apprentice ....Tenor
SERGEANT OF POLICE...Bass
MABEL⎫
EDITH ⎪
KATE ⎬ General Stanley's daughters............................Sopranos
ISABEL⎭
RUTH, a pirate maid-of-all-work..............................Contralto

Pirates, Police, etc.

Time and Place: The scene is laid on the coast of Cornwall; time, the present.

WHITE

DE WOLF HOPPER AS THE SERGEANT OF POLICE

The Pirates, as it is familiarly called, is one of the very few operas of note to have its first production in America. This unusual step was taken to protect the rights of the composers and publishers in American representations of the work.

The first act was written and the entire opera scored in this country, and the work was not published until after Messrs. Gilbert and Sullivan had returned to England. This prevented the work from being virtually stolen, as was Pinafore, the authors having been cheated out of their royalties on that opera because of the many unauthorized versions.

Gilbert's delightfully whimsical story tells of *Frederic*, apprenticed when a child to the *Pirates of Penzance*, who were very gentle with orphans for the reason that they themselves were orphans!

ACT I

The *Pirates* are celebrating the twenty-first birthday of *Frederic*, who, tiring of a piratical career, is about to leave them to seek another occupation. *Ruth*, a "female pirate," begs him to marry her, and as she is the only woman he has known, he consents, after she has assured him that she is "a fine figure of a woman."

Shortly afterward *Frederic* meets *General Stanley's* daughters, who have come to this rocky shore on an outing, and falls in love with *Mabel*, the youngest. The *Pirates* capture *Mabel* and her sisters and propose to marry them (the ladies meanwhile doing very little struggling with the handsome pirates!), but when their father arrives and tells them he also is an orphan, they relent and release the girls.

ACT II

In the second act the *General*, with a highly exaggerated sense of honor, is lamenting because he has deceived the *Pirates* by telling them he is an orphan. *Frederic*, who is about to lead an expedition (composed of brave policemen!) to exterminate the *Pirates*, comes to bid *Mabel* good-bye.

The *Pirate King* and *Ruth* arrive and show *Frederic* the apprentice papers which bound him to the *Pirates* until his twenty-first birthday, and call attention to their discovery of the fact that as he was born in leap year on the 29th of February, he has had but five birthdays, and consequently is still a member of the band until sixteen more leap years have rolled around! A strong sense of duty influences him to consent to return to the *Pirates* and serve out his unexpired term of something like sixty years! He also considers it his duty, now that he is a pirate once more, to tell them of the *General's* falsehood, and they swear vengeance.

In an attempt to carry off the *General* the pirates are captured by the policemen, but ask for their liberty on the ground that they are really English noblemen "gone wrong." On promising to give up their piratical career they are pardoned, and this releases *Frederic*, who is now free to marry *Mabel*.

The Victor offers here, in condensed form, six of the best numbers from the opera.

Gems from Pirates of Penzance

Chorus of Pirates—Solo, "Poor Wand'ring One"—Solo, "Is There Not One Maiden Breast"—Solo, and Chorus, "A Policeman's Lot"—Chorus, "With Catlike Tread "—Finale.

By the Victor Light Opera Company   31808   12-inch, $1.00

(Italian)	(French)	(English)
IL PROFETA	**LE PROPHÈTE**	**THE PROPHET**
(*Eel Pro-feh'-tah*)	(*Leh Pro-feh't'*)	

OPERA IN FIVE ACTS

Text by Scribe. Music by Giacomo Meyerbeer. First presented in Paris, April 16, 1849. First London production July 24, 1849. First American production at the New Orleans Opera, April 2, 1850. First New York production November 25, 1854. Revived at the Manhattan Opera in 1909 with d'Alvarez, Lucas and Walter-Villa.

Characters

JOHN OF LEYDEN, (*Ly'-den*) the Prophet, chosen leader of the Anabaptists . . Tenor
BERTHA, his sweetheart . . . . Soprano
FIDÈS, (*Fee'-dayz*) mother of John of Leyden . . . . Mezzo-Soprano
COUNT OBERTHAL, ruler of the domain about Dordrecht . . . . Bass
ZACHARIAH, 　 　 　 　 　 　 　 　 　 　 　 　 　 　 　 　 　 　 　 {Bass
JONAS, 　 　 three Anabaptist preachers . . . . {Tenor
MATHISEN, 　 　 　 　 　 　 　 　 　 　 　 　 　 　 　 　 　 　 　 {Bass

Nobles, Citizens, Peasants, Soldiers, Prisoners.

Scene and Period: Holland and Germany; in 1543, at the time of the Anabaptist uprising.

COPY'T DUPONT

ALVAREZ AS THE PROPHET

Meyerbeer's great work is certainly entitled to be called a grand opera, for it is grand to the utmost in theme, character and scenes; and with its brilliant and impressive music, at the time of its production sixty years ago was a model of its kind, as opera-goers demanded melodramatic action, tuneful music and opportunity for ballet; and all these requirements are fully met with in Le Prophète.

The plot is based on the Anabaptist fanaticism of the sixteenth century, which agitated a large part of Germany and Holland, and the leader of which was one Bockelson, commonly called John of Leyden.

ACT I

SCENE—*A Suburb of Dordrecht, Holland*

The story furnished by the librettists describes *John* as the son of the widow *Fidès*, an innkeeper of Leyden. At the opening of the opera he is about to wed *Bertha*, an orphan. She, being a vassal of the *Count Oberthal*, is obliged to ask his permission before marrying, and goes with *Fidès, John's* mother, to beg the Count's consent. The Count, struck with the young girl's beauty, covets her for himself, refuses his consent and orders *Fidès* and *Bertha* into the castle.

ACT II

SCENE—*The Inn of John in the Suburbs of Leyden*

Three Anabaptists enter and being astonished at the resemblance of *John* to the portrait of the guardian saint, *David*, at Munster, they try to induce him to become their leader. He refuses, but tells them of a strange dream he has had.

JOHN: Under the vast dome of a splendid temple
I stood—the people at my feet were prostrate—
The royal coronal adorn'd my brow!

The Anabaptists declare that Heaven has spoken in the dream, and promise that he shall yet be a ruler; but *John's* thoughts turn to his beloved *Bertha,* and in the beautiful *Pastorale* he tells them that another and sweeter life calls to him.

SCHUMANN HEINK AS FIDES

JOHN:
Oh, there's a sweeter empire, far,
Which long has been my guiding star,
Oh, thou my joy, my greatest gain,
If in thy faithful heart I reign!
For me, the proudest kingdom,

Less than this thatch'd roof
My hopes would bless,
Sweet home of calm felicity,
Where I would gladly live and die,
Where Bertha will forever prove
Alike my bosom's queen and love!

Bertha, who has escaped from the castle, now runs in, asking *John* to save her. She is concealed by him as the Count's soldiers enter and threaten to kill *Fidès* unless *John* delivers up the maiden. To save his mother's life he is forced to yield, and sees his bride carried off to become the Count's mistress.

Fidès, in her gratitude, sings this most dramatic and intense of Meyerbeer's airs, which has attained a world-wide popularity.

Ah, mon fils! (Ach, mein Sohn!) (Ah, My Son!)

By Ernestine Schumann-Heink, Contralto   (*In French*)   88187   12-inch, $3.00
By Margarete Ober, Contralto   (*In German*)   74397   12-inch, 1.50

FIDÈS:
Ah, my son! Blessed be thou!
Thy loving mother to thee was dearer
Than was Bertha, who claim'd thy heart!
Ah, my son! For thou, alas,
Thou dost give for thy mother more than life,
For thou giv'st all the joy of thy soul!
Ah, my son! now to heav'n my pray'r ascends
for thee;
My son, blessed be forever more!

From Operatic Anthology, by permission of
G. Schirmer. (Copy't 1899.)

OBER AS FIDÈS

John, left by his mother to bitter thoughts, hears the Anabaptists in the distance, and resolves to join them as a means of vengeance on the Count. The three conspirators enter and are addressed by *John :*

JOHN:
When in my dreams I thought of supreme
power,
Did you not say follow us,
And you shall reign?
FIRST ANABAPTIST:
And again we offer thee
A crown to be a king.
JOHN:
What must I do for this?
Speak, and I will quickly follow you.
FIRST ANABAPTIST:
Groaning beneath the yoke of tyranny,
The sons of our land await with ardor
The coming of the one to set them free.
In the name of the Prophet, who is promised
them
By Heaven, and who is found in thee.

JOHN:
Can I then destroy my enemies?
ANABAPTISTS:
At thy word they shall be
Destroyed in an instant.
JOHN:
And shall I be able to destroy Oberthal?
ANABAPTISTS:
In an instant.

The compact is soon made and they depart, leaving some blood-stained garments to lead *Fidès* to believe *John* has been slain by the Count's assassins.

ACT III

SCENE—*Camp of Anabaptists in the Westphalia Forest*

The city of Munster is about to be besieged by the rebels, and before proceeding to the charge, *John,* now the *Prophet,* and in command of the rebels, makes them kneel and pray for victory. They chant the *Miserere,* and *John* sings this noble *Inno* or hymn.

Re del cielo e dei beati (Triumphal Hymn, "King of Heaven")

By Francesco Tamagno, Tenor (*Piano acc.*)   (*In Italian*)   95005   10-inch, $5.00
By Antonio Paoli, Tenor, and La Scala Chorus   (*Italian*)   91080   10-inch, 2.00
By Luigi Colazza, Tenor (*Double-faced—See p. 409*)   (*Italian*)   16578   10-inch, .75

JOHN:
King of Heaven and of the angels,
I will praise Thee,
Like David, Thy servant.
A voice I heard—"Array thyself,
And safely on I will guide thee."
Praise to the Omnipotent!
Yes, victory is on our side,

Let's unfurl the sacred flag,
He whom we serve is Lord
Of Heaven and earth.
Let's sing and march away.
The eye of Heaven will watch over us,
A supreme power will guide us!
With songs of joy—with shouts of glory—
On—on to Munster!

ACT IV
SCENE I—*A Public Square in Munster*

The insurgents have captured the city. The *Prophet* is received with mixed feelings, some denouncing him as an impostor. *Fidès*, reduced to beggary, meets *Bertha*, who has escaped from the Count and come to Munster to seek *John*. *Fidès* tells her *John* is dead, and *Bertha*, thinking the *Prophet* is responsible, swears to have vengeance.

SCENE II—*The Munster Cathedral*

This magnificent cathedral scene is one of Meyerbeer's most brilliant compositions. It forms a striking contrast to the rest of the opera, so gloomy with religious and political fanaticism, and as a piece of glittering pageantry with gorgeous decoration, pealing bells, solemn chants, and the stately Coronation March, has seldom been equaled.

Coronation March
By Arthur Pryor's Band
31503 12-inch, $1.00

The great symphonic march which occurs in this scene is by far the most striking instrumental number in Meyerbeer's opera. It is brilliant and powerful, with superb instrumentation, and always produces a marked effect on the listener.

As *John* passes into the church, *Fidès* sees him, and in a transport of joy greets him as her son. He declares she is mad, knowing it is death to both if he acknowledges her. She finally realizes the situation, confesses that she is mistaken, and is led away to prison.

JOHN DENYING HIS MOTHER—ACT IV

FIDÈS:
Yes, the light comes to my darkened eyes.
People, I have deceived you—
It is not my son!—I have no longer a son.

PEOPLE:
Hail to the great Prophet.

FIDÈS (*aside*):
O grief, to save his life
I must deny him.
Have pity on him, Lord!

PEOPLE:
A miracle! A miracle!
The power of his voice has restored her reason!

ACT V
SCENE I—*The Crypt of the Palace at Munster*

The first scene takes place in the prison vaults beneath the palace, where *Fidès*, feeling certain that *John* will contrive to see her, patiently awaits his coming. She at first denounces him as an ungrateful son, then prays that Heaven may lead him to repent.

Prison Scene
By Ernestine Schumann-Heink, Contralto (*In French*) 88095 12-inch, $3.00

FIDÈS (*alone*):
O! my cruel destiny! Whither have you led me?
What, the walls of a prison! they arrest my footsteps.
I am no longer free.
Bertha swore my son's death, he denied his mother;
On his head let the wrath of Heaven fall!

(*Her wrath subsides.*)
Though thou hast abandoned me,
But my heart is disarmed,
Thy mother pardons thee.
Yes, I am still a mother.
I have given my cares that thou may'st be happy,
Now I would give my life,
And my soul exalted, will wait for thee in heaven!

An officer enters and announces the arrival of the Prophet.

JOHN THE PROPHET

Fidès then begins the second part of her great scene.

FIDÈS (*joyfully*):
He comes!
I shall see him, delightful hope!
Oh, truth! daughter of heaven,
May thy flame, like lightning,
Strike the soul of an ungrateful son.
Celestial flame restore to him calmness!
Restore, bless'd Heaven, his guardian angel!
Immortal grace, Oh! conq'ring come;
With thy pure love his heart reprove;
Tho' he be guilty, save him now
From that dark abyss which threatens to
engulf him;
Let thy light pierce this ingrate son,
Conscience riv'n, his soul soften,
Like brass in furnace fierce,
That he may ascend and reign in Heav'n!

When *John* enters, *Fidès* denounces the bloody deeds of the Anabaptists and calls on her son to repent and renounce his false robes.

FIDÈS:
But thou, whom the world detests,
Yes, thou, braving Heaven's behests;
Thou, whose fell hand is reeking with blood;
Go thou, my son no longer now!
Far from my heart, far from my eyes—
Blood-stain'd, go!

John confesses his sins and pleads for forgiveness, finally kneeling and receiving her blessing, just as a faithful officer enters and informs *John* that the Anabaptists are plotting to deliver him to the Emperor's forces, which are marching on the city.

Bertha enters through a secret passage, revealed to her by her grandfather, who was once keeper of the palace. She has resolved to blow up the palace and the false Prophet, and is horrified to learn that *John* is the *Prophet*. She denounces him for his crimes, and declaring she has no longer reason to live, stabs herself.

John, in despair, resolves to die with his enemies, and sending away his mother, plans to have the palace set on fire, and goes to the banquet hall.

SCENE II—*The Great Hall of the Palace*

After the Emperor's forces have entered, crying, "Death to the Prophet," *John* orders the gates closed. An explosion occurs and the palace falls, carrying down to death *John* and all his enemies.

OBERTHAL:
You are my prisoner!
JOHN:
Nay, ye are all *my* captives!

(*An explosion takes place, the walls fall and flames spread on every side.*)

JOHN (*to Gione and Oberthal*):
Thou, traitor! and thou, tyrant! shalt perish
with me;
Justice has sealed our doom;
I am the instrument,
We, all guilty, are all punished!

(*A woman with dishevelled hair rushes through the ruins into John's arms. He recognizes his mother.*)
JOHN:
My mother!
FIDÈS:
Yes, receive my pardon; I will die with thee!
FIDÈS AND JOHN:
Welcome, sacred flame!
To yon celestial sphere may our souls take
flight!
Adieu!
(*As the flames mount about them the curtain falls.*)

DOUBLE-FACED PROPHET RECORDS

{Fantasie from Prophet	By Pryor's Band}	35125	12-inch, $1.25
{ Barber of Seville Selection	By Pryor's Band}		
{Re del cielo (King of Heaven)	By Luigi Colazza, Tenor}	16578	10-inch, .75
{ William Tell Ballet Music—Part III	By Pryor's Band}		

I PURITANI   THE PURITANS
(*Ee Poo-ree-tah'-nee*)

OPERA IN THREE ACTS

Book by Count Pepoli; music by Vincenzo Bellini. First presented at the *Théâtre Italien,* Paris, January 25, 1835, with a famous cast—Grisi, Rubini, Tamburini and Lablache. First London producton, King's Theatre, May 21, 1835, under the title of *Puritani ed i Cavalieri.* First New York production, February 3, 1844. Produced at the New Orleans Opera, March 3, 1845. Revived in 1906 at the Manhattan Opera, with Pinkert, Bonci and Arimondi, and in 1908 with Tetrazzini, Severina, Constantino and de Segurola.

Characters

LORD GAUTIER WALTON, Puritan ....Bass
SIR GEORGE, Puritan ....Bass
LORD ARTHUR TALBOT, Cavalier................................. Bass
SIR RICHARD FORTH, Puritan ....Baritone
SIR BRUNO ROBERTSON, Puritan ....Tenor
HENRIETTA OF FRANCE, widow of Charles I.....................Soprano
ELVIRA, daughter of Lord Walton.... .... Soprano

Chorus of Puritans, Soldiers of Cromwell, Heralds and Men-at-Arms of Lord Arthur, Countrymen and Women, Damsels, Pages and Servants.

Scene and Period: England in the neighborhood of Plymouth, in the period preceding the impeachment and execution of Charles I by Parliament.

Previous to Mr. Hammerstein's revival in 1906, *Puritani* had not been given in America since the production of 1883, with Gerster as *Elvira.* This is not strange, as the opera on the whole is somewhat dreary, only the few numbers the Victor has collected being really worth hearing.

The plot is rather a foolish one: the libretto being one of the poorest ever written for Bellini, but the music is delightful and fascinating. However, we will briefly sketch the story, as it will add to the enjoyment of the lovely melodies of Bellini which the Victor has recorded. The only available translation is a very unsatisfactory one, but nevertheless a few quotations are given.

The action occurs in England in the time of the Stuarts, during the civil war between the Royalists and the Puritans. *Lord Walton,* the Puritan Governor-General, has a daughter *Elvira,* whom he wishes to marry to *Richard Forth,* a Puritan colonel, but the young girl loves an enemy, *Lord Arthur.*

ACT I

SCENE I—*Exterior of a Fortress near Plymouth*

At the beginning of Act I, *Forth,* learning that *Elvira* loves *Arthur,* and that her father refuses to force her into an unwelcome marriage, is disconsolate and gives vent to his feeling in a famous air, best known as *Ah per sempre* ("To me forever lost"). The Battistini record, however, takes its title from the second part of the number.

Bel sogno beato di pace (Blissful Dream)
By Mattia Battistini, Baritone   (*In Italian*)   88352   12-inch, $3.00

FORTH:
Ah! to me forever lost,
Flow'r of love, and hope the dearest!
Life, to me thou now appearest,
Gloomy and with tempests cross'd.
Oh, happy and lovely dream of peace and joy!
Oh, change thou my fate, or change my heart!
Ah, what a keen torment, in the day of grief,
Becomes the memory of a vanish'd love!

Bruno, a Puritan officer, enters and offers *Sir Richard* command of the army. He refuses, saying that his disappointment in love has unfitted him for so high an honor.

SCENE II—*Elvira's Room in the Castle*

The next scene shows *Elvira's* apartment, where her uncle, *Sir George,* in a fine air, tells her that he has persuaded her father to consent to her marriage with *Arthur.*

Sorgea la notte (The Night Was Growing Dark)

By Perelló de Segurola, Bass (*Double-Faced*) (*In Italian*) 55007 12-inch, $1.50

COPY'T MISHKIN

ANCONA AS SIR RICHARD

The night was growing dark,
And Heav'n and earth were silent,—
Favorable the sad hour,
Thy pray'rs gave courage to my soul,
And to thy sire I went.

Thus I began,—"My brother"—
"Your angel-like Elvira
Is for the valiant Arthur pining—
Should she another wed,
Oh, wretched one! she dies!"

Said thy father
"She is to Richard promised!"
"Thy unhappy child," repeated I, "will die."
"Oh! say not so," he cried,
"I must yield, let Elvira live,—
Ah! may she be happy—
Let her live in love!"

Elvira is overjoyed, and expresses her gratitude. Trumpets are now heard, and *Elvira's* surprise is complete when *Lord Arthur* arrives, attended by squires and pages, and bearing nuptial presents, prominent among which is a splendid white veil, soon to play an important part in the events to come.

Shortly after his arrival *Arthur* discovers that the widow of *Charles I* is in the castle under sentence of death, and his sense of duty toward the late Queen impels him to contrive her escape by concealing her in *Elvira's* veil, the guards thinking it is the bride. The escape is soon discovered and *Elvira,* supposing that her lover has deserted her on the eve of her bridal day, becomes insane. All denounce *Arthur* and swear to be revenged.

ACT II

SCENE—*The Puritan Camp*

Act II shows the camp of the Puritan forces. *Sir George* announces that Parliament has condemned *Arthur* to death for aiding in the escape of the late Queen. *Elvira* enters, demented, and sings her famous air, much like the Mad Scene in Lucia.

Qui la voce (In Sweetest Accents)

By Marcella Sembrich, Soprano (*In Italian*) 88105 12-inch, $3.00
By Frieda Hempel, Soprano (*In Italian*) 87179 10-inch, 2.00

She recalls her first meeting with *Arthur* and repeats the vows he swore.

ELVIRA:
It was here in accents sweetest,
He would call me—he calls no more!
Here affection swore he to cherish,
That dream so happy, alas! is o'er!
We no more shall be united,
I'm in sorrow doomed to sigh,
Oh, to hope once more restore me,
Or in pity I die! (*Her mood changes.*)
'Tis no dream, my Arthur, oh, my love!
Ah, thou art smiling—thy tears thou driest,
Fond Hymen guiding, I quickly follow!
(*Dancing toward Richard*)
Come to the altar!

Elvira's father and Sir George try in vain to calm her, but she knows them not and continues to call for her lover in another florid air:

Vien diletto (Come, Dearest, Come)

By Frieda Hempel, Soprano   88470 12-inch, $3.00

Elvira's uncle, hoping that the sight of her lover will restore her reason, begs *Sir Richard* to pardon the young man. *Richard* consents, provided he returns helpless and in peril, but if he comes bearing arms against his country he shall die. *Sir George* agrees to this, and in the splendid *Sound the Trumpet* they pledge themselves to fight together for their country.

Suoni la tromba (Sound the Trumpet)

By Pasquale Amato, Baritone, and Marcel Journet, Bass

(*In Italian*)   89056   12-inch, $4.00

This favorite duet, often sung in concert, has been aptly described as a "stentorian" number. It is undeniedly a most vigorous piece of declamation, and if the loyalty of *Sir George* and *Sir Richard* can be judged by the vigor of the usual rendition, they are loyal indeed!

> SIR RICHARD AND SIR GEORGE:
> Sound, sound the trumpet loudly!
> Bravely we'll meet the foemen,
> 'Tis sweet affronting death!
> Bold love of country aiding.
> The victor's wreath unfading,
> Will unto us be proudly
> Restor'd by Love and Faith!
> Morn! rising on a nation,
> Whose only trust is freedom—
> Will bring us eternal fame!
> Earth's tyrants who dissemble,
> At the war-message tremble,
> Midst the world's execration
> They sink in endless shame!

The Puritans then renew their pledge as to *Arthur,* saying:

> SIR GEORGE:
> All is now concluded,
> If Arthur is defenceless—
> RICHARD:
> He'll find support and succor.
> SIR GEORGE:
> If he in arms returns—
> RICHARD:
> He comes to shame and vengeance!

ACT III

SCENE—*A Garden near Elvira's House*

The rise of the curtain discloses *Arthur,* who is fleeing from the enemy, and has come to the castle in the hope of seeing *Elvira* once more before he leaves England forever. She comes from the castle and at the sight of *Arthur* her reason suddenly returns. The lovers are reconciled after *Arthur* explains that it was in the service of his Queen that he had fled from the castle. They sing a lovely duet:

Vieni fra queste braccia (Come to My Arms)

By Maria Galvany, Soprano, and Francesco Marconi, Tenor

(*In Italian*)   89046   12-inch, $4.00

Forgetting their present danger, they think only of their love and that they are in each other's arms again.

> ARTHUR:
> Come, come to my arms,
> Thou my life's sole delight!
> And thus press'd to my heart,
> We'll no more disunite!
> Thrill'd with anxious love and fear,
> On thee I call—for thee I sigh;—
> Come, and say the love is dear
> That soareth to boundless height!

The sound of a drum is heard, and *Elvira* again becomes delirious, which so alarms *Arthur* that he thinks not of escape and is captured by the Puritan forces. The sentence of death is read to him and he is being led to his execution, when a messenger arrives from *Cromwell* saying that the *Stuarts* were defeated and a pardon had been granted to all captives. *Elvira's* reason returns, and the lovers are finally united.

(*Curtain*)

(Italian)   (English)
REGINA DI SABA   QUEEN OF SHEBA
(Ray-jee'-nah dee Sah'-bah)

OPERA IN FOUR ACTS

Text by Mosenthal, founded upon the Biblical mention of the visit of the Queen of Sheba to Solomon. Music by Goldmark. First production 1875, in Vienna. In New York December 2, 1885, with Lehmann and Fischer. English version given by the National Opera Company in 1888. Given November 29, 1889, at the Metropolitan with Lehmann, which was the last New York production until the revival in 1905, with Walker, Rappold, Knote and Van Rooy

Characters

KING SOLOMON . . . . Baritone
HIGH PRIEST . . . . Bass
SULAMITH, his daughter . . . . Soprano
ASSAD, Solomon's favorite . . . . Tenor
QUEEN OF SHEBA . . . . Mezzo-Soprano
ASTAROTH, her slave (a Moor) . . . . Soprano

Priests, Singers, Harpists, Bodyguards, Women of the Harem, People.

Scene: Jerusalem and vicinity.

Mosenthal's story tells of the struggle of *Assad,* a courtier of *Solomon,* against fleshly temptation, and of his final victory which involves the sacrifice of the happiness of his betrothed, *Sulamith.*

For this text Goldmark furnished some of the most beautiful and sensuous music in the entire range of opera, and it is an interesting detail that after he had finished his opera and had submitted it to the Imperial Opera, Vienna, it was not accepted on the ground that it was too "exotic"! Later, through the influence of Princess Hohenlohe, it was presented and was a great success.

ACT I

The wisdom and fame of *Solomon* having reached even distant Arabia, the *Queen of Sheba* decides to visit him, and a favorite courtier, *Assad,* has been sent to meet her and escort her to the city. When *Assad* arrives with the Queen, his betrothed, *Sulamith,* is astonished to find him pale and embarrassed, and trying to avoid her. *Assad* afterward confesses to *Solomon* that he had met a beautiful woman at Lebanon and had fallen in love with her. When the *Queen of Sheba* arrives and removes her veil, *Assad* is astounded to recognize in her the mysterious woman who had captured his senses. Involuntarily he rushes toward her, but she coldly repulses him and passes on with the King.

ACT II

In Act II the Queen discovers that she loves *Assad,* and seeing him in the garden, bids her maid attract his attention with a weird Oriental song. *Assad* starts when he hears the mysterious air, as it seems to bring back memories of the night at Lebanon. He sings his beautiful air, *Magic Tones.*

Magiche note (Magic Tones!)
By Enrico Caruso, Tenor   (*In Italian*)   87041   10-inch, $2.00

A lovely melody, sung at first in *mezzo-voce,* develops gradually until the intense and passionate climax is reached.

The Queen and *Assad* soon meet and confess their love for each other, but are interrupted by the arrival of the night guard.

ACT III

In the next scene the Court assembles for the wedding of *Sulamith* and *Assad,* but *Assad* insults his bride and declares his love for the Queen. He is banished from Jerusalem and finally dies in the arms of *Sulamith,* who is crossing the desert on her way to a convent.

SOLOMON RECEIVING THE QUEEN—ACT I

(French)   (English)
LA REINE DE SABA   QUEEN OF SHEBA
(Lah Ran deh' Sah-bah')

OPERA IN FOUR ACTS

Text by Jules Barbier and Michel Carré. Music by Gounod. First performed at the Operá, Paris, February 28, 1862. An English version called *Irene*, by Farnie, was given in London at the Concert Palace, August 12, 1865. First American production at the New Orleans Opera, January 12, 1889.

Characters in the Opera

KING SOLOMON . . . . Bass
BALKIS, Queen of Sheba . . . . Soprano
ADONIRAM, a sculptor . . . . Tenor
BENONI, his assistant . . . . Tenor
PHANOR,   ⎫   ⎧Baritone
AMRU,   ⎬ workmen . . . . ⎨ Tenor
METHUSALL, ⎭   ⎩ Bass
SARAHIL, maid to the Queen . . . . Contralto
SADOC . . . . Soprano

The action takes place in Jerusalem.

La Reine de Saba is one of the four operas which Gounod composed between his *Faust* (1859) and *Romeo* (1867). None of these works have been very successful, but they contain much beautiful music.

ACT I
SCENE I—*The Studio of Adoniram*

The curtain rises, disclosing *Adoniram* at work on an important group of statuary. *Benoni* enters and informs him that the *King* desires his presence, as the *Queen of Sheba* is expected to arrive at any moment. As *Adoniram* prepares to leave the studio his workmen demand higher wages, but he refuses them and they go out muttering threats.

SCENE II—*Square in front of the Temple*

The *Queen* arrives and is welcomed by *King Solomon* and the people. *Adoniram* is presented to her as one of Palestine's great artists, and she seems greatly impressed by the handsome young sculptor.

ACT II

SCENE—*Moulding Room of Adoniram's Studio*

King Solomon and the *Queen* have promised to come and see the final casting of *Adoniram's* masterpiece, and he is preparing for this event when *Benoni* enters hurriedly and reveals the plot of the workmen, who have stopped the channels so that the melted bronze cannot flow. His information comes too late, and the molten mass overflows, apparently ruining the statue.

ACT III

SCENE—*Open place on the Feiche*

Adoniram meets the *Queen of Sheba* here, and she confesses her love for him. He is at first inclined to repel her advances, but soon falls under the spell of her fascinations and clasps her in his arms. He tells her that he also is of her race, the Nimrod. The faithful *Benoni* hurriedly enters in search of *Adoniram*, telling him that in spite of the plot of the workmen the moulding of his statue has been successful.

ACT IV

SCENE—*The Great Hall of Solomon's Palace*

Adoniram is received by *Solomon* and the Court and proclaimed the greatest sculptor of the time. All leave the hall except *Solomon* and the *Queen*, who gives a sign to her maid, *Sarahil*, to bring a draught which she presents to *Solomon*. He soon falls asleep at the feet of the *Queen*, who takes the ring from his finger and leaves the Palace.

ACT V

SCENE—*The Valley of Hebron*

Adoniram and the *Queen* have planned to fly together, and are already approaching the meeting place, when three of *Adoniram's* discontented workmen, bent on revenge, set upon and stab him. The *Queen* hurries to his side and falls on his body, cursing his murderers and *Solomon*.

The Victor has selected two numbers from Gounod's opera which are worthy of preservation—the first being the splendid recitative and air, *Lend Me Your Aid,* sung by Evan Williams; the second the *Sous les pieds* by Journet and Witherspoon.

Queen of Sheba Records

Lend Me Your Aid

By Evan Williams, Tenor
(*In English*) 64096 10-inch, $1.00

Lend me your aid, Oh race divine,
Fathers of old to whom I've pray'd,
Spirits of pow'r, be your help mine,
Lend me your aid, Fathers of old
To whom I've pray'd, O lend your aid!
Oh grant that my wild dream be not vain,
That future time shall owe to me
A work their bards will sing in their strain,
Tho' Chaos still an iron sea!

From the caldron the molten wave
Soon will flow into its mould of sand,
And ye, O sons of Tubal Cain,
Fire, Oh fire my soul, and guide my hand!
Lend me your aid, Oh race divine,
Fathers of old to whom I've pray'd,
Spirits of pow'r, be your help mine,
Lend me your aid!

Sous les pieds d'une femme (She Alone Charmeth My Sadness)

By Marcel Journet, Bass	(*In French*) 74269	12-inch, $1.50
By Herbert Witherspoon, Bass	(*In French*) 74277	12-inch, 1.50

(Italian)   (English)

IL RÈ PASTORE   THE SHEPHERD KING

DRAMATIC CANTATA IN TWO ACTS

MELBA

Text by Metastasio; music by Mozart. First production Salzburg, April 23, 1775. The libretto is the one used for Bono's opera of the same name, given in Vienna in 1751.

Characters

ALESSANDRO, King of Macedonia.

AMINTA, shepherd descendant of the Kings of Sidon and lover of Elisa.

ELISA, shepherdess.

TAMIRI, fugitive princess, daughter of the tyrant Stratone.

AGENOR, noble of Sidon, lover of Tamiri and friend of Alessandro.

The opera of "Il Rè Pastore" was written by Mozart in honor of the Archduke Maximilian, the composer having been ordered to produce the work for the entertainment of the Archduke during his visit to Salzburg in 1775.

The story tells of the capture of Sidon, the execution of the usurper *Stratone* by *Alessandro*, King of Macedonia, who places on the throne the rightful king, *Aminta*, who has been living as a shepherd. *Alessandro* plans that the new king shall marry *Tamiri*, daughter of *Stratone*, but *Aminta* is already in love with *Elisa*, a shepherdess, and rather than give her up he refuses the crown. The King, pleased with *Aminta's* fidelity, gives his consent to the marriage with *Elisa* and establishes the couple upon the throne. He also gives *Tamiri* to her lover *Agenor*, and promises them the next kingdom he shall conquer.

The aria *L'amero saro costante*, which Melba has sung for the Victor, was a great favorite with Jenny Lind. The beauty of Mozart's music is enhanced by the pure vocalization of Melba, and no fitter vehicle of expression for the composer's beautiful melody than the perfect vocal organ of this great singer could be imagined. The double cadenza at the conclusion for voice and instrument is an intricate and striking one, and provides a strong and effective climax to Melba's performance of this fine air. Kubelik's playing of the violin part is a masterly performance.

L'amero saro costante (My Love is Ever True)

By Nellie Melba, Soprano, and Jan Kubelik, Violinist (*In Italian*)

89074 12-inch, $4.00

WHITE   KUBELIK

416

KARNAC CHALLENGES MYLIO—ACT I

(French)   (English)

LE ROI D'YS   THE KING OF YS

OPERA IN THREE ACTS AND FIVE TABLEAUX

Text by Édouard Blau; music by Édouard Lalo. First production at the Opéra Comique, Paris, May 7, 1888, with Talazac, Bouvet, Cobalet, Fournets, Deschamps and Simonnet. The opera made a great success and was awarded the *Acádemie* prize of three thousand francs. It had its hundredth representation in Paris, May 7, 1889, and is still in the repertory of the Opéra Comique. First, and probably only American production, at the New Orleans Opera, January 23, 1890, with Furst, Balleroy, Geoffroy, Rossi, Leavinson and Beretta.

Characters

THE KING.. ....

MARGARET, ⎱ his daughters.......................................
ROZENN, ⎰

MYLIO, a Knight..

PRINCE OF KARNAC, at war with the King............................

People, Soldiers, Gentlemen of the Court, Ladies, Horsemen, Retainers

Time and Place: Armorica (Ancient Brittany); Middle Ages.

After a life of constant struggle and much hard work, Lalo, at the age of sixty-five, succeeded in having his Le Roi d'Ys produced in Paris, where it met with much success; but it was only in recent years that this composer's true position in music has been recognized. A bust was recently erected at Lille, his birthplace, and at the foot of the pedestal are represented *Rozenn, Margaret* and *Mylio,* the three chief characters in Le Roi d'Ys, which is regarded in France as the composer's best work.

Blau's libretto is based on an old legend about the flooding of the ancient Armorican city of Is, or, as Blau called it, "Ys." The King of Ys is at war with his neighbor, the *Prince of Karnac.* His daughters, *Margaret* and *Rozenn,* both loved a Knight, *Mylio,* but he is supposed to have died in battle. The King has bargained with *Karnac,* proposing that he shall wed *Margaret,* and thus end the exhausting war. The Princess does not relish the thought of this alliance, and when *Mylio* proves to be still alive she decides to wed him even at the cost of her father's kingdom. *Karnac* is enraged at the insult and challenges *Mylio* to a duel. The King agrees to give his other daughter, *Rozenn,* to the victor. *Mylio* wins and *Margaret,*

THE STATUE OF SAINT CORENTIN WARNING KARNAC—ACT II

furious that her sister should possess *Mylio*, induces *Karnac* to flood the city by opening the sluice gates which keep out the sea. When the water begins rising the King and his family flee to high ground, *Karnac* taking the reluctant *Margaret* with him. As they watch the floods begin to destroy the city and drown the inhabitants, the Princess, remorseful, confesses her guilt and precipitates herself into the flood. Her sacrifice saves the city, however, as Saint Corentin rises from the sea and commands the waters to recede.

The Victor offers a splendid record of one of the principal airs from this little-known opera, by Edmond Clement, one of the greatest of French tenors.

Vainement, ma bien aimee   (In Vain, My Beloved)
By Edmond Clement, Tenor   (*In French*)   **74264   12-inch, $1.50**

THE MARRIAGE OF ROZEN AND MYLIO—ACT III

HANS MAKART

THE THEFT OF THE RHINEGOLD

(German)   (English)
DAS RHEINGOLD   THE RHINEGOLD
(*Dahss Rine'-goldt*)

MUSIC DRAMA IN FOUR SCENES

Words and music by Richard Wagner. First produced at Munich, September 22, 1869.
First American production January 4, 1889, with Fischer and Alvary. Annual performances
given at the Metropolitan in recent years with many famous artists: Soomer, Reiss, Jörn,
Goritz, Burrian, Ober, Fremstad, Ruysdael, Witherspoon, Matzenauer, Homer, etc.

Characters

WOTAN, (*Vo'-tahn*)	⎫	Baritone
DONNER, (*Dohn'-ner*)	⎪ Gods	Bass
FRÖH, (*Froh*)	⎪	Tenor
LOGI, (*Low'-jee*)	⎭	Tenor
FASOLT, (*Fah-zohlt*)	⎫ Giants	Bass
FAFNER, (*Fahf'-ner*)	⎭	Bass
ALBERICH, (*Ahl'-ber-ik'h*)	⎫ Nibelungs (Gnomes)	Baritone
MIME, (*Mee'-meh*)	⎭	Tenor
FRICKA, (*Frik'-ah*)	⎫	Soprano
FREIA, (*Fry'-ah*)	⎪ Goddesses	Soprano
ERDA, (*Air'-dah*)	⎭	Contralto
WOGLINDE, (*Vog-lin'-d'h*)	⎫	Soprano
WELLGUNDE, (*Vell-goon'-d'h*)	⎪ Nymphs of the Rhine	Soprano
FLOSSHILDE, (*Floss-hill'-d'h*)	⎭	Contralto

Rheingold is not a "society" opera. Played in complete darkness and with no inter-
missions during the two hours required for its presentation, it is a work only for real music-
lovers who understand something of the story and appreciate Wagner's wonderful music.

This first part of the *Ring* is an introduction to the *Trilogy* proper, and a full understanding of its incidents is necessary to properly appreciate the other *Ring* operas.

SCENE I—*The Bottom of the Rhine*

The stage is in semi-darkness, representing the murky depths of the Rhine, and the
light glimmering on the surface of the water above shows but faintly the three Rhine
maidens guarding the *Rheingold*.

They sing their quaint song, as they float about the treasure rock:

MOTIVE OF THE RHINE MAIDENS

FERD. LEEKE

FASOLT:
Should we not find
The Rheingold fair and red,
Freia is forfeit!
(Rheingold, Act I.)

Alberich, prince of the *Nibelungs,* a strange race of dwarfs who dwell deep in the earth, observes the beauty of the maidens and tries to make love to them. They laugh at him and evade with ease his clumsy endeavors to catch them. Suddenly, as the sun rises, the gleam of the *Rhinegold* is seen. *Alberich,* dazzled by the splendor of this glow, asks what it is, and the maidens foolishly inform him that whoever can secure this treasure and form it into a ring can become lord of all the world. One condition, however, is that the possessor cannot wield this power unless he renounces forever the joys of love.

Alberich, having failed in his amorous attempts towards the *Naiads,* now conceives an ambition for power. He cries, "Then love I renounce forever," and swimming to the rock, he tears the gold from its place and flees, while from the complete darkness which ensues comes the dwarf's mocking laughter and the wailing of the maidens who are moaning for their lost treasure.

SCENE II—*A Mountain Top, Showing the Castle of Walhalla*

During this darkness the scene changes and as the stage becomes lighter we see *Walhalla,* the abode of the gods, a wonderful castle built for *Wotan* by the giants. *Wotan* and his wife are lying asleep on a flowery bank, but soon wake and see the castle which has been built while they slept. *Wotan* is overjoyed

HUGO BRAUNE

WOTAN:
'Tis ended—the infinite work!
A heavenly mansion * * *
Stands it in sight
Grand and glorious pile!

(Act I.)

at the glorious sight, but the more practical *Fricka* reminds him of the price which he had agreed to pay the giants for this godly dwelling; this being the surrender of *Freia,* goddess of youth and beauty. *Wotan* tells her that he never intended to keep his agreement, the god *Loge* having promised to show him a way to evade payment.

Freia now hastily enters, closely pursued by the giants *Fasolt* and *Fafner,* who call upon *Wotan* to deliver the goddess to them as agreed. *Wotan* repudiates his promise, saying that it was made only in jest.

WOTAN:
How sly to take for truth
What only in sport we had settled!
This beauteous goddess, light and bright,
What use to you are her charms?

Fröh and *Donner, Fricka's* brothers, enter, also *Loge,* and a long argument ensues, *Wotan* finally realizing that he must give up *Freia* to

GORITZ AS ALBERICH AND REISS AS MIME

HANS MAKART   FREIA (GODDESS OF YOUTH)

FRICKA: "See how distressed
Sadly the fair one stands!"

the giants. *Loge,* however, tells them of the *Rhinegold,* saying that if this treasure could be stolen from *Alberich* by *Wotan,* it might be accepted by the giants in place of *Freia.* *Wotan* refuses to entertain this plan and the giants seize *Freia* and carry her off, declaring that if the *Rhinegold* is not in their hands by night the original bargain must stand, and *Freia* be lost to the gods forever.

Left alone, the gods realize the serious predicament they are in, especially as it is seen that, deprived of their youth goddess, they are suddenly aging. *Wotan* thereupon decides to secure the *Nibelungs'* gold, and goes with *Loge* in search of *Alberich.* A vapor arises from the earth, concealing the stage, and when it disappears the scene has changed.

SCENE III—*Alberich's Cave*

Alberich, since he has acquired the *Rhinegold,* has become more arrogant and cruel than ever, and compels *Mime* and the other *Nibelungs* to continually toil and slave to bring him in more gold. At the beginning of the scene he is berating *Mime* for loitering over his task of making a *Tarnhelm,* or magic cap, fashioned from the *Rhinegold,* and which gives the wearer the power to become invisible. *Wotan* and *Loge* now enter on this scene and are rudely greeted by *Alberich,* who demands their business, and holding out the *Ring* bids them tremble at his power. They at first craftily flatter him, but he is surly and says that naught but envy could have brought them here. *Wotan* is angry and is about to voice his wrath when the crafty *Loge* makes him a sign to be quiet and begins to taunt *Alberich,* doubting his power. *Alberich* is so enraged that he offers to change himself into any shape required to prove the magic of the *Tarnhelm,* and immediately becomes a huge dragon. *Loge* affects extreme terror, at which *Alberich* laughs and resumes his human shape again. The god then cunningly asks him to change to a toad, which shape he has no sooner assumed than *Loge* puts his foot on the toad and seizes the *Tarnhelm,* thus robbing *Alberich* of his power. His natural form returns and they bind him and start for the upper earth. The scene changes again to the mountain summit.

SCENE IV—*Same as Scene II*

Wotan and *Loge* enter, dragging the helpless *Alberich,* who is beside himself with rage. They demand that he give them his hoarded store of gold as the price of his freedom. He reluctantly obeys and summons the *Nibelungs,* who instantly swarm up from below carrying the hoard. He then asks to be set free, but *Wotan* demands also the *Ring.* *Alberich* is horrified, but is finally compelled to add it to the pile of gold. He then sings his bitter and ironical air, *Bin ich nun frei?*

PAINTED BY ECHTER

THE CAPTURE OF ALBERICH—SCENE III

PAINTED BY MAKART   BATTLE OF THE GIANTS—SCENE IV

He lays a frightful curse on the Ring, predicting that it will bring misery and death to each possessor until it is restored to him again, and then vanishes.

Wotan, who has paid little attention to his cursing, dons the Ring, gazing at it in admiration. The giants now return for their pay, and demand that enough gold shall be piled around *Freia* to hide her completely from sight. This is done, but when all the gold is piled up *Fafner* says there is still one small crevice visible, and insists that it be filled with the Ring. *Wotan* refuses, and the giants are about to seize *Freia* again, when *Erda*, the earth goddess, rises and delivers her appeal to *Wotan*.

Weiche, Wotan, weiche! (Waver, Wotan)

By Ernestine Schumann-Heink,
   Contralto (*Wotan's* responses by
   Mr. Witherspoon)
   (*In German*) 88092 12-inch, $3.00

By Margarete Ober, Contralto
   (*Wotan's* responses by Reinald
   Werrenrath)
   (*In German*) 74396 12-inch, 1.50

She warns him solemnly that the Ring is cursed and charges him to give it up.

ERDA (*stretching her hand*):
  Waver, Wotan, waver!
  Quit the Ring accursed!
  (*She continues her solemn warning*)
  Ruin and dismalest downfall wait thee in its
    wealth.
WOTAN:
  Who speaks such menacing words?
ERDA:
  Whatever was, was I; what is, as well;
  What ages shall work—all I show;
  The endless world's All-wise one, Erda, opens
    thine eyes.
  Three, the daughters born to me
  E'er the world was made; all I notice
  Nightly thou know'st from the Nornir.
  But hither in dire danger haste I to thy help.
  Hear me! Hear me! Hear me!
  All that exists, endeth!
  A dismal day dawns for the Æsir:
  O render wisely the ring!
  (*She begins to sink slowly into the earth.*)
WOTAN:
  A secret spell speaks in thy words:
  Wait and impart more wisdom.
ERDA (*disappearing*):
  I've warned thee now; thou wott'st enough;
  Pause and ponder truth!
  (*She completely disappears.*)

ERDA:
Waver, Wotan! (Scene IV.)

423

Wotan at last yields and throws the Ring on the heap of gold. The giants, as if to prove the curse, immediately begin to quarrel about its possession, and *Fasolt* is killed by *Fafner;* after which the murderer coolly proceeds to collect the gold and then departs.

Donner, the god of thunder, now calls up a storm and causes a magic rainbow bridge to form, making a passage to the castle.

Abendlich strahlt der Sonne Auge (The Evening Light) (Wotan's Invocation)

By Marcel Journet, Bass (*In German*) 74268 12-inch, $1.50

Wotan then sings the famous invocation to the castle of Valhalla, which gleams with great brilliance, illumined by the setting sun. The god, absorbed in contemplation of the castle, sings:

HOMER AS ERDA

WOTAN:
See how at eve the eye of sun-
light
With glorious touch gilds tur-
ret and tow'r!
In the morning glamour, man-
ful and glad,
It bided masterless, mildly
beck'ning to me.
From morning till evening
thro' mighty ills
I won no way to its wonders!
The night is nigh; from all
annoy
Shelter it shows us now.
So-hailed be the fort; sorrow
and fear it heals!

As the gods proceed across the bridge to *Walhalla* the voices of the Rhine maidens can be heard from below, still bewailing the loss of their gold.

RHINE-NYMPHS (*from below*):
Rhinegold! Rarest gold!
O might but again
In the wave thy pure magic
wake!
What is of worth dwells but
in the waters!
Base and bad those who are
throned above.

(*As the gods slowly cross the bridge to the castle, the curtain falls.*)

PANEL BY HUGO BRAUNE

THE GODS ENTER WALHALLA—SCENE IV

DOUBLE-FACED RHINEGOLD RECORD

Selection from the Opera   By Conway's Band
"Entrance of Giants," Scene II—Change of Scene III—"Donner's Song,"
Scene IV—Wotan, "To Greet the Home"—Rhine Daughters—Finale
of the opera.

Gotterdammerung Fantasia (*Wagner*)   By Arthur Pryor's Band

35315   12-inch, $1.25

MONTERONE DENOUNCES THE JESTER—ACT I

RIGOLETTO

OPERA IN THREE ACTS

Text by Piave, adapted from Victor Hugo's drama *Le Roi s'Amuse*. Music by Giuseppe Verdi. First produced in Venice, March 11, 1851. First London production at Covent Garden, May 14, 1853; at the *Italiens*, Paris, January 19, 1857. Produced at the New Orleans Opera March 19, 1860, and in New Orleans on February 6, 1861, Patti sang in the opera for the first time. First New York production November 2, 1857, and since that time the opera has seldom been absent from the American stage. A notable performance occurred November 23, 1903, at the Metropolitan Opera House, when Caruso made his American début. November 4, 1912, Ruffo made his début in the United States at the Metropolitan Opera House, Philadelphia, in *Rigoletto*.

Characters

RIGOLETTO, a hunchback, jester to the Duke......................Baritone
DUKE OF MANTUA, a titled profligate ....Tenor
GILDA, (*Jeel'-dah*) daughter of Rigoletto...........................Soprano
SPARAFUCILE, (*Spahr-ah-foo-chee-leh'*) a hired assassin ....Bass
MADDALENA, (*Mad-dah-lay'-nah*) his sister ....Contralto
COUNT MONTERONE (*Mon-ter-oh'-nay*) ....Baritone
COUNT CEPRANO...Bass
Courtiers, Pages, Servants.

Scene and Period: Mantua and vicinity; sixteenth century.

The story tells of the gay and unprincipled *Duke of Mantua*, who is assisted in his crimes by his jester, *Rigoletto*, a hunchback. The father of one of the *Duke's* victims is mocked by *Rigoletto* and launches upon him a father's awful curse, which stuns and sobers the jester, as he, too, has a daughter, *Gilda*, unknown to the court.

On his way home *Rigoletto* meets a professional assassin, *Sparafucile*, who offers, for a price, to kill any enemy he may have. *Rigoletto* says he may need him later. The *Duke*, in the guise of a young student, has already met *Gilda*, not knowing who she is, and the young girl has fallen in love with him. When *Rigoletto* has left the house the *Duke's*

RUFFO AS RIGOLETTO

SETTING OF ACT I AT THE METROPOLITAN

courtiers abduct *Gilda* and take her to the Palace. The father's rage is terrible to witness, and he goes to the Palace, but too late to save his daughter. She pleads for the *Duke's* life, but *Rigoletto* swears to kill him, and arranges with the assassin, *Sparafucile,* to accomplish the deed. The *Duke* is lured to a lonely inn by *Sparafucile's* attractive sister, *Maddalena,* and is about to be murdered when *Maddalena,* who has taken a fancy to him, begs for his life. *Sparafucile* consents provided a substitute should happen along before midnight. *Gilda,* whom *Rigoletto* had brought hither (disguised as a page) in order that she might witness the fickleness of her lover, has been listening to the conversation, and now resolves to save the *Duke's* life at the cost of her own. She enters the hut, is stabbed by *Sparafucile,* who delivers the body to *Rigoletto* according to agreement. *Rigoletto* is about to cast the body into the river when he hears the *Duke's* voice in the distance. The wretched man opens the sack, sees his daughter and falls senseless on her body.

ACT I
SCENE I—*Ballroom in the Duke's Palace*

As a fête is in progress in the ducal residence, the *Duke* confides to one of his courtiers that he is about to make a new conquest. For some months he has seen a young and beautiful girl at church, but knows nothing of her except that she is visited often by a man who is supposed to be her lover. The *Duke* then sings his first air, *Questa o quella.*

COPY'T DUPONT

CARUSO AS THE COUNT

Questa o quella ('Mid the Fair Throng)
By Enrico Caruso, Tenor
    (*In Italian*) 87018 10-inch, $2.00
By Florencio Constantino, Tenor
    (*In Italian*) 64069 10-inch, 1.00
By John McCormack, Tenor
    (*In Italian*) 64344 10-inch, 1.00

This melodious number is perhaps the best of the *Duke's* solos, though usually cast somewhat in the background by the popular *La donna e mobile.* In it the *Duke* announces himself as a man of pleasure, sets forth his code of morals, and boasts of his conquests.

HEMPEL AS GILDA

RENAUD AS RIGOLETTO

DUKE:
'Mid the fair throng that sparkle around me,
    Not one o'er my heart holds sway;
Though a sweet smile one moment may
    charm me,
    A glance from some bright eye its spell
    drives away.
All alike may attract, each in turn may please;
    Now with one I may trifle and play,
Then another may sport with and tease—
    Yet all my heart to enslave their wiles
    display.
As a dove flies, alarm'd, to seek shelter,
    Pursued by some vulture, to bear it aloft
    in flight,
Thus do I fly from constancy's fetter:
    E'en women's spells I shun—all their efforts
    I slight.
A husband that's jealous I scorn and despise,
And I laugh at and heed not a lover's sighs;
If a fair one take my heart by surprise,
I heed not scornful tongues or prying eyes.

After making another enemy in the person of the *Count Ceprano*, by his marked attention to the latter's wife, the *Duke* departs. *Marullo* enters and eagerly announces to the courtiers a rich discovery. *Rigoletto*, the *Duke's* jester, is in love! The courtiers refuse to believe this, as *Rigoletto* is known as a confirmed woman-hater. *Marullo* insists that the jester makes frequent visits to a young girl. The nobles, who all hate *Rigoletto* for his cruel tongue, are eager to turn this knowledge into a means of revenge, and agree to meet *Ceprano* the next evening for a rare adventure.

The voice of the aged *Count Monterone*, whose daughter is one of the recent victims of the *Duke*, is now heard outside demanding admittance. He throws aside the guards who seek to stop him, and entering, denounces the *Duke* for his crimes.

Ch'io le parli (I Will Speak to Him)

By Francesco Cigada, Baritone; Aristodemo Sillich, Bass; La Scala Chorus
    (In Italian) *68190 12-inch, $1.25

Rigoletto ridicules and mocks the old man, who calls him a "vile buffoon," and then, in an awful rage, utters so terrible a curse upon him,—the curse of a father,—that all are horrified.

Rigoletto is stunned and sobered by this terrible malediction, for he, too, has a daughter, unknown to the court; and love for his child and respect for her dead mother are the sole redeeming traits in his cruel nature.

Monterone is removed by the guards, and the scene changes to the street in front of *Rigoletto's* house.

SCENE II—*A Street; Rigoletto's Cottage on one side, opposite the Palace of Count Ceprano*

The jester enters, brooding with superstitious fear over the curse which had been laid upon him. He is accosted by *Sparafucile*, a professional assassin, who offers so to rid him of an enemy if he has one. *Rigoletto* looks at him thoughtfully and says that if he has need of his services he will inform him. *Sparafucile* departs and *Rigoletto* delivers his famous monologue.

HALL

SPARAFUCILE OFFERS HIS SERVICES
ACT I, SCENE II

* *Double-Faced Record—See page 440.*

Monologo—Pari siamo (We Are Equal)

By Titta Ruffo, Baritone   (*In Italian*)   92041   12-inch, $3.00

By Ernesto Badini, Baritone   (*In Italian*)   *45032   10-inch, 1.00

He looks at the retreating form of the bravo and says:

COPY'T MISHKIN

SAMMARCO AS RIGOLETTO

RIGOLETTO:
Yon assassin is my equal—
He stabs in darkness,
While I with a tongue of malice
Stab men by daylight!
(*He thinks of Monterone's curse.*)
He laid a father's curse on me. . . .
(*Continuing in a burst of rage.*)
Oh hideous fate! Cruel nature!
Thou hast doom'd me to a life of torment.
I must jest, I must laugh,
And be their laughing stock!
Yonder the Duke, my master,
Youthful and brilliant, rich and handsome,
Tells me, between sleeping and waking:
"Come, buffoon, I would laugh now!"
Oh shame, I must obey him!
Oh life accursed! How I hate ye,
Race of vile and fawning courtiers!
'Tis my only joy to taunt ye!
For if I am vile, 'tis to your vice I owe it!
(*He thinks of his home and daughter.*)
In that blest abode my nature changes!
(*Again he remembers the curse.*)
How heavy was that old man's curse!
Still I hear it; 'tis ringing in my ears!
My soul is troubled—fear I some misfortune?
Ah, no, this is folly!

The jester enters the court-yard and is affectionately greeted by *Gilda*, who comes from the house. She notes his anxious looks and begs him to confide in her. She asks him about her mother, whom she but dimly remembers. *Rigoletto* avoids her question and sings a pathetic air, in which he begs her to refrain from questions regarding their past life. The duet (given here in two parts) then follows:

Deh non parlare al misero (Recall Not the Past)

By Mme. Magrini, Soprano, and Titta Ruffo,
Baritone   (*In Italian*)   89058   12-inch, $4.00

"Figlia! Mio padre!" (My Daughter!)

By Frieda Hempel, Soprano, and Pasquale Amato,
Baritone   (*In Italian*)   89082   12-inch, $4.00

RIGOLETTO:
My daughter!
GILDA:
My dear father!
RIGOLETTO:
Only when near to thee
Does my oppressed heart know joy.
GILDA:
Oh, what affection!

FARRAR AS GILDA

RIGOLETTO:
My only life art thou!
What other earthly happiness have I?
(*Sighing.*)
GILDA:
Why do you sigh?
Open your heart to your daughter.
If any secret you have, to her confide it,
Reveal to her your rightful name.
RIGOLETTO:
What matters it to thee?

GILDA:
If you are not willing
Of our family to speak—
RIGOLETTO (*interrupting her*):
Do you ever go out?
GILDA:
I go only to church.
RIGOLETTO:
In that thou dost right.
GILDA:
If of yourself you will not speak,
At least tell me something of my mother,

* *Double-Faced Record—See page 440.*

RIGOLETTO:
"If anyone here knocks, you must not open!"

RIGOLETTO:
Recall not the past!
Speak not of one whose loss to thee
All earth can boast could ne'er restore;
Her angel form methinks I see.
Who lov'd me, though deform'd and poor.
Pity, oh! Gilda; spare me!

GILDA:
Father, dear father, calm yourself,
Or my heart will surely break.
To me your name pray tell;
The grief that saddens you impart.

RIGOLETTO:
'Twere useless myself to discover;
Suffice it that thy father I am.
Some in the world there are who fear me,
In others, perhaps, envy I excite.
But one there is who has curs'd me!

GILDA:
Country, family, possess you none?

RIGOLETTO:
Thou art my country, family and friends!
The whole universe thou art to me!

GILDA:
Ah! if happier I could make you,
What joy to my heart it would bring!

He embraces her tenderly, then, recalling the curse, solemnly enjoins her to keep within the house and never venture into the town. *Gilda* says she has only been to Mass each Sunday, but does not tell him of the student with whom she had exchanged fond glances. *Rigoletto* summons the maid, *Giovanna,* and questions her, beginning another lovely duet, full of pathos.

Veglia o donna (Safely Guard This Tender Blossom)
By Maria Galvany and Titta Ruffo (*In Italian*) 91500 10-inch, $3.00
He warns the maid to always closely guard her mistress from any danger.

RIGOLETTO:
Safely guard this tender blossom,
Which to thee I now confide;
In her guileless heart and bosom
May no thought of ill betide;

GILDA:
Ah! such fear for me revealing,
Father dear, why thus display?
One from whom there's no concealing
Guides me ever on my way.

Rigoletto bids his daughter a tender farewell and takes his departure. The *Duke*, again dressed as a student, now enters, having previously purchased the silence of *Giovanna*. *Gilda* is alarmed, not thinking her innocent flirtation in the church would lead to this, and bids him begone, but he reassures her, beginning a fine duet.

E il sol dell' anima (Love is the Sun)
By Giuseppina Huguet and Fernando de Lucia
(*In Italian*) 92056 12-inch, $3.00
By Alice Nielsen and Florencio Constantino
(*In Italian*) 74063 12-inch, 1.50

He soothes her fears, telling her he loves her with a pure devotion.

DUKE:
Love is the sun by which passion is lighted,
Happy the mortal who feels its power;
Each pleasure once priz'd without it seems blighted;
With it we heed not what fate may shower.
Feeling celestial, no joy terrestrial
Ever to me can such sweet joys impart.
Ah! may no blight ever this heart from thee sever;
Rest in my bosom, ne'er to depart!

COPY'T DUPONT

ABOTT AS GILDA

431

ACT I, SCENE II

Footsteps are now heard, and after a tender farewell he leaves, first telling her that his name is Walter Malde.

Gilda remains pensively gazing at the gate through which the pretended student has departed. In rapturous soliloquy she sings:

GILDA:
Walter Malde! That romantic name!
Already it is on my heart engraven!

Walter, I love thee.
Ev'ry fond, tender thought for thee I cherish!

Caro nome (Dearest Name)

By Luisa Tetrazzini, Soprano	(*In Italian*)	88295	12-inch, $3.00
By Marcella Sembrich, Soprano	(*In Italian*)	88017	12-inch, 3.00
By Nellie Melba, Soprano	(*In Italian*)	88078	12-inch, 3.00
By Graziella Pareto, Soprano	(*In Italian*)	76007	12-inch, 2.00
By Marie Michailowa, Soprano	(*In Russian*)	61141	10-inch, 1.00

Then the lovely air, *Caro nome*, begins.

GILDA:
Carv'd upon my inmost heart
Is that name forevermore
Ne'er again from thence to part,
Name of love that I adore,
Thou to me are ever near,
Ev'ry thought to thee will fly,
Life for thee alone is dear,
Thine shall be my parting sigh!
(*Gilda enters the house, but reappears on the balcony.*)
Oh, dearest name!
Oh name beloved!

(*She disappears, but can be heard from within.*)
Oh! name beloved!
Dear name, within this breast,
Thy mem'ry will remain!
My love for thee confess'd,
No power can restrain!
Carved upon my inmost heart
Is that name for evermore.
Ev'ry thought to thee will fly,
Thine shall be my parting sigh,
Oh Walter mine!

Night has now fallen and the courtiers, led by *Ceprano*, enter, wearing masks. *Rigoletto* returns and is much alarmed to see them in this neighborhood, but his fears are allayed when they announce that they have come to carry off *Ceprano's* wife, as he is well aware that the *Duke* has had designs on that lady for some time past. He tells them *Ceprano's* palace is on the opposite side and offers to help them. They insist that he must be disguised and contrive to give him a mask which covers his eyes and ears, and lead him in a circle back to his own balcony, giving him a ladder to hold. *Gilda* is seized, her mouth gagged with a handkerchief, and she is carried away.

Rigoletto, suddenly finding himself alone, becomes suspicious, tears off his mask and finds himself at his own balcony. Frantic with fear he rushes in, finds his daughter gone, and falls in a swoon as the curtain descends.

THE ABDUCTION OF GILDA

ACT II
SCENE—*A Hall in the Duke's Palace*

Parmi veder le lagrime (Each Tear That Falls)
By Enrico Caruso, Tenor   (*In Italian*)   88429   12-inch, $3.00

The *Duke*, after his tender parting with *Gilda*, in the previous act, had again returned to the *Jester's* house, only to find it deserted and the young girl gone. Not knowing that his courtiers had carried her off under the very nose of *Rigoletto*, he bewails the unhappy fate which has robbed him of his latest conquest. As we hear him sing his pathetic lament, we forget his real nature and almost sympathize with the unhappy lover!

The courtiers enter and tell the *Duke* that they have captured *Rigoletto's* mistress. He expresses his appreciation of the adventure, not knowing they had abducted the young girl he had just left, and asks for particulars. They sing their chorus, *Scorrendo unite*,

Scorrendo unite remota via (On Mischief Bent)
By New York Grand Opera Chorus   (*In Italian*)   64049   10-inch, $1.00

which gives the details of the huge joke they have played on *Rigoletto* by making him assist in the capture of his own mistress.

COURTIERS:
Unto a lonely abode directed,
When shades of evening were falling fast,
By dark'ning shadows we were protected
Until our game we spied at last;
With timid footsteps she scarce came nigh us,
We were preparing our prey to seize
When Rigoletto just then came by us,

With angry brow and ill at ease.
And that the joke might be all the madder,
We said Ceprano's wife should be our prey,
We then desir'd him to hold the ladder;
His eyes were bandag'd, he did obey.
We swiftly mounted to the room,
And the startled beauty bore away!

When the *Duke* learns that *Gilda* is in an adjoining room he joyfully goes to her, saying that her fears will be soothed when she discovers he is the *Walter Malde* she loves.

Then occurs one of the most dramatic scenes in the opera, and the greatest opportunity for *Rigoletto*.

Povero Rigoletto! (Poor Rigoletto!)
By Pasquale Amato, with Bada, Setti and Chorus   88340   12-inch, $3.00

The jester's voice is now heard outside, singing a careless air. He enters, affecting indifference, but trying to find some clue to *Gilda's* whereabouts. A page enters with a message for the *Duke* and the courtiers tell him their master cannot be disturbed. *Rigoletto* listens, his fears becoming confirmed, and he exclaims:

VICTOR BOOK OF THE OPERA—VERDI'S RIGOLETTO

RIGOLETTO:
Ah, she must be here then!
In yonder chamber!
COURTIERS: If a sweetheart you've lost,
Go somewhere else to seek her!
RIGOLETTO (*with terrible emphasis*):
Give me my daughter!
COURTIERS (*in astonishment*):
What, his daughter!

RIGOLETTO:
Yes, my daughter!
The maid whom you last night
From my roof carried hither.
Ah, she is there, I know it!
(*Rushes toward the door, but the courtiers bar his passage and a terrible struggle occurs.*)
She is there! stand back, I tell ye!

His rage, now terrible to witness, is expressed in the second part, *Cortigiani, vil razza.*

Cortigiani, vil razza dannata (Vile Race of Courtiers)

By Pasquale Amato, Baritone   (*In Italian*)   88341   12-inch, $3.00
By Titta Ruffo, Baritone, and La Scala Chorus   (*Italian*)   92066   12-inch,   3.00
By Emilio Sagi-Barba, Baritone   (*In Spanish*)   74161   12-inch,   1.50
By Renzo Minolfi, Baritone   *16573   10-inch,   .75

He at first denounces them as abductors and assassins, then breaking down, asks for pity.

RIGOLETTO:
Race of courtiers, vile rabble detested,
Have ye sold her, whose peace ye molested?
Where is she? do not rouse me to madness—
Though unarm'd, of my vengeance beware,
For the blood of some traitor I'll pour!
(*Again making for the door.*)
Let me enter, ye assassins, stand back!
That door I must enter!
(*He struggles again with the courtiers but is repulsed and gives up in despair.*)
Ah, I see it—all against me—have pity!

Ah, I weep before ye, Marullo, so kindless?
Others' grief never yet saw thee mindless,
Tell, oh tell where my child they have hidden,
Is't there?—say in pity—thou'rt silent! alas!
(*In tears.*)
Oh, my lords, will ye have no compassion
On a father's despairing intercession?
Give me back my belov'd only daughter,
Have pity, oh give me back my child,
In pity, oh hear me implore!

This affecting scene is ended by *Gilda*, who now enters, in tears, and embraces her father.

RIGOLETTO (*overjoyed*):
Gilda, my daughter!
My lost one—my treasure!
Angel, I've found thee!
Come tell me, 'twas but jesting?
(*To the courtiers.*)
I who was weeping rejoice now.
(*To Gilda.*)
But why art thou weeping?

GILDA (*hiding her face*):
Dishonor, oh my father!
RIGOLETTO: Horror! what say'st thou?
GILDA:
Father, oh hide me from ev'ry eye but thine!
RIGOLETTO (*imperiously, to the courtiers*):
Hence, I command, and leave us!
If the worthless duke ye serve dares approach,
I forbid him to enter!
Say that, I charge ye!

The courtiers, somewhat ashamed, obey, and *Gilda* begins her pitiful confession.

Tutte le feste al tempio (On Every Festal Morning)

By Marcella Sembrich and
G. Mario Sammarco
89042   12-inch, $4.00
By Olimpia Boronat, Soprano
(*In Italian*)   88242
12-inch,   3.00
By Laura Mellerio and
Ernesto Badini   (*In Italian*)
*45000   10-inch,   1.00
By Giuseppina Huguet,
Soprano   (*In Italian*)
*62083   10-inch,   .75

GILDA:
On ev'ry festal morning
Near to the holy altar,
I saw a youth observing me,
Beneath whose gaze mine did falter,
Though not a word he said to me,
My heart his meaning well did know!
Last night he stood before me,
Fondly he vow'd to love me,
And I gave him vow for vow.

RIGOLETTO:
"Daughter, let me comfort thee!"

* *Double-Faced Record—See page 440.*

434

RIGOLETTO (*despairingly*):
Ah! that thou be spared my infamy
I've wearied Heaven with praying,
That every good may light on thee
Far from the world's betraying,
Ah, in my hopeless misery,
My saint I have enshrined thee,
In horror and anguish here I must find thee,
Thy future all turned to woe!
(*To Gilda.*)
Daughter, come, let me comfort thee in thy sorrow—

GILDA:
Father!

RIGOLETTO:
Weep here, weep, on my heart thy tears may flow.

GILDA:
Father, in thee an angel doth comfort bestow.

Piangi fanciulla (Weep, My Child)

By Maria Galvany, Soprano, and Titta Ruffo, Baritone
(*In Italian*) 92502
12-inch, $4.00

By A. Cassani, Soprano, and F. Federici, Baritone *45032
10-inch, 1.00

GILDA'S DESPAIR—ACT II

Following the duet *Rigoletto* exclaims:

RIGOLETTO:
I think what remains yet for me to accomplish:
This fatal abode we must leave on the instant.

GILDA:
Yes, my father, let us go!

RIGOLETTO (*aside*):
Oh, how all our fate has been changed in a day!

The *Count Monterone* now passes through the hall under guard. He pauses before the *Duke's* portrait and exclaims:

MONTERONE:
Oh, then, 'twas in vain in my anger I cursed thee!
No thunder from Heaven yet hath burst down to strike thee.
With pleasure triumphant thy days yet are crowned.
(*Exit, guarded.*)

Rigoletto, gazing after *Monterone*, grimly says that vengeance will not be long delayed.

Si, vendetta (Yes, My Vengeance)

By Maria Galvany, Soprano, and Titta Ruffo, Baritone
(*In Italian*) 91501 10-inch, $3.00
By Laura Mellerio and Ernesto Badini
(*In Italian*) *45000 10-inch, 1.00

* *Double-Faced Record—See page 440.*

SPARAFUCILE'S DEN—ACT III

He in turn gazes on the *Duke's* portrait and sings fiercely:

RIGOLETTO:
But, 'twill not be long thus, the avenger is nigh.
(*Impetuously.*)
Yes, my vengeance hath doomed thee.
Heartless fiend, 'tis my sole consolation,
That ere the flames of Hell entomb thee,
Thou shalt feel a father's wrath.

GILDA:
Oh my father, a joy ferocious
In thy words doth tell of danger—

RIGOLETTO:
To vengeance!

GILDA (*timidly*):
Heav'n doth know his crime atrocious,
Oh, might I avert its wrath—

RIGOLETTO:
To vengeance!

GILDA:
(In my heart there's nought of anger.)

RIGOLETTO:
Yes, to vengeance fierce I doom thee—
Thou shalt feel a father's wrath!

GILDA:
Oh, forgive him!
Ah, might I avert the wrath of Heaven!
(*They depart.*)

ACT III

SCENE I—*A Lonely Spot on the River Mincio*

A house, half in ruins, at one side. The front of the house, open to the spectator, shows a rustic inn on the ground floor; a broken staircase leads from this to a loft, where stands a rough couch. On the side towards the street is a door, and a low wall extends backwards from the house. The Mincio is seen in the background, behind a ruined parapet; beyond, the towers of Mantua. It is night. Sparafucile is in the house, seated by a table polishing his belt, unconscious of what is spoken outside.

Rigoletto and *Gilda*, the latter in male attire, now approach the inn. *Rigoletto* pityingly asks his daughter if she still can love the *Duke*. She confesses that she does, and he exclaims:

RIGOLETTO:
Thou lov'st him?

GILDA:
Always.

RIGOLETTO:
Still to love him is mere infatuation.

GILDA:
I love him.

RIGOLETTO:
Ah, tender heart of woman!
Oh, base despoiler!
Thou, my child, shalt yet have vengeance.

GILDA:
Nay, rather pity.

RIGOLETTO:
And if I could convince thee that he is worthless, wouldst thou still then love him?

GILDA:
Perhaps. Ah, he does love me!

RIGOLETTO (*leads her towards the house to look through a fissure in the wall*):
Come here, and look within.

She does so, and is startled to see the *Duke*, who comes in disguised as a soldier. He demands some wine, and while *Sparafucile* is serving him, sings his famous *La donna e mobile*.

La donna è mobile (Woman is Fickle)

By Enrico Caruso, Tenor	(*In Italian*)	87017	10-inch,	$2.00
By Florencio Constantino, Tenor	(*In Italian*)	64072	10-inch,	1.00
By Giovanni Martinelli, Tenor	(*In Italian*)	64382	10-inch,	1.00
By Giuseppe Acerbi, Tenor	(*In Italian*)	*62083	10-inch,	.75

This familiar canzone, beginning

La don-na è mo-bi-le qual piu-ma al ven-to, mu-ta d'ac-cen-to e di pen sie-ro
Wom-an is fick - le, false al-to-geth-er, Mov'd like the fea-ther borne by the bree-zes

is perhaps the best known of all the airs of the opera. Its spontaneous melody pictures the gay, irresponsible character of the young noble who thus sings of changeable womankind.

DUKE:
Woman is fickle, false altogether,
    Moves like a feather borne on the breezes;
Woman with guiling smile will e'er deceive you,
    Often can grieve you, yet e'er she pleases,
Her heart's unfeeling, false altogether;
    Moves like a feather borne on the breeze,
Borne on the breeze, borne on the breeze!

Wretched the dupe is, who when she looks kindly,
    Trusts to her blindly. Thus life is wasted!
Yet he must surely be dull beyond measure,
    Who of love's pleasure never has tasted.
Woman is fickle, false altogether,
    Moves like a feather, borne on the breeze!

At the close of the *Duke's* song *Sparafucile* enters with the wine. He knocks twice on the ceiling and a young girl comes down. The *Duke* tries to embrace her but she laughingly escapes him. Now occurs the great Quartet, one of the most famous of concerted pieces.

CONSTANTINO AS THE DUKE—ACT III

Quartet—Bella figlia dell'amore (Fairest Daughter of the Graces)

By Bessie Abott, Soprano; Louise Homer, Contralto; Enrico Caruso, Tenor; Antonio Scotti, Baritone
    (*In Italian*) 96000 12-inch, $6.00

By Marcella Sembrich, Mme. Severina, Enrico Caruso and Antonio Scotti
    (*In Italian*) 96001 12-inch, 6.00

By Lucrezia Bori, Soprano; Josephine Jacoby, Mezzo-Soprano; John McCormack, Tenor; Reinald Werrenrath, Baritone
    89080 12-inch, 4.00

By Giuseppina Huguet, Emma Zaccaria, Carmelo Lanzirotti and Francesco Cigada
    (*In Italian*) *68067 12-inch, 1.25

By Victor Opera Quartet
    (*In Italian*) 70073 12-inch, 1.25

By Huguet, Zaccaria, Lanzirotti, and Cigada *35456 12-inch, 1.25

* *Double-Faced Record—See page 440.*

PHOTO HALL
THE QUARTET—ACT III

By Kryl's Bohemian Band
*35239 12-inch, $1.25

By Pryor's Band
*16276 10-inch, .75

By Pietro Deiro
Accordionist
*35367 12-inch, 1.25

Among the musical gems with which the score of Rigoletto abounds, none is so well known and universally admired as this fine number, sung by the *Duke, Gilda, Maddalena* and *Rigoletto*. It is undoubtedly the most brilliant and musicianly of all Verdi's concerted pieces, and the contrasting emotions—the tender addresses and coquetry on the one side, and the heart-broken sobs of *Gilda* and the cries for vengeance of her father on the other—are pictured with the hand of a genius.

No less than five vocal records of this great number, in various classes, also three instrumental renditions, are offered by the Victor.

The situation at the opening of the act is a most dramatic one. The *Duke,* gay and careless, is making love to *Maddalena,* all unconscious that the assassin hired by *Rigoletto* is waiting for his opportunity.

He sings, beginning the quartet:

DUKE:
Fairest daughter of the graces,
I thy humble slave implore thee,
With one tender word to joy restore me,
End the pangs, the pangs of unrequited love.
Of my anguish see the traces,
Thee I treasure all above.
With one tender word to joy restore me,
End the pangs, the pangs of unrequited love!

MADDALENA (*repulsing him*):
I appreciate you rightly,
All you say is but to flatter.
Ah, I laugh to think how many
Yet your tender tale may move!

Rigoletto, who desires to prove to *Gilda* that her lover is false, bids her look through the window of the inn at the scene within. The unhappy girl, convinced, exclaims:

GILDA:
Ah, to speak of love thus lightly!
Words like these to me were spoken,
He is false; my heart is broken!

RIGOLETTO:
Silence, thy tears will not avail thee,
It were baseness to regret him!
Thou must shun him and forget him.
(*With fierce joy.*)
Thy avenger I will prove
The strength to punish will not fail me
That I vow to every power that rules above!

COPY'T DUPONT
HOMER AS MADDALENA

The *Duke* now goes to his bedroom and is soon asleep. *Rigoletto* bids his daughter go to Verona with all speed and he will meet her there. She reluctantly departs and *Rigoletto* pays *Sparafucile* half his price, the remainder to be paid on the delivery of the body of the *Duke* at midnight. *Rigoletto* goes away just as *Gilda,* who has disobeyed her father, returns and tries to see what is going on inside the house. *Sparafucile* enters the house and *Maddalena,* who has taken a fancy to the *Duke,* begs her brother to spare his life, delicately suggesting that he kill *Rigoletto* and take the money from him. *Spara-*

* *Double-Faced Record—See page 440.*

fucile is indignant and protests that he has never yet failed in his duty to his employers. *Maddalena* pleads with him and he finally says if another guest should enter he will kill him instead of the *Duke*.

SPARAFUCILE:
If some one should enter ere midnight has sounded, I promise that he for thy favorite shall die!

GILDA:
Oh, what a temptation! my fate! I have found it, In silence and darkness, to save him and die!

During this dramatic scene a storm is raging, and in addition to the stage effects of thunder and lightning Verdi has the chorus humming in chromatic thirds to illustrate the moaning of the wind. This scene is given here in a most impressive record.

PHOTO BERT

GILDA FINDS HER LOVER FALSE

Tempesta—Somiglia un Apollo (He's Fair as Apollo)

By Linda Brambilla, Soprano; Maria Cappiello, Mezzo-Soprano; Aristodemo Sillich, Bass; and La Scala Chorus (*In Italian*) *68190 12-inch, $1.25

Gilda hears this terrible agreement and the broken-hearted girl resolves to sacrifice her own life to save that of her false lover. She knocks at the door, is seized and stabbed by the bandit and her body wrapped in a sack. *Rigoletto* soon returns, pays the remainder of the price agreed upon, and receives the body. *Sparafucile*, fearing that *Rigoletto* will discover the substitution, offers to throw the body into the river. The Jester says he will do it himself and bids the bravo depart.

Left alone, the Jester gazes on the body with a horrible satisfaction, saying:

RIGOLETTO:
He is there, pow'rless! Ah, I must see him! Nay, 'twere folly! 'tis he surely! I feel his spurs here. Look on me now ye courtiers! Look here and tremble, Here the buffoon is monarch!

Yes, my foot is upon him! My grief has vanish'd, 'Tis turned to joy triumphant; Thy tomb shall be the waters, This coarse sack thy shroud and grave cloth! Away, now!

He is about to drag the sack towards the river, when he hears the voice of the *Duke* leaving the inn on the opposite side.

DUKE:
Woman is fickle, false altogether, etc.

RIGOLETTO (*tearing his hair*):
That voice! Am I mad? What fiend deludes me? No, no, no! here I hold him! (*Calling to the house.*) Hola, thou thief, thou bandit! (*The Duke's voice dies in the distance.*) Then whom have I within here? I tremble—the form is human! (*With utmost horror, recognizing Gilda.*) My daughter, oh, Heav'n, my daughter! Ah, no! Not my daughter! She is in Verona! 'Tis a dream!

Then begins the wonderful final duet, a fitting end to such a noble and powerful work, and a number which is unfortunately omitted in American performances of the opera. However, the Victor customer, more fortunate than the opera-goer, may hear it at his pleasure.

* *Double-Faced Record—See page 440.*

Lassù in cielo (In Heaven Above)

By Graziella Pareto and Titta Ruffo (*In Italian*) 92506 12-inch, $4.00
By Huguet and Minolfi (*Double-Faced—See below*) (*Italian*) *68067 12-inch, 1.25

RIGOLETTO:
'Tis Gilda!
(*Kneeling.*)
Child of sorrow! my angel, look on thy father!

The assassin deceived me. Hola!
(*Knocks desperately on the door of the house.*)
No answer! despair! my daughter! my Gilda!
Oh, my daughter!

The young girl, who is not yet dead, opens her eyes and cries feebly:

GILDA:
Ah, who calls me?
RIGOLETTO:
Ah, she hears me! She lives then!
Oh, thou, my heart's only treasure,
Behold thy father despairing!
Who was't that struck thee?
GILDA:
Oh, my father, for him that I cherish,
I deceived thee, and for him I perish.
RIGOLETTO:
Heaven's avenging wrath has undone me,
Turn thine eyes, oh my angel, upon me,
Speak, oh speak to me, who hath bereft me?
GILDA:
Father, oh ask not,
Bless thy daughter and forgive her.

RIGOLETTO:
Child, in pity, oh speak not of dying;
Stay thou to bless me, oh leave me not alone.
GILDA (*feebly*):
There we wait, my father, for thee!
RIGOLETTO:
Ah, no, no, leave me not!
Live, my child.
Canst thou leave me alone, despairing?
GILDA:
Ah, no—forgive my betrayer, my father.
From yonder sky—there we wait—my father,
for— (*She dies.*)
RIGOLETTO:
Gilda! my Gilda! I've lost her!
(*He recalls the curse.*)
Ah! 'twas a father cursed me!
(*Tears his hair and falls senseless on the body.*)

(*Curtain*)

DOUBLE-FACED AND MISCELLANEOUS RIGOLETTO RECORDS

Paraphrase de Concert (Verdi-Liszt)
By Vladimir de Pachmann, Pianist 74261 12-inch, $1.50

Ch 'io le parli (I Will Speak to Him)
By Cigada, Sillich and La Scala Chorus (*In Italian*)
Tempesta—Somiglia un Apollo (He's Fair as Apollo)
By Brambilla, Cappiello, Sillich and Chorus } 68190 12-inch, 1.25

Quartet—Bella figlia dell' amore (Fairest Daughter of the
Graces) By Giuseppina Huguet, Emma Zaccaria, Carmelo
Lanzirotti and Francesco Cigada (*In Italian*)
Lassù in cielo (In Heaven Above) By Giuseppina
Huguet, Soprano, and Renzo Minolfi, Baritone (*In Italian*) } 68067 12-inch, 1.25

Quartet By Kryl's Bohemian Band
Trovatore Selection (Home to Our Mountains) Vessella's Band } 35239 12-inch, 1.25

Quartet Accordion By Pietro Deiro
Light Cavalry Overture Accordion By Pietro Deiro } 35367 12-inch, 1.25

Bella figlia dell' amore (Fairest Daughter of the Graces)
(Verdi) (*Italian*) By Huguet-Zaccaria-Lanzirotti-Cigada
Trovatore—Miserere (*Italian*) By Giacomelli, Martinez-Patti and Cho } 35456 12-inch, 1.25

Monologo—Pari siamo By Ernesto Badini (*In Italian*)
Piangi fanciulla By Cassani and Federici (*In Italian*) } 45032 10-inch, 1.00

Tutte le feste al tempio By Mellerio and Badini (*In Italian*)
Si, vendetta By Mellerio and Badini (*In Italian*) } 45000 10-inch, 1.00

Gems from Rigoletto
Chorus, "Pleasure Calls Us"—Solo and Chorus, "Carved Upon My Heart"
(*Caro Nome*)—Duet, "Love is the Sun"—Solo, "Woman is Fickle"—Quartet,
"Fairest Daughter"—Finale
By the Victor Opera Company (*In English*) 31886 12-inch, 1.00

Cortigiani, vil razza dannata (Vile Race of Courtiers)
By Renzo Minolfi, Baritone (*In Italian*)
Lakme—Fantaisie aux divins By M. Rocca, Tenor (*In French*) } 16573 10-inch, .75

Tutte le feste al tempio (On Every Festal Morning)
By Giuseppina Huguet, Soprano (*In Italian*)
La donna è mobile By Giuseppe Acerbi, Tenor (*Italian*) } 62083 10-inch, .75

Rigoletto Quartet By Arthur Pryor's Band
Peacemaker March By Arthur Pryor's Band } 16276 10-inch, .75

RINALDO

(*Ree-nahl'-doh*)

OPERA IN THREE ACTS

Text by Adam Hill; Italian text by Rossi, founded on the episode of *Rinaldo* and *Armida* in Tasso's *Gerusalemme liberata*. Music by George Frederick Handel.

Rinaldo was produced at a time when Italian music had become the fashion in London, and the composer followed the plan then in vogue, to write the dialogue in recitative form. This opera was written by Handel in the amazingly brief time of fourteen days, and first performed at Queen's Theatre, February 24, 1711. The work was put on to signalize the coming of Handel to London, and was a magnificent production for that period. Only the year before the composer had been induced to leave the Court of Hanover for that of England; and upon his arrival in London Mr. Aaron Hill, the enterprising manager of the new Haymarket Theatre, engaged him to supply an Italian opera. Hill planned *Rinaldo*, Rossi wrote the Italian libretto, and Handel hurriedly dashed off the music.

HANDEL

The opera ran for fifteen consecutive nights—an unprecedented feat for that age—and was mounted with a splendor then quite unusual. Among other innovations, the gardens of *Armida* were filled with living birds, a piece of realism hardly outdone even in these days.

Characters in the Opera

RINALDO, a knight..Soprano
ARMIDA, an enchantress.....................................Soprano
ALMIRENA, Godfrey's daughter...............................Soprano
ARGANTE, a Pagan king......................................Bass
GODFREY, a noble...Bass
EUSTAZIO...Alto

The action takes place in Palestine at the time of the Crusade.

Rinaldo is a Knight Templar who loves *Almirena,* daughter of *Godfrey.* The enchantress, *Armida,* also loves *Rinaldo,* and in a jealous rage seizes *Almirena* and conceals her in a magic garden. *Armida's* lover, a Pagan King named *Argante,* complicates matters by himself falling in love with *Almirena.* *Rinaldo* finally rescues *Almirena,* and the sorceress and her lover are captured and converted to Christianity.

Among the many arias of great beauty with which the score abounds is the *Lascia ch'io pianga,* in which *Almirena* laments her capture by the sorceress. This striking number is delivered by Schumann-Heink with great beauty of tone coloring and impressive power in the most dramatic passages. The melody is a beautiful one.

Lascia ch'io pianga ('Mid Lures! 'Mid Pleasures!)

By Ernestine Schumann-Heink, Contralto   (*In Italian*)   **88189**   **12-inch, $3.00**

ALMIRENA: Armida, thou enchantress,
With thy craft, dark and fiendish,
Hast stolen from my sad heart
The bliss of Heaven;
And here a doom eternal
Suffer I ever,
The prey of pow'rs infernal!
Alas! naught's left to me

But grief with bitter tears!
'Mid lures, 'mid pleasures,
Hopeless I languish
Vainly deploring my freedom lost!
Heaven, who canst measure
My pain and anguish,
Thee I'm imploring
By ill fate toss't!

(French)   (English)

ROBERT LE DIABLE   ROBERT THE DEVIL
(Roh-ber leh Dee-ah'-bl)

OPERA IN FIVE ACTS

Words by Scribe and Delavigne; music by Giacomo Meyerbeer. First presented at the Académie, Paris, November 22, 1831, with Adolphe Nourrit as the original *Robert;* in London, in English, at Drury Lane, 1832; in Italian at Her Majesty's Theatre, May 4, 1847 (first appearance of Jenny Lind). First American production at the Park Theatre, New York, April 7, 1834. Revived at the Astor Place Theatre, December, 1851, and November 30, 1857, with Formes in the cast; 1875 given at the New Stadt Theatre, with Ilma di Murska. First New Orleans production December 24, 1836.

Cast

ROBERT, Duke of Normandy......................................Tenor
BERTRAM, the Unknown ....Bass
ISABELLA, Princess of Sicily....................................Soprano
ALICE, foster sister of Robert..................................Soprano

Knights, Courtiers, Heralds, Pilgrims, Peasants, Chaplains, Priests, Nuns, etc.

OLD PRINT   ALICE AND BERTRAM—ACT II

Robert the Devil is one of the longest of all operas (*William Tell* being the longest), lasting four hours and forty-five minutes when given without cuts.

Although Meyerbeer had produced several operas, mostly unsuccessful, it was not until the production of Robert le Diable in 1831 that the genius of the composer became known. The opera met with an unparalleled success and really made the fortune of the Paris Opéra with its splendid scenic effects, brilliant instrumentation, vigorous recitative and its heroic and partly legendary story.

Robert, Duke of Normandy, who was called *Robert the Devil* because of his courage in battle and his successes in love, is banished by his subjects and goes to Sicily, where he continues to struggle with an Evil Spirit, which seems to tempt him to every kind of excess. *Alice,* his foster sister, suspects that his supposed friend *Bertram,* is in reality this evil influence. At the close of Act I *Robert,* led on by *Bertram,* gambles away all his possessions, and failing to attend the Tournament, loses the honor of a knight and greatly displeases the *Lady Isabella,* whom he loves.

The second act shows the entrance to the Cavern of Satan, wherein a company of Evil Spirits are collected, and where occurs the great scene for *Bertram* and the chorus of fiends.

Valse Infernal, "Ecco una nuova preda" (I Have Well Spread My Toils)

By Marcel Journet and Chorus   (*In French*)   74282   12-inch, $1.50

Bertram promises the Demons that he will complete the ruin of *Robert* and the fiends rejoice at the prospect of adding another soul to their company.

BERTRAM:
I have well spread my toils, another soul to capture!
One more gained! glorious conquest,
At which demons must rejoice!
(*A subterraneous noise is heard; darkness falls. Bertram, under the control of the evil one, feels an unholy joy.*)
King of fallen angels! ruler mine! * * *
He is here! * * * He awaits me! * * *
I hear the noise

Of their infernal joy * * * the fallen spirits seek
To drown their remorse in hellish mirth!
INFERNAL CHORUS (*from the cavern*):
Ye demons, who Heaven and its laws defy,
The sound of your revels now mounts to the sky,
Your voices lift high!
Praise the master who reigns over us,
Sing aloud in lusty chorus!
Praise the Master, yes praise!

Alice, who has come to the vicinity of the cave to meet her lover, overhears this infernal bargain and determines to save him. *Robert*, dejected over the loss of his honor and wealth, meets *Bertram*, who promises that all shall be restored to him if he will have the courage to visit the ruined abbey and secure a magic branch, which can give wealth, power and immortality.

Du rendezvous (This is Our Meeting Place)
By Edmond Clement and Marcel Journet   (*In French*)   76020   12-inch, $2.00

Le Bonheur est dans l'inconstance (What is Life Without Change?)
By Edmond Clement and Marcel Journet   (*In French*)   76021   12-inch, $2.00

The next scene shows the ruins, where *Bertram* invokes the aid of the buried nuns in completing the downfall of *Robert*. He speaks of the founding of the convent and of the false nuns who lie buried here, and calls upon them to arise.

BERTRAM:
Here are the nuns of the ancient monastery,
To Heaven's cause bequeathed by St. Rosalie,
Here lie buried the false daughters

Whose unholy devotion was offered to other gods.
Nuns, who beneath this cold stone repose,
For an hour forsake your sepulcher beds,
King of Hell, it is I who calls you.

THE RUINED ABBEY—ACT III

The spectres arise, and when *Robert* appears they dance around him and lead him to the grave of *St. Rosalie*, where he is shown the magic branch. Overcoming his fears, he grasps it, and by its power defeats the multitude of demons who arise from the infernal regions to prevent his escape.

In the next scene *Robert* uses the branch to become invisible, and goes to *Lady Isabella's* room to carry her off. In this scene occurs the famous air for *Isabella*, "Oh, Robert, My Beloved."

Robert, O tu che adoro (Oh, Robert, My Beloved!)
By Margarete Matzenauer, Mezzo-Soprano   (*Italian*)   88365   12-inch, $3.00

She appeals to his better nature in this lovely cavatina:

ISABELLA:
Oh, Robert, oh, my beloved!
I live alone, yes, alone for thee
My anguish thou see'st,
On thyself have mercy, and pity on me!
Ah, the ties that once bound thee
Now no more canst thou feel?
Once I receiv'd thy homage,

Now at thy feet I kneel!
Mercy on thyself,
Oh, have mercy and pity on me!
Robert, who alone I cherish,
Thou for whom I'd gladly perish,
My anguish thou see'st,
On thyself have mercy, and pity on me!

Moved by her entreaties, he yields to the promptings of his good angel and breaks the branch, thus destroying the spell.

In the last act *Bertram* renews his efforts to induce *Robert* to sign an eternal contract. Tired of life, he is about to yield when *Alice* appears and tells him of the last words of his mother, warning him against the *Fiend*, who is in reality *Robert's* father. The clock strikes twelve, and the baffled *Fiend* disappears, while the cathedral door opens showing the *Princess* waiting for the reformed *Robert*.

SCENE FROM ROBIN HOOD—ACT II

ROBIN HOOD
COMIC OPERA IN THREE ACTS

Libretto by Harry B. Smith; music by Reginald de Koven. First performance in Chicago, June 9, 1890, by the Bostonians, who sang the opera more than four thousand times. Recently revived at the New Amsterdam, New York, by the de Koven Opera Company.

Characters

ROBERT OF HUNTINGTON, known as Robin Hood..................Tenor
SHERIFF OF NOTTINGHAM..Bass
SIR GUY OF GISBORNE, his ward................................Tenor
LITTLE JOHN ⎫   ⎧Baritone
WILL SCARLET ⎪ Outlaws ....⎪Bass
ALLAN-A-DALE ⎬   ⎨Contralto
FRIAR TUCK ⎭   ⎩Bass
LADY MARIAN FITZWATER, afterwards Maid Marian.............Soprano
DAME DURDEN, a widow.......................................Contralto
ANNABEL, her daughter......................................Soprano

Villagers, Milkmaids, Outlaws, King's Foresters, Archers and Peddlers.

Time and Place: Nottingham, England, in the twelfth century.

At the beginning of the opera a merrymaking is in progress at the marketplace in Nottingham. The three outlaws, *Little John, Will Scarlet* and *Friar Tuck,* enter and sing of their free life in the Forest of Sherwood, and finally the handsome, dashing *Robin Hood* appears, declaring that he is the *Earl of Huntington,* and demanding that the *Sheriff* shall so proclaim him. The *Sheriff,* however, protests that the youth has been disinherited by his own father, who before the birth of *Robin Hood* was secretly married to a peasant girl, who died when her child was an infant. The child is *Sir Guy of Gisborne,* the rightful heir to the earldom and the *Sheriff's* ward, whom he is planning to marry to *Lady Marian,* ward of the Crown. However, the young girl and *Robin Hood* are already deeply in love and exchange vows of eternal faith, much to the indignation of *Sir Guy.* *Lady Marian* protests against her marriage to *Sir Guy,* hoping that on the return of the *King* from the Crusades she will be released, while *Robin Hood* plans with the help of the *King* to prove his right to the earldom.   The outlaws sympathize with the pair and invite *Robin Hood* to join them, promising him he shall be their king and rule them under the Greenwood Tree, to which proposal *Robin Hood* at length agrees.

In the last act the dashing king of the outlaws brings the message which saves *Maid Marian* from the hated marriage with *Sir Guy,* and the opera ends amid general rejoicings at the triumph of *Robin Hood* and the gentle *Marian* over the plotting *Sheriff* and his ward.

Gems from Robin Hood—Part I
"Hey, for the Merry Greenwood"—"Brown October Ale"—
"Come Dream So Bright"—"Tinkers' Chorus"—"Oh, Promise
Me"—"Come Along to the Woods"
Victor Light Opera Company 31768 12-inch, $1.00

Gems from Robin Hood—Part II
"Ho, Ho, Then for Jollity"—"Ye Birds in Azure Winging"—
"Armorer's Song"—"A Hunting We'll Go"—"Ah! I Do Love
You"—"Sweetheart, My Own Sweetheart"—"Love, Now We
Never More Will Part"
Victor Light Opera Company 31868 12-inch,   1.00

Gems from Robin Hood—Part I		
Victor Light Opera Co.	35413	12-inch, 1.25
Gems from Robin Hood—Part II		
Victor Light Opera Co.		

Oh, Promise Me		
By Harry Macdonough, Tenor	16196	10-inch, .75
Sing Me to Sleep (Greene)		
By Elsie Baker, Contralto		

Oh, Promise Me By Alan Turner	17189	10-inch, .75
Dearie By Elsie Baker, Contralto		

Oh, Promise Me *Violin-'Cello-Harp* Venetian Trio		
Silver Threads Among the Gold Violin-Flute-Harp-Bells	17816	10-inch, $0.75
Neapolitan Trio		

Favorite Airs from the Opera By Pryor's Band	16919	10-inch, .75
Prince of Pilsen Selection (Luders) By Sousa's Band		

Armorer's Song By Wilfred Glenn, Bass	17268	10-inch, .75
Till the Sands of the Desert Grow Cold By Wilfred Glenn, Bass		

Armorer's Song By Eugene Cowles, Bass	4737	10-inch, .60

WAKEFIELD AS
ALLAN-A-DALE

WHITE

SCENE FROM ROBIN HOOD—ACT III

(French)
LE ROI DE LAHORE
(Rooah'-d'h Lah-ohr')

(English)
THE KING OF LAHORE

OPERA IN FIVE ACTS

Libretto by Louis Gallet; music by Jules Massenet. First production at the Grand Opéra, Paris, April 27, 1877; and at Covent Garden, Royal Italian Opera, June 28, 1879.

Cast

ALIM, King of Lahore..Tenor
SCINDIA, his minister..Baritone
TIMUR, a priest ....Bass
INDRA ....Bass
SITA ....Soprano
KALED, confidant of the King..............................Mezzo-Soprano

Time and Place : India ; the eleventh century, during the incursion of the Mohammedans.

This early work of Massenet's is founded upon an Indian subject, and deals with the Mussulman invasion. It is noted for its brilliant ballet, illustrative of an Indian paradise.

Sita, niece of the high priest, *Timur,* is beloved by *Alim,* King of Lahore. His rival, *Scindia,* accuses her of profaning the Temple and she is condemned to death, but is saved by the King, who asks her hand in marriage.

In the second act *Alim,* at war with the Mussulmans, is betrayed to the enemy by *Scindia,* and is killed in battle, while *Scindia* seizes his throne and carries away *Sita.*

Alim is transported to the celestial realm of India, but is not contented, and begs the divinities to allow him to return to earth. His request is granted on condition that he does not resume his rank and returns to India when *Sita* dies. On his return he finds that *Scindia* has secured the throne and forced *Sita* to become his wife. *Alim* declares himself, but *Scindia* denounces him as an impostor. *Alim* is obliged to flee, but *Sita* goes with him, and when they are about to be captured she kills herself. *Alim,* in fulfillment of his vow, also dies, and the lovers are united in celestial India.

Promesse de mon avenir (Oh, Promise of a Joy Divine)
By Emilio de Gogorza, Baritone   (In French)   88172   12-inch, $3.00

The most famous of the numbers is of course this superb air for baritone in the fourth act, which La Salle sang in the first production with great success. A portion of the fine translation by Dudley Buck, from the Schirmer "Operatic Anthology" (Copy't G. Schirmer), is given here by permission.

SCINDIA:
The Sultan's barb'rous horde, who had so
  gladly riven
From us fair Lahore,
By our own might have from the field been
  driven.
From care my people free,
Loudly sound forth my praises!

O promise fair of joy divine, Sita,
Thou dream of all my life,
O beauty torn from me by strife,
At last, thou shalt be mine! O Sita!
O fair one, charm my loving heart,
And ne'er again from me depart!

* * * * * * * * * * *

Sita, my queen thou soon shalt be!
To thee the world its glory offers,
To thee a king his crown now proffers;
Come, Sita, O come! ah! be mine!

A fine rendition of this air is given here by Mr. de Gogorza, whose beautiful voice and perfect French diction are well exhibited.

THE LOVERS' FIRST MEETING

ROMÉO ET JULIETTE   ROMEO AND JULIET
(French)   (English)

(Roh'-may-oh ay Joo-lee-et')

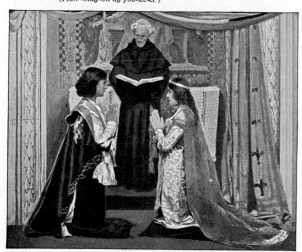

THE MARRIAGE

OPERA IN FIVE ACTS

Words by Barbier and Carré, after Shakespeare's drama. Music by Charles Gounod. First produced at the *Théâtre Lyrique,* Paris, April 27, 1867. First London production July 11, 1867. First Milan production at La Scala, December 14, 1867. Presented in America, 1868, with Minnie Hauk.

Some famous American productions occurred in 1890, with Patti, Ravelli, del Puente and Fabri; in 1891, with Eames (début), the de Reszkes and Capoul; in 1898, with Melba, Saleza, de Reszke and Plançon; and more recently with Farrar as *Juliet.*

Gounod's sweetly sentimental setting of this great tragedy of love and death has achieved a popularity second

FARRAR AS JULIET

only to his Faust. Some critics have called the music too insipid, but very few who have heard the splendid arias for *Juliet* will agree with this opinion.

Characters

JULIET, (*Joo-lee-et'*) daughter of Capulet .. Soprano
STEPHANO, (*Stef'-ah-noh*) page to Romeo. . Soprano
GERTRUDE, Juliet's nurse . . . . Mezzo-Soprano
ROMEO . . . . Tenor
TYBALT, (*Tee-bahl'*) Capulet's nephew . . . . . Tenor
BENVOLIO, (*Ben-voh'-lee-oh*) friend of Romeo. Tenor
MERCUTIO, (*Mer-kew'-shee-oh*) friend of Romeo
Baritone
PARIS, (*Pah-ree'*) Capulet's kinsman . . . . . Baritone
GREGORIO, Capulet's kinsman . . . . Baritone
CAPULET, (*Cap-u-leh'*) a Veronese noble
Basso-Cantante
FRIAR LAURENCE . . . . Bass
THE DUKE OF VERONA . . . . Bass
Guests; Relatives and Retainers of the Capulets and Montagues.

The action takes place at Verona.

PHOTO REUTLINGER
ALDA AS JULIET

Romeo and Juliet overflows with charming music, Gounod having written for the lovers some of the most emotional passages ever composed, and the opera has even been called "a love duet with occasional interruptions." It is, of course, not another Faust,—no composer could write two such works,—but it is a most beautiful setting of the story of the ill-fated Italian lovers, and will always be listened to with pleasure.

Several of the Shakespearean personages have been omitted from the opera cast by the librettists, and a new character, that of the page *Stephano,* has been added.

ACT I

SCENE—*Ballroom in Capulet's House, Verona*

The curtain rises on a scene of festivity. *Capulet,* a Veronese noble, is giving a masked fête in honor of his daughter *Juliet's* entrance into society.

Juliet is presented to the guests by her father, and *Capulet,* in a rousing air, calls on his guests to make merry.

When the guests have gone to the banquet hall, *Juliet* lingers behind and gives expression to her girlish joy in the famous waltz.

Valse (Juliet's Waltz Song)

By Louise Tetrazzini, Soprano
(*In Italian*) 88302 12-inch, $3.00
By Emma Eames, Soprano
(*In French*) 88011 12-inch, 3.00
By Blanche Arral, Soprano
(*In French*) 74151 12-inch, 1.50

It is maintained by some critics that this waltz is too showy and brilliantly effective to be sung by a modest young girl at her first ball. However, Gounod has written such an uncommonly pretty waltz of exquisite melody, that most hearers are too delighted to inquire very closely into questions of dramatic fitness.

COPY'T DUPONT
FARRAR AS JULIET

449

JULIET:
Song, jest, perfume and dances.
Smiles, vows, love-laden glances
All that spells or entrances
In one charm blend
As in fair dreams enfolden
Born of fantasy golden,

Sprites from fairyland olden,
On me now bend.
Forever would this gladness
Shine on me brightly as now,
Would that never age or sadness
Threw their shade o'er my brow!

Three records of this delicate waltz, with its ear-haunting melody, are offered for a selection. Mme. Tetrazzini gives it with much animation, its difficult requirements being met with a perfect ease and grace.

Mme. Eames, whose *Juliet* is remembered with pleasure, sings the number with much charm; while another fine rendition is contributed by Mme. Arral.

Juliet is about to leave the room when *Romeo* enters, having ventured masked into the house of his enemy. He is much impressed with the young girl's beauty and grace, and contriving to speak with her, asks her to remain a moment. They sing the first of their duets, the opening portion of which is full of airy repartee. As the number progresses a mysterious attraction seems to draw the youth and maiden toward each other, and the duet becomes an impassioned love scene.

Ange adorable (Lovely Angel)

By Geraldine Farrar, Soprano, and Edmond Clement, Tenor
(*In French*)   88421   12-inch, $3.00

By Alice Nielsen and Florencio Constantino   (*In French*)   74108   12-inch, 1.50

ROMEO:
Angel that wearest graces the fairest,
Forgive, if to touch I dare,
The marble whiteness of thy hand
That Heav'n hath formed so fair!
Claim, then, unsparing, that for my daring
I one soft kiss be fined.
Kiss, that effaces unworthy traces,
This hand hath left behind.
JULIET:
Thy hand, good pilgrim, this fine but
    wrongeth
For thou dost blame it o'ermuch,
To pure devotion surely belongeth,
Saintly palm that thou may'st touch.
Hands there are, sacred to pilgrim's greeting,

But, ah me! I not such as this,
Palm unto palm, not red lips meeting,
Is a holy palmer's kiss!
ROMEO:
To palmer and to saint, have not lips too
    been given?
JULIET:
Yes; but only for prayer!
ROMEO:
Then grant my pray'r, dear saint, or faith
    may else be driven,
Unto deepest despair!
JULIET:
Know, the saints ne'er are moved,
And if they grant a pray'r, 'tis for the
    prayer's sake!

ROMEO:
Then move not, sweetest saint,
Whilst the effect of my pray'r, from thy lips
    (*He kisses her*)
I shall take!
JULIET:
Ah! now my lips from thine burning,
Have the sin that they have taken!
ROMEO:
O give that sin back again,
To my lips their fault returning.
JULIET:
No, not again! No, not again!
ROMEO:
O give the sin to me again!

ABOTT AS JULIET

Tybalt, a hot-headed member of the *Capulet* family, recognizes *Romeo* through his mask, and threatens to kill him for his presumption in coming to the house of his enemies. *Capulet* restrains *Tybalt* and the dancing recommences.

ACT II

SCENE—*Capulet's Garden; Juliet's Apartments Above*

This scene is taken almost literally from Shakespeare, the only variation being the entrance of *Gregorio* and the servants, which serves merely to divide the long love duet.

Romeo, who is braving the displeasure of his enemies in the hope of seeing *Juliet* again, appears, and gazing at the balcony, sings his lovely serenade.

Ah! leve toi soleil (Arise, Fairest Sun)

By Herman Jadlowker, Tenor
(*In French*) **76025** 12-inch, $2.00

ROMEO:

Rise, fairest sun in heaven!
Quench the stars with thy brightness,
That o'er the vault at even
Shine with a feeble lightness,
Oh! rise again! Oh! rise again!
And banish night's dark shades.
She is watching, ah! ever untwining
From their bonds her tresses shining!
Now she speaketh. Ah! how charming!
By her beauty's brilliant ray,
As burneth, ashamed and jaded,
A lamp by the light of day!
At her window, on her fair hand,
See now she leaneth her cheek.
On that hand, were I a glove,
That I might touch that cheek!

Juliet appears on the balcony and *Romeo* conceals himself. She speaks to the stars of her new-found happiness.

JULIET:

Ah, me—and still I love him!
Romeo, why art thou Romeo?
Doff then thy name, for it is no part,
My love, of thee! What rose we call
By other name would smell as sweetly;
Thou'rt no foe, 'tis thy name!

A long scene between the lovers is interrupted by *Gregorio* and some retainers, who are

THE BALCONY SCENE

searching for *Romeo*. He hides himself again, and on their departure the duet is resumed.

Ne fuis encore (Linger Yet a Moment)

By Alice Nielsen, Soprano, and Florencio Constantino, Tenor
(*In French*) **64091** 10-inch, $1.00

ROMEO AND JULIET:

Ah! go not yet, but stay thee!
Let me once more kiss thy dear hand, I pray thee!

JULIET:

Silence! a step is near us.
Someone I fear will hear us,
Let me at least take my hand from thy keeping.
Good night, love.

ROMEO:

Good night, love.

BOTH:

Good night! Dearest, this fond good night is such sweet sorrow
That I would say good night, till it be dawn!

ROMEO:

Soft be thy repose till morning!
On thine eyes slumber dwell, and sweet peace
In thy bosom: would I were sleep and peace
So sweet to rest!

FROM THE PAINTING BY PAPPERITZ

ROMEO AND JULIET

FROM A PAINTING

ROMEO AND JULIET IN THE FRIAR'S CELL

ACT III

SCENE I—*The Cell of Friar Laurence*

Romeo and *Juliet* meet by appointment in the Friar's cell to ask him to marry them. He at first protests but finally consents, hoping the union will bring the rival houses together in friendship. The marriage takes place, and *Juliet* returns home with her nurse.

SCENE II—*A Street in Verona*

Stephano enters, seeking his master. Observing the residence of *Capulet,* he decides to sing a song, thinking *Romeo* may still be lingering near the house.

Gregorio appears, angry at being waked up, and scolds the noisy youth, finally recognizing him as the companion of *Romeo* on the previous night. They fight, but are interrupted by *Mercutio* and *Tybalt,* who begin to quarrel with *Gregorio.* *Romeo* enters and tries to act as peacemaker, but is insulted and forced to fight, killing *Tybalt.* The action comes to the ears of the *Duke of Verona,* who happens to be passing with his suite, and he banishes *Romeo* from the kingdom. The unhappy youth yields to the decree, but secretly vows to see *Juliet* again

PHOTO BYRON

THE DEATH OF TYBALT

452

ACT IV
SCENE—*Juliet's Room*

Romeo has made his way into *Capulet's* house at imminent risk of death, and has penetrated to the room of his bride. As the curtain rises he is taking leave of her, and in another exquisite duet she begs him not to go. He finally departs after a tender farewell, just as *Capulet* and *Friar Laurence* enter to tell her that it was *Tybalt's* dying wish that she should marry *Paris*. Left alone with the good priest she tells him she will die rather than be separated from *Romeo*. The *Friar* tells her to have patience, as he has a plan by which they are to be reunited. He then gives *Juliet* a potion, commanding her to drink it when her marriage with *Paris* seems imminent, and tells her she will go into a death-like trance. He continues:

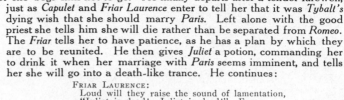

COPY'T MISHKIN
CONSTANTINO AS ROMEO

FRIAR LAURENCE:
Loud will they raise the sound of lamentation,
"Juliet is dead! Juliet is dead!" For so
Shall they deem thee reposing. But
The angels above will reply, "She but sleeps!"
For two-and-forty hours thou shalt lie in death's seeming,
And then, to life awaking as from a pleasant dreaming,
From the ancient vault thou shalt haste away!

The good priest leaves her and shortly afterward, seeing her father and *Paris* approaching, she drinks the contents of the phial, and growing faint, apparently expires in *Capulet's* arms.

ACT V
SCENE—*The Tomb of Juliet*

The curtain rises, showing the silent vault of the *Capulets*, where *Juliet* is lying on the bier still in her trance. *Romeo*, who has failed to receive *Friar Laurence's* message, and believes *Juliet* is dead, now forces the door with an iron bar and enters.

He sees his bride apparently dead, and flings himself on her body. After a mournful air in which he bids her farewell, he drinks poison, but is soon startled to see signs of life in the body of *Juliet*. Forgetting the poison he had taken, he embraces her joyfully and they sing their final duet:

JULIET:
Ah! methought that I heard
Tones that I lov'd, soft falling!
ROMEO:
'Tis I! Romeo—thine own—
Who thy slumbers have stirr'd,
Led by my heart alone,
Thee, my bride, unto love
And the fair world recalling!
(*Juliet falls into his arms.*)

ROMEO:
Come, let's fly hence!
JULIET:
Happy dawn!
ROMEO AND JULIET:
Come, the world is all before us,
two hearts, yet one!
Grant that our love—
Be now and ever
Holy and pure, till our life shall end.

Suddenly remembering the fatal draught, *Romeo* cries out in horror:

ROMEO:
Alas! I believed thee dead, love, and—
I drank of this draught!
(*Shows the phial.*)
JULIET:
Of that draught! It is death!
(*Taking the phial.*)
Ah! thou churl
To drink all! No friendly drop thou'st left me,
So I may die with thee!
(*She flings the phial away, then remembering the dagger, draws it out.*)
Ah! here's my dagger still!

Now, happy dagger, behold thy sheath!
(*She stabs herself. With a supreme effort Romeo half raises himself to prevent her.*)
ROMEO:
Hold! Hold thy hand!
JULIET:
Ah, happy moment.
My soul now with rapture is swelling,
Thus to die, love, with thee.
(*She lets fall the dagger.*)
Yet one embrace! I love thee!
(*They half rise in each other's arms.*)
O heav'n grant us thy grace!
(*They die.*)

DOUBLE-FACED ROMEO AND JULIET RECORDS

{ Romeo and Juliet Selection   By Arthur Pryor's Band }
{ Introduction to Act I, "The Capulet's Ball"—Interlude, Act IV—   }
{ Capulet's Solo, "The Altar is Prepared"—Ballet—Nuptial Procession } 35234 12-inch, $1.25
{ *Samson and Delilah Selection* (*Saint-Saëns*) *Arthur Pryor's Band* }

(French)

SAMSON ET DALILA

(*Sam-sohn ay Dah-lee-lah*)

(English)

SAMSON AND DELILAH

OPERA IN THREE ACTS

Text by Ferdinand Lemaire; music by Camille Saint-Saëns (*Sah'-Sahnz'*). First production at Weimar, under Liszt, December 2, 1877. In France at Rouen, 1890. Performed at Covent Garden, in concert form, September 25, 1893. First American production at New Orleans, January 4, 1893, with Renaud and Mme. Mounier. First New York production February, 1895, with Tamagno and Mantelli (one performance only). Revived by Oscar Hammerstein, November 13, 1908, and again in 1911, with Gerville-Reache, Dalmores and Dufranne.

Cast of Characters

DELILAH . . . . Mezzo-Soprano
SAMSON . . . . Tenor
HIGH PRIEST OF DAGON . . . . Baritone
ABIMELECH, Satrap of Gaza . . . . First Bass
AN OLD HEBREW . . . . Second Bass
PHILISTINE MESSENGER . . . . Tenor
FIRST PHILISTINE . . . . Tenor
SECOND PHILISTINE . . . . Bass

Chorus of Hebrews and Philistines.

Time and Place: 1150 B. C.; Gaza in Palestine.

Camille Saint-Saëns has been for two generations the foremost figure in music in France. Poet, astronomer, traveler, excelling in every branch of the art of music, he is undoubtedly the most versatile musician of our time. He has held a commanding position on the concert stage since 1846, when at the age of ten he gave a concert in Paris. On October 15, 1906, he played one of his own concertos at the Philharmonic concert in Berlin. Sixty years before the public! In all the history of music there is no more wonderful career than that of the composer of Samson, who a few years ago visited America for the first time, and this year comes to us again, although he is 80 years of age.

COPY'T DUPONT

TAMAGNO AS SAMSON

Samson et Dalila may be called a biblical opera, almost an oratorio, and the polished beauty and grace of this great composition has caused it to be pronounced Saint-Saëns' masterpiece. The religious and militant flavor of the Jewish nation is finely expressed in the score, and the exquisite love music is more or less familiar by its frequent performance on the concert stage.

ACT I

SCENE—*A Public Square in Gaza*

The opera has no overture. The first scene shows a square in the city of Gaza, where a crowd of Hebrews are lamenting their misfortunes, telling of the destruction of their cities and the profanation of their altars by the Gentiles.

Samson speaks to the people and bids them take courage.

DALMORES AS SAMSON

SAMSON (*coming out from the throng*):
Let us pause, O my brothers,
And bless the holy name of the God of our
    fathers!
For now the hour is here when pardon shall
    be spoken.
Yes, a voice in my heart is the token.
'Tis the voice of the Lord, who by my mouth
    thus speaketh.
Our prayers to him have risen,
And liberty is ours.
Brothers! we'll break from bondage!
Our altars raise once more
To our God, as before!

The Hebrews are cheered by *Samson's* words, but their mood soon changes when a number of Philistines enter and revile them. A fight occurs, and *Samson* wounds *Abimelech*. The High Priest of Dagon comes out of the Temple and curses *Samson*.

From the Temple now comes *Delilah,* followed by the Priestesses of Dagon, bearing flowers and singing of Spring. *Delilah* speaks to *Samson* and invites him to the valley where she dwells. He prays for strength to resist her fascinations, but in spite of himself he is forced to look at her as she dances with the maidens. As the young girls dance *Delilah* sings to *Samson* the lovely *Song of Spring.*

(*French*)   (*German*)

Printemps qui commence—Der Fruhling erwachte (Delilah's Song of Spring)

By Ernestine Schumann-Heink, Contralto	(*In German*)	88417	12-inch, $3.00
By Gerville-Réache, Contralto	(*In French*)	88244	12-inch, 3.00
By Julia Culp, Contralto	(*In French*)	74430	12-inch, 1.50

DELILAH: Spring voices are singing,
Bright hope they are bringing,
All hearts making glad.
And gone sorrow's traces,
The soft air effaces
All days that are sad.
The earth glad and beaming,
With freshness is teeming,
In vain all my beauty:

I weep my poor fate!
(*She gazes fondly at Samson.*)
When night is descending,
With love all unending,
Bewailing my fate,
For him will I wait.
Till fond love returning,
In his bosom burning
May enforce his return!

Samson shows by his hesitation and troubled bearing that *Delilah* has shaken his resolutions, and as the curtain falls he is gazing at her, fascinated.

ACT II

SCENE—*Delilah's Home in the Valley of Soreck*

Delilah, richly attired, is awaiting the coming of *Samson,* and muses on her coming triumph over his affections, and the plot to secure his downfall. In a fine air she calls on Love to aid her.

Amour viens aider (Love, Lend Me Thy Might)

By Louise Homer, Contralto   (*In French*)   88201   12-inch, $3.00

DELILAH:
O Love! in my weakness give power!
Poison Samson's brave heart for me!
'Neath my soft sway may he be vanquished;
Tomorrow let him captive be!
Ev'ry thought of me he would banish,
And from his tribe he would swerve,

Could he only drive out the passion
That remembrance doth now preserve.
But he is under my dominion;
In vain his people may entreat.
'Tis I alone that can hold him—
I'll have him captive at my feet!

After a scene between *Delilah* and *Dagon,* who urges her not to fail in her purpose *Samson* arrives, impelled by a power he cannot resist.

Delilah greets him tenderly, and when he bitterly reproaches himself for his weakness, she sings that wonderfully beautiful song of love and passion.

COPY'T MISHKIN

GERVILLE-RÉACHE AS DALILA

Mon coeur s'ouvre à ta voix (My Heart at Thy Sweet Voice)

By Louise Homer, Contralto
  (*In French*) 88199 12-inch, $3.00
By Schumann-Heink, Contralto
  (*In German*) 88190 12-inch, 3.00
By Jeanne Gerville-Réache, Contralto
  (*In French*) 88184 12-inch, 3.00
By Elsie Baker, Contralto
  (*In English*) *16192 10-inch, .75
By Michele Rinaldi with Vessella's Band
  Cornet *17216 10-inch, .75

This lovely air of *Delilah,* perhaps the most beautiful contralto air ever written, and the most familiar of the numbers in the opera, is in the repertoire of almost every contralto.

DELILAH:
 My heart at thy sweet voice opens wide like the flower
  Which the morn's kisses waken!
 But, that I may rejoice, that my tears no more shower,
  Tell thy love still unshaken!
 O, say thou wilt not now leave Delilah again!
 Repeat thine accents tender, ev'ry passionate vow,
  O thou dearest of men!
        (Copy't 1892, G. Schirmer.)

Five records of this well-known air are listed here.
Delilah now asks that *Samson* confide to her the secret plans of the Hebrews, and when he refuses she calls the Philistines, who are concealed, and *Samson* is overpowered.

ACT III
SCENE I—*A Prison at Gaza*

Samson is shown in chains, blinded and shorn of his hair. As he slowly and painfully pushes a heavy mill which is grinding corn, he calls on Heaven to forgive his offence. A file of guards enter and conduct him to the Temple.

SCENE II—*A Magnificent Hall in the Temple of Dagon*

The High Priests and Philistines, with *Delilah* and the Philistine maidens, are rejoicing over the downfall of their enemies. The music of the opening chorus and the Bachanal has been given here in a fine record by a famous Spanish band.

Coro y Bacanal (Chorus and Bachanal)

By Banda Real de Alabarderos de Madrid *62660 10-inch, $0.75

They have sent for *Samson* to make sport of him. *Delilah* approaches him and taunts him with his weakness. He bows his head in prayer, and when they have wearied of their sport *Samson* asks the page to lead him to the great pillars which support the Temple. He offers a last prayer to God for strength to overcome his enemies, then, straining at the pillars, he overthrows them. The Temple falls amid the shrieks and groans of the people.

DOUBLE-FACED SAMSON AND DELILAH RECORDS

Samson and Delilah Selection Pryor's Band			
"The Breath of God," Act I—Chorus of the Philistines, Act III—"My Heart at Thy Sweet Voice," Act II	35234	12-inch,	$1.25
Romeo and Juliet Selection (Gounod) *Pryor's Band*			
My Heart at Thy Sweet Voice—By Elsie Baker (*In English*)	16192	10-inch,	.75
Manon—Laughing Song By Edith Helena (*In English*)			
My Heart at Thy Sweet Voice *Cornet*			
By Michele Rinaldi with Vessella's Band	17216	10-inch,	.75
Farewell to the Forest (Mendelssohn) (2.) Spring Song (Pinsuti)			
By Victor Brass Quartet			
Chorus and Bachanal By Banda Real de Alabarderos	62660	10-inch,	.75
Minuet from 2nd Symphony (Haydn) *By Banda Real*			

*Double-Faced Record—See above list.

(Italian)

IL SEGRETO DI SUSANNA
(*Eel Seh-gray'-toh dee Soo-zan'-nah*)

(English)

THE SECRET OF SUZANNE
(*Soo-zan'*)

OPERA IN ONE ACT

Text by Kalbeck; music by Ermanno Wolf-Ferrari. First production Munich, November 4, 1909; in America, at the Metropolitan, March, 1911, with White, Sammarco and Daddi.

Characters

COUNT GIL (aged thirty)......................................Baritone
COUNTESS SUZANNE, his wife (aged twenty)................ ....Soprano
SANTE, a servant (aged fifty)..............................Acting part

Time and Place : A drawing room in Piedmont ; 1840.

Il Segreto di Susanna is a playful conceit, with a very simple little plot. *Count Gil* is very much in love with his wife, but is averse to cigarette smoke, and *Countess Suzanne*, who is a devotee of the cigarette, takes the opportunity to smoke during her husband's absence.

MARIO SAMMARCO AND MLLE. LIPKOWSKA AS THE COUNT AND SUZANNE

On his return he smells the smoke and questions the servant, who denies being the guilty party. The *Count* immediately concludes that his beautiful wife is receiving attentions from some Piedmont gallant. His wife's efforts to pacify him are unsuccessful, and in a huff he leaves the house. On his departure *Suzanne* lights a cigarette, but on her husband's sudden return she throws it into the fire. The testy *Count* notices the fresh smoke and rushes about the apartment in jealous rage, determined to capture the culprit. Failing to find any one, he once more goes out. As *Suzanne* attempts to enjoy another cigarette, the *Count* peeps through the window, and seeing the smoke, rushes in triumph into the room. *Suzanne* hides the cigarette behind her, and the *Count,* trying to reach the imaginary man whom the lady is concealing, burns his hand! The secret is out, the *Count* forgives *Suzanne, Suzanne* forgives the *Count,* and husband and wife smoke a cigarette together.

Three of the best airs are offered—the charming duet of *Suzanne* and the *Count,* the *Via ! cosi,* in which *Suzanne* entreats her husband not to go away angry; and the song of *Suzanne,* which tells of the delights of smoking.

Il dolce idillio (Dost Thou Remember ?)
By Geraldine Farrar and Pasquale Amato   (*In Italian*)   89057   12-inch, $4.00

Via ! cosi non mi lasciate (Do Not Go Like This)
By Geraldine Farrar, Soprano   (*In Italian*)   87136   10-inch, $2.00

Oh gioia, la nube leggera (What Joy to Watch)
By Frances Alda, Soprano   (*In Italian*)   74388   12-inch, $1.50

(Italian)

SEMIRAMIDE

(Seh-mih-rah-mee'-dah) *

TRAGIC OPERA IN TWO ACTS

Text by Rossi; music by Gioachino Antonio Rossini. It is founded on Voltaire's tragedy *Semiramis*. First produced at the Fenice Theatre, Venice, February 3, 1823; in London at the King's Theatre, July 15, 1824. In French, as *Semiramis*, it appeared in Paris, July 9, 1860. First American production occurred in New York, April 25, 1826. First New Orleans production May 1, 1837. Some notable American revivals were in 1855 with Grisi and Vestvalli; in 1890 with Adelina Patti as *Semiramide;* and in 1894 with Melba and Scalchi.

Cast of Characters

SEMIRAMIDE, or SEMIRAMIS, Queen of Babylon....Soprano
ARSACES, commander in the Assyrian army, afterward the son of Ninus and heir to the throne..Contralto
THE GHOST OF NINUS.............................Bass
OROE, chief of the Magi...........................Bass
ASSUR, a Prince of the blood royal.................Bass
AZEMA, Princess of the blood royal..............Soprano
IDRENUS, of the royal household....................Tenor
MITRANES, of the royal household...............Baritone

Magi, Guards, Satraps, Slaves

FROM HARPER'S WEEKLY, 1855

GRISI AS SEMIRAMIDE

Semiramide is perhaps the finest of Rossini's serious operas, but although it was a great success in its day, its splendid overture and the brilliant *Bel raggio* are about the only reminders of it which remain.

The story is based on the classic subject of the murder of *Agamemnon* by his wife, called *Semiramis* in the Babylonian version. It is a work which the composer completed in the astonishingly short time of one month, but which shows his art at its ripest.

The action takes place in Babylon; *Semiramide,* the Queen, assisted by her lover *Assur,* has murdered her husband, *King Ninus,* who, in the second act, rises in spirit from the tomb and prophesies the Queen's downfall.

Overture

By Police Band of Mexico City	*35167	12-inch, $1.25
By Arthur Pryor's Band	31527	12-inch, 1.00

The overture opens with an unusually brilliant introduction, followed by a beautiful chorale for brass which is one of the most admired portions of the work. The familiar melody which forms the principal theme of the overture then appears as a clarinet passage. It begins:

The finale is rather long drawn out for modern ears, but is a fine example of its kind, and the overture is a most showy one, very popular on band and orchestra programs. Two splendid records of this famous number are presented here, and a comparison of the playing of these two great organizations is most interesting.

* Double-Faced Record—See page 459.

The *Bel raggio,* a favorite cavatina with all prima donnas, and a brilliant and imposing air, occurs in the first act.

The scene shows the Temple of Belus, where a religious festival is in progress. *Semiramide* is about to announce an heir to the throne and has secretly determined to elect *Arsaces,* a young warrior, with whom she has fallen in love, unaware that he is in reality her own son.

FROM HARPER'S WEEKLY, 1850

ALBONI AS ARSACES

Bel raggio lusinghier (Bright Gleam of Hope)

By Marcella Sembrich, Soprano
(*In Italian*) 88141 12-inch, $3.00

SEMIRAMIDE:
Here hope's consoling ray
Bids sorrow hence away,
And joy calls from above!
Arsaces to my love soon will return dejected,
But ere while with grief I dropp'd my head,
Now once more beams my smile!
Hence all my doubts have fled,
No more I feel the sway of grief and anguish
    dread!
Yes! now hope's consoling ray
Bids dark sorrow hence away,
And calls down joy from above,
Awhile in this breast to stay.
Arsaces will return!
Vision enchanting, my spirit haunting,
With fond emotion thou fill'st my heart,
Ah, bright smiles the morn
When dark waves of sorrow
Like some wild ocean sink and depart!

FROM HARPER'S WEEKLY

TAMBURINI AS ASSUR

Rossini, who objected to the ornamentation of his music by famous singers, is said to have written this air in so elaborate a fashion as to make further additions impossible. But even as left by Rossini, *Bel raggio* is not sufficiently elaborate to show the skill of a Sembrich, and the additions with which the *diva* has embellished it not only make it more dazzling, but belong also to the true spirit of the air.

Thus the inspiring declamatory passages, with their brilliant runs, receive a lavish addition of the singer's splendid high notes, notably the high B on the *alfin perme brillo,* and the astonishing arpeggio up to C sharp on the *dal mio pensier* which follows.

The ensuing *cantabile* is sung with all the *legato* and grace which it requires, its principal figure being also additionally embellished.

DOUBLE-FACED SEMIRAMIDE RECORD

{ Overture   By Police Band of
    Mexico City
    Marche Slave (Op. 31)
        By Arthur Pryor's Band }   35167 12-inch, $1.25

Siegfried Discovers the Sleeping Brünnhilde

(German)

SIEGFRIED

(*Zeeg'-freed*)

MUSIC DRAMA IN THREE ACTS
Second Opera of the Rhinegold Trilogy

Words and music by Wagner. First produced at Bayreuth, August 16, 1876. It was given in French at Brussels, June 12, 1891, and subsequently at the Opéra in Paris. In London (in English) by the Carl Rosa Company, in 1898. First American production in New York, November 9, 1887, with Lehmann, Fischer, Alvary and Seidl-Kraus.

Characters

SIEGFRIED..Tenor
MIME (*Mee'-meh*)...Tenor
THE WANDERER (WOTAN).....................................Baritone
ALBERICH (*Ahl'-ber-ik'h*)....................................Baritone
FAFNER (*Faf'-ner*)...Bass
ERDA (*Air'-dah*)..Contralto
BRÜNNHILDE (*Bruen-hill'-d'h*).........................Mezzo-Soprano

---

There is little of tragedy and much of lightness and the joy of youth and love in this most beautiful of the Ring Cycle, which tells of the young *Siegfried,*—impetuous, brave, joyful and handsome; and *Brünnhilde,* the god-like maid—unselfish, lovely, innocent, who finds she is but a woman after all.

After *Sieglinde* had been saved from the wrath of *Wotan* by *Brünnhilde* (related in the last part of *Walküre*), she wanders through the forest and dies in giving birth to the child *Siegfried,* who is found and brought up by *Mime,* the *Niblung.*

In the first two acts of Siegfried the hero is shown in his forest home, where he mends his father's sword, and with it slays the dragon. Having accidentally tasted the dragon's blood, he becomes able to understand the language of the birds, which tells him of *Brünnhilde,* the fair maiden who sleeps on the fire-encircled rock. He follows the guidance of one of the birds, cuts through the spear of *Wotan,* who endeavors to stop him, and penetrates the flames. On the top of the rock he beholds the sleeping *Valkyrie* covered with her shield. He removes the armor, and *Brünnhilde* lies before him in soft, womanly garments. She is the first woman he has ever seen, and he kneels down and kisses her long and fervently. He then starts up in alarm; *Brünnhilde* has opened her eyes. He looks at her in wonder, and both remain for some time gazing at each other. She recognizes him as *Siegfried,* and hails him as the hero who is to save the world. This part of the trilogy ends in a splendid duet.

PANEL BY BRAUNE

SIEGFRIED AND THE SWORD

ACT I. SCENE—*A Forest. At One Side a Cave*

Mime, the *Niblung,* brother of *Alberich,* found *Sieglinde* in the forest after she had escaped from *Wotan,* and brought up her child, knowing that it was *Siegfried,* who was destined to kill *Fafner* and regain the Ring. The opera opens with an air by *Mime,* who is discovered at the anvil in his forest smithy trying to forge a sword for *Siegfried.*

Siegfried and the Dragon

Zwangvolle Plage! (Heartbreaking Bondage)

By Albert Reiss, Tenor   (*In German*)   74235   12-inch, $1.50

Mr. Reiss' wonderful character study of the dwarf gains each year in the sardonic and malignant side of *Mime's* nature, but is always amusing, nevertheless.

Siegfried, in forest dress, with a horn around his neck, bursts impetuously from the woods. He is driving a great bear and urges it with merry roughness towards *Mime,* who drops the sword in terror and hides behind the forge. Taking pity on the frightened dwarf, *Siegfried* drives the bear back into the wood, and seeing the sword, breaks it over the anvil, as he has broken all of the others. He questions *Mime* about his childhood, and the dwarf tells him reluctantly about his mother and about the sword his father had broken in his last fight. *Siegfried* demands that *Mime* shall mend his father's sword without delay, and goes back into the forest.

Wotan now enters and in answer to *Mime's* questions says he is the *Wanderer,* and speaks to *Mime* of the sword, telling him that only he who knows no fear will be able to forge the broken weapon.

DAS GAB MIR DEINE MUTTER: — SIEH'HER, EIN ZERBROCHENES SCHWERT

PANEL BY BRAUNE

MIMI: Accursed steel! I cannot restore it! (Siegfried, Act I.)

After the *Wanderer* has departed, *Siegfried* returns, and *Mime,* who is now beginning to be afraid of the youth, tells him that it was his mother's wish that he should learn fear. "What is this fear?" says *Siegfried,* and *Mime* attempts to describe it.

MIME: Feltest thou ne'er in forest dark,	Balefullest shudders shake thy whole body,
Feltest thou then, no grisly gruesomeness grow	In thy breast bursting and big
o'er thy fancy?	Beat thy hammering heart?

Siegfried regretfully admits that he has never felt any such sensation. *Mimi,* in despair, then tells him of the Dragon which dwells near by. *Siegfried* eagerly asks *Mime* to conduct him hither, but says he must have his sword mended first, and, when *Mime* refuses, he forges it himself. When it is finished, to try the blade, he strikes the anvil a mighty blow and splits it in half, while *Mime* falls on the ground in extreme terror. *Siegfried* brandishes the sword and shouts with glee as the curtain falls.

ACT II. SCENE—*The Dragon's Cave in the Forest*

Fafner, who has changed himself into a dragon, the better to guard his gold, dwells within a cave, keeping constant watch. *Alberich* is spying near by, hoping to regain the treasure by killing the hero whom he knows will overcome the Dragon. The *Wanderer* enters and warns *Alberich* of the approach of *Siegfried.* *Alberich*

FERD. LEEKE

SIEGFRIED (*To the bird*):
Once more say to me,
Lovely singer,
May I then waken
The marvelous bride?

(Siegfried, Act II.)

wakes the Dragon and offers to save its life in return for the Ring. *Fafner* contemptuously refuses, and makes light of the hero's prowess. *Wotan* departs, laughing at the discomfited *Alberich*, who hides as *Siegfried* and *Mime* approach. The latter is still trying to terrorize *Siegfried* with awful descriptions of the Dragon, but *Siegfried* laughs at him and finally drives him away.

The young hero, left alone, sits down under a tree and meditates about his mother, whom he pictures as gentle and beautiful. His dreaming is ended by the song of the birds, and he regrets that he cannot understand their language. He answers their song with a blast of his horn, which disturbs *Fafner* and the Dragon utters an awful roar, which, however, only makes the youth laugh. The Dragon rushes upon him, but *Siegfried* jumps aside and buries his faithful sword in the reptile's heart.

Having accidentally tasted of the Dragon's blood by carrying his stained hand to his lips, he finds to his astonishment that he is able to understand the song of the bird, which tells him to go into the cave and secure the Ring. *Siegfried* thanks the warbler and goes into the cavern. *Mime* comes back and, seeing the dead *Fafner*, is about to enter the cave when *Alberich* stops him and a heated argument occurs. This scene has been given for the Victor by two celebrated impersonators of these rôles, Goritz and Reiss.

HOFFERT

KRAUS AS SIEGFRIED

Wohin schleichst du ? (Whither Slinkest Thou ?)

By Otto Goritz, Baritone, and Albert Reiss, Tenor
(*In German*) 64215 10-inch, $1.00

ALBERICH:
Wither slinkest thou, hasty and sly, slippery scamp?

MIME:
Accursed brother, what brings thee here?
I bid thee hence.

ALBERICH:
Graspest thou, rogue, towards my gold?
Dost lust for my goods?

MIME:
Yield the position! This station is mine.
What stirrest thou here?

ALBERICH:
Startled art thou from stealthy concerns, that I've disturbed?

MIME:
What I have shaped with shrewdest toil shall not be shaken.

ALBERICH:
Was't thou that robbed the golden Ring from the Rhine?
Or charged it with great and choice enchantment around?

MIME:
Who formed the Tarnhelm which to all forms can turn?
By thee 'twas wanted; its worker wert thou too?

ALBERICH:
What couldst thou ere, fool,
By thyself have fancied and fashioned?
The magic Ring made the dwarf meet for the task.

MIME:
Where now is thy Ring?
The giants have robbed thee, thou recreant!
What thou hast lost, by my lore, belike, I will gain.

ALBERICH:
By the boy's exploit
Shalt thou, booby, be bettered?
Thou shalt have it not,
For its holder in truth is he.

KNOTE AS SIEGFRIED

The Master's Vision

MIME:
I nourished him,
And his nurse now shall he pay:
For toil and woe long while have I waited
  reward.

ALBERICH:
For a bantling's keep
Would this beggarly, niggardly boor,
Bold and blustering,
Be well nigh as a king?
To rankest of doge booteth the ring
Far rather than thee:
Never, thou rogue, shall reach thee the magic
  round!

MIME:
Then hold it still and heed it well,
Thy hoarded Ring.
Be thou head, and yet hail me as a brother!
For my own Tarnhelm,
Excellent toy, I'll tender it thee!
'Twill boot us twain,
Twin we the booty like this.

ALBERICH (*laughing scornfully*):
Twin it with thee?
And the Tarnhelm too?

MIME (*beside himself*):
Wilt not bargain? Wilt not barter?
Giv'st thou to me no booty?

ALBERICH:
Not an atom, not e'en a nail's worth!

MIME (*furiously*):
In the Ring and Tarnhelm
Ne'er shalt thou triumph!
Nought talk we of shares!
Siegfried, the caustic boy,
Shall crush thee, brother of mine!

ALBERICH:
The Tarnhelm he holds!—

MIME:
Aye, and the Ring!—
(*With an evil laugh*):
Let him the Ring to thee render!
I ween full soon I shall win it.
(*He slips back into the wood.*)

SIEGFRIED

ALBERICH:
And yet to its lord
Shall it alone be delivered!
(*He disappears in the cleft.*)

They hide themselves as *Siegfried* comes from the cave with the Ring, the value of which he does not yet comprehend. The bird's voice is again heard explaining its history, and revealing the intended treachery of *Mime*. When the dwarf approaches, *Siegfried* is able, by the magic of the Ring, to read his thoughts. Horrified to learn that *Mime* is planning to kill him, he strikes down the dwarf and throws his corpse in the cave, rolling the body of the Dragon before the entrance.

Wearied by his adventures, *Siegfried* reclines under the tree and asks the bird to sing again. This time the songster reveals to him that *Brünnhilde* lies sleeping, waiting for the hero who is able to reach the fire-encircled spot.

THE BIRD:
Hey! Siegfried has slain now the sinister
  dwarf!
I wot for him now a glorious wife.
In guarded fastness she sleeps,
Fire doth emborder the spot:
O'erstepped he the blaze,
Waked he the bride.
Brünnhilde then would be his!

SIEGFRIED (*starting impetuously to his feet*):
O lovely song! Sweetest delight!
How burns its sense my suffering breast!
But once more say to me, lovely singer,—
May I the furnace then break through?
And waken the marvelous bride?

THE BIRD:
The bride is won,
Brünnhilde awaked by faint-heart ne'er:
But by him who knows not fear.

He laughs with delight, saying, "Why, this stupid lad who knows not fear,—it is I!" and follows the bird, who flies ahead to guide him to *Brünnhilde's* fiery couch.

ACT III

SCENE—*A Wild Region at the Foot of a Rocky Mountain*

The act opens with a long scene between *Erda* and *Wotan*. The god summons his earth goddess wife and tries to consult her regarding the coming deliverance of the world through *Siegfried* and *Brünnhilde*. The goddess, however, is confused and bewildered by *Wotan's* eager questions and fails to give counsel, asking only to be allowed to return to her sleep. *Wotan*, wearying of the struggle against fate, renounces his sway over the world, realizing that the era of love must supplant the rule of the gods.

THE AWAKENING OF BRÜNNHILDE—ACT III

Siegfried approaches and *Wotan* attempts to bar his way as a final trial of his courage. The youth, however, makes short work of the weary god, shatters his spear at a single stroke, and continues on his way singing:

SIEGFRIED:
Ha! Heavenly glow! brightening glare!
Roads are now opening radiantly round me!
In fire will I bathe,
Through fire will I fare to my bride!
Oho! Oho! Aha! Aha! Gaily! Gaily!
Soon greets me a glorious friend!

As the hero plunges fearlessly through the fire the flames gradually abate, and when he reaches the sleeping *Brünnhilde* they die out completely. *Siegfried* approaches the unconscious maiden with awe and removes her helmet. He is speechless with admiration, and naively asks if the strange emotion which he feels can be fear. Finally, when he presses an ardent kiss on her lips she awakes and greets him joyfully as the hero *Siegfried* who is to save the world. After a long scene in which *Siegfried's* ardent wooing is gently repressed by *Brünnhilde*, he finally seizes her in his arms. Frightened, she repulses him, crying:

BRÜNNHILDE:
No god e'en has touched me!
As a maiden ever heroes revered me:
Virgin I hied from Valhalla!—
Woe's me! Woe's me!
Woe for the shame, the shunless disgrace!
My wak'ning hero deals me this wound!

Siegfried pleads his love and asks her to be his bride, but she begs him to spare her in a wonderful plea, *Deathless Was I*, sung here by Mme. Gadski.

Ewig war Ich (Deathless Was I) (Brünnhilde's Appeal to Siegfried)
By Johanna Gadski, Soprano

(In German) 88186 12-inch, $3.00

BRÜNNHILDE:
Deathless was I, deathless am I,
Deathless to sweet sway of affection—
But deathless for thy good!
O Siegfried, happiest hope of the world!
Life of the universe! Lordliest hero!
Leave me in peace!
Press not upon me thy ardent reproaches!
Master me not with thy conquering might!
Saw'st e'er thy face in crystal floods?
Did it not gladden thy glance?

When into wavelets the water was roused,
The brook's glassy surface broken and flawed,
Thy face saw'st thou no more:
Nought but ripples swirling round!
So disturb me no more, trouble me not:
Ever then thou wilt shine
In me an image reflected,
Fair and lovely, my lord!—
O Siegfried! Siegfried! Light of my soul!
Destroy not thy faithful slave!

But the impetuous hero resumes his wooing, and love finally conquers the god-like maiden. She laughs in a transport of love, exclaiming:

BRÜNNHILDE:
O high-minded boy! O blossoming hero!
Thou babe of prowess,
Past all that breathe!
Gladly love do I glow with,
Gladly yield to thee blindly,

Gladly glide to destruction,
Gladly go down to death!
Far hence, Walhall' lofty and vast,
Let fall thy structure of stately tow'rs;
Farewell, grandeur and pride of gods!

and throws herself into *Siegfried's* arms as the curtain falls.

(Russian)

SNEGOUROTCHKA

(French)   (English)

LA FILLE DE NEIGE   THE SNOW MAIDEN

OPERA IN FOUR ACTS AND A PROLOGUE

Text by Ostrovsky, based on the old folk-lore tale of the *Snow Maiden*. Music by Nicolai Andreyevich Rimsky-Korsakoff. First production St. Petersburg, March, 1882. Produced at the Private Opera, Moscow, 1911. In Paris, at the *Opéra Comique*, June, 1908. The work has not yet been given in America.

Characters

SNEGOUROTCHKA, the Snow Maiden..........................Soprano
MISGUIR, her lover...Baritone
SHEPHERD LEHL ....Contralto
CZAR BERENDEY..Tenor
BOBY...Bass
BOBYLYCKA, his wife...Soprano
KOUPAVA, betrothed to Misguir...............................Contralto

---

The scene is laid in Berendey, an imaginary province of Russia.

THE SNOW MAIDEN
(SNEGOUROTCHKA)

Those who have enjoyed Mme. Gluck's beautiful interpretation of *The Snow Maiden* air will like to know something of this Russian opera, and we therefore give a brief sketch of the plot.

The opera abounds in picturesque scenes, representing Winter and Spring, and the poetic little story is supposed to take place in the happy country of Berendey, an unknown province of an imaginary Russia, ruled by a benevolent old *Czar* who has devoted his life to the happiness of his people, governing his kingdom by the law of love.

The beautiful, unknown *Snegourotchka*, daughter of old *Winter* and the fairy *Spring*, is found one cold morning by some villagers, abandoned in the forest, and the old drunkard, *Boby*, and his wife, *Bobylycka*, adopt her without knowing her parentage. *Misguir*, a merchant, falls in love with her, abandoning his sweetheart *Koupava*, but *Snegourotchka*, as her name indicates, is made of ice, and her coldness and indifference discourage all the young men who are infatuated with her beauty. Even the handsome shepherd *Lehl*, who sings such wonderful songs, gives up in despair and offers his heart to *Koupava*. The old *Czar* is grieved that this coldness has entered his kingdom, and offers the hand of the *Snow Maiden* and a handsome gift besides to any one who can win her love. *Snegourotchka* finds it impossible to love, and appeals to her mother, the fairy *Spring*, who invokes the aid of the flowers—the carnation lending its grace, the rose its heart and the jasmine its languor. This influence gradually touches the heart of the *Snow Maiden*, and she finds herself falling in love with the handsome *Misguir*. They both attend the festival of lovers and present themselves to the good *Czar* as a betrothed couple. But, alas, at the first kiss from her lover the little snowflake melts and disappears, while *Misguir*, in despair, throws himself into the river.

This dainty little shepherd song is the gem of the opera—a tender, melodious air which Miss Gluck sings exquisitely in perfect English.

Song of the Shepherd Lehl
By Alma Gluck, Soprano

(*In English*) 64209 10-inch, $1.00

BOYER & BERT

SCENE FROM THE SNOW MAIDEN

THE SLEEP-WALKING SCENE—ACT III, SCENE II

(Italian)   (English)

LA SONNAMBULA—THE SOMNAMBULIST

(Lah Son-nahm'-boo-lah)

OPERA IN THREE ACTS

Libretto by Felice Romani; music by Vincenzo Bellini. Produced at the *Teatro Carcano,* Milan, March 6, 1831; Paris, October 28, 1831; and at the King's Theatre, London, July 28th of the same year. At Drury Lane in English, under the Italian title, May 1, 1833. First performance in New York, in English, at the Park Theatre, November 13, 1835, with Brough, Richings, and Mr. and Mrs. Wood. First New Orleans performance, January 14, 1840. First performance in Italian in New York, Palmo's Opera Company, May 11, 1844. Revived in 1905 at the Metropolitan with Caruso, Sembrich and Plançon; at the Manhattan Opera, 1909, with Tetrazzini, Trentini, Parola and de Segurola.

Characters

COUNT RUDOLPH, lord of the village . . . . .Bass
TERESA, milleress. . . . . .Mezzo-Soprano
AMINA, orphan adopted by Teresa, betrothed to Elvino. . . . . .Soprano
ELVINO, wealthy peasant. . . . . .Tenor
LISA, inn-keeper, in love with Elvino. . . . . .Soprano
ALESSIO, peasant, in love with Lisa . . . . .Bass

Peasants and Peasant Women.

The scene is laid in a Swiss village.

How our grandfathers and grandmothers doted on this fine old opera by Bellini! In the '30's it was a novelty by a young and gifted composer; by 1850 it was part of every opera season and shone through a halo of great casts—Malibran, Pasta, Jenny Lind, Gerster, Campanini, Grisi—and in the '60's and '70's it continued to be popular. Then came the Wagnerian era, and the pretty little pastoral work was all but forgotten until the recent revival, which greatly delighted Metropolitan audiences.

ACT I

SCENE—*A Village Green*

The peasants are making merry in honor of the marriage of *Amina* and *Elvino.* *Lisa,* the hostess of the inn, enters and gives way to bitter reflections. She also loves *Elvino,* and her jealousy finds expression in a melodious air, *Sounds So Joyful.* *Alessio,* a villager who fancies *Lisa,* tries to console her, but she repulses him. *Amina* and her friends enter, followed soon after by *Elvino,* and the marriage contract is signed. *Elvino* places the ring on his bride's finger, and they sing a charming duet, *Take Now This Ring.*

Prendi l'anel ti dono (Take Now This Ring)

By Maria Galvany and Fernando De Lucia (*In Italian*) 89045 12-inch, $4.00
By Emilio Perea, Tenor (*In Italian*) *62092 10-inch, .75

The nuptial celebration is interrupted by the sound of horses' hoofs, and a handsome and distinguished stranger enters, inquires the way to the castle, and learning that it is some distance, decides to remain at the inn. He looks around him, appearing to recognize the scene, and sings his fine air, *Vi ravviso*.

Vi ravviso (As I View These Scenes)

By Perello de Segurola, Bass
(*In Italian*) *62092 10-inch, $0.75

COUNT:
As I view the scene, how familiar that mill-
   stream, yon fountain, those meadows!
Oh remembrance of scenes long vanish'd,
Soft enchantment long lost and banish'd,
Where my childhood serenely glided,
Where the joyous moments flew;
Oh how peaceful have ye abided,
While those days nought can renew!

JENNY LIND AS AMINA

The stranger inquires the reason for the festivities, and is presented to the pretty bride, in whom he is much interested. He tells the peasants that in his childhood he lived with the lord of the castle, and now brings news of the lord's only son, who disappeared some years since.

Amina's mother, *Teresa,* now says that as night is falling they must go within, as the phantom may appear. The stranger is told that a spectre has been often seen of late, and he scoffs at the tale, but the peasants, in an effective chorus, describe the appearance of the ghost.

Ah! fosco ciel! (When Daylight's Going)

By La Scala Chorus (*In Italian*) *62642 10-inch, $0.75

The stranger now desires to retire and is shown to his room. *Amina* and *Elvino* remain, and the latter reproaches his bride for her interest in the guest; but at the sight of her tears he repents his suspicions, and the act closes with a duet by the reconciled lovers.

ACT II
SCENE—*The Apartment of the Stranger*

The guest muses that he might have done worse than stop at this little inn—the people are courteous, the women pretty, and the accommodations good. *Lisa* enters and asks if he is comfortable, calling him "my lord," the villagers having suspected that he is *Count Rudolph.* The Count, although somewhat annoyed that his identity is revealed, takes it good-naturedly, and even flirts a little with the buxom landlady. She coyly runs away, dropping her veil as she does so.

Amina now appears at the window, walking in her sleep. She unlatches the casement and steps into the room, saying in her sleep, "Elvino, dost thou remain jealous? I love but thee." The Count is at first astonished, but soon sees that the young girl is asleep. Just here *Lisa* peeps into the room, and seeing *Amina,* runs off scandalized. *Amina,* in her dream, again goes through the marriage ceremony, and entreats *Elvino* to believe that she loves him, finally throwing herself on the bed in a deep sleep. The Count is somewhat puzzled at the situation, and finally deciding to leave the young girl in possession of the room, goes out by the window.

Elvino and the villagers, who have been summoned by *Lisa,* now enter and are astonished to see *Amina* asleep in the Count's room. She wakes at the noise, bewildered, and runs to *Elvino,* who repulses her roughly. She is met with cold looks on every hand, and sinks down in despair, crying bitterly. Rousing herself, she begins the duet, *D'un pensiero.*

* *Double-Faced Record—See page 473.*

D'un pensiero (Hear Me Swear, Then)

By Giuseppina Huguet, Soprano; Aristodemo Giorgini, Tenor;
and Chorus (*In Italian*) 88255 12-inch, $3.00

AMINA:
Not in thought's remotest dreaming,
Was a crime by me intended;
Is the little faith now granted,
Fit return for so much love?

ELVINO:
Heav'n forgive ye, this guilt redeeming;
May thy breast be ne'er thus rended;
With what love my soul was haunted,
Let these burning tear-drops prove!

Finding all turned against her except her mother, she runs to the maternal arms, while *Elvino* rushes from the room. The curtain falls.

ACT III

SCENE I—*A Shady Valley near the Castle*

Amina and *Teresa* enter on their way to the castle to plead with the Count to clear the girl's good name. Seeing *Elvino, Amina* makes another effort to convince him she is still true, but he reproaches her bitterly, takes the ring from her finger, and rushes away.

SCENE II—*A Street in the Village. Teresa's mill on the left*

The villagers enter and inform *Lisa* that *Elvino* has transferred his affections to her. He enters and confirms the good news, and they go toward the church. The Count stops them, and assures *Elvino* that *Amina* is the victim of a dreadful misunderstanding. *Elvino* refuses to listen to him and bids *Lisa* follow him to the church, but they are again interrupted by *Teresa*, who has learned of the proposed marriage, and now shows *Lisa's* veil which she had found in the Count's room. "Deceived again," cries *Elvino*, and asks if any of these women are to be trusted.

Rudolph assures him again that *Amina* is guiltless, and *Elvino* desperately says, "But where is the proof?" "There," cries the Count, suddenly pointing to *Amina*, who in her night dress comes from a window in the mill roof, carrying a lamp. All watch her breathlessly, fearing to wake her lest she fall. She climbs down to the bridge over the wheel, and descends the stairs. The first of the two lovely airs for *Amina* in this act now occurs.

Ah! non credea mirarti (Could I Believe)

By Luisa Tetrazzini, Soprano	(*In Italian*)	88305	12-inch, $3.00
By Graziella Pareto, Soprano	(*In Italian*)	76003	12-inch, 2.00
By Alma Gluck, Soprano	(*In Italian*)	74263	12-inch, 1.50

Ah! non credea is sung by the sleeper as she descends from her dangerous position, while her lover and friends watch in terror, fearing to awaken her. It opens with a beautiful *cantabile* in the key of A minor, its pathos being fully in keeping with the plight of *Amina*, who, being discarded by her lover and doubted by her friends, weeps over her short-lived love and happiness. Regarding the flowers which her lover had given her, she exclaims:

AMINA:
Ah! must ye fade, sweet flowers,
Forsaken by sunlight and showers,
As transient as lover's emotion
That lives and withers in one short day!

But tho' no sunshine o'er ye,
These tears might yet restore ye,
But estranged devotion
No mourner's tears have power to stay!
—From the Ditson Edition.

Elvino can restrain himself no longer, and rushes to *Amina*, who wakes, and seeing *Elvino* on his knees before her, utters a cry of delight and falls in his arms.

The opera then closes with the joyous, bird-like air, *Ah! non giunge*, which is a fitting close to this charming work, with its graceful and tender music and peaceful pastoral scenes.

Ah, non giunge (Oh, Recall Not One Earthly Sorrow)

By Luisa Tetrazzini, Soprano	(*In Italian*)	88313	12-inch, $3.00
By Marcella Sembrich, Soprano	(*In Italian*)	88027	12-inch, 3.00

AMINA:
Do not mingle one human feeling
With the rapture o'er each sense stealing;
See these tributes, to me revealing
My Elvino, true to love.

Ah, embrace me, and thus forgiving,
Each a pardon is now receiving;
On this bright earth, while we are living,
Let us form here a heaven of love!

DOUBLE-FACED SONNAMBULA RECORDS

Vi ravviso	By Perello de Segurola, Bass	(*In Italian*)	62092	10-inch, $0.75
Prendi l'anel ti dono	By Emilio Perea, Tenor	(*In Italian*)		
Ah! fosco ciel!	By La Scala Chorus	(*In Italian*)	62642	10-inch, .75
Lohengrin—Coro Nuziale	By La Scala Chorus	(*In Italian*)		

THE VENETIAN SCENE AT THE OPÉRA-COMIQUE

(French)   (English)
CONTES D'HOFFMANN   TALES OF HOFFMAN
(Kongt Doff'-mahn)

(German)
HOFFMAN'S ERZÄHLUNGEN
(Air-tsay'-loong-en)

OPERA IN THREE ACTS
WITH PROLOGUE AND EPILOGUE

Text by Jules Barbier. Music by Offenbach. First performance in Paris, February 10, 1881. First United States production October 16, 1882, at Fifth Avenue Theatre, by Maurice Grau's French Opera Company on their first appearance in America. Revived at the Manhattan Opera House, New York, November 27, 1907, and by the Metropolitan Opera Company in 1911, with Hempel, Bori, Fremstad, de Segurola, Ruysdael and Rothier.

Cast

THE POET HOFFMAN	Tenor
NICLAUS, his friend	Soprano
OLYMPIA, GIULIETTA, the various ladies with whom Hoffman falls	
ANTONIA, STELLA, in love	Sopranos
COPPELIUS, his opponents. (These three rôles are usually sung	
DAPERTUTTO, by the same artist)	Baritone
MIRACLE,	
LUTHER, an innkeeper	Bass
SCHLEMIL, Giulietta's admirer	Bass
SPALANZANI, an apothecary	Tenor
COUNCILLOR CRESPEL, father of Antonia	Bass

Offenbach's delightful and fantastic *opéra comique*, first produced at Paris in 1881, has been a success wherever performed, although it was tabooed in Germany for many years after the disastrous fire at the Ring Theatre in Vienna, which occurred during the presentation of the opera at that house. Its American successes are familiar to opera-goers, especially the brilliant and altogether admirable Hammerstein production, which drew large and delighted audiences for several years.

THE PROLOGUE

This introductory scene occurs in Nuremberg at Luther's tavern, a popular student resort. *Hoffman,* the favorite of all, enters with his friend *Nicholas* and joins in the merry-making. In response to calls for a song, *Hoffman* sings the *Ballad of Klein-Zach,* and then volunteers to relate his three love affairs. This proposal is greeted with enthusiasm, and as *Hoffman* begins by saying "The name of my first was Olympia," the curtain falls. When it rises, the first tale of *Hoffman* is seen in actual performance.

PROLOGUE—THE LEGEND OF KLEINSACK

ACT I

Spalanzani, a wealthy man with a mania for automatons, has perfected a marvelous mechanical figure of a young girl which he calls *Olympia,* pretending it is his daughter. *Hoffman* and *Nicholas* call upon him, and during *Spalanzani's* absence, *Hoffman* discovers *Olympia,* and falls in love at sight. Unable to take his eyes from the doll-like perfection of the figure, he expresses his infatuation in a beautiful air.

C'est elle ('Tis She!)

By Charles Dalmores, Tenor (*In French*) 87089 10-inch, $2.00

Dalmores makes a great success in the part of *Hoffman.* This rôle calls for a handsome appearance, a gallant bearing, and enduring vocal powers, and this tenor fills these requirements admirably. He sings this beautiful air with graceful fluency and much warmth of tone.

PHOTO CHERI-ROUSSEAU

OLYMPIA, THE MECHANICAL DOLL

Nicholas tries in vain to prevent his friend from making a fool of himself, but *Hoffman,* owing to the magic glasses *Spalanzani* has induced him to wear, sees only a lovely woman instead of an automaton; but is undeceived when he dances with the figure and she falls to pieces before his astonished eyes.

ACT II

COPY'T MISHKIN

DALMORES AS HOFFMAN

This adventure concerns the *Lady Giulietta,* who resides in Venice. Among her many friends are *Hermann* and *Nathaniel,* and the latter, fearing the power of the lovely coquette, tries to get *Hermann* away, but he insists that he is proof against her fascinations. *Dapertutto,* the real lover of the lady, hearing this boast, induces *Giulietta* to try her arts on the young man. She succeeds, and *Hoffman,* madly in love, challenges *Giulietta's* protector, *Schlemil,* and kills him in a duel. *Hoffman* rushes back to his charmer's residence only to find that she has fled with her chosen admirer.

This second tale introduces that lovely gem, the *Barcarolle,* with its languorous, fascinating rhythm and charming melody.

LE THÉÂTRE   TALES OF HOFFMAN—ACT III—THE BARCAROLLE

Barcarolle—Belle Nuit (Oh, Night of Love)

By Geraldine Farrar and Antonio Scotti	(In French)	87502	10-inch, $3.00
By Alma Gluck and Louise Homer	(In French)	87202	10-inch, 2.00
By Maud Powell, Violinist		64457	10-inch, 1.00
By Victor Concert Orchestra		*17311	10-inch, .75
By Lucy Marsh and Marguerite Dunlap	(In English)	60096	10-inch, .75
By Mr. and Mrs. Wheeler	(In English)	*16827	10-inch, .75
By the Victor Orchestra, with duet for two violins		5333	10-inch, .60
By the Vienna Quartet		5754	10-inch, .60

This popular Offenbach number, which is given as a duet in the Venetian scene and afterwards as an instrumental intermezzo, is one of the best known examples of the *barcarolle*. As the name implies, it was originally a song or chant used by the Venetian gondoliers.

The music, in 6-8 time, portrays admirably the swaying of the boat

and its dreamy melancholy suggests the calm of a perfect moonlight night.

O Night of Love

Beauteous night, O night of love,
Smile thou on our enchantment;
Radiant night, with stars aglow,
O beauteous night of love!
Fleeting time doth ne'er return
But bears on wings our dreaming,

Far away where we may yearn,
For time doth ne'er return.
Sweet zephyrs aglow,
Shed on us thy caresses—
Night of love, O night of love!

From Ditson Edition—Copy't 1909

In this act is also the air sung by *Dapertutto* to the sparkling diamond, which he says never yet failed to tempt a woman.

LE THÉÂTRE
GIULIETTA

Air de Dapertutto (Dapertutto's Air)

By Marcel Journet, Bass   (In French)   74103   12-inch, $1.50

Journet delivers this song of the swaggering, garrulous Venetian bravo with much spirit.

* Double-Faced Record—See page 477.

ANTONIA

ACT III

The third adventure of *Hoffman* introduces us to an humble German home where *Antonia*, a young singer, has become the victim of consumption. She is forbidden to sing by her father, but a *Dr. Miracle*, who is the secret enemy of the family, urges her on, and *Hoffman*, who knows nothing of the poor girl's affliction, sees her literally sing herself to death, and she dies in his arms.

Romance—Elle a fui (The Dove Has Flown)

By Lucrezia Bori, Soprano

(*In French*) 88525 12-inch, $3.00

The pathetic air sung by the unfortunate young singer, *Antonia*, whose life is finally sacrificed to her art.

THE EPILOGUE

The epilogue shows again the tavern of the prologue, where *Hoffman* is apparently just concluding his third tale. Having tried three kinds of love—the love that is inspired by mere beauty, the sensuous love, and the affection that springs from the heart—he says he has learned his lesson, and will henceforth devote himself to art, the only mistress who will prove faithful. He bids farewell to another of his flames, *Stella*, an opera singer, and as the curtain falls is left alone, dreaming, while the Muse appears and bids him follow her.

MISCELLANEOUS HOFFMAN RECORDS

{ **Gems from Tales of Hoffman**   **By Victor Opera Company**
      Chorus, "Our Good Host"—Solo, "Song of Olympia"—Chorus,
      "Hear Him His Tales Disclose"—Solo, "Ah, Now Within My Heart"
      —Barcarolle, "Oh, Night Divine"—Chorus, "See She Dances"—
      Finale, "Fill Up Our Glasses"
    Gems from Mignon   *By Victor Light Opera Company* }
	35337	12-inch, $1.25

{ Barcarolle—*Waltz* (*For Dancing*) **By Victor Military Band** *Passing of Salome—Waltz* *By Victor Military Band* }	35383	12-inch, 1.25
Tales of Hoffman Selection **By Victor Concert Orch.**	31820	12-inch, 1.00
{ Barcarolle **By Victor Concert Orchestra** *Cavalleria Rusticana—Intermezzo* *By Victor Concert Orchestra* }	17311	10-inch, .75
{ Barcarolle—O, Night of Love **By Mr. and Mrs. Wheeler** *Fatinitza Selection* (*von Suppe*) *By Pryor's Band* }	16827	10-inch, .75

EPILOGUE—HOFFMAN AND THE MUSE

TANNHÄUSER AND VENUS

TANNHÄUSER
(*Tahn'-hoy-zer*)

ROMANTIC OPERA IN THREE ACTS

Words and music by Richard Wagner. First presented at the Royal Opera, Dresden, October 20, 1845; at the *Opéra*, Paris, March 13, 1861. First London production at Covent Garden, in Italian, May 6, 1876. First American production at the Metropolitan Opera House, April 4, 1859, in German. First Italian production at the New Orleans Opera in 1877.

Characters

HERMANN, Landgrave of Thuringia...............................Bass
TANNHÄUSER, ⎫ Tenor
WOLFRAM VON ESCHENBACH, ⎟ Baritone
WALTHER VON DER VOGELWEIDE, ⎬ Minstrel Knights............ Tenor
BITEROLF, ⎟ Bass
HEINRICH DER SCHREIBER, ⎟ Tenor
REINMAR VON ZWETER, ⎭ Bass
ELIZABETH, Niece of the Landgrave...........................Soprano
VENUS..Soprano
A Young Shepherd..Soprano
Four Noble Pages.................................Soprano and Alto
Chorus of Thuringian Nobles and Knights, Ladies, Elder and Younger
Pilgrims, and Sirens, Naïads, Nymphs and Bacchantes.

Scene and Period: Vicinity of Eisenach; beginning of the thirteenth century.

THE STORY

There are a great many people who like to go to the opera, but who do not care for Wagner's Ring Operas, with their Teutonic myths and legends, and their long and sometimes undeniably tedious scenes. But *Tannhäuser*, with its poetry, romance and passion, and above all its characters, who are real human beings and not mysterious mythological gods, goddesses and heroes, appeals strongly to everyone.

To show the wonderful vogue of this work, it is estimated that more than one thousand performances of the opera take place annually throughout the world; and in Germany during the decade 1901-1910 it was given 3,243 times.

The story is quite familiar, but the chief events will be noted here in brief. It tells of conflict between two kinds of love: true love of the highest human kind as distinguished from mere sensuous passion; and relates how the higher and purer love triumphed in the end.

Tannhäuser, a knight and minstrel, in an evil moment, succumbs to the wiles of *Venus* and dwells for a year in the Venusberg. Tiring of these monotonous delights, he leaves the goddess and returns to his home, where he is warmly received and told that the fair *Elizabeth,* niece of the *Landgrave,* still mourns for him. He is urged to compete in the Tournament of Song not far distant, the prize being the hand of *Elizabeth.* The theme of the contest is The Nature of Love, and when *Tannhäuser's* turn arrives the evil influence of the Venusberg is apparent when he delivers a wild and profane eulogy of passion. Outraged by this insult the minstrels draw their swords to slay him. Coming to his senses, too late, he repents, and when a company of Pilgrims pass on their way to Rome, he joins them to seek pardon for his sin. In the last act we see *Elizabeth,* weary and worn, supported by the noble *Wolfram,* who

FIRST PROGRAM OF TANNHÄUSER, 1845

SETTING OF ACT III AT THE METROPOLITAN

FERD. LEEKE

WOLFRAM:
Oh, royal maid.
May I not guide thee homeward?
(Tannhauser, Act III.)

PHOTO GERLACH   GADSKI AS ELIZABETH

also loves her, watching for the Pilgrims to return, but *Tannhäuser* is not among them. *Elizabeth* is overcome with disappointment and feebly returns to her home.

Tannhäuser now appears, in a wretched plight, on his way to re-enter the Hill of Venus. He tells *Wolfram* that he appealed to the Pope for pardon, but was told that his redemption was as impossible as that the Pope's staff should put forth leaves. *Wolfram's* remonstrances are in vain, and *Tannhäuser* is about to invoke the goddess, when a chant is heard and the Pilgrims appear, announcing that the Pope's staff had blossomed as a sign that the sinner was forgiven. *Tannhäuser* kneels in prayer as the mourners pass with the body of *Elizabeth*, who, overcome by her bitter disappointment, had suddenly passed away.

Overture—Part I
By Arthur Pryor's Band
31382   12-inch, $1.00

Overture—Part II
By Arthur Pryor's Band
31383   12-inch,   1.00

{Overture—Part I	By La Scala Orchestra}	68205 12-inch, 1.25
{Overture—Part II	By La Scala Orchestra}	

This overture, with its sombre opening chorus, its weird music of the Venus Mount, and the final return of the penitents, when the chant is accompanied by a striking variation for clarinets, is one of the greatest works of Wagner. It has become quite familiar by its frequent repetitions in orchestra and military band concerts, and no concert piece is more admired.

The overture depicts the struggle between good and evil, and as Liszt has said, is a poem on the same subject as the opera and equally comprehensive.

The sombre religious motive appears first:

beginning softly and gradually swelling to a *fortissimo*. Then, as it is dying away, it is suddenly interrupted by the Venusberg motive:

with its rising tide of sensual sounds. This motive continues with terrible persistence, leading into *Tannhäuser's* hymn to *Venus*, after which the enchanting Venus motive returns and is developed with various changes. The tide now changes again and the majestic pilgrim theme predominates, finally reaching a climax in the final hymn of triumph.

VENUS:
"Canst thou so soon weary of the blisses,
That love immortal hath cast around thee!"

ACT I

SCENE I—*The Hill of Venus—Nymphs, Sirens, Naïads and Bacchantes dancing or reclining on mossy banks*

The rising of the curtain discloses *Venus* reclining on a couch gazing tenderly at *Tannhäuser*, who is in a dejected attitude. The goddess asks him why he is melancholy, and he tells her he is weary of pleasure and would see the earth again. She reproves him fondly:

VENUS:
What! art thou wav'ring? Why these vain lamentings?
Canst thou so soon weary of the blisses
That love immortal hath cast 'round thee?
Can it be—dost thou now repent that thou'rt divine?
Hast thou soon forgotten how thy heart was mourning,
Till by me thou wert consoled?
My minstrel, come, let not thy harp be silent;
Recall the rapture—sing the praise and bliss of love
In tones that won for thee love's self to be thy slave!
Of love sing only, for her treasures are all thine!

He rouses himself and sings the *Praise to Venus,* but it is a forced effort, and throwing down his harp he exclaims:

TANNHAUSER:
For earth I'm yearning,
In thy soft chains with shame I'm burning,
'Tis freedom I must win or die—
For freedom I can all defy;
To strife or glory forth I go,
Come life or death, come joy or woe,
No more in bondage will I sigh!
Oh queen, beloved goddess, let me fly!

Venus in a rage, then tells him to go if he will, but predicts his return and disappears with all her train, while the scene instantly changes.

SCENE II—*A Valley*

Tannhäuser suddenly finds himself in a beautiful valley near the Wartburg. On the peaceful scene there break in the notes of a shepherd's pipe, and tinkling sheep bells sound from the heights. A company of Pilgrims pass, singing their chant, while the little shepherd pauses in his lay, and begs them utter a prayer for him in Rome. This entire scene is effectively given by Mme. Runge and the Nebe Chorus, while several additional records of the Pilgrims' Chorus are provided.

Pilgrims' Chorus

By Gertrud Runge, Soprano, and Nebe Qt.	*(German)*	68352	12-inch,	$1.25
By Pryor's Band		31160	12-inch,	1.00
By Pryor's Band	*(Double-faced—See page 488)*	16537	10-inch,	.75
By Victor Brass Quartet	*(Double-faced—See page 488)*	17133	10-inch,	.75
By Victor Male Chorus	*(Double-faced—See page 488) (English)*	17563	10-inch,	.75

TANNHAUSER (*kneeling in ecstasy*):

Almighty, praise to Thee!
Great are the marvels of Thy mercy!
Oh, see my heart by guilt oppress'd—

I faint, I sink beneath the burden!
Nor will I cease, nor will I rest,
Till heav'nly mercy grant me pardon!

The *Landgrave* and several minstrels now enter, and seeing a knight kneeling in prayer, accost him. They are amazed and delighted to see that it is the long lost *Henry,* their brother knight. They question him, but he gives evasive replies. The Knights urge him to return with them, and speak the name of *Elizabeth, Wolfram* telling him that he is beloved by the *Landgrave's* fair niece.

WOLFRAM:

When for the palm in song we were contending,
And oft thy conq'ring strain the wreath had won,
Our songs anon thy victory, suspending,
One glorious prize was won by thee alone!
Was't magic, or a pow'r divine,
That wrought thro' thee the wondrous sign,
Thy harp and song in blissful hour
Enthrall'd of royal maids the flower!
For ah, when thou in scorn hadst left us,
Her heart was closed to joy and song,
Of her sweet presence she bereft us,
For thee in vain she wearied long.
Oh! minstrel bold, return and rest thee,
Once more awake the joyous strain!

Tannhäuser joyfully consents to return and promises to compete in the forthcoming Tournament of Song, the prize for which is to be the hand of *Elizabeth.* The remainder of the hunting train of the *Landgrave* now arrives, and as *Tannhäuser* is being greeted by his friends, the curtain falls.

PHOTO BENQUE

RENAUD AS WOLFRAM

ACT II

SCENE—*The Great Hall in the Wartburg*

Elizabeth enters, full of joy over the return of *Tannhäuser,* and greets the Hall in a noble song.

Dich, theure Halle (Hail, Hall of Song)

By Johanna Gadski *(German)* 88057 12-inch, $3.00

ELIZABETH:

Oh, hall of song, I give thee greeting!
All hail to thee, thou hallowed place!
'Twas here that dream so sweet and fleeting,
Upon my heart his song did trace.
But since by him forsaken
A desert thou dost seem—
Thy echoes only waken
Remembrance of a dream.
But now the flame of hope is lighted,
Thy vault shall ring with glorious war;
For he whose strains my soul delighted
No longer roams afar!

Mme. Gadski sings this glorious air in a surpassingly beautiful fashion.

Tannhäuser enters and kneels at the feet of *Elizabeth,* who in blushing confusion bids him rise.

Verzeiht wenn ich nicht weiss (Forgive, I Scarcely Know What I am Saying)

By Johanna Gadski *(German)* 88442 12-in., $3.00

PHOTO GERLACH

FARRAR AS ELIZABETH

With that frankness which seems characteristic of Wagner's heroines, the young girl makes no secret of her partiality for the Knight, and a long scene between the lovers ensues, interrupted by the entrance of the *Landgrave*, who greets *Tannhäuser* cordially and welcomes him to the contest.

BRAND, BAYREUTH
THE HALL OF SONG—ACT II

The Knights and Ladies now assemble to the strains of the noble *Fest March*, given here in splendid fashion by Sousa's Band.

Fest March

By Sousa's Band	31423	12-inch, $1.00
By Sousa's Band *(Double-faced—See page 488)*	16514	10-inch, .75

When the company is seated, the *Landgrave* rises and makes the address of welcome.

LANDGRAVE:

Minstrels assembled here, I give you greeting,
Full oft within these walls your lays have sounded;
In veiled wisdom, or in mirthful measures
They ever gladdened every list'ning heart.
And though the sword of strife was loosed in battle,
Drawn to maintain our German land secure,
Unto the harp be equal praise and glory!
The tender graces of the homestead,
The faith in what is good and gracious—
For these you fought with word and voice;
The meed of praise for this is due.
Your strains inspiring, then, once more attune,
Now that the gallant minstrel hath returned,
Who from our land too long was parted.

To what we owe his presence here amongst us
In strange, mysterious darkness still is wrapp'd;
The magic power of song shall now reveal it,
Therefore hear now the song you all shall sing.
Say, what is love? by what signs shall we know it?
This be your theme. Who so most nobly this can tell,
Him shall the Princess give the prize.
He may demand the fairest guerdon:
I vouch that whatsoe'er he ask is granted.
Up, then, arouse ye—sing, oh, gallant minstrels!
Attune your harps to love—great is the prize.
Ere ye begin, let all receive our thanks!

Four pages, who have drawn lots from a gold cup, now announce that *Wolfram* is to begin the contest. He rises and delivers his *Eulogy of Love*.

Wolfram's Ansprache (Wolfram's Eulogy of Love)
By Otto Goritz, Baritone   (*In German*) 74215 12-inch, \$1.50

The singer gives his conception of love, which he describes as pure and ethereal, comparing it to a crystal spring.

WOLFRAM:

Gazing around upon this fair assembly,
How doth the heart expand to see the scene!
These gallant heroes, valiant, wise and gentle—
A stately forest soaring fresh and green.
And blooming by their side in sweet perfection,
I see a wreath of dames and maidens fair;
Their blended glories dazzle the beholder—
My song is mute before this vision rare!
I raised my eyes to one whose starry splendor
In this bright heaven with mild effulgence beams,
And gazing on that pure and tender radiance,

My heart was sunk in prayerful holy dreams.
And lo! the source of all delights and power
Was then unto my listening soul revealed,
From whose unfathomed depths all joy doth shower—
The tender balm in which all grief is healed.
Oh, may I never dim its limpid waters,
Or rashly trouble them with wild desires!
I worship thee kneeling, with soul devoted:
To live and die for thee my heart aspires!
(*After a pause.*)
I know not if these feeble words can render
What I have felt of love both true and tender.

Tannhäuser, who has shown signs of impatience during this recital, now jumps to his feet, flushed and eager, while the company looks at him in astonishment.

TANNHAUSER:

Oh, minstrel, if 'tis thus thou singest,
Thou ne'er hast known or tasted love!
If thou desire an unapproached perfection—
Behold the stars—adore their bright reflection—
They were not made to be belov'd:

(*Ardently.*)
But what can yield to soft caresses,
And, fram'd with me in mortal mould
Gentle persuasion's rule confesses,
And in these arms I may unfold—
This is for joy, and knows no measure,
For love's fulfillment is its pleasure!

At this definition of love, strange for such an occasion, *Biterolf,* a hotheaded Knight, rises and challenges *Tannhäuser,* who excitedly retorts that such a grim wolf as *Biterolf* can know nothing of the delights of love! He then, in wild exultation, sings his blasphemous *Praise of Venus,* saying

TANNHAUSER:

Dull mortals, who of love have never tasted
Go forth! Venus alone can show ye love!

At this the Knights rush toward him with drawn swords, exclaiming:

KNIGHTS:

Ye all have heard,
His mouth hath confess'd
That he hath shared the joys of Hell,
In Venus' dark abode that dwell,
Disown him—curse him—banish him!
Or let his traitor life-blood flow!

Elizabeth throws herself in front of the unhappy *Tannhäuser,* who stands as if in a trance. She begs for his life in a touching plea.

WITHERSPOON AS THE LANDGRAVE

Zuruck, von ihm ! (Away from Him !)
By Johanna Gadski, Soprano   (*In German*) 88443 12-inch, \$3.00

ELIZABETH:

Away from him! 'Tis not for you to judge him!
Shame on you! He is one against you all!
I pray for him—spare him, oh, I implore ye!
Let not the hope of pardon be denied!
To life renew'd his sinking faith restore ye.
Think that for him, too, once the Saviour died!
Oh, let a spotless maid your grace implore!

Let Heav'n declare through me what is its will—
The erring mortal, who hath fallen
Within the weary toils of sin.
How dare ye close the heav'nly portal!
On me, a maiden young and tender,
Yon knight hath struck a cruel blow—
I, who so deeply, truly loved him,
Am hurl'd in dark abyss of woe!

The *Landgrave* pronounces judgment and declares *Tannhäuser* banished, suggesting that he join the band of Pilgrims about to start for Rome. In the distance is heard the Pilgrims' chant, and the strains seem to bring the erring knight to his senses. He cries: "To Rome!" and dashes from the hall.

ACT III

SCENE—*The Valley beneath the Wartburg—at one side a Shrine*

As the curtain rises *Elizabeth* is seen kneeling at the shrine in prayer. *Wolfram* comes down by the path, and observing her, sadly notices her changed appearance, and muses of his own hopeless love. The song of the Pilgrims is heard in the distance, and *Elizabeth* eagerly rises and scans the approaching band. *Tannhäuser* is not among them, and the despairing maiden kneels again at the shrine, and offers her prayer to the Virgin.

Elisabeth's Gebet (Elizabeth's Prayer)

By Geraldine Farrar, Soprano
(*In German*) 88053 12-inch, $3.00
By Emmy Destinn, Soprano
(*In German*) 88488 12-inch, 3.00
By Elizabeth Wheeler, Soprano
(*In English*) *35096 12-inch, 1.25

This prayer of the sainted *Elizabeth* is one of the most beautiful and touching of the master's compositions. "He will return no more!" cries the unhappy girl, and falls on her knees.

ELIZABETH:

Oh, blessed Virgin, hear my prayer!
Thou star of glory, look on me!
Here in the dust I bend before thee
Now from this earth, oh, set me free!
Let me, a maiden pure and white,
Enter into thy kingdom bright!
If vain desires and earthly longing

FROM AN OLD PRINT

ELIZABETH AND WOLFRAM—ACT III

Have turn'd my heart from thee away,
The sinful hopes within me thronging,
Before thy blessed feet I lay;
I'll wrestle with the love I cherish'd,
Until in death its flame hath perish'd.
If of my sin thou will not shrive me,
Yet in this hour, oh grant thy aid!
Till thy eternal peace thou give me,
I vow to live and die thy maid.
And on thy bounty I will call,
That heav'nly grace on him may fall!

She remains for a long time in prayerful rapture; as she slowly rises she glances at *Wolfram,* who is approaching. She bids him by gesture not to speak to her, but he asks that he may escort her.

Elizabeth again expresses to him by gesture that she thanks him from her heart for his faithful love; her way, however, leads to Heaven, where she has a high purpose to fulfill; she wishes him not to accompany or follow her now. She slowly ascends the height and disappears gradually from view.

Wolfram gazes sadly after her for a long time, then seats himself at the foot of the hill, begins to play upon his harp, and finally sings the noble and beautiful ode to the evening star.

PHOTO GERLACH ELIZABETH AT THE CROSS

* *Double-Faced Record—See page 488.*

(German)   *(French)*

O du mein holder Abendstern   O douce étoile

(English)

Song to the Evening Star

By Emilio de Gogorza, Baritone	*(In German)*	88154	12-inch,	$3.00
By Maurice Renaud, Baritone	*(In French)*	91067	10-inch,	2.00
By Marcel Journet, Bass	*(In German)*	74006	12-inch,	1.50
By Reinald Werrenrath, Baritone	*(In German)*	*35160	12-inch,	1.25
By Reinald Werrenrath, Baritone	*(In German)*	31462	12-inch,	1.00
By Alan Turner, Baritone	*(In English)*	*17446	10-inch,	.75
By Victor Sorlin, 'Cellist		*16813	10-inch,	.75

WOLFRAM:
Like Death's dark shadow, Night her gloom
   extendeth,
Her sable wing o'er all the vale she bendeth;
The soul that longs to tread yon path of light,
Yet dreads to pass the gate of Fear and Night,
I look on thee, oh, star in Heaven the fairest,
Thy gentle beam thro' trackless space thou
   bearest;
The hour of darkness is by thee made bright,
Thou lead'st us upward by pure light.
O ev'ning star; thy holy light
Was ne'er so welcome to my sight,
With glowing heart, that ne'er disclos'd;
Greet her when she in thy light reposed;
When parting from this vale a vision,
She rises to an angel's mission.
*(He continues to play, his eyes raised to
Heaven.)*

Tannhäuser now appears, wearing a ragged
Pilgrim's dress, his face pale and drawn, and
supporting himself with difficulty by means of
a staff. *Wolfram* greets him with emotion and
learns that he is still unforgiven and has resolved to re-enter the Venusberg.

   The unhappy *Tannhäuser* tells of the *Pope's*
refusal of a pardon:

FROM THE PAINTING BY KAULBACH

THE DEATH OF ELIZABETH

TANNHÄUSER:
Rome I gained at last; with tears imploring,
I knelt before the rood in faith adoring.
When daylight broke, the silv'ry bells were
   pealing;
Through vaulted roof a song divine was
   stealing;
A cry of joy breaks forth from thousand
   voices—
The hope of pardon ev'ry heart rejoices.
I told what mad desires my soul had dark-
   ened,
By sinful earthly pleasure long enslav'd—
To me it seem'd that he in mercy harken'd—
A gracious word in dust and tears I crav'd.
Then he who thus I prayed replied:
"If thou hast shared the joys of Hell
If thou unholy flames hast nurs'd
That in the hill of Venus dwell,
Thou art forever more accurs'd!
And as this barren staff I hold
Ne'er will put forth a flower or leaf,
Thus shalt thou never more behold
Salvation or thy sin's relief!"

TANNHÄUSER:
Rome I gained at last; * * *
Then he who thus I prayed replied:
"If thou hast shared the joys of Hell,
Thou art forever more accursed!"

* *Double-Faced Record—See page 488.*

Wolfram, in horror, urges him to remain, but *Tannhäuser* refuses until *Wolfram* mentions the name of *Elizabeth*. The unhappy man, in sudden repentance, sinks to his knees, while in the distance is seen a company of minstrels bearing the body of *Elizabeth*, who has suddenly passed away. As the procession approaches, a company of Pilgrims enter and announce that the staff of the Pope had put forth green leaves as a sign that *Tannhäuser* was pardoned.

The *Minstrel*, supported by *Wolfram*, gazes on the saintly face of the dead *Elizabeth*, then expires, while the Pilgrims and minstrels with great emotion exclaim:

> The Lord Himself now thy bondage hath riven—
> Go, enter in with the blest in His Heaven!

(Curtain)

DOUBLE-FACED AND MISCELLANEOUS TANNHÄUSER RECORDS

Elizabeth's Prayer By Elizabeth Wheeler, Soprano				
A Night in Venice Mr. and Mrs. Wheeler	35096	12-inch,	$1.25	
Lied des Hirtenknaben und Chor der Pilger				
(In German) Runge and Nebe Qt				
Lied des Hirtenknaben und Chor der Pilger (Part II)	68352	12-inch,	1.25	
(In German) Runge and Nebe Qt				
O du mein holder Abendstern By Reinald Werrenrath				
Treue Liebe—Ach, wie ist's moglich dann Emil Muench, Tenor	35160	12-inch,	1.25	
Overture—Part I By La Scala Orchestra				
Overture—Part II By La Scala Orchestra	68205	12-inch,	1.25	
Selection from the Opera By Arthur Pryor's Band				
Madame Butterfly Selection, No. 2 By Arthur Pryor's Band	35331	12-inch,	1.25	
Fest March By Sousa's Band				
La Marseillaise—National Air of France By Sousa's Band	16514	10-inch,	.75	
The Evening Star By Victor Sorlin, 'Cellist				
Last Rose of Summer By Elizabeth Wheeler, Soprano	16813	10-inch,	.75	
The Evening Star (In English) By Alan Turner				
The Rosary (Nevin) By Alan Turner	17446	10-inch,	.75	
Pilgrims' Chorus By Pryor's Band				
Lohengrin—Coro delle nozze (In Italian) By La Scala Chorus	16537	10-inch,	.75	
Pilgrims' Chorus By Victor Brass Quartet				
Don Carlos—Grand March (Verdi) By Sousa's Band	17133	10-inch,	.75	
Pilgrims' Chorus (In English) By Victor Male Chorus				
Trovatore—Anvil Chorus (In English) By Victor Male Chorus	17563	10-inch,	.75	

BYRON

THE REDEMPTION OF TANNHÄUSER

THAÏS

(*Tah-ees'*)

OPERA IN THREE ACTS

Libretto by Louis Gallet, based on the novel of Anatole France; music by Jules Massenet. First production at the Opéra Comique, Paris, 1894, and the opera has since been given in nearly every music capital of Europe. First American production November 25, 1908, at the Manhattan Opera House, New York.

Characters

THAÏS, actress and courtesan.................Soprano
ATHANAEL, a Cenobite monk.................Baritone
NICIAS, a wealthy Alexandrian.................Tenor
PALEMON, an aged Cenobite monk.................Bass
ALBINE, an abbess.................Mezzo-Soprano
CROBYLE, } slave girls.................Sopranos
MYRTALE, }

Monks, Nuns, Citizens, Servants, Dancers, etc.

DALMORES AS NICIAS

*Time and Place :   Alexandria and the Egyptian desert;
early Christian era.*

Thaïs the Egyptian, a woman of wonderful beauty and a courtesan, who was converted by *Pafnucio* and led by him into the righteous path, is the subject of this lyric opera. The librettist has given the name of *Athanael* to *Pafnucio*, who is a young and handsome monk living with an assemblage of holy men, called Cenobites, in the desert of Thebes.

ACT I

DUFRANNE AS ATHANAEL

SCENE I—*The Camp of the Cenobites near the Nile*

At the opening of the opera *Athanael* has just returned from Alexandria, haunted by the story of the famous courtesan, *Thaïs*, whom he feels it his duty to save. Against the advice of the head Cenobite, *Palemon*, he calls his brother monks together and announces his intention of returning to Alexandria to convert the courtesan to the higher life.

SCENE II—*The House of Nicias at Alexandria*

Athanael arrives and is warmly greeted by *Nicias*, who knew the monk years before. The traveler tells his old friend he has come to the capital to teach *Thaïs* the better life, but *Nicias* only laughs at him and scoffs at the idea. However, he has his slaves dress the monk in rich robes, and when *Thaïs* arrives she is soon curious about the handsome stranger, whose severe demeanor arouses her interest. The monk tells her he has come to Alexandria to teach her salvation and the life everlasting, but she says she believes only in joy and love and pleasure. In horror at the revelry which is planned for the evening, *Athanael* leaves, declaring he will see *Thaïs* at her home and show her the true light.

ACT II

SCENE I—*Thaïs' Apartments*

The second act takes place in the luxurious home of *Thaïs*. *Athanael* enters, steeling himself against the seductive charms of *Thaïs,* and eloquently pleads with her for the new and higher love and the life to come. *Thaïs* is at first frightened and then defiant, but *Athanael* declares that she will yet repent, and that he will await her coming.

SCENE II—*A Street in Alexandria*

The next scene is in the square at dawn, where *Thaïs* comes to *Athanael*, renounces her life of pleasure, and tells him she will follow wherever he leads. He urges her to put a torch to all her earthly possessions, and she permits him to set fire to her palace. *Nicias* now appears with his joyous companions, singing and dancing. In the midst of the revelry they discover *Thaïs* in her sombre garments, and becom-

FROM A PAINTING CONVERSION OF THAIS

ing infuriated over her departure, and the firing of her house, threaten to hang *Athanael*. *Nicias*, realizing the seriousness of the situation, diverts his followers by scattering gold coins among them, and in the scramble which follows *Thaïs* and *Athanael* make their escape.

ACT III
SCENE I—*A Desert Oasis*

In Act III the pair are seen on their way to a convent. *Thaïs* is almost exhausted with fatigue, and *Athanael* tenderly supports her. *Saint Albine* and the *White Sisters* come to meet

them, and the monk delivers *Thaïs* over to them to remain with them till the end of life. *Thaïs* is happy with a great spiritual peace, but *Athanael*, who has grown to love her with an earthly love, is troubled at the thought of parting with her forever.

SCENE II—*The Cenobites' Camp*

Athanael, returned to his retreat, no longer finds there the peace of former days, and endures mental torture, continually thinking of *Thaïs*. He has a vision in which she appears to him first as the courtesan and then as a nun dying in the convent. Awakening in terror, he rushes out in the darkness and makes his way again to the retreat of *Thaïs*.

SCENE III—*The Convent of the White Sisters*

Athanael arrives, finds *Thaïs* ill, and in a frenzy of love implores her to return to the earthly life, but *Thaïs* has a vision of heavenly bliss and is deaf to his entreaties, dying with a glow of happiness on her face, while *Athanael* falls to the ground in despair.

No opera of Mr. Hammerstein's producing made such a deep impression on opera-goers as did Massenet's wonderful and mystic work, although its beauties were almost intangible and hard to realize without many hearings and

MAIRET THAIS AND ATHANAEL—ACT II

MAIRET   THE DEATH OF THAIS—ACT IV

an intimate acquaintance with the text. The lovely *Meditation,* however, always made an instant impression on every hearer and received enthusiastic approval, being played as an intermezzo between the scenes of the opera. But *Thaïs* audiences heard no such renderings of this intermezzo as have been given here by Powell, Elman and Kreisler. Two other fine records by Pilzer and Rattay, in the popular double-faced class, are also offered. Mr. Ruffo gives notable renditions of two of the best airs. The great air from Act I, in which *Athanael* tells the Cenobites of his vision of life in the wicked city, is sung by Mr. Whitehill with a noble quality of voice and much dramatic force. A very fine record of the *D'acqua aspergimi,* the duet between *Thaïs* and *Athanael* in Act III, by Janni and Battistini, is also presented.

THAÏS RECORDS

Voilà donc la terrible cité (That Awful City I Behold)
By Clarence Whitehill, Baritone   (*In French*)   74364   12-inch, $1.50

Aime fanciullo ancora (Whilst Yet a Simple Youth)
By Titta Ruffo, Baritone   (*In Italian*)   87137   10-inch, $2.00

Ecco la terrible città (That AwfulCity I Behold)
By Titta Ruffo, Baritone   (*In Italian*)   87143   10-inch, $2.00

D'acqua aspergimi (With Holy Water Anoint Me)
By Mme. Janni, Soprano,
and Mattia Battistini, Baritone
(*In Italian*)   88353   12-inch, $3.00

Meditation (Intermezzo Religieuse)
By Maud Powell, Violinist
     74135   12-inch, $1.50
By Fritz Kreisler, Violinist
     74182   12-inch,   1.50
By Mischa Elman, Violinist
     74341   12-inch,   1.50

Meditation (*Intermezzo Religieuse*)
By Howard Rattay, Violinist   35147   12-inch, $1.25
Lohengrin Selection (*Wagner*)
By Pryor's Band

Meditation (*Intermezzo Religieuse*)
By Maximilian Pilzer, Violinist   35306   12-inch,   1.25
Humoresque (*Dvorak*)
By Maximilian Pilzer, Violinist

MAIRET

DELMAS AS ATHANAEL

IMPERIAL OPERA, VIENNA

ROYAL OPERA HOUSE, BERLIN

FAMOUS OPERA HOUSES OF EUROPE

THE TE DEUM—ACT I

(Italian)

TOSCA

(*Toss'-kah*)

OPERA IN THREE ACTS

Text by Illica and Giacosa after Sardou's drama. Music by Giacomo Puccini. First produced at the Constanzi Theatre, Rome, January 14, 1900. First London production at Covent Garden, July 12, 1900. Given in Constantinople, September 8, 1900; Madrid, December 15, 1900. During 1901, brought out in Odessa, January 1st; Lisbon, January 29th; Santiago, July 29th; Cairo, November 26th. First in Germany at Dresden, October 21, 1902; in France, at Paris, October 13, 1903 (in French), and October 31, 1904, in Italian. Given at Budapest, May 10, 1906; Berlin, January, 1907; Vienna, October 26, 1909. First American production at Buenos Aires, June 16, 1900; in the United States, February 4, 1901, at the Metropolitan, the cast including Ternina, Cremonini, Scotti and Gilibert. Also produced in English by Henry W. Savage. The opera has become a fixture in the American opera repertoire.

Characters

FLORIA TOSCA, (*Floh'-ree-ah Toss'-kah*) a celebrated singer..............Soprano
MARIO CAVARADOSSI, (*Mah'-ree-oh Cav-a-rah-doss'-ee*) a painter............Tenor
BARON SCARPIA, (*Scar'-pee-ch*) chief of the police ....Baritone
CESARE ANGELOTTI, (*See-zahr'-ay Ahn-jel-lot'-tee*) ....Bass
A SACRISTAN...Baritone
SPOLETTA, (*Spo-let'-tah*) a police agent.................................Tenor
SCIARRONE, a gendarme..Bass
A JAILOR..Bass

Judge, Cardinal, Officer, Sergeant, Soldiers, Police Agents, Ladies, Nobles, Citizens.

Scene and Period: Rome, June, 1800.

493

The Story

Tosca is Puccini's fifth opera, and by far the most popular, next to Mme. Butterfly, which probably holds first place in the affections of opera-goers. The opera is a remarkable example of Puccini's skill in adjusting both instrumental and voice effects to the sense of the story, interpreting both the characters and the situations.

The plot is gloomy and intensely tragic, following closely the Sardou melodrama, but is relieved somewhat by the beauty of the musical setting, which confirmed Puccini's place in the first rank of modern operatic composers. The three acts of the opera are crowded with sensational events and highly dramatic situations.

The work has neither introduction nor overture. The first scene occurs in the church of *San Andrea*, where the painter, *Mario Cavaradossi*, is at work on the mural decorations. Here he has been accustomed to meet his fiancée, the beautiful *Floria Tosca*, a singer. While awaiting her, he contemplates the Magdalene he is at work on, the face being that of the unknown beauty who had frequently prayed at the altar.

Suddenly a political refugee, *Angelotti*, who has just escaped from the castle, appears, recognizes his friend *Cavaradossi*, and asks his assistance. The painter gives him food and sends him to his (*Cavaradossi's*) villa, just as *Tosca* arrives.

FARRAR AS TOSCA

Her lover's confused manner arouses her curiosity, and when she sees the likeness on the easel, she is jealous. He soothes her, and after her departure hurries out to guide *Angelotti*, a cannon shot from the castle meanwhile announcing the escape of the fugitive.

Scarpia and his police enter in search of the prisoner, who has been traced to the church. *Cavaradossi* is suspected as an accomplice, and *Scarpia*, who is secretly in love with *Tosca*, plans his ruin, with a view to removing from his path a dangerous rival.

In the second act *Scarpia*, putting into execution his schemes, orders *Mario's* arrest, and when the painter is brought in, sends for *Tosca* and contrives that she shall hear the cries of her lover as he is being tortured to induce him to reveal *Angelotti's* hiding place. Unable to endure *Mario's* agony, she tells *Scarpia* where the refugee is concealed. *Mario* is sent to prison, and *Scarpia* tells *Tosca* that unless she looks with favor on him, her lover shall die within an hour. To save his life she consents, but demands that they be allowed to depart in safety the next day. A mock execution is planned by *Scarpia*, who writes out a pass for the lovers. As he gives it to *Tosca*, she stabs him and runs to *Mario* with the release.

In Act III the mock execution takes place as planned, but through *Scarpia's* treachery, it proves to be a real one, and *Mario* is killed. *Tosca* afterwards throws herself from the castle parapet as they attempt to arrest her for *Scarpia's* murder.

COPY'T DUPONT

CARUSO AS MARIO—ACT I

ACT I

SCENE—*Interior of the Church of St. Andrea*

Mario Cavaradossi, the painter, enters the church, where he has been at work on a Madonna. As he uncovers the portrait, the Sacristan, who is assisting *Mario,* is surprised to discover in the face of the painting the unknown beauty whom he had noticed of late in the church. *Mario* smilingly confesses that while she had prayed he had stolen her likeness for his Madonna. Then taking out a miniature of his betrothed, *Tosca,* he sings a lovely air in which he compares her dark beauty with the fair tresses and blue eyes of the unknown worshipper, calling it "a strange but harmonious contrast."

LE THÉÂTRE   TOSCA AND MARIO IN THE CHURCH—ACT I

Recondita armonia (Strange Harmony)

By Enrico Caruso,
Tenor (*In Italian*)
87043 10-inch, $2.00
By Giovanni Martinelli,
Tenor (*In Italian*)
64420 10-inch, 1.00

His musings are interrupted by the hurried entrance of a man in prison garb, panting with fear and fatigue, whom *Mario* recognizes as an old friend, *Angelotti,* a political prisoner. *Mario,* in response to his friend's appeal for assistance, hastily closes the outer door, and conceals *Angelotti* in the chapel, just as *Tosca's* voice is heard impatiently demanding admittance.

He admits her, but is anxious and ill at ease, fearing to intrust even *Tosca* with so dangerous a secret, but she notices his preoccupation and is somewhat piqued because he is not as attentive as usual. She is at first jealous and asks him if he is thinking of another woman; but soon repents, and in the charming love scene which follows endeavors to smooth his brow by planning an excursion for the morrow.

She sings of the delights of the proposed visit to the villa, and the romantic forest where they will wander and forget the cares and troubles of their professional life.

He listens but seems absent-minded, and she continues her recital of the joys of their secluded little retreat among the hills. *Mario* says she is an enchantress, and in this duet they exchange anew their vows of love.

Non la sospiri la nostra casetta (Our Cottage Secluded)

By Ruszcowska, Soprano; Cunego, Tenor
(*In Italian*) **88272 12-inch, $3.00**

Tosca now perceives the Madonna and recognizes the face as that of the *Attavanti,* sister of *Angelotti.* Her jealousy revives, and she declares that *Mario* has fallen in love

COPY'T DUPONT

EAMES AS TOSCA

with the blue eyes. Beginning another duet, he swears that none but *Tosca's* eyes are beautiful to him.

Mario promises to meet her at the stage door that evening, and she bids her lover a tender farewell and departs.

The painter hurries to the chapel and bids *Angelotti* escape, showing him the path to the villa, where he will be safe. A cannon shot from the fortress tells that the escape of the prisoner has been discovered.

He is no sooner gone than the Sacristan and choir enter, followed soon after by *Scarpia* and his police, who have traced *Angelotti* to the church. The *Attavanti's* fan and *Mario's* empty basket are found in the chapel, and when the Sacristan says it should contain the painter's lunch, *Scarpia* suspects *Mario* of aiding the prisoner.

Tosca now returns, still doubting her lover, and *Scarpia*, divining the state of affairs, decides to add fuel to the flame of jealousy. He approaches her respectfully and sings his first air, *Divine Tosca*.

COPY'T DUPONT

MARTIN AS MARIO—ACT I

Tosca Divina (Divine Tosca!)
By Gustav Berl-Resky, Baritone
(*In Italian*) *16745 10-inch, $0.75

He praises her noble character and devout habits. She is inattentive and scarcely hears him, until he insinuatingly says that she is not like other women who come here to meet their lovers. She asks him what he means and *Scarpia* shows her the fan which he had found in the church. *Tosca* is now convinced that *Mario* has been deceiving her, and in a jealous rage she leaves the church, weeping.

Te Deum
By Pasquale Amato, Baritone, and Metropolitan
Opera Chorus (*In Italian*) 88489 12-inch, $3.00
By Giuseppe Maggi, Bass, and La Scala Chorus
(*In Italian*) *55008 12-inch, 1.50

The act closes with a *Te Deum*, sung in celebration of the defeat of Bonaparte, and the scene at the fall of the curtain is a most impressive one, the solemn strains of the service sounding through the church, while *Scarpia* kneels, apparently in reverence, but secretly plotting his diabolical crimes.

ACT II
SCENE—*A Room in Scarpia's Apartments in the Farnese Palace*

When the curtain rises *Scarpia* is shown at his supper, restless and agitated, awaiting the report of his police, who have been sent to arrest *Mario* and *Angelotti*. Hearing *Tosca's* voice in the apartments of the Queen below, where she is singing at a *soiree*, he sends her a note saying he has news of her lover. He is certain she will come for *Mario's* sake, and sure that his plans will succeed. He then sings his celebrated soliloquy. *Scarpia* loves such a conquest as this—no tender vows in the moonlight for him! He prefers taking what he desires by force, then when wearied he is ready for further conquest. This, in short, is his creed—God has created divers wines and many types of beauty —he prefers to enjoy as many of them as possible!

COPY'T MISHKIN

SAMMARCO AS SCARPIA

Mario is brought in by the police, who report that *Angelotti* cannot be found. *Scarpia* is furious, and tries to force *Mario* to reveal the hiding place of

---

* *Double-Faced Record—See page 501.*

PHOTO TESTA

THE TORTURE—ACT II

the fugitive; but he refuses to speak, and is ordered into the torture chamber adjoining. *Tosca* comes in answer to *Scarpia's* summons and is told that *Mario* is being tortured into a confession. Unable to bear the sound of his groans, she reveals the hiding place of *Angelotti*. *Scarpia*, in triumph, orders the torture to cease, but sends *Mario* to prison, telling him he must die. *Tosca* tries to go with him but is forced to remain.

Then begins the great scene of the opera, which *Scarpia* begins by offering to save *Mario's* life. She scornfully asks him his price, and he proposes that *Tosca* shall accept his attentions in order to save her lover's life. He then sings his famous *Cantabile*.

Cantabile Scarpia (Scarpia's Air) (Venal, My Enemies Call Me)
By Antonio Scotti, Baritone 88122 12-inch, $3.00

Gia mi struggea (You Have Scorned Me)
(Last Part of Cantabile)
By Ernesto Badini (*In Italian*) 45016 10-in., $1.00

He tells her that he has long loved her and had sworn to possess her. She scorns him, but when he tells her that *Mario* shall die in an hour and exults in his power, her spirit is broken, and weeping for shame, she sings that loveliest and most pathetic of airs, *Vissi d'arte*.

PHOTO GARO

SCOTTI AS SCARPIA

Vissi d'arte e d'amor (Love and Music)

By Nellie Melba, Soprano	(*In Italian*)	88075	12-inch, $3.00
By Geraldine Farrar, Soprano	(*In Italian*)	88192	12-inch, 3.00
By Emma Eames, Soprano	(*In Italian*)	88010	12-inch, 3.00
By Emmy Destinn, Soprano	(*In Italian*)	88487	12-inch, 3.00
By Lucille Marcell, Soprano	(*In Italian*)	76018	12-inch, 2.00
By Frances Alda, Soprano	(*In Italian*)	74400	12-inch, 1.50
By Maria Bronzoni, Soprano	(*In Italian*)	45017	10-inch, 1.00

THE MURDER OF SCARPIA—ACT II

One of the most interesting comparisons to be found in the Victor's opera list is in a hearing of these seven renditions, by seven famous *Toscas*—Melba, the Australian; Farrar and Eames, the Americans; Destinn, the Bohemian; Alda, the New Zealander; Marcell, the Frenchwoman; and Bronzoni, the Italian, the latter record being doubled with *Mario's* 3d Act air.

This highly impassioned number is given its full dramatic value by Mme. Melba, whose performance of the ill-fated *Floria Tosca* is always an impressive one. Farrar, in her rendition, delivers this touching appeal of the unfortunate *Tosca* with much pathos and simplicity. It is probably the most perfect and beautiful of all the Farrar records. The air is also a fine test of Mme. Eames' dramatic ability, and this scene is one in which she has made one of her greatest triumphs.

The unhappy woman asks what she has done that Heaven should forsake her. *Scarpia,* who is watching her intently, calls her attention to the sound of drums, summoning the escort for the condemned prisoners, and demands her answer. She yields, bowing her head for shame. *Scarpia* is overjoyed, and when she insists that *Mario* shall be set free he consents, but says a mock execution is necessary.

It is agreed that after this pretended execution, *Mario* shall have his liberty, but *Tosca* demands a safe escape from the country for them both. While *Scarpia* is writing the document, *Tosca* contrives to secure the dagger from the table, and as *Scarpia* approaches to give it to her and then take her in his arms, she stabs him, crying that thus she gives him

TOSCA AND THE DAGGER—ACT II

DESTINN AS TOSCA

the kiss he desired. In a prolonged and highly dramatic scene she takes the paper from *Scarpia's* dead fingers, then washes her hands in a bowl on the table, places the two candles at the dead man's head and the cross on his bosom, then goes out, turning for a last look at the lifeless body as the curtain falls.

ACT III

(*A terrace of San Angelo Castle, outside the prison cell of Cavaradossi. View of Rome by night*)

The music of the opening act is most effective, with its accompaniment of pealing church bells. This entire prelude is given by an Italian orchestra under the direction of Sabaino, doubled with the Te Deum of Act I, by Giuseppi Maggi, Bass, and the Chorus of La Scala, Milan.

MARTINELLI AS MARIO

MARIO AND TOSCA—ACT III

Prelude

By La Scala Orchestra
*55008   12-inch, $1.50

Mario is brought out from his cell, is shown the official death warrant, and told he has but one hour to live. He asks permission to write a note to *Tosca,* and is given paper and pen. He begins to write, but engrossed with memories of the past, he pauses and sings passionately of his loved one, who he expects never to see again.

E lucevan le stelle (The Stars Were Shining)

By Enrico Caruso, Tenor
    (*In Italian*) 87044 10-inch, $2.00
By Riccardo Martin, Tenor
    (*In Italian*) 87050 10-inch, 2.00
By Franco de Gregorio, Tenor
    (*In Italian*) *45017 10-inch, 1.00
By Giovanni Martinelli
    Tenor (*In Italian*)
            64393 10-inch, 1.00
By Paul Althouse, Tenor
    (*In Italian*) *45055 10-inch, 1.00

Double-Faced Record—See page 501.

CLICHÉ BOYER

THE EXECUTION—ACT III

Mario at first recalls their former meetings on starlight nights in quiet gardens; then, feeling the bitter regret of loss of life and all that he holds dear, the voice rises in passages of tragical import and power as the air proceeds. The regret, the grief and the hopelessness of the situation are depicted with intense pathos, the closing portion of the air effectively expressing the extremity of passionate grief.

Tosca now enters, and joyfully telling *Mario* he is to be free, shows him the safe conduct, telling him how she had killed *Scarpia*. He gazes at her with compassion and regrets that these hands—such tender and beautiful hands—should be compelled to foul themselves with a scoundrel's blood. She then explains that a mock execution has been arranged, and instructs him to fall down when the volley is fired, and when the soldiers are gone they are to escape together.

In a beautiful duet, recorded here in two parts, they rejoice in their hopes for the future.

Amaro sol per te m'era il morire (The Bitterness of Death)

By Elena Ruszcowska, Soprano, and Egidio Cunego, Tenor
(*In Italian*) 88274 12-inch, $3.00

Trionfa di nuova speme (A New World)

By Elena Ruszcowski and Egidio Cunego (*In Italian*) 87069 10-inch, $2.00

The squad of soldiers now enter and the pretended execution takes place as planned; the shots are fired and *Mario* falls as if dead. *Tosca* waits till the firing party is gone, whispering to her lover not to get up until the footsteps have died away. "Now, *Mario*, all is safe," she cries, but is astounded that he does not obey her. She rushes to him, only to find that *Scarpia* had added another piece of treachery to his long list, having secretly ordered *Mario* to be killed. She throws herself on his body in an agony of grief.

Spoletta and soldiers now come running in and announce the murder of *Scarpia*; but when they attempt to arrest *Tosca* she leaps from the castle wall and is killed,

THE DEATH OF MARIO—ACT III

DOUBLE-FACED AND MISCELLANEOUS TOSCA RECORDS

{ Te Deum—Finale to Act I	Maggi and Chorus	(In Italian) }	55008	12-inch,	$1.50
{ Preludio—Atto III	By Italian Orchestra				
{ Già mi struggea	By Ernesto Badini, Baritone	(In Italian) }	45016	10-inch,	1.00
{ Manon Lescaut—Donna non vidi mai	Egidio Cunego	(In Italian)			
{ Vissi d'arte e d'amor	Maria Bronzoni, Soprano	(In Italian) }	45017	10-inch,	1.00
{ E lucevan le stelle	By De Gregorio, Tenor	(In Italian)			
{ E lucevan le stelle	By Paul Althouse, Tenor	(In Italian) }	45055	10-inch,	1.00
{ Pagliacci—Vesti la giubba	By Paul Althouse, Tenor	(In Italian)			
{ Tosca—Tosca Divina	By Berl-Resky, Baritone	(In Italian) }	16745	10-inch,	.75
{ Preghiera—Alla mente confusa (Tosti)	Berl-Resky	(In Italian)			

PHOTO BOYER

TOSCA'S SUICIDE—ACT III

FARRAR AS VIOLETTA—ACT III

(Italian)

LA TRAVIATA

(Lah Trah-veeah'-tah)

OPERA IN THREE ACTS

Text by Piave, founded on Dumas' "Lady of the Camelias," but the period is changed to the time of Louis XIV. Score by Giuseppe Verdi. First presented in Venice, March 6, 1853; London, May 24, 1856; Paris, in French, December 6, 1856; in Italian, October 27, 1864. First American production December 3, 1856, with Brignoli and La Grange. Recent productions at the Metropolitan with Caruso, Melba, Tetrazzini, Lipkowska, McCormack and Sammarco. Many notable productions in America in recent years, among the most recent being the Metropolitan production of 1905, for Caruso and Sembrich; that of 1908 (début of Amato) and 1909 (début of Lipkowska); the Hammerstein revivals for Tetrazzini and Melba; and the recent Metropolitan production with Hempel.

Characters of the Opera

VIOLETTA VALERY, a courtesan.................................Soprano
FLORA, friend of Violetta..................................Mezzo-Soprano
ANNINA, confidante of Violetta....................................Soprano
ALFREDO GERMONT, lover of Violetta............................Tenor
GIORGIO GERMONT, his father....................................Baritone
GASTONE, Viscount of Letorieres.................................Tenor
BARON DOUPHOL, a rival of Alfred..............................Baritone
DOCTOR GRENVIL, a physician....................................Bass
GIUSEPPE, servant to Violetta....................................Tenor

Chorus of Ladies and Gentlemen, friends of Violetta and Flora.
Mute Personages: Matadors, Picadors, Gypsies, Servants, Masks, etc.

Scene and Period: Paris and environs, about the year 1700.

Verdi's La Traviata is based upon a well-known play by Alexandre Dumas, *La Dame aux camelias*, familiar in its dramatic form as *Camille*. It is one of the most beautiful works of its class, and is full of lovely melodies; while the story of the unfortunate *Violetta* has caused many tears to be shed by sympathetic listeners.

FRANCESCO PÍAVE
(1810-1876)
LIBRETTIST OF
TRAVIATA

VERDI AT THE TIME OF THE
FIRST TRAVIATA PRO-
DUCTION

The opera met with but indifferent success at its first production. Several ludicrous incidents aroused the laughter of the audience, the climax being reached when the *Violetta* (Mme. Donatelli), who happened to be very stout, declaimed in feeble accents that she was dying of consumption! This was too much for the Venetian sense of humor, and the house exploded with mirth, utterly spoiling the final scene.

The opera was then revised, eighteenth century costumes and settings being substituted for the modern ones first used; and the new version was produced in various cities with success, the London season being particularly brilliant.

The plot, being quite familiar, will be but briefly sketched here. *Violetta*, a courtesan of Paris, is holding a brilliant revel in her home. Among the guests is a young man from Provence, *Alfred*, who is in love with *Violetta*, and after much persuasion, the spoiled beauty agrees to leave her gay life and retire with him to an humble apartment near Paris. After a few brief months of happiness, the lovers are discovered by *Alfred's* father, who pleads with *Violetta* to release his son from his promises. She yields for his sake, and resumes her former life in Paris. *Alfred*, not knowing the real cause of her desertion, seeks her out and publicly insults her. Too late he discovers the sacrifice *Violetta* has made, and when he returns, full of remorse, he finds her dying of consumption, and she expires in his arms.

Prelude to Act I

By La Scala Orchestra	*68027	12-inch, $1.25
By Vessella's Italian Band	*17729	10-inch, .75

The prelude, one of the loveliest bits in the opera, is played in fine style by the famous orchestra of La Scala, and by Vessella's Italian Band.

ACT I

SCENE—*Drawing-room in the House of Violetta*

A gay revel is in progress at the house of *Violetta*, and the act opens with a lively chorus, followed by a rousing drinking song, given by *Alfred*, in which *Violetta* joins.

Libiam nei lieti calici   (A Bumper We'll Drain)

By Alma Gluck, Soprano; Enrico Caruso, Tenor; and
Metropolitan Opera Chorus   (*In Italian*) 87511 10-inch, $3.00

By Amelia Rizzini, Soprano; Emilio Perea, Tenor; and
La Scala Chorus   (*In Italian*) *62415 10-inch, .75

ALFRED:
A bumper we'll drain from the wine-cup flowing,
That fresh charms to beauty is lending,
O'er fleeting moments, so quickly ending,
Gay pleasure alone should reign.

VIOLETTA:
Enjoy the hour, for rapidly
The joys of life are flying—
Like summer flow'rets dying—
Improve them while we may!
The present with fervor invites us.
Its flattering call obey.

CHORUS:
Enjoy then the wine-cup with songs of pleasure
That make night so cheerful and smiling,
In this charming paradise, beguiling,
That scarcely we heed the day.

Double-Faced Record—See page 510.

MELBA

The dance commences, and all go into the ballroom except *Violetta* and *Alfred*, who remain for a charming love scene. In a beautiful duet the lovers speak of their first meeting.

Un di felice (Rapturous Moment)

By Marie A. Michailowa, Soprano, and A. M. Davidow,
Tenor   (*In Russian*)   61138   10-inch, $1.00
By Emma Trentini, Soprano, and Gino Martinez-Patti,
Tenor   (*In Italian*)   *62067   10-inch,   .75

Alfred now bids her a tender farewell and takes his departure, and *Violetta* sings her great air, one of the most brilliant of all colorature numbers.

{ Ah, fors' è lui (The One of Whom I Dreamed)
{ Sempre libera (The Round of Pleasure)

By Luisa Tetrazzini, Soprano	(*In Italian*)	88293	12-inch,	$3.00
By Marcella Sembrich, Soprano	(*In Italian*)	88018	12-inch,	3.00
By Nellie Melba, Soprano	(*In Italian*)	88064	12-inch,	3.00
By Frieda Hempel, Soprano	(*In Italian*)	88471	12-inch,	3.00
By Lucy Marsh, Soprano	(*In Italian*)	70094	12-inch,	1.25
By Giuseppina Huguet, Soprano (Part I)	(*In Italian*)	*62084	10-inch,	.75
By Giuseppina Huguet, Soprano, and Pietro Lara, Tenor (Part II)	(*In Italian*)	*62084	10-inch,	.75

The aria occurs at the close of the act. *Violetta*, wonderstruck at finding herself the object of a pure love, begins the soliloquy, *E strano*, saying:

How wondrous!
His words deep within my heart are graven!
No love of mortal yet hath moved me.

Shall I dare disdain it,
And choose the empty follies that now surround me?

She then sings the plaintive air, *Ah, fors' è lui*, and gives herself up to the spell of awakening love:

VIOLETTA:
  Ah, was it he my heart foretold, when in the throng of pleasure,
  Oft have I joy'd to shadow forth one whom alone I'd treasure.
  He who with watchful tenderness guarded my waning powers,
  Strewing my way with flowers,
  Waking my heart to love!
  Ah, now I feel that 'tis love and love alone,
  Sole breath of all in the life, the life universal,
  Mysterious power, guiding the fate of mortals,
  Sorrow and sweetness of this poor earth.

The animated last movement follows, as the unhappy woman shakes off the illusion and once more vows to devote her life to pleasure.

  What folly! what folly!
  For me there's no returning!
  In ev'ry fierce and wild delight.
  I'll steep my sense and die!
  I'll fulfill the round of pleasure,
  Joying, toying from flower to flower,
  I will drain a brimming measure from the cup of rosy joy.
  Never weary, each dawning morrow
  Flies to bear me some new rapture
  Ever fresh delights I'll borrow,
  I will banish all annoy!

PHOTO CLERKE, LONDON

MELBA AS VIOLETTA

Victor customers have no fewer than seven renditions of this great air at their command and are likely to be embarrassed in their attempts to choose between them.

Melba's singing of this air is marked not only by great brilliancy, but by dramatic fervor, and she makes a marked contrast between the sadness of the prelude and the forced gayety of the finale. Both portions of the aria (formerly issued in two parts) now are included in one record.

Hempel's singing of this dazzling number is given with such purity and mellowness of voice, and such a brilliancy of vocalization that we can but wonder at the perfection of art which makes such a record possible.

Mme. Tetrazzini chose this opera for her first appearance both in London and New York, and the choice was an admirable one, as Verdi's work exhibits all the soprano's fine qualities—not only her wonderful coloratura but the warmth and color which she possesses in a high degree. Many operatic sopranos regard the part of *Violetta* merely as a background for a vocal display. Tetrazzini, on the other hand, while not neglecting the opportunities for coloratura, brings to the part a human tenderness and a pathos which are most affecting. Her rendering of this familiar *Ah, fors' è lui* is a most musical one, with its astonishing feats of execution; and the ease with which she trills an E *in alt* can only be described as amazing.

Mme. Sembrich in her turn fully realizes the composer's ideal in the presentation of this florid and ornamental air, and seldom has a more satisfying rendition been heard.

Other fine renderings are provided by Miss Marsh and Mme. Huguet.

ACT II

SCENE—*Interior of a Country House near Paris*

Alfred enters and soliloquizes upon his new-found happiness.

ALFRED: Three months have already flown
Since my belov'd Violetta
Left for me her riches and admirers.
Yet now contented in this retreat, so quiet,
She forgets all for me.

He then sings his *Dei miei bollenti*, a lovely air, in which he speaks of his wild youth, and the peace and happiness which have come to him through his love for *Violetta*.

Dei miei bollenti spiriti (Wild My Dream)

By Aristodemo Giorgini
(*In Italian*)   76011   12-inch, $2.00
By Herman Jadlowker
(*In Italian*)   76024   12-inch,   2.00
By Alberto Amadi, Tenor
(*In Italian*) *63314   10-inch,   .75

ALFRED: Fever'd and wild my dream of youth,
No star on high to guide me,
She shone on me with ray benign,
And trouble fled away!
When low she whisper'd: "Live for me, on
earth I love but thee,"
Ah, since that bright, that blessed day,
In Heaven, 'mid joys celestial,
In Heaven I seem to be!

COPY'T MISHKIN

CONSTANTINO AS ALFRED—
ACT II, SCENE I

Alfred learns from *Violetta's* faithful maid that she has been obliged to sell her jewels for their support. He is much ashamed and leaves for Paris to secure some money.

Violetta returns and is surprised at *Alfred's* sudden departure. A visitor is announced, who proves to be *Germont*, the father of *Alfred*. He has been greatly distressed at his son's entanglement, and comes to beg *Violetta* to release the young man from his promises. She is much moved, and her bearing makes a favorable impression on *Germont*, especially when he learns that she has sold her property for *Alfred's* sake.

Pura siccome un angelo (Pure as an Angel)

By Battaglioli and Badini   (*In Italian*) *45001   10-inch, $1.00
By Renzo Minolfi, Baritone   (*In Italian*) *62415   10-inch,   .75

*Double-Faced Record—See page 510.

Non sapete (Ah, You Know Not)

By Giulia Battaglioli, Soprano, and Ernesto Badini, Baritone

(*In Italian*) *45028 10-inch, $1.00

In this air *Germont* pleads for his own daughter, whose engagement to a youth of Provence will be broken if *Alfred* does not return home. *Violetta* at first refuses, saying that her love for *Alfred* is above all other considerations, but when *Germont* says:

> Be to my home and lov'd ones
> Our angel, good, consoling.
> Violetta, oh, consider well
> While yet there may be time.
> 'Tis Heav'n itself that bids me speak,
> These words in faith sublime!

she finally yields, agreeing to leave *Alfred* forever, and they sing a melodious duet:

Dite alla giovine (Say to Thy Daughter)

By Maria Galvany and Titta Ruffo   (*In Italian*) 92503 12-inch, $4.00
By Frieda Hempel, Soprano, and Pasquale Amato, Baritone

(*In Italian*) 89079 12-inch, 4.00

VIOLETTA:
Say to this child of thine, young, pure and lovely,
Thou hast a victim found, whose life of sadness
Had but one single ray of rapture and gladness,
Which she will yield to her, then gladly die.

GERMONT:
Weep on, thou hapless one,
Weep on; I witness thy trial
In what I ask of thy self-denial.
Bear up, thou noble heart, triumph is nigh.

Imponte (Now Command Me)

By Frieda Hempel, Soprano, and Pasquale Amato, Baritone

(*In Italian*) 89081 12-inch, $4.00

This is a continuation of the scene between *Violetta* and *Germont*. *Violetta* has decided to sacrifice herself for the sake of *Alfred's* future, and says to *Germont* courageously:

VIOLETTA:
Now, command me—but how shall I proceed?

GERMONT:
Say you do not love him.

VIOLETTA:
He'll not believe me.

GERMONT:
Well, leave him.

VIOLETTA:
He will follow.

GERMONT (*puzzled*):
Well, then—

VIOLETTA (*suddenly thinking of a plan*):
Embrace me, embrace me as thine own child—
'Twill give me strength. (*They embrace.*)
(*Firmly.*)
He soon shall be restored, though broken-hearted.
Do you wait in the garden and console him.
(*She points to the garden and sits down to write.*)

GERMONT:
What will you do, my child?

VIOLETTA:
Nay, ask me not;
I fear you would oppose me!

GERMONT:
Generous woman! How can I e'er repay thee?

VIOLETTA (*turning piteously to Germont*):
I shall die, but my memory
He'll have no cause to curse.
This bitter sacrifice
I make for the sake of my lover,
But ever whilst I live
None else shall have my heart!

GERMONT:
No, generous one, thou must not die,
But live to be rewarded;
For e'en by Heaven thy deeds will be
As noble ones regarded.
The sacrifice is great, indeed,
Of thy most loving heart;
Thou'st done a noble deed,
And acted well thy part.

VIOLETTA:
Ah! some one comes! Go now.

GERMONT:
How shall I ever repay you?

VIOLETTA:
Perhaps I no more may see thee.

GERMONT:
May'st thou be happy! Farewell!
(*Germont goes out.*)

Beautiful, indeed, is the singing of these two great artists in the duet, one of the most effective that Verdi has written.

---

* *Double-Faced Record—See page 510.*

MME. GUIONIE AS VIOLETTA

Germont expresses his gratitude, embraces the weeping *Violetta* and departs, while the unhappy woman writes to *Alfred* of her decision and returns to Paris.

When the young man returns he is driven to despair by *Violetta's* note, and repulses his father, who pleads with him to return. *Germont* then sings his most beautiful number, the *Di Provenza*.

Di Provenza il mar (Thy Home in Fair Provence)

By G. Mario Sammarco, Baritone
          (*In Italian*)   88314   12-inch, $3.00
By Pasquale Amato, Baritone
          (*In Italian*)   88474   12-inch, 3.00
By Ernesto Badini, Baritone
          (*In Italian*) *45001   10-inch, 1.00

In this touching appeal he asks his son to return to his home in Provence and to his father's heart.

GERMONT:
From fair Provence's soil and sea,
Who hath won thy heart away?
From thy native sunny clime,
What strange fate caus'd thee to stray?
Oh, remember in thy woe

All the joy that waits for thee,
All the peace thy heart would know,
Only there, still found may be.
Ah, thy father old and worn,
What he felt thou ne'er canst know,
In thine absence, so forlorn

Seem'd his home, with grief and woe.
But I find thee now again,
If my hope doth not mislead,
If yet honor doth remain
With its voice not mute or dead,
Heav'n sends me aid!

Alfred refuses to yield to his father's plea, and departs for Paris in search of *Violetta*.

SCENE II—*A Richly Furnished Salon in Flora's Palace. On the Right a Gaming Table*

As the curtain rises *Flora* and her friends are discussing the separation of the lovers and *Flora* says she expects *Violetta* will soon arrive with the *Baron*. *Alfred* enters, and remarking with assumed indifference that he knows nothing of *Violetta's* whereabouts, begins to gamble and wins heavily.

The *Baron* appears, accompanied by *Violetta,* who is agitated at the sight of *Alfred,* but he pretends not to see her and challenges the *Baron* to a game, again winning large amounts. Supper is announced and all leave the room except *Violetta* and *Alfred,* who linger behind. He charges her with her falseness, and, in furtherance of the promise made to *Germont,* she pretends to him that she loves the *Baron. Alfred* then loses all control over himself, and throwing open the doors, he calls to the guests to re-enter.

Questa donna conoscete (Know Ye All This Woman?)

By Alberto Amadi, Tenor   (*In Italian*) *63314   10-inch, $0.75

Pointing to *Violetta, Alfred* cries wildly:

ALFRED:
All she possess'd, this woman here,
Hath for my love expended.
I, blindly, basely, wretchedly,
This to accept, condescended.

But there is time to purge me yet
From stains that shame, confound me.
Bear witness all around me
That here I pay the debt!

and completes the insult by throwing at her feet the money he had just won.

At this moment *Alfred's* father, *Germont,* enters, and is horrified at the scene which confronts him. Then follows the splendid finale, one of the greatest of Verdi's concerted numbers.

Alfredo, di questo core (Alfred, Thou Knowest Not)

By Giuseppina Huguet, Soprano; G. Pini-Corsi, Tenor; Ernesto Badini,
   Baritone; and Chorus   (*In Italian*) 58392 12-inch, $1.00

Double-Faced Record—See page 510.

CONSTANTINO AS ALFRED—
ACT II, SCENE II

The emotions of the various characters are expressed by the librettist as follows:

GUESTS:
Oh, to what baseness thy passions have led
To wound thus fatally one who has loved thee!

GERMONT:
Of scorn most worthy himself doth render
Who wounds in anger a woman tender!
My son, where is he? No more I see him;
In thee, Alfred, I seek him; but in vain!

ALFRED (aside):
Ah! yes, 'twas shameful! a deed abhorrent!
A jealous fury—love's madd'ning torrent.
But now that fury is all expended,
Remorse and horror to me remain.

BARON:
This shameful insult against this lady
Offends all present; behold me ready
To punish the outrage!

VIOLETTA (reviving):
Ah, lov'd Alfredo, this heart's devotion
Thou canst not fathom yet—its fond emotion!
When, hereafter the truth comes o'er thee
May Heaven in pity then spare thee remorse!
(Germont goes out supporting Alfred, who is
almost in a state of collapse. The fainting
Violetta is led away by her friends, and the
guests begin to disperse as the curtain falls.)

ACT III

(*Violetta's apartment. She is asleep on the couch, while her maid dozes by the fire*)

As the curtain rises the doctor's knock is heard, and *Dr. Grenvil, Violetta's* physician, enters and attends his patient, afterwards telling the maid that she has not long to live. Left alone, *Violetta* reads again a letter she has received from Germont.

"*Thou hast kept thy promise. The duel took place and the Baron was wounded, but is improving. Alfredo is in foreign countries. Your sacrifice has been revealed to him by me, and he will return to you for pardon. Haste to recover; thou deserveth a bright future.*"

Georgio Germont.

"Alas, it is too late," she exclaims, and sings her beautiful and pathetic "Farewell."

Addio del passato (Farewell to the Bright Visions)

By Lucrezia Bori, Soprano	(*In Italian*)	87178	10-inch, $2.00
By Alice Nielsen, Soprano	(*In Italian*)	64068	10-inch, 1.00
By Marie Michailowa, Soprano	(*In Russian*)	61178	10-inch, 1.00

VIOLETTA:
Farewell to the bright visions I once fondly cherish'd,
Already the roses that deck'd me have perish'd;
The love of Alfredo is lost, past regaining,
That cheer'd me when fainting, my spirit sustaining.

Pity the stray one, and send her consolation,
Oh, pardon her transgressions, and send her salvation.
The sorrows and enjoyments of life will soon be over,
The dark tomb in oblivion this mortal form will cover!

Alfred now enters, filled with remorse, and asks forgiveness, which is freely granted; and *Violetta*, forgetting her illness, plans with *Alfred* to leave Paris forever. They sing this melodious duet, "Gay Paris We'll Leave With Gladness."

Parigi o cara (Far from Gay Paris)

By Lucrezia Bori, Soprano, and John McCormack, Tenor	(*In Italian*)	88453	12-inch, $3.00
By Alice Nielsen and Florencio Constantino	(*In Italian*)	74075	12-inch, 1.50
By Amelia Rizzini, Soprano, and Emilio Perea, Tenor	(*In Italian*)	*62067	10-inch, .75

Double-Faced Record—See page 510.

MLLE. VIX AS VIOLETTA IN THE OPÉRA-
COMIQUE PRODUCTION

ALFRED:
Gay Paris, we'll leave with gladness,
Our lives united, fly we from sadness.
Joy shall repay thee for each dark sorrow,
Thy cheek so faded shall bloom again.

VIOLETTA:
Gay Paris, dearest, we'll leave with gladness,
Our lives united, fly we from sadness.
Life, light and breath from thee will I borrow,
O'er coming years, love, bright smiles shall
reign.

At the close of the duet *Violetta's* overtaxed
strength gives way, and she collapses in her lover's
arms. He notices for the first time her paleness,
and is much alarmed, sending the maid to call the
doctor. *Dr. Grenvil* soon enters, accompanied by
Germont, and after an affecting scene, in which
Germont blames himself for all that has occurred,
Violetta expires, and the curtain falls on a sorrowful tableau.

DOUBLE-FACED AND MISCELLANEOUS TRAVIATA RECORDS

Prelude **By La Scala Orchestra** *L'Africana—Marcia Indiana* **By La Scala Orchestra**	68027	12-inch,	$1.25
Traviata Selection **By Pryor's Band** Ball Scene, Act I—"Far From the Busy Throng," Act III—Chorus of Matadors—Drinking Song, Act I *Trovatore Selection* **By Pryor's Band**	35076	12-inch,	1.25
Alfredo, di questo core **(Alfred, Thou Knowest Not!)** **By Huguet, Pini-Corsi and Badini** *Ruy Blas—O dolce volutta* **By Grisi and Lara** *(In Italian)*	68070	12-inch,	1.25
Gems from "Traviata"—Part I **Victor Opera Co.** Chorus, "Drinking Song"—Duet, "The One of Whom I Dreamed" *(Ah, fors' e lui)*—Solo, "Thy Home in Fair Provence" *(Di Provenza)*—Solo, "I'll Fulfill the Round of Pleasure" *(Sempre libera)*—Chorus of Matadors	35433	12-inch,	1.25
Gems from "Traviata"—Part II **Victor Opera Co.** Chorus of Matadors—Duet, "May He be Spared the Anguish" *(Cono sca il Sacrifizio)*—Solo, "Farewell to the Bright Visions" *(Addio)*—Duet, "Far from Gay Paris" *(Parigi o cara)*—Chorus, Finale			
Non sapete **(Ah, You Know Not)** **By Battaglioli and Badini** *Manon—Gavotta* **By Giuseppina Huguet** *(In Italian)*	45028	10-inch,	1.00
Di Provenza il mar **(In Fair Provence)** **By Ernesto Badini** *(In Italian)*	45001	10-inch,	1.00
Pura siccome un angelo **By Battaglioli and Badini** *(In Italian)*			
Ah, fors' è lui **By Giuseppina Huguet** *(In Italian)* Sempre libera **By Huguet and Lara** *(In Italian)*	62084	10-inch,	.75
Un di felice, eterea **By Trentini and Martinez-Patti** Parigi o cara **By Amelia Rizzini, Soprano, and Emilio Perea, Tenor** *(In Italian)*	62067	10-inch,	.75
Traviata—Entr' acte **Orchestre Symphonique** *Colombe, La—Entr' acte (Gounod)* **Orchestre Symphonique**	17661	10-inch,	.75
Prelude **Vessella's Italian Band** *Aida—Prelude* **Vessella's Italian Band**	17729	10-inch,	.75
Pura siccome un angelo **By Renzo Minolfi** *(In Italian)* Libiam nei lieti calici **(A Bumper We'll Drain)** **By Rizzini, Perea and Chorus** *(In Italian)*	62415	10-inch,	.75
Dei miei bollenti spiriti **By Alberto Amadi** *(In Italian)* Questa donna conoscete **By Alberto Amadi** *(In Italian)*	63314	10-inch,	.75

FROM A PANEL BY STASSEN   SCENES FROM TRISTAN

(German)   (English)

TRISTAN UND ISOLDE—TRISTAN AND ISOLDE
(*Tris'-tahn oondt Ees-zol'-deh*)

OPERA IN THREE ACTS

Words and music by Richard Wagner, the plot being derived from an old Celtic poem of the same name, written by Gottfried of Strasburg, who flourished in the thirteenth century—though Wagner has changed the narrative sufficiently to make it his own. *Tristan* is one of the most popular of legendary heroes and has been treated of by numerous writers, among them Tennyson, Matthew Arnold and Swinburne.

Wagner's *Tristan und Isolde* was first presented in Munich, June 10, 1865. First London production June 20, 1882. First American performance in New York, December 1, 1886, with Lehmann, Brandt and Fischer. Produced at the New Orleans Opera December 21, 1895. Some notable American productions occurred in 1895 with Sucher, Alvary, Brema and Fischer; in 1896 with the de Reszkes, Nordica and Brema; in 1901 with Ternina and Van Dyke; and in 1910 with Homer, Fremstad, Knote and Van Rooy, this being Gustav Mahler's American début.

ISOLDE:
  Tristan! Traitor beloved!
TRISTAN:
  Isolde! Woman divine!
      (Tristan and Isolde, Act I)

Characters

TRISTAN, a Cornish knight, nephew of King Mark . . Tenor
KING MARK of Cornwall . . . . Bass
ISOLDE, Princess of Ireland . . . . Soprano
KURVENAL, Tristan's devoted servant . . . . Baritone
MELOT, (*May'-lot*) one of King Mark's courtiers . . . . Tenor
BRANGÄNE, (*Bran-gay'-neh*) Isolde's friend and
    attendant . . . . Soprano
A Shepherd, a Steersman, a Sailor Lad ; Chorus of Sailors,
    Knights, Esquires and Men-at-Arms.

Although completed in 1859, Tristan was not produced
until six years later. Through the strenuous efforts of King
Ludwig II of Bavaria, it was ultimately brought out in
Munich with distinct artistic success—Schnorr, the tenor,
scoring brilliantly in
the rôle of *Tristan*.
Previous to this time,
however, it had been
underlined for per-
formance in Vienna, but
was abandoned after
fifty-seven rehearsals. Both the Prelude and the Love
Death were performed in concerts before the production
of the opera in Munich. The Prelude was played for
the first time at Prague, March 12, 1859, and again at
Leipsic, June 1, 1859. Wagner himself frequently conducted the Prelude and Love Death in the concerts
given by him in 1863.

The opera did not find its way to America until it was
more than twenty years old, but since that time has
grown steadily in popularity.

This great drama of love and hatred, with its wonderful music, is now quite generally admitted to be the
finest of the master's operas. Written at the time of
Wagner's own love affair (with Mathilde Wesendonck),
it is supposed that
he sought to em-
phasize the fact
that love cannot always be bound by conventions.

Tristan, a Cornish knight, has a quarrel with
Morold, an Irish chieftain who had been sent to collect
tribute, and kills him; and after the custom of the
time, sends back his head, which is given to his af-
fianced, an Irish princess, *Isolde*. *Tristan* himself had
received a dangerous wound which fails to heal, and
he resolves to assume the name of *Tantris* and seek the
assistance of *Isolde*, who is famed for her knowledge of
the art of healing. *Isolde*, however, recognizes him by
a notch in his sword, which fits exactly a piece of metal
she had extracted from the head of *Morold*. She plans
to kill him, but falls in love instead, while he merely
sees in her a good wife for his uncle, *King Mark*.

COPY'T DUPONT

GADSKI AS ISOLDE

PHOTO MATZENE

DALMORES AS TRISTAN

Preludio (Prelude)

By La Scala Orchestra 68210 12-inch, $1.25

The first act shows the deck of the ship which is
conveying *Isolde* and *Tristan* to Cornwall, she having
accepted *King Mark*'s proposal, made through his

ISOLDE: "So, this, then, is the end!
Tristan, farewell!" (Tristan and Isolde, Act I)

VAN DYCK AS TRISTAN

nephew. During the voyage, however, the refusal of *Tristan* to see her, the exultation of the sailors over the killing of *Morold* (which freed Cornwall from its subjection to *Isolde's* royal father), and detestation of the loveless marriage she is about to contract, infuriate the Princess, and she resolves to die and drag *Tristan* down to death with her. She tells *Tristan* she is aware of his crime in killing her lover, and demands vengeance. He admits her right to kill him and offers his sword, but she bids her maid, *Brangäne,* prepare two cups of poison from her casket. *Brangäne,* unwilling to see her mistress die, secretly substitutes for the poison a love potion, the effect of which is immediate, and the lovers sink into each other's arms just as the ship approaches the shore and the King arrives to claim his bride.

Act II takes place in the garden outside *Isolde's* chamber. The King has gone on a hunting expedition, but *Brangäne* fears that it is merely a ruse, and thinks the King's courtier, *Melot,* suspects the true state of affairs. *Brangäne* then confesses that she intentionally substituted the philtre for the poisoned cup intended for *Tristan.*

BRAGÄNE:
Fatal folly!
The fell pow'r of that potion!
That I framed
A fraud for once
Thy orders to oppose!

Had I been deaf and blind,
Thy work were then thy death!
But thy distress,
Thy distraction of grief,
My work has contrived them,
I own it!

This confession meets with but faint reproaches from *Isolde,* who gives herself up wholly to the intoxication of the potion, and sings with growing exaltation:

Dein Werk (Thy Act?)
By Johanna Gadski, Soprano

(*In German*)   88165   12-inch, $3.00

ISOLDE:
Thy act?
O foolish girl!
Love's goddess dost thou not know?
The witch whose will the world obeys;
Life and death she holds in her hands,
She waketh hate into love!
The work of death

I took into my own hands;
Love's goddess saw
And gave her good commands.
Planning our fate in her own way.
How she may bend it, how she may end it,
Still hers am I solely;
What she may make me, whereso'er take me
So let me obey her wholly!

ISOLDE GIVING THE SIGNAL, ACT II.   (COLOGNE FESTIVAL PRODUCTION)

ISOLDE: "Ah look again! it hath the grace of dawn, the stars are flushed with crimson, and the sky holds some new light I know not!" (Tristan and Isolde—Act II)

Refusing to heed *Brangäne's* warning, *Isolde* gives the signal for *Tristan's* coming by extinguishing the torch. He appears, and a long love scene ensues, interrupted by the return of the King, who surprises the lovers in a fond embrace. *Mark* bitterly reproaches his nephew, and *Melot*, shouting "treason," stabs *Tristan*, inflicting a fatal wound.

The third act shows *Tristan* dying of the wound at his castle in *Bretagne*, whither he has been carried by his faithful servant, *Kurvenal*, who has sent for *Isolde*, knowing that she alone can cure his master's wound by means of her healing arts.

Despairing of her coming, *Tristan* in his delirium tears off his bandages and is at the point of death when *Isolde* arrives, and dies in her arms. *King Mark* and his courtiers, closely pursuing *Isolde*, now arrive and are attacked by *Kurvenal*, who kills *Melot* and is himself slain by *Mark's* soldiers. *Mark*, seeing *Tristan* dead and *Isolde* senseless on his body, repents his rage and gives way to grief. *Isolde* revives, and when she realizes that *Tristan* is dead, her grief bursts forth in the heartrending *Love-Death motive:*

THE LOVE DEATH:

So stür-ben wir, um un - - - ge-trennt,

Then she sings this wondrous death song, so full of touching sadness and inexpressible sweetness, and expires upon his body.

Isolde's Liebestod (Isolde's Love-Death)

By Johanna Gadski,		*(In German)*	88058	12-inch, $3.00
By Victor Herbert's Orchestra	*(Double-faced—See below)*		55041	12-inch, 1.50
By La Scala Orchestra	*(Double-faced—See below)*		68210	12-inch, 1.25

PANEL BY STASSEN   ISOLDE'S LIEBESTOD

ISOLDE (*unconscious of all around her, turning her eyes with rising inspiration on Tristan's body*):
Mild and softly he is smiling;
How his eyelids sweetly open!
See, oh comrades, see you not
How he beameth ever brighter—
How he rises ever radiant
Steeped in starlight, borne above?
See you not how his heart
With lion zest, calmly happy
Beats in his breast?
From his lips in Heavenly rest,
Sweetest breath he softly sends.
Harken, friends!
Hear and feel ye not?
Is it I alone am hearing
Strains so tender and endearing?
Passion swelling, all things telling,
Gently bounding, from him sounding,
In me pushes, upward rushes
Trumpet tone that round me gushes.
Brighter growing, o'er me flowing,
Are these breezes airy pillows?
Are they balmy beauteous billows?
How they rise and gleam and glisten!
Shall I breathe them? Shall I listen?
Shall I sip them, dive within them?
To my panting breathing win them?
In the breezes around, in the harmony sound,
In the world's driving whirlwind be drown'd—
And, sinking, be drinking—
In a kiss, highest bliss!
(*Isolde sinks, as if transfigured, in Brängane's arms upon Tristan's body. Profound emotion and grief of the bystanders. Mark invokes a blessing on the dead. Curtain.*)

DOUBLE-FACED TRISTAN AND ISOLDE RECORDS

⎰ Isolde's Liebestod (Isolde's Love Death)	By Herbert's Orch ⎱		55041	12-inch, $1.50
⎱ *Träume* (Dreams) (*Wagner*)	*By Victor Herbert's Orchestra* ⎰			
⎰ Prelude	By La Scala Orchestra ⎱		68210	12-inch, 1.25
⎱ Isolde's Love-Death	By La Scala Orchestra ⎰			

GADSKI AS ISOLDE

LANDE

IL TROVATORE—FIRST SCENE

(Italian)
IL TROVATORE

(Eel Troh-vah-toh'-reh)

(English)
THE TROUBADOUR

OPERA IN FOUR ACTS

Words by Salvatore Cammanaro, the story being suggested by a Spanish drama of the same name. Music by Giuseppe Verdi. Produced at the Teatro Apollo, Rome, January 19, 1853; at the *Théâtre des Italiens*, Paris, December 23, 1854; at the *Opéra*, Paris, as Le Trouvère, January 12, 1857; at Covent Garden, London, May 17, 1855; in English as *The Gypsy's Vengeance*, Drury Lane, March 24, 1856. First New York production, in Italian, April 30, 1855, with Brignoli, Steffanone, Amodio and Vestvali. First Philadelphia production at the Walnut Street Theatre, January 14, 1856, and at the Academy of Music, February 25, 1857. Produced at the New Orleans Opera April 13, 1857. A German version was given at the Metropolitan Opera House in 1889. Some notable revivals occurred in 1908 with Caruso, Eames and Homer; and again, in 1914, with Destinn, Ober, Martinelli, Amato and Rothier.

Characters

LEONORA, *(Lee-oh-noh'-rah)* a noble lady of the Court of an Aragon Princess . . Soprano
AZUCENA, *(Ahz-you-say'-nah)* a wandering Biscayan gypsy . . . . Mezzo-Soprano
INEZ, *(Ee'-nez)* attendant of Leonora . . . . Soprano
MANRICO, *(Man-ree'-koh)* a young chieftain under the Prince of Biscay,
  of mysterious birth, and in reality a brother of Count di Luna . . . . . . Tenor
COUNT DI LUNA, *(dee Loo'-nah)* a powerful young noble of the Prince
  of Arragon . . . . Baritone
FERRANDO, a captain of the guard and under di Luna . . . . Bass
RUIZ, a soldier in Manrico's service . . . . Tenor
AN OLD GYPSY . . . . Baritone
  Also a Messenger, a Jailer, Soldiers, Nuns, Gypsies, Attendants, etc.

Scene and Period: Biscay and Aragon ; middle of the fifteenth century.

519

ACT I

SCENE I—*Vestibule in Aliaferia Palace*

As befits a tragic work, *Il Trovatore* opens in an atmosphere of romance and mystery. The retainers of *Count di Luna* await the arrival of their master, and to beguile the time *Ferrando* relates the history of the Count's childhood and the loss of his brother.

Abbietta zingara (Swarthy and Threatening)

By Torres de Luna and La Scala Chorus (*In Italian*) *62416 10-inch, $0.75

The brother, as an infant, came under the evil eye of a witch, who was seized and condemned to the stake.   This witch had a daughter, who determined to avenge her mother's fate, with the result that the Count's younger son disappeared; and after the witch's burning there was discovered upon the pile of charred embers the bones of a child.   This story is told in the *Abbietta* to a fierce rhythmical tune, expressing all shades of horror.

ALAN TURNER AS THE COUNT
(COVENT GARDEN OPERA; MODENA, ITALY, OPERA; CHICAGO OPERA, ETC.)

FERRANDO:
With two sons, heirs of fortune and affection,
Liv'd the Count in enjoyment;
Watching the younger for his safe protection
A good nurse found employment.
One morning, as the dawn's first rays were
    shining,
From her pillow she rose,—
Who was found, think ye, near the child
    reclining?
(*Impressively.*)
Sat there a gypsy-hag, witch-like appearing;
Of her dark mysteries, strange symbols
    wearing.
O'er the babe sleeping—with fierce looks
    bending,
Gaz'd she upon him, black deeds intending!
Horror profound seized the nurse at that
    dark vision;
And the dark intruder was soon expelled.
Soon they found the child was failing,
Coming darkness appall'd him,
The hag's dark spell enthrall'd him!
(*All appear horrified.*)
Sought they the gypsy, on all sides turning,
Seiz'd and condemn'd her to death by burning.
One child, accursed, left she remaining,
Quick to avenge her, no means disdaining.
Thus she accomplished her dark retribution!
Lost was the Count's child; search unavailing;
But on the site of the hag's execution
They found, 'mid the embers,
The bones of a young infant,
Half consumed and burning!

In the second part *Ferrando* concludes his narrative, which is mingled with the comments of the listeners, who tell of the reputed appearance of the witch in ghostly shape.

Sull' orlo dei tetti (As a Vampire You May See Her)

By Torres de Luna, Bass, and La Scala Chorus
*16655 10-inch, $0.75

To the voice of the narrator is added the awe-stricken whispers of the chorus, which afterwards swell into a cry of fierce denunciation. The foreboding bell and an instru-

LANDE

IL TROVATORE—ACT I, SCENE II

Double-Faced Record—See page 530.

mental diminuendo complete the picture, which makes a fitting conclusion to a grue-some story. The clock strikes twelve, and with cries of "Cursed be the witch infernal!" the retainers disperse.

SCENE II—*The Gardens of the Palace*

The fair *Leonora* now appears with her faithful companion, *Inez*. She confides to *Inez* her interest in the unknown knight whom she had first seen at the Tournament.

Tacea la notte placida (Peaceful Was the Night)

By Luisa Tetrazzini, Soprano	(*In Italian*)	88420	12-inch,	$3.00
By Edith Helena, Soprano	(*In English*)	*35214	12-inch,	1.25
By Lucia Crestani, Soprano	(*In Italian*)	*16655	10-inch,	.75

In this wistful air, so unlike the weird music preceding it, she speaks of the *Troubadour* who serenades her, and of the feelings which have been inspired in her breast by his song.

LEONORA:

How calm, how placid, was the night!
The cloudless sky, how clear, how bright!
The moon in splendor shed her light,
And all was hushed in peace around!
Suddenly, on the midnight air,

In tones so sweet and thrilling,
Breathing to Heav'n an earnest pray'r,
My heart with deep joy filling,
I heard a voice oft heard before,
My long-loved knightly Troubadour!

The ladies go into the house just as the *Count*, who is also wooing the fair *Leonora*, appears to watch under her window. He has barely taken his station when the lovely song of the *Troubadour* is heard:

Deserto sulla terra (Naught on Earth is Left Me)

By Nicola Zerola, Tenor (*In Italian*) 64172 10-inch, $1.00

In this beautiful serenade, one of the gems of the opera, the *Trouba-dour* sings of his lonely life and the one hope that remains to him.

MANRICO:

Lonely on earth abiding,
Warring 'gainst fate's cruel chiding,
Hope doth one heart implore,
To love the Troubadour!

But that fond treasure gaining,
In faith and love obtaining,
High o'er all kings would soar,
The happy Troubadour!

The Count is filled with rage as *Manrico* appears and confesses his love in song, and when *Leonora* comes forth to greet her lover, the anger of *di Luna* bursts in a storm upon them both, in the strain with which this number opens.

Di geloso amor sprezzato (Now My Vengeance)

By Maria Bernacchi, Soprano; Luigi Colazza, Tenor; Ernesto
Caronna, Baritone (*In Italian*) *16808 10-inch, $0.75

Manrico defies him and they agree to fight to the death. *Leonora* implores her lover to stay, but is unable to restrain the jealous passion which inspires the rivals, and after the powerful and exciting trio they rush out with drawn swords, while *Leonora* falls senseless.

ACT II

SCENE I—*A Gypsy Camp in the Biscay Mountains*

We are now in the gypsy encampment at early morning, as the shad-ows of night are passing away before the dawn. The men are beginning work, and in this, the famous *Anvil Chorus,* they hammer as they sing.

La zingarella (Anvil Chorus)

By La Scala Chorus	(*In Italian*)	*62418	10-inch,	$0.75
By Victor Orchestra		*17231	10-inch,	.75
By Victor Male Chorus	(*In English*)	*17563	10-inch,	.75
By Victor Male Chorus	(*In English*)	1258	10-inch,	.60

The swinging tune is accompanied by the ring of blows on the anvil, and the rough voices of the men and the sound of the hammers make a truly impressive musical picture.

CHORUS OF GYPSIES:

See how the shadows of night are flying!
Morn breaketh, Heav'n's glorious arch un-
  veiling:
Like a young widow, who, weary of sighing,
Lays by her garments of sorrow and wailing.
Rouse up, to labor!
Take each his hammer.

MEN:

Who makes the gypsy's, a life with pleasure
laden?
WOMEN:

Who makes the gypsy's, a life with pleasure
laden, who?
ALL:

The gypsy maiden!

*Double-Faced Record—See page 530.

Azucena, the gypsy, who now appears, proves to be none other than the witch's daughter spoken of in the first act. In the highly dramatic song allotted to her she relates to *Manrico* the dreadful story of the death of her mother, who had been burned at the stake as a witch by the father of the present *Count di Luna.*

COPY'T MCINTOSH

HOMER AS AZUCENA

Stride la vampa (Fierce Flames Are Soaring)

By Louise Homer, Contralto
        (In Italian)   87033   10-inch, $2.00
By Lina Mileri, Contralto
        (In Italian) *16808 10-inch, .75

In the aria she mentally lives again through the scene of her mother's execution, each horrible detail of which is indelibly imprinted upon her memory.

This wild contralto air in the minor, with its deep, rich, and ever-changing tones, is well suited to so grim a recital.

Upward the flames roll; the crowd presses fiercely on,
Rush to the burning with seeming gladness;
Loud cries of pleasure from all sides re-echoing!
By guards surrounded—forth comes a woman!
While, o'er them shining, with wild, unearthly glare,
Dark wreaths of flame curl, ascending to heaven!
Upward the flames roll! on comes the victim still;

Robed in dark garments, ungirt, unsandal'd;
Fierce cries of vengeance from that dark crowd arise;
Echo repeats them from mountain to mountain.
O'er them reflecting, with wild, unearthly glare.
Dark wreaths of flame curl, ascending to heaven!

The rendition of this thrilling air by Mme. Homer is a most dramatic and impressive one; while an excellent lower-priced record is furnished by Mme. Mileri.

Questioned by *Manrico, Azucena* tells him the story of her past. In obedience to her mother's last cry for vengeance, she stole the Count's young child, and threw it on the flames where her mother was consumed. But she soon discovered that in her frenzy she had destroyed her own infant, and preserved the child of the noble. Wild as was the previous air, this proves a still more dramatic setting of the conclusion of the story. The orchestral accompaniment crashes, wails and sobs, the voice rises and falls in hatred or terror, until at last the gypsy sinks exhausted with the stress of emotion that her tale has excited.

Condotta ell'era in ceppi (In Chains to Her Doom They Dragged Her)

By Lina Mileri, Contralto   (In Italian) *35176 12-inch, $1.25

The story has set *Manrico* thinking. "If your son perished," he asks, "whose child am I?" But the gypsy, with a born instinct for dissimulation, avoids the question, still claiming him as her son. She reminds him of the almost fatal wounds received in an attack from the *Count di Luna* and his men, from which she had nursed him back to life.

AZUCENA:
To me thy life's protection thou owest.
At midnight, on the field of battle
My cares revived the vital spark
Many hours did I tend thee, healing thy wounds,
So ghastly and numerous!

Mal reggendo all'aspro assalto (At My Mercy Lay the Foe)

By Louise Homer and Enrico Caruso   (In Italian)   89049 12-inch, $4.00
By Clotilde Esposito and Luigi Colazza (In Italian) *16550 10-inch, .75

In the opening strain of this air, *Manrico* tells of his single combat with the *Count*, in which by an irresistible impulse, after felling his antagonist to earth, he spared the noble's life. The voice of the gypsy then bids him never again to allow their enemy to escape, but to unhesitatingly administer the death-blow. *Manrico's* story of the duel is expressed by a

LANDE

THE CONVENT NEAR CASTELLOR—ACT II

bold martial air, the gypsy's incitements to vengeance being heard at the same time, leading to the vigorous climax of the duet.

SCENE II—*The Cloisters of a Convent*

In this scene we return to the fortunes of the *Count* and *Leonora.* She, believing the *Troubadour* to have been killed, presumably in a recent duel with his rival, has determined to enter a convent. *Di Luna* appears in front of the convent with the intention of carrying her away before the ceremony shall have taken place, and sings his famous air, "Il balen."

Il balen del suo sorriso (The Tempest of the Heart)

By Emilio de Gogorza, Baritone	(*In Italian*)	88175	12-inch, $3.00
By Francesco Cigada, Baritone	(*In Italian*)	*16812	10-inch, .75
By Alan Turner, Baritone	(*In English*)	*16521	10-inch, .75

This solo almost wins the *Count* our sympathy, in spite of ourselves, so genuine and heartfelt an expression of the tender passion it is.

COUNT:
Of her smile, the radiant gleaming
Pales the starlight's brightest reflection,
While her face with beauty beaming,
Brings me fresh ardor, lends to my affection.

Ah! this love within me burning,
More than words shall plead on my part,
Her bright glances on me turning,
Calm the tempest in my heart!

The convent bell is heard tolling as a signal for the final rites which make *Leonora* a nun. The *Count,* in a burst of passion, declares they must seize her before she reaches the altar.

Per me ora fatale (This Passion That Inspires Me)

By Ernesto Caronna, Baritone, and La Scala Chorus
(*In Italian*) *16814 10-inch, $0.75

This declaration is expressed in a vigorous air.

COUNT (*furiously*):
Oh, hour of fate to me,
Hasten thy lagging moments.
The joy that I anticipate
Is of more than mortal worth!

No rival can I have;
No one dare my love to thwart!
For me hath fate design'd her,
And to me she shall belong!

They conceal themselves among the trees as the chant of the nuns is heard.

Ah! se l'error t'ingombra ('Mid the Shades of Error)

By Francesco Cigada, Baritone, and La Scala Chorus
(*In Italian*) *16550 10-inch, $0.75

They sing of the coming retirement of *Leonora* from the world, while from their place of concealment the *Count* and his retainers speak of their coming triumph.

CHORUS OF NUNS:
Ah! when the shades of night,
Oh, daughter of Eve, shall close on thee,
Then wilt thou know that life
Is but a shadow, a fleeting dream;—
Yes, like the passing of a shadow
Are all our earthly hopes!

Come, then, and let this mystic veil
From human eye enshroud thee;
Hence let care and worldly thought
For evermore be banish'd.
To Heaven now turn thee, and Heaven
Will open to receive thee!

* *Double-Faced Record—See page 530.*

COUNT:
　Triumphant hour impending,
　Thy moments urge with speed elating,
　The joy my heart's awaiting,
　Is not of mortal birth,
　In vain doth Heaven, contending
　With rival claims, oppose me,
　If once these arms enclose thee,
　No power in heav'n or earth,
　No pow'r shall tear thee from me!
FERRANDO AND RETAINERS:
　How bold! Let's go—conceal ourselves
　Amid the shades in haste.
　How bold!—Come on—and silence keep,
　The prize he soon will hold!

As the nuns appear, conducting the penitent, the Count's retainers rush out and seize *Leonora*.

The calculations of *di Luna* are once more upset, for just as he interrupts the ceremony, *Manrico* unexpectedly appears. *Leonora*, overjoyed to find her lover still living, begins the great trio.

E deggio e posso crederlo (Blessed Vision)
By Grisi, Sangiorgi, Cigada and Chorus
(*In Italian*) *35176 12-inch, $1.25

Leonora foregoes her religious vows, and the lovers, for the time united, make their escape, to the chagrin of the baffled Count, while his men are defeated by *Manrico's* followers.

ACT III
SCENE I—*The Camp of di Luna*

COPY'T DUPONT
MARTIN AS MANRICO

Squilli e cheggi la tromba (Soldiers' Chorus)
By New York Grand Opera Chorus　(*In Italian*) 64050 10-inch, $1.00

Act III opens with the chorus of *di Luna's* men—called the *Soldiers' Chorus*. In spite of the wealth of melody already heard in this work, here is yet another marvelous number, which works up to a powerful climax, and then dies away softly, as these *Trovatore* choruses so frequently do.

SOLDIERS:
Now let the trumpet in war tones resounding,
Call to arms, with courage bold, we'll march undaunted.
Haply, to-morrow, our proud foes confounding
On those walls shall our banners be planted.

Ne'er more brilliant were prospects victorious
Than the hopes which our hearts now elate.
Thence, we'll gather renown, bright and glorious
Pleasure, honor and profit there await us.
Honor and booty for us there await.

Giorni poveri vivea (In Despair I Seek My Son)
By Ida Mameli, Soprano; Renzo Minolfi, Baritone; Cesare Preve,
Baritone; La Scala Chorus　(*In Italian*) *35177 12-inch, $1.25

A scouting party from the Count's troops have fallen in with *Azucena*, and now bring her to the Count as a possible spy. Inquiries as to her past immediately connect her with the episode of the Count's childhood, and *Ferrando* declares her to be the murderess of *di Luna's* lost brother. *Azucena* in her extremity, cries out the name of *Manrico*, and the Count, finding she claims the *Troubadour* as her son, vows upon her a double vengeance, and she is bound and dragged away. The gypsy's pleading, the Count's threatening anger and triumph, with the accompanying chorus, combine to make a moving and dramatic *ensemble*.

SCENE II—*Manrico's Castle*

The scene changes to the castle wherein *Manrico* and *Leonora* are at last enjoying a brief honeymoon, though in expectation of an attack from the baffled *Count di Luna*. Here *Manrico* sings a tender farewell to his beloved ere he departs to repel his rival's assault.

Ah, si ben mio (The Vows We Fondly Plighted)
By Enrico Caruso, Tenor	(*In Italian*)	88121	12-inch,	$3.00
By Giovanni Martinelli, Tenor	(*In Italian*)	74439	12-inch,	1.50
By Giorgio Malesci, Tenor	(*In Italian*)	*16809	10-inch,	.75

* *Double-Faced Record—See pages 529 and 530.*

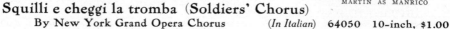

SLEZAK AS MANRICO

This beautiful lyrical number is a delightful relief after so much that is forcible and dramatic.

MANRICO:
'Tis love, sublime emotion, at such a moment
Bids thy heart still be hopeful.
Ah! love; how blest our life will be
Our fond desires attaining,
My soul shall win fresh ardor,
My arm new courage gaining.
But, if, upon the fatal page
Of destiny impending,
I'm doom'd among the slain to fall,
'Gainst hostile arms contending,
In life's last hour, with fainting breath,
My thoughts will turn to thee.
Preceding thee to Heaven, will death
Alone appear to me!

Quietness soon departs, for the news comes that the attacking party have captured *Azucena,* and are piling up faggots around the stake at which she is to be burnt. Maddened at the approaching outrage upon one whom he believes to be his mother, *Manrico* prepares to rush to her assistance. The air with chorus which forms the climax to this scene is full of martial fire.

Di quella pira (Tremble, Ye Tyrants)

By Francesco Tamagno, Tenor
        (*In Italian*)   95006   10-inch, $5.00
By Antonio Paoli, Tenor, and La Scala
   Chorus   (*In Italian*)   92032   12-inch, 3.00
By Enrico Caruso, Tenor   (*In Italian*)   87001   10-inch, 2.00
By Nicola Zerola, Tenor   (*In Italian*)   64170   10-inch, 1.00
By Giovanni Valls, Tenor, and La Scala Chorus
        (*In Italian*) *16809   10-inch, .75

It is led up to by a very powerful introductory passage, and the high notes at the end, delivered in robust tones, never fail of their effect.

MANRICO:
Ah! sight of horror! See that pile blazing—
Demons of fury round it stand gazing!
Madness inspiring, Hate now is raging—
Tremble, for vengeance on you shall fall.

Oh! mother dearest, though love may claim me,
Danger, too, threaten, yet will I save thee;
From flames consuming thy form shall snatch'd be,
Or with thee, mother, I too will fall!

Caruso's singing of this number is absolutely electrifying in its effect on the listener, the two famous high C's being easily taken and with the full power of his great voice.

Tamagno's *Manrico* was a figure of noble proportions, and he endowed it with all his splendid vitality. Such a high C had never before been heard, and it electrified the audiences. The record of *Di quella pira* is a faithful reproduction of the great singer's rendition of the famous aria. Paoli, the famous Milan tenor, also gives a vigorous performance of this great air.

Other fine renditions, at a lower price, are given by Zerola and by Signor Valls, assisted by La Scala Chorus.

THE RAMPARTS OF ALIAFERIA—ACT IV

* Double-Faced Record—See page 530.

The Death of Leonora

ACT IV

SCENE I—*Exterior of the Palace of Aliaferia*

The last act brings us outside the palace of *Aliaferia*, wherein *Manrico*, defeated by *di Luna's* men, and the gypsy, are confined in the dungeons. Hither *Leonora* has wended her way to be near her lover, and she now sings the plaintive *D'amor*.

D'amor sull' ali rosee (Love, Fly on Rosy Pinions)

By Luisa Tetrazzini, Soprano	(*In Italian*) 88426	12-inch, $3.00
By Lucia Crestani, Soprano	(*In Italian*) *16810	10-inch, .75

This sad but melodious air reveals her heartfelt grief for the sorrows which she cannot relieve.

LEONORA:
In this dark hour of midnight
I hover round thee, my love!
Ye moaning breezes round me playing,
In pity aid me, my sighs to him conveying!
On rosy wings of love depart,
Bearing my heart's sad wailing,
Visit the prisoner's lonely cell,

Console his spirit failing.
Let hope's soft whispers wreathing
Around him, comfort breathing,
Recall to his fond remembrance
Sweet visions of his love;
But, let no accent reveal to him
The sorrows, the griefs my heart doth move!

And now comes Verdi's most famous operatic scene, the great *Miserere*.

Miserere (I Have Sighed to Rest Me)

By Enrico Caruso, Tenor; Frances Alda, Soprano; Chorus of the Metropolitan Opera	(*In Italian*) 89030	12-inch, $4.00
By Destinn and Martinelli	(*In Italian*) 88530	12-inch, 3.00
By Olive Kline, Soprano; Harry Macdonough, Tenor; and Victor Chorus	(*In English*) *35443	12-inch, 1.25
By Ida Giacomelli, Soprano; Gino Martinez-Patti, Tenor; La Scala Chorus	(*In Italian*) *35456	12-inch, 1.25
By Stevenson, Macdonough and Chorus	(*In English*) *16013	10-inch, .75
By Arthur Pryor and Emile Keneke (*Trombone-Cornet*)	*16371	10-inch, .75
By Walter Rogers and Arthur Pryor (*Cornet-Trombone*)	*16794	10-inch, .75

Leonora is terror-stricken at the solemn tolling of a deep-toned bell and the mournful chorus of priests chanting for the soul of a doomed prisoner.

CAMPANINI AS MANRICO

PRIESTS:
Pray that peace may attend a soul departing,
Whither no care or thought of earth can follow;
Heav'nly mercy allays the pangs of parting,
Look up beyond this life's delusions hollow.

Then follows an impressive series of chords in the orchestra, leading to a sobbing lament of *Leonora*.

LEONORA:
What voices of terror! For whom are they praying?
With omens of fear unknown, they darken the air,
New horrors assail me, my senses are straying,
My vision is dim, is it death that is near?

In upon this there breaks the beautiful air of the *Troubadour*, sung within the prison, followed by a joyful cry of devotion from his beloved.

MANRICO:
Ah! I have sighed to rest me; deep in the quiet grave—
Sighed to rest me, but all in vain I crave.
Oh fare thee well, my Leonora, fare thee well!

These fragments, first given separately, are next combined and heard together, forming a most impressive scene of touching beauty, for which the opera of *Il Trovatore* will ever be remembered.

The entrance of *di Luna* brings from *Leonora* a prayer for mercy for the prisoner. The appeal is unheeded, or rather it appears to increase the triumph which belongs to the *Count's* vengeance. The appeal of the unhappy woman and the fierce joy of the gratified noble are powerfully expressed in this magnificent duet.

* *Double-Faced Record—See pages 529 and 530.*

Mira d'acerbe lagrime (Oh, Let My Tears Implore Thee)

By Johanna Gadski, Soprano, and Pasquale Amato, Baritone
(In Italian)   89069   12-inch, $4.00
By Emma Eames, Soprano, and Emilio de Gogorza, Baritone
(In Italian)   89022   12-inch,   4.00
By Celestina Boninsegna, Soprano, and Francesco Cigada, Baritone
(In Italian)   91077   10-inch,   2.00
By Maria Bernacchi and Ernesto Caronna   (In Italian) *16810   10-inch,   .75

In the extremity of despair, *Leonora* makes one last effort. If the *Count* will spare the one she loves, she will consent to become *di Luna's* wife. She swears to perform her promise, at the same time intending to take poison as soon as *Manrico* is free. *Di Luna's* wrath is now changed into joy, while *Leonora*, forgetting her own fate, is filled with happiness at the thought of the *Troubadour's* release. This situation gives opportunity for another wonderful duet of a most thrilling character.

Vivra! Contende il giubilo (Oh, Joy, He's Saved)

By Johanna Gadski, Soprano, and Pasquale Amato, Baritone
(In Italian)   89070   12-inch, $4.00
By Boninsegna and Cigada   (In Italian)   91071   10-inch,   2.00
By de Angelis and Cigada   (In Italian) *16811   10-inch,   .75

In this number the *Count* expresses his rapture at the success of his conquest, while *Leonora* exclaims, aside: "Thou shalt possess but a lifeless bride." As the scene changes they enter the tower to secure the release of *Manrico*.

SCENE II—*The Prison Cell of Manrico*

Yet a third duet—the famous *Home to Our Mountains*. The scene has changed to the prison interior, where *Azucena* and *Manrico* are together, and the gypsy, with the second-sight of her race, predicts her approaching end.

Ai nostri monti (Home to Our Mountains)

By Louise Homer, Contralto, and Enrico Caruso, Tenor
(In Italian)   89018   12-inch, $4.00
By Schumann-Heink and Caruso   (In Italian)   89060   12-inch,   4.00
By Vessella's Italian Band   *35239   12-inch,   1.25
By Marguerite Dunlap, Contralto, and Harry Macdonough,
Tenor   (In English) *35443   12-inch,   1.25
By Clotilde Esposito and Luigi Colazza   (In Italian) *16811   10-inch,   .75
By Miss Morgan and Mr. Macdonough   (In English) *16407   10-inch,   .75

This familiar duet is considered by many to be the gem of Verdi's opera. *Manrico* is watching over the couch of *Azucena,* whose strength is exhausted, and who is full of vague terrors; and he endeavors to soothe her fears.

MANRICO:
If any love remains in thy bosom,
If thou art yet my mother, oh, hear me!
Seek thy terrors to number,
And gain repose from thy sorrows in soothing slumber.

AZUCENA:
Yes, I am grief-worn and fain would rest me,
But more than grief have sad dreams oppressed me;
Should that dread vision rise in slumber
Rouse me! its horrors may then depart.

MANRICO:
Rest thee, oh mother! I'll watch o'er thee,
Sleep may restore sweet peace to thy heart.

A fierce and avenging gypsy no longer, but a broken woman whose consuming passions of remorse and revenge have died away, she dreams of the happy days gone by.

AZUCENA (*dreaming*):
Home to our mountains, let us return, love,
There in thy young days peace had its reign:
There shall thy song fall on my slumbers,
There shall thy lute, make me joyous again.
MANRICO:
Rest thee, my mother, kneeling beside thee,
I will pour forth my troubadour lay.

AZUCENA:
O sing and wake now thy sweet lute's soft numbers,
Lull me to rest, charm my sorrows away.
BOTH:
Lull { me / thee } to rest!

* *Double-Faced Record—See pages 529 and 530.*

Matters now move swiftly to a climax. *Leonora* arrives on the scene, bringing *Manrico* the news of his freedom. The joy of meeting is all too soon destroyed when the prisoner finds his liberty to have been purchased at the cost of a happiness which is to him dearer than life itself. He accuses *Leonora* of betraying his love.

Ha quest' infame (Thou Hast Sold Thyself)

By Ida Giacomelli, Soprano; Lina Mileri, Contralto; Gino
Martinez-Patti, Tenor　　　　　　　(*In Italian*)　*35177　12-inch, $1.25

Here *Azucena*, who cares nothing for his passion, counsels flight. This gives the elements of the closing trio: *Manrico's* reproaches, *Leonora's* ineffectual protestations, and the gypsy's voice through all, singing dreamily of her mountain home. With these mingled voices dying away into soft harmonies the musical portion of the opera draws to a close.

MANRICO:
Thou giv'st me life? No! I scorn it! 'Twas from my rival thou purchased thy
Whence comes this power? what price has mission!
  bought it? Ah! thou hast sold him thy heart's affection!
Thou wilt not speak? oh, dark suspicion! Barter'd a love once devoted to me!

Leonora, who had already taken the poison, now sinks dying at *Manrico's* feet, and he pleads forgiveness as he learns the truth. *Di Luna* now enters, and furious at finding himself cheated of his promised bride, orders the *Troubadour* to instant execution. *Manrico* is taken out by the guards and beheaded.

At the moment of his death, the gypsy awakes, and not seeing *Manrico*, realizes that he has gone to his execution. She drags the *Count* to the window and cries to him: "You have killed your brother!" *Di Luna* utters a wild cry of remorse and falls senseless as the curtain slowly descends.

DOUBLE-FACED AND MISCELLANEOUS TROVATORE RECORDS

Gems from "Trovatore"

"Soldiers' Chorus"—Solo, "Tremble, Ye Tyrants" (*Di quella pira*)—Solo,
"Tempest of the Heart" (*Il balen*)—Duet, "Home to Our Mountains"—Solo,
"I Have Sigh'd to Rest Me"—Ensemble, "Miserere"
　　　　　By Victor Opera Company　(*In English*)　31888　12-inch, $1.25

Condotta ell'era in ceppi (In Chains to Her Doom)
　　　　　By Lina Mileri, Contralto　(*In Italian*)
E deggio e posso crederlo (Oh, Blessed Vision)　　　　　　35176　12-inch, 1.25
　　　　　By Grisi, Sangiorgi, Cigada and Chorus　(*In Italian*)

Giorni poveri vivea　(In Despair I Seek My Son)　　By
　Ida Mameli, Soprano; Renzo Minolfi, Baritone; Cesare
　Preve, Baritone; La Scala Chorus　　　　　(*In Italian*)　35177　12-inch, 1.25
Ha quest' infame　(Ah, Thou Hast Sold Thyself)　　By
　Ida Giacomelli, Soprano; Lina Mileri, Contralto; Gino
　Martinez-Patti, Tenor　　　　　　　　(*In Italian*)

Trovatore Selection　　　　　　By Arthur Pryor's Band
　Introduction, Act III—"Fierce Flames," Act II—Introduction, Act I
　—"At Thy Mercy," Act II　　　　　　　　　　　　35076　12-inch, 1.25
　Traviata Selection　　　　　　*By Arthur Pryor's Band*

Miserere　By Olive Kline, Soprano; Harry Macdonough,
　Tenor; and Victor Chorus　　　　　　(*In English*)　35443　12-inch, 1.25
　Home to Our Mountains　By Marguerite Dunlap, Contralto, and
　　Harry Macdonough, Tenor

Miserere　By Giacomelli, Martinez-Patti and Chorus
　　　　　　　　　　　　　　　　　(*In Italian*)　35456　12-inch, 1.25
　Rigoletto—Bella Figlia　By Huguet, Zaccaria, Lanzirotti and
　　Cigada　　　　　　　　　　　(*In Italian*)

* *Double-Faced Record—See above list.*

Tacea la notte (Peaceful Was the Night) By Edith
   Helena, Soprano   (In English)
   Lucia—Mad Scene *By Edith Helena, Soprano* (In English)   35214   12-inch, $1.25

Home to Our Mountains   By Vessella's Italian Band
   Rigoletto—Quartet (Verdi)   *By Kryl's Bohemian Band*   35239   12-inch, 1.25

Anvil Chorus   Victor Orchestra
   Forge in the Forest (Michaelis) (Descriptive piece with anvil
   effects)   *Arthur Pryor's Band*   17231   10-inch,   .75

Abbietta zingara (Swarthy and Threatening)   By Torres
   de Luna, Bass, and La Scala Chorus   (In Italian)
Sull' orlo dei tetti (As a Vampire You May See Her)   62416   10-inch,   .75
      By Torres de Luna and La Scala Chorus (In Italian)

Sull' orlo dei tetti de Luna and La Scala Chorus (In Italian)
Tacea la notte placida (Peaceful Was the Night)   16655   10-inch,   .75
      By Lucia Crestani, Soprano (In Italian)

Di geloso amor sprezzato (Now My Vengeance)
      By Bernacchi, Colazza and Caronna (In Italian)
Stride la vampa (Fierce Flames Are Soaring)   16808   10-inch,   .75
      By Lina Mileri, Contralto (In Italian)

Mal reggendo all'aspro assalto (At My Mercy Lay the
   Foe)   By Clotilde Esposito and Luigi Colazza (In Italian)
Ah! se l' error t' ingombra ('Mid the Shades of Error)   16550   10-inch,   .75
      By Francesco Cigada and Chorus (In Italian)

Il balen del suo sorriso (The Tempest of the Heart)
      By Francesco Cigada, Baritone (In Italian)
   Martha—Porter Song   *By Carlos Francisco* (In Italian)   16812   10-inch,   .75

Tempest of the Heart   By Alan Turner (In English)
   Carmen—Toreador Song   *By Alan Turner* (In English)   16521   10-inch,   .75

Per me ora fatale (This Passion That Inspires Me)
      By Ernesto Caronna, Baritone (In Italian)
   Pagliacci—Opening Chorus, Son qua La Scala Chorus (In Italian)   16814   10-inch,   .75

Ah, si ben mio (The Vows We Fondly Plighted)
      By Georgio Malesci, Tenor (In Italian)
Di quella pira (Tremble Ye Tyrants)   By Giovanni   16809   10-inch,   .75
   Valls, Tenor, and La Scala Chorus   (In Italian)

D'amor sull ali rosee By Lucia Crestani, Soprano (In Italian)
Mira d'acerbe lagrime (Oh, Let My Tears Implore Thee)   16810   10-inch,   .75
      By Maria Bernacchi and Ernesto Caronna (In Italian)

Miserere   By Stevenson and Macdonough (In English)
   I Would That My Love   *By Stevenson and Macdonough*   16013   10-inch,   .75

Miserere   By Pryor and Keneke (Trombone-Cornet)
   Spring Song (Mendelssohn)   *By Victor String Quartet*   16371   10-inch,   .75

Miserere   By Rogers and Pryor (Cornet-Trombone)
   Chant sans paroles (Tschaikowsky)   *By Vienna String Quartet*   16794   10-inch,   .75

Vivra! contende il giubilo (Oh, Joy, He's Saved)
      By Angela de Angelis and Francesco Cigada (In Italian)
Ai nostri monti (Home to Our Mountains) By Clotilde   16811   10-inch,   .75
   Esposito, Soprano, and Luigi Colazza, Tenor (In Italian)

Home to Our Mountains   By Corinne Morgan,
   Contralto, and Harry Macdonough, Tenor (In English)
   Bohemian Girl—Heart Bow'd Down By Alan Turner (In English)   16407   10-inch,   .75

Di geloso amor sprezzato (Now My Vengeance)
      By Bernacchi, Colazza and Caronna (In Italian)
La zingarella (Anvil Chorus) La Scala Chorus (In Italian)   62418   10-inch,   .75

Anvil Chorus   Victor Male Chorus (In English)
   Tannhäuser—Pilgrims' Chorus   *Victor Male Chorus* (In English)   17563   10-inch,   .75

THE TRUMPETER OF SÄCKINGEN
OPERA IN THREE ACTS AND A PROLOGUE

WERNER THE TRUMPETER AND MARGARET VON SÄCKINGEN

Text by B. Bunge; music by Victor Nessler. First production Leipsic, 1884. Presented at the Metropolitan Opera House, New York, November 23, 1887, with Robinson and Fischer, and revived there in 1889. Given at the Harlem Opera House, November, 1890, by the Emma Juch Opera Company.

Characters

THE BARON VON SCHONAU ... Bass
MARIA, his daughter ...... Soprano
COUNT WILDENSTEIN .... Bass
COUNTESS WILDENSTEIN .. Contralto
DAMIAN, son of the Count .... Tenor
WERNER KIRCHOFER ..... Baritone
KONRADIN, foot soldier .... Bass

Time and Place: Heidelberg and Säkkingen; seventeenth century.

Nessler has taken Scheffel's poem and built the charming little metrical romance into an operatic production. The story tells of a young student of Heidelberg, *Werner Kirchofer,* who, with his comrades, is banished from the university for serenading an English princess. The youths join the army, and in due time *Werner* reaches the town of Säckingen, where the peasants are on the eve of an uprising against the nobles. He manages to protect the *Countess of Wildenstein* and her niece, *Maria,* from the insults of the rabble, and later becomes trumpeter in the castle of *Maria's* father, the *Baron von Schonau. Werner* and *Maria* fall in love with each other, but it has already been planned that the young girl shall marry *Damian,* the son of the *Count of Wildenstein,* who is expected at the castle shortly. The *Countess* surprises *Werner* making love to *Maria,* and the *Baron* angrily orders the bugler from the castle. As *Werner* is departing, the Hauenstein peasants rebel against the *Baron* and attack the castle. The trumpeter, gathering the besieged forces together, succeeds in driving off the assailants. In the meantime, *Damian* and his father have arrived, and during the conflict the young man shows himself to be a coward. *Count Wildenstein* happily recognizes *Werner* as his long lost son, who had been stolen as a child by gypsies, and the *Baron,* reconciled, gives the *Trumpeter of Säckingen* his daughter *Maria* for a bride.

A record of the best known air from this popular German opera is offered.

GORITZ AS THE TRUMPETER

Es hat nicht sollen sein (It Was Not So to Be)

By Otto Goritz, Baritone
(*In German*) 74212 12-inch, $1.50

531

LES VÊPRES SICILLIENNES
(Leh Veh-per See-see-lee-en')

I VESPRI SICILIANI   SICILIAN VESPERS
(Ee Ves'-pree See-chee-lee-ah'-nee)

OPERA IN FIVE ACTS

Text by Scribe and Duveyrier. Music by Verdi. First given at the *Académie*, Paris, June 13, 1855. First performance in Italy at Parma, *Teatro Regio*, December 26, 1855. A revised version was given at La Scala, Milan, in 1856, as *Giovanna di Guzman ;* and at Naples, January, 1857, under the title of *Batilde di Turenna.* The first London production was at Drury Lane, 1859, with Tietiens, Mongini and Vialetti. The work was presented in New York at the Academy of Music, November 7, 1859, with Colson, Brignoli and Ferri, and revived there in November, 1868.

Characters

GUY DE MONTFORD, Viceroy.....................................Baritone
ARRIGO, a Sicilian officer...Tenor
DUCHESSE HÉLÈNE, a prisoner ....Soprano
JOHN OF PROCIDA, a Sicilian conspirator..........................Bass

Verdi's *Sicilian Vespers* followed the composer's *Traviata* and was written for the Paris Opéra, being produced there June 13, 1855. It is a brilliant work, but has never been popular, and much wonder has often been expressed that Verdi, in writing for the French stage, should have selected so inappropriate a subject as the Sicilian massacre of the French!

But the young composer could hardly help himself, as the libretto was offered to him by the great Scribe, then in the height of his glory. The French, however, kindly overlooked the plot and welcomed the composer's fine music most generously.

The scene is laid in Sicily at the time of the French invasion, and tells of the slaughter of the French at vespers, Easter Monday, 1282. This massacre was caused by the Viceroy's brutal attitude toward the Sicilians.

Arrigo is in love with *Hélèna,* and the plot turns on his attempt to rescue her. He is afterward discovered to be the son of the Viceroy.

The Victor offers a fine record of the splendid Bolero sung in the opera by *Hélène,* and given here by Mme. Tetrazzini.

Mercè, dilette amiche (Thanks, Beloved Companions)

By Luisa Tetrazzini, Soprano   *(In Italian)*   88504   12-inch, $3.00

My thanks, beloved companions,
    For these delightful flow'rs.
Your friendly gift but typifies,
    Your own sweet gen'rous dow'rs.
Oh, welcome, dear alliance,
    Which love for me is making,
Since ye around me twine the wreaths,
    My warmest thanks awaking.
Sicilian mountains clad with vines,
    A splendid day shall dawn,
Too long these awful feuds have raged,
    Hate's heart-corrupting spawn.
The day that brings my festal rite,
    Shall seal your glory too,
At thought of love, my heart beats fast,
    In realms of joy, my lot is cast!

THE RIDE OF THE VALKYRIES

(German)
DIE WALKÜRE
(Dee Vahl-kuer'-reh)

(English)
THE VALKYRIE
(Vahl-kee'-ree)

MUSIC-DRAMA IN THREE ACTS

Text and music by Richard Wagner. Completed in 1856, but not given until June 25, 1870, at Munich. First London production, in English, at Covent Garden, October 16, 1895. First New York production at the Academy of Music, April 2, 1877, with Mme. Pappenheim, Canissa, Listner, Bischoff, Blum and Preusser. Not heard again in New York until January 30, 1885, when Dr. Leopold Damrosch revived the work at the Metropolitan, with Brandt, Schott and Materna. Since that time the work has seldom been absent from the Metropolitan, the latest production being that of 1915, with Kurt, Gadski, Matzenauer, Berger, Ruysdael and Braun. Among the artists who have appeared in the opera during the past thirty years may be mentioned the following: as *Sieglinde* — Fremstad, Ternina, Nordica, Morena, Saltzmann-Stevens, Osborn-Hannah; as *Brünnhilde* — Ternina, Gadski, Walker, Leffler-Burckhard, Matzenauer, Nordica, Litvinne, Weidt; as *Siegmund* — Burrian, Burgstaller, Dalmores, Urlus, Kraus; as *Wotan* — Van Rooy, Griswold, Whitehill, Feinhals and Goritz.

Characters

SIEGMUND (*Zeeg'-moond*)..Tenor
HUNDING (*Hoond'-ing*) ....Bass
WOTAN (*Voh'-tahn*)..Baritone
SIEGLINDE (*Zeeg-lin'-d'h*) ....Soprano
BRÜNNHILDE (*Bruen-hill'-d'h*) ....Soprano
FRICKA (*Frik'-ah*)..Soprano
VALKYRIES—Gerhilda, Ortlinda, Valtrauta, Sverleita, Helmviga, Siegruna, Grimgerda, Rossvisa.

533

Brünnhilde Bearing a Wounded Warrior to Walhalla

HUGO BRAUNE HOJO-TO-HO!—HOJO-TO-HO!

Walküre is the second in the series of music-dramas composing the *Niebelung Ring,* and to most opera-goers perhaps the most melodious and pleasing. The story is beautiful and compelling, the situations by turn thrilling and pathetic, while the glorious music written by the master to accompany the adventures of his mythical personages is easily understood and appreciated by the average listener.

Wotan has been warned by *Erda,* the *Earth Goddess,* that if *Alberich* regains the *Ring* the gods must perish. Brooding over this impending fate, *Wotan* descends to earth and weds the goddess; this union resulting in nine splendid daughters, the *Walküre,* who are to aid in the salvation of the gods. Riding forth each day among the tumult and the strife which prevail on the earth as a result of the Curse of the Ring, they carry to *Walhalla,* on their flying horses, the bravest of the warriors who fall in battle. These revived heroes keep themselves ready to defend *Walhalla* from the *Niebelungs.* But in order to regain the Ring, a brave hero is necessary, who shall be free from the universal curse and who can take it from *Fafner,* now changed into a dragon the better to guard the treasure. With this in mind *Wotan* visits the earth again and weds a mortal who bears him twins, *Siegmund* and *Sieglinde.* While these children are quite young, the brutal *Hunding* finds their cottage, burns it, kills the mother and carries off *Sieglinde,* whom he afterward forces to become his bride.

The father and son return and swear vengeance on *Hunding.* *Wotan* (known as *Volse* on earth) returns to *Walhalla,* leaving the young *Siegmund* to fight alone and become a self-reliant hero. This is the situation when the action begins.

PHOTO WHITE FIRST ACT SCENE AT THE METROPOLITAN

FERD. LEEKE

BRÜNNHILDE:
Was it so shameful, what I have done,
That for my deed, I so shamefully am scourged?
(Walkure, Act III.)

ACT I

SCENE I—*Interior of Hunding's Hut in the Forest—a Large Tree rises through the Roof*

The prelude represents a fearful storm in the forest, in the midst of which *Siegmund* rushes in exhausted, and falls by the fire. *Sieglinde* gives him refreshment and feels drawn to him by some strange attraction. While they are conversing, *Hunding* enters, and after questioning the stranger, recognizes in him his mortal enemy. He says, "Thou shalt have shelter from the storm to-night, but to-morrow thou diest!" and goes to his room, bidding *Sieglinde* prepare his evening drink. She does so but puts a drug in it to make him sleep soundly, and returns to *Siegmund*, unable to control her interest in the mysterious youth who has so strangely affected her.

Then occurs the lovely *Liebeslied*, the gem of this beautiful first act.

Siegmund's Liebeslied (Siegmund's Love Song)

By Riccardo Martin, Tenor
(*German*) 88276 12-in., $3.00

By George Hamlin, Tenor
(*German*) 74111 12-in., 1.50

By Tollefsen Trio (*Violin-'Cello-Piano*) *17749 10-in., .75

SIEGLINDE AND SIEGMUND—ACT I

The hut, which has been in semi-darkness, is suddenly illuminated by the blowing open of the great door at the back, and without can be seen the beauty of the spring night after the storm. The full moon shines in upon them, so that they see each other clearly for the first time. *Siegmund*, in ecstasy, rhapsodizes Spring and Love:

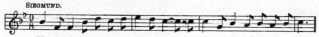

SIEGMUND.

Win-ter stür-me wi-chen dem Won-ne-mond, in mil-dem Lich-te leuchtet der Lenz.
Winter storms have waned, to the winsome moon, In mild as-cen-dance smileth the Spring.

He takes her hand, seats her beside him on the rude bench, and continues:

SIEGMUND:

With balmy breezes, soft and soothing,
Wonders weaving, on he wends,
Through wood and meadow wafts his breathing,
Wide and lustrous laughs his eye;
In songs of birds his silv'ry voice resounds,
Wondrous fragrance he outbreathes;
From his living blood the loveliest flowers are blooming
Leaf and spray spring forth at his voice.
With gentle sceptre's sway he ruleth the world;
Winter and storm wane as his strength awakes:

By dint of his hardy striving
The stoutest doors he is cleaving,
Which, stubborn and strong, once held us from him!
To greet his sister swiftly he flies;
Thus Love the spring hath allured.
Within our bosoms Love lay asleep
That now laughs out to the light
The bride and the sister is freed by the brother;
Destroyed the walls that held them apart;
Joyous meet now the youthful pair;
United are Love and Spring!

Copy't Oliver Ditson Co.

*Double-Faced Record—See page 545.

SIEGMUND AND SIEGLINDE

Although the true charm of this poetry can be realized best by those on intimate terms with the German tongue, this excellent translation from the Ditson *Wagner Lyrics for Tenor* will add to the enjoyment of the record.

Du bist der Lenz (Thou Art the Spring)

By Johanna Gadski, Soprano
(*In German*) 87167 10 $2.00

This exquisite number is sung after the *Liebeslied*.

SIEGMUND:
Joyous meet now the youthful pair;
United are Love and Spring!
SIEGLINDE (*pushing back the locks from his brow and gazing at him in wonder*):
Thou art the Spring,
For thee have I sighed
'Neath the frost-fettered winter's frown.
Tow'rd thee leapt my heart with Heavenly thrill,
When thy radiant glance on me rested.
Foreign seemed all till now,
Friendless I and forsaken;
I counted strange and unknown

What was hid, clear as the day
Dawned on my eyes,
The dulcet refrain fell on my ear,
When in winter's frosty wildness
A friend first awaited me.

Each and all that came near.
But thee, now, I thoroughly knew;
When these eyes fell on thee
Wert thou mine own one.
What my heart long had held,

Sieglinde then tells *Siegmund* the story of the Sword—how at her wedding a stranger had suddenly appeared and thrust into the trunk of the tree a magic sword which should belong only to him who could take it out. The stranger had secretly told *Sieglinde* that no one but *Siegmund* would have power to remove it.

Siegmund rises eagerly, and going to the tree withdraws the sword with a mighty effort. The reunited brother and sister embrace each other and agree to fly from the power of *Hunding*. The curtain falls as they pass out into the moonlit forest.

The love scenes between *Sieglinde* and *Siegmund* should be considered in their allegorical and poetical sense, and not judged by modern ethical standards. Wagner intended this episode to represent the union of Love and Spring.

ACT II

SCENE I—*A Wild and Rocky Pass*

Wotan and his favorite *Valkyrie* daughter, *Brünnhilde*, are discovered in full armor. He tells her to go to the rescue of the *Volsung* (*Siegmund*), whom *Hunding* is pursuing.

WOTAN:
Make ready thy steed, warrior maid,
Soon will come battle and strife;
Brünnhilde, haste to the field,
Give aid to Volsung to-day!

The *Valkyrie* eagerly prepares for her flight, and sings her famous *Battle Cry*.

REMBRANDT
WOTAN AND BRÜNNHILDE

538

THE WONDERFUL SETTING OF ACT II AT THE METROPOLITAN

Ho, yo, to, ho! (Brünnhilde's Battle Cry)

By Johanna Gadski, Soprano　　　　　(*In German*)　87002　10-inch, $2.00

Gadski is always a statuesquely beautiful *Brünnhilde,* and her voice glorifies this music, in which many persons, insensible to the poetic depth and power of the story, hear only noisy declamation. In this first scene especially, she brings into beautiful relief the joyful nature of the *Valkyrie,* and her cries are full of eager, happy vitality. Some idea of the difficult nature of this famous *Battle Cry* may be had from these few measures:

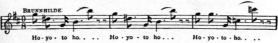

Mme. Gadski, however, surmounts these difficulties with ease, and the aria is a really wonderful specimen of both singing and recording.

BRÜNNHILDE:
> Ho-yo-to-ho! Ho-yo-to-ho! Hei-aha!
> But listen, father! care for thyself;
> For a storm o'er thee will break;
> Fricka, thy busy wife, approacheth in her
> 　ram-impelled car.
> Ha! how she swings her golden whip!
> The frighten'd goats are fainting with fear,
> Wheels rattling and rolling whirl her here to
> 　the fight.
> At such a time away I would be,
> Tho' my delight is in scenes of war!
> Take heed that defeat be not thine,
> For now I must leave thee to fate!

Brünnhilde is right—*Wotan* is in for a scolding, as *Fricka* now appears in an extremely bad humor. *Hunding* has appealed to her, the guardian of marriage, for help, and she insists that *Siegmund* be punished. *Wotan* protests that this true love romance should not be interfered with, but the wrathful wife reminds him that the whole

GADSKI AS BRÜNNHILDE

PAINTED BY DELITZ

Wotan's Farewell

difficulty is but the result of his own infidelity, and he is finally forced to swear that *Siegmund* shall be punished.

Fricka then triumphantly calls to *Brünnhilde* that *Wotan* has further instructions for her. *Brünnhilde* finds her father in deep dejection, and when she questions him he confides to her his efforts to find a hero who shall banish the curse, but says his quest has been in vain. He bids her see that victory goes to *Hunding*. She protests, but he sternly commands obedience and leaves her.

Siegmund and *Sieglinde* now appear, fleeing from the wrath of *Hunding*. *Sieglinde's* strength has failed her, and she falls down exhausted. *Brünnhilde* comes to the lovers and tells *Siegmund* he must die. He scorns her prophecy and says his sword will not fail him. *Hunding's* voice is now heard, and in a sudden wave of sympathy *Brünnhilde* resolves to defend the young lovers.

Siegmund rushes to meet *Hunding,* and amid flashes of lightning the warriors can be seen in deadly combat, while *Brünnhilde* is visible flying above *Siegmund* and protecting him. *Wotan,* seeing the situation, then appears and causes *Siegmund* to fall by his opponent's sword, but also strikes down *Hunding.*

Brünnhilde retreats in terror from her father's wrath, and runs to protect *Sieglinde.* She lifts the helpless maiden on her horse and they disappear.

PHOTO MATZENE GERVILLE-REACHÉ AS FRICKA

ACT III

SCENE I—*The Summit of a Rocky Mountain*

The act opens with the wonderful *Ride of the Valkyries,* one of the most striking of all the master's compositions. This is graphically pictured in the splendid record by Vessella's Band and in the La Scala Record.

Cavalcata (Ride of the Valkyries)

By Vessella's Italian Band
*35369   12-inch $1.25

By La Scala Orchestra
*62693   10-inch,   .75

In the *Ride of the Valkyries* Wagner pictures the wild and warlike nature of the "warrior maids." It is one of the most tremendous compositions in existence. The wild shouts of the goddesses as they ride their winged steeds through the air to the Rock, the warlike cries of *Brünnhilde* and the neighing of the war horses are splendidly portrayed.

THE DEATH OF SIEGMUND

Double-Faced Record—See page 545.

The *Valkyries* see *Brünnhilde* flying toward them, evidently in great distress. She alights and asks her sisters to shield her from the wrath of *Wotan,* who is riding in pursuit; but they dare not help her.

BRÜNNHILDE:
Shield me! Oh, help in hardest need!

THE VALKYRIES:
Why fleest thou in all haste?
Art thou in fear? So flee but culprits who fear!

BRÜNNHILDE:
I am for the first time pursued in flight;
Host-father hunts me down!

She then bids *Sieglinde* flee alone, telling her that she is destined to bear a son who shall be the hero *Siegfried.*

Fort denn eile (Fly Then Swiftly)

By Margarete Matzenauer, Contralto (*In German*)
87102 10-inch, $2.00

HUGO BRAUNE

WOTAN IN PURSUIT OF BRÜNNHILDE

BRÜNNHILDE:
Fly then swiftly, and speed to the east!
Bravely determine all trials to bear.
Hunger and thirst, thorns and hard ways,
Smile through all pain while suffering pangs!

This only heed and hold it ever:
The highest hero of worlds hidest thou,
O wife,
In sheltering shrine!
(*She produces the pieces of Siegmund's sword from under her breastplate and hands them to Sieglinde.*)
For him keep these shreds of shattered sword-blade;
From his father's death-field by fortune I saved them:
Anon renewed this sword shall he swing;
And now his name I declare—Siegfried, of vict'ry the son!

SIEGLINDE:
O marvelous sayings! maiden divine!
What comfort o'er my mind thou hast cast!
For his sake I live and save this belov'd one!
May my blessing frame future reward!
Fare thee well! Be Sieglinde's sorrow thy weal!
(*She hastens away. The rocky peak is enveloped in black thunder-clouds; a fearful tempest roars up from the back; between the peals of thunder Wotan's voice is heard.*)

The *Valkyries* hurriedly conceal *Brünnhilde* in their midst as *Wotan* springs from his horse in a furious rage.

WOTAN:
Where is Brünnhilde? Where the rebellious one?
Dare ye to veil her from Wotan's vengeance?
(*Brünnhilde comes out from the group and faces her father, saying*):

BRÜNNHILDE:
Here stand I, father, to suffer my sentence!

WOTAN:
I sentence thee not; thou hast shaped the stroke for thyself.
Wish-maid art thou no more.
One time a Valkyrie wert thou,
Remain henceforth but merely thyself!

COPY'T DUPONT   VAN ROOY AS WOTAN

542

BRÜNNHILDE (*violently startled*):
Thou disownest me? Thine aim I divine!

WOTAN:
From heavenly clans art thou excluded,
Bann'd, degraded from thy blessed degree;
For broken now is our bond; exiled for aye
Art thou banished from bliss.

He then tells her that she must be put in a deep sleep, and shall be wakened by the first man who passes. She pleads with him in a beautiful appeal.

Brünnhilde's Bitte (Brünnhilde's Appeal)

By Johanna Gadski, Soprano
(*In German*) 88183 12-inch, $3.00

BRÜNNHILDE:
Was it so shameful, what I have done,
That for my deed I so shamefully am
  scourged?
Was it so base to warp thy command, that
  thou
For me such debasement must shape?
Was't such dishonor what I have wrought
That it should rob me of honor for aye?
O speak, father! see me before thee: soften
  thy wrath;
Wreak not thine ire, but make to me clear
  the mortal
Guilt that with cruel firmness compels thee to
Cast off thy favorite child!

JOURNET AS WOTAN

Wotan, deeply moved, softens his stern decree, and consents that she shall be won only by a great hero who can brave the flames with which she is to be surrounded. He then bids her farewell in the splendid *Abschied*.

Wotan's Abschied (I) (Wotan's Farewell, Part I)

By Clarence Whitehill, Baritone
(*German*) 64278 10-in., $1.00

WOTAN:
Farewell, my brave and beautiful child!
Thou once the light and life of my heart!
Farewell! Farewell! Farewell!
Loth I must leave thee; no more in love
May I grant thee my greeting;
Henceforth my maid no more with me rideth,
Nor waiteth wine to reach me!
When I relinquish thee, my beloved one,
Thou laughing delight of my eyes,
Thy bed shall be lit with torches more
  brilliant
Than ever for bridal have burned!
Fiery gleams shall girdle the fell,
With terrible scorchings scaring the timid
Who, cowed, may cross not Brünnhilde's
  couch
For one alone freeth the bride;
One freer than I; the God!

BRÜNNHILDE:
O speak, father! see me before thee: soften
thy wrath!

Brünnhilde sinks, wrapt and transfigured, on *Wotan's* breast; he holds her in a long embrace. She throws her head back again and gazes with solemn emotion into her father's eyes.

WHITEHILL AS WOTAN

Wotan's Abschied (II) (Wotan's Farewell, Part II)

By Clarence Whitehill, Baritone
(In German) 74305 12-inch, $1.50

WOTAN:
Those eyes so lustrous and clear,
Which oft in love I have kissed,
When warlike longings won my lauding,
Or when with lisping of heroes leal thy
honied lips were inspired;
Those effulgent, glorious eyes,
Whose flash my gloom oft dispelled,
When hopeless cravings my heart discouraged,
Or when my wishes t'wart wordly pleasure
from wild warfare were turning—
Their lustrous gaze lights on me now as my
lips imprint this last farewell!
On happier mortal here shall they beam;
The grief-suffering god may never henceforth
behold them!
Now heart-torn, he gives thee his kiss,
And taketh thy godhood away!

He imprints a long kiss on her eyes; she sinks back in his arms with closed eyes, her powers gently departing. He tenderly helps her to lie upon a low mossy lounge, closes her helmet and completely covers her with the great steel shield of the *Valkyrie.* He slowly moves away, then directs the point of his spear toward a huge stone, and summons the *God of Fire.*

WOTAN: Loki, hear! Listen and heed!
Appear, wavering spirit, and
spread me thy
Fire round this fell!
Loki! Loki! Appear!

A stream of fire issues from the stone, which swells to an ever brightening glow of flame; bright flames surround *Wotan,* leaping wildly.

Magic Fire Spell (Feuerzauber)

By Vessella's Italian Band
*35387 12-inch, $1.25

By Julius L. Schendel, Pianist
*35448 12-inch, 1.25

By Alfred Grünfeld, Pianist
58006 12-inch, 1.00

VAN DYCK AS SIEGMUND

The leave-taking and the breaking out of the flames are musically pictured in one of those marvelous bits of writing which only Wagner could produce. This wonderful music is given in a masterly manner by Vessella's players and two records of the beautiful Brassin transcription are given by two well-known pianists. The number begins with the passage just preceding *Wotan's* summons to *Loge.*

MATERNA AS BRÜNNHILDE
(BAYREUTH, 1876)

Double-Faced Record—See page 545.

Then follows a long modulation ending in E major, when the fire motive

begins and continues with all its varied changes and modulations to the close of the opera.

Wotan directs, with his spear, the fiery flood to encircle the rocks.

WOTAN:
He who my spear in spirit feareth,
Ne'er springs through this fiery bar!

He casts a last look on *Brünnhilde* and disappears through the fire.

FRICKA IN HER RAM CHARIOT

(*The curtain falls.*)

DOUBLE-FACED DIE WALKURE RECORDS

Magic Fire Scene	By Vessella's Italian Band	35387 12-inch, $1.25	
Rienzi Overture (*Wagner*)	By Pryor's Band		
Magic Fire Spell (Transcription by Brassin)	By Julius L. Schendel, Pianist	35448 12-inch, 1.25	
(1) Rustle of Spring (*Sinding*) (2) Papillon (*Grieg*)	By Julius L. Schendel, Pianist		
Ride of the Valkyries	By Vessella's Italian Band	35369 12-inch, 1.25	
Gotterdammerung—Siegfried's Funeral March By Vessella's Band			
Ride of the Valkyries	By La Scala Orchestra	62693 10-inch, .75	
Lohengrin—Prelude, Act III	By La Scala Orchestra		
Siegmund's Love Song (*Violin-'Cello-Piano*) By Tollefsen Trio		17749 10-inch, .75	
Romance (*Rubinstein*) (*Violin-'Cello-Piano*)	By Tollefsen Trio		

HUGO BRAUNE   WOTAN SUMMONING THE FIRE GOD

ACT I

WERTHER

LYRIC DRAMA IN FOUR ACTS AND FIVE TABLEAUX

Libretto by Edouard Blau, Paul Milliet and George Hartman, founded upon Goethe's melancholy and romantic story of his own life, *The Sorrows of Werther*. Music by Massenet. First produced at the Imperial Opera House, Vienna, February 16, 1892, with Van Dyck and Renard. First Paris production at the Opéra Comique, January 16, 1893, with Mme. Delna. First Milan production December, 1894. Given at the New Orleans Opera, November 3, 1894. First American production in New York at the Metropolitan Opera House, April 20, 1894, with Eames, Arnoldson and Jean de Reszke in the cast. Revived at the New Theatre by the Metropolitan Opera Company, 1910, with Farrar, Clement, Gluck and Dinh-Gilly; and at the Boston Opera in 1913.

Characters

WERTHER . . . . Tenor
ALBERT, the bailiff. . . . . Baritone
SCHMIDT,⎫his friends. . . . . ⎰Bass
JOHANN, ⎭ . . . . ⎱Tenor
CHARLOTTE, his daughter . . . . Soprano
SOPHIE, her sister. . . . . Mezzo-Soprano
BUHLMANN . . . . Baritone
KATCHEN . . . . Mezzo-Soprano

Six younger children of the bailiff.

Time and Place : In the vicinity of Frankfort, Germany, 1772.

FARRAR AS CHARLOTTE IN WERTHER

As the curtain rises, *Charlotte,* surrounded by her brothers and sisters, is engaged in preparing the noonday meal. *Werther,* a serious-minded and romantic young man, comes to the house with his friend *Albert,* who is betrothed to *Charlotte.* The charming domestic picture appeals to *Werther* greatly, and he promptly falls in love with the young girl. When *Werther* finds an opportunity to tell *Charlotte* of his love, she confesses that she returns his affection, but feels it her duty to marry *Albert* to fulfill a promise made to her dying mother, and begs him to leave the village.

After *Charlotte* and *Albert* are married *Werther* returns and tells *Charlotte* that he still loves her. She admits that he still possesses her affections, but entreats him to spare her and go away forever. *Werther* then writes a message to *Albert,* telling him he has resolved to go on a long journey, and asking him for his brace of pistols. *Charlotte,* greatly alarmed at this request, follows *Werther,* but is too late, as she finds him mortally wounded, and he dies in her arms. Overcome with grief, she faints on the body of her lover, while in strange contrast to this affecting scene the pealing of bells and the joyous voices of little children singing Christmas carols are heard in the distance.

Two of the best selections from the opera, by Clement and Battistini, are offered here.

Lied d'Ossian (Ossian's Song)
By Edmond Clement, Tenor   (*In French*)   64234   10-inch, $1.00

Ah! non mi ridestar! (Do Not Waken Me!)
By Mattia Battistini, Baritone   (*In Italian*)   88354   12-inch, $3.00

BOYER

SCENE FROM ACT II

ILLUS. ZEITUNG, LEIPZIG

(French)

GUILLAUME TELL
(Gee-yaum Tell)

(Italian)   (English)

GUGLIELMO TELL   WILLIAM TELL
(Gool-yel'-moh Tell)

OPERA IN FOUR ACTS

Words by Etienne Jouy, Hippolyte Bis and Armand Marast, taken from Schiller's drama of the same name. Music by Gioachino Rossini. First presented at the *Académie,* Paris, August 3, 1829, with Adolph Nourrit as the original *Arnold.* Produced in Italy, at Lucca, September 17, 1831. First London production, in English, at Drury Lane, 1830, and in Italian at Her Majesty's, 1839. First New York production September 26, 1825, at the Park Theatre. Produced at the New Orleans Opera December 13, 1842. Revived at the Academy of Music by Leonard Grover's German Opera Company, Formes making his first appearance in opera in America. Produced at the Metropolitan December 3, 1888, with Fischer, and March 31, 1890, with Tamagno. Again revived, after twenty-five years, at the Century Opera House September 22, 1914. *Tell* is one of the longest of all operas, lasting four hours and fifty minutes, when given without cuts.

Characters

WILLIAM TELL,		Bass
ARNOLD, suitor of Matilda,	Swiss Patriots...................	Tenor
WALTER FÜRST,		Bass
MELCTHAL, Arnold's father.......................................		Bass
GESSLER, Governor of Schwitz and Uri............................		Bass
LEUTHOLD, a shepherd...		Bass
MATILDA, daughter of Gessler.................................		Soprano
HEDWIGA, Tell's wife...		Soprano
JEMMY, Tell's son...		Soprano

Chorus of Peasants of the Three Cantons; Knights, Pages and Ladies of the train of Matilda; Hunters, Soldiers and Guards of Gessler.

Scene and Period : Switzerland; thirteenth century.

PROGRAM OF WILLIAM TELL
PREMIERE, PARIS OPERA, 1829

THE PLOT

The story of *Tell*, the distinguished patriot, and chief instrument of the revolution which delivered the Swiss cantons from the German yoke in 1207, has been taken by Rossini for the theme of one of his most admired operas, the dramatic interest being heightened by the introduction of love scenes and other episodes.

In the libretto by Jouy and Marast *Gessler* is endowed with a beautiful and amiable daughter, *Matilda*, who has been saved from a watery grave by *Arnold*, son of *Melcthal*, the patriarch of the country, and a determined opponent of the tyrannies of *Gessler*. As a matter of course, mutual attachment ensues, and leads to the troubles which might have been expected from so ill-sorted a connection.

At the opening of the opera we learn that an agent of *Gessler's* has attempted an outrage on the daughter of a herdsman, and has been slain by her father, *Leuthold*. Obliged to fly the country after this act of vengeance, it becomes necessary to cross Lake Lucerne while the weather is so adverse that none of the boatmen will row the old man across the tempestuous waters. *William Tell* finally undertakes the rescue, and by so doing incurs the mortal hatred of *Gessler*.

As time progresses, the people become more and more disaffected; and the father of *Arnold*, suspected of inciting them to acts of insubordination, is seized by *Gessler* and executed. The son's feelings are thus subjected to a severe conflict between his love for *Matilda*, *Gessler's* daughter, his duty to his country, and his desire to avenge his father's death. He, however, renounces his love, and joins the band of patriots now marshaled under *William Tell*. Events are brought to a climax by *Gessler* causing a cap to be elevated on a pole, and requiring all passers-by to bow to it. *Tell* firmly refuses to do so, and is thereupon subjected to the ordeal of the apple, being required, under pain of death, to shoot at an apple placed on the head of his son. Although the distance was considerable, he was able to strike the apple off without injuring the child. The tyrant, perceiving another arrow concealed under *Tell's* cloak, asks him for what purpose it was intended. To which he boldly replies, "To have shot you to the heart, if I had killed my son!" The enraged governor orders him to be hanged; but the Swiss, animated by

CAUTIN-BERGER

THE TYRANT GESSLER

such fortitude and patriotism, fly to arms, attack and vanquish *Gessler*, who is shot by *Tell*. *Matilda* and *Arnold* are united, and the independence of the country is assured.

THE OVERTURE

This overture, which is played probably as often as any other single work at concerts the world over, was called by Berlioz "a symphony in four parts." It is a fitting prelude to a noble work and abounds in beautiful contrasts.

The opening Andante depicts the serene solitude of Nature at dawn, and the music is enchantingly reposeful. From the slowly-climbing figure on the 'cello:

the wayward, elusive air resolves after a time into a more definite rhythmic tune, soon lapsing into dreamy meditation, which continues to the close of the movement. Although this first part is virtually a 'cello solo, the orchestral background is exceedingly beautiful, the close being especially effective with its sustained shake on the richest string of the 'cello, while the orchestra slips gently away, downwards, climbing up to serenity again just at the last. The tranquil mood of the Andante is rudely interrupted by the beginning of the second movement—a string passage suggesting the distant mutterings of a storm. This comes nearer and nearer, until the full fury of the storm bursts upon the ear. The *fortissimo* passage continues until the storm seems to have spent its force and the strain dies down into refreshing clamness once more.

To the *Storm* succeeds a beautiful pastoral with a delicious melody for the English horn, and as Berlioz says, "with the gamboling of the flute above this calm chant producing a charming freshness and gayety." As the last notes of the melody die away, the trumpets enter with a brilliant fanfare on the splendid finale, a fitting climax to a great work.

{Part I—At Dawn	By Pryor's Band}	16380	10-inch,	$0.75
{Part II—The Storm	By Pryor's Band}			
{Part III—The Calm	By Pryor's Band}	16381	10-inch,	.75
{Part IV—Finale	By Pryor's Band}			
{Part I—At Dawn	By Pryor's Band}	35120	12-inch,	1.25
{Part II—The Storm	By Pryor's Band}			
{Part III—The Calm	By Pryor's Band}	35121	12-inch,	1.25
{Part IV—Finale	By Pryor's Band}			
{Part I—At Dawn	By Victor Concert Orchestra}	17815	10-inch,	.75
{Part II—The Storm	By Victor Concert Orchestra}			

PASTORAL SCENE IN THE SWISS OUTDOOR PRODUCTION OF WILLIAM TELL

ACT I

SCENE—*A Village in the Canton of Uri*

The curtain rises on a peaceful scene, showing a charming village with the house of *William Tell* in the foreground. *Tell* and his family are engaged in rural occupations, and the fishermen, while they prepare to put out the boats, sing a lovely *barcarolle*.

Accours dans ma nacelle (Come, Love, in My Boat)
M. Regis, Tenor (*Double-faced—See p. 556*) (*In French*) *45026 10-inch, $1.00

FIRST ACT SCENE

FISHERMEN:
Come hither, my dearest love!
In my little boat embark;
Ah! hither come, and with thy
smile
My loving heart rejoice.
Though leave I must, Eliza, dear,
Do not let me alone depart;
See how the shining sky above
A brilliant day doth augur.
Gentle as the bending rosebud,
Born in the morning's early dew,
Heaven's threaten'd tempests
wild
Will thy presence, love, appease;
When by your side I'm seated,
What new life my soul receives!
There's a Providence above us
Our heart's affections will pro-
tect.

A horn sounds as the sig-
nal for the beginning of the annual Shepherds' Festival, at
which three marriages are to
be celebrated by *Melcthal,*
the patriarch of the village. *Arnold, Melcthal's* son, is saddened at the signal, thinking of his own love, *Matilda,* who is the daughter of the tyrant *Gessler.*

Tell confides to *Arnold* some of his plans for overthrowing the power of *Gessler,* and asks *Arnold* to assist.

AN INTERESTING AL FRESCO PRODUCTION OF WILLIAM TELL IN SWITZERLAND

Chè finger tanto invano   (Vain is the Attempt!)
By Antonio Paoli and Francesco Cigada   (*In Italian*)   92048   12-inch, $3.00

ARNOLD:
What dost thou desire?
TELL:
To recall you, Arnold, to your duty.
ARNOLD (*aside*):
Ah! Matilda, dearly do I love thee;
But from my heart the passion I must root,
If my country and my honor so demand.
TELL (*aside*):
If to us unfaithful he has been,

This grief his repentance doth attest.
(*To Arnold*):
If true to ourselves, we must conquer.
If our valor fail us not,
The tyrant will surely fall.
ARNOLD:
When the hour of danger comes,
Faithfully I will stand by you.

TWO SCENES FROM THE PASTORAL PRODUCTION AT CANTERETS, FRANCE

The young man hesitates between duty to his country and his love for the tyrant's daughter, but finally casts his lot with *Tell,* and goes to bid a last farewell to *Matilda.*

The festival now begins, but is interrupted at intervals by the sound of hunting horns, showing that *Gessler* and his huntsmen are in the mountains near by. The young couples are wedded, and all are rejoicing in their happiness when the festival is rudely interrupted by *Leuthold,* a shepherd, who rushes in crying, "Save me from the tyrant." He explains that one of *Gessler's* officers had abducted his daughter, and to rescue her he had killed the villain. He begs the fishermen to row him across the lake to safety. They refuse, not daring to offend the tyrant, and because of the storm which is raging. *Tell* appears, rushes to the boat with *Leuthold* and puts out on the raging lake just as the soldiers of *Gessler* appear. Baffled of their revenge, they burn the village, devastate the fields, and strike down the aged *Melcthal.*

ACT II

SCENE—*A deep valley in the Alps. On the left the Lake of the Four Cantons. Twilight*

Matilda appears and muses upon her love for *Arnold.* Her lover now joins her, and an effective love scene ensues, which is interrupted by the approach of *Tell* and *Walter,* and *Matilda* departs. *Tell* has seen the young man talking to the daughter of his mortal enemy, and accuses him of being false to the Swiss. *Arnold* confesses that he loves *Matilda,* but says he will renounce her if his country demands the sacrifice.

They then break to *Arnold* the news that *Gessler* has put his father to death, and feelings of vengeance drive from his mind all thought of *Matilda.* In a fine trio the three patriots call upon Heaven to aid their righteous cause.

Troncar suoi di (His Life Basely Taken)

By Antonio Paoli, Tenor; Francesco Cigada, Baritone; Aristodemo Sillich, Bass
(*In Italian*)   92051   12-inch, $3.00

> ARNOLD:
> His life the tyrant wickedly hath taken,
> And yet my sabre in its sheath reposeth;
> Alas! my father his son's aid was needing,
> While I Helvetia was e'en then betraying.
> Heavens! never again shall I behold him!
> TRIO:
> May glory our hearts with courage exalt
> Our cause propitious Heaven will aid;
> The shade of your father our souls will
>   inspire!
> Vengeance it calls for, and not lamentation;
> Although departed, he doth seem to say,
> Happy in his destiny hath he been;
> His remains a martyr's tomb shall hallow,
> Of virtue such as his the fit recompense.

Berlioz writes of his attempt to analyze this great trio: "What! Analyze the awful despair of a son who learns his father is brutally slain? Note the details of a flute or second violin passage! No,—I can only cry, 'Wonderful, superb, heart-rending!'"

The men of the cantons now assemble, and in a splendid finale swear to conquer or die.

Domo, o ciel, da uno straniero (By a Vile Foreigner Subdued)

By Nestore Della Torre, Baritone
(*In Italian*)   76013   12-inch, $2.00

The curtain falls to a magnificent outburst of patriotism, "To arms! To arms!"

ACT III

SCENE—*The Grand Square of Altorf—Gessler's Castle in the background. In the Foreground a Pole surmounted by a Cap*

Gessler and his barons are seated on a throne at one side of the Square, while various amusements are given for their entertainment. It is here that the superb ballet, one of the most beautiful ever composed, is introduced.

William Tell Ballet Music—Parts I and II	By Pryor's Band	*35042	12-inch, $1.25
William Tell Ballet Music—Part III	By Pryor's Band	*16578	10-inch, .75

Double-Faced Record—See page 556.

Tell Saves Leuthold from the Tyrant

TELL REFUSES TO BOW TO THE TYRANT

Gessler, who, with much satisfaction, has been watching the populace bow to the cap which he has had placed on a pole as a symbol of his authority, suddenly notices that *Tell* and his son fail to pay honor to the standard, and he orders them seized and brought before him. He asks if the boy is *Tell's* son, and when *Tell* replies, "My only son," a fiendish idea strikes the tyrant. He orders *Tell* to shoot an apple from the boy's head on pain of instant death for both. *Tell* refuses, but *Jemmy* urges his father to obey, saying, "Father, remember your skill! Fear not, I will not move!"

Tell embraces his boy, and selecting an arrow, manages to conceal another in his coat. He casts a fierce look at the tyrant, then aims with care and strikes the apple fairly in the centre. When he realizes *Jemmy* is safe, *Tell* faints and the concealed arrow is discovered. "For whom was the second arrow?" demands *Gessler.* "For you, tyrant, if I had harmed my child!"

Gessler then orders both put to death, but *Matilda,* who has entered, demands the life of the boy and takes him under her protection. *Tell* is taken to prison amid the curses of the Swiss.

GORITZ AS WILLIAM TELL

ACT IV

SCENE—*The Ruined Village of Act I*

Arnold, who knows nothing of the capture of *Tell,* has come to his native village to bid farewell to the home of his boyhood. He gazes at the desolate cottage and sings his charming and pathetic air, *Oh, Blessed Abode.*

O muto asil (Oh, Blessed Abode)

By Francesco Tamagno, Tenor	(*In Italian*) 95009	10-inch, $5.00
By M. Gautier, Tenor	(*In French*) *45007	10-inch, 1.00
By Leon Beyle, Tenor	(*In French*) *45026	10-inch, 1.00

This number, one of the most effective of those allotted to *Arnold,* is reposeful and offers a fine contrast to the tumult of the last scene.

ARNOLD:
I will ne'er abandon my resolve,
My heart's thirsting for revenge!
William the tyrant has in chains imprison'd!
The hour of battle impatiently I wait!
What silence in this lone place doth reign;
I listen,—my own steps alone I hear!

Oh! bless'd abode, within whose walls
  Mine eyes first saw the light,
Once so belov'd, yet now thy halls,
  Bring mis'ry to my aching sight.
In vain I call; no father's greeting,
Which fancy now to me's repeating,
Will e'er again these ears be meeting,
Then home once lov'd, forevermore, farewell!

Double-Faced Record—See page 556.

A company of Swiss patriots enter hurriedly and tell *Arnold* of recent events at Altdorf. He calls on them to follow him to the rescue of *Tell,* and all depart.

PAINTED BY KAULBACH

WILLIAM TELL'S ESCAPE

SCENE II—*Lake of Four Cantons.*
A Storm is Gathering

Tell's wife is resting here on her way to demand of *Gessler* her husband and son. Suddenly she hears her son's voice and is overjoyed to see him brought to her by *Matilda.* She clasps him in her arms, and anxiously inquires for her husband. *Matilda* says that *Tell* has been removed from Altdorf Prison, and taken across the lake. She has no sooner spoken than *Tell* appears, having escaped from the boat and sent an arrow through the tyrant's heart. *Arnold* and the patriots appear, rejoicing that *Gessler* has been slain and that the Swiss are free once more.

The storm breaks, and as if to announce liberty to Switzerland the sun bursts forth, revealing the glittering, snowy peaks of the Alps in all their dazzling beauty. An invocation to Freedom comes from every throat:

TELL:
Let us invoke, with hearts devout,
Thee, oh Freedom, to sway each heart!
Thou gav'st us pow'r to strike and conquer,
Do thou ne'er depart!

ALL:
Thou gav'st us pow'r to strike and conquer!
We are free, do thou ne'er depart!

DOUBLE-FACED AND MISCELLANEOUS WILLIAM TELL RECORDS

Overture, Part I—At Dawn By Victor Concert Orchestra		17815	10-inch, $0.75
Overture, Part II—The Storm By Victor Concert Orchestra			
Overture, Part I—At Dawn	By Pryor's Band	16380	10-inch, .75
Overture, Part II—The Storm	By Pryor's Band		
Overture, Part III—The Calm	By Pryor's Band	16381	10-inch, .75
Overture, Part IV—Finale	By Pryor's Band		
Overture, Part I—At Dawn	By Pryor's Band	35120	12-inch, 1.25
Overture, Part II—The Storm	By Pryor's Band		
Overture, Part III—The Calm	By Pryor's Band	35121	12-inch, 1.25
Overture, Part IV—Finale	By Pryor's Band		
Ballet Music, Part I	By Pryor's Band	35042	12-inch, 1.25
Ballet Music, Part II	By Pryor's Band		
Ballet Music, Part III	By Pryor's Band	16578	10-inch, .75
Profeta—Re del cielo By Luigi Colazza, Tenor (In Italian)			
William Tell Fantasie Xylophone	By Wm. H. Reitz	17120	10-inch, .75
Omena Intermezzo (Hartz) Banjo	By Fred Van Eps		
Asile hereditaire (Oh! Blessed Abode)		45007	10-inch, 1.00
By M. Gautier, Tenor (In French)			
Les Huguenots—Plus blanche By M. Gautier, Tenor (In French)			
Accours dans ma nacelle—Barcarola (Come, Love, In My		45026	10-inch, 1.00
Boat) By M. Regis, Tenor (In French)			
Asile hereditaire (Oh! Blessed Abode)			
By Leon Beyle, Tenor (In French)			

THE STAGE SCENE IN ACT I

ZAZA

OPERA IN FOUR ACTS

Libretto adapted by the composer from a play by Simon and Berton; music by Ruggiero Leoncavallo. First production in Milan, 1900. First American production at the Tivoli Opera House, San Francisco, November 27, 1903. Revived in November, 1913, at the New Tivoli, San Francisco, under the direction of Leoncavallo himself.

Characters

ZAZA......................A concert hall singer
ANAIDE...........................Her mother
FLORIANA..................A concert hall singer
NATALIE...........................Zaza's maid
SIGNORA DUFRESNE ....His wife
MILIO DUFRESNE ....A wealthy Parisian
CASCART..................A concert hall singer
BUZZY...........................A journalist
MALARDOT......The proprietor of the concert café
LARTIGNON..................A monologue artist
DUCLOU........................Stage manager
MICHELIN..........................A journalist
MARCO................Valet of Signor Dufresne
Singers, Dancers, Scene Shifters, Firemen, Property Men, etc.

Time and Place : Paris ; the present time.

PHOTO BERT   ZAZA AND DUFRESNE

Zaza has had some success in London, Paris and Berlin, but has never been given in New York, although several Zaza excerpts were given at the Leoncavallo concerts in 1906, when the composer visited America. The story is quite familiar to American audiences, however, through the performances of the play of that name, which has been heard in many countries and many languages, and the musical version follows closely the original play.

CARRERE AS ZAZA

SAMMARCO AS CASCART

The rising curtain discloses a stage set in two sections, at one side the dressing room of *Zaza*, and at the other the end of a stage setting. *Zaza*, a concert hall singer, is in love with *Dufresne*, and boasts to *Buzzy*, the journalist, that she will have his love in return. She exerts all her charms, and *Dufresne* finally falls in love with the fascinating singer.

The second act takes place in the reception room of *Zaza's* house. *Dufresne* tells *Zaza* that he must leave her to go to America for several months. She pleads with him not to go, and he finally consents to postpone his trip, but tells her he must go to Paris at once on business. *Cascart*, an old lover of *Zaza's*, enters and hints that *Dufresne* may have other reasons for the trip, and speaks of seeing him in Paris with another woman. *Zaza's* jealousy is aroused, and she announces her intention of following him to Paris.

The third act shows a room in *Dufresne's* house in Paris. *Zaza* enters, accompanied by her maid, and, discovering a letter addressed to *Signora Dufresne*, she realizes that he is married. His little girls enter, and finally *Signora Dufresne* herself, who gazes with astonishment at the visitor. *Zaza* merely says she has made a mistake in the house and goes away.

DUFRESNE DENOUNCING ZAZA—ACT IV

The scene of the last act is again *Zaza's* house in the suburbs. *Cascart*, who has learned of the singer's visit to Paris, pleads with her to give up *Dufresne*, but she only laughs at the suggestion and *Cascart* reminds her sternly that it is a matter of duty. *Cascart* leaves and *Dufresne* is announced. He greets *Zaza* in the old affectionate way, but she informs him she knows of his marriage, but that she forgives his deception. She declares she has told *Signora Dufresne* of their intimacy, and in a rage he curses her. She then sends him away, crying she is cured of her love, after assuring him that her first story was untrue, and that *Signora Dufresne* really knows nothing of the affair.

The rôle of *Cascart* is one of Titta Ruffo's best, and his rendition of the great air, *Buona Zaza, del mio buon tempo*, from the second act, is a magnificent one.

The second selection made by the baritone is the air from Act IV, sung by *Milio* just before the parting of the lovers. It is a highly effective number, emotional yet very melodious. Those who hear these fine airs are likely to regret that the work has not been adequately presented here.

Buona Zaza, del mio buon tempo
By Titta Ruffo, Baritone   (*In Italian*)   87114   10-inch, $2.00

Zaza, piccola zingara (**Zaza, Little Gypsy**)
By Titta Ruffo, Baritone   (*In Italian*)   87125   10-inch, 2.00